EIGHTH EDITION

KEYS FOR WRITERS

Ann Raimes

Susan K. Miller-Cochran
University of Arizona

Australia • Brazil • Mexico • Singapore • United Kingdom • United States

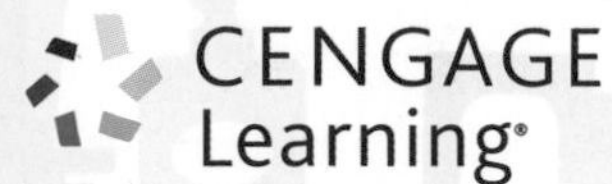

***Keys for Writers,* Eighth Edition**
Ann Raimes, Susan K. Miller-Cochran

Product Director: Monica Eckman
Product Manager: Laura Ross
Content Developer: Stephanie Carpenter
Senior Content Developer: Leslie Taggart
Content Development Manager: Janine Tangney
Product Assistant: Claire Branman
Marketing Manager: Kina Lara
Content Project Manager: Rebecca Donahue
Senior Art Director: Marissa Falco
Manufacturing Planner: Betsy Donaghey
IP Analyst: Ann Hoffman
IP Project Manager: Reba Frederics
Production Service: Thistle Hill Publishing Services
Compositor: Cenveo® Publisher Services
Text Designer: Cenveo® Publisher Services
Cover Designer: Roycroft Design
Cover Image: Alexzel/Shutterstock.com

Library of Congress Control Number: 2016945328

Student Edition:
ISBN: 978-1-305-95675-9

Loose-leaf Edition:
ISBN: 978-1-305-95908-8

Cengage Learning
20 Channel Center Street
Boston, MA 02210
USA

Cengage Learning is a leading provider of customized learning solutions with employees residing in nearly 40 different countries and sales in more than 125 countries around the world. Find your local representative at **www.cengage.com.**

Cengage Learning products are represented in Canada by Nelson Education, Ltd.

To learn more about Cengage Learning Solutions, visit **www.cengage.com.**

Purchase any of our products at your local college store or at our preferred online store **www.cengagebrain.com.**

Printed in China
Print Number: 02 Print Year: 2018

PREFACE

Because of the presence of digital media in our lives, we are all writing more than ever before. Now, for most of us, daily writing is brief, purposeful, and informal—so much so that students facing an important writing task raise all kinds of questions of what is expected and what to do to meet those expectations. Recent technological changes and our present-day culture of rapid written communications have certainly made writing less of an unfamiliar and scary enterprise than it was once, but when much is at stake, such as a grade or a promotion at work, the specter of what instructors and bosses expect still looms large.

The eighth edition of *Keys for Writers* preserves the aim of helping student writers bridge the gap between what they already know and do in their everyday writing and what academic readers and readers in the workplace expect. This handbook still helps students plan and edit their writing and make it fit into academia. There are still many examples that show how to construct effective sentences, paragraphs, and essays. And, to follow the tradition of earlier editions, the needs of multilingual writers are taken into account both in part 9, Writing across Languages and Cultures, and throughout the text in the many *Notes for Multilingual Writers.*

An important feature of this new edition is that examples are more plentiful and more prominent throughout the text. The four new *Key Examples* offer extended application of the *Critical Thinking Framework* that was introduced in the previous edition, cuing students to notice elements of critical thinking at key points in their writing and research processes. The *Assignment Guide: Keys to Common Genres* also provides students with concise, step-by-step instructions for fifteen common genres that they might encounter in their academic and professional careers. The *Assignment Guides* are fully cross-referenced to guide students to examples of the genres throughout the book.

This new edition of *Keys for Writers* is also updated with multiple examples of how to document sources using the 2016 MLA guidelines for documentation. Source shots in chapter 12 provide students with clear examples of how to put the new guidelines into action in their own research and writing.

The success of the previous editions of *Keys for Writers* tells us to keep this handbook's distinctive navigation and its two (yes, only two) color-coded, numbered, and descriptively labeled rows of tabs; the coaching tone that students see as lively but respectful; and the concise explanations and examples of grammar and style that have guided and delighted many users. Yet *Keys for Writers* has also changed because both teachers and students have conveyed in person, have mailed, and have e-mailed invaluable suggestions to help the book keep pace with current trends in writing and be as accurate and timely as a handbook should be. We are grateful for those shared ideas and are happy to incorporate them.

The result is that you are reading a handbook that provides solid instruction and lively examples in an updated design, keeps up with change, guides you through the critical thinking process, insists on authentic examples of student writing, and conveys the challenges of writing for multiple audiences in multiple settings and sometimes in multiple media. We'd like to hear your reactions. You can write to us in care of (c/o) Laura Ross at Cengage Learning, 20 Channel Center Street, Boston, MA 02210.

Cengage Learning has prepared the following expanded summary of what's new in the eighth edition, a summary of the features that have been hallmarks of this book and that continue in the new edition, and a guide to its comprehensive supplements package, which includes several exciting additions and is described in this Preface beginning on page vi.

New to the Eighth Edition

Keys for Writers offers the following new coverage and features:

New *Key Examples* offer extended examples to help with critical thinking Building on the handbook's *Critical Thinking Framework*, we now feature four extended examples, prompting students to consider rhetorical context. Topics include critical reading (with examples of active reading and more passive reading), source evaluation (featuring two sources a student has critically evaluated), source synthesis (with examples of a strong and weak synthesis of two sources), and revision (making use of a heuristics for working through the five C's for stylistic revision).

New *Assignment Guides* deliver help for considering audience, purpose, voice, and medium in fifteen genres The *Assignment Guide: Keys to Common Genres* walk students through common features and organizational strategies for fifteen commonly assigned writing genres. Each guide is fully cross-referenced to full or partial examples of each of the fifteen academic genres found elsewhere in the book or in MindTap.

MLA style sections reflect the latest 2016 MLA updates Newly designed source shots in chapter 12 clearly label each of the necessary elements as students encounter them in the source and then show how to organize them into a citation. These source shots are placed together in 12c to offer consistent templates for students to follow as they work with their own sources.

Part openers on "The Value of Writing in Different Careers" Each part begins with a tab that draws students into the chapters, with an emphasis on real people writing in the real world.

More examples for establishing cause and effect Section 2g is now called "Nine examples of paragraph development" because it has added "Establish cause and effect," complete with an example.

Formative feedback on student writing examples In chapters 4 and 5, new purple annotations in student sample arguments allow students to see more formative feedback, not just descriptions.

More on transitions Two additional examples illustrate "Context links" and "Transitional words and expressions" (both in 2f).

Continuing Proven Features

This text's intuitive, color-coded, two-part organization; laminated tabbed part dividers; quick reference features such as *Key Points* boxes and the *Critical Thinking Framework*; abundant examples and models; friendly writing style; and uncluttered design continue in this new edition, making information easy for student writers to find, understand, and apply.

Two rows of color-coded divider tabs The unusual simplicity and clarity of only two rows of tabs make it easy to find information quickly. The first row of tabs is red, for writing and research issues; the second row is gold, for sentence-level issues.

Practical *Key Points* boxes These handy boxes open or appear within most major sections of the handbook to provide quick-reference summaries of essential information. Eighth edition *Key Points* boxes include A Critical Thinking Framework (part 1); What Every Librarian Wishes You Knew (part 2); How to Cite and List Sources in MLA Style (part 3); DOIs and URLs: Locating and Citing Electronic Sources (part 4); Guidelines for College Essay Format (Printed) (part 5); Checklist for Word Choice (part 6); Forms of Personal Pronouns (part 7); Titles: Quotation Marks or Italics/Underlining? (part 8); and Articles at a Glance: Four Basic Questions about a Noun (part 9).

Source Shots for Citation The handbook's popular *Source Shots* appear in parts 3 and 4 and clearly show students where they are likely to find elements needed to cite common sources from their research in MLA, APA, CSE, and Chicago styles. Clearly labeled citation models show at a glance what types of information students need to include and how to format, arrange, and punctuate that information when documenting sources in all covered styles.

Thorough coverage of style *Keys for Writers* continues to devote a full part (Part 6, Style: The Five C's) to the important area of style, covering sentence- and word-related style issues in a unified presentation. The popular coverage advises students in straightforward, memorable fashion to Cut, Check for Action, Connect, Commit, and Choose the Best Words.

Thorough, consolidated, and clear coverage of grammar Part 7, Common Sentence Problems, gives students one central place to turn to when they have grammar questions. Grammar coverage is not divided confusingly over several parts, as in other handbooks. A section on students' frequently asked grammar questions begins in part 7.

Distinctive approach to English as a new language, Englishes, and vernaculars Superior coverage for multilingual writers takes a "difference, not deficit" approach presented within *Language and Culture* boxes, an extensive "Editing guide to multilingual transfer patterns" (57d), an "Editing guide to vernacular Englishes" (57e), and *Note for Multilingual Writers* integrated throughout the text.

Exercises on writing, research, and grammar Exercises at the ends of all of the writing, research, and grammar sections of the text (including Part 9: Writing across Languages and Cultures) allow students to practice important concepts. Answers to these exercises are found on the *Instructors Resource Manual*, located online. Additional exercises are also found in many of the supplements, both print and online, described below.

Coverage of writing and communicating throughout college and beyond college *Keys for Writers* prepares students for a range of writing and communicating tasks they may encounter in college as well as in the community and the workplace. Part 1 and the *Assignment Guides* support students' writing in different academic disciplines, and part 5 provides model documents, Web pages, presentations, and other resources for writing, communicating, and document design in a range of media for diverse audiences.

A Complete Support Package

Keys for Writers is accompanied by a wide array of supplemental resources developed to create the best teaching and learning experience inside as well as outside the classroom, whether that classroom is on campus or online.

Online Resources

MindTap® English for Raimes/Miller-Cochran's *Keys for Writers*, eighth edition, engages your students to become better thinkers, communicators, and writers by blending your course materials with content that supports every aspect of the writing process.

- Interactive activities on grammar and mechanics promote application in student writing.
- An easy-to-use paper management system helps prevent plagiarism and allows for electronic submission, grading, and peer review.
- A vast database of scholarly sources with video tutorials and examples supports every step of the research process.
- Professional tutoring guides students from rough drafts to polished writing.
- Visual analytics track student progress and engagement.
- Seamless integration into your campus learning management system keeps all your course materials in one place.
- MindTap lets you compose your course, your way.

The **Instructor's Resource Manual,** provides teaching suggestions, suggested answers to exercises, and a sample course syllabus to assist instructors in teaching the course. The Instructor's Resource Manual and other resources for teaching can be accessed in MindTap.

Acknowledgments

The *Keys* handbooks have always made a point of using authentic student writing. For giving permission to use their work, we offer many thanks to the following people, all of whom were responsive, helpful, and a pleasure to work with:

Tiffany Brattina, Charles Bentley Brooks, Jr., Andrew Dillon, Brian Cortijo, Yulanda Croasdale, Ashley Hanson, Bibi Bhani K. Khalsa, Maria Saparauskaite, Daniel Sauve, Hannah Lynne Sims, Patricia Suchan, Catherine Turnbull, Jared Whittemore, and Natasha Williams.

The following composition instructors were instrumental in suggesting changes in this new edition. We are grateful to them for sharing their wisdom and experience in detailed reviews:

Brooke Archila, Madisonville Community College; Emily J. Beard-Bohn, Saginaw Valley State University; Candace Boeck, San Diego State University; Jennifer Boyle, Davidson County Community College; Sydney Brown, Grossmont College; Nancy Cheeks, California State University, Northridge; Jennifer Ferguson, Cazenovia College; Lisa Ford, Tompkins, Cortland Community College; Robert Goldberg, Prince George's Community College; Jeff Gray, East Los Angeles College; Gregory Hagan, Madisonville Community College; Stefan Hagemann, Edgewood College; Jon Inglett, Oklahoma City Community College; Reagan King, Southwest Texas Junior College; Nancy Lee-Jones, Endicott College; Christina Marty, University of Wisconsin–Fox Valley; Michèle Moragné e Silva, St. Edward's University; Bridget Murphy, North Hennepin Community College; Carolyn Nolte, Nebraska Wesleyan University; Dixie Shaw-Tillmon, The University of Texas at San Antonio; Kay Siebler, Missouri Western State University; Mary Thompson, Sussex County Community College; Michelle Williamson, Davidson County Community College; Lee Wright, Saginaw Valley State University

We are also grateful to the following dedicated instructors who helped at earlier stages of composition:

Victoria Aarons, Trinity University; Jacob Agatucci, Central Oregon Community College; John Alcorcha, MTI College; Robert Arend, San Diego Miramar College; Kara Ayik, University of California, Merced; Craig Bartholomaus, Metropolitan Community College of Kansas City; Jenny Billings Beaver, Rowan-Cabarrus Community College; Brooke

Bognanni, Community College of Baltimore County; Aby Boumarate, Valencia College; Laura Bowles, University of Central Arkansas; Dara Brannan, Evangel University; Janice Brantley, University of Arkansas at Pine Bluff; Robert Canipe, Catawba Valley Community College; Judith Carter, Amarillo College; Sherry Cisler, Arizona State University; Bruce Coscia, Cleveland Institute of Electronics; Thomas Desmond, University of Massachusetts Lowell; Katherine Dillion, Harding University; Michael Emery, Cottey College; Mackinzee Escamilla, South Plains College; Beth Farnsworth, Bradford School; Debra Farve, Mt. San Antonio College; Kevin Ferns, Woodland Community College; Ulanda Forbess, North Lake College; Patricia Gallo, Delaware Technical Community College; Phillip Gibson, Henderson State University; Debra Glasper, San Joaquin Valley College–Hesperia; Steve Goldberg, Wayne County Community College; Cynthia Gomez, Hodges University; Joshua Grasso, East Central University; Ismail Hakim, Richard J. Daley College; Clinton Hale, Blinn College; Andrea Hart, Everest University Online; Karry Hathaway, Harford Community College; Laura Headley, Monterey Peninsula College; Jennifer Holmes, Concorde Career College; Teresa Horton, Baker College; Michelle Huston, Lincoln College of New England; Spring Hyde, Lincoln College; Danen Jobe, Pikes Peak Community College; Bettina Jones, Duquesne University; Douglas King, Gannon University; James Kirkpatrick, Central Piedmont Community College; Rita Kranidis, Montgomery College; Suzanne Labadie, Oakland Community College; Erica Lara, Southwest Texas Junior College; Bianca Lee, Mt. San Antonio College; Kristine Leibhart, Mid-Plains Community College; Anna Maheshwari, Schoolcraft College; Sheila McAvey, Becker College; Jimidene Murphey, Wharton County Junior College; Chris Murray, Texas A&M University; Harold Nelson, Minot State University; Lonetta Oliver, St. Louis Community College-Florissant Valley; Jerome Olson, Middlesex County College; Diana Ostrander, Anoka Technical College; Randall Otto, Thomas Edison State University; Nicole Peters, University of Washington; Kevin Petersen, University of Massachusetts Lowell; Sharon Prince, Wharton County Junior College; Joan Reeves, Northeast Alabama Community College; Gabrielle Rose Simons, Hamline University; Elizabeth Saffarewich, Colby-Sawyer College; Howard Sage, Hunter College; Margaret Sherve, Minot State University Mary Ann Simmons, James Sprunt Community College; Michele Singletary, Nashville State Community College; Mickey Marsee, UNM Los Alamos; Nanette Tamer, Stevenson University; Joan Tucker, Northeast Alabama Community College; Kristen Weinzapfel, North Central Texas College; Kathryn West, Bellarmine University; Natalie

Williams-Munger, Golden Gate University; Gaye Winter, Mississippi Gulf Coast Community College; Rick Woten, Thomas Edison State College; Susan Wright, William Paterson University

The publisher plays a large role in the development and publication of a new edition. Thanks go to Monica Eckman, Product Director, Nicole Morinon, Product Team Manager, and Laura Ross, Product Manager, for their support and encouragement throughout the process; to Stacey Purviance, Marketing Director, and Kina Lara, Marketing Manager, for their assistance in helping us identify and understand the needs of students and their teachers; to Leslie Taggart, Senior Content Developer, and Stephanie P. Carpenter, Content Developer, for heroic patience and wisdom as we collaborated on this revision; and to both Jennifer Feltri-George, Senior Content Project Manager, and Rebecca Donahue, Content Project Manager, for coping so ably with production details, snags, and deadlines. Grateful acknowledgments are also due to others on the *Keys* team for their help and expertise: at Cengage Learning, Claire Branman, Breanna Robbins, and all at Cenveo Publisher Services, especially Andrea Archer and Angela Urquhart.

The authors would also like to include additional words of personal thanks. First, we offer appreciation to the students we have been privileged to work with over the years. We hope those students who use this book find it comprehensive and useful in their college courses.

Ann Raimes: Heartfelt thanks go to Susan Miller-Cochran for taking over the work on *Keys for Writers* with this new edition. I know the handbook is in good hands now that I am fully retired.

Susan Miller-Cochran: A special thank you is due to my husband, Stacey Cochran, and my children, Sam and Harper, who have continued to be extraordinarily generous in their support of my work on this edition. I also have deep gratitude for Ann Raimes, who has trusted me to carry on the tradition of her clear, helpful, user-friendly handbooks. I am tremendously honored to follow in her footsteps.

1 The Writing Process

WRITING IN YOUR CAREER

The Chef, the Writer

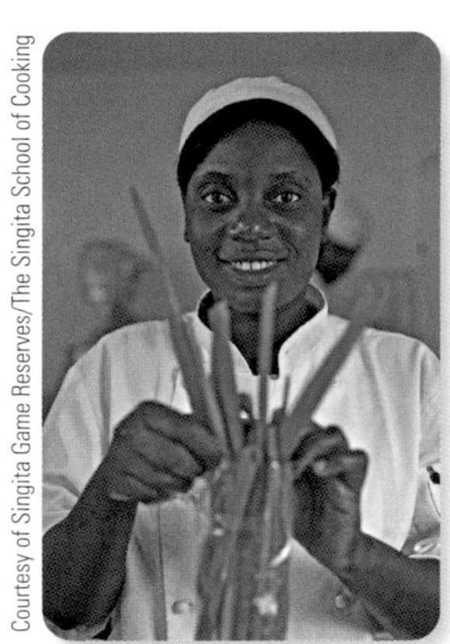
Courtesy of Singita Game Reserves/The Singita School of Cooking

Rhonda Williams is training to be a chef, and she was surprised when she stopped to think about how large a role writing plays in her work. Early in her training, Williams depended on recipes with clear and concrete descriptions; whether it was the creamiest hollandaise sauce or the tangiest lemon curd, the recipe could make the difference between culinary success or disaster. And the importance of writing in the world of food doesn't end with the recipe. Chefs have to communicate the "art" of their food through the descriptive words used on the menu. A typical writing task for a chef is to create a menu. Williams knows that a customer spends only about three minutes reading the menu, so she will need to assess her audience to create a menu that informs, entertains, and persuades. Presentation must be flawless. Compare the two menu entries from *A Taste for Writing* that follow. Who is the audience? What kind of restaurant is it? Do these menus achieve their purpose with this presentation? Notice the importance of the different font styles used to convey the menu styles.

Bistro Urbano

Quattro-Formaggi Macaroni. Fontina, mild cheddar, mozzarella, and smoked gouda sauce with freshly made pasta. Tossed with asparagus, tomatoes, and olive oil. $18.95

Flourless dark chocolate truffle cake served with raspberry compote and a cognac glaze. $6.50

DOWNTOWN DINER

CLASSIC MAC & CHEESE...$8.95

AUNTIE LAURA'S HOMEMADE CHOCOLATE CAKE..............................$3.50

1 The Writing Process

1 Critical Thinking, Reading, and Writing

1a Getting started

Starting on a writing project can be hard if you think of a piece of writing only as a permanent document that others will judge. As you get started on a writing project, it can help to remember that writing is a conversation. When you write, you write for someone. With some writing tasks, you might write only for yourself, and other times you might write for another individual (a teacher, a supervisor, a friend) or for a group of people (a class, a work group, an admissions committee). How and what you write are influenced by your knowledge, by your reading and thinking about a subject, and also by the expectations of the audience you are writing for. Keeping that audience in mind, along with your purpose for writing, can help you get started in the writing process.

MindTap®

Understand the goals of this part, and complete a warm-up activity.

Read, highlight, and take notes online.

1b Understanding context: Purpose, audience, voice, and medium

A helpful way to think about your writing is to understand your writing context. There are four elements to keep in mind for understanding the context of a writing project: purpose, audience, voice, and medium.

Your purpose Ask yourself: What is your main purpose for writing in a particular situation, beyond aiming for an A in the course? Here are some possibilities that are common in academic writing:

- to explain an idea or theory or to explore a question (expository writing)
- to analyze the structure or content of a text (analytical writing)
- to report on a process, an experiment, or lab results (technical or scientific writing)
- to provide a status update on a project at work (business writing)

- to persuade readers to understand your point of view, change their minds, or take action (persuasive or argumentative writing)
- to record and reflect on your own experiences and feelings (expressive writing)
- to tell a story, whether imaginative or real (narrative writing)

The purpose of your writing will determine your options for presenting your final text.

KEY POINTS

Four Questions about Context

Your answers to the following four questions shape the writing you do in significant ways.

- What is your purpose?
- Who is your audience?
- What is unique about your voice on this subject?
- What medium of delivery will you use?

Your audience A good writer keeps readers in mind at all times. Achieving this connection, however, often proves challenging because not all readers have the same characteristics. Readers come from different regions, communities, ethnic groups, organizations, and academic disciplines, all with their own linguistic and rhetorical conventions.

This means that you as a writer have several shifting selves, depending on your audience. In other words, you write differently when you text a friend, post a message on *Instagram*, write an essay for a college instructor, or apply for a grant, an internship, or a job.

Your voice Academic writing, as well as business writing and news reporting, is characterized by an unobtrusive voice. The writer is obviously there, having confronted ideas and sources and having decided what to say about them, but the person behind the writing needs to come across as someone who knows what he or she is writing about and expresses the ideas with an authority that impresses readers. The content takes precedence.

Your voice in writing is the way you come across to readers. What impression do you want them to form of you as a person—of your values and opinions? One of the first considerations is whether you want to draw attention to your opinions as the writer by using the first person pronoun *I* or whether you want to take the more neutral approach of keeping that *I* at a distance. Many academic disciplines have specific expectations for when and how you use *I*. Even if you try to remain neutral by not using *I*, though, as is often recommended for academic and especially for scientific writing, readers will still see you behind your words. Professor Glen McClish at San Diego State University has pointed out how the voice—and, consequently, the effect—of a text such as the following changes significantly when the first fourteen words, including the first person pronouns, are omitted:

> *In the first section of my paper, I want to make the point that* the spread of technology is damaging personal relationships.

The *I* phrases may be removed to make the sentence seemingly more neutral and less wordy. However, the voice also changes: what remains becomes more forceful, proffered confidently as fact rather than as personal opinion.

Regardless of whether you use the word *I* in a particular piece of writing, beware of the leaden effect of using *I*-avoiding phrases such as "it would seem" or "it is to be expected that" and of overusing the pronoun *one*. William Zinsser in *On Writing Well* points out that "good writers are visible just behind their words," conveying as they write "a sense of I-ness." He advises at least thinking of *I* as you write your first draft, maybe even writing it, and then editing it out later. It's worth a try.

LANGUAGE AND CULTURE

Using *I* in Academic Writing

When readers read for information, it is generally the information that appeals to them, not the personality of the writer. Views differ on whether *I* should be used in academic writing, and if so, how much it should be used. Scholarly journals in the humanities several decades ago used to edit out uses of *I*. Not anymore. In the sciences and social sciences, however, a neutral voice is still preferred unless there is a reason to give specific information about the writer. To be safe, always ask your instructor whether you can use *I*.

Your use of media What are you working toward? a print document? a document with embedded images or other media? a multimedia presentation? an online document with hyperlinks, images, sound, or video? As you work through the process of choosing and developing a topic for a defined purpose and audience, consider simultaneously the communication means available to you, especially if you are presenting your work online or with the help of presentation software. Always bear in mind how you can enhance your ideas with the design of your document and the use of images, graphs, or multimedia tools.

As you choose media, consider how to make your work accessible for all readers. For example, you might want to:

- Consider whether readers have a reliable high-speed connection before you post large image files online.
- Increase the type size, provide a zoom function, and either limit the number of visuals or describe them in words for readers with visual impairment.
- Pay attention to color in the visuals. Colors with high contrast work better for some viewers.
- Use online sites such as *AChecker*, *WAVE*, or *Webagogo* to test your documents for accessibility.

1c Reading and writing in context: A framework for critical thinking

Texts in academic, personal, and professional settings all have contexts that influence how we interpret, respond to, use, or ignore them. Understanding that context, both when you're reading and when you're writing, is a key to critical thinking. The word *critical* isn't negative and does not indicate that you are finding fault with something. Instead, *critical thinking* refers to the careful, reflective consideration that writers give to a text when they are reading closely and writing deliberately. In this sense, the ability to understand the context of a piece of writing (either one that you're reading or one that you're writing) and to consider the ways in which the purpose, audience, voice, and medium shape the text is a key component of critical thinking.

1d Reading and writing in college

Academic writing such as reports, essays, and research papers, and everyday writing such as letters, lists, and online messages, are *genres*, or types, of writing. Other genres include creative pieces such as novels,

KEY POINTS

A Framework for Critical Thinking

As you read and write, especially for academic purposes, you might find the following framework useful for critically considering the relationship between context and writing:

PURPOSE

- What is/was the text meant to accomplish? Is that purpose explicit or implied?
- What possibilities are there for creating a text that could meet that purpose?
- Are there specific expectations the text must meet to achieve its intended purpose? If so, what are they?

AUDIENCE

- Who is the audience for this piece of writing? Is there more than one audience? If so, are their interests similar or competing?
- What does the audience expect in terms of content, language use, tone, style, format, and delivery method?
- If expectations are not met, what is the impact on the audience?

VOICE

- What unique perspective does the author bring to this piece of writing? How is that unique perspective communicated?
- How explicitly does/should the author make reference to his or her perspective? Does the author use *I*, and if so, when and why?
- What is the author's tone in the piece of writing? For example, is it playful, serious, accusing, encouraging, hopeful, factual? What effect does that tone have on the piece of writing?

MEDIUM

- How could the writing be delivered to its intended audience to meet its purpose (for example, as a blog post, printed essay, Web site, newspaper article, academic journal article, MP3 file, or *YouTube* video)?
- What formatting rules should the text follow in that medium?
- How can the text be made most accessible to the intended audience?
- What would the impact be of delivering the text in another medium?

As you read, you could use these questions as a guide for understanding and interpreting the text. When you write, you can use these questions to help you make decisions at important points in the writing process. These questions can be useful for writing that you do in many contexts, including professional settings and college courses.

poems, and plays as well as professional writing like memos, résumés, proposals, and presentations. An awareness of the genre in which you are writing and reading is important because it is tightly tied to all elements of context: the purpose for writing, an understanding of the audience for the writing, the voice or tone used, and the medium through which the writing is presented. It puts your writing and reading tasks into perspective, which may make the task seem more manageable and even may save you time.

When reading, for example, an understanding of genre can help you determine which of three common reading strategies would be best to use in different contexts:

Skimming	Reading for Information	Close Reading
Find what's relevant. **Key question:** Should I read this more closely?	Understand important facts. **Key question:** What do I need to understand and remember?	Examine how the context of a piece of writing impacts how it is written and understood. **Key question:** What is the relationship between the context of the reading and how it is written?

When reading genres such as online messages or personal letters, you might not go beyond skimming or reading for information. If you're reading an academic text, however, you might start with skimming, and then you might move to one or both of the other reading strategies, depending on your reason for reading the text. If you're preparing for an exam, you might stick to reading for information as a study strategy. If you're reading a novel or a literary analysis for an English class, however, a close reading would be more appropriate.

How does understanding genres help with your writing tasks? By paying attention to *conventions*—the writing practices associated with a genre—you do a better job of meeting readers' expectations and thus stand a better chance of achieving your intended purpose. If you ignore conventions, readers might be distracted and might miss the message you are trying to convey. In a text message, direct message, or tweet, for example, writers use abbreviations, cultural references, shortcuts, and code words that are conventions online:

Smiley 123: hey sup?

Nicagalxoxo: hey did u c fallon last night?

Smiley 123: no, need 2 hulu

Nicagalxoxo: i was rotfl

Many students know this code from using it in daily life. If that same exchange were written in academic language, it would sound ridiculous. Similarly, there is a code for academic writing, which leads to very different and more formal texts. The later chapters in this book will help you become familiar with these conventions for academic writing.

KEY POINTS

How to Be a Close Reader of Text and Images

➊ Do multiple readings.
Read more than once; examine a text or an image slowly and carefully, immersing yourself in the work and annotating to record your reactions. Start by skimming, and then go back and examine the text more closely, paying attention to context.

➋ Look for common ground.
Note where you nod in approval at points made in the text or image.

➌ Question and challenge.
Take on the role of a debater in your head. Ask yourself: Where does this idea come from? What biases does the writer reveal? What interesting information does the writer or creator provide—and is it convincing? Does the writer use sound logic? Is the writer fair to opposing views? Does the writer even take opposing views into account?

➍ Write as you read.
Write comments and questions in the margins of a page, between the lines in an online document saved to your word processor, on a blog, or on self-stick notes. In this way, you start a conversation with anything you read. If you have made the text you are reading look messy, that's a good sign.

➎ Remember that readers will read critically what you write.
It is not enough just to *read* critically. Be aware that your own writing has to stand up to readers' careful scrutiny and challenge, too.

KEY EXAMPLE

Critical Reading

While reading the following passage about the effects of drinking milk on children and young adults, a student annotates the passage as she reads it, considering different elements of context. The passage is from an article in the academic journal *Pediatrics*. Her comments, questions, and challenges establish her role in the conversation.

Writing to doctors in a pediatrics journal, so they're drawing on research from other respected sources (audience)

Article in an academic journal (medium), so this piece will reach other doctors

Is there some way the government benefits? This looks suspicious.

Over the past 20 years, the National Institutes of Health, the National Academy of Sciences, and the US Department of Agriculture have made recommendations for calcium intake for children and adults for the intended purpose of osteoporosis prevention. Recommended intakes have escalated gradually, and dairy products have been promoted often in federal nutrition policy documents as a "preferred" calcium source.

Authors don't insert their own opinion but report what others have said (voice).

So, is drinking milk harmful to me? Or is there just no evidence that it's necessary?

Look up — epidemiologic

This looks like it will be the purpose of the article.

However, because the level of dairy product consumption in the United States is among the highest in the world, accounting for 72% of dietary calcium intake, and osteoporosis and fracture rates are simultaneously high, numerous researchers have called into question the effectiveness of nutrition policies aimed at osteoporosis prevention through dairy consumption. Findings from recent epidemiologic and prospective studies in women, children, and adolescents also have raised questions about the efficacy of the use of dairy products and other calcium-containing foods for the promotion of bone health.

—Amy Joy Lanou, Susan E. Berkow, and Neal D. Barnard, "Calcium, Dairy Products, and Bone Health in Children and Young Adults: A Reevaluation of the Evidence"

Now imagine that the student had read the same passage but had used a highlighter to indicate important parts and wrote general, unspecific notes instead of writing more detailed annotations, as in the following example.

Over the past 20 years, the National Institutes of Health, the National Academy of Sciences, and the US Department of Agriculture have made recommendations for calcium intake for children and adults for the intended purpose of osteoporosis prevention. Recommended intakes have escalated gradually, and dairy products have been promoted often in federal nutrition policy documents as a "preferred" calcium source. Important

However, because the level of dairy product consumption in the United States is among the highest in the world, accounting for 72% of dietary calcium intake, and osteoporosis and fracture rates are simultaneously high, numerous researchers have called into question the effectiveness of nutrition policies aimed at osteoporosis prevention through dairy consumption. Findings from recent epidemiologic and prospective studies in women, children, and adolescents also have raised questions about the efficacy of the use of dairy products and other calcium-containing foods for the promotion of bone health. Interesting Surprising ?

—Amy Joy Lanou, Susan E. Berkow, and Neal D. Barnard, "Calcium, Dairy Products, and Bone Health in Children and Young Adults: A Reevaluation of the Evidence"

Questions

1. As you compare the two examples of annotating a text, consider the ways in which the first example might be more helpful to a writer. How might the writer use the annotations later? Explain your thoughts to a classmate.
2. What issues do you see with the highlighting and minimal note-taking in the second example? What challenges might a writer have when relying on those notes later to write a paper?
3. Can you imagine a situation in which elements of the annotations and highlighting in the second example might be useful to a writer? In what kind of writing situation might highlighting with minimal note-taking be useful?
4. What strategies have you used in the past to annotate texts? What strategies were useful? What strategies might you try the next time you are asked to read something carefully and critically?

2 Drafting in Stages

MindTap®
Read, highlight, and take notes online.

Writing itself helps you develop ideas, make connections, and raise questions. That is, in writing, you do not just *display* what you know; you also *discover* what you know and think. How is that possible? It's possible because writing is not a linear or step-by-step procedure but a frequently messy *process*—a sort of adventure—one that you control but that often surprises you with your own insights as you progress through a sequence of several overlapping and recurring activities that comprise the writing process (Figure 2.1):

Figure 2.1 Overlapping and recurring activities in the writing process

2a Using critical thinking to find a topic

Whether you have to choose your own idea for a topic or have had a topic assigned, you need strategies other than staring at the ceiling or waiting for inspiration to fly in through a window. Professional writers use a variety of prewriting techniques to generate ideas at various stages of the process. In her article "Oh Muse! You Do Make Things Difficult!" Diane Ackerman reports that poet Dame Edith Sitwell used to lie in an open coffin, French novelist Colette picked fleas from her cat, statesman Benjamin Franklin soaked in the bathtub, and German dramatist Friedrich Schiller sniffed rotten apples stored in his desk.

PURPOSE | AUDIENCE
VOICE | MEDIUM

See the full model on page 7.

Extreme methods aside, perhaps you have developed your own original approach for generating the ideas that will help you choose and develop a topic. If what you do now does not seem to produce good results, though, or if you are ready for a change, try starting by thinking about the context of your writing. Focusing on your purpose, your audience, your voice, and your medium can help you narrow the options to make them feel more manageable.

If you have not had a topic assigned to you, think about the things that matter to you most when choosing a topic. This is a way of considering your voice as part of the context for your writing. Writers do their best work when they write about things they care about. Reflect on issues raised in your college courses; read newspapers and magazines for current issues; consider campus, community, city, state, and nationwide issues; and look at the Library of Congress Subject Headings to get ideas. If you can, begin with an idea that has caught your interest and has some connection to your life. Think about why you are interested in it, what unique perspective you have on the subject, and whether you will be able to sustain your interest to complete the project.

In addition to thinking about what will spark your interest most, read the prompt for your writing assignment very carefully. What guidelines does your instructor give for topic selection? Are there specific requirements that might limit what you could write about? Look for key words about what your instructor is asking you to do. Look for words such as the following, each of which asks the writer to do something slightly different:

- define
- describe
- compare
- contrast
- provide an example
- analyze
- annotate
- summarize

KEY POINTS

Online Resources for Generating Ideas and Planning

Web directories assembled by librarians and academic institutions provide reliable sources for finding good academic subjects. The *Librarians' Index to the Internet, Academic Info*, and *Voice of the Shuttle*, a University of California at Santa Barbara directory for humanities research, are among the best.

The Purdue University Online Writing Lab and other online resources also include information on generating ideas and planning.

Adapting to an assigned topic that does not interest you Don't panic or resign yourself to boredom if you are assigned a topic that does not interest you. If you spend time reading as much as you can on the topic, something is bound to capture your attention. Ask yourself, Is there an angle I could take on the issue or a part of the topic I could focus on to make it more interesting to me? You may have to go beyond the obvious approaches to a topic. Imagine, for instance, a biology student who is assigned to write a literary analysis of Nathaniel Hawthorne's *The Scarlet Letter*. She notices that there are many references to medicinal herbs and poisons in the novel, and she decides to explore how they are used as metaphors in the narrative. Suddenly she realizes that she can do a close reading of the novel from the perspective of a scientist.

You might try challenging the point of view of one of your sources, taking the opposite position. Or you can set yourself the task of showing readers exactly why the topic has not grabbed people's interest—maybe the literature and the research have been just too technical or inaccessible. If you can, find a human angle.

For more on topics, see 4c.

Drawing from journals, blogs, and online conversations Your own *daily journal* can be far more than a personal diary. Many writers carry a notebook, either paper or electronic, and write in it every day, jotting down observations, references, quotations, questions, notes on events, and ideas about assigned texts or topics, as well as specific pieces of writing in progress. Your daily journal can also serve as a review for final examinations or essay tests, reminding you of areas of special interest or subjects you did not understand.

A *double-entry journal* provides a formalized way for you to think critically about readings, lectures, and other data you collect. Two pages or two columns, or two open windows in your word processor, provide the space for interaction. On the left side, write summaries, quotations, data you've collected, and accounts of readings, lectures, and class discussions. The left side, in short, is devoted to what you read, hear, or observe. On the right side, record your own comments, reactions, and questions about the material. Doing so gives you a way to visualize the conversation between you and your sources.

A *blog* gives you the opportunity to think aloud in public. Not only can others read your posting, but they can respond to it as well. Other than this social element, a blog can be similar to a writer's journal. The unedited blog titled "The *Life* of a Salesman" (Figure 2.2) was posted on a writing course blog site by Tiffany Brattina, a student at Seton Hill University in Greensburg, Pennsylvania. Here she works out a personal,

March 16

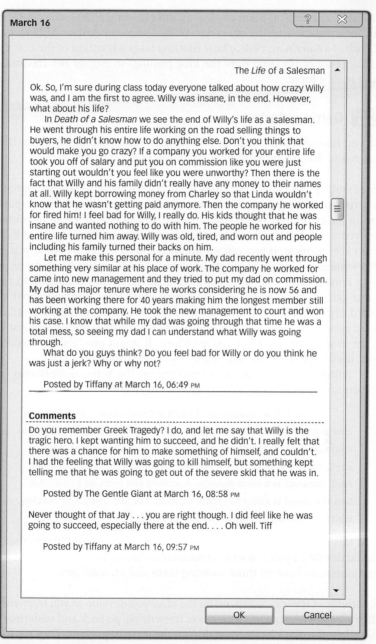

The *Life* of a Salesman

Ok. So, I'm sure during class today everyone talked about how crazy Willy was, and I am the first to agree. Willy was insane, in the end. However, what about his life?

In *Death of a Salesman* we see the end of Willy's life as a salesman. He went through his entire life working on the road selling things to buyers, he didn't know how to do anything else. Don't you think that would make you go crazy? If a company you worked for your entire life took you off of salary and put you on commission like you were just starting out wouldn't you feel like you were unworthy? Then there is the fact that Willy and his family didn't really have any money to their names at all. Willy kept borrowing money from Charley so that Linda wouldn't know that he wasn't getting paid anymore. Then the company he worked for fired him! I feel bad for Willy, I really do. His kids thought that he was insane and wanted nothing to do with him. The people he worked for his entire life turned him away. Willy was old, tired, and worn out and people including his family turned their backs on him.

Let me make this personal for a minute. My dad recently went through something very similar at his place of work. The company he worked for came into new management and they tried to put my dad on commission. My dad has major tenure where he works considering he is now 56 and has been working there for 40 years making him the longest member still working at the company. He took the new management to court and won his case. I know that while my dad was going through that time he was a total mess, so seeing my dad I can understand what Willy was going through.

What do you guys think? Do you feel bad for Willy or do you think he was just a jerk? Why or why not?

Posted by Tiffany at March 16, 06:49 PM

Comments

Do you remember Greek Tragedy? I do, and let me say that Willy is the tragic hero. I kept wanting him to succeed, and he didn't. I really felt that there was a chance for him to make something of himself, and couldn't. I had the feeling that Willy was going to kill himself, but something kept telling me that he was going to get out of the severe skid that he was in.

Posted by The Gentle Giant at March 16, 08:58 PM

Never thought of that Jay . . . you are right though. I did feel like he was going to succeed, especially there at the end. . . . Oh well. Tiff

Posted by Tiffany at March 16, 09:57 PM

OK Cancel

Figure 2.2 A student's blog on a course site

original, and critical point of view as, after missing a class, she considers an interpretation of the character Willy Loman in Arthur Miller's play *Death of a Salesman*. Notice how Brattina takes advantage of the conventions of the genre (that is, of the blog posting) to engage her classmates and build a topic.

2b Getting started

If you have difficulty getting started with your writing once you have narrowed down a possible topic, try some of these strategies.

Freewriting If you do not know what to write about or how to approach a broad subject, try doing five to ten minutes of *freewriting* either on paper or on the computer. When you freewrite, you let one idea lead to another in free association, without concern for correctness. The important thing is to keep writing. If you cannot think of a word or phrase while you are freewriting, simply write a note to yourself inside square brackets, or put in a symbol such as #. On a computer, use the Search command to find your symbol later, when you can spend more time thinking about the word. If you feel like you're too focused on grammar, spelling, and surface-level issues, try changing your font to white or turning off the monitor for a bit so you can't see what you're writing. It might give you the freedom you need to get some ideas down that you can work with.

Jimmy Wong did some freewriting on the topic of uniforms (an excerpt from a classmate's paper appears in 3d):

> When I think of uniforms I think of Derek Jeter and A-Rod and how cool they look as they leap for a baseball, spin around and throw it straight to first to get someone out. But does the uniform add anything to the skill? I'd say not, but it probably adds a lot of other stuff. Baseball is a team game so a uniform can work as a reminder that the game is about the team winning, not just one player scoring well and earning a place in the Hall of Fame.

Just this short piece, done very quickly, gave Wong an indication that he could develop a piece of writing focused on the unity-building effect that uniforms can have on those wearing them and on outsiders.

Looping One way to expand on the ideas you develop as you freewrite is to try *looping*. After a few minutes of freewriting, go back and underline or highlight the one idea that you think is the most important. Then try free-writing on that idea for a few minutes. You might try this activity several times to narrow down a broad topic and to figure out what is most interesting to you or what might be the most promising focus for your writing.

Brainstorming Another way to generate ideas is by *brainstorming*—making a list of ideas as you think of them. Brainstorming is enhanced if you do it collaboratively in a group, discussing and then listing your ideas (see also 2i, Writing with others). You can then, by yourself or with the group, scrutinize the ideas, arrange them, reorganize them, and add to or eliminate them.

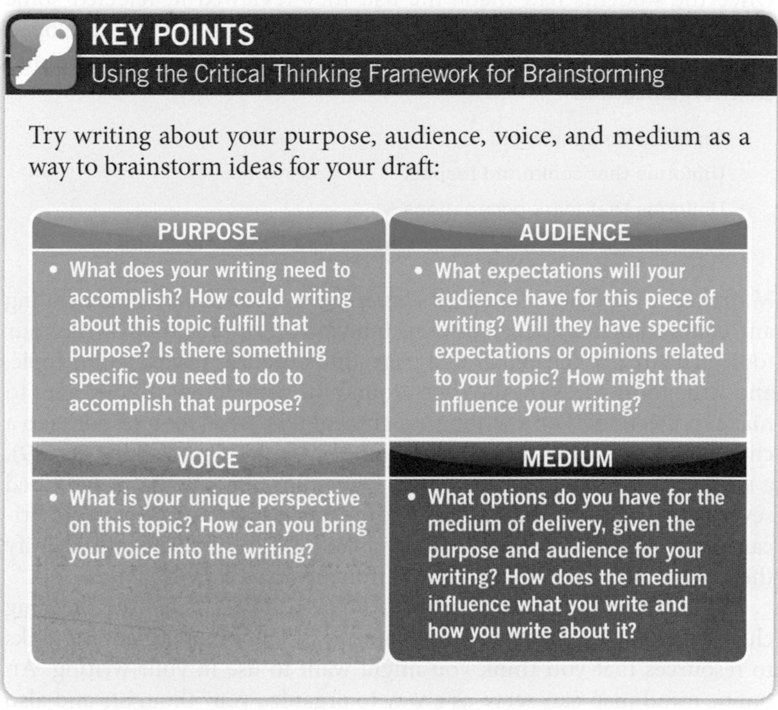

KEY POINTS

Using the Critical Thinking Framework for Brainstorming

Try writing about your purpose, audience, voice, and medium as a way to brainstorm ideas for your draft:

PURPOSE

- What does your writing need to accomplish? How could writing about this topic fulfill that purpose? Is there something specific you need to do to accomplish that purpose?

AUDIENCE

- What expectations will your audience have for this piece of writing? Will they have specific expectations or opinions related to your topic? How might that influence your writing?

VOICE

- What is your unique perspective on this topic? How can you bring your voice into the writing?

MEDIUM

- What options do you have for the medium of delivery, given the purpose and audience for your writing? How does the medium influence what you write and how you write about it?

Before they were assigned a chapter from *Uniforms: Why We Are What We Wear* by Paul Fussell, a group of students working collaboratively made the following brainstorming list on the topic of what uniforms signify:

Pink for girls, blue for boys—perpetuating stereotypes

Uniforms in parochial schools and in many British schools

Men's suits and ties

Uniforms for prisoners and wardens

Team uniforms; nurse uniforms

Municipal employee uniforms

The uniform of fashion—ripped jeans fashionable

Official vs. nonofficial uniforms

Advantages of uniforms—but for whom?

Keep them in line. Keep them recognizable.

Armed services

How do we treat uniforms—respect, contempt, pity, indifference?

Once the students had made the list, they reviewed it, rejected some items, expanded on others, and grouped items. Thus, they developed subcategories that led them to possibilities for further exploration and essay organization:

Uniforms for spectators

Uniforms that command respect

Uniforms that mark occupations

Fashion as a uniform of social markers—part of an "in-group"

Mapping *Mapping*, also called *clustering*, is a visual way of generating and connecting ideas. It can be done individually or in a group. Write your topic in a circle at the center of a page, think of ideas related to the topic, and write those ideas on the page around the central topic. Draw lines to make connections. For a writing assignment that asked for a response to a chapter in Paul Fussell's book *Uniforms* (see Source Shot 2, pp. 238–239), a student created the map shown in Figure 2.3. She saw that it indicated several possibilities for topics, such as the increasing casualness of American society and the power of uniforms to both camouflage and identify their wearers. You can see an excerpt from her draft in 3d.

Web-based applications such as *MindMeister* can be useful for doing clustering activities, mapping out your ideas, and even embedding links to resources that you think you might want to use in your writing. An online mind map can serve as a way to organize your thoughts and also to track your research.

Using journalists' questions Journalists check for thorough coverage of their stories by making sure they answer six questions, though not in any set order: Who did it? What happened? When did it happen? Where did it occur? Why did it happen? How did it turn out? If you are telling the story of an event, either as a complete essay or as an example in an essay, asking the journalists' six questions will help you think comprehensively about your topic.

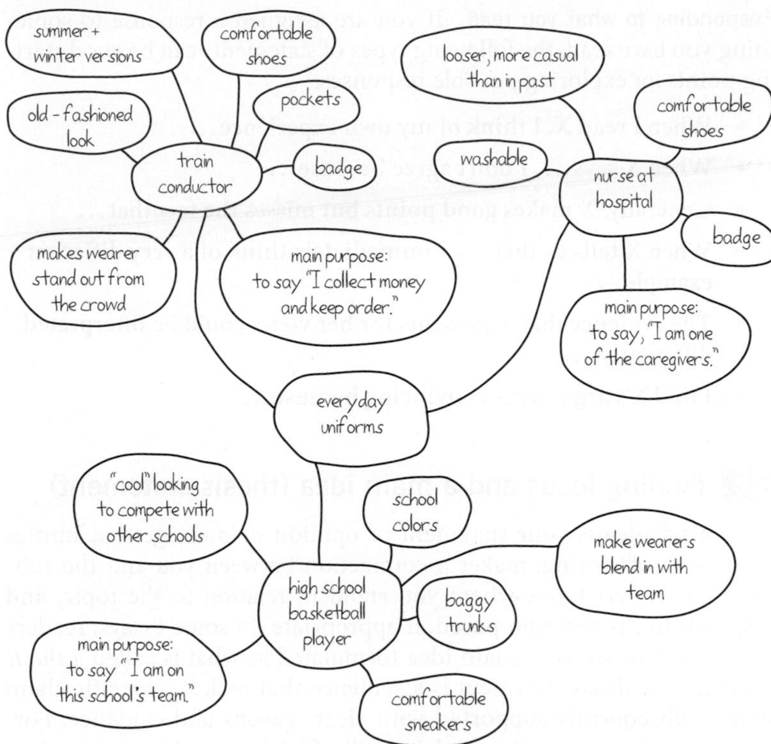

Figure 2.3 A map created for a chapter of Paul Fussell's book *Uniforms*

Including descriptions Whatever your topic, ask questions about color, light, location, movement, size, shape, sound, taste, and smell. Doing so can help you discover an interesting angle on your topic. Putting these details in writing can also eventually help readers "see" your topic—whether it is a person, place, object, or scientific experiment—exactly as you see it.

Making comparisons You can better understand a topic—and help your audience understand it, too—by describing what it might be similar to and different from. For example, how is learning to write like learning to ride a bike—or not?

Assessing cause and effect Try approaching your topic by asking what causes or produces it and what effects or results emerge from it. For example, what are the causes and effects of dyslexia? inflation? acid rain? hurricanes? salmonella? asthma?

Responding to what you read If you are assigned a response to something you have read, the following types of statements can be good starting points for exploring possible responses:

- **When I read X, I think of my own experience...**
- **When X says..., I don't agree because...**
- **Generally, X makes good points but misses the fact that...**
- **When X tells us that..., I immediately think of a very different example:...**
- **The evidence that X presents for her views could be interpreted differently:...**
- **I find X's arguments convincing because...**

2c Finding focus and a main idea (thesis statement)

Your main idea is your statement of opinion or message that unifies your piece of writing, makes a connection between you and the subject, lets readers know where you stand in relation to the topic, and responds to the question posed, if appropriate. In some essays, readers may expect to see your main idea formulated as what is called a *thesis statement*. A thesis statement is a sentence that makes a specific claim that is subsequently supported with clear reasons and evidence. Formal essays that are stating a claim will often have a thesis statement, but essays that don't have a persuasive purpose may have only a main idea but not an identifiable thesis statement. See 4c for help in understanding the difference between effective and ineffective thesis statements.

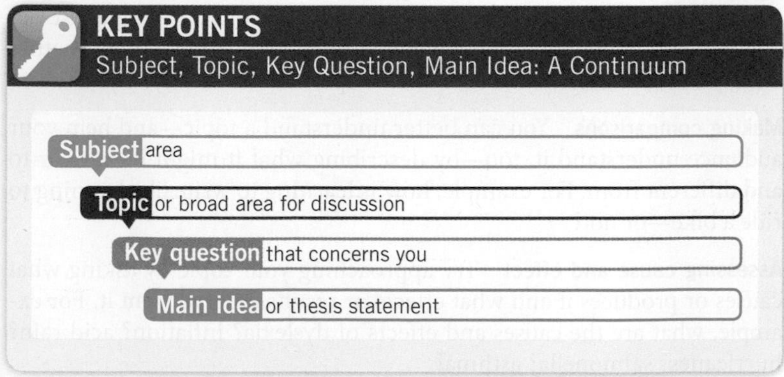

KEY POINTS
Subject, Topic, Key Question, Main Idea: A Continuum
Subject area
Topic or broad area for discussion
Key question that concerns you
Main idea or thesis statement

From subject to topic to main idea After analyzing some readings on social networking, discussing Web sites, and making notes, students were given the task of working together in groups to formulate a progression from subject to question to main idea based on what they had read about social networking and issues of privacy. This is what one group produced:

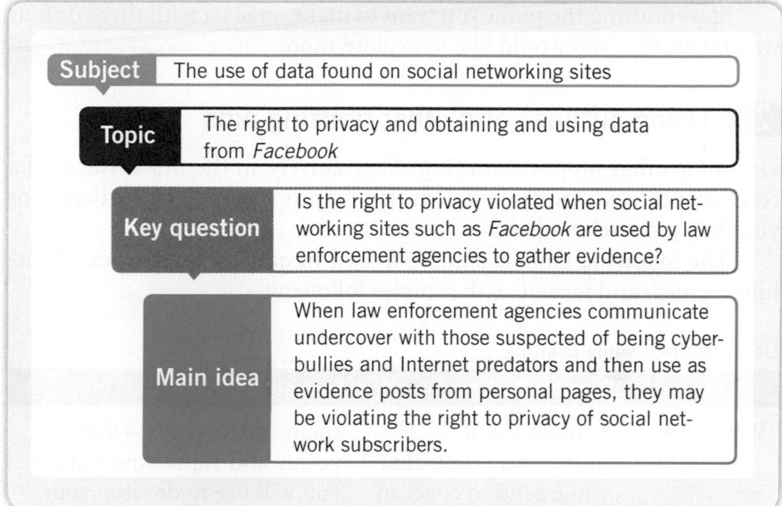

Subject
The use of data found on social networking sites
Topic
The right to privacy and obtaining and using data from Facebook
Key question
Is the right to privacy violated when social networking sites such as Facebook are used by law enforcement agencies to gather evidence?
Main idea
When law enforcement agencies communicate undercover with those suspected of being cyberbullies and Internet predators and then use as evidence posts from personal pages, they may be violating the right to privacy of social network subscribers.

If you choose a topic and a question that are too broad, you will find it difficult to generate a main idea (or thesis) with focused ideas and examples. Whenever you find yourself thinking, for instance, "There's so much to say about social life online that I don't know where to start," narrow your topic. If you begin by choosing a topic and a question that are too narrow, you probably will not find enough material and will end up being repetitive. Above all, stay flexible. You may want to revise your topic or your question as you discover more information.

Progressing from topic to main idea It is not enough to say, "I am writing about *Facebook*," although that may be what you start with. This simply names your topic. It does *not* indicate what you might explore about *Facebook*. Are you going to address the hazards that teens need to be aware of when they enter a social networking site? the way teens can gain friends but also expose themselves? the places where predators lurk? Are you going to analyze *Facebook* postings? its effects on predatory behavior? the ethics of using postings to catch predators? In short, work toward considering the most important point you want to make about the right to privacy and social networking sites. Maybe you will compare *Facebook* with another social networking site, such as *Instagram,* or perhaps you will interview parents to get their reactions to their children's participation. Or maybe you will explore how the networks provide outlets for students who need an alternative to parental authority. Whichever road you take, play with your first general idea until it gels more for you and you find something that makes a point you know you can describe, explain, and support.

Start drafting the point you want to make, or start with three or four statements that you would like to explore more.

2d Using outlines and other drafting aids

Outlining often supports drafting. Alternatively, in the initial stages of a research project, a purpose statement or a proposal may work better for you than a scratch outline.

The following table is a guide to two frequently used types of outlines, *scratch* and *formal,* with samples following.

Using Outlines while Drafting

	Scratch Outline	Formal Outline
What it is	a rough list of numbered points that you intend to cover in your essay	spells out, in order, what points and supportive details you will use to develop your main idea or thesis and arranges them to show the overall form and structure of the essay
What it helps you do	lets you see what ideas you already have, how they connect, what you can do to support and develop them, and what further planning or research you still need to do	serves as a check on the logic and completeness of what you have written, revealing any gaps, repetition, or illogical steps in the development of your essay
When you use it	early in the process and at midpoints if integrating major revisions	early in the process, but you are likely to find that making an outline with a high level of detail is more feasible after you have written a draft
Starting point	chosen topic	thesis statement or main idea

Scratch outline One student in a class discussing social networking sites made the following scratch outline:

Subject: The use of data found on social networking sites

Topic: The right to privacy and obtaining and using data from *Facebook*

Question: Is the right to privacy violated when social networking sites such as *Facebook* are used by law enforcement agencies to gather evidence?

Possible main idea: Law enforcement agencies that use social networking sites to pursue cyberbullies and suspected terrorists may be violating a citizen's right to privacy.

Points:

1. Information stored on home computers and private servers may be protected by privacy law.
2. Information stored on external servers such as *Facebook* may not be considered private.
3. Social networking sites such as *Facebook* have guidelines and privacy policies.
4. Evidence from updates, tweets, IP addresses, uploaded photographs, and Web sites that track relationships is currently being used by law enforcement agencies.
5. Law enforcement agencies that engage in analytical or undercover operations using social networking sites and similar media avoid violations of privacy when they are pursuing crimes against cyberbullies and suspected terrorists.

Possible directions: Ways law enforcement can use social networking sites; visibility of sites' privacy policies; ethics of using false identities online; ways to prevent youth from sharing too much online; legal risks for minors?

Formal outline When the same student began to work on a new draft, however, he developed a more nuanced and more focused thesis. Note how to structure an outline:

Main points: I, II, III, etc.

2nd level: A, B, C, etc.

3rd level: 1, 2, 3, etc.

4th level: a, b, c, etc.

The following shows an outline of just one main point, with complete sentences for the first two levels. When you create your own outline, be sure you have at least two items in each of the levels: if you have an "a," then you must have a "b," for example.

Thesis: Law enforcement agencies that use social networking sites to pursue cyberbullies and suspected terrorists may be violating a citizen's right to privacy.

I. *Facebook* has historically cooperated with law enforcement agencies by providing user-generated information that has been used in criminal investigations.
   A. Personal profiles have provided contact and employment information.
   B. Status updates and blog entries have provided insight into an individual's whereabouts and activities.
   C. Photographs have been used to establish location information, personal relationships, and even character.
      1. The use of dated photographs to establish or refute alibis
      2. Joshua Lipton drunk driving case
   D. Messaging and status updates can be linked to a device and the time and place it was used.
      1. Rodney Bradford's avoidance of robbery charges because he updated his status from his father's computer at the time of the crime
      2. How Jonathan G. Parker checked his *Facebook* status at the scene of the crime

Other strategies for drafting Writing offers opportunities that speech can never provide: the ability to revise your ideas and the way you present them. Writing drafts allows you to work on a piece of writing until it meets your goals. Try the following ideas for drafting:

- **Plan the steps and set a schedule.** Work backward from the deadline, and assign time in days or hours for each of the following tasks: deciding on a topic, generating ideas, making a scratch outline, writing a draft, getting feedback, analyzing the draft, making large-scale revisions, finding additional material, editing, proofreading, formatting, and printing. Be certain to include additional time for revisiting any of these stages if needed.
- **Manage writer's block.** If you feel yourself suffering from what is called *writer's block*, try to ignore any self-imposed rigid rules that hinder you, such as "Always stick with a complete outline" or "Check everything and edit as you write." Editing too early may prevent you from thinking about ideas and moving forward.

- **Don't start at the beginning.** Don't automatically begin by writing the introduction. Begin by writing the essay parts for which you already have some specific material. Then you will know what you need to introduce.
- **Pace yourself.** Write in increments of twenty to thirty minutes to take advantage of momentum. When you take a break, have a set time that you will get back to writing and a specific place that you will begin writing again in the document.
- **Put your first draft to work.** Write your first draft as quickly and fluently as you can, and print it double-spaced. Write notes to yourself in capitals or surrounded by asterisks to remind yourself to add or change something or to do further research. Sometimes seeing your writing in print can help you identify possibilities for revision or expansion that you cannot see on the screen.
- **Be specific.** Avoid obvious, vague, or empty generalizations (such as "All people have feelings"). Be specific, and include interesting supporting details. Keep in mind that claims always need evidence.
- **Use Comment and AutoCorrect.** Word processing programs have a Comment function that allows you to type notes that appear only on the screen, not in a printout, provided you set the Print options to ignore them. These notes are easily deleted from later drafts. In addition, if you use a term frequently (for example, the phrase "bilingual education"), abbreviate it (as "b.e.") and use a tool like AutoCorrect and Replace to substitute the whole phrase throughout your draft as you type.
- **Resist the lure of Copy and Paste.** Copying a passage from an online site and pasting it into your own document may seem like a good solution when you are facing a looming deadline and surfing for good Web sources. However, the penalties for plagiarism are far worse than those for lateness (see 9a). So the bottom line here is *don't do it.*

2e Paragraph and topic sentences

Paragraphs A good paragraph makes a clear point, supports your main idea, and focuses on one topic. Some paragraphs, however, may have more to do with function than with content. They serve to take readers from one point to another, making a connection and offering a smooth transition from one idea to the next. These transitional paragraphs are often short.

To indicate a new paragraph, indent the first line one-half inch from the left margin or, in business and online documents, begin it at the left margin after a blank line.

KEY POINTS

When to Begin a New Paragraph

Both logic and aesthetics dictate when it is time to begin a new paragraph. Think of a paragraph as something that gathers together in one place ideas that connect to each other and to the main purpose of the piece of writing. You should begin a new paragraph:

1. to introduce a new point (one that supports the claim or main idea of your essay)
2. to expand on a point already made by offering new examples or evidence
3. to break up a long discussion or description into manageable chunks that are easier to read

Topic sentences A *topic sentence* in a body paragraph lets readers know explicitly what the main idea of the paragraph is. Readers should notice a logical flow of ideas as they read through a paragraph and as they move from one paragraph to another through an essay.

When you write a paragraph, imagine readers saying, "Look, I don't have time to read all this. Just tell me in one sentence (or two) what point you are making here." Your reply would express your main point. Each paragraph in an academic essay generally contains a controlling idea expressed in a sentence (called a *topic sentence*) and does not digress or switch topics in midstream. Its content is unified. A *unified paragraph*, in academic writing, includes one main idea that the rest of the paragraph explains, supports, and develops.

The following paragraph is devoted to one broad topic—tennis—but does not follow through on the topic of the *trouble* that the *backhand* causes *average* players (key terms highlighted in yellow). The unity of the paragraph could be improved. What is Grand Slam winner Serena Williams doing in a paragraph about average players? What relevance does her powerful serve have to the average player's problems with a backhand? The writer would do well to revise by cutting out the two sentences about Serena Williams (sentences highlighted in blue).

> The backhand in tennis causes average weekend players more trouble than other strokes. Even though the swing is natural and free flowing, many players feel intimidated and try to avoid it. Serena Williams, however, has a great backhand, and she often wins difficult points with it. Her serve is a powerful weapon, too. When faced by a

> backhand coming at them across the net, midlevel players can't seem to get their feet and body in the best position. They tend to run around the ball or forget the swing and give the ball a little poke, praying that it will not only reach but also go over the net.

When placed first, as it is in the paragraph on the troublesome backhand, a topic sentence makes a generalization and serves as a reference point for the rest of the information in the paragraph. When placed after one or two other sentences, the topic sentence focuses the details and directs readers' attention to the main idea. When placed at the end of the paragraph, the topic sentence serves to summarize or draw conclusions from the details that precede it.

Some paragraphs, such as the short ones typical of newspaper writing or the one-sentence paragraphs that make a quick transition, do not always contain a topic sentence. Sometimes, too, a paragraph contains such clear details that the point is obvious and does not need to be explicitly stated. However, in academic essays, a paragraph in support of your essay's claim or thesis (main point) will usually be unified and focused on one clear topic, regardless of whether you state it in a topic sentence.

2f Using transitions and links for coherence

However you develop your individual paragraphs, readers expect to move with ease from one sentence to the next and from one paragraph to the next, following a clear flow of argument and logic. When you construct an essay or paragraph, do not force readers to grapple with "grasshopper prose," which jumps suddenly from one idea to another without obvious connections. Instead, make your writing *coherent*, with all the parts connecting clearly to one another with transitional expressions, context links, parallel structures, and word links.

Transitional words and expressions Make clear connections between sentences and between paragraphs either by using explicit connecting words like *this*, *that*, *these*, and *those* to refer to something mentioned at the end of the previous sentence or paragraph or by using transitional expressions. Ta-Nehisi Coates uses the phrase "this tangle of perils" to connect sentences and ideas from a previous paragraph to the next paragraph in the following passage from his article about incarceration rates in the United States:

> Robert Sampson, a sociologist at Harvard who focuses on crime and urban life, notes that in America's ghettos, "like things tend to go together." High rates of incarceration, single-parent households, dropping out of school, and poverty are not unrelated vectors. Instead, taken together, they constitute

what Sampson calls "compounded deprivation"—entire families, entire neighborhoods, deprived in myriad ways, must navigate, all at once, a tangle of interrelated and reinforcing perils.

Black people face this tangle of perils at its densest. In a recent study, Sampson and a co-author looked at two types of deprivation—being individually poor, and living in a poor neighborhood. Unsurprisingly, they found that blacks tend to be individually poor and to live in poor neighborhoods. But even blacks who are not themselves individually poor are more likely to live in poor neighborhoods than whites and Latinos who are individually poor. For black people, escaping poverty does not mean escaping a poor neighborhood. And blacks are much more likely than all other groups to fall into compounded deprivation later in life, even if they managed to avoid it when they were young.

—Ta-Nehisi Coates, "The Black Family in the Age of Mass Incarceration"

KEY POINTS
Transitional Expressions

Adding an idea also, in addition, further, furthermore, moreover

Contrasting however, nevertheless, nonetheless, on the other hand, in contrast, still, on the contrary, rather, conversely

Providing an alternative instead, alternatively, otherwise

Showing similarity similarly, likewise

Showing order of time or order of ideas first, second, third (and so on), then, next, later, subsequently, meanwhile, previously, finally

Showing result as a result, consequently, therefore, thus, hence, accordingly, for this reason

Affirming of course, in fact, certainly, obviously, to be sure, undoubtedly, indeed

Giving examples for example, for instance

Explaining in other words, that is

Adding an aside incidentally, by the way, besides

Summarizing in short, generally, overall, all in all, in conclusion

For punctuation with transitional expressions, see 45e.

Although transitional expressions are useful to connect one sentence to another or one paragraph to another, do not overuse these expressions. Too many of them, used too often, make writing seem heavy and mechanical.

Context links A new paragraph introduces a new topic, but that topic should not be entirely separate from what has gone before. Let readers know the context of the big picture. If you are writing about the expense of exploring Mars and then switch abruptly to the hazards of climbing Everest, readers will be puzzled. You need to state clearly the connection with your main idea: "Exploration on our own planet can be as hazardous and as financially risky as space exploration." For example, when Winifred Gallagher pivots from a paragraph in which she quotes a passage from *War and Peace* to discussing one scientist's conception of the brain's three parts, she needs to help her readers make sense of the shift. Gallagher links the scientist's subject (and the topic of her chapter) to the "inner experience" of the novel's characters, Prince Andrei and Natasha:

> The type of complex inner experience that cascades from Andrei's focus on Natasha is of particular interest to the Northwestern University cognitive scientist Don Norman. According to his conceptual model, the brain has three major parts. . . .
>
> —Winifred Gallagher, *Rapt* (p. 37)

Word links You can also provide coherence by using repeated words or connected words, such as pronouns linked to nouns; words with the same, similar, or opposite meanings; or words linked by context. Note how Deborah Tannen maintains coherence not only by using transitional expressions (*for example, furthermore*) but also by repeating words and phrases (blue) and by using certain pronouns (red)—*she* and *her* to refer to *wife*, and *they* to refer to *Greeks*.

> Entire cultures operate on elaborate systems of indirectness. For example, I discovered in a small research project that most Greeks assumed that a wife who asked, "Would you like to go to the party?" was hinting that **she** wanted to go. **They** felt that **she** wouldn't bring it up if **she** didn't want to go. Furthermore, **they** felt, **she** would not state **her** preference outright because **that** would sound like a demand. Indirectness was the appropriate means for communicating **her** preference.
>
> —Deborah Tannen, *You Just Don't Understand*

2g Nine examples of paragraph development

Whether you are writing a paragraph or an essay, you will do well to keep in mind the image of skeptical readers who are always inclined to say something challenging, such as "Why on earth do you think that?" or "What could possibly lead you to that conclusion?" Show readers that your opinion is well founded and supported by experience, knowledge, logical arguments, the work of experts, or reasoned examples, and provide vivid, unique details. Here are illustrations of some rhetorical strategies you can use to develop ideas in paragraphs and essays. They may serve as prompts to help you generate ideas.

Give examples Examples that develop a point make writing interesting and informative. The following paragraph about Harry S. Truman (president of the United States, 1945–53) as a young boy follows an account of his happy childhood. It begins with a topic sentence that announces the controlling idea: "Yet life had its troubles and woes." The author then gives examples of some "troubles and woes" that young Harry faced. Beginning with a generalization and supporting it with specific illustrative details is a common method of organizing a paragraph, known as *deductive organization.*

> Yet life had its troubles and woes. On the summer day when his Grandfather Truman died, three-year-old Harry had rushed to the bed to pull at the old man's beard, trying desperately to wake him. Climbing on a chair afterward, in an attempt to comb his hair in front of a mirror, he toppled over backward and broke his collarbone. Another time he would have choked to death on a peach stone had his mother not responded in a flash and decisively, pushing the stone down his throat with her finger, instead of trying to pull it out. Later, when Grandpa Young [Harry's mother's father] lay sick in bed and the little boy approached cautiously to inquire how he was feeling, the old pioneer, fixing him with a wintry stare, said, "How are you feeling? You're the one I'm worried about."
>
> —David McCullough, *Truman*

In addition, you may decide to illustrate an idea in your text by using a visual image as an example.

Tell a story Choose a pattern of organization that readers will easily grasp. Organize the events in a story chronologically so that readers can follow the sequence. In the following paragraph, Dawn Braithwaite tells a story that leads to the point that people with disabilities often face ignorance and insensitivity. Note that she uses *inductive organization*, beginning with background information and the specific details of the story in chronological order and ending with a generalization.

> Jonathan is an articulate, intelligent, thirty-five-year-old man who has used a wheelchair since he became a paraplegic when he was twenty years old. He recalls taking an ablebodied woman out to dinner at a nice restaurant. When the waitress came to take their order, she patronizingly asked his date, "And what would he like to eat for dinner?" At the end of the meal, the waitress presented Jonathan's date with the check and thanked her for her patronage.

Although it may be hard to believe the insensitivity of the waitress, this incident is not an isolated one. Rather, such an experience is a common one for persons with disabilities.

—Dawn O. Braithwaite, "Viewing Persons with Disabilities as a Culture"

Describe with details appealing to the senses To help readers see and experience what you feel and experience, describe people, places, scenes, and objects by using sensory details that re-create those people, places, scenes, or objects for readers. In the following paragraph from a memoir about growing up to love food, Ruth Reichl tells how she spent days working at a summer camp in France and thinking about eating. However, she does much more than say "The food was always delicious" and much more than "I looked forward to the delicious bread, coffee, and morning snacks." Reichl appeals to our senses of sight, smell, touch, and taste. We get a picture of the campers, we smell the baking bread, we see and almost taste the jam, we smell and taste the coffee, and we feel the crustiness of the rolls. We feel that we are there—and we wish we were.

When we woke up in the morning the smell of baking bread was wafting through the trees. By the time we had gotten our campers out of bed, their faces washed and their shirts tucked in, the aroma had become maddeningly seductive. We walked into the dining room to devour hot bread slathered with country butter and topped with homemade plum jam so filled with fruit it made each slice look like a tart. We stuck our faces into the bowls of café au lait, inhaling the sweet, bitter, peculiarly French fragrance, and Georges or Jean or one of the other male counselors would say, for the hundredth time, "*On mange pas comme ça à Paris*." Two hours later we had a "*gouter*," a snack of chocolate bars stuffed into fresh, crusty rolls. And two hours later there was lunch. The eating went on all day.

—Ruth Reichl, *Tender at the Bone: Growing Up at the Table*

Develop a point by providing facts and statistics The following paragraph supports with facts and statistics the assertion made in its first sentence (the topic sentence) that the North grew more than the South in the years before the Civil War.

While southerners tended their fields, the North grew. In 1800, half the nation's five million people lived in the South. By 1850, only a third lived there. Of the nine largest cities, only New Orleans was located in the lower South. Meanwhile, a tenth of the goods manufactured in America came from southern mills and factories. There were one hundred piano makers in New York alone in 1852. In 1846, there was not a single book publisher in New Orleans; even the city guidebook was printed in Manhattan.

—Geoffrey C. Ward, *The Civil War: An Illustrated History*

Here, too, visuals such as tables, charts, and graphs would help present data succinctly and dramatically.

Define key terms Sometimes, writers clarify and develop a topic by defining a key term, even if it is not an unusual term. Often, they will explain what class something fits into and how it differs from others in its class; for example, "A duckbilled platypus is a mammal that has webbed feet and lays eggs." In his book on diaries, Thomas Mallon begins by providing an extended definition of his basic terms. He does not want readers to misunderstand him because they wonder what the differences between a diary and a journal might be.

> The first thing we should try to get straight is what to call them. "What's the difference between a diary and a journal?" is one of the questions people interested in these books ask. The two terms are in fact hopelessly muddled. They're both rooted in the idea of dailiness, but perhaps because of *journal*'s links to the newspaper trade and *diary*'s to *dear*, the latter seems more intimate than the former. (The French blur even this discrepancy by using no word recognizable like *diary*; they just say *journal intime*, which is sexy, but a bit of a mouthful.) One can go back as far as Dr. Johnson's *Dictionary* and find him making the two more or less equal. To him a diary was "an account of the transactions, accidents, and observations of every day; a journal." Well, if synonymity was good enough for Johnson, we'll let it be good enough for us.
>
> —Thomas Mallon, *A Book of One's Own: People and Their Diaries*

Analyze component parts Large, complex topics sometimes become more manageable to writers (and readers) when they are broken down for analysis. The *Columbia Encyclopedia* online helps readers understand the vast concept of life itself by breaking it down into six component parts:

> Although there is no universal agreement as to a definition of *life*, its biological manifestations are generally considered to be organization, metabolism, growth, irritability, adaptation, and reproduction.... Organization is found in the basic living unit, the cell, and in the organized groupings of cells into organs and organisms. Metabolism includes the conversion of nonliving material into cellular components (synthesis) and the decomposition of organic matter (catalysis), producing energy. Growth in living matter is an increase in size of all parts, as distinguished from simple addition of material; it results from a higher rate of synthesis than catalysis. Irritability, or response to stimuli, takes many forms, from the contraction of a unicellular organism when touched to complex reactions involving all the senses of higher animals; in plants response is usually much different than in animals but is nonetheless present.

> Adaptation, the accommodation of a living organism to its present or to a new environment, is fundamental to the process of evolution and is determined by the individual's heredity. The division of one cell to form two new cells is reproduction; usually the term is applied to the production of a new individual (either asexually, from a single parent organism, or sexually, from two differing parent organisms), although strictly speaking it also describes the production of new cells in the process of growth.
>
> —*Columbia Encyclopedia*, ed. Paul Lagasse, © 2006 Columbia University Press. Reprinted with the permission of the publisher.

Classify into groups Dividing people or objects into the classes or groups that make up the whole gives readers a new way to look at the topic. In the following paragraphs, Laurie Helgoe develops her essay on personality by classifying people into two categories and providing back and forth comparisons between the two types of personalities.

> Although introverts and extraverts may seem like they come from different planets, introversion and extraversion exist on a continuous dimension that is normally distributed. There are a few extremely extraverted folk, and a few extreme introverts, while most of us share some extravert and some introvert traits.
>
> Although there is no precise dividing line, there are plenty of introverts around. It's just that perceptual biases lead us all to overestimate the number of extraverts among us (they are noisier and hog the spotlight). Often confused with shyness, introversion does not imply social reticence or discomfort. Rather than being averse to social engagement, introverts become overwhelmed by too much of it, which explains why the introvert is ready to leave a party after an hour and the extravert gains steam as the night goes on.
>
> —Laurie Helgoe, "Revenge of the Introvert"

Compare and contrast When you examine similarities and differences among people, objects, or concepts, block style and point-by-point style achieve different purposes:

Block style	Point-by-point style
You can deal with each subject one at a time, perhaps summarizing the similarities and differences at the end. This organization works well when each section is short and readers can easily remember the points made about each subject.	You can select and organize the important points of similarity or difference, referring within each point to both subjects.

The following example uses the point-by-point approach in comparing John Stuart Mill (Figure 2.5), a British philosopher and economist, and Harriet Taylor (Figure 2.4), a woman with whom Mill had a close intellectual relationship. The author, Phyllis Rose, organizes the contrast by points of difference, referring to her subjects' facial features, physical behavior, ways of thinking and speaking, and intellectual style. (A block organization would deal first with the characteristics of Taylor, followed by the characteristics of Mill.)

Library of the London School of Economics

Figure 2.4 Harriet Taylor

> You could see how they complemented each other by the way they looked. What people noticed first about Harriet were her eyes—flashing—and a suggestion in her body of mobility, whereas his features, variously described as chiselled and classical, expressed an inner rigidity. He shook hands from the shoulder. He spoke carefully. Give him facts, and he would sift them, weigh them, articulate possible interpretations, reach a conclusion. Where he was careful, she was daring. Where he was disinterested and balanced, she was intuitive, partial, and sure of herself. She concerned herself with goals and assumptions; he concerned himself with arguments. She was quick to judge and to generalize, and because he was not, he valued her intellectual style as bold and vigorous where another person, more like her, might have found her hasty and simplistic.
>
> —Phyllis Rose, *Parallel Lives: Five Victorian Marriages*

Bettmann/Corbis

Figure 2.5 John Stuart Mill

Establish cause and effect Explaining the relationship between cause and effect can help readers understand why something has occurred or can lay the groundwork for proposing a solution to a problem. In the following paragraphs, Jane McGonigal identifies the causes of true relaxation and the effects that result from misunderstanding what causes "fun":

> Virtually every activity that we would describe as a "relaxing" kind of fun—watching television, eating chocolate, window-shopping, or just chilling out—doesn't make us feel better. In fact, we consistently report feeling worse afterward than when we started 'having fun': less motivated, less confident, and

less engaged overall. But how can so many of us be so wrong about what's fun? Shouldn't we have a better intuitive sense of what actually makes us feel better?

We certainly have a strong intuitive sense of what makes us feel bad, and negative stress and anxiety are usually at the top of the list. . . . [R]esearchers believe that when we consciously seek out relaxing fun, we're usually trying to reverse these negative feelings. When we seek out passive entertainment and low-engagement activities, we're using them as a counterbalance to how stimulated and overwhelmed we feel.

But by trying to have easy fun, we actually often wind up moving ourselves too far in the opposite direction. We go from stress and anxiety straight to boredom and depression. We'd be much better off avoiding easy fun and seeking out hard fun, or hard work that we enjoy, instead.

—Jane McGonigal, *Reality Is Broken*

2h Writing introductions and conclusions

Introductions Readers like to know a little about a topic, about why it is even worth discussing, before you pronounce your opinion on it. Think of your introduction as a way to establish your purpose for writing and to make an important connection with your intended audience. If you find it difficult to write an introduction because you are not yet clear about your claim or how you will support it, wait until you have written the body of your essay. You may find it easier to introduce the actual text you have composed than something you have not yet written.

When you write an essay in the humanities, keep the following points in mind. Other disciplines have slightly different ways of introducing writing, depending on the conventions of the genre.

KEY POINTS

How to Write a Good Introduction

Options

- Make sure your first sentence stands alone and does not depend on readers being aware of the essay title or an assigned question. For instance, avoid beginning with "This story has a complex plot."
- Provide context and background information.
- Indicate what claim you will make in your essay, or at least indicate the issue that your main idea concerns.

(Continued)

(Continued)

- Define any key terms that are pertinent to the discussion.
- Establish the tone of the paper: informative, persuasive, serious, humorous, personal, impersonal, formal, informal.
- Engage the interest of readers to make them want to explore your topic with you. Tell them something they may not know or something to surprise them, such as an unlikely fact or statistic, a challenging question, a pithy quotation, interesting background details, a joke, an intriguing opinion, a startling verbal image, or a description of a problem.

What to Avoid

- Avoid being overly general and telling readers the obvious, such as "Crime is a big problem" or "In this fast-paced world, TV is a popular form of entertainment" or "Since the beginning of time, the sexes have been in conflict."
- Do not refer to your writing intentions, such as "In this essay, I will. . ."
- Do not make extravagant claims, such as "This essay will prove that bilingual education works for every student."
- Do not restate the assigned essay question.

Consider these attention-grabbing beginnings of books or chapters:

- **"You gonna eat that?" The woman is eyeing the tray the flight attendant has just set before me. I can't tell if she wants reassurance that I find it as repellent as she does or if she is simply hungry and hopeful that I will hand my food over. I loosen my seatbelt, swivel in my narrow seat, and see that her face holds a challenge. Is she daring me to eat the food?**

  —Ruth Reichl, *Garlic and Sapphires*

- **Faced with working-class life in towns such as Winchester, I see only one solution: beer.**

  —Joe Bageant, *Deer Hunting with Jesus: Dispatches from America's Class War*

- **It is a truth universally acknowledged, that a single man in possession of a good fortune, must be in want of a wife.**

  —Jane Austen, *Pride and Prejudice*

- **It was a bright cold day in April, and the clocks were striking thirteen.**

—George Orwell, *1984*

- **Every day in the United States, roughly 200,000 people are sickened by a foodborne disease, 900 are hospitalized, and fourteen die.**

—Eric Schlosser, *Fast Food Nation*

Brainstorming may help you come up with catchy openings. A brainstorming session, for example, produced the following openers for an essay on fashion:

A description — **Everyone stared at him as he walked in. His jeans were torn, his sneakers stained and ripped, his jacket a shapeless rag, his tee shirt sweaty. He was the coolest guy in the room.**

A memorable quotation — **The flamboyant author Oscar Wilde advises, "One should either be a work of art or wear a work of art."**

A startling fact — **How far obedience to fashion can be taken was shown in China when for hundreds of years women were truly fashionable when they had undergone the torture and permanent disfigurement of having their feet bound so they could fit into unnaturally tiny shoes.**

An anecdote — **I keep clothes I have rarely worn for a time when they might come back into fashion and I can maybe wear them again. I still have bright green pants with vast bell bottoms and a purple jacket with football-quarterback shoulders in my closet. The sad thing is that a fashion never returns in exactly the same style or colors. When I put on the pants, my friends just laugh and say "Nice Halloween costume!"**

A question — **"Who are you wearing?" Such a question, the one most often heard on the red carpet before the Oscars, would have been unintelligible a few decades ago.**

An interesting observation — **Identical twins can live apart for twenty years without ever having been in touch and yet at any moment can be wearing the same colored dress, shoes of the same make, hair cut in the same style.**

Conclusions Think of your conclusion as completing a circle. You have taken readers on a journey from a presentation of the topic in your introduction, to your main point, to supporting evidence and discussion, with specific examples and illustrations. Remind readers of the purpose of the journey. Recall the main idea of the paper, and make a strong statement about it that will stay in their minds. Readers should leave your document feeling satisfied, not turning the page and looking for more.

Each academic discipline has slightly different ways of concluding a piece of writing, depending on the conventions of the genre. When you write an essay in the humanities, keep the following points in mind.

KEY POINTS

How to Write a Good Conclusion

Options

- Frame your essay by reminding readers of something you referred to in your introduction and by reminding readers of your main idea. End on a strong note: a quotation, a question, a suggestion, a reference to an anecdote in the introduction, a humorous insightful comment, a call to action, or a look to the future.
- Leave readers with a sense of completion of the point you are making.

What to Avoid

- Do not use the obvious "In conclusion."
- Do not apologize for the inadequacy of your argument ("I do not know much about this problem") or for holding your opinions ("I am sorry if you do not agree with me, but . . .").
- Do not repeat the identical wording you used in your introduction.
- Do not introduce a totally new direction. If you raise a new point at the end, readers might expect more details.
- Do not contradict what you said previously.
- Do not be too sweeping in your conclusions. Do not condemn the whole medical profession, for example, because one person you know had a bad time in one hospital.

2i Writing with others

Writing is not necessarily a solitary process. In the academic or business world, you will often have to work collaboratively with one or more classmates or colleagues. You might be part of a group, a team, or a committee assigned to draft a proposal or a report. You might be expected to produce a document reflecting the consensus of your team or group. Or you might need to draft and circulate a document and then incorporate into it the comments of many people.

In group settings, you can make sure that every member contributes by assigning each person a set of specific tasks. These tasks may include making lists of ideas, drafting, analyzing the draft, revising, editing, assembling visuals, and preparing the final document. You also can divide a project into parts and assign each person a section to draft. Schedule regular meetings, and expect everyone to come with a completed written assignment. Build on strengths within the group. For example, ask the member skilled in document design and computer graphics to prepare the visual features of the final document.

Word processing programs and e-mail provide useful tools for collaboration. You can work on a text, make and highlight changes, insert comments, and attach the revised text to an e-mail message to a colleague, who can then accept or reject the changes. *Google Drive* also provides a useful tool for working with others, allowing you to upload a document that others can then access, change, and add to. Group members can even edit the document simultaneously.

However, make sure that you work collaboratively only when doing so is expected or permitted. An instructor who assigns an essay will not always expect you to work on it with your sister, classmate, or tutor.

Revising, Editing, and Proofreading

MindTap®
Read, highlight, and take notes online.

Revising—making changes to improve a piece of writing—is an essential part of the writing process. It is not a punishment inflicted on inexperienced writers. Even Leo Tolstoy, author of the monumental Russian novel *War and Peace,* commented: "I cannot understand how anyone can write without rewriting everything over and over again."

Take a look at one manuscript page from chapter 1 of this text, shown in Figure 3.1. You'll notice that, even though both authors of this text are professional writers and teachers, we worked with our editor to revise and edit a page of this book in significant detail.

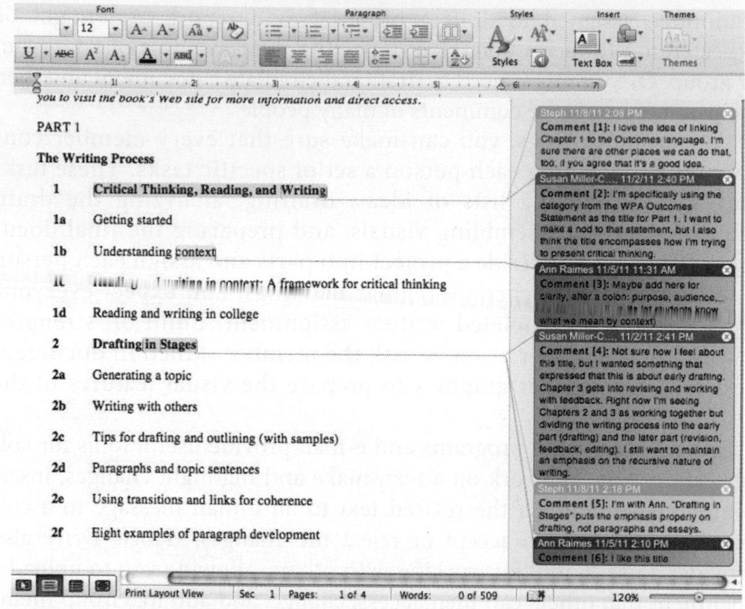

Figure 3.1 This screenshot captures part of the revision process for this book: a conversation among its authors and editor.

KEY POINTS

Computer Tools for Revising an Essay

- **Copy and paste first sentences.** Select the first sentence of each paragraph, and use the Copy and Paste features to move the sequence of sentences into a new file. Then examine these first sentences to check for a logical progression of ideas, repetition, or omission.
- **Use different file names.** Write multiple drafts, and save every draft under a separate file name that clearly labels the topic and the draft. Some people prefer to save deleted sections in a separate "dump" file so that they can retrieve deleted parts.
- **Use the Find feature.** The Find feature helps you locate words and phrases that you tend to overuse. Use it to look for instances of *there is* or *there are*, for example, and you will see if you are using either phrase too often.
- **Use the Insert Comment feature.** The Insert Comment feature allows you to write a note to yourself in the middle of a draft and see it highlighted on your screen. You can then choose to print your document with or without the comments showing.

3a Revising content

It is often tempting just to correct errors in spelling and grammar and see the result as a new draft, but revising entails more than simply fixing errors. Reworking a draft to reconsider ideas and logic and to add interest is what revision is all about. Use these proven strategies to improve your writing in substantial ways:

- **Wait.** Don't start revising until you have completed a significant part of your draft.
- **Create distance.** Put aside a draft for at least a few hours or days, and then read it again with fresher, more critical eyes.
- **Consider the context of your writing.** Remind yourself of your intended purpose, your audience's expectations, the elements of your voice that are important to have in the draft, and how the choice of medium might influence the piece of writing.

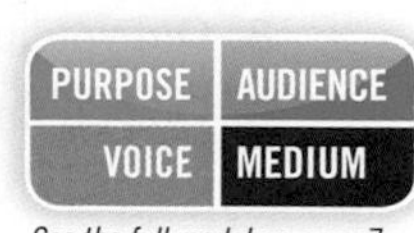

See the full model on page 7.

- **Highlight key words in the assignment.** Mark passages in your draft that address those key words. If you fail to find any, that could signal where you need to revise.
- **Read your draft aloud.** Mark any places where you hesitate and have to struggle to understand the point. Go back to them later. Alternatively, ask somebody else to read a copy of the draft aloud to you and note where he or she hesitates or seems confused.
- **Make an outline.** Outlining what you have written will help you to discover gaps or repetitions.
- **Use the "Triggers for Revision" Key Points box.** These points will alert you to things to look for as you read your draft.

KEY POINTS
Triggers for Revision

Any of the following should alert you to a need for revision:

1. Is the introductory paragraph weak or boring?
2. Do you have a worried frown, a pause, or a thought of "Huh? Something is wrong here" in any spot as you read your draft?
3. Do you find a paragraph that never makes a point?
4. Are there any paragraphs that seem unrelated to the thesis of the essay?

(Continued)

(Continued)

5. Do you read a phrase, a sentence, or a passage that you cannot immediately understand? (If you have trouble grasping your own ideas, readers surely will have trouble, too.)
6. Do you use generalizations excessively—*everyone, most people, all human beings, all students/lawyers/politicians,* and so on? (Instead, use specific examples: *the students in my political science course this semester.*)
7. Do you have a feeling that you would have difficulty summarizing your draft? (Maybe it is too vague?)
8. Did you just read the same point earlier in the draft?
9. Do you fail to find a definite conclusion?

3b Giving and getting feedback

Ask a friend, colleague, or tutor to read your draft with a pencil in hand or the Track Changes feature turned on in the word processor, noting passages that work well and placing a question mark next to those that do not. Ask the reader to tell you what main point you made and how you supported and developed it. This process may reveal any lack of clarity or indicate gaps in the logic of your draft. The reader does not have to be an expert English teacher to give you good feedback. If you notice worried frowns (or worse, yawns) as the person reads, you will know that something in your text is puzzling, disconcerting, or boring. Even that simple level of feedback can be valuable.

If you are asked to give feedback to a classmate or a colleague, use the following guidelines.

KEY POINTS

Giving Feedback to Others

1. Don't think of yourself as an English teacher armed with a red pen. Instead, ask the writer who the intended audience is, and try to read the piece from that perspective.

2. Start by providing positive reactions to ideas and clarity. Look for parts that make you think, I agree, I like this, or This is well done.
3. As you read, mark one or two passages that make you pause and send you back to reread. If you can, write a comment next to those passages that indicates what you would like to have clarified ("I would like to know more about . . ." or "I wasn't sure what you meant by . . .").
4. Try to avoid comments that sound like accusations ("You were too vague in paragraph 3"). Instead, ask questions of the writer ("Could you give a specific example in paragraph 3?"). Questions invite a response, and they'll help the writer revise.

Here is a sample peer response form that can be used to provide feedback.

Draft by ____________________ Date ____________________

Response by ____________________ Date ____________________

1. Who is the audience and what is the purpose for this piece of writing? Consider offering a suggestion if either the audience or purpose is not clearly established.
2. What do you see as the writer's main point in this draft?
3. Which part of the draft interests you the most? Why?
4. Where do you feel you would like more detail or explanation? Where do you need less?
5. Do you find any parts unclear, confusing, or undeveloped? Mark each such spot and write a question in the margin to the writer.
6. Which medium did the author choose for presenting his or her work? Is the medium appropriate, or would you suggest an alternative?
7. Suggest one change that you think would improve the draft the most.

KEY POINTS

Using Track Changes

The Track Changes feature in *Microsoft Word* allows you to see and keep track of changes you make to your own document or to a document that you receive electronically to work on collaboratively. This feature lets you see clearly on the screen and on the printed page the changes you have made. Settings allow you to choose the color of your text inserts and label your comments with whatever initials or name you specify. The Accept Changes and Reject Changes options allow you to accept or reject the changes either individually or all at once.

3c Editing surface features

Once you have developed a solid draft and revised for issues of content and context, you should turn your attention to editing for surface features. Surface features are smaller-order concerns such as grammar, mechanics, and formatting. Paying attention to these issues will help you polish your draft for presentation to your audience.

Drafting and revising a title A good title captures readers' attention, makes them want to read on, and lets them know what to expect in a piece of writing. You might have a useful working title as you write, but after you finish writing, brainstorm several titles and pick the one you like best.

Working title	**The Benefits of Travel**
Revised title	**Beyond Eco-Tourism in Costa Rica**
Working title	**Effects of the Economic Recession in the United States**
Revised title	**Portraits of Persistence: Two Case Studies of Women Searching for Employment during the Recession**

Correcting grammar, punctuation, and spelling Examine your draft for grammar, punctuation, and spelling errors. Often, reading your essay aloud will help you find sentences that are tangled, poorly constructed, or not connected. If you pay attention to your own reading, your hesitations and restarts will flag possible problem areas that are not well constructed or gracefully phrased. Looking carefully at every word and its function in a sentence can also alert you to grammatical problem areas. Part 7 will help you with Standard English and methods for correcting common errors.

KEY POINTS

Computer Tools for Editing

- A **spelling checker** will flag any word it does not recognize, and it is very good at catching typographical errors, such as *teh* for *the* or *responsability* for *responsibility*. However, it will not consistently identify minor grammatical errors, such as missing plural or *-ed* endings. Nor will it flag an omitted word or find a misspelled word that forms another word, such as *then* for *than*, *their* for *there*, or *affect* for *effect*.
- An online **thesaurus** will prompt you with synonyms and words close in meaning to a highlighted word; check suggested words in a dictionary for their connotations to be sure you're choosing the most precise word.
- The **word count** feature of word processing programs is handy when you are given a word limit; it provides an immediate, accurate count.

NOTE FOR MULTILINGUAL WRITERS

Beware of Grammar-Check Programs

Never make a change in your draft at the suggestion of a grammar-check program before verifying that the change is really necessary. A student from Ukraine wrote the grammatically acceptable sentence "What he has is pride." Then, at the suggestion of a grammar-check program, he changed the sentence to "What he has been pride." The program had not recognized the sequence "has is."

See 35b for more on the uses and dangers of grammar-check programs.

3d A student's annotated drafts

Student Catherine Turnbull was assigned to read a chapter of Paul Fussell's book *Uniforms: Why We Are What We Wear* and respond to it. After she wrote a first draft, she read it aloud to a group of classmates and took note of their comments. She also received feedback from her instructor in a conference. Turnbull's first draft of her first two paragraphs and her conclusion shows her notes and annotations for revision.

FIRST DRAFT

Shift from self to topic—get readers interested

Think up better title

Reader Response Essay: Nonmilitary Uniforms

I read the wedding gown chapter from Paul Fussell's assigned book. This chapter covered the history of the white tradition, cost, fanciness, and saving the dress afterwards, etc. This chapter and the idea of the book made me look at the uniforms of people around me. While wedding dresses are intended to be incredibly special and are basically heavy, tight, and uncomfortable, many "real" uniforms are intended to be comfortable, casual, and are team- or job-related.

Say how? Move to end? Expand this point.

Change this

My first example is my aunt, a nurse at a hospital. She wears colorful, baggy, easy-wash scrubs most days, like pajamas with pockets, badge, and a stethoscope. Her name and credentials (RN) are on her badge. She wears super-comfortable shoes because she has to walk miles in the course of making her rounds, day or night. Her uniform says, I am part of the hospital team and am hear to help you. sp

add more details

[Two more paragraphs were included, one on her brother's basketball uniform and another on a train conductor's uniform.]

Move to beginning. Make stronger

~~In sum~~, Paul Fussell writes on wedding dresses in his uniform book, but they are not really uniforms in the sense most working people mean the term. More commonly, uniforms are functional and comfortable garments, symbolizing an active day-to-day role played for the larger good. They make you one with your team and also stand out from the rest of the general populace. Unlike a wedding dress, an average uniform is not so special that it needs special storage. It is what people do and their roles in society that are special.

thesis

choppy

SECOND DRAFT

Comfortable Shoes: Everyday Uniforms
and the People Who Fill Them

Title revised to include word *everyday*

New intro: third person

How many people would call a bridal gown a uniform? Paul Fussell makes this somewhat startling claim in a chapter in a recent book in which he examines the so-called uniform of the formal wedding gown, its history, cost, and traditions, particularly the way it is often stored carefully away for future generations (167–69). He may justify his classification of the wedding dress as a uniform, but that is not the way most people mean the term. Surely it is more common to see uniforms as functional and comfortable garments, symbolizing an active day-to-day role played for a larger good.

Cites author and page

Thesis moved here from last ¶ of first draft

Deletes reference to "my first example"

My aunt, for instance, a nurse at Boston City Hospital, wears colorful, baggy, cotton medical scrubs to work, like pajamas with pockets, a badge, and a stethoscope. She says this outfit is easy to wash, which is important in the hygienic hospital setting. She wears the most comfortable rubber-soled shoes she can find since her job involves a lot of walking in the course of a day, making her rounds. Her name and credentials (RN) are on her badge, letting people know her official status and role as well-trained caregiver. In the past, nurses might have had to dress in white or wear more formal outfits and hats, but today the code is relaxed, with an emphasis on comfort and ease of laundering. Still, no matter how casual, her uniform definitely communicates the message, "I am an experienced member of the hospital team. I am here to help you."

New descriptive details emphasize importance of uniforms

[Turnbull included two more paragraphs.]

Paul Fussell stretches the definition of uniform when he includes wedding gowns. He correctly points out that wedding dresses conform to many set features, but even so they are meant to be as out of the ordinary and beautiful as possible. They are usually expensive, heavy, and snugly fitting, made with impractical fabrics and beads. In contrast, however, most everyday uniforms are loose, comfortable, and inexpensive; they identify wearers as part of a particular team with a particular mission, thus making them stand out from the crowd. Unlike a wedding dress, an average uniform is not so valuable that it needs to be preserved in a special garment bag. It is what people *do* in their uniforms and the roles they have taken on within their larger community that has special value.

Makes a strong point about Fussell

Synthesis of role of uniforms in 3 adjectives

Ends with a strong claim

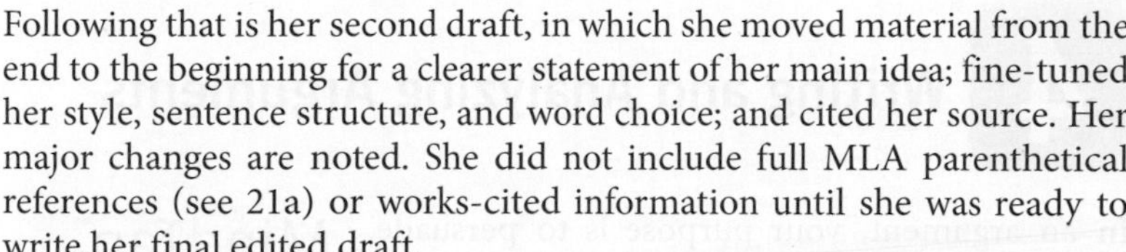

Following that is her second draft, in which she moved material from the end to the beginning for a clearer statement of her main idea; fine-tuned her style, sentence structure, and word choice; and cited her source. Her major changes are noted. She did not include full MLA parenthetical references (see 21a) or works-cited information until she was ready to write her final edited draft.

3e Proofreading

Even after editing carefully with help from computer tools and this handbook, you still need to write a final draft and format it according to the conventions of the discipline you are studying or your instructor's directions. Sections 21a and 21b show how to format a document for page or screen, and chapter 22 shows how to include visuals.

Before you submit or post a written assignment, proofread it carefully one more time to make sure no errors remain.

KEY POINTS
Proofreading Tips

All of these tips will help you spot remaining errors.

- Do not try to proofread on the computer screen. Print out a hard copy.
- Make another copy of your manuscript and read it aloud while a friend examines the original as you read.
- Put a blank piece of paper under the first line of your text. Move it down line by line as you read, focusing your attention on one line at a time.
- Read the last sentence first, and work backward through your text. This strategy will not help you check for meaning, logic, pronoun reference, fragments, or consistency of verb tenses, but it will focus your attention on the spelling, punctuation, and grammatical correctness of each individual sentence.
- If possible, put away your manuscript for a few hours or longer after you have finished it. Proofread it when the content is not so familiar.

Chapters 21, 22, and 25–27 show you how to format and design your document for print or online presentation.

Writing and Analyzing Arguments

MindTap®

Read, highlight, and take notes online.

In an argument, your purpose is to persuade. You present your opinions on an issue as clearly and convincingly as you can. A well-formed argument—one that will persuade readers that your point of view is based on solid evidence—presents a carefully chosen and developed claim (a thesis) along with compelling reasons and supporting evidence specifically geared to the intended audience. The best arguments establish common ground as they consider and address opposing views in a manner that allows those who may have been opposed to save face as they change their minds. A good argument is strategically arranged and written in a voice likely to appeal to an audience's logical, ethical, and emotional inclinations. With such tact and strategy, it is no wonder that argument is called the *art* of persuasion.

But argument is also a *science* of persuasion when you consider that behind a good argument is a writer who has gone through the rigorous process of considering and weighing his or her own assumptions, biases, and quick conclusions. In his introduction to John Brockman's *What Have You Changed Your Mind About?* Brian Eno points out that as an intellectual invention, science is "a construction designed to neutralize the universal tendency to see what we expected to see and overlook what we didn't expect." Although the brilliance of the human brain, he continues, allows us to discern "complex ideas from insubstantial data," the downside is that it all too easily allows us to reach a familiar but wrong conclusion rather than an unfamiliar but right conclusion.

When you write and analyze arguments, you challenge that tendency in yourself and invite others to do the same through a careful weighing of evidence and reason.

Understanding the process of constructing a well-formulated argument goes beyond writing essays for your composition class. As you become more practiced in the process of writing and analyzing arguments in your courses, you become more aware of the arguments all around you—in magazine articles, advertisements, blogs, visually displayed information, letters to publishers, scientific explanations, political opinions, newsletters, and business reports. Understanding the structures and strategies that form arguments is the very essence of what it means to be a critical thinker, reader, and writer.

4a Using critical thinking to read and write arguments

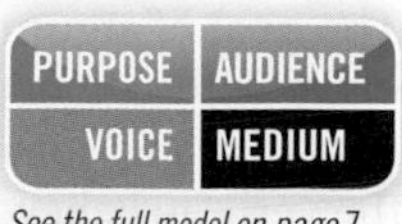

See the full model on page 7.

Whatever your topic, approach it by considering the context of the argument you are developing. Considering your purpose, audience, voice, and use of media will give you a framework for thinking critically as you read, research, and write.

It is a good habit to step back and read an argument critically, whether it is your own or someone else's, to identify its merits and faults. As you read, develop a system of inquiry. Do not assume that because something is in print, it is accurate. Assume that readers will use the same care when they read an argument that *you* write. So put yourself in critical readers' shoes when you evaluate your own arguments. Here are questions to ask while you are analyzing an argument, either your own or someone else's:

1. **What is the writer's purpose?** Is the writer expressing an opinion, arguing for a course of action, making an evaluation, or arguing against another claim?
2. **Who is the writer's audience?** What choices, if any, has the writer made to present the argument persuasively to the intended audience?
3. **Who is the writer?** What is the writer's background and credentials? What is the writer's bias? Is the writer credible?
4. **How reliable are the writer's statements?** Are the writer's statements measured, accurate, fair, and to the point? Do readers feel the need to interject a challenge, using "but..."?
5. **What assumptions does the writer make?** If a writer argues for a college education for everyone, is the underlying assumption that a college education automatically leads to happiness and success?
6. **Does the writer support claims with evidence?** Is the writer relying on extreme language or name-calling rather than presentation of evidence? Does the writer fail to support any part of the claim?
7. **Where does the evidence come from?** Can readers trust the sources? Is the evidence persuasive to the writer's intended audience?
8. **What medium has the writer chosen to deliver the argument?** Is the choice of medium appropriate for the argument? Does it constrain the argument in any way? Would another medium be more appropriate or accessible?

4b Developing an effective argument

The goal of argument is to persuade. We often associate the word *argument* with combat and confrontation, but the Latin root of the word *argue* means "to make clear." The Greek word *persuasion* derives from the verb "to believe." So, in the process of formulating and constructing a good argument, your work lies in making your claim so clear to readers that they may come to believe what you do. Readers need to recognize that the claim you make about your topic rests on solid, reliable evidence and that you have provided a fair, unbiased approach to this evidence. In reading your argument, readers will discover that you have good reasons for your position.

KEY POINTS

The Features of a Good Argument

A good argument

- deals with a controversial, debatable issue
- is not based on strong gut reactions or beliefs but on careful analysis of reliable information
- stands up to a critical reading
- takes a position on, and makes a clear claim about, the topic
- supports that position with detailed and specific evidence (such as reasons, facts, examples, descriptions, and stories)
- establishes common ground with listeners or readers and avoids confrontation
- takes opposing views into account and either refutes them or shows why they may be unimportant or irrelevant
- is engaged and vital, a reflection of the writer's careful, critical thinking rather than just a collection of others' opinions

4c Choosing a topic and developing a claim (thesis)

Choosing a topic Choose an issue that is fresh. Avoid topics such as the death penalty, drug laws, and abortion, which have been written about so often that original or interesting arguments are hard to develop. In addition, choose an issue in which you are interested and invested, but be wary of topics that you might have trouble looking at from multiple perspectives, such as religious and political topics.

Knowing what a thesis statement looks like—and why you need one Suppose someone were to ask you, "What is the main point that you want to communicate to readers in your piece of writing?" The sentence you would give in reply is your *thesis statement*, also known as a *claim*. Your thesis, or claim, tells readers what stand you are going to take on a topic. It won't take you far to say, for instance, "I am interested in writing about sustainable/ethical food sources" if you stop right there and hope that somehow ideas will shoot right out at you. What aspects of sustainable and ethical food practices interest you, and what are the issues? Which readers do you regard as your primary audience? Which geographical areas will you discuss? Will you be concerned with the present or the future? What do you intend to propose about food practices—both about producing food and consuming it? In short, what point will you end up making (purpose) and for which readers (audience)? You don't have to know exactly where to put your thesis statement in your essay right now, but having a thesis will focus your thoughts as you read and write.

A good thesis statement may be one or more of the following:

1. a strong, thought-provoking, or controversial statement

   ▸ **Although food costs can be kept low by producing food in large quantities and shipping it long distances, the benefits are outweighed by the risks to the environment.**

2. a call to action

   ▸ **The best way to promote sustainable production of food is to support legislation that encourages the use of locally grown crops.**

3. a generalization needing support

   ▸ **Ethical production of food sources should focus on humane treatment of animals raised for consumption.**

4. an analytical statement that sets up the structure of the essay

   ▸ **Two examples illustrate the complexity of issues surrounding the humane treatment of animals produced for consumption and the importance of supporting humane treatment: the production of veal and the production of foie gras.**

Keep a working thesis in front of you on a self-stick note or an index card as you write your first draft, but be flexible. You are the boss as you write. You can change and narrow your thesis whenever you like. Many readers will expect to discover your point within the introductory paragraphs of your essay, but your thesis may, in fact, not take shape in your mind until you have read, written, and revised a great deal. A clear thesis may not emerge for you until the end of your first draft, pointing the way to the focus and organization of your next draft.

Formulating an arguable claim (thesis) The position you take on a topic constitutes your thesis or claim. Avoid using any of the following as claims, because they are not debatable:

- a neutral statement, which gives no hint of the writer's position
- an announcement of the paper's broad subject
- a fact, which is not arguable
- a truism (a statement that is obviously true)
- a personal or religious conviction that cannot be logically debated
- an opinion based only on your own feelings
- a sweeping generalization

Here are some examples of nondebatable claims, each with a revision that makes it more debatable.

Neutral statement	**There are unstated standards of beauty in the workplace.**
Revised	**The way we look affects the way we are treated at work and the size of our paychecks.**
Too broad	**This paper is about violence in video games.**
Revised	**Violence in video games has to take its share of blame for the violence in our society.**
Fact	***Plessy v. Ferguson* was overturned in 1954 by *Brown v. Board of Education.***
Revised	**The overturning of *Plessy v. Ferguson* by *Brown v. Board of Education* has not led to significant advances in integrated education.**
Truism	**Bilingual education has advantages and disadvantages.**
Revised	**A bilingual program is more effective than an immersion program at helping students grasp the basics of science and mathematics.**
Personal conviction	**Racism is the worst kind of prejudice.**
Revised	**The best weapon against racism is primary and secondary education.**

Opinion based only on feeling	**I think jet-skiing is a dumb sport.**
Revised	**Jet-skiing should be banned from public beaches.**
Sweeping generalization	**Women understand housework.**
Revised	**The publication of a lengthy guide to housekeeping and its success among both men and women suggest a renewed interest in the domestic arts.**

Avoiding loaded terms In your claim, avoid sweeping and judgmental words—for instance, *bad, good, right, wrong, stupid, ridiculous, moral, immoral, dumb,* and *smart.*

Seeing your thesis as a signpost or indication of where you have been In much academic writing in the humanities and social sciences, a thesis is stated clearly in the essay, usually near the beginning. View your thesis statement as a signpost—both for you as you write your draft and, later, for readers as they read your essay. A clear thesis prepares readers well for the rest of the essay. If you use key words from your thesis as you write, you will keep readers focused on your main idea.

KEY POINTS
A Good Working Thesis

- **answers a question** that is guiding your argument and writing
- **narrows your topic** to a single main idea that you want to communicate
- **makes your point** clearly and firmly in one sentence or two
- **states not simply a fact but, rather, an opinion or a summary conclusion** from your observations
- **makes a generalization that can be supported** by details, facts, and examples within the assigned limitations of time and space
- **stimulates curiosity and interest in readers** and prompts them to wonder, Why do you think that?

Sometimes, though, you may choose to imply your thesis and not state it explicitly. In such a case, you make your thesis clear by the examples, details, and information you include. An essay that details all the beneficial—or harmful—changes to a neighborhood may not need a bald statement that, for example, the South Congress area of Austin has made great strides. You may also choose to state your thesis at the end of your essay instead of at the beginning, presenting all the evidence to build a case and then making the thesis act as a climax and logical conclusion about the outcome of the evidence.

On not falling in love with your thesis Many writers begin with a tentative working thesis and then find that they come to a new conclusion at the end of the first draft. If that happens to you, start your second draft by focusing on the thesis that emerged during the writing of the first draft. Be flexible: it's easier to change a thesis statement to fit new ideas and newly discovered evidence than to find new evidence to fit a new thesis. Note that your final thesis statement should provide a clear answer to a question. Flexibility during the writing process is not the same as indecision in the final product.

LANGUAGE AND CULTURE

Arguments across Cultures: Making a Claim and Staking a Position

Often, writers who have developed their writing skills in one language notice distinct differences in the conventions of writing in another language, particularly with respect to the explicit statement of opinion in the thesis.

The types of arguments described in this section are those common in academic and business settings in North America and the Western world. Writers state their views directly, arguing for their viewpoints. The success of their arguments lies in the credibility and strength of the evidence they produce in support of their arguments. But such an approach is not universal. Other cultures may prefer a less direct approach that begins by exploring and evaluating all options rather than by issuing a direct claim. One of the basic principles of writing well—knowing your audience's expectations—is especially relevant to writing arguments for cultures different from your own.

4d Supporting a claim with reasons and evidence

Supporting your claim means telling readers what reasons, statistics, facts, examples, and expert testimony bolster and explain your point of view. If readers ask "Why do you think that?" about your claim, then the support you offer answers that question in detail.

Reasons Imagine someone saying to you, "Okay. I know your position on this issue, but I disagree with you. What led you to your position?" This is asking you to provide the reasons for your conviction. To begin to answer the question, add at least one "because clause" to your claim.

> **Claim:** Colleges should stop using SAT scores to determine admissions.
>
> **Reason:** (because) SAT scores are biased toward certain demographic groups.
>
> **Claim:** Organized hunting of deer is necessary in suburban areas.
>
> **Reason:** (because) With a diminishing natural habitat, deer are becoming an otherwise uncontrollable hazard to people and property.
>
> **Claim:** A large coal-fired cement factory in a rural scenic region could be an ecological disaster.
>
> **Reason:** (because) Its operation would threaten water, wildlife, and the residents' health.

Once you have formulated a tentative claim, make a scratch outline listing the claim and developing and expanding your reasons for supporting it. As you develop your reasons, consider what your audience will find most convincing. After you have determined some tentative reasons, you will then need to find specific and concrete evidence to explain and support each one.

Concrete evidence You need reasons for supporting your claim, but reasons are not enough. You also need to include specific evidence that supports, illustrates, and explains your reasons. Imagine readers saying, after you give one of your reasons, "How do you know that's true?" Your evidence will make your argument more persuasive by supporting your reasons.

Add to the outline any items of concrete evidence you will include to illustrate and explain your reasoning. What counts as evidence? Facts, statistics, stories, examples, and testimony from experts can all be used as evidence in support of your reasons.

LANGUAGE AND CULTURE

Evidence Used to Support an Argument

The way arguments are structured, the concept of *expertise*, and the nature of evidence regarded as convincing may vary from one culture to another. In some cultures, for example, the opinions of religious or political leaders may carry more weight than the opinions of a scholar in the field. Be sure to consider your audience and what evidence they will accept and find persuasive.

4e Four questions for constructing an argument (Toulmin)

The four questions in the Key Points box, derived from Stephen Toulmin's *The Uses of Argument*, will provide you with a systematic way to construct a logical argument.

KEY POINTS

Four Questions to Ask about Your Argument

1. **What is your claim?** (What is the point you want to make?)
2. **What do you have to go on?** (What reasons can you give for your claim, and what evidence supports those reasons?)
3. **What connections hold your argument together?** (What assumptions—Toulmin calls them *warrants*—would your audience have to accept in order to find your argument persuasive?)
4. **What is getting in the way of your argument?** (What qualifications do you need to include, using *but, unless*, or *if*, or adding words such as *usually, often, several, mostly*, or *sometimes* to provide exceptions to your assumptions?)

Here is an example showing how the Toulmin questions can be used to develop the claim and supporting reasons introduced in 4d:

Claim	**Colleges should stop using SAT scores in their admissions process.**
Support	**(because) SAT scores are biased toward certain demographic groups.**
Assumptions	**Colleges use SAT scores to predict success in college.**
	Colleges should not use measures that are demographically biased.
Qualifier	**. . . unless the colleges use a variety of measures to predict student success.**
Revised claim	**Colleges that use SAT scores to predict college success should consider other measures of student success to balance proven test bias.**

Examine your assumptions Pay special attention to examining assumptions that link a claim to the reasons and evidence you provide. Consider whether readers will share those assumptions or whether you need to explain, discuss, and defend them. Your audience matters. For example, the claim "Internet marketing should be monitored closely because it can violate personal privacy" operates on the assumption that monitoring will catch and reduce abuses. The claim "Internet marketing should be encouraged and supported because it can benefit the economy" operates on the assumption that benefiting the economy is an important goal. These different assumptions will appeal to different readers, and some may need to be persuaded of the assumptions before they attempt to accept your claim or the reasons you give for it.

Note that if your claim is "Internet pop-up ads should be encouraged because they are useful," you are saying little more than "Internet pop-up ads are good because they are good." Readers are certain to object to such circular reasoning and to reject your claim. That is why it is important to ask question 3 from the Key Points box on page 58. That question leads you to examine what assumptions your audience would have to accept in order to find your argument persuasive.

4f Appeals, common ground, and opposing views

You can choose from several approaches to persuade readers as you develop and support your argument. Appeals, common ground, and refutations of opposing positions can all act as support for your argument.

Ask who your readers are First, consider the readers you are writing for. Assess what they might know, what assumptions they hold, what they need to know, how they can best be convinced to accept your position, and what strategies will persuade them to respect or accept your views.

If you are writing for readers who have no specific prior knowledge, biases, or expertise—a *general audience*—remember to include background information: the place, the time, the context, and the issues. Do not assume that general readers know a great deal more than you do.

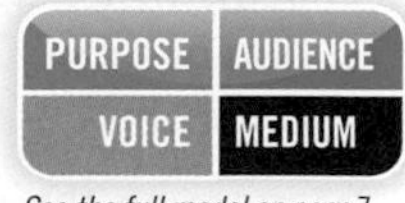

See the full model on page 7.

Appeal to readers Aristotle classified the ways that writers appeal to readers in arguments. Your knowledge of your readers will help you decide what types of appeal to use. Within one extended argument, you may find it necessary to use more than one type of appeal to reach all readers' needs. The examples of the appeals that follow, for example, were used by Peggy Orenstein in a *New York Times Magazine* article in which she argued against a trend in US kindergartens toward increased instruction and testing ("Kindergarten Cram: Toss Out the No. 2 Pencils and Let Them Play." 3 May 2009, p. 13).

Rational appeal (Logos) A rational appeal bases an argument's conclusion on facts, examples, and authoritative evidence. Such an appeal is appropriate for educated readers and is useful when readers are uninformed or hostile.

> *Rational appeal:* Orenstein presents authoritative evidence that assigning homework and testing young children neither predicts nor improves their academic success. In addition, instruction and testing in reading and math take up the time previously allotted to free play, which has proven instrumental not only in children's intellectual development but also in their emotional, psychological, social, and spiritual development. To underscore just how much of a decline in play there is, Orenstein cites a survey of kindergarten teachers. It found that kindergartners spent less than 30 minutes a day playing in comparison to two to three hours a day being instructed or tested in math and reading. In a visual illustration of survey results, a simple, colorful graph effectively displays the shrinking free play of Los Angeles kindergarten classes.

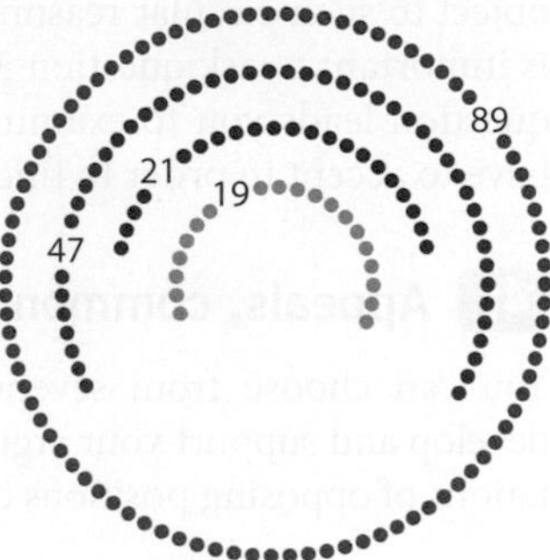

Figure 4.1 A visual illustration of survey results

(For more on the use of visual arguments, see 4i. For more on creating and using tables, charts, and graphs, see chapter 22.)

Appeal to credibility (Ethos) In an appeal to credibility, you represent yourself or any sources you refer to as reliable, experienced, thoughtful, objective, and fair, even when you are considering opposing views. Such an appeal is appropriate for formal situations in business and academic worlds. In advertising, too, ethical appeals often include testimony from famous people, regardless of whether they are experts—for example, Ben and Jerry's uses celebrities such as Stephen Colbert and Jimmy Fallon to promote their ice cream.

> *Appeal to credibility*: Orenstein presents as experts in early childhood education the Alliance for Childhood, a nonprofit research and advocacy group and draws from their report, "Crisis in the Kindergarten." She cites as a reliable source Daniel Pink, a writer on the changing world of work who argues that without the "imagination economy" fostered by among other things, "playfulness," the United States' continued viability in the twenty-first century is at risk. She addresses and refutes opposing views by invoking Jean Piaget, the twentieth century's groundbreaking child psychologist, who famously challenged the American penchant for speeding up children's development.

Emotional appeal (Pathos) In an emotional appeal, you try to gain the empathy and sympathy of readers by assessing their values, and you attempt to persuade them by using descriptions, anecdotes, case studies, and visuals to appeal to those values. Such an appeal is less common in academic writing than in journalism and other media. It is appropriate when readers are regarded as either already favorable to particular ideas or apathetic toward them. Emotional appeals can also be compelling in introductions or conclusions as ways to either grab readers' attention or leave them with a powerful image or thought.

> *Emotional appeal:* Orenstein shares personal anecdotes to establish a bond with her readers. She wants for her child what the *New York Times Magazine*'s readers want for their children. Although she and her readers want their children to grow up ethical, thoughtful, and responsible, they are concerned with how their early education will impact their ability to compete in a future job market. She confesses to her readers, "I wonder how far I'm willing to go in my commitment to the cause: would I embrace the example of Finland—whose students consistently come out on top in international assessments—and delay formal reading instruction until age 7?" Orenstein ends her article on a note that will seal her readers' empathy: her daughter, now enrolled in a school that does not assign homework until fourth grade, has complained that she doesn't have homework like "all the other kids."

Within one extended argument, you will probably find it necessary to use all types of argument to reach the maximum number of readers, each with individual expectations, preferences, and quirks.

Establish common ground Remember that readers who are turned off by exaggerations or extreme language have the ultimate power to stop reading and ignore what you have to say.

KEY POINTS

Ways to Establish Common Ground with Readers

1. **Avoid extreme views or language.** Do not label someone's views as *ridiculous, ignorant, immoral, fascist,* or *crooked,* for example.
2. **Write to convince, not to confront.** Recognize shared concerns, and consider the inclusive use of *we*.
3. **Steer clear of sarcastic remarks** such as "The mayor's office has come up with the splendid idea of building a gigantic parking garage right in the middle of a popular and historic city park."
4. **Use clear, everyday words** that sound as if you are speaking directly to readers.
5. **Acknowledge valid arguments from your opponents,** and work to show why the arguments on your side carry more weight.
6. **If possible, propose a solution** with long-term benefits for everyone.

Refute opposing views It is not enough to present your own reasons and evidence for your claim. When you take into account any opposing arguments and the reasons and evidence that support those arguments, you present yourself as objective and evenhanded, furthering your appeal to credibility. Examine opposing arguments; describe the most common or convincing ones; evaluate their validity, applicability, and limitations; and explain what motivates people to take those positions. Then discuss why you see your reasons and evidence as more pertinent and convincing than those in opposing arguments.

Be careful to argue logically and rationally without insulting your opponents. Take pains to explain rationally why your views differ from theirs. You may choose to do this by following each one of your own points with a discussion of an opposing view. Or you may prefer to devote an entire section of your essay to dealing with opposing views.

4g Structuring an argument

Written arguments are typically structured to follow one of four basic patterns: (1) general to specific, (2) specific to general, (3) problem and solution, and (4) cause and effect.

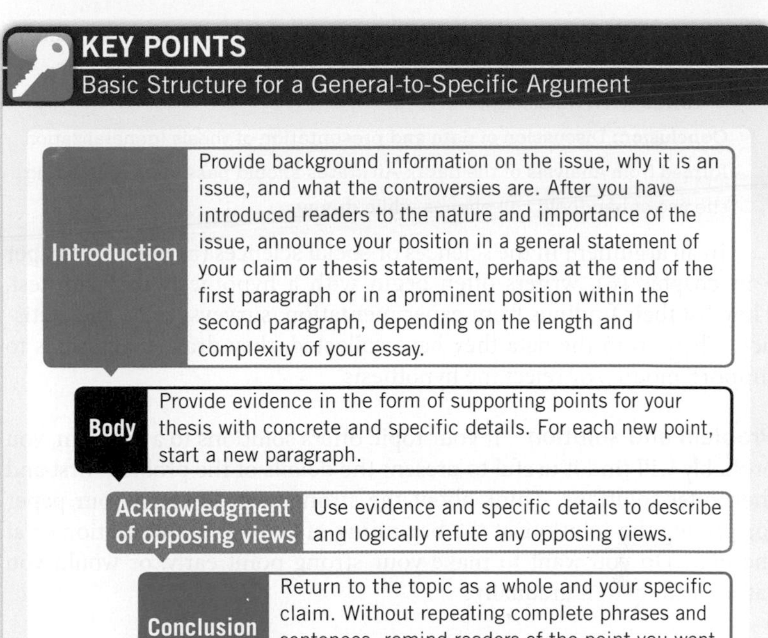

KEY POINTS
Basic Structure for a General-to-Specific Argument
Introduction
Provide background information on the issue, why it is an issue, and what the controversies are. After you have introduced readers to the nature and importance of the issue, announce your position in a general statement of your claim or thesis statement, perhaps at the end of the first paragraph or in a prominent position within the second paragraph, depending on the length and complexity of your essay.
Body
Provide evidence in the form of supporting points for your thesis with concrete and specific details. For each new point, start a new paragraph.
Acknowledgment of opposing views
Use evidence and specific details to describe and logically refute any opposing views.
Conclusion
Return to the topic as a whole and your specific claim. Without repeating complete phrases and sentences, remind readers of the point you want to make. End on a strong note.

General to specific The general-to-specific structure is used frequently in the humanities and arts. It moves from the thesis to support and evidence. Obviously, writers experiment with many variations on this structure, but it is one you can use as a reliable starting point.

Specific to general Alternatively, you may choose to begin with data and points of evidence and then draw a conclusion from that evidence, provided the evidence is relevant and convincing. A basic specific-to-general argument on the topic of driving while using a cell phone looks like this:

Introduction: background, statement of problem and controversy

Data:

1. Cell phone users admit to being distracted while driving (cite statistics).
2. Many accidents are attributable to cell phone use (cite statistics).
3. Several states have passed laws against using handheld cell phones while driving.

4. The National Safety Council attributes at least 28 percent of all traffic accidents (1.6 million accidents) to cell phone use and texting while driving (www.nsc.org).

Conclusion: Discussion of data and presentation of thesis (generalization formed from analysis of the data): All states should pass laws prohibiting the use of handheld cell phones while driving.

In an argument in the sciences or social sciences (as in sample paper 5 in chapter 16), writers often begin with a hypothesis they can test. They list their findings from experimentation, surveys, facts, and statistics. Then, from the data they have collected, they draw conclusions to support, modify, or reject the hypothesis.

Problem and solution If your topic offers solutions to a problem, you probably will find it useful to present the details of the problem first and then offer solutions. Think about the strongest position in your paper for placing the solution: at the beginning of your solutions section or at the end? Do you want to make your strong point early, or would you rather lead up to it gradually?

Cause and effect Writers of arguments in history, art history, and social movements often examine the causes and effects of events and trends to enhance their point of view. The reasoning behind an analysis of causes and effects is far from simple, involving many variables and interpretations. Take care not to reduce your analysis to one simple cause, and avoid the logical fallacy of assuming that one event causes another simply because it precedes it.

4h Logical reasoning, logical fallacies

Reasoning logically As you evaluate the logic of your arguments, assess whether they are valid examples of deductive or inductive reasoning and ensure that they do not fall prey to logical fallacies.

Deductive reasoning The classical Aristotelian method of constructing an argument is based on a reasoning process (a syllogism) that moves from true premises to a certain and valid conclusion.

Major premise	**Coal-fired factories can cause significant damage to the environment.**
Minor premise	**The proposed cement plant will use coal for fuel.**
Conclusion	**The proposed cement plant could cause significant damage to the environment.**

Even if the major premise is not stated, readers must nevertheless accept it as the truth:

Major premise not stated **Since the new proposed cement plant will be coal-fired, it could cause significant damage to the environment.**

The premises must be true for a conclusion to be valid.

Inductive reasoning An inductive argument begins with details that lead to a *probable* conclusion. Inductive arguments are used often in the sciences and social sciences. Researchers begin with a tentative hypothesis. They conduct studies and perform experiments; they collect and tabulate data; they examine the evidence of other studies. Then they draw a conclusion to support, reject, or modify the hypothesis. The conclusion, however, is only probable and not necessarily certain. It is based on the circumstances of the evidence. Different evidence at a different time could lead to a different conclusion. Conclusions drawn in the medical field change with the experiments and the sophistication of the techniques—eggs are called good for you one year but bad the next. That is because the nature of the evidence changes.

Recognizing logical fallacies Faulty logic can make readers mistrust you as a writer. Watch out for some common flaws in logic (called *logical fallacies*) as you write and check your drafts.

Sweeping generalizations Generalizations can sometimes be so broad that they fall into stereotyping. Avoid them.

- **All British people are stiff and formal.**
- **The only thing that concerns students is grades.**

Readers will be right to wonder what evidence has led to these conclusions. Without any explanation or evidence provided, the conclusions will simply be dismissed. Beware, then, of the trap of words like *all*, *every*, *only*, *never*, and *always*.

Hasty conclusion with inadequate support To convince readers of the validity of a generalization, you need to offer enough evidence—usually more than just one personal observation. Thoughtful readers can easily spot a conclusion that is too hastily drawn from flimsy support.

- **My friend Arecelis had a terrible time in a bilingual school. It is clear that bilingual education has failed.**
- **Bilingual education is a success story, as the school in Chinatown has clearly shown.**

Non sequitur *Non sequitur* is Latin for "it does not follow." Supporting a claim with evidence that is illogical or irrelevant causes a non sequitur fallacy.

- **Maureen Dowd writes so well that she would make a good teacher.** (The writer does not establish a connection between good writing and good teaching.)
- **Studying economics is a waste of time. Money does not make people happy.** (Here the writer does not help us see any relationship between happiness and the study of a subject.)

Causal fallacy You are guilty of a causal fallacy if you assume that one event causes another merely because the second event happens after the first. (The Latin name for this logical flaw is *post hoc, ergo propter hoc:* "after this, therefore because of this.")

- **The number of A's given in college courses has increased. This clearly shows that faculty members are inflating grades.** (But does the number of A's clearly show any such thing? Or could the cause be that students are better prepared in high school?)
- **Teachers who give high grades get good student evaluations.** (Could the positive evaluations be caused by something else? Might students with high grades also give bad evaluations?)

Examine carefully any statements you make about cause and effect.

Ad hominem attack *Ad hominem* (Latin for "to the person") refers to unfair ethical appeals to personal considerations rather than to logic or reason. Avoid using arguments that seek to discredit an opinion through criticizing a person's character or lifestyle.

- **The new curriculum should not be adopted because the administrators who favor it have never even taught a college course.**
- **The student who is urging the increase in student fees for social events is a partygoer and a big drinker.**

Argue a point by showing either the logic of the argument or the lack of it, not by pointing to flaws in character. However, personal considerations may be valid if they pertain directly to the issue, as in, "The two women who favor the abolition of the bar own property on the same block."

Circular reasoning In an argument based on circular reasoning, the evidence and the conclusion restate each other, thus proving nothing.

- **Credit card companies should be banned on campus because companies should not be allowed to solicit business from students.**
- **That rich man is smart because wealthy people are intelligent.**

Neither of these statements moves the argument forward. They both beg the question; that is, they argue in a circular way.

False dichotomy or false dilemma Either/or arguments reduce complex problems to two simplistic alternatives without exploring them in depth or considering other alternatives.

- **After September 11, 2001, New York could do one of two things: increase airport security or screen immigrants.**

This proposal presents a false dichotomy. These are not the only two options for dealing with potential terrorism. Posing a false dilemma like this will annoy readers.

4i Using and analyzing visual arguments

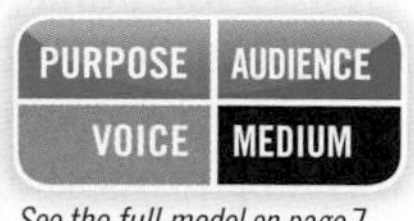

See the full model on page 7.

We commonly think of arguments as spoken or written, but we encounter visual arguments every day. Because of their immediacy and subtle appeals to viewers' reason, emotions, and morals, visual arguments can be as compellingly persuasive as written arguments, if not more so. Whether their purpose is to strengthen an argument or to illustrate an argument in its complexity, writers often choose to supplement their essays with visuals. When you write an argument, consider adding to the impact of your thesis by including visual support.

Using visuals in arguments You can supplement your written arguments with visual arguments: maps, superimposed images, photographs, charts and graphs, political cartoons—vivid images that will say more than many words can to readers.

An argument essay that argues for the health benefits of milk, for example, would make a strong visual impact if it included an image such as the example of tennis stars Venus and Serena Williams in the "Got Milk?" campaign shown in Figure 4.2. The ad implies that milk consumption contributes to their athletic achievements.

Visual arguments make their appeals in ways that are similar to written arguments by appealing to logic, showcasing the character and credentials of the author, or appealing to viewers' emotions. But, unlike written arguments, which present arguments, reasons, and evidence in a linear and logical manner, arguments made in cartoons, advertisements, and works of art can simultaneously pit our logic against our ethics while moving us emotionally.

Figure 4.2 Venus and Serena Williams in the "Got Milk?" campaign

Analyzing visual arguments Photographs of hurricane devastation or of starving children in Africa are carefully chosen to appeal to viewers for donations and can distract viewers from asking important questions like "What exactly will my money be used for?" Analyzing a visual for its unspoken argument or point of view is part of the critical thinking process that underlies good reading and writing.

KEY POINTS

Using Visuals

1. Use visuals in your argument when:
   - the visual serves to strengthen or illustrate your argument
   - your paper focuses on a visual topic (an analysis of an ad, a cartoon, a work of art)
   - your paper relies on visual images for its evidence and support of your argument
2. Choose an appropriate visual in your argument that:
   - has a concrete connection to your argument
   - appeals to readers' reason, emotions, and/or ethics

3. Integrate the visual into your paper by:
    - connecting the visual to your text with a comment
    - locating the visual close to the text that describes it
    - including a caption with the figure number and title or a brief description
    - providing complete documentation in your works-cited page

Figure 4.3 Dr. Phil McGraw in the "Got Milk?" campaign

Consider, for example, the advertisement in Figure 4.3, also from the popular "Got Milk?" campaign. The ad features Dr. Phil McGraw, a mental health professional and former clinical psychologist, who hosts the popular television talk show, *Dr. Phil*. The text to the left of Dr. Phil's image uses his catch-phrase "Get real" to make a claim about milk's potential for helping people lose weight. Dr. Phil says "Get real. About losing weight" above a thumbnail picture in the lower left-hand corner of the ad of Dr. Phil's book, *The Ultimate Weight Solution*. Are the connections among Dr. Phil's credibility, milk, and his book logical ones? Just as written arguments challenge readers to question assumptions and implications, visual arguments push viewers to think critically about the implications and intended effects of images. If a picture is worth a thousand words, it is still up to us to interpret what those words are.

Creating multimedia arguments Present-day technology allows for a new way to express ideas. No longer limited to using type on a page, writers now can use screens to present an interaction of words, color, music, sound, images, and movies to tell a story and make a point.

In preparing a multimedia presentation, consider, then, the effectiveness of juxtaposing images and conveying emotion and meaning through colors and pictures as well as through words. If you use media imaginatively, you can do what writing teachers have long advised: Show, don't just tell.

An outstanding example of a multimedia visual argument was created by undergraduates at the University of Southern California for a course in Near Eastern and Mediterranean archeology. The students chose the ancient city of Troy as the subject of their presentation. Using excavation records, archeological findings, and Homer's texts (as well as architectural modeling software, audio, and virtual reality techniques), the students reconstructed "the citadel as it may have appeared at the time of the Trojan War in the thirteenth century B.C." You can see the story of this fascinating project on *YouTube* at www.youtube.com/watch?v=E0qOzjT2BSY.

4j Sample paper 1: A student's argument essay

Here is a draft of Bibi Bhani Khalsa's argument paper on whether the consumption of milk is necessary, or even healthy, for humans.* The draft is annotated to point out the strategies in her argument. Note how she presents her thesis, supports it, considers and refutes opposing views, and varies her appeals to readers. For her final draft, she included her name and page number as a running head on every page.

Does Everybody Need Milk?

Draws in audience with use of *we* and reference to common experiences

We are bombarded with commercials from the dairy industry telling us that milk is one of the best sources of nutrition and is essential for good health. One popular advertising slogan is "Everybody needs milk." Posters and billboards display this slogan with various pictures: a baby, a muscular man, and even Uncle Sam. We have been told cow's milk is a "perfect food" that helps build healthy bodies and strong bones. Commercials and nutritional guidelines have long told us that we should all consume dairy products daily, beginning at birth, as the advertisement in Fig. 1 shows. Is this true or a myth perpetuated by the dairy industry? We need to know the facts about dairy products so we can make informed decisions about whether or not to consume them. Through

*Used by permission of Bibi Bhani Khalsa.

Blue = description of content, Purple = feedback for writer

Image courtesy of The Advertising Archives

Fig. 1 Carnation Milk ad from the 1940s. Source: Carnation Milk. Advertisement. *Advertising Archives*, www.advertisingarchives.co.uk/index.php?service=search&action=do_quick_search&language=en&q=30529282.

my research I've discovered that many people, including respected physicians, believe that cow's milk products can be harmful to our health and that there are safer ways to get high-quality nutrition. I've also learned that organic and raw milk are superior to conventional dairy products, but they may not be suitable for everyone. I will prove through compelling evidence that, contrary to propaganda from the dairy industry, everybody does not need milk.

Your thesis is stated very clearly.

On its Web site the National Dairy Council lists the eight nutrients and their daily values that are contained in an eight-ounce glass of milk and recommends "3 servings of milk or milk products each day" ("Three Servings of Milk"). Citing data from the USDA and other reputable government organizations, the website reminds us

Blue = description of content, Purple = feedback for writer

that "Milk's essential nutrients can be difficult to replace in a healthy dietary pattern" and lists the following nutrients that are provided in significant amounts in an 8-ounce glass of milk: protein, calcium, phosphorus, potassium, vitamin D, riboflavin, vitamin B12, and vitamin A ("Three Servings of Milk"). Now consider this statistic cited by Irene Jakobsson and Tor Lindberg in an article in the journal *Pediatrics*: it is estimated that "in one third of breast-fed infants, infantile colic is related to cow's milk consumption by the mother" (270). Further, in a European telephone survey of more than 44,000 contacts, 5 million claimed to be allergic to milk (Fiocchi et al. 1120). If so many people have problems with milk, is it really good for us or even a natural source of nutrition for humans?

Includes counterargument

If we observe nature, we see that no other animal consumes the milk of another species. The nutritional elements in cow's milk are suited for calves and not humans (Sears, "Milk Allergies"). Dr. Robert Kradjian, former chief of General Surgery at Seton Medical Center in California, notes that cow's milk has three to four times as much protein as human milk, is five to seven times higher in minerals, and has far fewer essential fatty acids than human milk. He explains that biochemists and physiologists have learned that each species' milk contains the specific elements required for the optimal growth and development of that kind of mammal (Kradjian). Dr. William Sears says that the protein in milk "is suited for bovine intestines" and that it can cause irritation and damage to humans' intestinal lining. When these proteins are absorbed into the circulatory system, they are attacked by the immune system as foreign substances. This reaction can lead to symptoms such as runny nose, rashes, and wheezing and can also cause frequent ear infections, colds, and behavioral changes. Sears says it has been estimated that, when tested, about "75 percent of infants under one year of age were allergic to cow's milk" ("Milk Allergies").

By drawing on several experts from the medical field, you help develop your ethos.

Another famous pediatrician, Dr. Benjamin Spock, also warns against dairy consumption. In the ninth edition of his book *Dr. Spock's Baby and Child Care,* he recommends that vegetables, fruits, grains, and beans should make up the bulk of children's diets and that meat, fish, and dairy products should be limited or avoided. Green leafy

Blue = description of content, **Purple = feedback for writer**

vegetables and beans, he says, contain calcium that is as easily if not more easily absorbed than the calcium in milk is. Whereas milk generally lacks iron, vitamins, complex carbohydrates, and fiber, vegetables and beans are a good source of these nutrients. Spock gave up dairy products himself at age 88 and within two weeks was cured of chronic bronchitis (380). Similarly, Alisa Fleming, author of *Go Dairy Free*, describes her suffering from numerous health problems until an alternative doctor suggested she give up dairy products. She did so, and within days all her symptoms disappeared (6). In my own experience, I've had fewer colds and illnesses since I began following a vegan diet (no meat, fish, eggs, or dairy).

The list of concerns about milk continues. According to Dr. Spock, dairy products contribute to a number of children's health problems since "cow's milk itself . . . is *not* safe for infants" (*Spock's Baby* 321). He points out that in addition to containing little iron itself, milk can cause iron deficiency by interfering with a child's ability to absorb iron (*Spock's Baby* 376). The proteins in cow's milk, he says, are a common cause of colic (*Spock's Baby* 322). Spock also notes that the American Academy of Pediatrics has confirmed evidence that links cow's milk consumption to "constipation, ear infections, and even (in rare cases) type-1 diabetes" (*Spock's Baby* 385). On his Web site Sears tells his readers that studies show "a statistical correlation between young children drinking milk and the later onset of insulin-dependent diabetes" ("Medical Problems"). Spock recommends that after being weaned from breast milk, children should be given soy or rice milk products (*Spock's Baby* 387). There are many great alternatives to dairy products that are much better for our health.

Uses transitions to provide a road map for readers.

Some of these sources are quite dated. Can you find more recent sources to support your argument?

Another concern about dairy products is the hormones they contain. To stimulate milk production, most cows are injected with bovine growth hormone (BGH), a genetically engineered drug. Fifty years ago the average yearly milk production of a cow was 2,000 pounds while today many cows produce up to 50,000 pounds of milk a year (Kradjian). According to an article in *Science* discussing an FDA review of genetically engineered milk, the presence of BGH in milk increases the concentration of IGF-1, an insulin-like growth factor (Juskevich and Guyer 875). This is sobering evidence that should give us pause before

Blue = description of content, **Purple = feedback for writer**

eating that bowl of ice cream or sinking our teeth into a slice of double-cheese pizza.

Other toxic substances found in cow's milk include antibiotics, chemicals, pesticides, and white blood cells, also known as pus. The FDA does not adequately test for these contaminants. According to Kradjian, "authorities test for only 4 of the 82 drugs in dairy cows." Cows frequently get udder infections, or mastitis, which are treated with antibiotics. "Mastic milk" has been found to contain pus cells, which Kradjian argues is acceptable to the FDA.

Continues to consider and refute opposing views

In spite of all this, don't we still need milk to build strong bones and prevent osteoporosis? An article published in *Pediatrics* in 2005 that was based on numerous studies states that there is no conclusive evidence to prove daily consumption of dairy products is beneficial to bone health in children and young adults (Lanou et al. 740). In addition, the Harvard Nurses' Health Study of more than 78,000 women over a period of 18 years showed that increasing milk consumption did not result in lower risk of bone fracture (Feskanich et al. 994–95). To decrease the risk of osteoporosis, the Physicians Committee for Responsible Medicine (PCRM) recommends consuming less animal protein and sodium, eating more fruits and vegetables, exercising, and getting calcium from green leafy vegetables and beans ("Health Concerns").

If all this isn't enough to make us reconsider the benefits of milk, there is more. Depending on the cow's feed, milk can be a source of cholesterol, hydrogenated and saturated fats, and trans fatty acids (Sears, "Fat Content"). The high level of cholesterol and saturated fat in many dairy products increases the risk of heart disease ("Health Concerns"). So why not just consume low-fat or non-fat dairy products? First of all, low-fat milk is not really low in fat: 24 to 33% of its calories come from fat (Kradjian). Secondly, I've observed that even those who use skim or low-fat milk or don't drink milk at all usually won't pass up foods such as pizza, Mexican food, macaroni and cheese, butter, and ice cream. Dairy products are ubiquitous.

For those who can't go without dairy, here are some safer options: organic and raw milk products. *Organic* can mean various things; it can mean the cows were not given antibiotics, were not

Blue = description of content, **Purple = feedback for writer**

given hormones, or were fed organic grain ("Dairies"). Organic milk is better than conventional milk, but organic raw (unpasteurized) milk is better still. Pasteurizing milk means heating it, which can "destroy almost all of the nutritive value of cow's milk," according to Edward Group, founder of The Global Healing Center. Dr. William Campbell Douglass II writes:

> There are many indications that raw milk consumption can relieve allergies, asthma, digestive disorders—even autism. That's a lot of power in one glass of milk. So it's no wonder that smart folks everywhere are ignoring the warnings and seeking out the small, organic dairies that sell raw milk ("Raw Milk's Popularity").

His book *The Raw Truth about Real Milk* talks about milk in historical terms and connects modern illnesses to pasteurization. Dr. Thomas Cowan, a family practitioner in New Hampshire, also supports the use of raw milk. He harkens back to the "pre-processed food era" in the US before the 1930s when people drank fresh raw milk. He claims there were very few cases of coronary artery disease and prostate or breast cancer then. According to Cowan, the problem with dairy products is pasteurization, not the milk itself ("Raw Milk"). Kradjian, however, warns that raw milk may be contaminated with E. coli, salmonella, and staphylococcus bacteria (Kradjian). And even raw milk is better suited for calves than for human beings. We really don't need milk at all.

Uses counterargument to bring closure to section and provide transition into conclusion

We have been conditioned through advertising and education to believe that dairy products are essential to build strong bones and bodies. But when we examine the facts, we see that this assertion is far from the truth. Everybody does *not* need milk, and many do much better without it. Milk allergies and lactose intolerance are widespread. Heart disease, diabetes, osteoporosis, and several forms of cancer have been linked to dairy consumption ("Health Concerns"). Do we really want to risk our children's health and our own when there are much safer ways to get the nutrition we need? If you do choose to eat dairy products, find a source of uncontaminated, organic raw milk. And if you want milk on your cereal or in your coffee, use the kind made from soy, whole grains, or nuts.

This might be more effective as a statement instead of opening the door for your audience to answer no.

Blue = description of content, **Purple = feedback for writer**

Works Cited

Cowan, Thomas. "Raw Milk." *AnthroMed Library*, Physicians' Association for Anthroposcopic Medicine (PAAM), 2009, www.anthromed.org/Article.aspx?artpk=512.

"Dairies: Conventional to Organic and Everything in Between." *Dairy Good*, National Dairy Council, 8 Jan. 2016, dairygood.org/content/2014/conventional-to-organic-and-everything-in-between-our-nations-dairy-farms.

Douglass, William Campbell, II. "Raw Milk's Popularity Growing by Leaps and Bounds." *Daily Dose with Jack Harrison*, 14 May 2008, jacksdailydose.com/2008/05/14/raw-milks-popularity-growing-by-leaps-and-bounds/.

---. *The Raw Truth about Milk*. Rhino Publishing, 2007.

Feskanich, Diane, et al. "Milk, Dietary Calcium, and Bone Fractures in Women: A Twelve-Year Prospective Study." *American Journal of Public Health*, vol. 87, no. 6, 1997, pp. 992-97. *Academic Search Complete,* ISSN:0090-0036.

Fiocchi, Alessandro, et al. "DRACMA (Diagnosis and Rationale for Action against Cow's Milk Allergy): A Summary Report." *Journal of Allergy and Clinical Immunology*, vol. 126, no. 6, pp. 1119-28. dx.doi.org/10.1016/j.jaci.2010.10.011.

Fleming, Alisa. *Go Dairy Free: A Guide and Cookbook for Milk Allergies, Lactose Intolerance, and Casein-Free Living*. Fleming Ink, 2008.

Group, Edward. "Pasteurized vs. Raw Milk: Which One Is Healthier for You and Your Family?" *Global Healing Center*, 28 Sept. 2009, www.globalhealingcenter.com/natural-health/raw-milk-vs-pasteurized-milk/.

"Health Concerns about Dairy Products." *PCRM: Physicians Committee for Responsible Medicine*, www.pcrm.org/health/diets/vegdiets/health-concerns-about-dairy-products.

Jakobsson, Irene, and Tor Lindberg. "Cow's Milk Proteins Cause Infantile Colic in Breast-Fed Infants: A Double-Blind Crossover Study." *Pediatrics*, vol. 71, no. 2, 1983, pp. 268-71. *Academic Search Complete,* ISSN: 0031-4005.

Blue = description of content, Purple = feedback for writer

Juskevich, Judith C., and C. Greg Guyer. "Bovine Growth Hormone: Human Food Safety Evaluation." *Science*, vol. 249, no. 4971, 24 Aug. 1990, pp. 875-84. *JSTOR*, www.jstor.org.ezproxy1.library.arizona.edu/stable/2877952.

Kradjian, Robert. "The Milk Letter: A Message to My Patients." *Notmilk*, Robert Cohen, www.notmilk.com/kradjian.html.

Lanou, Amy Joy, Susan E. Berkow, and Neal D. Barnard. "Calcium, Dairy Products, and Bone Health in Children and Young Adults: A Reevaluation of the Evidence." *Pediatrics*, vol. 115, no. 3, pp. 736-43. *Academic Search Complete*, DOI:10.1542/peds.2004-0548.

Sears, William. "Facts about Fat." *Ask Dr. Sears*, William Sears and Martha Sears, 2011, www.askdrsears.com/topics/feeding-eating/family-nutrition/facts-about-fats/17-more-fat-facts-you-should-know.

---. "Medical Problems." *Ask Dr. Sears*, William Sears and Martha Sears, 2011, www.askdrsears.com/topics/feeding-eating/feeding-infants-toddlers/milk/medical-problems.

---. "Milk Allergies." *Ask Dr. Sears*, William Sears and Martha Sears, 2011, www.askdrsears.com/topics/feeding-eating/feeding-infants-toddlers/milk/milk-allergies.

Spock, Benjamin. *Dr. Spock's Baby and Child Care.* 9th ed., Pocket Books, 2011.

"Three Servings of Milk Delivers a Unique Nutrient Package." *National Dairy Council*, 1 Jan. 2016, www.nationaldairycouncil.org/Content/2015/Three-Servings-of-Milk-Delivers-A-Unique-Nutrient-Package.

Blue = description of content, **Purple = feedback for writer**

Writing in Academic Disciplines

MindTap® Read, highlight, and take notes online.

Writing is required in many, if not most, college courses. In fact, colleges and universities that emphasize the importance of writing often have initiatives or programs that are commonly referred to as Writing across the Curriculum (WAC) or Writing in the Disciplines (WID), which encourage instructors in a broad array of disciplines to require writing in their courses.

5a Writing in all your courses

Writing can be a way to explore what you know, to discover new ideas, and to assess what you have learned. Instructors in many of your courses in college may use writing for these purposes, to help you learn and master the subject matter in the course. You can expect to write both low-stakes (usually ungraded or with a minor amount of credit) and high-stakes (carrying more assessment weight) assignments in your college courses. When you are given a writing assignment in a college course, be sure to determine how much weight is given to the assignment and what the instructor's expectations are.

5b Writing to join academic conversations

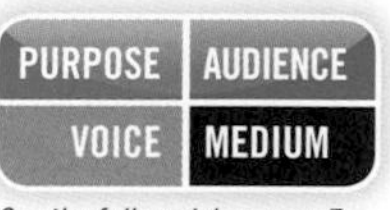

See the full model on page 7.

One semester you may be writing about *Hamlet*, and the next semester you may be exploring the census, writing about Chopin's music, discussing geological formations, researching the history of the civil rights movement, or preparing a paper on Sigmund Freud and dreams. You may be expected to write scientific laboratory reports or to manipulate complex statistical data and to use a style of documentation different from one you learned in an English course. Find out which style of writing and documenting is expected in each of your courses. Each discipline has specific expectations for the genres that are most common.

KEY POINTS

The Cultures of the Academic Disciplines

When you take a course in a new discipline, you are joining a new academic community with established conventions and ways of thinking and writing. Use the following strategies to get acquainted with the discipline's conventions.

- Listen carefully to lectures and discussions; note the specialized vocabulary used in the discipline. Make lists of new terms and definitions.
- Read the assigned textbook and note the conventions that apply in writing about the field.
- Use subject-specific dictionaries and encyclopedias to learn about the field. Examples include the *Encyclopedia of Religion* and the *Encyclopedia of Sociology*.
- When given a writing assignment, make sure you read samples of similar types of writing in that discipline.
- Look at published writing in that field by reading articles from scholarly journals.
- Talk with your instructor about the field, its literature, and readers' expectations.

5c Sample paper 2: A student's analysis of academic essays across disciplines

If you take a look at how publications from different disciplines cover the same event, you'll get a good idea of the ways various disciplines use language and evidence differently. That's exactly what Charles Brooks does in this essay about the Chernobyl nuclear disaster. Because the disaster happened in 1986, it wasn't necessarily important that he locate recent articles, but he assesses the focus, organization, language use, and tone of academic essays in three disciplines to understand what the expectations are for writing in those disciplines.

Charles Brooks

Professor Shawna Jones

ENG 101

24 April 2016

Differences in Chernobyl Articles

Introduction provides a basic overview of the differences between the three disciplinary areas

Generally speaking, there are three disciplines into which academic pursuits can fall. Natural sciences concern themselves with the physical world, and include subjects such as biology, physics, or engineering. Social sciences focus their pursuits on humans and how they interact with each other and the world around them. Psychology, anthropology, and economics can all be categorized as social sciences. The third academic discipline encompasses fields such as art, language, and philosophy, and is known as the humanities. The humanities explore the way humans experience the world. Each of these disciplines demands a different style of writing for their audiences.

In order to examine the differences between the published research in each of these disciplines, I consider three articles written about the same general topic, but from the perspective of each academic discipline. The natural science article, "Chromosome Alterations in Cleanup Workers Sampled Years after the Chernobyl Accident," written by Elizaveta Neronova, Natalia Slozina and Alexey Nikiforov, was published by *Radiation Research* in 2003. In the December 2007 edition of *Acta Psychiatrica Scandinavica*, a social sciences article entitled "Chernobyl Exposure as Stressor during Pregnancy and Behaviour in Adolescent Offspring" was published and credited to authors Anja C. Huizink, Danielle M. Dick, Elina Sihvola, Lea Pulkkinen, Richard J. Rose, and Jaakko Caprio. Finally, "Lessons of Chernobyl: The Cultural Causes of the Meltdown" is a humanities article written by Sergei P. Kapitza and published in *Foreign Affairs* in 1993. All of these articles are written about some aspect of the Chernobyl accident of 1986, but they differ in their foci, their organization, and the diction used by the authors.

This introduction to your topic would be useful before you list the three articles.

Blue = description of content, **Purple = feedback for writer**

One aspect of an academic article that will always differ between the disciplines is its specific focus. One could even venture to say that an article's focus determines the discipline whose writing style it will follow. "Chromosome Alterations" reports on an experiment which tested chromosome alterations in Chernobyl cleanup workers and found that "different types of unstable chromosomal aberrations were found in Chernobyl cleanup workers many years after their exposure to low-dose radiation" (Neronova et al. 50). This article falls under natural science because it explores how the radioactive environment has physically affected a particular group of people. The article "Chernobyl Exposure" certainly explores Chernobyl's effects on people, but not physically. Instead, this social sciences article looked at "the potential harmful effect of in utero exposure to the Chernobyl disaster in April 1986, and maternal anxiety associated with that exposure, on symptoms of behaviour disorder observed at age 14" (Huizink et al. 439). The focus on emotional response to radiation exposure is typical of research done in the social sciences. The third article, "Lessons of Chernobyl," does not place its focus on the effects of Chernobyl, but rather explores the causes. This is not the main difference, however. The aspect of this article that sets it apart most from its scientific brethren is the lack of experimentation. The article features a thoughtful discussion about whether the Chernobyl disaster was an inevitable outcome produced by the Soviet culture of that time.

Defines how the natural sciences explore questions about the natural world

Can you say more about why that is typical of the social sciences?

While an article's focus directly reflects its discipline, focus is not the only distinguishing feature of an academic article. When reading an academic article, one rarely makes note of the article's organization even though the organization plays an instrumental role in the way the reader experiences the article. All three of these articles are divided into headed sections, but the similarity between the social and natural science articles is more significant. These two articles share the exact same headings: Introduction, Materials and Methods, Results, Discussion, Acknowledgments, and References. This organization and these headings are indicative of lab reports. These articles, as is the case with most social and natural science research, are reporting the

Blue = description of content, Purple = feedback for writer

procedure and results of experiments that were conducted. It is important that professionals in these disciplines use this standardized format to report their experimental findings, because the objective of these reports is not only exposition, but also confirmation and potential replication. These reports are meant to provide other scientists with a guide to replicate the experiment and possibly the results. There is a slight addition to these headings within "Chernobyl Exposure." Each of the sections mentioned above is further divided into subsections. For instance, the "Material and Methods" section is divided into the following headings: Sample, Procedure, and Statistical Analyses. While these extra subheadings are not necessary, they do present the reader with a more organized, lucid experience with the article.

Explores both the similarities and differences between research in different disciplines

While the humanities article is organized into headed sections, it does not follow the scientific formula. Humanities writers are afforded much more freedom in their organization because they have different objectives than the writers of scientific articles. Instead of presenting data acquired through experiments, humanities articles often explore ideas or present an argument. In the case of "Lessons of Chernobyl," the idea that Soviet culture was responsible for the Chernobyl disaster is explored in depth, but without one referential staple of the science articles: documentation. While Kapitza does include two footnotes, one describing his own qualifications and another providing extra detail, he does not give any sources for his material. This lack of references does not leave the reader doubting the article's credibility, however. Upon further examination, Kapitza's mini-biographical footnote reveals that he is a "Professor of Physics at the Institute for Physical Problems, [of the] Russian Academy of Sciences" (7). This implies that Kapitza was a part of the Soviet culture he describes, and likely involved in the Soviet nuclear program. This would make references a moot point, because the article is a personal account of what he experienced and observed.

Your clarification of the prior point is a nice transition into the final section.

Although this particular article is free of sources and a documentation style, one cannot assume that all humanities research is so. Likewise, one cannot assume that all humanities articles share the same tonal and diction attributes. A humanities writer can

Blue = description of content, **Purple = feedback for writer**

exercise much more freedom with language. Tone and attitude can be incorporated, and sentence structure can be varied. Kapitza writes, "Apart from disregarding all formal instructions and rules, the engineers and administrators involved displayed a total lack of understanding of nuclear power reactor physics" (Kapitza 9). This sentence demonstrates the subjectivity that can, and often does, present itself in writing in the humanities. Kapitza uses strong language and an almost condescending tone to place blame on the "engineers and administrators." Kapitza is also free to use figurative language, like hyperbole: ". . . every possible safety rule was broken . . ." (9). All of these freedoms of language combine to make humanities articles a generally more enjoyable reading experience, at least to the general public, than literature from the scientific disciplines.

Writers hoping to get their research published in the natural or social sciences can expect much stricter standards for their writing style. Authors in the sciences are expected to be as objective as possible. While science writers are limited to a certain tone, they are free to use as much technical jargon as they see fit. These articles are meant for other professionals in a given field, and thus the reader should not require any further explanation. The article in *Radiation Research* includes this sentence: "To estimate cytogenetic damage from ionizing radiation in Chernobyl cleanup workers, unstable chromosomal aberrations in peripheral blood lymphocytes were studied" (Neronova et al. 47). If this had been written for the general public, much of the preceding sentence would require explanation. This sentence also exemplifies the passive voice that is used throughout the natural sciences article, especially in the "Materials and Methods" section of the article. Passive voice is often used in natural science articles because it places the emphasis on the object receiving the action instead of the performer of the action, which is insignificant in natural science experiments.

Identifies language and style features typical of the natural sciences

In contrast, an article written in the social sciences will have much more active voice, because nothing in a psychological experiment is insignificant. Seemingly insignificant details, such as the type of chair the participants sit in, can skew the results. The authors of the social science article, "Chernobyl Exposure," write,

This is not always the case, so you might want to hedge this claim by saying "often."

Blue = description of content, **Purple = feedback for writer**

"Because the distribution of symptom counts was skewed, we used Poisson regression analyses, yielding an incidence rate ratio (IRR) and its 95% confidence interval (CI)" (Huizink et al. 441). This sentence is a great example of both passive and active voice, but also first person point-of-view and a bit of technical jargon.

First person perspective was barely used in "Chromosome Alterations," and even then only in the "Discussion" section of the article. This is not the case in "Chernobyl Exposure"; while first person is used sparingly, it appears throughout the article. The jargon used in this social science article is not quite as frequent as it was in "Chromosome Alterations," but would still raise questions in readers outside of the field.

Because of the technical jargon, objective tone, standardized organization, and highly specific subject matter, one could label "Chromosome Alterations" and "Chernobyl Exposure" as being "reader unfriendly," while "Lessons of Chernobyl" is more "reader friendly" because of its broad focus, flowing organization, and varied writing style. While this may be the case to the general reader, each of these articles has a specific purpose, and each of these articles fulfills its purpose effectively for their specific audiences.

New page in final MLA draft

Works Cited

Huizink, Anja C., et al. "Chernobyl Exposure as Stressor during Pregnancy and Behaviour in Adolescent Offspring." *Acta Psychiatrica Scandinavica*, vol. 116, no. 6, 2007, pp. 438–46. *Academic Search Complete,* DOI:10.1111/j.1600-0447.2007.01050.x.

Kapitza, Sergei P. "Lessons of Chernobyl: The Cultural Causes of the Meltdown." *Foreign Affairs*, vol. 72, no. 3, 1993, www.foreignaffairs.com/articles/russian-federation/1993-06-01/lessons-chernobyl-cultural-causes-meltdown.

Neronova, Elizaveta, et al. "Chromosome Alterations in Cleanup Workers Sampled Years after the Chernobyl Accident." *Radiation Research*, vol. 160, no. 1, 2003, pp. 46-51. *JSTOR,* www.jstor.org/stable/3581233.

Blue = description of content, **Purple = feedback for writer**

5d Writing and researching in the humanities and arts

Courses in the humanities generally focus on questions about interpretation and understanding the human experience. Classes you might take in the humanities could include literature, history, music, philosophy, and religion, to name a few.

Writing in the humanities is generally driven by a clear thesis or claim, supported by reasons and evidence. The evidence is often drawn from texts such as novels, poems, essays, works of art, or historical artifacts. The following guidelines will help you effectively write papers in your humanities courses.

GUIDELINES

- Consult primary sources first, such as original works of literature, or attend original performances, such as plays, films, poetry readings, and concerts.
- Form your own interpretations of works. The first person *I* is used in personal and expository writing in the humanities more than in other disciplines. Consult your instructor, though, before using the first person.
- Use secondary sources (works of criticism) only after you have formed your own interpretations and have established a basis for evaluating the opinions expressed by others. Secondary sources can provide additional support for an interpretation.
- Look for patterns and interpretations supported by evidence, not for one right answer to a problem.
- Use the present tense to refer to what writers have said: *Emerson points out that. . . .*
- Use MLA guidelines (chapters 11–13) or *The Chicago Manual of Style* (chapters 19–20) for documentation style. These documentation styles are most common in the humanities.

5e Writing about literature

When you are asked to write about literature, pay careful attention to the content and form of the work of literature by reading the work more than once and highlighting significant passages. Then use the Key Points box on pages 86–87 to help you systematically analyze the work.

Here are some basic guidelines for writing about literature, followed by more specific guidelines for analyzing fiction, nonfiction, poetry, and drama.

- **Assume a larger audience than just your instructor.** Think of readers as people who have read the work but have not thought of the issues you did.
- **Make sure that you formulate a thesis.** Do not devote a large part of your essay to summary; assume that readers have read the work. Occasionally, though, you may need to include a brief summary of the whole or parts of the work to orient readers. Make sure you tell them not only what is in the work but also how you perceive and interpret important aspects of the work.
- **Turn to the text for evidence, and do so often.** Text references, in the form of paraphrase or quotation, provide convincing evidence to support your thesis. But do not let your essay turn into a string of quotations.

KEY POINTS

Ten Ways to Analyze a Work of Literature

1. **Plot or sequence of events** What happens and in what order? What stands out as important?
2. **Theme** What is the message of the work, the generalization that readers can draw from it? A work may, for example, focus on making a statement about romantic love, jealousy, sexual repression, courage, ambition, revenge, dedication, treachery, honor, lust, greed, envy, social inequality, or generosity.
3. **Characters** Who are the people portrayed? What do you learn about them? Do one or more of them change, and what effect does that have on the plot or theme?
4. **Genre** What type of writing does the work fit into—parody, tragedy, love story, epic, sonnet, haiku, melodrama, comedy of manners, or mystery novel, for example? What do you know about the features of the genre, and what do you need to know? How does this work compare with other works in the same genre? What conventions does the author observe, violate, or creatively vary?
5. **Structure** How is the work organized? What are its major parts? How do the parts relate to each other?

6. **Point of view** Whose voice speaks to readers and tells the story? Is the speaker or narrator involved in the action or an observer of it? How objective, truthful, and reliable is the speaker or narrator? What would be gained or lost if the point of view were changed?
7. **Setting** Where does the action take place? How are the details of the setting portrayed? What role, if any, does the setting play? What would happen if the setting were changed?
8. **Tone** From the way the work is written, what can you learn about the way the author feels about the subject matter and the theme? Can you, for example, detect a serious, informative tone, or is there evidence of humor, sarcasm, or irony?
9. **Language** What effects do the following have on the way you read and interpret the work: word choice, style, imagery, symbols, and figurative language?
10. **Author** What do you know, or what can you discover through research, about the author and his or her time, and about the author's other works? Does what you discover illuminate this work?

Writing about prose As you read novels, short stories, memoirs, biographies, and autobiographies, consider these basic questions for thinking about what you read: What happened? When and where did it happen? Who did what? How were things done? Why? Then extend your inquiry by considering the ten options for analyzing literature in the preceding Key Points box in addition to the following:

- **Narrator** What is the author's attitude to, and depiction of, the narrator: omniscient, deceived, observant, truthful, biased, crazy?
- **Style** What do you notice in regard to the author's word choice, sentence length and structure, and significant features?
- **Imagery** What effect do the figures of speech, such as similes, metaphors, and others, have on you? (see pp. 88–89 and section 32e)
- **Symbols** Are there objects or events in the work that have special significance?
- **Narrative devices** How, if at all, does the author use foreshadowing, flashback, leitmotif (a recurring theme), alternating points of view, turning point, and dénouement (outcome of plot)?

Writing about poetry In addition to using some of the suggestions relating to prose, consider the following factors when you analyze a poem:

stanza: lines set off as a unit of a poem

rhyme scheme: system of end-of-line rhymes that you can identify by assigning letters to similar final sounds—for example, a rhyme scheme for couplets (two-line stanzas), *aa bb cc;* and a rhyme scheme for a sestet (a six-line stanza), *ababcc*

meter: number and pattern of stressed and unstressed syllables (or *metric feet*) in a line. Common meters are trimeter, tetrameter, and pentameter (three, four, and five metric feet, respectively). The following line is written in iambic pentameter (five metric feet, each with one unstressed and one stressed syllable):

> Bright Stár/wŏuld Í/wĕre stéd-/făst ás/thŏu árt —John Keats

foot: unit (of meter) made up of a specific number of stressed and unstressed syllables

Writing about drama As you prepare to write about a play, use any of the relevant points listed for prose and poetry, and in addition, focus on the following dramatic conventions:

structure of the play: acts and scenes

plot: episodes, simultaneous events, chronological sequence, causality, climax, and turning point

characters: analysis of psychology, social status, and relationships

setting: time, place, and description

time: real time depicted (all action takes place in the two hours or so of the play) or passage of time

stage directions: details about clothing, sets, actors' movements, expressions, and voices; information given to actors

scenery, costumes, music, lighting, props, and special effects: purpose and effectiveness

presentation of information: recognition of whether the characters in the play know things that the audience does not or whether the audience is informed of plot developments that are kept from the characters

Figurative language The writers of literary works often use figures of speech to create images and intensify effects.

metaphor: implied comparison, with no *like* or *as*

The still, sad music of humanity —William Wordsworth

The winter of our discontent —William Shakespeare

simile: type of metaphor, but with two sides stated

Like as the waves make towards the pebbled shore,
So do our minutes hasten to their end. —William Shakespeare

The weather is like the government, always in the wrong. —Jerome K. Jerome

Playing for teams other than the Yankees is "like having a crush on Cinderella but dating her ugly stepsisters." —David Wells (when a Yankees pitcher)

irony: mismatch of words and meaning, meaning the opposite

Yet Brutus says he was ambitious;
And Brutus is an honourable man. —William Shakespeare, Julius Caesar

metonymy: substitution of one term for another that is closely associated with it

Democrats don't like Wall Street bailouts.
Republicans don't like Wall Street bailouts.
The American people are disgusted by Wall Street bailouts. —Elizabeth Warren

The *pen* is mightier than the *sword.*

synecdoche: use of a part for the whole or the whole for a part

The ranch owner rode into town with thirty *head* of cattle and two hired *guns.*

oxymoron: contradiction, as in "clean coal"

alliteration: repetition of consonant sounds

He bravely breach'd his boiling bloody breast. —William Shakespeare

assonance: repetition of vowel sounds

And feed deep, deep upon her peerless eyes —John Keats

onomatopoeia: sound of word associated with meaning

murmuring of innumerable bees —Alfred, Lord Tennyson

personification: description of a thing as a person

Deep, dying groans the aged year breathed forth —Alice Moore-Dunbar Nelson

zeugma: a word that modifies more than one other word in different senses, forming different and often humorous logical connections

The art dealer departed in anger and a Mercedes.

He came out in a top hat and a rash.

For more on using figurative language, see 32e.

KEY POINTS

Common Conventions in Writing about Literature

- **Tense** Use the present tense to discuss works of literature even when the author is no longer alive.
- **Authors' Names** Use an author's full name the first time you mention it: *Jesmyn Ward*. Thereafter, and always in parenthetical citations, use only the last name: *Ward*, not *Jesmyn*.
- **Author/Narrator Distinction** Make a clear distinction between the author and the narrator. The narrator is the person telling a story or serving as the voice of a poem and does not necessarily express the author's views. Often, the author has invented the persona of the narrator. Keep the terms distinct.
- **Titles of Works** Underline or italicize the titles of books, journals, and other works published as an entity and not as part of a larger work. Use quotation marks to enclose the title of a work forming part of a larger published work: short stories, essays, articles, songs, and short poems.
- **Quotations** Integrate quotations into your text, and use them to help make your point. Avoid a mere listing and stringing together: "Walker goes on to say. . . . Then Walker states. . . ." When you are quoting two or three lines of poetry, separate lines with a slash (/). When you are using long quotations (more than three lines of poetry or four typed lines of prose), indent the lines one-half inch, but do not add quotation marks; the indentation signals a quotation.

5f Sample paper 3: A student's literature paper

The following draft of an essay was written by sophomore Brian Cortijo for a course on multicultural American literature. The assignment was to compare and contrast two collections of stories according to the way they present a concept of identity and to focus on the texts themselves without turning to secondary sources. Cortijo was writing for his instructor and classmates, all of whom were familiar with the stories, so summary was unnecessary. He decided to focus on three of the ten areas in the Key Points box on pages 86–87: theme, setting, and language, specifically symbols. The draft is documented according to MLA style; in a later draft, the writer added a paper identification and a page break for the works-cited list. For more on this and MLA format for a final draft, see 21a and chapters 11–13.

Identity and the Individual Self

While distinct in their subject matter, the collections of stories presented in Sherman Alexie's *The Lone Ranger and Tonto Fistfight in Heaven* and Edwidge Danticat's *Krik? Krak!* are strikingly similar in the responses they evoke and in their ability, through detached or seemingly detached narratives, to create a sense of collective selfhood for the peoples represented in those narratives. Through connected stories, repetition of themes and events, shifting of narrative voice and honest, unapologetic discussion of the problems and the beauty of their personal experiences, Danticat and Alexie provide frank, cohesive portrayals of a Haitian and Native American peoplehood, respectively.

Introduces the works with complete names of authors

Refers to setting and theme

After first mention, uses last names only

Your thesis provides a useful outline of how readers will expect argument to progress.

While it may not be the intention of these authors to address such a collective identity, it is clear that each is working from some conception of what that identity is, if not what it should be. Each author has symbols and characters that are used to display the identity in all its glory and shame, all its beauty and horror. For Alexie, both characters and objects are used, each for its own purpose. Most notable among these are Thomas Builds-the-Fire, a symbol of spirituality; Norma, who remains uncorrupted by the life

Points out how theme is addressed

You're consistently referring to published work in the present tense. Great job!

Analyzes symbols

Blue = description of content, **Purple = feedback for writer**

Integrates quotation smoothly

imposed on the Indian peoples; and the seemingly ubiquitous drum, a symbol of religion that, if played, "might fill up the whole world" (23). Danticat, by contrast, concentrates more on objects than on characters to embody the ideals and the fears of the identity she is constructing through her narrative. The most prominent among these symbols are the bone soup, braids, and, more generally, hair.

Your references to the text and characters are helpful for the development of your argument.

Danticat's use of the bone soup in her last story, "Caroline's Wedding," and of the braids in her "Epilogue: Women Like Us" is of paramount importance to any claim of Haitian peoplehood, or Haitian womanhood, that she might try to make. The use of these elements is indicative of the loving imposition and inclusion of past generations into one's own, as well as the attempt to pass down all that has gone before to those who will one day bear the burden of what that past means. Thus, Hermine's soup is her daughter Gracina's soup as well, not because she eats of it but because those bones—that ancestry—are a part of her and she will one day be responsible for passing them (and it) on. Likewise, Danticat's reader in the epilogue must know her history and her lineage, not only to know how to braid her daughter's hair but for whom those braids are tied.

Your transitions help connect the various parts of your argument.

Not surprisingly, as both books deal greatly with ancestry, they also deal with the transition and maintenance of an identity over time. Both authors assert that the collective self represented by the past is part and parcel of that embodied by the future—bound to it and inseparable. The one serves to define the other. Likewise, there is a call to make the efforts and struggles of the past worthwhile—to do better, if simply for the sake of one's ancestors.

Gives specific references

In *Tonto*, Alexie goes as far as to suggest that time is unimportant, if even existent, with respect to reality. Watches and keeping track of time are of no consequence. One's past will always be present, and the future always ahead, so there is no need to dwell on either, but that does not mean that they do not matter. A person lives in the now, but every "now" was once the future and will become the past (22). Alexie makes extensive use of the period of five hundred years, as though that is a length of time perceptible to the human consciousness, if appreciated more by the Indian.

Danticat's twisting of time is less blatant than Alexie's, but that may be because it is not necessary to speak of things in terms of hundreds of years. A few generations suffice, and the connections between her characters rely so heavily on the similarities between their stories that their relations are obvious. The suicide of the new mother in the first story is mirrored perfectly in the last, though they might take place fifty years apart. The question and answer game played by the sisters forces one to wonder whether Caroline and Grace's mother went through an experience similar to Josephine's mother's. Then there is Marie, who finds and claims the dead baby Rose, who very well may be the daughter of Josephine, who is connected to at least two of the other tales. Beyond the characters themselves, the reuse of the symbols of hair and the bloody water is striking. The Massacre River, which took the lives of many who attempted to cross it, is named (44), but it is also implied in the bloody stream of Grace's dream with her father, even though the character may know nothing of it. After years, generations, and physical separation, the events at that river seem to pervade the collective consciousness of the Haitian people.

Focuses on structure of work

Provides specific details about characters

Points out relevance of symbols

Clearly, these authors make no attempt to glorify the identity that they are helping to define. What is vital to the presentation of these collective identities is that they are transcendent of both time and location and that they are honest, if not visceral, in their telling. As beautifully told as these pieces of fiction are, they aim for truth and are unapologetic in presenting the faults and difficulties inherent in that truth. By telling these tales honestly and without pretense, Alexie and Danticat help to reveal what many may not be willing to admit or acknowledge about others or about themselves—the importance, beauty, and complexity of a collective selfhood.

Draws threads together with term "collective identities"

You've ended on a strong note that affirms your claim about collective identity.

Works Cited

Alexie, Sherman. *The Lone Ranger and Tonto Fistfight in Heaven*. HarperCollins, 1994.

Danticat, Edwidge. *Krik? Krak!* Vintage Books, 1996.

New page in final MLA draft

Follows MLA for citing books

Blue = description of content, **Purple = feedback for writer**

5g Writing and researching in the natural and applied sciences

Most writing in the natural sciences (such as astronomy, biology, chemistry, and physics) and applied sciences (agriculture, engineering, environmental studies, computer science, and nursing, for example) concerns itself with empirical data—that is, with the explanation and analysis of data gathered from a controlled laboratory experiment or from detailed observation of natural phenomena. Frequently, the study will be a replication of a previous experiment, with the new procedure expected to uphold or refute the hypothesis of that previous experiment.

GUIDELINES

- Be prepared to write according to a set format, using sections with headings such as Abstract, Introduction, Methods, Results, Discussion, and Conclusion.
- Focus on empirical data.
- Avoid personal anecdotes.
- Report firsthand original experiments and calculations.
- Present a hypothesis.
- Give background information in the introductory section of your paper, sometimes called "Review of Literature."
- Use the present perfect tense to introduce a survey of the literature: *Several studies have shown that. . . .*
- Use the past tense for details of specific studies: *Cocchi et al. isolated the protein fraction. . . .*
- Use the passive voice more frequently than in other types of writing, especially to avoid using the first person *I*: *The muscle was stimulated. . . .*
- Use APA (chapters 14–16) or CSE (chapter 17) documentation style, or follow specific style manuals in scientific areas.

KEY POINTS

A Model for the Organization of an Experimental Paper in the Sciences

1. **Title page:** running head, title, author's name, and institution
2. **Table of contents:** a list of the sections in the paper, necessary for a long paper or for a paper posted online

3. **Abstract:** a summary of your research and your conclusions (about 100 to 175 words)
4. **Introduction:** why the study is necessary, review of other studies, your research questions and hypothesis
5. **Method:** description of the system of inquiry used to answer the research question, with headed subsections on participants, apparatus, and procedures
6. **Results:** reporting of statistics, survey data, or observation data collected with tables, charts, and graphs where appropriate
7. **Discussion:** interpretation of the results and evaluation from the perspective of your hypothesis
8. **Conclusion and recommendations:** implications of the results of the study and suggestions for further research; might also include discussion of limitations of the study
9. **References:** a list of the works cited in the paper
10. **Tables and figures:** a list of any visuals included in the paper; check with your instructor about placing them at the end or within your text

Abstract The following abstract from a paper titled "*Longaeva*: The Scientific Significance of the Ancient Bristlecone Pine" was written by Andrew Dillon for a first-year course on "Volcanoes of the Eastern Sierra Nevada" at Indiana University.* You can read excerpts from Dillon's paper in chapter 18.

> More than any other species of tree, the bristlecone pine (*Pinus longaeva*), of the White Mountains in California, helps scientists to understand the environmental conditions of the past. With some living specimens attaining ages nearing 5,000 years, and dead matter persisting for another several thousand, these ancient trees have provided climatologists, geologists, and dendrochronologists with a continuous tree-ring chronology that dates back to the last Ice Age. This paper examines the complex physiology and habitat of the species and considers what scientists have learned from the bristlecone about the earth's history. Research from the past half century illuminates the magnificence of bristlecone pine as living evidence of past millennia.

---

*Used with permission of Andrew Dillon.

Excerpt from a student's lab report The following annotated excerpt is from Natasha Williams's lab report on microbial genetics conjugation, written for a cell biology course.

Discussion

Major section heading centered

Conjugation involves transfer by appropriate mating types. F+ and Hfr are donor cells with respectively low and high rates of genetic transfer. F- cells are recipients. Contact between the cell types is made by a conjugation bridge called an F pilus extending from the Hfr cell. The donor chromosome appears to be linearly passed through the connecting bridge. Sometimes this transfer is interrupted. The higher the frequency of recombination, the closer the gene is to the beginning of the circular DNA. In this way one can determine the sequence of genes on the chromosome.

Passive voice common in lab reports

Use of *one* for general reference

Table 1 shows consistently that histidine is the last amino acid coded with the smallest number of recombinants, and arginine is the second to last coded with the next smallest number of recombinants. However, the results obtained for proline and leucine/threonine vary.

Discussion of table included in paper

5h Writing and researching in the social sciences

The social sciences (anthropology, business, economics, geography, political science, psychology, and sociology) examine how society and social institutions are constructed, how they work (or don't work), and how humans behave within structures and organizations.

Two types of writing prevail in the social sciences. Some writers use empirical methods that are similar to those used in the natural sciences to gather, analyze, and report data, with a focus on people, groups, and their behavior. Ethnographic studies are common, for example, in which researchers take detailed notes as they observe a situation they want to analyze—the behavior of fans at a baseball game, for instance.

GUIDELINES

- Understand that the research method you choose will determine what kind of writing is necessary and how you should organize the writing.
- Decide whether your purpose is to describe accurately, measure, inform, analyze, or synthesize information.
- Decide what kind of data you will use: figures and statistics from experimental research, surveys, the census, or questionnaires; observational data from case studies, interviews, and on-site observations; or your reading.
- For an observational study, take careful field notes that describe accurately everything you see. Concentrate on the facts rather than interpretations. Save the interpretive possibilities for the sections of your paper devoted to discussion and recommendations.
- Examine research studies in the field, evaluate their methodologies, compare and contrast results with those of other studies, and draw conclusions based on the empirical evidence uncovered. Devote a section of the paper to a review of the literature.
- Look for accurate, up-to-date information, and evaluate it systematically against the stated criteria.
- Use sections and headings in your paper. See the APA paper in chapter 16 written as a research paper in a first-year composition course.
- Report facts and data. Add comments and expressions such as *I think* only when this is a specific requirement of the task.
- Use the past tense to refer to another researcher's work: *Smith's study (2011) showed that. . . .*
- Use the passive voice when it is not important for readers to know the identity of the person performing the action: *The participants were timed. . . .*
- Present statistical data in the form of tables, charts, and graphs whenever possible (chapter 22).
- Follow the APA *Publication Manual* or whichever style manual is recommended.

Turn to chapter 16 for an example of a complete documented paper in the social sciences.

5i Writing for community service projects

Community service learning projects link a college to the community. For such projects, students volunteer for community service, which is often related to the content of a discipline or a particular course. They then must demonstrate what they learned from the community service experience. You'll probably do three main types of writing for community service projects:

1. You'll work with the site supervisor to outline the goals, activities, and desired outcomes of the community service project.
2. During the community service work, you'll prepare reports to a supervisor, daily records, summaries of work completed, and documents such as flyers and brochures (22c).
3. In the course, you'll write reflective reports that describe the objectives of the community service, the project's success, and your experiences.

To reflect fully on the work you do, keep an ongoing journal of your activities so that you can provide background about the setting and the work, and give specific details about the problems you encounter and their solutions. Link your comments to the goals of the project.

5j Writing under pressure: Essay exams and short-answer tests

One of the highest-stakes and highest-stress writing situations in college is the essay exam. Essay exams and short-answer tests are a challenge because you have to organize your thoughts and write quickly on an assigned topic, and the end result is usually worth a considerable percentage of your grade in a course. Having a solid strategy to approach essay exams is important.

For short-answer tests In short-answer tests, use your time wisely. So that you know how long you should spend on each question, count the number of questions and divide the number of minutes you have for taking the test by the number of questions (add 1 or 2 to the number you divide by, to give yourself time for editing and proofreading). Then, for each answer, decide which points are the most important ones to cover in the time you have available. You cannot afford to ramble or waffle during short-answer tests. Get to the point quickly, and show what you know. To increase your confidence, answer the easiest question first.

For essay exams and short-answer tests Always read the questions carefully, and make sure you understand what each question asks you to do. Test writers often use the following verbs when specifying writing tasks:

analyze: divide into parts, and discuss each part
argue: make a claim, and give your reasons
classify: organize people, objects, or concepts into groups
compare: point out similarities
contrast: point out differences
define: give the meaning of
discuss: state important characteristics and main points
evaluate: define criteria for judgment, and examine good and bad points, strengths and weaknesses
explain: give reasons or make clear by analyzing, defining, contrasting, illustrating, and so on
illustrate: give examples from experience and from reading
relate: point out and discuss connections

KEY POINTS

Guidelines for Essay Exams

1. **Prepare.** Prior to a content-based essay test, review the assigned materials and your notes; assemble facts; underline, annotate, and summarize significant information in your textbooks and other assigned materials; predict questions on the basis of the material your instructor has covered in detail in class; and draft some answers.
2. **Highlight or underline key terms in the assigned questions.**
3. **Think positively about what you know.** Work out a way to emphasize the details you know most about. Stretch and relax.
4. **Make a scratch outline to organize your thoughts.** Jot down specific details as evidence for your thesis.
5. **Focus on providing detailed support for your thesis.** In an exam, this is more important than an elaborate introduction or conclusion.
6. **Check your essay for content, logic, and clarity.** Make sure you answered the question.

Exercises on the Writing Process

EXERCISE 1 Write about your own writing process 1a–1b

Think about your most recent written assignment. Write an account of what the assignment was, how you generated ideas, how you wrote it, where you did your writing, and what technology you used as you were writing (such as a computer or a pen and paper). How much time was given between the assignment and the due date, and how did you use that time? How did you feel as you completed the assignment? Be thorough and frank in describing your writing process. The point is to examine the way you write. Read your account aloud to a group of classmates, and then discuss any differences between their accounts and yours.

EXERCISE 2 Write for different audiences 1b

Write three passages that respond to the following question: "When is it okay to lie to someone?" Write one passage for your eyes alone (a diary entry or a freewrite), one for an e-mail message to a close friend (for more on writing e-mail messages, see 23a), and one for a college instructor. Keep each version short—no more than two paragraphs each. How do the versions differ, and why?

EXERCISE 3 Explore a topic in several ways 2a–2b

Work with a group of students to select a broad topic (such as the environment, heroes, immigration, aging, or fast food). Each person in the group will explore the topic using two of the following methods:

- writing a blog post to initiate an online discussion
- freewriting
- brainstorming and grouping ideas
- mapping
- writing answers to the journalists' questions

Read each other's explorations, and discuss which methods generated good ideas.

EXERCISE 4 Revise thesis statements 2c

The following thesis statements are too narrow, too broad, or too vague, or they are factual statements that are not debatable. Revise each one to make it an appropriate thesis statement for a three- to five-page essay.

1. Gun control is a controversial issue.
2. Literacy is an important issue that must be dealt with.
3. Plants enhance the beauty of a home.
4. People with disabilities can face employment discrimination in several ways.

5. Alcoholism affects children.
6. Advertisers of food products use color-enhanced images to entice consumers into purchasing their products.
7. The media are responsible for causing eating disorders, lowering self-esteem, and encouraging unrealistic ideals of beauty.

EXERCISE 5 Write thesis statements 2c

Read the following list of topics, and, together with a group of classmates, refine the topics into thesis statements for a three- to four-page argumentative or persuasive essay. Use the four levels outlined in the following example:

Example

Level 1:	Subject	Reality TV shows
Level 2:	Narrowed topic	Reality TV shows such as *The Amazing Race*
Level 3:	Key question	Why did they become popular?
Level 4:	Tentative thesis	Reality TV shows such as *The Amazing Race* enjoy widespread popularity and high ratings because of viewers' interest in the contestants, challenging activities, and financial prizes.

1. Level 1: Subject Your college's registration process
2. Level 1: Subject America's system of movie ratings

   [Note: G (general audience, all ages admitted); PG (parental guidance suggested); PG-13 (parents strongly cautioned); R (restricted—under seventeen requires accompanying parent or adult guardian); NC-17 (no one seventeen or under admitted)]
3. Level 1: Subject Women in combat
4. Level 1: Subject Alternative energy sources for automobiles

EXERCISE 6 Write a scratch outline and a formal outline 2d

Choose one of the thesis statements you wrote in Exercise 5, and write a scratch outline. Bring your outline to class, and, as a group, select one scratch outline to develop together into a formal outline.

EXERCISE 7 Identify topic sentences in paragraphs 2e

Read each of the following paragraphs. Then determine whether the topic sentence is at the beginning or at the end, or is implied.

1. Lisa wrote a list of all items they needed. She then went to the store, purchased essentials, and upon returning, packed the overnight bags for the family weekend getaway trip to upstate New York in the Catskills. Her husband, Charlie, confirmed the reservations at the resort and wrote down the directions. Their son Dave, who had recently received his driver's license, got the car washed and filled the tank with regular

unleaded gas. Everyone in the family pitched in. Teamwork is essential in planning a trip.

2. On Wednesday, I ran for a bus and made it. The dentist said I had no cavities. The phone was ringing when I arrived home and even after I dropped my key a couple of times, I answered it and they were still on the line. The Avon lady refused me service saying I didn't need her as I already looked terrific. My husband asked me what kind of a day I had and didn't leave the room when I started to answer.

—Erma Bombeck, *If Life Is a Bowl of Cherries, What Am I Doing in the Pits?*

3. There are only three ways to make money. One is to go out and work for it. However, few among us can work forever, and there will likely come a time in our lives when working for a paycheck may not be an option. The second way to make money is to inherit it or to win the lottery. Again, not something we all can count on. The third way, and the only one that is available to all of us for an unlimited amount of time, is to invest what we earn during our working years wisely, so that the money we work so hard for goes to work for us. —Suze Orman, *The Courage to Be Rich*

EXERCISE 8 Experiment with different methods of development 2g

Choose a topic that interests you. First, write a paragraph about some aspect of your topic using one of the following methods of development:

1. one extended illustration
2. facts and statistics
3. an account of a process
4. definition of terms

Then write another paragraph on another aspect of your topic using a second method of development from the preceding list. In groups, discuss how different aspects of your topic worked with the two methods of development that you chose. Did one method of development work better or less well than the other, and if so, why?

EXERCISE 9 Use the Track Changes feature to work collaboratively 3b

Select one or two paragraphs (about ten to twelve lines) of an assignment that you have written for a course, and paste the text into your word processing program. Then e-mail the document to another student. Your partner will open the document in Word, use the Track Changes feature to make changes to the text, and send it back to you. Decide whether to accept or reject each change. Print out the final version, and discuss it with your partner.

EXERCISE 10 Evaluate thesis statements 4c

Which of the following statements work well as a thesis statement to focus an essay of three to five pages in length, and which do not? Give reasons for your assessment.

1. Adding a sixth day of classes is more effective in helping students than extending the hours of the present five-day class schedule.
2. Although solar panels and wind farms offer promising energy alternatives, the economic relationships among countries using fuel oil make alternative energy sources highly unlikely to succeed.
3. Although art and music therapies differ in their approaches, there are compelling similarities between these methods.
4. In order to assist the increasing population of young homeless people, new policies are needed to improve the quality of shelters, create back-to-work employment programs, and fund medical and mental health treatment.
5. Although several studies reveal that placebos are effective in healing ill patients, physicians need to conduct more research into how and why placebos work.
6. Understanding personality types provides us with insights into ourselves and the world.
7. "Mindfulness" or "paying attention" to the world around us is a vital skill to develop because it enriches our lives, sharpens our memory skills, keeps us safe, and helps us become more aware eyewitnesses.

EXERCISE 11 Find details to use in support of a thesis 4d

For each of the following thesis statements, discuss with other students which types of supporting details you would choose to support the thesis, and provide evidence to make a convincing case to readers (for example, facts and statistics, examples, stories, descriptions, definitions, instructions). Create a list of the types of supporting details that would be effective for each thesis statement, and include any specific details that would illustrate the point.

1. The current adoption systems must be reformed so that couples seeking to adopt a child avoid long delays, unnecessary extensive paperwork, and costly fees.
2. Community centers in ethnic neighborhoods play an important role in helping new immigrants assimilate into America by providing job assistance, English language instruction classes, and interaction with other immigrants who have successfully struck a balance between assimilation and preservation of their heritage.
3. "Recycle, Reduce, and Reuse" are three activities citizens can do on a daily basis to help protect our environment from the hazards of pollution and solid waste.

4. Although law enforcement authorities claim that video surveillance of neighborhood streets protects residents from crime, video surveillance infringes on our civil liberties and should not be used.
5. Internships help students explore their intended careers, make important contacts, and gain valuable work experience.

EXERCISE 12 Examine an argument for logic 4h

For each of the following statements, determine whether the argument is logical or contains a logical fallacy. If it contains a logical fallacy, identify the logical fallacy and explain why it is a fallacy.

1. The new vice president of sales is untrustworthy because many years ago he was arrested for civil disobedience while in college.
2. Married couples without children often experience societal pressure to have or adopt children.
3. Mary can either matriculate as a full-time student in the fall or wait until the following fall to attend classes.
4. Keeping a diary is cathartic because writing on a daily basis releases bottled-up emotions.
5. All men like sports.

EXERCISE 13 Experiment with figurative language 5e

In groups of two or three, write five sentences about your favorite food, object, activity, sport, or sports figure using at least four of the following stylistic devices: simile, metaphor, alliteration, personification, and irony.

EXERCISE 14 Identify key terms in essay questions 5j

Underline key terms that writers should address when they respond to the following essay exam questions from various courses.

1. In chapter 10, we explored the controversial issues surrounding the death penalty. Write a 350-word essay arguing for or against the death penalty, making reference to some or all of these issues. You have the entire class period.
2. Define *coup d'ètat*.
3. Compare and/or contrast the major characteristics of the Romantic period in Britain with the Augustan period in Britain. Be sure to refer to at least two writers whom you believe are representative of each period.
4. What are the various ways rocks can be classified?
5. Discuss the key issues presented by both candidates during the last mayoral election.
6. Evaluate the significance of Maslow's "Hierarchy of Needs."
7. Explain the effects of current immigration policies on families and children.

MindTap®

- **Practice skills that you have learned in this part and receive automatic feedback.**

Assignment Guide: Keys to Common Writing Genres

WRITING IN YOUR CAREER

The Accountant, the Writer

Eric Audras/Glowimages.com

Numbers and *Excel* programs—that's the stuff many of us think accountants are made of. But actually, one of the main jobs of an accountant is the audit. You can think of an audit as a genre, a type of writing with its own conventions and audience expectations. Audits require evidence of purchases, income, expenditures, and so forth. This evidence allows the accountant (or a staff of accountants) to form an opinion that can be tested according to the prevailing standards of the profession. The audit uses both oral and written communication skills. In fact, a large part of the auditing process can even involve fact-gathering interviews with employees during which questions must be framed as neutral and reasonable lines of inquiry. As proof that evidence has been gathered and tested in accordance with accounting principles and procedures that are governed by laws, auditors create "elaborate written records," according to Melanie McKay and Elizabeth Rosa in *Communicating and Auditing: A Step-by-Step Guide*. They take the forms of descriptions, narratives, summaries, and analyses and tell the story of how the audit was conducted. These written records have to show that the auditor has gathered and evaluated evidence within an environment of honest and thorough communication. The following example of appropriate and inappropriate descriptions of findings is found in the *Communicating and Auditing* manual to train accountants.

Procedure: Trace all outstanding checks appearing on a bank reconciliation as of a certain date to checks cleared in the bank statement of the subsequent month.

INAPPROPRIATE DESCRIPTION OF FINDINGS	Nothing came to my attention as a result of applying the procedure.

The inappropriate description is a conclusion drawn by the accountant without supporting evidence.

APPROPRIATE DESCRIPTION OF FINDINGS	All outstanding checks appearing on the bank reconciliation were cleared in the subsequent of month's bank statements.

The appropriate description shows how the evidence supports the findings in the audit.

Assignment Guide: Keys to Common Writing Genres

Assignment Guide: Keys to Common Writing Genres

You will certainly encounter many different kinds of writing during your academic and professional careers. Perhaps you already have. In 1d, we explain that types of writing—such as résumés, reports, essays, research papers, letters, lists, and online messages—are considered *genres*. Every genre has specific common features or conventions that readers expect the writer to follow, and they help the writer engage in effective communication. For example, a résumé generally includes contact information at the top of the first page, often in a larger font, and lists the person's most recent experience first. Following these conventions not only helps readers understand how to read the writing but also makes it easy for a potential employer to find relevant information. Likewise, a literary analysis generally states a thesis, or primary claim, in the first paragraph or toward the beginning of the analysis. Following this convention helps readers determine the primary argument that the author is going to develop in the analysis.

Effective writers pay attention to the expectations of the genres in which they are writing. Following conventions not only helps their readers find the information they need but also helps establish the writers' ethos as reliable and authoritative. At times, writers may choose not to follow all of the conventions for a genre, but they do so for particular purposes, not out of ignorance.

In this section, you'll find concise, useful information for following the conventions of common genres. For each genre, we include the following:

- **Guidelines and starting questions** provide help for thinking about how the context of your writing (purpose, audience, voice, medium) affects the choices you might make when writing a particular genre.
- **Keys Points** offer specific help for writing the genre, divided into three parts:
    - **Key Elements** list the common features expected in the target genre.
    - **Keys for Organization** describe common strategies used for structuring the target genre.
    - **Key Steps for Writing** list specific tasks that effective writers complete when writing the target genre.

These guidelines are a starting point, but you must consider your own rhetorical context as you follow them. Are there specific guidelines your teacher or an employer has asked you to follow? Use the instructions you've been given, if any, in tandem with the guidelines in this section to approach common genres effectively.

Literacy Narratives

A literacy narrative typically tells the story of a writer's experience with reading and writing. Some types of literacy narratives, such as technological literacy narratives or professional literacy narratives, tell of a writer's development in other areas. In all of these areas, it may be useful to think of literacy as something broader than the ability to read and write.

Purpose

An author might write a literacy narrative as an assignment for school, to accompany applications for positions, or to share an experience or lesson learned. Literacy narratives sometimes appear as part of a larger piece, too, to provide a personal illustration of a point.

- What is your purpose for writing this literacy narrative?
- What motivates you to write about your literacy development and experiences?

Audience

Literacy narratives can be written for a wide range of audiences. Imagine a commencement speaker telling the story of her literacy development to a group of graduates from a College of Education, or a college applicant telling the story of how he met the challenges of dyslexia to excel in high school. The audience you are addressing can affect the details you choose to share and how you shape the significance of your story.

- Who is the audience for your literacy narrative?
- What details would be most interesting to your audience?
- How much does your audience already know about the setting of your story? What background information might you need to provide?

Voice

Literacy narratives are incredibly personal, so your perspective and voice should be evident throughout your narrative. Literacy narratives are almost always written in the first person. Because they highlight personal stories, authors must always be careful to explain details that might seem evident to the author but might not be as evident to others listening to or reading the narrative. The tone of your narrative should fit your rhetorical context.

- How can you shape your literacy narrative to reflect who you are as a writer?

Medium

Literacy narratives can be written in print, but they can also be written in digital formats such as blog posts, videos, images, or interactive timelines. The choice of medium is related to the purpose and audience for the literacy narrative.

- What medium is most appropriate for your literacy narrative?

KEY POINTS
Writing Literacy Narratives

Key Elements of Literacy Narratives

- An interesting story
- A clear indication of the importance of the story to the writer
- Rich description that helps readers imagine the details of the story and that helps support the main point

Keys for Organization of Literacy Narratives

- *Chronological:* Because you are telling a story, it might make sense to organize the details chronologically and tell the story as you experienced it.
- *Flashback:* If the end result of the story is compelling, you might start the story there and then go back to the beginning of the story and show readers how you arrived at the end point.
- *Framing:* You could choose an image, theme, person, event, or something else that demonstrates the meaning of the story to you and use that image at the beginning and end of your story, framing your narrative.

Key Steps for Writing a Literacy Narrative

- Choose a compelling topic, perhaps an event that was important in your literacy development, or a progression of themes in your life that could be a cohesive story.
- Determine the significance of the story to you.
- Consider the setting, people, and events that you need to describe, and brainstorm as many details as you can that illustrate the significance of the story.
- Draft a compelling beginning that will draw readers into your story and will help them connect with it, and end with a conclusion that helps emphasize the significance of your story.

MindTap®

A sample literacy narrative is available online.

Summary and Response

A summary and response offers a condensed version of one or more texts and the author's analysis, interpretation, or reaction with references to the author's experience.

Purpose

Writers summarize and respond to texts for a variety of reasons. A student might write a summary of, and response to, sources found on a research topic of interest. A film reviewer, by contrast, might write a summary of a recent film and her response to it for a film blog. In an academic journal, a professor might write a review essay that summarizes a recently published book and responds to its quality.

- What is your purpose for writing this summary and response?
- What motivates you to write your summary and response?

Audience

Summaries and responses appear in a variety of places for many different audiences. A student writing a summary of, and response to, sources must consider her instructor's specific criteria for the assignment, but a film review blogger would think about the expectations of an online audience who is deciding whether or not to go see a film. Depending on the nature of the blog, the reviewer might be writing for an audience that has certain expectations for the film. Imagine a film reviewer writing about a new film adaptation of a Marvel comic book on a blog for comic enthusiasts. Her review would need to connect to the readers of the blog and their love of the print comic in her review of the film.

- Who is your audience for your summary and response? What do they already know about the text?
- Will your summary and response be assessed by someone? If so, what criteria do you need to follow?

Voice

Depending on the kind of response you are writing, your perspective and experience can be very important to your summary and response. The summary should remain factual and neutral, but the response might include your reaction to the text.

- What unique perspective do you bring to your summary and response? What experiences can you draw on as you write your response?

Medium

A summary and response could be presented in a variety of media, to include a word-processed document, a blog post, a microblog (*Twitter, Facebook, Tumblr*), a podcast, a slide presentation, or a video. The choice of medium is related to the purpose and audience for the summary and response. If you are summarizing a documentary and responding to it for a class, you might choose to create a video that includes small sections from the film as evidence, assuming you follow copyright regulations for fair use.

- What medium is most appropriate for your summary and response?

KEY POINTS

Writing a Summary and Response

Key Elements of a Summary and Response

- Your summary should be brief, accurate, and discuss the main points of the text or texts. Do not include details of the texts, but focus on the most important findings or developments in the texts.
- Your response might take several different forms, depending on the rhetorical context of your writing. You could
    - analyze the quality of the texts, using a set of specific criteria
    - offer an interpretation of the texts
    - draw on your experience to affirm or refute claims made in the texts

Keys for Organization of a Summary and Response

- *Summary and then response:* You might choose to organize your summary and response by writing your summary first and then using the remainder of the space to discuss your response to the text. This organization might work best if your audience is unfamiliar with the text and the clarity of your summary is important.
- *Point-by-point:* Another possibility is to organize your summary and response according to the main points you would like to make in your response. As you introduce each point, you provide the relevant summary to support your discussion of your response. This organization might work best if your emphasis is on your response and there are several specific points you would like to make about different elements of the text.

Key Steps for Writing a Summary and Response

- If you are summarizing and responding to more than one text, look for the key points that the texts have in common to focus your summary. Your response might then focus on the differences among the texts or on the significance of the similarities you've identified.
- Spend time thinking about what you have to say about the text. What knowledge or experiences can you draw on? What perspective do you bring that is unique?

MindTap®

A sample summary and response is available online.

Rhetorical Analyses

A rhetorical analysis breaks down the rhetorical context of a text (print, digital, visual, audio, or other) with the goal of understanding what it says and how it communicates its message.

Purpose

Researchers write rhetorical analyses of texts to understand the context and the rhetorical moves being made in a text. When analyzing the context, a writer might look at the purpose, audience, voice, and medium of the text. If analyzing textual features, a writer might look at several elements to include the organization and structure of the text, the kind of language used, and the rhetorical or persuasive appeals made.

- What is your purpose for writing this rhetorical analysis?
- What could you learn from understanding the context of this text?

Audience

A researcher might write a rhetorical analysis to help her understand the context of a text she is using in her research. A student might write a rhetorical analysis to demonstrate a deeper understanding of the context or rhetorical elements of a text. A writer might also write a rhetorical analysis to explain features of a text to colleagues or fellow students.

- Who is your audience for your rhetorical analysis? How much information about the content of the text do you need to provide?
- Will your rhetorical analysis be assessed by someone? If so, what criteria do you need to follow?

Voice

One of the more challenging aspects of a rhetorical analysis is to focus on textual elements and not merely summarize content. If you are analyzing a persuasive piece, for example, you should maintain a neutral stance toward the issue and focus on the kinds of persuasive appeals the author makes instead of whether or not you agree with the author's position.

- What strategies can you use to focus on the rhetorical elements of the text?
- What potential bias should you be aware of as you write so that you can maintain a neutral stance?

Medium

Rhetorical analyses could be presented in a variety of media. Often they appear in print, but they could easily be written in a digital format, especially if the writer intends to link or embed other media to demonstrate rhetorical elements of the text. For example, a rhetorical analysis of Martin Luther King's "I Have a Dream" speech from the March on Washington might include images, audio, or video from various parts of the speech.

- What medium is most appropriate for your rhetorical analysis?

KEY POINTS

Writing Rhetorical Analyses

Key Elements of Rhetorical Analyses

- Identification of the rhetorical context of a text and/or rhetorical features present in a text including those listed under "Purpose" on the facing page
- Evidence from the text to support any claims
- Discussion of the effects of the rhetorical choices of the writer, with a focus on how the writer achieves those effects
- Documentation of any quotations or references from the text in the analysis

Keys for Organization of Rhetorical Analyses

- *Thesis-driven:* Many rhetorical analyses are thesis-driven. In other words, they make a claim (thesis) about the text and how it is written, and then they support that claim with evidence.
- *Thematic:* Some rhetorical analyses are thematic in nature, or they analyze a series of specific rhetorical elements. This organizational style might be most common in a classroom setting where the writer is assigned to analyze a specific set of elements in a text.

Key Steps for Writing Rhetorical Analyses

- Choose a text that you find intriguing to analyze.
- After closely reading the text, decide which elements of the text you want to analyze, focusing on the rhetorical context and/or rhetorical features.
- Read the text again, taking notes on the elements you have chosen to analyze.
- Construct a claim you can make about the text based on the notes you took during your close reading.
- Draft your analysis, choosing evidence from your notes to support your claim.
- Remember to include an introduction that describes your text and states your claim, along with a conclusion that summarizes key points from your analysis.

▶ **You can find an example of a rhetorical analysis in section 5c.**

Visual Analyses

A visual analysis is an interpretation of how an image communicates meaning with its audience.

Purpose

Writers develop visual analyses to understand how images evoke responses from an audience and communicate messages through the use of techniques such as size, color, texture, focus, framing, gaze, and caption, which can vary depending on the type of image.

- What is your purpose for writing this visual analysis? What would you like to understand about how it communicates meaning?
- What initially drew your attention to this image?

Audience

Visual analyses can have a variety of audiences. A scholar might write a visual analysis to share a new interpretation with other scholars interested in the same image or theme. An advertising intern might write a visual analysis for executives at an advertising firm to explain how some advertising campaigns have connected more effectively with their target audiences. A student might write a visual analysis for an instructor to fulfill course requirements and to demonstrate knowledge of the theories that might be used to interpret the image.

- Who is your audience for your visual analysis?
- Will your visual analysis be assessed by someone? If so, what criteria do you need to follow?

Voice

Authors of visual analyses bring unique perspectives to their interpretations that can influence how they understand the message being conveyed. For example, a veteran analyzing a magazine photo from a military conflict might draw upon personal experience to interpret the image.

- What unique interpretation do you bring to your visual analysis?
- What evidence do you need to provide to support your analysis? What kinds of sources, perspectives, or research should you include as further support for your interpretation?

Medium

Visual analyses are often presented in print, but they can also be effectively published in digital form. An informal visual analysis of an advertisement might be published in a blog posting or on *Twitter,* with a link to the ad, for example. If a visual analysis is published in print, it can help reproduce all or part of the image, but you must be careful to pay attention to copyright regulations (see section 22d for information on images and copyright issues).

- What medium is most appropriate for your visual analysis?
- Can your audience see/experience the image you are analyzing? If not, how can you describe the image sufficiently so that readers who can't see the image can understand your analysis?

KEY POINTS
Writing Visual Analyses

Key Elements of a Visual Analysis

- Identification of the rhetorical context of the image
- A clear claim about the author's interpretation of the image
- Evidence from the image to support any claims, to include reference to specific techniques that are relevant to the interpretation. If you are analyzing a camera shot, for example, you might refer to an extreme close-up that emphasizes a specific element of a subject.

Keys for Organization of a Visual Analysis

- *Thesis-driven:* Many visual analyses are thesis-driven. In other words, they make a claim (thesis) about the image and what it communicates, and then they support that claim with evidence.
- *Thematic:* Some visual analyses are thematic in nature, or they analyze a series of specific elements of the image. This organizational style might be most common in a classroom setting where the writer is assigned to analyze a specific set of elements in an image.

Key Steps for Writing a Visual Analysis

- Choose an image that you find intriguing to analyze.
- After closely observing the image, decide which elements you want to analyze.
- Study the image again, taking notes on the elements you have chosen to analyze.
- Construct a claim you can make about the image based on the notes you have taken.
- Draft your analysis, choosing evidence from your notes to support your claim.
- Remember to include an introduction that describes the image and states your claim, along with a conclusion that summarizes key points from your analysis.

▶ **You can find help analyzing the argument of an image in section 4i.**

Literary Analyses

A literary analysis is a close reading of a piece of literature that offers an interpretation of that work and supports the interpretation with evidence from the text and sometimes from other scholars.

Purpose

Scholars write literary analyses to share their interpretations of a piece of literature. The aim is often to persuade other readers of the validity of their interpretation and to contribute to the ongoing conversation about a literary work. Sometimes they are sharing a new interpretation of a work that has been analyzed before, and sometimes they are introducing a piece of literature that is new or has been neglected in prior scholarship and are offering an interpretation of it.

- What is your purpose for writing this literary analysis?
- What has already been written about the literary work you are analyzing?

Audience

A scholar might write a literary analysis to share a new interpretation with other scholars interested in the same text. A student might write a literary analysis to fulfill course requirements and to demonstrate knowledge of a literary text for an instructor.

- Who is your audience for your literary analysis?
- Will your literary analysis be assessed by someone? If so, what criteria do you need to follow?

Voice

Literary analyses use the specific language of literary studies, discussed in 5e (especially on pp. 87–90). Literary works are always referred to in the present tense. As you write, address an audience that is larger than your instructor, assuming they have read the work but perhaps have not interpreted it in the way you have.

- What unique interpretation do you bring to your literary analysis?
- What evidence do you need to provide to support your analysis? What kinds of sources, perspectives, or research should you include as further support for your interpretation?

Medium

Literary analyses are most often presented in print form, but some are also designed in a digital format. The choice of medium is related to the purpose and audience for the literary analysis. A digitally presented literary analysis might use technology to show different, competing interpretations of the same text or to present digital representations of rare texts that are hard to access.

- What medium is most appropriate for your literary analysis?

KEY POINTS
Writing Literary Analyses

Key Elements of a Literary Analysis

- A claim or thesis that interprets some aspect of the literary work
- Evidence from the primary literary text to support the claim or thesis
- Evidence from other sources also written about the same piece of literature (optional, depending on the requirement of your instructor)
- Consistent documentation style for both in-text citations and a reference list
- A reference list, bibliography, or works-cited list

Keys for Organization of a Literary Analysis

- State your claim or thesis near the beginning of the literary analysis, usually at the end of an opening paragraph.
- Organize the paragraphs in the body of the literary analysis to develop the parts of the claim or thesis in the order in which they are written.
- Conclude your literary analysis by summarizing key points from your argument for readers.

Key Steps for Writing a Literary Analysis

- Read your text carefully, writing notes and questions about elements of the text you find interesting and consulting section 5e to be sure you are using literary terms correctly.
- Based on your close reading, draft a claim or thesis that will serve as the focus of your interpretation.
- If required by your instructor, search for other sources that analyze your literary work, and look for claims they make that might serve as support for your claim or counterarguments that you should refute.
- Draft your analysis, paying careful attention to the keys for organization stated previously.

▶ **You can find an example of a literary analysis in section 5f.**

Abstracts

An abstract is a concise summary of the research questions, methodology, and findings of a research study.

Purpose

Scholars write abstracts to provide a brief description of a research study for readers who are deciding whether reading the full article would be beneficial to their own research. Abstracts appear at the beginning of many published scholarly articles, and they also appear in databases, giving researchers quick summaries of full studies before they go to the trouble of retrieving and reading a full article. Abstracts are also sometimes written as proposals for potential publications or conference presentations.

- What is your purpose for writing this abstract?
- What information about your study is most important to communicate?

Audience

The audience for an abstract is usually other researchers interested in the same subject, research questions, and/or methodologies as the author. Because brevity is important in an abstract, some background information that would appear in the article would be excluded, especially if the audience might already be familiar with the information.

- Who is your audience for your abstract?
- How much does your audience already know about your research subject?

Voice

Abstracts are short, so choosing precise language is important. Because abstracts describe a study that has been completed, they are written in the past tense and generally do not use the first person. They use a formal, academic tone, and often they include jargon that is specific to an area of study or a profession.

- What language choices can you make to summarize the study as efficiently as possible?
- How will you convey the role your research plays in the ongoing conversation about the subject?

Medium

Abstracts are published in multiple media, even if they were originally written for an article that is published in print. Because the same abstract can appear in print, in an online library database, or in an online version of a journal, be sure to include predictable keywords that will help readers find your study in a search.

- In what media will your abstract appear?
- What keywords should you be sure to include in your abstract so that it will show up in search results?

KEY POINTS
Writing Abstracts

Key Elements of Abstracts

- Reference to key prior research that informed the study, giving readers an idea of what ongoing conversations about the subject the research study continues
- Explanation of the relevance of the study, connecting the study to other work that has been done and/or ongoing conversations in a field of study
- Description of the research question and methodology used to collect and analyze data
- Brief summary of the findings of the study

Keys for Organization of Abstracts

- In the opening sentence, include important terms that help readers know what your study is about.
- Toward the beginning of the paragraph, mention any relevant work that your study builds upon.
- Before you describe any results, mention how you collected and analyzed data.
- Close your abstract with a description of what your study examines and what your conclusions are.

Key Steps for Writing Abstracts

- When you are drafting your abstract, consider the most important points from each of the major sections of your study. Doing so can give you an easy outline for your abstract and ensure that you don't forget to include important aspects of your research.
- Use the past tense when describing results of your study. Even if you draft the abstract before you have finished the study, your intended audience will read your abstract after the study is completed. You are not describing what they *will* read; rather, you are describing what you have already accomplished.
- Abstracts are generally written in the third person and often contain passive voice to avoid the first person. This is one time in academic writing when passive voice is often expected and serves a useful purpose.

▸ **You can find an example of an abstract in section 5g.**

Research Proposals

A research proposal describes a study that a researcher proposes to complete, often written to request funding or support for the study.

Purpose

Scholars write research proposals for a variety of reasons. An established researcher might draft a research proposal to request funding or support for a research project. A student might write a research proposal to request permission to pursue a particular topic in his or her research.

- What is your purpose for writing this research proposal?
- What information about your study is most important to communicate?

Audience

The audience for a research proposal is usually the person or people who will make a decision about the future of the study. The audience might be a funding agency, an instructor, an advisory committee, or an institutional review board. Different audiences have unique criteria they use for review, based on the kind of decision they need to make about the research study. A funding agency, for example, might be concerned about the importance of the study, the ability of the researcher to complete the study, and the way that funding would be used in the research.

- Who is your audience for your research proposal?
- What would your audience want to know about your proposed study to make a favorable decision about your proposal?

Voice

Maintaining a professional, authoritative tone when you are writing your research proposal can help you establish credibility by showing that you know about the subject you are researching, you are capable of completing the research successfully, and you are a careful researcher and writer.

- What conventions should you follow in your research proposal to maintain a professional, authoritative tone?
- How can you establish that you are capable of successfully completing your research project?

Medium

The medium in which a research proposal is written and published is usually determined by where the author will send it for a decision. An instructor might ask that you print your research proposal on paper to turn it in. A funding agency might ask you to submit your research proposal through an online form with strict limitations on word count and formatting.

- What medium is most appropriate for your research proposal?
- What requirements for drafting and formatting your research proposal do you need to follow?

KEY POINTS
Writing Research Proposals

Key Elements of Research Proposals

- An introduction that describes the importance of the topic
- A review of other relevant research that has already been conducted on the subject, showing where there might be a gap in the research that your study could fill
- A clear research question or questions that will guide the study
- A description of the proposed methodology
- A timeline for conducting the study
- A budget, if the research proposal is asking for funding
- A list of any sources used in the research proposal, formatted according to the appropriate style guide

Keys for Organization of Research Proposals

- Research proposals typically follow the order of preceding elements. In this way, they broadly follow the same organization as the first three parts of an experimental paper in the sciences, as described in section 5g: they provide an introduction, description of methodology, and any preliminary results that the researcher might have (not required, but important to report if available).
- Budgets are required only if the research proposal asks for funding, and they appear at the end of the proposal if they are included.

Key Steps for Writing Research Proposals

- Compile a detailed, comprehensive list of what has been written about your subject already. Consider using a bibliographical system like *Zotero* or a social bookmarking application like *Diigo* to keep track of your sources.
- Look for gaps in the research that your study could fill, and narrow your topic to a specific question or set of questions that address the gap.
- Develop a plan for a study that will allow you to gather data to respond to your research question. Your research method should be appropriate to the questions you are asking. For example, if you ask "How often do students on campus recycle materials in their dorms?" you might answer this question by collecting survey data from students and also doing observations of recycling habits.
- Keep in mind that your study needs to be something you can actually accomplish. Develop a timeline that is reasonable and show that you have access to the data you propose to collect. Section 6b provides a worksheet that can help you estimate how long a typical research project will take.

MindTap®

A sample research proposal is available online.

Annotated Bibliographies

An annotated bibliography is a list of sources on a specific subject or issue that includes citations and summaries of each source.

Purpose

Researchers write annotated bibliographies for a variety of purposes: to organize and keep track of the sources they've found, to better understand the relationships among different perspectives on a topic, and to demonstrate knowledge of existing research, among others.

- What is your purpose for writing this annotated bibliography?
- What could you learn from compiling sources about your topic?

Audience

A researcher might write an annotated bibliography for herself to track sources in her research. She might also have a primary audience of other scholars interested in the topic of the annotated bibliography. A student writer might be writing for a teacher who will be assessing the annotated bibliography.

- Who is your audience for your annotated bibliography?
- Will your annotated bibliography be assessed by someone? If so, what criteria do you need to follow?

Voice

Researchers always bring a unique perspective to their work, and that might be influenced by personal experience with the topic or a bias toward a particular position. Often researchers need to be sure to include multiple perspectives in an annotated bibliography, not just their own.

- What unique perspective do you bring to your annotated bibliography? Do you have prior knowledge of your topic or experience with it?
- What kinds of sources should you be certain to include to provide multiple perspectives?

Medium

Annotated bibliographies can be presented in print form, but they can also be written in digital formats such as hypertext documents, social bookmarking applications (like *Diigo*), or within a project management system (like *Zotero*). The choice of medium is related to the purpose and audience for the annotated bibliography. If you are giving an oral presentation about a subject, for example, a printed annotated bibliography of your sources will allow your audience to refer to your sources as you mention them.

- What medium is most appropriate for your annotated bibliography?

KEY POINTS
Writing Annotated Bibliographies

Key Elements of Annotated Bibliographies

- A title that includes reference to the topic of the annotated bibliography

  The Effects of Sleep Habits on the Academic Success of College Freshmen

- A beginning statement of the scope of the annotated bibliography

  This annotated bibliography compiles studies of the sleep habits of college students that help shed light on the potential effects of sleep on academic success, happiness, and overall health and wellness.

- Bibliography entries (one for each source) that include
  - A full citation
  - A summary of the source
  - (sometimes) An evaluation or commentary on the source

Keys for Organization of Annotated Bibliographies

- *Alphabetical:* Most documentation styles (such as MLA and APA) recommend using an alphabetical organization as a default approach.
- *Topical:* If your annotated bibliography is long, you might organize it according to themes or topics to help readers.
- *Chronological:* If the order in which sources are published is important for your topic, you might organize your annotated bibliography chronologically. For example, an annotated bibliography about a scientific or technological topic might lend itself well to a chronological organization.
- *Source type:* If your instructor has asked you to find specific kinds of sources and show a variety of source types, you might organize your annotated bibliography to highlight the medium in which you found your source.

Key Steps for Writing an Annotated Bibliography

- Draft an introduction that explains the scope of the annotated bibliography.
- Find sources to include, and skim them to choose the most relevant ones.
- Read the selected sources in more detail, and write concise summaries of them.
- Write citations for your sources, and compile the citations and summaries.
- Consider how you will organize the sources in your annotated bibliography.
- Make any necessary revisions to the introduction based on the sources you have included and the organizational method you have chosen.

▶ **You can find an example of an annotated bibliography entry in section 9e.**

Literature Reviews

A literature review is designed to give readers an overview of the research that has been published on a given topic, and it also often points out what research should be conducted to investigate the issue further.

Purpose

Researchers write literature reviews for a variety of purposes: to understand a topic better, to demonstrate knowledge of the topic, to develop their own ideas, and to present a case for new research that needs to be done on a topic, among others.

- What research has been conducted and published about this topic, and what needs to be done next?
- What is your purpose for writing this literature review?
- As you compile sources about your topic and weave them together into an overview of the topic, what do you hope to learn about the research that has been conducted?

Audience

A researcher might write a literature review for other researchers in the same area of interest to help them see a significant gap in the existing research. This allows a researcher to develop a case for why a particular study is important to conduct—because it would fill that gap. Authors might also write literature reviews for instructors to demonstrate knowledge, or they might write for supervisors at work to summarize what has been written about a subject.

- Who is your audience for your literature review?
- Will your literature review be assessed by someone? If so, what criteria do you need to follow?

Voice

Literature reviews often tell the story of research that has been conducted on a particular subject. Writers of literature reviews bring a unique perspective to their work, and that might be influenced by personal experience with the topic or a bias toward a particular position or outcome. Often writers need to be sure to include sources representing multiple perspectives in a literature review, not just their own, to show how the story of the topic unfolds.

- What unique perspective do you bring to your literature review? Do you have prior knowledge of your topic or experience with it?
- What kinds of sources, perspectives, or research should you be certain to include to provide a thorough overview of the research published on your topic?

Medium

Literature reviews can be presented in print form, but they can also be written in a digital format such as a hypertext document or a digital, interactive timeline. The choice of medium is related to the purpose and audience for the literature review. For example, if you want to depict visually how a conversation about a topic has unfolded and when certain pieces published, a digital timeline might be the best option—especially if you can link out to many of those sources because they are available online.

- What medium is most appropriate for your literature review?

KEY POINTS
Writing Literature Reviews

Key Elements of Literature Reviews

- A collection of sources on your topic (the number of sources depends on how comprehensive you aim for your literature review to be)
- A claim or thesis, perhaps showing a gap in the research or highlighting a point of conflict in the published research on the topic
- Discussion of the relationships among sources, rather than just summaries of the sources
- Consistent documentation style for both in-text citations and a reference list
- A reference list, bibliography, or works-cited list

Keys for Organization of Literature Reviews

- Literature reviews are written in a prose format, with paragraphs organized to tell the story of the research written on an issue.
- Track your sources carefully as you collect them, perhaps using a software program like *Zotero* or *Diigo* to help you maintain a list of sources.
- If the order in which research is published is important for your topic, you might organize your literature review chronologically.
- If your literature review includes a large number of sources, you might organize it according to themes or topics to help readers follow the connections.

Key Steps for Writing Literature Reviews

- Find sources to include, and skim them to choose which are relevant to include.
- Read the selected sources in more detail, and map the connections between them, looking for
    - cross references
    - dates of publication
    - common research questions and data sets
- Begin drafting, using paragraph breaks to show relationships between sources and the progression of ideas and research.
- Include an introduction that establishes the scope of the literature review and a conclusion that emphasizes the gap in the research that you have found.

MindTap®

A sample literature review is available online.

Persuasive Arguments

A persuasive argument makes a claim about an issue that people can reasonably debate, and it supports that claim with evidence.

Purpose

Writers develop persuasive arguments for a wide range of purposes. They might want to analyze the causes of a problem, speculate about the effects of a particular policy, argue for a specific solution to a problem, or explain why a policy needs to be changed, to name a few.

- What is your purpose for writing this persuasive argument?
- What motivates you to write about this issue?

Audience

Effective arguments are written for specific audiences. Sometimes the audiences are large, but sometimes they are very small—perhaps only one person. The choice of audience shapes the argument; the same topic can be argued differently by the same writer for different audiences. A writer concerned about a current educational policy might choose to publish an editorial about it or write a statement about it to be read at a school board meeting or delivered to a school administrator.

- Who is your audience for your persuasive argument?
- What perspective does your audience already hold on your issue, and how might that affect the way you present your claim and evidence?
- Will your persuasive argument be assessed by someone? If so, what criteria do you need to follow?

Voice

The most effective arguments are written by authors who care deeply about the issues they write about. Because these writers are highly invested in their writing, they must also be aware of other perspectives on the issue so they can present reasonable and persuasive arguments that reach their audiences. If your perspective on your issue differs considerably from that of your audience, you should consider how to present your claim and back it up with evidence that your audience will find credible and persuasive.

- What unique perspective do you bring to your persuasive argument? Do you have prior knowledge of your topic or experience with it?
- What kinds of evidence should you be certain to include that your audience will find credible?

Medium

Persuasive arguments can be presented in print form, but they can also be written in digital formats such as hypertext documents (or full Web sites), blog posts, microblogs (*Twitter, Facebook, Tumblr*), infographics, slide presentations, images, or videos. The choice of medium is related to the purpose and audience for the persuasive argument. If you are presenting an argument that includes data to a school board and you have access to technology, you might choose to write a *PowerPoint* presentation.

- What medium is most appropriate for your persuasive argument?

KEY POINTS

Writing Persuasive Arguments

Key Elements of Persuasive Arguments

- A clear and arguable claim (for help with writing an effective claim, see 4c)
- An effort to establish common ground with readers and appeal to their values (for help with establishing common ground, see 4f)
- Convincing reasons and persuasive evidence from sources the target audience will find credible (for help with developing reasons and finding evidence, see 4d and 4e)
- Consideration of other perspectives, with clear counterarguments where necessary (for help with writing counterarguments, see 4f)

Keys for Organization of Persuasive Arguments

- *General to specific:* Begins with a clear claim and moves to the reasons and evidence
- *Specific to general:* Begins with data and evidence and draws a conclusion from that evidence
- *Problem and solution:* Presents a problem first that establishes the reasons for the problem with evidence and then offers a solution that directly addresses the problem
- *Cause and effect:* Examines the causes and effects of events and trends to make an argument about the origin or to speculate about the future effects of an issue
- For more about structuring an argument, see 4g.

Key Steps for Writing a Persuasive Argument

- Choose an issue that is important to you and that reasonable people could research but perhaps come to different conclusions.
- Consider the rhetorical context for your argument.
- Gather information about your issue from a variety of sources and perspectives.
- Construct a claim that you can support with evidence that you have found.
- Determine an effective organizational strategy for your argument.
- Include an introduction that will gain readers' interest in the issue and a conclusion that will offer memorable closure and perhaps a call to action.

▸ **You can find extended information about developing arguments in chapter 4 and an example of a persuasive argument in section 4j.**

Lab Reports

A lab report describes the methods and interprets the results from a research study that has collected data to respond to a research question and test a hypothesis.

Purpose

Lab reports serve a variety of purposes. Scientists, engineers, and other scholars write lab reports to share the methods and results of their research with others in the same field. Students write lab reports to demonstrate to instructors that they have followed appropriate procedures and have drawn accurate conclusions from the data.

- What is your purpose for writing this lab report?
- What information do you need to include in your lab report to achieve your intended purpose?

Audience

The audience for a lab report is usually somewhat knowledgeable about the subject. The audience might be researchers in the same field or researchers in related fields who read the study because it looks at a common interest from a different perspective. Another knowledgeable audience would be an instructor who is interested in whether or not you conducted your study appropriately. Often other scholars will read a lab report so that they can replicate, adapt, or build upon the study and test the results; therefore, clear, accurate descriptions of methodology and data collected are essential.

- Who is your audience for your lab report? What expectations will your audience have?
- Will someone be assessing your lab report? If so, what criteria will be used?

Voice

The disciplinary fields that most often produce lab reports (natural sciences, social sciences, engineering) value neutrality in research, so avoid using the first person in your lab report even though it might feel strange because you are the person who collected the data. Many lab reports use passive voice to avoid the first person in descriptions of the research methods. Try to minimize the influence of your own perspective and bias as you collect and describe results in a lab report.

- Where in your lab report will you need to pay close attention to the potential influence of your perspective and bias?

Medium

Lab reports can be published in both print and digital formats, but they often follow similar conventions of organization and formatting.

- What medium is most appropriate for your lab report?
- What requirements for presentation of your lab report do you need to follow?

KEY POINTS
Writing Lab Reports

Key Elements of Lab Reports

- A descriptive title
- An abstract that provides a summary of the study and its findings
- An introduction to the study that includes a clear statement of its importance and connects it to other research that has already been published
- A detailed description of the methods used for data collection
- A summary of the data collected
- Analysis and discussion of the data
- A list of all references, formatted according to the appropriate documentation style
- Appendices, if needed, which might include surveys used, raw data, interview questions and protocol, or other information that is too detailed or lengthy to include in the main body of the report

Keys for Organization of Lab Reports

- Lab reports usually follow a standard organization that is often described with the acronym IMRAD, and the sections of the report often have titles that refer to the five primary parts of the report. The titles might vary slightly, but the content and organization are fairly standard.
- *Introduction:* Includes a justification of the importance of the study and a review of relevant research
- *Methods:* Includes a description of the methods used for data collection, participants in the study, materials used
- *Results:* Includes a summary of the data collected
- *Analysis:* Interpretation of what the results might mean
- *Discussion:* Often combined with the analysis, describes what conclusions researchers might come to from the results gathered in the study and what the implications are for the subject and for future research

Key Steps for Writing Lab Reports

- Know your subject well, and read studies that others have conducted about your subject.
- Write a clear research question, and, if appropriate, pose a hypothesis about the results you expect to find.
- Plan how you will analyze your data before you begin collecting it.
- Keep clear, accurate, detailed records of your data.
- Pay attention to the requirements for how your lab report should be formatted for final presentation or publication, and follow those requirements as much as you can while drafting.

▶ **You can find an excerpt from a student's lab report and more information about writing in the natural sciences and social sciences in sections 5g and 5h.**

Portfolio Reflections

A portfolio reflection is a self-assessment of written work completed over a period of time.

Purpose

An author might write a portfolio reflection to assess and reflect on what was learned over the course of a semester by examining the writing completed. In this case, the analysis would focus on areas of growth as a writer. An author might also write a portfolio reflection when compiling materials for a job application. Rather than focus on areas of growth, the author might emphasize how various pieces in the portfolio demonstrate specific areas of expertise.

- What is your purpose for writing this portfolio reflection?
- What writing should you examine to complete your portfolio reflection?
- What criteria should you use to assess your work?

Audience

Portfolio reflections are written for a variety of audiences. Often they are written at the culmination of an educational experience: a course, a program, a degree. In these cases, the audience is usually a group of educators interested in what you have learned and how the work in your portfolio demonstrates your growth. If the portfolio reflection accompanies an application, the audience might be a selection committee or a potential employer. In these circumstances, they are looking for evidence that you meet criteria for selection and perhaps that your work stands out in a group of applicants.

- Who is the audience for your portfolio reflection?
- What elements of your work will be most interesting to your audience?
- What criteria will your audience expect you to use as you assess your work?

Voice

Portfolio reflections are personal, and they usually are written in the first person. Depending on your rhetorical context, you might adopt a more vulnerable tone, focusing on areas in which you have improved and still hope to improve. In other contexts, your tone might be more self-promoting, emphasizing the areas of strength in your portfolio.

- What tone is most appropriate for you to adopt in your portfolio reflection? How would you like to represent the work in your portfolio?

Medium

Because portfolios can include work that might be digital, print, or a combination of both, portfolio reflections can also be either print or digital. Many portfolios are compiled online, so portfolio reflections in these cases might be documents added to online portfolios or they might be digital reflections that link out to elements of the portfolio itself.

- What medium is most appropriate for your portfolio reflection?

KEY POINTS
Writing Portfolio Reflections

Key Elements of Portfolio Reflections

- Primary claim about your overall performance or development
- Indication of the criteria used for evaluation in the reflection
- Specific assessment of each piece included in the portfolio

Keys for Organization of Portfolio Reflections

- The organization of the reflection should reflect the organization of the portfolio itself. If there are specific categories, assignments, or types of writing included in the portfolio, organize your reflection in a similar way.
- Begin with an overall assessment and then move to specific details by referring to pieces included in the portfolio as evidence for your overall assessment.
- Unless you are instructed otherwise, mention each item included in your portfolio in the reflection.

Key Steps for Writing a Portfolio Reflection

- Compile materials to include in the portfolio.
- Determine the criteria to be used for self-assessment.
- Examine each piece to be included, using the criteria to take notes about your performance.
- Look for trends across the pieces in your portfolio. Are there areas where you see growth? Areas of consistent strength or weakness? What evidence can you point to?
- Draft an introduction to your reflection that highlights an overall assessment of your work.
- Include details from each of the elements of your portfolio to support the overall assessment.

▶ **You can find instructions for compiling a portfolio of your writing as well as a student's e-portfolio in chapter 25.**

Job Application Letters

A job application letter outlines an applicant's qualifications for a position and draws connections between those qualifications and the job advertised. It usually accompanies a résumé as part of a job application package.

Purpose

Writers draft job application letters when they are applying for a specific job. A job application letter is often the first chance an applicant has to make a good impression on a prospective employer, and it is usually intended to get an applicant in the door for an interview. Job application letters should always be written for specific jobs, so consider the specific qualifications for the job to increase your chances of landing an interview.

- What can you determine about the review process for the job for which you are applying?
- What qualifications are required and desired for this job, and how can you address them in your letter?

Audience

The audience for a job application letter is generally quite narrow, including a specific person or set of people who make hiring decisions. Depending on the size and hiring practices of the company, your job application letter might first be reviewed by a committee, by the person who would be your direct supervisor, or by a person in a Human Resources department, to name a few. The audience for your job application letter will likely be reviewing many letters, so get to the point quickly, and consider how to make your letter stand out from the others in a positive way.

- Who is your audience for your job application letter? What can you learn about the person or people who will be reviewing your letter from information available online or elsewhere?
- What does the audience for your job application letter value? What will they be searching for in a candidate?

Voice

The tone of a job application letter should be professional and appropriate to the job for which you are applying. You will also want to make your letter stand out in a stack of job application letters, so consider how you can highlight your unique voice and perspective.

- What unique qualifications and experience should you highlight to make your letter stand out from the others?

Medium

Job application letters are often delivered digitally, but whether or not they are printed on paper or sent as a digital file, they are almost always written in a standard print-based format.

- What format should you follow for your job application letter?
- What medium should you use for delivery of your job application letter?

KEY POINTS

Writing Job Application Letters

Key Elements of Job Application Letters

- An appropriate salutation. Address the letter to a specific person in the company. If you cannot determine who that might be from the job posting, consider e-mailing or calling the contact in the job posting.
- An explanation of your interest in the job
- A description of your qualifications, focusing on those qualifications that make you a good candidate for this particular position
- Contact information for the company to contact you for an interview, ideally in several forms (phone number, e-mail, mailing address)

Keys for Organization of Job Application Letters

- Use standard block formatting for a business letter (see the example in section 26c).
- In the first paragraph, identify the job for which you are applying and mention where you saw the job posting.
- Clearly highlight your qualifications for the position in the letter, and consider organizing the paragraphs of your letter according to specific required and desired qualifications listed in the job posting.
- Close your letter by thanking reviewers for their time and expressing your interest in speaking further about the position.

Key Steps for Writing Job Application Letters

- Look for all of the possible connections between your experience and the requirements for the job. Don't forget to look beyond formal work and educational experience; sometimes the most persuasive application letters show how unusual life experiences make a candidate uniquely qualified for a job.
- Carefully address all of the required qualifications for the job, mentioning and explaining specific items included on your résumé. Do not just tell readers to "see my résumé."
- Carefully balance the need to promote your qualifications while remaining professional. In addition to showing you are qualified for the job, you are also demonstrating that you are pleasant to work with.
- Edit and proofread your job application letter carefully. Your letter must contain no errors, and it should be your best representation of your communication skills.

▸ **You can find an example of a job application letter in section 26c.**

Résumés

A résumé is a brief summary of education and work experience, usually given to a prospective employer as part of a job application or professional portfolio.

Purpose

Job applicants write résumés to communicate to a prospective employer what they have accomplished and when. Résumés provide details of education, work experience, honors or awards, interests, and special skills relevant to a specific job.

- What is your purpose for writing this résumé?
- How can you tailor your résumé to accomplish your specific purpose?

Audience

The audience for a résumé is most often a prospective employer, and the résumé provides specific details about experience often referred to in a job application letter. The first audience for a résumé might be a prospective supervisor, a hiring committee, a Human Resources employee, or even a computer program that will scan the résumé to look for specific search terms relevant to a job posting.

- Who is your audience for your résumé? What can you find out about that audience?
- What conventions will your audience be expecting you to follow for the organization and content of your résumé? Are there specific terms you should be sure to include—keywords that software will be scanning for?

Voice

Résumés are written in concise language to communicate a great deal of information in a small amount of space. Avoid elaborate language and full sentences, opting for clear, precise wording and grammatically parallel phrases and descriptions.

- What details are most important to include in your résumé? How can you phrase them concisely without losing essential details?

Medium

Résumés can be presented on paper, posted on the Web, or delivered electronically through e-mail or a dropbox. Because résumés are often searched electronically first before a person reads them, choosing a plain white or off-white paper, a sans serif font, and clean, simple formatting can help preserve readability of your résumé. To maintain the formatting of a résumé being sent as a file, save it as a PDF instead of a .doc, .docx, or .rtf unless directed differently.

- What medium is most appropriate for your résumé?

KEY POINTS

Writing Résumés

Key Elements of Résumés

- Name and contact information
- Information about education, degrees, and certifications, with names of institutions, years attended, and titles of degrees and certifications
- Relevant prior work experience, with brief information about job responsibilities and accomplishments
- List of special skills or honors
- A mention that references are available upon request (or a list of references, if requested)

Keys for Organization of Résumés

- Format the document to include plenty of white space to make the résumé more readable, but limit yourself to one or two pages.
- Include all contact information at the top.
- List education first and then work experience.
- Special skills, honors, or other information should be listed after education and work experience in order of relevance.
- Mention of references should come at the end of the résumé.

Key Steps for Writing Résumés

- Brainstorm details about your work experience and your job responsibilities, considering all information that would be relevant for your desired position. Your résumé for one position might not be identical to your résumé for another position, depending on the skills and experience you would like to highlight.
- Consider including language proficiency and technological capabilities in a section on special skills. Even if not mentioned in a job posting, these skills are often valued by prospective employers.
- Single-space all sections of the résumé, and include an extra line between sections.
- Use a table format to place headings on the left-hand side of the page and descriptions on the right-hand side.

▶ **You can find additional instructions for writing a résumé in section 26a and an example of a résumé in section 26b.**

Memos

A memo is a message conveying specific information from one person to another person or group of people in a business setting. You can find additional information about writing memos in section 27d.

Purpose

People write memos to convey messages in business settings. Memos generally report on information briefly, or they might raise a question or ask permission to follow a course of action, or they might outline a policy.

- What is your purpose for writing this memo?
- Why does the information need to be conveyed in writing?

Audience

Memos are written for specific people in a business setting. As you write, consider what the audience already knows about the message you are conveying and what contextual information they might need. Imagine an employee writing to an immediate supervisor to communicate quarterly sales for her division. The context for reporting sales data would not need to be explained in great detail, since the supervisor would likely be familiar with the context. Imagine now that the sales figures need to be communicated to management at a regional sales office. In this case, some background information about the context for the sales data might be needed.

- Who is your audience for your memo?
- What information does your audience need to understand the message of your memo? How much of that information can you assume your audience already knows?

Voice

Memos maintain a professional tone. They are specific, precise, and brief. Accuracy is important, and it is communicated both by conveying correct information and by writing a memo with few, if any, grammatical problems.

- What tone is most appropriate for your memo?
- How might you edit your writing to make it as specific, precise, and brief as possible?

Medium

Memos are sometimes printed and hand-delivered, but they are often delivered electronically (usually by e-mail). When you are choosing a medium for your memo, you might think about what will convey the information most appropriately and what is considered general practice in your business setting.

- What medium is most appropriate for your memo?

KEY POINTS
Writing Memos

Key Elements of a Memo

- Standard headings, including a list of people to whom the letter is being sent (often on a CC: line). For an e-mail, be sure to complete the subject line.
- An opening paragraph that states the purpose of the memo
- Details that support or give more information to fulfill the stated purpose

Keys for Organization of a Memo

- Begin with a standard memo format for headings. You can use a template in your word processing program to find a default opening.
- State your main purpose in the first sentence.
- Use additional text to support and fulfill that purpose (perhaps divided into paragraphs if the memo is long).
- Single-space your memo.
- Consider bulleting lists or information that you would like to have stand out on the page.

Key Steps for Writing a Memo

- Determine what message you need to convey.
- Narrow your audience, and consider what your audience already knows about the situation, issue, or topic about which you are writing.
- Get to the point, ideally in the first sentence.
- Develop supporting information in the body of the memo, taking care to explain information for which the audience might not have any context.

MindTap®

A sample memo is available online.

2 The Research Process

2 The Research Process

WRITING IN YOUR CAREER

The Nurse, the Writer

Courtesy of Shelly Culbertson

When you think of health care, you probably don't think about writing. Nurse Shelly Culbertson did not, until she realized that writing not only was part of case management but also had important consequences and involved critical research. As a health care practitioner, Culbertson does primary research in the form of patient-client interviews and careful observation. As with all research, the better the questions are, the better the information. Documentation and word choice are extremely important because they help guide other medical professionals toward accurate assessments of every patient. As a nurse, Culbertson also does secondary research, reviewing sources such as patients' medical records and retrieving information that affects Medicare reimbursement and insurance payment criteria. She evaluates complex medical data and uses the hospital's software program to document her patients' clinical conditions. The clarity of her writing and level of detail has a direct impact on patients' diagnoses and treatments. This type of technical writing utilizes special medical terminology overflowing with acronyms and abbreviations. But make no mistake, the quality of the research and of the written presentation that Culbertson does directly affects her patients and the quality of care provided by the medical staff.

Glen Stubbe/MCT/Newscom

2 The Research Process

6 Research: A Conversation with Sources

MindTap®

Understand the goals of this part, and complete a warm-up activity.

Read, highlight, and take notes online.

What is research, and why do it? Imagine you have the flu, and you try to find out what the symptoms are and the best way to treat them. That's research. You want to buy a new smartphone, but you don't know anything about the features, brands, and prices. You search online, talk to salespeople, go to stores, ask friends what they recommend, and read consumer reviews. That's research, too. And when your English professor asks you to write a paper on, say, the role of government in protecting the environment, research helps you as you interview experts, find reliable print and online sources, consult government documents, and get help from librarians. Doing research is finding out as much as possible about an issue, formulating a research question, and then attempting to find answers to that question. Entering into the ongoing debates around an issue is a vital part of daily life; contributing to the discussion is an essential part of academic and scholarly work.

6a Knowing what is involved in researched writing

1. Know your research context Start by identifying the elements of your research context. Keeping your purpose, audience, voice, and medium in mind will help you make smart choices in your research, just as they will for any writing project.

See the full model on page 7.

2. Know the requirements, and set a realistic schedule Find out what the demands of the assignment are, such as length, due date, information to include, number and types of sources, documentation style, and manuscript format. Set a week-by-week or day-by-day schedule for the steps in the process, as in 6b.

3. Assemble the tools you will need Consider what will help you in your research. Do you need to create folders on your computer, identify tracking software, or set up space online so that you can access files from multiple spaces, for instance?

4. Do preliminary research to establish your topic Make sure you understand and answer the assigned question or address the assigned topic. If you select your own topic, check with your instructor to make sure it is appropriate. Do preliminary research online or in reference works to browse for topics and become familiar with the issues. Narrow the topic so that it is manageable for the number of pages you intend to write. Also be sure to choose a topic that will engage and sustain not only readers' interests but also your own, and make connections with your own experience whenever possible. If your topic is assigned, make sure you understand the terms used in the assignment.

5. Develop your research question Design a research question that establishes what you know and what you want to discover. The answer you find as you do research is likely to become your thesis (more on this in 4c and 6e).

6. Write a statement of purpose or a proposal A clearly articulated statement of purpose or a fuller research proposal will help you outline what you plan to do. Section 6f explains how to write both.

7. Determine types of sources and how to find them Decide which types of primary and secondary sources will give you the best results (use section 6c and chapter 7 to help you with this stage); then draw up a plan of action. Allow large blocks of time for locating sources. You'll find that this work cannot be done in just an hour or two.

8. Look for and evaluate sources, and keep full and accurate records Select only sources that fit the criteria for your research context, considering which will be most credible in that context. Record full bibliographical information for every source you consult (9e). Bookmark, download, or print your source material so that you can annotate it later. There are several computer applications and online tools that can help you save, tag, and annotate resources (such as *Mendeley* and *Zotero*); see 9f for more on reference tools.

9. Take precise notes (more on this in 10a–10e) Paraphrase and summarize as often as possible while taking notes. Be sure to use your own words and write down why the information is useful or how you might integrate it into your paper. Make sure you copy quotations exactly as they are written, using quotation marks or a colored font. In your notes, record all page numbers of print sources. Track Web addresses through a research application such as *Mendeley* or *Zotero* or in a specially named file for your paper; be sure to also record the date of access along with the address.

10. Establish your main idea or hypothesis Digest your material, and determine your focus. Your paper should not simply string together what others have said with no commentary from you. Especially in the humanities, use your research to help form opinions and arrive at conclusions about your topic. Readers want to find *you* and your ideas in your paper. If you are writing in an academic genre that requires a thesis, develop a preliminary one as soon as you can, and make lists of supporting evidence and specific details from what you know and what you read. In the natural and applied sciences and in the social sciences, it is more usual to form a hypothesis, present the evidence, and then draw conclusions (5g and 5h).

At some point, when you decide you have something to say about what you think and what your sources say, make a plan or a map, and start a rough first draft.

11. Write drafts: Revise, revise, revise Write more than one draft. As with almost all writing for college and beyond, revision is an essential step in the writing process. You should not expect to produce a perfect first draft. Consider making an outline from each draft to check on your coverage of the main points and the logic of your argument.

12. Organize your drafts Be sure to save copies of each draft as a new file so you can keep a record of the changes you have made. It's a good idea to develop a consistent naming convention so you can quickly see which file includes your most recent draft. You can also distinguish among your earliest rough drafts, your later revisions, and your final copyedited versions by using keywords like *rough*, *revised*, and *edited*, along with numbers, as shown in the sample course folder (Figure 6.1).

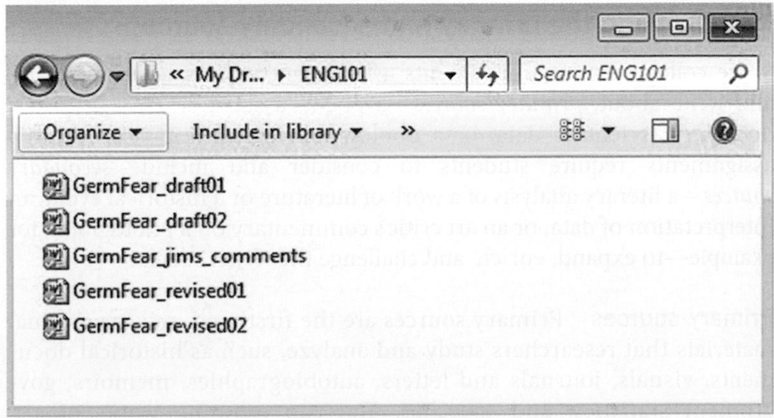

Source: Microsoft Corporation

Figure 6.1 Course folder with clearly labeled drafts

Be sure to follow any file-naming conventions that your instructor provides if you will be turning in your work electronically.

13. Acknowledge and document all your sources Avoid plagiarism by providing information in your text every time you not only quote but also refer to the ideas you find in a source (10c, 10d, 10e).

14. Prepare a list of works cited Follow a clear and consistent set of conventions (spacing, indentation, names, order, and punctuation of entries) when you prepare a list of works cited or references (chapters 12–13 and 15–20). Then compare your citations with your list. Make sure that every item on your list appears in your paper and that every work referred to in your paper appears on your list. Using a system of checkmarks in both places as you read a draft is an easy way to do this.

See Chapters 13, 16, 18, 20 for examples of lists of works cited or references.

6b Setting a schedule

Get started as early as you can. As soon as a project is assigned, set a tentative schedule for searching for sources, evaluating the sources, and drafting, working backward from the date the paper is due and splitting your time so that you know when you absolutely must move on to the next step. Figure 6.2 includes a sample schedule, showing blocks of time, which you can adapt for your own use. You will find that, in reality, several tasks overlap and the divisions are not neat. If you finish a block before the deadline, move on and give yourself more time for the later blocks.

6c Considering primary and secondary sources

Some college writing assignments ask student writers to engage with, and write about, *primary sources*—a poem, a short story, a historical document, scientific data, or a photograph. Many first-year research assignments require students to consider and include *secondary sources*—a literary analysis of a work of literature or a historical event, an interpretation of data, or an art critic's commentary on a photograph, for example—to expand, enrich, and challenge the writer's ideas.

Primary sources Primary sources are the firsthand, raw, or original materials that researchers study and analyze, such as historical documents, visuals, journals and letters, autobiographies, memoirs, government statistics, and speeches. You can examine works of art,

RESEARCH SCHEDULE

Starting date:

Date final draft is due:

Block 1: Getting started

Understand the requirements.

Select a topic, or narrow a given topic.

Determine the preliminary types of sources to use.

Do preliminary research to discover the important issues.

Organize research findings in computer files or online.

Write a research question.

Complete by ________

Block 2: Reading, researching, and evaluating sources

Find and bookmark or download sources.

Annotate and evaluate sources.

Write summaries and paraphrases, and make notes.

Set up a working bibliography.

Complete by ________

Block 3: Planning and drafting

Formulate a working thesis.

Write a purpose statement, proposal, and/or an outline.

Write a first draft.

Complete by

Block 4: Evaluating the draft and getting feedback

Put the draft away for a day or two but continue collecting useful sources.

Outline the draft, and evaluate its logic and completeness.

Plan more research as necessary to fill any gaps.

Get feedback from your instructor and classmates.

Complete by ________

Block 5: Revising, preparing list of works cited, editing, presenting

Revise the draft.

Prepare a list of works cited.

Design the format of the paper.

Edit the draft.

Proofread the final draft.

Complete by ________
(final deadline for handing in)

Figure 6.2 Sample research schedule, outlining the typical parts of a research process

literature, and architecture or watch or listen to performances and programs. You can study or initiate case studies or scientific experiments and take extensive field notes. You can also conduct interviews and use data collected from questionnaires. The use of such primary sources can bring an original note to your research and new information to readers.

Interviews Interview people who have expert knowledge of your topic. Plan a set of interview questions, but do not stick so closely to your script that you fail to follow up on good leads in your respondent's replies. Ask permission to record the interview; otherwise, you will have to take quick and accurate notes, particularly if you want to quote. Check the functioning of your recording device beforehand. Make note of the date, time, and place of the interview. Remember that developing good questions and performing the background research on your interviewee is equally important whether you are conducting interviews via e-mail or instant messaging or in person. Be sure to write a thank-you note to follow up after your interview.

Surveys and questionnaires Designing useful questionnaires is tricky because much depends on the number and sample of respondents you use, the types of questions you ask, and the methods you employ to analyze the data. Embark on survey research only if you have been introduced to the necessary techniques in a college course or have consulted experts in this area. You may also need permission to conduct research on human subjects. If you do choose to conduct a survey, you can also use low-cost, user-friendly online survey applications, such as *Google Forms* or *SurveyMonkey*.

Secondary sources Secondary sources are analytical works that comment on and interpret other works, such as primary sources. Examples include reviews, discussions, biographies, critical studies, analyses of literary or artistic works or events, commentaries on current and historical events, class lectures, and electronic discussions.

6d Consulting reference works to get started

Reference works provide basic information about a subject, often compiled from a variety of secondary sources. You can access many standard reference works online or through your library's home page. Use reference works only to get started with basic information, however, and for assistance as you explore a topic and find out what issues that topic involves. Then quickly move beyond them.

Encyclopedias Encyclopedias provide an overview of the issues involved in a complex topic. Some may also provide extensive bibliographies of other useful sources, so they can help you develop your research and formulate a research proposal if you are asked to provide one.

General print and online encyclopedias such as the *Columbia Encyclopedia*, *Encyclopaedia Britannica*, and subject-specific encyclopedias such as the *Internet Encyclopedia of Philosophy* or *Berkshire Encyclopedia of World History* can help you get started. Similarly, *Wikipedia* can be useful in early stages as long as you keep in mind that it is constantly being revised. Cross-check any information you find there with other sources, and do not include it as a source. Even the founder of *Wikipedia*, Jimmy Wales, has said, "You're in college; don't cite the encyclopedia." If you consult *Wikipedia*, you might just scroll to the end of the article to see the list of references and follow those for potential leads. In addition, your instructor may recommend not using *Wikipedia* at all.

Bibliographies (also known as *guides to the literature*) You can find lists of books and articles on a subject in online bibliographical databases such as the following: *Books in Print, International Medieval Bibliography, MLA International Bibliography,* and *New Books on Women, Gender and Feminism.*

Biographies Read accounts of people's lives in biographical works such as *Who's Who, American National Biography Online, Biography Index: A Cumulative Index to Biographic Material in Books and Magazines, Contemporary Authors, Dictionary of Literary Biography, African American Biographical Database, Chicano Scholars and Writers,* and *American Men and Women of Science.*

Directories Directories provide lists of names and addresses of people, companies, and institutions. They are useful for setting up interviews and contacting people when you need information. Examples are *Communication Media in Higher Education: A Directory of Academic Programs and Faculty in Radio-Television-Film and Related Media* and *The Computer Science Directory* (a resource of conference, professionals, publications, and institutes in computer science).

Dictionaries For etymologies, definitions, synonyms, and spelling, consult *The American Heritage Dictionary of the English Language*, 5th edition; *Oxford English Dictionary* (multiple volumes—useful for detailed etymologies and usage discussions); *Facts on File* specialized dictionaries; and other specialized dictionaries such as *Dictionary of Literary Terms* and *Dictionary of the Social Sciences*.

Dictionaries of quotations For a rich source of traditional quotations, go to *Bartlett's Familiar Quotations*; for more contemporary quotations, searchable by topic, go to *The Columbia World of Quotations* (both are available online). Also consult specialized dictionaries of quotations, such as volumes devoted to chess, law, religion, fishing, women, and Wall Street.

Collections of articles of topical interest and news summaries *CQ* (*Congressional Quarterly*) weekly reports, *Facts on File* publications, and *CQ Almanac* are available in print and online. *SIRS* (*Social Issues Resources Series*) also appears in print and online by subscription.

Statistics and government documents Among the many useful online sources are *Statistical Abstract of the United States, Current Index to Statistics, Handbook of Labor Statistics, Occupational Outlook Handbook,* US Census publications, *GPO Access, UN Demographic Yearbook, Population Index,* and *Digest of Education Statistics.*

Almanacs, atlases, and gazetteers For population statistics and boundary changes, see *The World Almanac, Countries of the World,* or *Information Please.* For locations, descriptions, pronunciation of place names, climate, demography, languages, natural resources, and industry, consult a gazetteer such as *Columbia-Lippincott Gazetteer of the World* and the *CIA World Factbook* series.

General critical works Read what scholars have to say about works of art and literature in *Contemporary Literary Criticism* and in the *Oxford Companion* volumes (such as *Oxford Companion to Art* and *Oxford Companion to African American Literature*).

For more information about finding sources beyond reference works, see chapter 7, pages 153–167.

6e Moving from research question to preliminary thesis

Designing a research question For a paper that draws on research, design a research question that gets at the heart of what you want to discover. Your question should contain concrete keywords that you can search rather than general terms or abstractions. The answer you find as you do research is likely to become your thesis (claim) or main idea. If you find huge amounts of material on your question and realize that you would have to write a book (or two) to cover all the issues, narrow your question.

Questions Needing Narrowing	Revised Questions
How important are families? *Too broad: important to whom and for what? No useful keywords to search.*	In what ways does a stable family environment contribute to an individual's future success?
What problems does the Internet cause? *Too broad: what types of problems? what aspects of the Internet?*	What types of Internet controls would protect individual privacy?
What are the treatments for cancer? *Too wide-ranging: volumes could be and have been written on this.*	For which types of cancer are the success rates of radiation therapy the most promising?

Formulating a preliminary thesis If your research question is "Should Internet controls be established to protect individual privacy?" as you read and do research, you will probably move toward either a "yes" or "no" answer to the question. At this point, you might formulate a preliminary thesis in the form of a statement of opinion, which will help drive the organization of your paper. Continue, however, to look for information that will help you move beyond just "yes" or "no" to develop an informed, specific response to your question.

KEY POINTS

Writing a Preliminary Thesis

1. **Make sure it is a statement.** A phrase or a question is not a thesis: "Internet controls" is a topic, not a thesis statement. "Are Internet controls needed?" is a question, not a thesis statement.
2. **Make sure it is not merely a statement of fact.** "About 50 percent of US residents are active users of the Internet" is a statement that cannot be developed and argued. A statement of fact does not let readers feel the need to read on to see what you have to say.

(Continued)

(Continued)

3. **Make sure it does more than announce the topic.** "This paper will discuss Internet controls" is inadequate because your thesis statement should give information about, or offer an informed opinion on, the topic: "Service providers, Internet users, and parents share the responsibility of establishing Internet controls to protect an individual's privacy."
4. **Change and refine your thesis as you do more research.** Revising your thesis is essential as you discover more about what your topic entails. Remember that this is a preliminary thesis, so it will likely change as you conduct your research.

6f Writing a purpose statement or a proposal

After you have done some preliminary research, you can write a simple statement of purpose. This statement may become more developed or even change completely as you learn more about your topic, but it will serve to guide your first steps in the research process. Your purpose statement should reflect as much as you can about your research context (purpose, audience, voice, and medium) and the direction you're taking. Here is an example:

PURPOSE | AUDIENCE | VOICE | MEDIUM

See the full model on page 7.

Medium — Purpose — Audience

> The purpose of this documented paper is to persuade film directors and critics that films based on real-life events—such as *Spotlight*—should give precedence to the development of a good story rather than to unembellished factual accuracy; after all, adults expect entertainment rather than education when they go to the movies.

Your instructor may also ask for an outline (2d) or for a fuller proposal with a working bibliography attached (9e). Once you have your brief purpose statement, you can use it as a basis for a proposal in narrative or list form, covering background information, establishing your connection to the topic, addressing more information about your purpose and audience, discussing your voice and unique perspective on the issue, and including your research question.

6g Tips for writing, revising, and editing researched writing

WHAT NOT TO DO

- Do not expect to complete a polished draft in one sitting.
- Do not write the title and the first sentence and then panic because you feel you have nothing left to say.
- Do not necessarily begin at the beginning, and especially do not think you must first write a dynamite introduction. That is why you need to set aside time to revise!
- Do not constantly imagine your instructor's response to what you write.
- Do not worry about coherence—a draft by its nature is something that you work on repeatedly and revise.

WHAT TO DO

- Wait until you have a block of time available before you begin writing a draft of your paper.
- Turn off your cell phone, log off social media, turn off the Wi-Fi connectivity on your laptop, close the door, and tell yourself you will not emerge from the room until you have written several pages.
- Promise yourself a reward when you meet your target—a short walk or a snack break, for instance.
- Assemble in one place your copy of the assignment, your purpose statement and thesis statement, all your copies of sources, your research notebook and any other notes, your working bibliography, and your proposal or outline. Yes, that's a lot! So start early.
- Write the parts you know most about first.
- Write as much as you can as quickly as you can. If you only vaguely remember a reference in your sources, just write what you can remember and be sure to leave yourself a note to come back to it, but keep writing, and don't worry about gaps: as so and so (who was it? Jackson?) has observed, malls are taking the place of city centers (check page reference).
- Write the beginning—the introduction—only after you have some ideas on paper that you feel you can introduce.

- Write at least something on each one of the points in your outline. Start by asking yourself: "What do I know about this point, and how does it support my thesis?" Write your response in your own words, and then check your notes and fill in the gaps later.
- Write until you feel you have put down on the page or screen your main points and you have made reference to most of your source material.

Jasminko Ibrakovic/Shutterstock.com

Figure 6.3 As you write, remember that writing consultants at campus writing centers may be able to help you take a fresh look at your draft.

If you can, set your draft aside and do not look at it for a while—at least a day. In the meantime, follow up on any research leads; find new sources; discuss your draft with your instructor, classmates, or a consultant at your campus writing center; and continue writing ideas in your research notebook. To revise your draft, make an outline of what you have written and ask yourself these questions:

- Have I covered the most important points?
- When I read the paper aloud, where do I hesitate to try to sort out the meaning? (Watch for those worried frowns!)
- Do I come across as someone with interesting, unique ideas on this topic? What opinions do I offer?
- Have I cited sources accurately and used summary, paraphrase, and quotation responsibly? (See chapters 9 and 10 for more on this important point.)
- Where do I need to provide more evidence from sources to support my claims?

How to Search for Sources

MindTap®
Read, highlight, and take notes online.

Conducting research involves looking for and collecting information on a topic to develop and refine your own views. When you conduct research for an academic project, you gather information that you need to evaluate as valid, reliable, and relevant to your research context. Then you cite this source information in your paper in ways that are specific to the discipline.

No matter how many sources you find and use, your paper should be a synthesis of the main issues you come across in your research. But a well-researched essay is not simply a mindless compilation of sources. Rather, your essay should establish your place in the ongoing conversation about the topic. Let it present you in interaction with your topic and engaged with the ways others have addressed that topic. In the sciences, the structuring of information is more important than the personal opinion of the writer. In the humanities, the writer's perspective is often more visible, so avoid the danger of listing an abundance of sources without coming to some conclusion or presenting your own point of view.

7a Starting the search for sources on a topic

Your library offers several useful starting points for a research project. This section lists categories of resources with examples of when you might find them useful. But the best resource of all remains a librarian, who can help you navigate these different resources and figure out where to start. Don't hesitate to talk to a librarian about the different resources available at your library.

Your library's catalog and interlibrary loan The online library catalog for your college or university is the best way to find books held in the library's permanent collection. Many libraries participate in interlibrary loan programs as well, so you can access resources at other libraries by ordering them and having them sent to your school or local library. For more information about how to find books using the library catalog, see 7b.

Online library subscription databases Databases of abstracts and full-text general and scholarly articles previously in print are a good place to start serious online searching on topics. For more information about using online databases to find scholarly articles, see 7c. Access these databases by keyword searching (7f).

Web directories Libraries, colleges, and other organizations provide valuable subject directories for researchers. These allow you to start with a subject area and drill down until you get to specific sites on specific topics.

- *Research Quickstart* has lists of sources in many academic subjects.
- *Michigan Electronic Library* (MeL) is a University of Michigan site that provides access to a range of sources.
- *Internet Public Library*, run by librarians, offers a guide to subject collections and an "Ask an IPL Librarian" feature, which allows you to e-mail a question about a research project to librarians for evaluation and a possible response within three days.
- *INFOMINE*, a University of California, Riverside, site, has scholarly resources in medical sciences, business, and visual arts, along with general references.
- *Voice of the Shuttle*, a University of California, Santa Barbara, site, lists research sources in the humanities.
- *Library of Congress* is important for the listing of its own collections.
- *Librarians' Internet Index* includes useful links to sites in cross-disciplinary subject areas, some of which present a specific viewpoint.
- *The WWW Virtual Library* provides a common access point to Web catalogs and directories maintained by different institutions throughout the world.
- *MLA International Bibliography* provides "a classified listing and subject index for books and articles published on modern languages, literatures, folklore, and linguistics."

Free catalogs from other libraries The Web gives you free access to the online resources of many libraries (actual and virtual) and universities, which are good browsing sites. Some useful sites are *Library of Congress*, *LibWeb*, *New York Public Library*, and *Smithsonian Institution Libraries*.

KEY POINTS

What Every Librarian Wishes You Knew

- **Libraries do more than store books.** You might think of a library as a place that holds books, but libraries do that and far more. These days they provide access to information available through multiple media. For this reason, many experienced researchers make the library their first stop for any new project.
- **Not everything is accessible online.** While you can probably access your library's databases online and perhaps even see what other books are on a shelf next to one you're interested in, some things are only available in person. Go to the physical library if you can, and spend some time learning about what is available.
- **Keywords should be chosen carefully.** Many students come to the library without having thought through the best way to phrase their search terms. Think of the specific words you should search for and any alternatives. Ask a librarian for help. Read through section 7f for ideas about choosing keywords for searching.
- **Good researchers visit a library early and often.** Don't go to the library at the last minute and expect to be able to conduct solid research. You'll need time to look through the resources available, assess whether they're credible, and determine what parts you want to use. Some resources may only be available through interlibrary loan, which can take several days.
- **Librarians are people, too.** Librarians are specialists in finding information of all types, and they want to help you. Go with a specific question, and ask for help. You'll be glad you did.

7b Using library catalogs to find books

Library catalogs offer the option of searching by title, author, subject, or keyword (7f). Exact wording and exact spelling are essential for each kind of search.

Subject searches To find sources focused on one topic, try subject searching. For that, you need to know the specific subject headings the catalogers used to identify and classify material, so consult a reference source such as *Library of Congress Subject Headings*, or ask a librarian for help. For example, you won't find *cultural identity* or *social identity* in *Library of Congress Subject Headings*, but you'll find a link to *group identity*, which includes searches for both terms. You could also look up *culture* and find a list of thirty-nine associated headings, such as "language and culture" and "personality and culture."

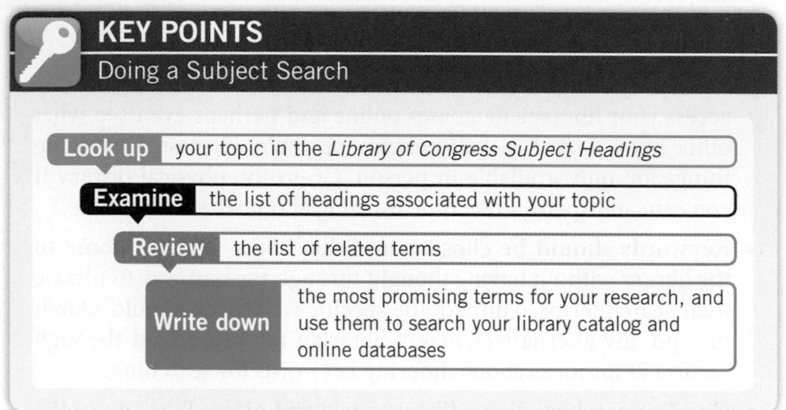

KEY POINTS
Doing a Subject Search
Look up your topic in the *Library of Congress Subject Headings*
Examine the list of headings associated with your topic
Review the list of related terms
Write down the most promising terms for your research, and use them to search your library catalog and online databases

In addition, these subject headings show related terms, which can suggest ways to narrow or broaden a topic and can help you in other searches, particularly in electronic keyword searches. The term *bilingualism*, for example, takes you to topics such as "air traffic control," "code switching," and "language attrition." An entry in a library catalog will appear with the subject descriptors, so if you find one good source, use its subject classifications to search further. A search in a library online catalog using the keywords *bilingual, education,* and *politics* comes up with 193 records. One of these sources (shown in Figure 7.1) provides some subject terms to help with further searching: *education and state, educational change,* and *educational evaluation.*

Information in the catalog The screens of electronic catalogs vary from one system to another, but most contain the name of the system you are using; the details of your search request and of the search, such as the number of records found; and detailed bibliographical information, which is useful for evaluating whether the book will be helpful in your research.

The screen shown in Figure 7.1 shows publication information and the library call number, as well as all the essential information you will

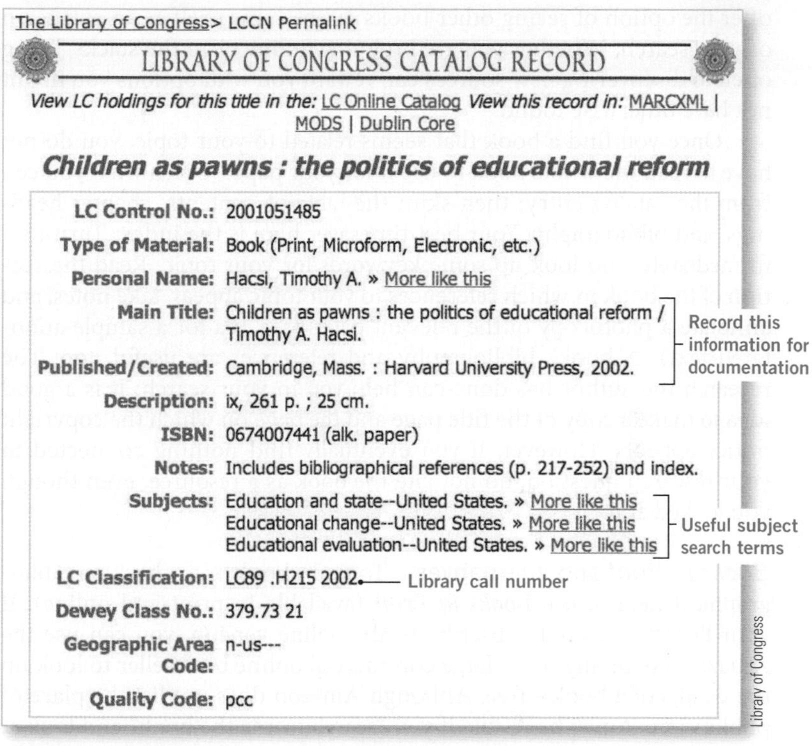

The Library of Congress> LCCN Permalink

LIBRARY OF CONGRESS CATALOG RECORD

View LC holdings for this title in the: LC Online Catalog *View this record in:* MARCXML | MODS | Dublin Core

Children as pawns : the politics of educational reform

LC Control No.:	2001051485
Type of Material:	Book (Print, Microform, Electronic, etc.)
Personal Name:	Hacsi, Timothy A. » More like this
Main Title:	Children as pawns : the politics of educational reform / Timothy A. Hacsi.
Published/Created:	Cambridge, Mass. : Harvard University Press, 2002.
Description:	ix, 261 p. ; 25 cm.
ISBN:	0674007441 (alk. paper)
Notes:	Includes bibliographical references (p. 217-252) and index.
Subjects:	Education and state--United States. » More like this Educational change--United States. » More like this Educational evaluation--United States. » More like this
LC Classification:	LC89 .H215 2002.
Dewey Class No.:	379.73 21
Geographic Area Code:	n-us---
Quality Code:	pcc

Figure 7.1 Example of a catalog record for a book

need to document the source at the end of your paper: the author, the title, the place of publication, the publisher, and the year of publication. It also lets you know the number of pages in the book, including the number of pages (ix: nine) of introductory material, and shows that the book contains a bibliography and an index, both of which are useful research tools. In addition, the subject terms shown here indicate the subjects the book addresses; these can help you structure further searches.

The call number shown in the catalog entry tells you where a book is located in the library stacks (the area where books are shelved). If a book looks promising, write down its call number immediately, along with the book's title, author(s), and publication information. In a library with open stacks, you will be able to browse through books on a similar topic on the same shelf or on one nearby. Many library catalogs now offer the option of seeing other books on the same shelf as an extension of your search. Whether you are browsing online or in the stacks, being open to discovering new sources can reward you with options you might not have otherwise found.

Once you find a book that seems related to your topic, you do not have to read the whole book to use it for your paper. Learn what you can from the catalog entry; then skim the table of contents, chapter headings, and bibliography. Your best timesaver here is the index. Turn to it immediately, and look up some keywords for your topic. Read the section of the book in which references to your topic appear, take notes, and annotate a photocopy of the relevant pages (see 10a for a sample annotated text). A book's bibliography and references are useful, too. The research the author has done can help you in your search. It is a good idea to make a copy of the title page and the page on which the copyright notice appears. However, if you eventually find nothing connected to your research question, do not cite the book as a resource, even though you looked at it.

***Books in Print* and alternatives** To find a book or to check on bibliographical details, use *Books in Print* (available in print and online). If your library does not subscribe to the online version, you can use the Amazon site or any other large commercial online bookseller to look up the details of a book—free. Although Amazon does not list the place of publication, it may be visible if you "search inside the book" and look at the copyright page. Complete works that are out of copyright are freely available for downloading at, for example, *Project Bartleby*, *Project Gutenberg*, *Oxford Text Archive*, and *University of Virginia Electronic Text Center. The Internet Archive* at www.archive.org also includes literary and nonliterary texts, as well as audio and moving-image archives.

7c Using online databases to find articles

Online databases and citation indexes owned or leased by libraries can be accessed in the library itself. Many libraries also make the databases they subscribe to available on the Internet through their home pages. For example, many libraries provide online access to the following:

- databases of abstracts in specific subject areas, such as *ERIC* (for education), *PAIS* (for public affairs), *PsycINFO* (for psychology), and *SocIndex* (for sociology)
- general databases of full texts of articles published in the last twenty or thirty years, such as *InfoTrac Expanded Academic ASAP, LexisNexis Academic*, EBSCO's *Academic Search Premier*, and *ProQuest SIRS*

(note that sponsors such as *EBSCO, InfoTrac, LexisNexis,* and *ProQuest* may each offer from ten to one hundred different databases covering different fields)

- databases of abstracts (with some full texts) of general, nonspecialized magazine articles, such as the *Wilson Readers' Guide to Periodical Literature*
- databases devoted to quantitative statistics, such as the *Millennium Development Goals Indicators Database*, or to images such as works of art at the J. Paul Getty Trust Web site
- the *JSTOR* database, providing access to less recent sources
- open-access databases, which are freely available online but are often easier to find via the library catalog. These databases may include full-text scholarly or scientific articles (*PubMed Central*), catalogs of government documents, and collections of bibliographies.

Access to databases on university library Web sites, from both library and home computers, is often limited to enrolled students, who need to verify their status when they log on. Check with your college library to learn which databases it subscribes to.

New issues of periodicals will be available on your library shelves. However, you'll find most of the recent articles you need by accessing online databases. Methods for searching databases are similar to those for finding books. (Refer to 7f for help with using keywords and subject categories to search for articles through a database.) For finding earlier works for a historical study—especially for works written before 1970—you'll need to use print indexes. Check which services your library subscribes to and the dates the indexes cover.

If the periodical index does not provide the full text, you will need to find out first whether your library owns the periodical and then in which form it is available. The catalog for your library will tell you on the screen which issues are available in the library and in which location and format: in files, in bound volumes, or, less commonly, in film form with pages shown in a strip (microfilm) or on a sheet (microfiche), which you will need to read with a special machine. For articles in journals not available in your library, ask about interlibrary loan.

7d Finding Web sources

The democratic nature of the Internet means that many Web pages have no editorial control, so although you will probably find a great deal of material, much of it can be inaccurate. On the plus side, you will find vast resources, current material, and frequent updates—all without leaving your computer. As you plan your research, consider which of the following Internet resources may be the most appropriate for your topic. A reference librarian can help you decide.

Online magazines and online scholarly journals Online scholarly journals have all of their articles read and approved by experts (peer reviewers), whereas online magazines will typically have editors but no scholarly peer reviewers. You'll find a useful directory at *Librarians' Internet Index*. Some scholarly journals have no print versions. Some online journals and magazines are available free; others allow you to view only the current issue at no cost. Many, however, require either a subscription through your library computer network or a personal subscription. Most university libraries include a directory of journals on their sites.

Online literary texts Literary texts that are out of copyright and in the public domain are increasingly available online. Try *Project Bartleby*, *Project Gutenberg*, *University of Virginia's Electronic Text Center*, or *The Internet Archive*. Be sure that the version of the text you are looking at is a reliable edition. Pay attention to the source that is making it available.

Online news sites The Web sites of major newspapers, magazines, and television networks provide up-to-date news information; some offer archived information but often only to subscribers. *CNN* and *MSNBC* are among the sources that offer open archives. *LexisNexis* also provides access to articles from many newspapers.

Nonprofit research sites Some nonprofit sites offer valuable and objective information. For example, see *Public Agenda Online, American Film Institute, Follow the Money*, and *San Francisco Bay Bird Observatory*.

Web home pages and hypertext links Universities and research institutes provide information through their own Web home pages, with hypertext links that take you with one click to many other sources. Individual Web pages can provide useful information, too, but they need careful evaluation because anyone can publish on the Web (see 8c for more on how to evaluate a potential source). Be sure to pay attention to context as well; Web sites don't always warn you when links take you to other sites that may be less authoritative.

E-mail discussion groups With e-mail, you have access to many discussion groups. Messages go out to a list of people interested in specific topics. Without charge, you can join a list devoted to a topic of interest.

However, many lists are not refereed or monitored, so you have to evaluate carefully any information you find.

For academic research, personal blogs and chat rooms provide information with widely varying reliability. Evaluating the credibility of a contributor's comments can be difficult. See chapter 8 for tips on evaluating the credibility of your sources.

Using URLs If you already know the Web address (the uniform resource locator, or URL) of a useful site, type it exactly, paying attention to underscores, dots, symbols, and capital or lowercase letters. Leave no spaces in a URL. Just one small slip can prevent access. Whenever you can, copy and paste a URL from a Web source so that you do not make mistakes when typing. If you ever get a message saying "site not found," check your use of capital and lowercase letters (and avoid inserting spaces as you type an address), and try again. Or try adding *l* to an .htm suffix or deleting *l* from .html. You may find, however, that the site really is no longer available. If a good resource appears to no longer exist, try putting the URL into the search engine at the Internet Archive, which keeps a permanent archive of a series of snapshots of the Web that began in 1996.

7e Finding visual sources

In a research paper, consider where tables and charts could present visual data concisely and clearly. Images may also help you strengthen an argument. Use visuals to illustrate and enhance a point or to present information clearly and economically. Do not use visuals merely to fill space or to look trendy, and check with your instructor if you are unsure whether visuals are allowed in your paper.

If you look at section 4i, as well as the sample papers in section 4j and in chapters 13, 16, and 18, you'll see how photographs and Web visuals work well to highlight or illustrate specific information or to capture the essence of an argument and thus make a point convincingly. Visuals can also be used effectively to convey quantitative information in a readily comprehensible form in tables, graphs, and charts (see chapter 22 for more on visuals of this type).

Finding appropriate visuals Several of the major search engines, including *Google, Bing, Ask*, and *Yahoo! Search,* offer specific image searches, and by using the advanced search forms there, you will be able to narrow your search to certain types of images, including those that are licensed for noncommercial use; adding that to your search parameters means you won't have to worry about copyright or whether to ask permission to use the image. Other useful sources that provide access to a large number of amateur photos are *Flickr* and *Instagram*.

Searching for images can often be difficult and frustrating because many "hits" may not interest you. Image searches use keywords or tags attached to the image, and often these are not very accurate or they do not describe the image the same way you would describe it. So, rather than doing a general image search, it may be more productive to look for images at the Web sites where you find relevant textual information in the first place. Many Web sites, including government sites like the US Bureau of the Census or nonprofit organizations like Public Agenda, make great efforts to present the information on their sites in a visually attractive form. In addition, the National Telecommunications and Information Administration is a good source for tables and charts analyzing Internet use; and the College Board and the UCLA Higher Education Research Institute provide annual studies of first-year students using many tables and graphs.

As a general rule, whichever style of documentation you use, you need to identify and label a visual source, such as a figure or a table, where you include it in your paper. Be sure to give credit to the original source of the image. Section 4j and chapters 13, 16, and 18 show examples of documenting visuals in MLA, APA, and CSE styles.

7f Using search engines and keywords

Search engines such as *Google* and *Bing* find their results in different ways, so if one does not work for you, try another. Also useful to researchers are Web directories (7a) and meta search engines such as *Dogpile* and *MetaCrawler*, which search the results of other search engines.

KEY POINTS

Tips for Using Search Engines

1. **Don't mistake popularity for quality.** Although the exact methods that commercial search engines use to find and rank sources are trade secrets, the number of links and visits to a page play a large role in determining which sites get listed first. However, the popularity of a Web site is not necessarily an indication of quality. Search engines do not assess the quality of the content. So make your search string as specific as possible to exercise greater

control of your results, and don't be afraid to look beyond the first page of hits your search returns.

2. **Be aware of "sponsored links."** These sites often appear on the very top of a result list or may even say "Ad" next to the link. The site's owner pays for it to appear at the top of the page, so its inclusion there is no indication of quality, popularity, or even relevance.
3. **Try using search engines that are intended for academic work.** You probably use a search engine such as *Google* for everyday Web searches using keywords or to search for images and videos. For your academic work, branch out and use *Google Scholar* and *Book Search*, the directories listed earlier in section 7a, and your library's online licensed databases, where no paid advertisements appear on the screen. To find material in journal and newspaper articles, use databases such as *Academic Search Premier, InfoTrac, LexisNexis*, and specialized subject-area databases; there you can find abstracts (when available) or full articles.
4. **Persist and be resourceful.** If a search yields only a few hits, try new keywords in new combinations. Also try variant spellings for names of people and places (such as *Chaikovsky, Tchaikovsky, Tschaikovsky*), and/or try a different search engine.

After you have decided which search engines to use for your particular task, you then have to decide how best to do the search.

TIPS FOR HOW TO DO EFFICIENT KEYWORD SEARCHES FOR ACADEMIC PURPOSES

- **Know the system of the database or search engine.** Use Search Tips or the Help tool to learn how to conduct a search. Some systems search for any or all of the words you type in, some need you to indicate whether the words make up a phrase, and others allow you to exclude search terms or search for alternatives. Before you begin a search, read the instructions on the database to learn how to perform both a simple search and an advanced search. Generally, begin a search by using keywords or subject terms if you know them. A keyword search of an online database of full-text articles will produce articles with subject terms attached, as in Source Shot 4 in section 12e, page 242. Use what the database provides to limit a search as to type of source, date, full-text articles or not, and scholarly, peer-reviewed articles, as shown in the screenshot in Figure 7.2.

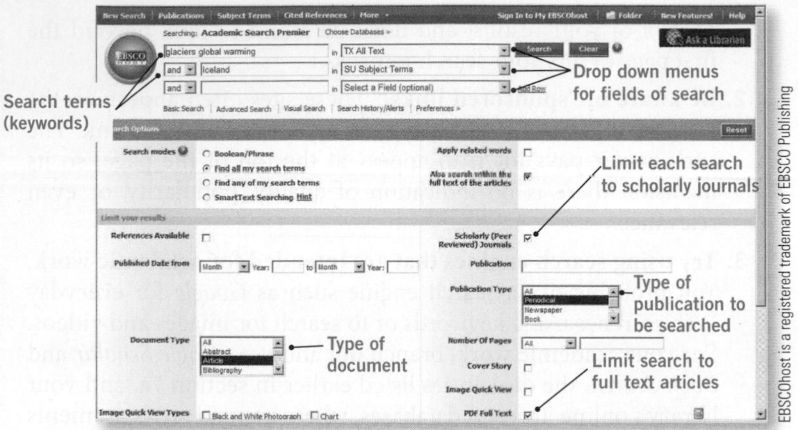

Figure 7.2 Advanced search screen: EBSCO *Academic Search Premier* database

- **Learn how to do Boolean searches.** Many database searches operate on the Boolean principle; that is, they use the "operators" *AND, OR,* and *NOT* in combination with keywords to define what you want the search to include and exclude. Imagine that you want to find out how music can affect intelligence. A search for "music AND intelligence" would find sources in the database that included both the word *music* and the word *intelligence.*

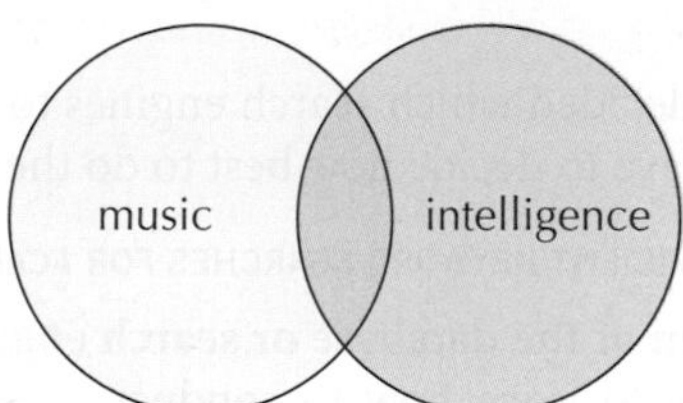

Figure 7.3

A search for "music AND (intelligence OR learning)" would expand the search. You would find sources in the database that included both the word *music* and the word *intelligence* or the word *learning*, as represented by the hash marks in Figure 7.4.

Some search engines let you use terms such as *NEAR* and *ADJ* (adjacent to) to find phrases close to each other in the searched text.

- **Know how to expand or narrow a search.** Many search engines, including *Google*, let you use signs such as + or – to include or prohibit a term, thereby expanding or narrowing your search. You do not need to insert the word *and.*

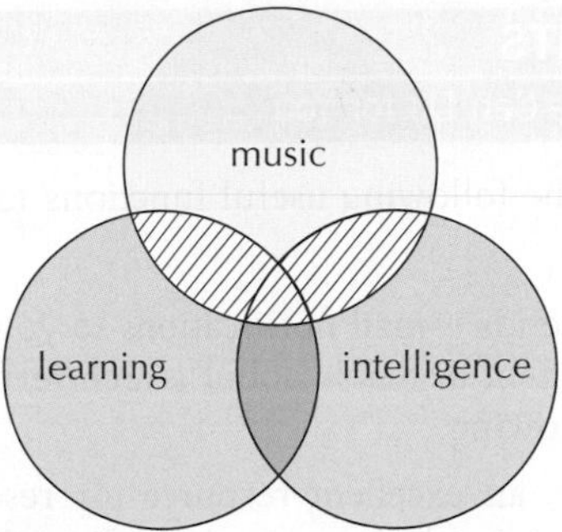

Figure 7.4

- **Use a wildcard character (* or ?) to truncate a term and expand the search.** The truncated search term *podiatr** will produce references to *podiatry*, *podiatrist*, and *podiatric*. In *Google*, however, the wildcard character * is used to stand for a whole word only, as in "Foot doctor is a *," but *Google* automatically uses "stemming" and searches for "podiatrist" as well as "podiatry" if you have entered the latter term only.
- **Narrow a search by grouping words.** Enclose search terms in quotation marks (or, in some cases, parentheses) to group the words into a phrase; this is a useful technique for finding titles, names, and quotations. A collection of keywords from a half-remembered quotation from Elie Wiesel ("to write is to sow and to reap") entered as a *Google* search without quotation marks does not produce a link to Elie Wiesel's text on the first page of hits. Putting quotation marks around this phrase, however, produces a link to the text of his book, *All Rivers Run to the Sea*, on the first page, and it includes the full quotation ("To cry is to sow, said the Maharal of Prague; to laugh is to reap. And to write is to sow and to reap at the same time.").
- **Be flexible.** If you don't get good results, try using synonyms. *Google* will include synonyms in the search, for example, if you type a tilde (~) immediately before the search term, as in ~ *addiction*. Or try a different search engine or database.

7g Getting the most out of *Google*

Your college instructor may direct you away from the popular search engine *Google* and toward engines more geared to finding academic sources. However, remember that *Google* can be far more versatile, direct, and productive than the results in its basic search engine indicate.

KEY POINTS

What *Google* Can Do for You

Google provides the following useful functions for researchers. Use them.

- ***Google Alerts*** sends e-mail notifications to you about new information and content available about search terms or news stories that you are following.
- ***Google Scholar***, an excellent resource for researchers, searches scholarly sources (such as research studies, dissertations, peer-reviewed papers) across many disciplines. You may also be able to customize the program to provide links to the full text of articles in your college library. Click "Scholar preferences," and enter the name of the library. You can then import local links into bibliographical programs your college may own, such as *EndNote* or *RefWorks*.
- ***Google Book Search*** helps you find books and provides details of the contents, even allowing you to search the full text of many books for specific content.
- ***Google Blog Search*** helps you find blogs that might provide interesting, current information about topics of interest.
- ***Google Earth*** allows you to search for maps, detailed satellite images, and 3D images.
- ***Google Advanced Search*** provides many options for tailoring your search to your precise needs (see Figure 7.5).
- ***Google Forms*** allows you to create surveys to collect and organize data. The surveys can include a wide range of question types (multiple choice, fill in the blank, paragraph text), and responses to the survey are displayed as a group or by individual response.

Using advanced searches Whenever you can, use a search engine's advanced search feature. This will allow you to specify results that use all the keywords in any order, just the exact phrase, or only one of the words, or that exclude unwanted words. Databases also often provide an

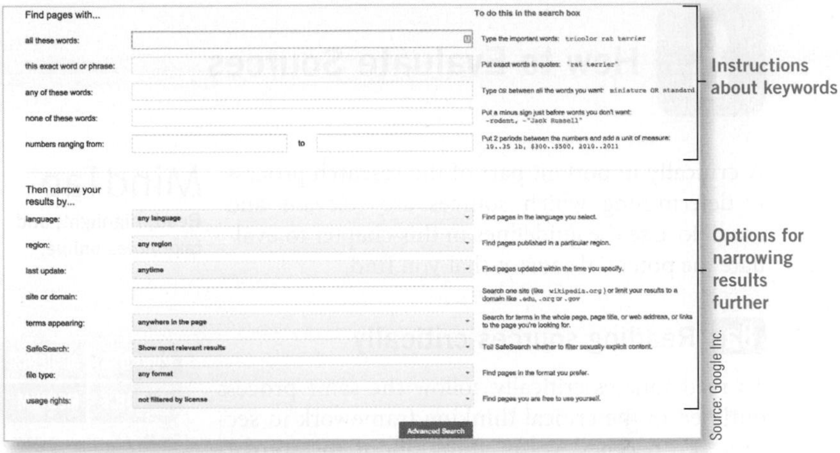

Instructions about keywords

Options for narrowing results further

Source: Google Inc.

Figure 7.5 ***Google Advanced Search***

advanced search feature that allows you to limit your search to retrieve only full-text or "peer-reviewed" articles (scholarly articles, scrutinized and approved for publication by reviewers familiar with the field). The screenshot in Figure 7.5 shows this feature.

In addition, a *Google Advanced Search* allows you to be specific about the order and number of keywords, number of results, language of the source, and the file type (*Word, Excel, PowerPoint, Acrobat*, and so on).

How to get information to come to you—research in your pajamas Not only can you find a vast amount of source material online, but also you can arrange to be notified when materials on your specific topic become available. For example, *Google Alerts* will e-mail search results directly to you, and *feedly* (feedly.com) allows you to keep up with Web sites' RSS feeds by notifying you of the latest news items, events, or discussion postings on a given topic during the time interval you specify. In addition, several journal databases, such as those sponsored by *EBSCO, SAGE,* and *CSA,* will run a search on a topic you specify as often as you request, even daily, and alert you via e-mail about articles that meet the criteria you establish. These RSS feeds mean that you get full-text research articles brought to you 24/7 without your having to remember to redo a search.

How to Evaluate Sources

A critically important part of the research process is determining which sources are relevant and credible. Use the guidelines in this chapter to evaluate the potential sources that you find.

MindTap®
Read, highlight, and take notes online.

Reading sources critically

See the full model on page 7.

To read sources critically, follow the same process outlined in the critical thinking framework in section 1c. In other words, think about the source's purpose, audience, voice, and medium as you

KEY POINTS
Reading Sources Critically

Respond to these questions from the critical thinking framework as you read your sources.

PURPOSE	AUDIENCE
What is the author's purpose in writing this piece? Is it meant to be persuasive, informative, or something else? What influence might that purpose have on the potential usefulness of the piece as a source in your own work?	What audience is the author addressing? How do you know? Does the intended audience have any impact on what information is included in, or excluded from, the piece? If so, how?
VOICE	**MEDIUM**
What are the credentials and reputation of the author? What is the place of publication? What or whom does the author represent? Is there a particular bias that the author demonstrates? If so, where do you see it, and what is its impact on the author's credibility?	In what medium was the piece published? Why do you think it was published in that medium? Was it peer reviewed or edited by someone else? Is the publication venue subject to rapid change (like an article in *Wikipedia*), or is it fairly static, like a printed book or an online journal article?

Here are some other things you might do as you read your sources critically:

- Ask questions about the ideas you read. An easy way to do this is to write your annotations in the margin. If you find yourself thinking "but . . ." as you read, go with that sense of doubt, and make a note of what troubles you.
- Be on the lookout for assumptions that may be faulty. If you are reading an article on home-schooling and the writer favors home-schooling because it avoids subjecting students to violence in schools, the unstated assumption is that all schools are violent places.
- Make sure the writer's evidence is adequate and accurate. For example, if the writer is making a generalization about all Chinese students based on a study of only three, you have cause to challenge the generalization as resting on inadequate evidence.
- Note how the writer uses language. Which terms does the writer use with positive—or negative—connotations, signaling the values the writer holds? Does the writer flamboyantly denigrate the views of others with such phrases as "a ridiculous notion" or "laughably inept policies"?
- Be alert for sweeping generalizations, bias, and prejudice: "Women want to stay home and have children." "Men love to spend Sundays watching sports."

read—its *context.* Understanding the context of the sources you are reading while keeping in mind your own research context will help you find sources that will be a good match—sources that readers will find credible, reliable, and relevant for your research goals.

Do your reading when you are able to write—not on the treadmill or while watching TV. Note any questions, objections, or challenges on the page, as in the annotated text shown in section 10a, on self-stick notes, on index cards, in a response file on your computer, or in a journal. Your critical responses to your reading will provide you with your own ideas for writing.

8b Recognizing a scholarly article

A scholarly article is not something you are likely to find in a magazine in a dentist's office. Scholarly articles are published in journals that are designed for specialists in a field. A scholarly article is reviewed by other scholars in the field for approval prior to publication, which is called "peer review." Scholarly articles also share several other characteristics.

KEY POINTS

How to Recognize a Scholarly Article

1. It is reviewed by other scholars (peer reviewers) for their approval before publication.
2. It refers to the work of other scholars and includes notes, references or a list of works cited, footnotes, and/or endnotes.
3. It names the author and may describe the author's affiliation and credentials.
4. It deals with a serious issue in depth. For example, a magazine might simply report on various findings and how they might apply to its targeted audience, but a scholarly journal would go further to discuss issues such as methodology, possible differing opinions, and potential future research directions.
5. It uses academic or technical language for informed readers.
6. If it is in print, it generally appears in journals that do not include colorful advertisements or eye-catching pictures. Source Shot 1 on page 236 shows a page from a scholarly journal.

(***Note:*** Not all scholarly articles will include all six of these criteria.)

Periodicals such as *Time*, *Newsweek*, and *The Economist* are serious, but they are not scholarly periodicals. Note that a scholarly article may appear in academic journals such as *College English* or the *New England Journal of Medicine*, or it may be found in a publication for the general population, such as *Psychology Today* or *Science*.

Online articles in HTML or other digital formats, aside from PDFs, do not necessarily provide the immediate signals of color, illustrations, and varied advertisements that would identify nonscholarly work in print publications. If you find an online article and wish to check its credibility, try doing the following:

- Follow links from the author's name (if available) to find a résumé and more information.

- In *Google Scholar*, use the author's name as a search term to see publications and citations by others.
- Do a search for the title of the periodical in which the article appears to find out that periodical's purpose and its requirements for submitting and publishing articles. In some library databases (*EBSCO*'s, for example), you can limit your search to articles that are peer reviewed; that is, they are read by other scholars working on similar topics and are found to contribute new and important knowledge before they are accepted for publication.

KEY POINTS

Databases of Journal Information

- *Genamics JournalSeek* provides links to the Web sites of journals to help you identify whether journals are scholarly.
- The Cornell University Web site *Distinguishing Scholarly Journals from Other Periodicals* provides definitions and examples of four categories of periodical literature: scholarly, substantive news and general interest, popular, and sensational.
- Many academic journals available online are listed in the *Directory of Open Access Journals*. All journals listed in this directory are freely available on the Internet.
- Another good resource for finding scholarly journals is the Web site for the Council of Editors of Learned Journals.

8c Evaluating potential sources

Before you make detailed notes about a source that you might use for your research, be sure it will provide suitable information to help answer your research question. As you evaluate your sources, pay careful attention to how something was vetted before it was published. Pay attention to whether the article was peer reviewed (such as a scholarly article) or was edited prior to publication (such as a magazine article). You'll find more help with evaluating Web sources on pages 173–175, and you'll find information about how to compile summaries and evaluations of sources into an annotated bibliography in section 9e.

Books Whether a book is in print or electronic form, find out who the publisher is, and do a quick Web search if you don't recognize the name. Is the book published by a university press or a recognized commercial publishing house? Is it a self-published book (perhaps published through services such as *Lulu, XLibris,* or Amazon's *CreateSpace*)? Check the date of publication, notes about the author, the table of contents, and the index. Skim the preface, introduction, chapter headings, and summaries to give yourself an idea of the information in the book and the book's theoretical basis and perspective. Do not waste time making detailed notes on a book that deals only tangentially with your topic or on an out-of-date book (unless your purpose is to discuss and critique its perspective or examine a topic historically). Ask a librarian or your instructor for help in evaluating the appropriateness of the sources you discover. If your topic concerns a serious academic issue, readers will expect you to consult scholarly books and/or articles and not limit your references to popular magazines, newspapers, and Web sites.

Periodical articles Whether your access to a periodical article is in print, on the Web, or through a library's online database, you'll need to consider similar criteria. Take into account the type of periodical it is, any organization with which it is affiliated, and the intended audience. Differentiate among the following types of articles (listed in descending order of reliability, with the most reliable first):

- scholarly articles (see 8b)
- articles, often long, in periodicals for nonspecialists but serious, well-educated readers, such as *New York Review of Books, Atlantic Monthly, The Economist, Scientific American,* and *Nation*
- shorter articles, with sources not identified, in popular magazines or online publications for a general audience, such as *Ebony, Time, Slate, Huff Post, Parents, Psychology Today,* and *Vogue,* or in newspapers
- articles with dubious sources, written for sensationalist tabloid magazines, such as *National Enquirer, Globe,* and *Star*

Newspaper articles and news articles The *New York Times, Washington Post,* and *Los Angeles Times,* for example, provide mostly reliable accounts of current events; daily editorial comments; and reviews of books, film, and art. Be aware that most newspapers (as well as televised news reports on such stations as *Fox News* and *MSNBC*) have political leanings, so perspectives on the same event may differ.

KEY POINTS

Questions to Evaluate a Source

1. **What does the work cover?** It should be long enough and detailed enough to provide adequate information.
2. **How objective is the information?** The author, publisher, or periodical should not be affiliated with an organization that has an ax to grind, unless, of course, your topic entails reading critically and making comparisons with other points of view.
3. **How current are the views?** Check the date of publication. The work should be up to date if you need a current perspective.
4. **How reputable is the publisher?** The work should be published by someone reputable in a source that is academically reliable, not one devoted to gossip, advertising, propaganda, or sensationalism. Look online for information about the publisher of the print book or journal or the host of the Web site. Is it a university press? an established commercial publisher? a self-publishing Web site? Is the host of the Web site affiliated with a particular company or organization? If you are looking at a journal, is there an editorial board? If you are looking at a Web site, what kinds of ads do you see? Does it look like someone is trying to make a profit?
5. **How reputable is the author?** The author should be an authority on the subject. Find out what else the author has written (in *Google*, in *Books in Print*, or at *Amazon*) and what his or her qualifications are as an authority.
6. **Is the piece well written?** A source filled with spelling and grammatical errors should not inspire confidence. If the language has not been checked, the ideas probably haven't been given much scrutiny or thought, either. However, postings to discussion lists, though often written spontaneously, can contain useful ideas to stimulate thinking on your topic.

Other sources found online What makes the Internet so fascinating is that it is wide open, free, and democratic. Anyone can "publish" anything, and anyone can read it. However, if you are looking for well-presented facts and informed opinion among the more than 1 billion domain names registered as of July 2015 (ISC Internet Domain survey), the Internet can pose a challenge.

- **Postings found in e-mail discussion lists, blogs, and wikis** Discussion list postings, blogs (Web logs), and wiki entries (additions to, or editing of, a Web text appearing in a wiki) will often appear in a list of a search engine's findings. Many professionally moderated lists and other targeted discussion lists can be useful sources of information, although quality can vary considerably. Treat with caution postings in e-mail bulletin boards, newsgroups, blogs, or synchronous (real-time) communications such as chat rooms. If you look at such postings as possible sources, be sure to read and take into consideration the responses to the post you're interested in.
- **Personal or organizational Web sites** Evaluate Web sites with particular care. Individuals on a rant, as well as serious government or research agencies, can establish a site. Because anyone can "publish" anything, and thousands or millions can read it, finding reliable information and well-presented, informed opinions on Web pages can pose a challenge. Learn to separate good information from junk.

Note: For more on the features to look for, evaluate, and record about Web sites, see the screenshot and examples of documentation in section 10i: One source, four systems of documentation.

KEY POINTS

Locating Key Information on Web Sites

1. **Scrutinize the domain name of the URL.** Reliable information can usually be found on .gov and .edu addresses that are institutionally sponsored (but also see item 2). With .com ("dot com"), .net, .info, or .org sources, always assess whether the source provides factual information or advocates a specific point of view on an issue.
2. **Assess the originator of an .edu source.** Is the educational institution or a branch of it sponsoring the site? A tilde (~) followed by a name in the URL generally indicates a posting by an individual, with no approval from the institution. So follow up by finding out what else the individual has published.

3. **Locate missing information.** If you can't readily find information on the actual Web site, a good way to begin an evaluation is to look the site up on www.betterwhois.com. This site will provide information on the author, date, sponsor, and address, and so supply clues about the reliability of the site.
4. **Check the About page or the Home page.** If you find your way to a Web page, always go to Home or About (if available) to find out about the larger site. Look for the title of the site, its stated purpose, and sponsor. Check, too, for bias. For instance, does the site aim to persuade, convert, or sell? If you reach a page via a search engine and no site name is visible or shown in About, delete the URL progressively back to each single slash, and click to see which part of the site you access.
5. **Follow the links.** See whether the links in a site take you to authoritative sources. If the links no longer work (you'll get a 404 message: "Site Not Found"), the home page with the links has not been updated in a while—not a good sign.
6. **Check for dates, updates, ways to respond, and ease of navigation.** A well-managed site will have recent updates, clear organization, up-to-date links, and easy-to-find contact information.

KEY EXAMPLE

Source Evaluation

A student who is starting to search for sources about the gun control debate and the number of mass shootings in the United States found the following two sources for a research paper. After carefully evaluating the sources using the guidelines in section 8c, the student decided that one of the sources seemed to be a stronger, more reliable source than the other. Take a look at the student's annotations of the sources. Do you agree?

Source 1:

Fingerhut, Hannah. "5 Facts about Guns in the United States." *FactTank: News in the Numbers,* Pew Research Center, 5 Jan. 2016, www.pewresearch.org/fact-tank/2016/01/05/5-facts-about-guns-in-the-united-states/.

Recent publication

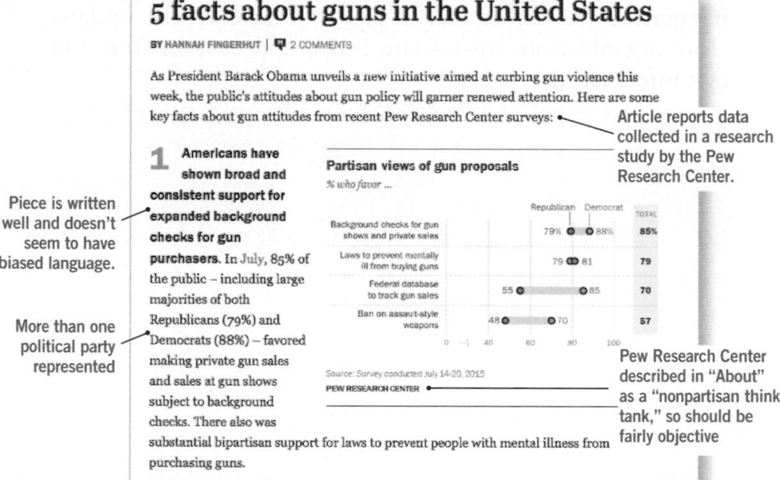

5 facts about guns in the United States

BY HANNAH FINGERHUT | 2 COMMENTS

As President Barack Obama unveils a new initiative aimed at curbing gun violence this week, the public's attitudes about gun policy will garner renewed attention. Here are some key facts about gun attitudes from recent Pew Research Center surveys:

1 Americans have shown broad and consistent support for expanded background checks for gun purchasers. In July, 85% of the public – including large majorities of both Republicans (79%) and Democrats (88%) – favored making private gun sales and sales at gun shows subject to background checks. There also was substantial bipartisan support for laws to prevent people with mental illness from purchasing guns.

Figure 8.1

Title of article reveals political bias.

Source 2:

Shapiro, Ben. "Democrats Push Gun Control, Refuse Armed School Guards." *Breitbart*, 2 Oct. 2015, www.breitbart.com/big-government/2015/10/02/democrats-push-gun-control-refuse-armed-school-guards/.

Piece was written recently, following highly publicized shooting in Oregon.

One link within article is to another page written by this author.

Umpqua Community College had one guard on shift at a time. Unarmed. But it did notify those on campus that it was a gun free zone, just like most campuses across America. And according to retired Umpqua Community College president Joe Olson, the college decided against an armed security guard in the last few months. "We talked about that over the last year because we were concerned about safety on campus," he said. "The campus was split 50-50. We thought we were a very safe campus, and having armed security officers on campus might change the culture."

Typically, those who oppose armed guards, or arming teachers on campuses, cite idiocies like "changing the culture" or "making children uncomfortable." Randi Weingarten, head of the National Education Association, has written, "Schools must be safe sanctuaries, not armed fortresses. Anyone who would suggest otherwise doesn't understand that our public schools must first and foremost be places where teachers can safely educate and nurture our students."

Use of "asinine" shows that this is more of a political rant.

This is asinine. The only way to keep students safe is to provide security, not hope that gunmen abide by "Gun-Free Zone" signs. In Israel, in order to prevent terrorist attacks, armed guards are posted in schools routinely. That has indeed prevented terrorist attacks. When I attended a Jewish high school in Los Angeles, located next to the Simon Wiesenthal Center, administration provided heavy security – and it worked. In 1999, during the summer months of my high school term, Buford Furrow, a white supremacist with a history of mental illness, stopped by the Wiesenthal Center and wanted to shoot it up – but there was security. So he promptly motored over to the North Valley Jewish Community Center, where there were no armed guards, and proceeded to shoot five people.

So yes, more guns at schools would be a useful measure.

Piece argues for a particular position instead of presenting unbiased data.

Figure 8.2

Questions

1. With a classmate, find another source that discusses the gun control debate. Does it share similarities with either of the preceding sources? What guidelines would help you determine if it is a reputable source to use?
2. Both of the sources the student found are Web sources. What special considerations might the student need to consider when looking at Web sources? Are there other things you might consider as you search online for sources?
3. What strategies have you used in the past to select and evaluate sources? Which strategies were useful? What strategies might you try the next time you start searching for sources for a research project?

9 How to Avoid Plagiarizing

MindTap®
Read, highlight, and take notes online.

The convenience and comfort of researching online are not without a downside. The ease of finding, copying, and downloading information from the Internet has its attendant dangers: researchers may lose sight of what is theirs and what isn't, they may forget where they read something, and the information may seem so abundant that surely it must appear to be there for the taking. Unfortunately, though, that is not the case, especially in the academic world, where presenting somebody else's words or ideas without acknowledging where those words and ideas come from is a punishable offense.

The word for the offense, *plagiarism*, is derived from a Latin verb meaning "to kidnap," and so, if you use someone else's words and ideas without acknowledging them, you are in effect cheating by "kidnapping," or stealing, those words and ideas. Readers do not want to be fooled into thinking that the ideas and words you wrote actually originated someplace else. For all audiences, but especially for academic readers, honesty counts for a great deal, so much so that many colleges encourage professors and students to run papers through a plagiarism-checking program such as *Turnitin.com* to ensure that no passages in the text match any in the database of the service.

This chapter describes the various types of plagiarism, and it stresses that acknowledging the work you have done by accurately tracking your research as you do it and citing your sources (who said it, where, and when) is always the way to go.

9a The seven sins of plagiarism

The Council of Writing Program Administrators, a professional organization of writing teachers and program directors, says that plagiarism occurs "when a writer deliberately uses someone else's language, ideas, or other (not common-knowledge) material without acknowledging its source." Such intentional use can take many forms.

Consequences Obviously, these "sins" vary in their severity and in the intention to deceive. The types of plagiarism described in items 4 through 6 of the Key Points box sometimes occur unintentionally, but they may be

KEY POINTS

Plagiarism's Seven Sins

1. **Intentional grand larceny** Presenting as your own work a whole essay bought from a paper mill, "borrowed" or commissioned from a friend, or intentionally copied and pasted from an online source
2. **Premeditated shoplifting** Taking passages from a book, article, or Web site and intentionally inserting them in your paper without indicating who wrote them or where you found them; differs from intentional grand larceny only because passages, not the entire paper, are copied
3. **Tinkering with the evidence** Making only a few word changes to source material and inserting the slightly altered version into your paper as if you wrote it, with no acknowledgment of the source, and trusting that those changes are enough to avoid charges of plagiarism
4. **Idea kidnapping** Using ideas written by others (even if you do use your own words) and neglecting to cite the source of the ideas
5. **Unauthorized borrowing of private property** Citing your source with a parenthetical reference or footnote/endnote but following its sentence structure and organization too closely or not indicating with quotation marks any of your source's exact words
6. **Trespassing over boundaries** Failing to indicate in your paper where ideas from a source end and your ideas take over (see 10d for more on this)
7. **Writing under the influence** Being too tired, lazy, or disorganized, or facing an imminent deadline, and turning to any of the six previous sins in desperation or ignorance

perceived as plagiarism nevertheless. You have to work hard at avoiding them, especially since the consequences of plagiarism can be severe, ranging from receiving an F on a paper or in a course to disciplinary measures or expulsion from college. In the world at large, plagiarism can lead to lawsuits and ruined careers. Those are reasons enough to do your own work and to learn to document your sources fully and correctly.

LANGUAGE AND CULTURE

Ownership Rights across Cultures

American academic culture takes seriously the ownership of words and text. It respects both the individual as author (and authority) and the originality of the individual's ideas. In some cultures, memorization and the use of classic texts are common in all walks of life. And worldwide, the ownership of language, texts, music, and videos is being called into question by the democratic, interactive nature of the Internet. In short, therefore, plagiarism is not something universal and easy to define. In American academic culture, basic ground rules exist for the "fair use" of another writer's work without payment, but easy access to music and media sources poses interesting questions about intellectual property and the opportunities to create and remix culture.

9b How to avoid even the suspicion of plagiarism

Research and clear documentation open a channel of communication between you and the audience. Readers learn what your views are and what has influenced those views. They will assume that anything not documented is your original idea and your wording.

Remember that citing any words and ideas that you use from your sources works to your advantage. Citing accurately reveals a writer who has done enough research to enter ongoing conversations in the academic world. In addition, citations show readers how hard you have worked, how much research you have done, and how the points you make are supported by experts. So be proud to cite your sources.

KEY POINTS

How to Avoid Plagiarizing

- Start your research early enough to avoid panic mode.
- Make a record of each source so that you have all the information you need for appropriate documentation. Consider using an online application such as *Zotero* to track your sources as you work.
- Set up a working annotated bibliography (9e).

- Take notes from the sources, using a systematic method of indicating quotation, paraphrase, and your own comments. For example, use quotation marks around quoted words, phrases, sentences, and passages; introduce a paraphrase with a tag, such as "Korones makes the point that . . ."; in your notes about a source, write your own comments in a different color. Then, later, you will see immediately which ideas are yours and which come from your source.
- Always acknowledge and document the source of any passage, phrase, or idea that you have used or summarized from someone else's work.
- Never use exactly the same sequence of ideas and organization of argument as your source.
- When you use a single key word from your source or three or more words in sequence from your source, use the appropriate format for quoting and documenting.
- Be aware that substituting synonyms for a few words in the source or moving a few words around is not enough to counter a charge of plagiarism.
- Keep in mind that paraphrasing without citing your source is plagiarism. (See section 10b for more information on how to paraphrase.)
- Don't use passages in your paper that have been written or rewritten by a friend or a tutor.
- Never even consider buying, downloading, or "borrowing" a paper or a section of a paper to turn in as your own work.

9c Know why, how, and what to cite

Why you need to cite sources

- Citing sources shows the audience that you have done your homework on an issue; you will receive respect for the depth and breadth of your research and for having worked hard to make your case.
- Citing responsible and recent sources lets the audience know that your arguments are both weighty and current.
- Citing sources draws readers into the conversation about the issue and educates them. It also allows them to see you as engaged in the ongoing intellectual conversation around the issue you are writing about. With full and accurate citations, readers can follow up on the same sources you used and so can learn more.

- Citation can be used to strengthen your argument, protect against counterclaims, or align your thinking with a particular scholar or institutional perspective. In other words, careful use of citations can make your writing and research stronger and more persuasive.
- Citing all sources fully and accurately is essential if you are to avoid even the suspicion of plagiarizing.

How to cite sources Citing a source means letting readers know whose words or ideas you are quoting, summarizing, or paraphrasing; where you found the information; and, in the case of Web sites, when it was published or posted online. Styles of documentation vary in whether they ask initially for author and page number (MLA) or author and year of publication (APA), with a detailed list at the end of the paper of all the sources cited. Other systems (*Chicago* and CSE) use numbering systems or footnotes in the paper, with a listing of source details at the end. See comparisons of a citation in each system in section 10i, and follow the detailed models in parts 3 and 4 for each of these systems.

How to cite visuals Provide a number and a source note for all tables and figures you include in your paper. In MLA style, place the visual close to the text it illustrates, with a credit line immediately beneath it. For APA papers, consult with your instructor. Some recommend including visuals within the text of a college paper; others adhere to strict APA style, with tables and figures placed at the end of the paper.

Chapters 4, 13, 16, and 18 show student papers with visuals.

What to cite Intentionally presenting another person's work as your own may be the most deceptive kind of plagiarism, but the effect is the same if you neglect to acknowledge your sources because of sloppy research and writing practices. In both cases, readers will not be able to discern which ideas are yours and which are not. Always provide full documentation of sources, with a citation in your text and an entry in your list of sources. The Key Points box shows you what you must always cite and also points out when citing is not necessary. If you are in doubt about whether you need to cite a source, it is always safer to cite it.

KEY POINTS

To Cite or Not to Cite

What to Cite

- exact words from a source (a key word or three or more words in succession), even facts, enclosed in quotation marks

- somebody else's ideas and opinions, even if you restate them in your own words in a summary or a paraphrase
- each sentence in a long paraphrase if it is not clear that all the sentences paraphrase the same source
- facts, theories, and statistics

What Not to Cite

- common knowledge, especially when it is available in many sources, such as the dates of the Civil War, birth and death dates, chronological events in the lives of authors and public figures, or allusions to nursery rhymes or folktales handed down through the ages

Note how James Stalker, in his article "Official English or English Only," does not quote directly but still cites Anderson as the source of the specialized facts mentioned in the following passage. His in-text citation follows MLA style:

> By 1745 there were approximately 45,000 German speakers in the colonies, and by 1790 there were some 200,000, nine percent of the population (Anderson 80).

9d Keeping track of sources

The first step toward avoiding plagiarism is keeping track of what your sources are and which ideas come from your sources and which come from you. You will find that one of the more frustrating moments for you as a researcher occurs when you find a note about an interesting point you read but you cannot remember where you found the passage or who wrote it or whether your notes represent an author's exact words. Avoid this frustration by keeping track as you go along.

- **Keep a working bibliography.** Some options: Make a bibliography card (one for each source; use one side only); save screens or printouts from a library catalog, database listing, or Web site; or use as a research organizing tool any bibliographical software provided by your library, such as *EndNote* or *RefWorks,* or available freely online, such as *Zotero* or *Mendeley*. Record all the relevant information for each source you read and plan to use, including reference works, and remember to record inclusive page numbers for all print sources as well as the date on which you access Web sites. You may want to include annotations (notes of varying length that provide more detail) in your working bibliography either for your own benefit or to fulfill assignment requirements that include an annotated bibliography. You'll find instructions for writing an annotated bibliography on pages 122–123 and a sample entry from one in section 9e.

- **Make copies of print material.** While you are in the library, scan or photocopy complete journal or magazine articles and a periodical's table of contents (which will provide the date and volume number). Scan or copy book sections or chapters, too, along with the title page and copyright page of the book. You will need this information for your list of works cited.
- **Make a copy or take a screenshot of every Web source you may use.** Material you find online can change quickly, so always print a source, take a screenshot, e-mail it to yourself, add it to your bibliographical software file (9f), or save it on a flash drive, making sure you use highlighting or a special font to distinguish your own comments and notes from the material you have copied and saved.
- **Use *Google's Bookmarks* feature to save important links.** When you log into *Google Bookmarks,* you can save links to useful sites so that you can easily find them again. By storing useful Web sites as Bookmarks to access later, you can easily move from one computer to another (if you need to use a networked computer in a lab instead of your personal computer, for instance) and still have access to all of your online sources.
- **Record complete online document information, the URL, DOI, and the date of your access.** Bookmarking will not always last with the URLs of subscription databases. If you do not take a screenshot of the whole site, record the name of the author, title, and date posted or updated (this information is sometimes available via the Properties or Page Info commands in your browser). Recording the DOI (Digital Object Identifier) is helpful as well. The DOI provides a consistent way of identifying something you find online regardless of how you access it (for more information, see section 15c). Copy and paste to save the URL exactly on your hard drive or flash drive, and note the date on which you access the online material. In addition, the citation style you use may require a URL or DOI for documentation purposes. See 10i for a screenshot and the information you need to look for on a Web site.
- **Highlight, copy, and paste.** As you read material on the Web, highlight a passage you find, copy it, and then paste it into your own file. Make sure that you indicate clearly in your new document that you

have included a direct quotation. Use quotation marks and/or a bigger or colored font or highlighting along with an author/page citation, as in the following example:

> Novelist John Lanchester has made a telling point about our image of self by having his narrator declare that we **"wouldn't care so much what people thought of us if we knew how seldom they did"** (62).

Save as much information as you can about the original document in your working bibliography.

9e Recording information and setting up a working bibliography

From the first steps of your research, keep accurate records of each source in a working bibliography, with or without annotations about each source. Record enough information so that you will be able to make up a list of references in whichever style of documentation you choose, although not all the points of information you record will be necessary for every style of documentation.

Keep your list of sources in a form that you can work with to organize them alphabetically, add and reject sources, and add summaries and notes. Note cards, computer files, or your own files kept in licensed bibliographical software such as *RefWorks* or *EndNote* (9f) have the advantage over sheets of paper or a bound research journal. They don't tie you to page order.

Here is a sample bibliographical record in a computer file for a magazine article accessed in an online subscription database.

> Flora, Carlin. "The Beauty Paradox." *Psychology Today,* vol. 47, no. 1, 2014, pp. 36-37. *Academic Search Complete,* ezproxy.library.arizona.edu/login?url=http://search.ebscohost.com/login.aspx?direct=true&db=a9h&AN=93288156&site=ehost-live.

Sample annotated bibliography entry Here is a sample from Jared Whittemore's annotated bibliography that he prepared for a paper on the community college system in California. He includes the bibliographical details for future reference and ease of relocating the source, adding also useful comments about the content of the source and its relevance to his purpose in including it in his paper.

> *Significant Historical Events in the Development of the Public Community College*. American Association of Community Colleges, 13 Feb. 2001, www.aacc.nche.edu/AboutCC/history/Pages/significantevents.aspx.

This site provides a timeline charting the significant events in the history of community colleges, from 1862 to 2001. The timeline includes historical events, such as the founding of the first community college in 1901, and tracks important legislation and publications relating to the development and improvement of the community college system. It provides a historical perspective on the implementation and advancements made in the system in more than a century.

9f Using bibliographical software and databases to help you keep records

Bibliographical software When you are asked to write research papers, you may find that your college library owns special software (such as *EndNote* or *RefWorks*) to help you search databases, store the results of your database searches, organize your research, insert citations while you write, and prepare a bibliography in one of many styles available. If your library does not provide access to software like *EndNote* or *RefWorks*, several free applications are available online such as *Zotero* and *Mendeley*.

Databases Several database screens, such as those sponsored by *EBSCO* (Figure 9.1), include useful features for writers of research papers.

From the Citation screen for an article, clicking on the "Cite" icon (fifth from the top) will take you to a screen that shows you how to cite the article in several documentation styles, including AMA, APA, *Chicago*, and MLA. The next icon down allows you to "Export" your saved citations to *EndNote*, *RefWorks*, and other bibliographical software. Try out these features with the article shown in Source Shot 4 on pages 242–243.

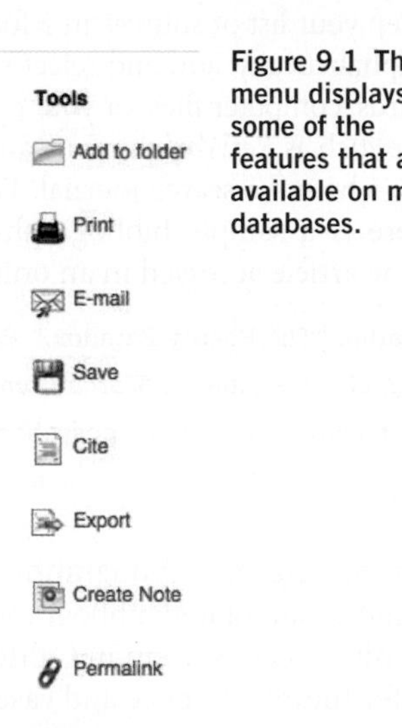

Figure 9.1 This menu displays some of the features that are available on many databases.

KEY POINTS

What Bibliographical Software Can (and Can't) Do

- Software can provide a way for you to record and easily save citations for sources you find in online databases.
- It will automatically create a bibliographical list or endnotes either in Cite While You Write (CWYW) mode or after completion of your text.
- It can prepare these lists in a variety of documentation styles, including those styles commonly required in college courses and covered in this handbook: MLA, APA, *Chicago*, and CSE. In fact, *EndNote* claims to offer 3,000 styles—more than enough for anyone.
- It does a lot, but it does not do everything. Take the time to learn the program. Using these programs requires a considerable initial investment of time and patience, but the investment will pay off eventually by making your citations in research papers much easier to manage. Read the documentation, and consult the Help menu whenever you need to.
- The software needs to be supplemented by your informed knowledge of the documentation system you are using. Do not let the program take over *all* the chores of recording the results of your research, inserting your citations, and preparing your list of works cited. You still need to be able to check citations for general accuracy and completeness, fix glitches, insert your anchors and hyperlinks in online papers, and handle the occasional abstruse reference yourself.

10 How to Use, Integrate, and Document Sources

10a Interacting with your sources: Annotating and making notes

MindTap®
Read, highlight, and take notes online.

Annotating your sources as you work helps you interact with the author's ideas, ask questions, write comments, and jot down your own ideas. You can annotate your online sources by printing them, saving them, or by using a social bookmarking tool such as *Diigo* to track your work. *Diigo* will allow you to post notes and highlight sections of text on any Web page.

Here is a passage from an article that a student read while researching a paper about plagiarism. As the author, Amy Robillard, tells the story of a colleague whose nephew sent him a plagiarized paper to read, she begins to explore how teachers respond emotionally to student plagiarism. The passage shows the annotations that a student made as she gave the article a critical reading.

Was his nephew lazy? confused by the assignment?

Is there a difference between how a teacher would respond and a family member?

> The bulk of our conversation centered on Aaron's anger at his nephew's actions. Some of his anger, of course, stemmed from the very fact that his nephew would plagiarize. But more anger seemed to be focused on the insult implied in his nephew's decision to send Aaron the paper to read before turning it in. Did his nephew really think Aaron wouldn't be able to tell the difference between the plagiarized work and the rest of the writing he'd been reading for him since he began college? Did he really think Aaron was that stupid? (12)
>
> —Robillard, Amy E. "We Won't Get Fooled Again: On the Absence of Angry Responses to Plagiarism in Composition Studies." *College English*, vol. 70, no. 1, 2007, pp. 10-31.

Because he's breaking the rules

No way to know that's what his nephew intended

Is this really how teachers feel?

Annotating is useful for comments, observations, and questions. You also may need to make notes when you do not have a copy that you can write on or when you want to summarize, paraphrase, and make detailed connections to other ideas and other sources. Write notes on the computer, on legal pads, in notebooks, or on index cards—whatever works best for you. On the computer, you can use *Word*'s Comment function to annotate a text or to insert your own comments within a text and highlight them in a color. Index cards—each card with a heading and only one note—offer flexibility: you can shuffle and reorder them to fit the organization of your paper. In your notes, always include the author's name, a short version of the title of the work, and any relevant page number(s). Include full source information in your working bibliography (9e). Then, when you write your paper, you will have at your fingertips all the information necessary for a including a citation.

10b Summarizing and paraphrasing

As you incorporate sources into your own writing, you can choose to summarize, paraphrase, or directly quote your sources. Summaries are useful for giving readers basic information about the work you are discussing. To summarize a source or a passage in a source, select only the main points as the author presents them, without your own commentary or interpretation. Be brief, and use your own words at all times. A good thing to remember is not to have the original source in front of you as you write. Read, understand, and put the passage away before you write your summary. Then, if you find that you absolutely need to include some particularly apt words from the original source, put them in quotation marks.

Use summaries in your research paper to let readers know the gist of the most important sources you find. When you include a summary in a paper, introduce the author or the work to indicate where your summary begins. At the end of the summary, give the page numbers you are summarizing. Do not include page numbers if you are summarizing the complete work or an online source; instead, indicate where your summary ends and your own ideas return (see 10d). When you write your paper, provide full documentation of the source in your list of works cited at the end.

Here is a passage from a *Psychology Today* article by Carlin Flora. A student's bibliographical citation for the article is shown in section 9e on page 185.

Original (paragraphs from a longer source)

> Beauty might be particularly beastly for women going after highly masculine jobs. Whereas attractiveness benefited men seeking traditionally masculine and traditionally feminine jobs, a 2010 study found it hurt women applying for a masculine job, such as a prison guard. Once women have scored a position, their attractiveness provides a boost only when the job is nonmanagerial. Yet attractiveness seems to have no effect on performance evaluations of men.
>
> "We have a conception of a beautiful woman, and 'leader' does not usually fit into that," says Lorri Sulpizio, Ph.D., coordinator of the Women's Leadership Academy at the University of San Diego.
>
> —Flora, Carlin. "The Beauty Paradox." *Psychology Today*, vol. 47, no. 1, 2014, pp. 36-37. *Academic Search Complete*, ezproxy.library.arizona.edu/login?url=http://search.ebscohost.com/login.aspx?direct=true&db=a9h&AN=93288156&site=ehost-live.

Summary (recorded in a computer file)

> Flora
> Summary
> "The Beauty Paradox"
>
> Carlin Flora reports that women who are considered physically attractive might have more difficulty securing and keeping jobs that are usually considered more masculine, especially if those positions involve managing other employees (37).

A *paraphrase,* in contrast, is similar in length to the original material. It presents the details of the author's argument and logic, but *it avoids plagiarism by not using the author's exact words or sentence structure.* You can paraphrase instead of quoting a source if you want to translate the information into language that is more appropriate for your intended audience. If you keep the source out of sight as you write a paraphrase, you will not be tempted to use any of the sentence patterns or phrases of the original. Even if you are careful to cite your source, your writing may still be regarded as plagiarized if your paraphrase resembles the original too closely in wording or sentence structure. You can use common words and expressions without quotation marks, but if you use longer or more unusual expressions from the source, always enclose them in quotation marks.

KEY POINTS

How to Paraphrase

- Keep the source out of sight as you write a paraphrase so that you will not be tempted to copy the sentence patterns or phrases of the original.
- Do not substitute synonyms for some or most of the words in an author's passage.
- Use your own sentence structure as well as your own words. Your writing will still be regarded as plagiarized if it resembles the original in sentence structure as well as in wording.
- Do not comment or interpret. Just tell readers the ideas that the author of your source presents.

- Check your text against the original source to avoid inadvertent plagiarism.
- Cite the author (and page number if a print source) as the source of the ideas, introduce and integrate the paraphrase, and provide full documentation. If the source does not name an author, cite the title.

You can use common words and expressions such as "traditionally masculine" or "performance," but if you use more unusual expressions from the source ("beauty might be particularly beastly"), you need to enclose them in quotation marks. In the first sample paraphrase shown here, nothing is quoted, but the words and structure resemble the original too closely.

Paraphrase too similar to the original (similarities are highlighted)

Flora

Paraphrase

"The Beauty Paradox"

Once women have secured a position, being attractive is usually an asset. If a woman is in a management position, however, it might become a problem. By contrast, attractiveness appears to have no effect on job evaluations of men (Flora 37).

Revised paraphrase

Flora explains the double standard that exists between men and women in management positions. For women, their attractiveness often becomes problematic in management, but a man's appearance does not seem to have any effect on his evaluations (37).

10c Quoting accurately

Quote sources only when the exact wording of the quotation is powerful or important to the point you are trying to make. Readers should immediately realize why you are quoting a particular passage and what the quotation contributes to the ideas you want to convey. They should also learn who said the words you are quoting and, if the source is a print source, on which page of the original work the quotation appears. Then they can look up the author's name in the list of works cited at the end of your paper and find out exactly where you found the quotation.

The Modern Language Association (MLA) format for citing a quotation from an article by one author is illustrated in this chapter and in part 3. For the use of quotation marks, see chapter 47. To learn how to cite a quotation the source itself cites, see section 11b, item J.

Decide what and when to quote Quote sparingly and only when the original words express the exact point you want to make, and express it succinctly and well. Ask yourself: Which point of mine does the quotation illustrate? Why am I considering quoting this particular passage rather than paraphrasing it? What do I need to tell my readers about the author of the quotation?

Quote the original exactly Any words you use from a source must be included in quotation marks and quoted exactly as they appear in the original, with the same punctuation marks and capital letters. (For quotations of longer than four lines, see the guidelines on pp. 194–195.) Do not change pronouns or tenses to fit your own purpose, unless you enclose changes in square brackets (as in the examples on pp. 193–194).

Not exact quotation	**Flora makes the point that "attractiveness has no effect on performance evaluations for men" (37).**
Exact	**Flora makes the point that "attractiveness seems to have no effect on performance evaluations of men" (37).**

If a quotation includes a question mark or an exclamation point, include it, and if a page number is necessary, put the final period after it: *Flora ends her article with a response to the question, "what are eye-catching aspiring leaders to do?" (37).*

How to indicate words omitted from a quotation

In the middle If you omit as irrelevant to your purpose any words or passages from the middle of a quotation, signal this by using the ellipsis mark, three dots separated by spaces:

> **Flora reports,** "Beauty might be particularly beastly for women going after highly masculine jobs . . . such as a prison guard" (37).

At the end If you omit the end of the source's sentence at the end of your own sentence, use three ellipsis dots and put the sentence period after any necessary parenthetical citation.

▸ **Compared to others, "the beautiful are treated more kindly and are perceived as more socially skilled, mentally healthy, and intelligent . . ." (Flora 36).**

At the beginning If you omit any words from the beginning of a quoted sentence, do not use an ellipsis.

▸ **Perhaps surprisingly, Flora reports that being attractive has "no effect on performance evaluations of men" (37)**

Omitting a sentence or a line of poetry If you omit a complete sentence (or more), use three dots after the previous period. For an omitted line of poetry, use a line of dots (see 49g).

Note: In MLA style, if your source passage itself uses ellipses, place your ellipsis dots within square brackets to indicate that your ellipsis mark is not part of the original text: [. . .].

How to split a quotation For variety, you may want to use your own words to split a quotation:

▸ **"Once women have scored a position," new research suggests, "their attractiveness provides a boost only when the job is nonmanagerial" (Flora 37).**

Don't rig the evidence It should go without saying that quoting means quoting an author's ideas without adding any of your own contextual material—or omitting any of the author's—that substantially changes the author's intent. For example, writing the following distorts the author's views and presents the evidence incorrectly, even though the words that are quoted are in the original article:

▸ **Carlin Flora reports that "the beautiful are . . . more socially skilled, mentally healthy, and intelligent than their less attractive counterparts" (36).**

How to add or change words to fit into your sentence If you add any comments or explanations in your own words or if you change a word of the original to fit it grammatically into your sentence or to spell it correctly, enclose the added or changed material in square brackets. Generally, however, it is preferable to rephrase your sentence, because bracketed words and phrases make sentences difficult to read. The first example shows a word in the quotation changed to make it fit the quoter's sentence structure, and the second is a personal interjected comment; the revised example does away with the awkward square brackets.

Awkward **Beauty is particularly tricky for female leaders who are "charismatic and [aim to increase] communication among coworkers" (Flora 36).**

Revised **Flora reports that women whose leadership style is marked by "being charismatic and increasing communication among coworkers" are particularly susceptible to bias (36).**

How to quote a long passage If you quote more than three lines of poetry or four typed lines of prose, do not use quotation marks.

- Begin the quotation on a new line.
- For MLA style, indent the quotation one-half inch from the left margin.
- For APA or *Chicago* style, indent the quotation one-half inch from the left margin.
- Double-space throughout.
- Do not indent from the right margin.
- If you quote from more than one paragraph, indent the first line of a new paragraph an additional one-quarter inch.
- Establish the context for a long quotation, and integrate it into your text by stating the point you want to make and naming the author of the quotation in your introductory statement.

Flora describes research conducted on the effect of attractiveness for women seeking certain kinds of jobs:

> Whereas attractiveness benefited men seeking traditionally masculine and traditionally feminine jobs, a 2010 study found it hurt women applying for a masculine job, such as a prison guard. Once women have scored a position, their attractiveness provides a boost only when the job is nonmanagerial. Yet attractiveness seems to have no effect on performance evaluations of men. (37)

Note: With a long, indented quotation with a parenthetical page citation, notice that the period goes before the parenthetical citation, not after it.

Avoid a string of quotations Use quotations, especially long ones, sparingly and only when they help you make a good argument. Readers do not want to see a collection of passages from other writers; they can read the original works themselves. Rather, they want your analysis of your sources and the conclusions you draw from your research. Quotations should not appear in a string, one after the other. If they do, your readers will wonder what purpose the quotations serve and will search for your voice in the paper.

Fit a quotation into your sentence When you quote, use the exact words of the original, and make sure that those exact words do not disrupt the flow of your sentence and send it in another direction, with, for instance, a change of tense.

A bad fit **I noticed in my last job that "the beautiful are treated more kindly and are perceived as more socially skilled, mentally healthy, and intelligent than their less attractive counterparts" (Flora 36).**

A better fit **I noticed in my last job that some of my more attractive co-workers were treated better, illustrating Flora's claim that "the beautiful are treated more kindly and are perceived as more socially skilled, mentally healthy, and intelligent than their less attractive counterparts" (Flora 36).**

10d Indicating the boundaries of a source citation in your text

Naming an author or a title in your text tells readers that you are citing ideas from a source, and citing a page number at the end of a summary or paraphrase lets them know where your citation ends. However, for one-page print or database articles and for Internet sources, a page citation is not necessary, so it is harder to indicate where your comments about a source end. You always need to indicate clearly where your summary or paraphrase ends and where your own comments take over. Convey the shift to readers by commenting on the source in a way that clearly announces a transition back to your own views. Use expressions such as *it follows that, X's explanation shows that, as a result, evidently, obviously,* or *clearly* to signal the shift.

Unclear citation boundary

> According to promotional material on a Sony Web site more than ten years ago, the company decided to release a cassette and a CD based on a small research study indicating that listening to Mozart improved IQ. The products showed the ingenuity of commercial enterprise while taking the researchers' conclusions in new directions.

Revised citation, with source boundary indicated

> According to promotional material on a Sony Web site more than ten years ago, the company decided to release a cassette and a CD based on research indicating that listening to Mozart improved IQ. Clearly, Sony's strategy demonstrated the ingenuity of commercial enterprise, but it cannot reflect what the researchers intended when they published their conclusions.

Another way to indicate the end of your citation is to include the author's or authors' name(s) at the end of the citation instead of (or even in addition to) introducing the citation with the name.

Unclear citation boundary

> For people who hate shopping, Web shopping may be the perfect solution. Jerome and Taylor's exploration of "holiday hell" reminds us that we get more choice from online vendors than we do when we browse at our local mall because the online sellers, unlike mall owners, do not have to rent space to display their goods. In addition, one can buy almost anything online, from CDs, cell phones, and books to cars and real estate.

Revised citation, with source boundary indicated

> For people who hate shopping, Web shopping may be the perfect solution. An article exploring the "holiday hell" of shopping reminds us that we get more choice from online vendors than we do when we browse at our local mall because the online sellers, unlike mall owners, do not have to rent space to display their goods (Jerome and Taylor). In addition, one can buy almost anything online, from CDs, cell phones, and books to cars and real estate.

10e Synthesizing sources

Large amounts of information are no substitute for a thesis or a clear main idea with relevant support. Your paper should *synthesize* your sources, not just tell about them one after the other. When you synthesize, you connect the ideas in individual sources to create a larger picture, to inform yourself about the topic, and to establish your own ideas on the topic. Leave yourself plenty of time to:

- read through your notes on your sources and think about what you have read
- connect with the material and form responses to it
- take into account new ideas and opposing arguments
- find connections among the facts and the ideas that your sources offer

For this last point, try drawing a map of your sources, or creating a timeline using online software, such as *Timeglider*, to show connections between your sources.

Avoid sitting down to write a paper at the last minute, surrounded by library books or stacks of photocopies. In this scenario, you may be tempted to lift material, but, if you do, you will produce a lifeless paper. Remember that the paper is ultimately your work, not a collection of other people's words, and that your identity and opinions as the writer should be evident.

10f Organizing your essay by ideas, not sources

As you consider how to incorporate your sources into your paper's organization, let your ideas, not your sources, drive your paper.

Avoid Organization Like This

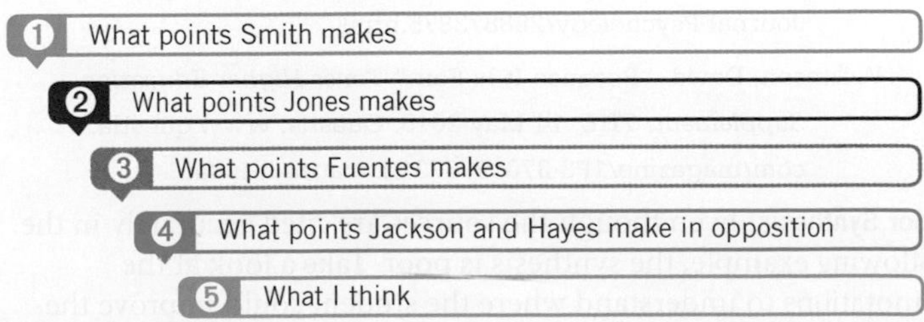

KEY EXAMPLE

Source Synthesis

As you incorporate sources into your own writing, avoid copying, pasting and "dumping" sources into your writing. Instead, read and understand what the sources say first so that you can figure out how the sources help you construct and then support a position or argument. Try completing these two steps to get you on the right track before you incorporate sources into your writing:

1. **Summarize your potential sources.** You don't need to write a detailed, formal summary, but you do need to understand what each source says well enough to figure out how it fits into a larger conversation about your topic. Follow the guidelines in section 10b to write a quick summary of each of your sources. Use your own words when you write the summaries, and if you use any quotations, be sure to keep quotation marks around the exact words of the original author.
2. **Determine the relationships between your sources.** As you think about how your sources relate to each other, try to put together the story they tell about your topic. Consider these questions: How do your sources relate to each other? When were they published? What positions on your topic do they represent? Do they refer to each other or to similar issues or incidents? You might try using an online application like *Timeglider* to construct a timeline based on when your sources were published.

A student's paper discussing workplace differences between men and women drew on the following two sources:

Nadler, Joel T., and Margaret S. Stockdale. "Workplace Gender Bias: Not Just Between Strangers." *North American Journal of Psychology,* vol. 14, no. 2, 2012, pp. 281-91, www.freepatentsonline.com/article/North-American-Journal-Psychology/288873875.html.

Wilkinson, David. "Because It Is Fair." *Times Higher Education Supplement: THE*, 14 May 2015. Questia, www.questia.com/magazine/1P3-3701976731/because-it-is-fair.

Poor Synthesis Even though the sources are cited accurately in the following example, the synthesis is poor. Take a look at the annotations to understand where the student could improve the synthesis:

Introduction to quote doesn't explain the source. Who is Wilkinson?

Is this rigging the evidence? It's hard to tell whether the meaning is the same as the original from this excerpt.

Several sources discuss reasons women often have lower pay for the same work. Wilkinson says, "it is known that women tend to bargain less for starting salaries than do men" (34).

Additionally, "women are statistically more likely to take time off . . . for parental leave, and to care for sick or elderly family members" (Wilkinson 34). "Studies indicate career-oriented women are more likely to delay relationships or children in order to advance their careers" (Nadler and Stockdale 282). To address these problems, McMaster University made the decision to increase women's salaries to the level of male faculty, and "We are paying women and men equally simply because it is fair" (Wilkinson 34).

String of quotations without any explanation or meaningful connection from the student author.

The sudden use of "we" in the quotation and the shift from past tense to present tense is confusing.

A Good Synthesis The following synthesis does a much better job of synthesizing the two sources into a meaningful paragraph. Take a look at the annotations to understand what the student did well:

Intro to the source explains where the data came from.

The way the quote is split helps readers understand what the study says.

In a review of research on pay differences between men and women, Joel Nadler and Margaret Stockdale report that "the attainment of top positions in fields, and benefits to go along with those top positions, bypass women for many reasons" (282). Research points to several reasons for this gender disparity, "women are more likely to perceive workplace pressure to make a choice between career and family" (Nadler and Stockdale 282). Another factor impeding women's advancement is cited by David Wilkinson, Provost of McMaster University: "women are statistically more likely to take time off" for a variety of reasons, including "parental leave, and to care for sick or elderly family members" (34). To address these problems, Wilkinson explains that his university raised the pay of many women to make pay equal between men and women. He clearly states, "We are paying women and men equally [at McMaster] simply because it is fair" (Wilkinson 34).

Inserted word in brackets helps give context for the statement.

Questions

1. What do you find most challenging about synthesizing sources into your own writing?
2. Take another look at the preceding example of a poor synthesis. With a classmate, try rewriting it to make it a good synthesis. What did you have to change, and why?
3. What strategies have you used in the past to summarize and synthesize sources? What strategies were useful? What strategies might you try the next time you are asked to incorporate sources into your writing?

The preceding organization is driven by sources, with the bulk of the paper dealing with the views of Smith, Jones, and the rest. Instead, let your main point and then the supporting evidence for subpoints determine the organization, as shown below:

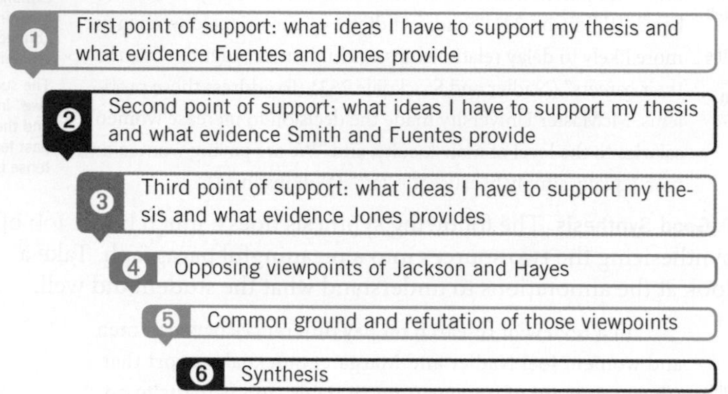

Improved Organization
1 First point of support: what ideas I have to support my thesis and what evidence Fuentes and Jones provide
2 Second point of support: what ideas I have to support my thesis and what evidence Smith and Fuentes provide
3 Third point of support: what ideas I have to support my thesis and what evidence Jones provides
4 Opposing viewpoints of Jackson and Hayes
5 Common ground and refutation of those viewpoints
6 Synthesis

To avoid producing an essay that reads like a serial listing of summaries or references ("Crabbe says this," "Tyger says that," "Tyger also says this"), spend time reviewing your notes and synthesizing what you find into a coherent and convincing statement of what you know and believe.

- Make lists of good ideas that your sources raise about your topic.
- Look for the connections among those ideas: comparisons and contrasts.
- Find links in content, examples, and statistics.
- Note connections between the information in your sources and what you know from your own experience.

If you follow these guidelines, you will take control of your material instead of letting it take control of you.

10g Introducing and integrating source material

Introduce information from your sources (summaries, paraphrases, and quotations) in a way that integrates them into the flow of your writing. They should not just pop up with no lead-in.

Source not introduced and integrated

> Women can have difficulty with securing jobs and keeping them if they are physically attractive. "Yet attractiveness seems to have no effect on performance evaluations of men" (Flora 37).

Source introduced and integrated

> In an article about how women can have difficulty securing and keeping their jobs if they are physically attractive, Carlin Flora describes that, by contrast, "attractiveness seems to have no effect on performance evaluations of men" (37).

If you quote a complete sentence, or if you paraphrase or summarize a section of another work, introduce the source material by providing an introductory phrase with the author's full name (for the first reference to an author) and a brief mention of his or her expertise or credentials. For subsequent citations, the last name is sufficient.

Ways to introduce source material

X has pointed out that	According to X,
X has made it clear that	As X insists,
X explains that	In 2016, X, the vice president
X suggests that	of the corporation, declared

Vary the introductory phrase The introductory verbs *say* and *write* are clear and direct. Occasionally, use one of the following verbs to express subtle shades of meaning: *acknowledge, agree, argue, ask, assert, believe, claim, comment, contend, declare, deny, emphasize, explain, insist, note, point out, propose, speculate,* or *suggest.*

10h Documenting to fit the discipline

Documentation is an integral part of a research paper. Conventions vary from discipline to discipline and from style manual to style manual—as illustrated by the inclusion of MLA, APA, CSE, and *Chicago* styles in parts 3 and 4—but the various styles of documentation are not arbitrary. The styles reflect what the disciplines value and what readers need to know.

In the humanities, for instance, many research findings offer scholarly interpretation and analysis of texts, so they may be relevant for years, decades, or centuries. Publication dates in the Modern Language Association (MLA) style, therefore, occur only in the works-cited list and are not included in the in-text citation. Such a practice also serves to minimize interruptions to the text.

The endnote/footnote system of the *Chicago Manual of Style* (along with the citation-sequence and citation-name systems of the Council of Science Editors–CSE) goes further, requiring only a small superscript number in the text to send readers to the list of sources.

Both the American Psychological Association (APA) and the CSE name-year style include the date of the work cited within the text citation itself, emphasizing that timeliness of research is an issue in the sciences and social sciences. In addition, abbreviations used in all three CSE styles (chapter 17) reflect the fact that scientists are expected to be aware of the major sources in their field.

All systems, however, aim to give enough information in the text for readers to be able to find full details of the source in a bibliographical list at the end of the work or in footnotes or endnotes.

10i One source, four systems of documentation

Note that on many sites, you may have difficulty finding a date of posting, a document title as well as a Web site name, or an exact identification of the author of the material, whether the author is an individual or an organization. Just record whatever you can find by a thorough search of the site, always scrolling down to the bottom of a page and consulting the Home or About pages, as well as the page properties or page information tools found in your browser. Also try using the root domain of the URL—the material just before the dot preceding the first single slash—to identify the owner who is responsible for its content, also referred to as the *publisher* or *sponsor* of the site. If the Home and About pages provide no useful information, consider whether you should use a source if you are unsure about the identity of the author, the author's credentials, or the owner and purpose of the site. You can also do a search to see who links to a site and what those referrers have to say about it as an additional aid to evaluation. (When using a search engine, if you put "link:" followed by a URL in the Search field and hit Return, the results will show you which sites link to that URL.)

If you find and record as many of the indicated items of information as you can (see Figure 10.1), you will then be able to cite a Web source in the four most common documentation styles.

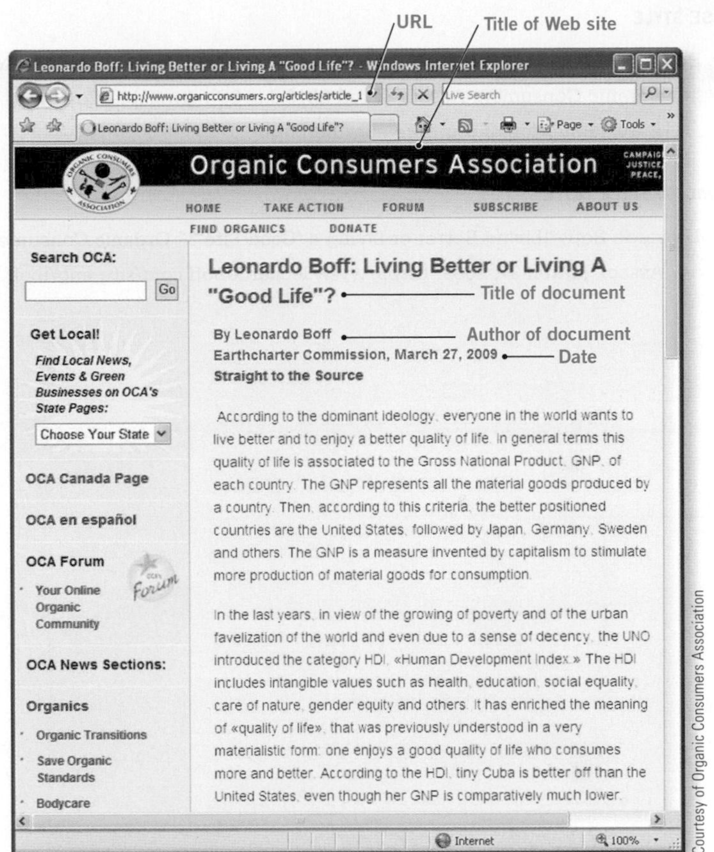

Courtesy of Organic Consumers Association

Figure 10.1 A Web page that includes information needed for documentation

MLA STYLE

Boff, Leonardo. "Living Better or Living a 'Good Life'?" *Organic Consumers Association*, 27 Mar. 2009, www.leonardoboff.com/site-eng/lboff.htm.

APA STYLE

Boff, L. (2009, March 27). Living better or living a "good life"? Retrieved from http://www.leonardoboff.com/site-eng/lboff.htm

CSE STYLE

2. Boff L. Living better or living a "good life"? [Internet]. 2009. Finland (MN): Organic Consumers Assoc.; [cited 2016 Jan 23]. Available from: http://www.leonardoboff.com/site-eng/lboff.htm

***CHICAGO* STYLE NOTE**

9. Leonardo Boff, "Living Better or Living a 'Good Life'?" Organic Consumers Assoc., March 27, 2009, http://www.leonardoboff.com/site-eng/lboff.htm

Exercises on the Research Process

EXERCISE 1 Select and revise thesis statements 6e

Which of the following would make a good thesis statement for a research paper? Show how the others could be improved to make them more effective thesis statements.

1. How to discipline children.
2. The advantages and disadvantages of spanking.
3. In this paper I will discuss how parents should bring up their children.
4. Doctors' advice on the issue of spanking.
5. Children who fear spanking will behave themselves.
6. Disciplining children should involve rewards, removal of privileges, and above all, discussion of right and wrong.

EXERCISE 2 Find and narrow a topic in a search directory 7a, 7e

Access an online library database such as *InfoTrac/Expanded Academic* or *EBSCO Host/Academic Search Complete*. In the Search box, start with a subject search of any broad category: for example, "family," "health," or "music." Look at the categories until you find one you are interested in. For example, a subject search of "family" yields "family and mass media" as one of the categories. Whatever broad category you decide to search, keep narrowing the subject to a topic you can explore in a short paper.

Click on the category, and access at least two sources. Then formulate a possible question that would focus your thinking and any research.

EXERCISE 3 Do a keyword search 7f

Go to *Google* at www.google.com, and do a keyword search to find reliable information on *one* aspect of *one* of the following topics. Discuss your results with classmates.

- nonallergenic dogs
- hamstring injuries
- the digital divide
- mononucleosis
- termites
- titanium

EXERCISE 4 Find and evaluate Web sources on a topic 8c

Use a search engine to do a Web search for information on either the topic "body building" or "dieting." Find one Web page that offers useful, serious information and another that you would reject as a source of balanced and objective information. Make a copy of each page, bring the copies to class, and explain your evaluation to your classmates.

EXERCISE 5 Detect plagiarism 9a–9c

The following passage is from page 142 of *His Excellency: George Washington* by Joseph Ellis:

> Whereas Cromwell and later Napoleon made themselves synonymous with the revolution in order to justify the assumption of dictatorial power, Washington made himself synonymous with the American Revolution in order to declare that it was incompatible with dictatorial power.

Consider which of the following passages use the source responsibly and avoid kidnapping its words or ideas. For each passage, explain what is or is not done correctly and what may be considered plagiarism. (If you want to review paraphrase and quotation before you do this exercise, turn to sections 10b–10d.) Then compare your results with those of your classmates, and discuss which of the seven sins you find represented here.

1. Joseph Ellis makes the point that whereas Cromwell and later Napoleon made themselves synonymous with the revolution in order to justify the assumption of dictatorial power, Washington made himself synonymous with the American Revolution in order to declare that it was incompatible with dictatorial power.
2. Joseph Ellis speculates that whereas Cromwell and later Napoleon made themselves synonymous with the revolution in order to justify the assumption of dictatorial power, Washington made himself synonymous with the American Revolution in order to declare that it was incompatible with dictatorial power (142).
3. As Joseph Ellis points out in *His Excellency: George Washington,* Washington was not like Cromwell or Napoleon, who led revolutions in order to become dictators themselves. Washington led the American Revolution in order that no American should ever become a dictator (142).
4. Joseph Ellis proposes that whereas Cromwell and Napoleon used their revolutions to justify their assumption of dictatorial power, Washington used the American Revolution to announce that it was incompatible with dictatorial power (142).
5. It is interesting to speculate that Cromwell and Napoleon each led revolutions to become dictators. Washington, on the other hand, led the American Revolution to deny dictatorship to himself and to all other Americans.
6. As Joseph Ellis notes, Washington differed from previous great revolutionary leaders who became dictators by seeing to it that the American Revolution, which he led, "was incompatible with dictatorial power" (142).
7. Cromwell and Napoleon identified with their revolutions so that they could become dictators, whereas Washington identified with the American Revolution so that no one could become an American dictator.

8. As Joseph Ellis observes, "Whereas Cromwell and later Napoleon made themselves synonymous with the revolution in order to justify the assumption of dictatorial power, Washington made himself synonymous with the American Revolution in order to declare that it was incompatible with dictatorial power" (142).
9. Joseph Ellis comments that while both Cromwell and Napoleon made themselves identical with the revolution so that they could give good reason for taking on despotic authority, Washington identified with the revolution at home to show that it was irreconcilable with tyranny (142).

EXERCISE 6 Write an annotated bibliography entry 9e

Choose a reading from one of your courses as the subject for an annotated bibliography entry. The entry should cite the reading's bibliographical details in MLA style and should include a brief summary of the reading. See part 3 for more on MLA style.

EXERCISE 7 Paraphrase 10b

While Michelle Guerra was working on a paper on the English-only controversy (whether languages other than English should be banned in schools, government offices and publications) and was looking for the history of the issue, she came across the following source.

ORIGINAL SOURCE

> If any language group, Spanish or other, chooses to maintain its language, there is precious little that we can do about it, legally or otherwise, and still maintain that we are a free country. We cannot legislate the language of the home, the street, the bar, the club, unless we are willing to set up a cadre of language police who will ticket and arrest us if we speak something other than English.
>
> —Stalker, James C. "Official English or English Only." *English Journal*, vol. 77, no. 3, Mar. 1988, pp. 18-23.

1. In the following paraphrase, underline the words and structures that resemble the original too closely.
2. Revise the paragraph so that the original source is paraphrased appropriately.

PARAPHRASE OF STALKER, P. 21

As Stalker points out, if any group of languages, Greek or other, decides to keep its language, there is not much any of us can do, with laws or not, and still claim to be a free country. We cannot pass legislation about the language we speak at home, on the street, or in restaurants, unless we also want to have a group of special police who will take us off to jail if they hear us not speaking English (21).

EXERCISE 8 Quote 10c

The following sentences incorporate quotations from the paragraph by Ben Harder. Correct any errors or inaccuracies in the quotation, and make sure the quotation fits smoothly into the sentence. Some sentences may not need any editing.

> Using good bacteria to obstruct bad ones—a strategy known as bacterial interference—is one application of so-called probiotics, a field with growing medical promise. The name suggests a twist on antibiotics, which kill disease-causing microbes. Some probiotic bacteria do their work by competing for resources and space with pathogens inside the body and, in effect, elbowing the bad bugs out of the way.
>
> —Harder, Ben. "Germs That Do a Body Good." *Science News*, vol. 161, no. 3, Jan. 2002, pp. 72-74.

Example Harder calls the word *probiotics* "a twist on antibiotics . . . " (72).

1. Harder says, "The use of good bacteria to obstruct bad ones is one application of probiotics . . . " (72).
2. Harder discusses one strategy of probiotic bacteria, which fight "for resources and space with pathogens inside the body and, in effect, elbowing the bad bugs out of the way" (72).
3. According to Harder, "probiotics is a field with growing medical promise" (72).
4. Harder explains that "antibiotics, which kill disease-causing microbes" (72).
5. Harder notes that probiotic bacteria can "[compete] for resources and space with pathogens inside the body . . . " (72).

EXERCISE 9 Summarize, paraphrase, and indicate a clear citation boundary 10d

1. The following excerpt is from a textbook chapter on how political power is represented in art. Summarize the excerpt. Then compare your summary with those of your classmates.

> Images of contemporary political leaders are fundamentally different from those of the past, just as the concept of "rule" has evolved. Today, almost no rulers openly consider themselves to be of divine descent, and many are not royalty. And with photography, pictures of rulers come to us not as artworks, but as a flood of newspaper or television images. There is a great difference between images that are produced under the ruler's direction and those over which the ruler has little or no control.
>
> —Lazzari, Margaret, and Dona Schlesier. *Exploring Art: A Global, Thematic Approach.* 4th ed., Cengage Learning, 2011. p. 276.

2. Paraphrase the following excerpt from the same textbook chapter. Then compare your paraphrase with those of your classmates.

> In 1934, Adolf Hitler commissioned the film *Triumph of the Will,* directed by Leni Riefenstahl, to glorify his rule, his military strength, and the Nazi order

of Aryan supremacy. A work of brilliant propaganda, Riefenstahl's film established Hitler as the first media hero of the modern age.

Given unlimited funding by Hilter, Riefenstahl had a staff of more than 130 people, sixteen cameras, four sound trucks, and cranes and dollies for dramatic shots. Skillfully edited into the film were speeches, parades, cheering crowds, and the lush music of the popular German composer Richard Wagner. Although the film was a documentary covering a six-day rally celebrating Hitler at Nuremberg, the imagery was entirely staged.

—Lazzari, Margaret, and Dona Schlesier. *Exploring Art: A Global, Thematic Approach.* 4th ed., Cengage Learning, 2011. p. 276.

3. Revise the following two passages to create clear citation boundaries between the writer's summary or paraphrase and her own commentary.
   a. Lazzari and Schlesier point out that Adolf Hitler was the first twentieth-century leader to use filmmaking to reinforce his powerful persona. China's Mao Zedong and Korea's Kim Jong-Il later relied on similar propaganda.
   b. Lazzari and Schlesier observe, for example, that Leni Riefenstahl's "documentary" *Triumph of the Will* does not record real-life events but was carefully planned and staged. Americans watching Democratic and Republican delegates cheer and applaud at their national conventions must remember the producer's sometimes cynical role in creating a TV-ready show of enthusiasm.

EXERCISE 10 Use document styles to suit the discipline 10h, 10i

1. On the Web, find an article related to your area of concentration. Record the information described in section 10i (author name, article title, Web site title, sponsor or publisher, posting date, page numbers, date of access, and URL).
2. Determine which documentation style you will use for research projects in your area of concentration. Confirm this with your instructor or a course syllabus, if necessary.
3. Using the four sample listings in 10i as an example, draft a listing for the Web site in the appropriate documentation style.

MindTap®

▶ **Practice skills that you have learned in this part and receive automatic feedback.**

3 MLA Documentation

WRITING IN YOUR CAREER

The Arts Professional, the Writer

Photo courtesy of Preethi Burkholder

Documentation is a key area of concern for those in the arts. Individuals who work in the arts also preserve the arts, and whole branches of the arts are devoted to documenting the who, what, when, and where of precious and historical objects. Contemporary artists, who often work in ephemeral media, must also take great pains to preserve their work through clear documentation. The business of art is no different. Whether you are an arts administrator, an arts educator, or an artist yourself, grant writing is the economic lifeblood of the industry. Individual artists may apply directly to government agencies or to private foundations for money to fund their projects. Museums, art councils, and other nonprofit organizations do the same. Funding agencies have explicit requirements for documentation and format. In the competition for funding, proposals that lack the required documentation in the required format will be rejected. For more on grant writing, see the article "How to Write a Successful Grant Proposal" (1 Feb. 2008), by Preethi Burkholder on *www.artistsnetwork.com*. In her article, she shows how to establish a need and then present a project as a way to meet that need. Additionally, take a look at the Research Proposal guidelines in the Assignments Guides. Research proposals are often written for the purpose of securing funding through a grant or other means.

From Preethi Burkholder's grant proposal for an art project

During the last thirty years there has been a general understanding in the United States that alcoholism is a progressive family disease, and that it is treatable. This medical advancement has transformed lives of alcoholics and their families to step outside of their self-inflicted cells and to enjoy things in life besides alcohol. Unfortunately, the majority of alcoholics and their families live in denial and transmit dysfunctional elements caused by the disease to the next generation.

"Living in a Box" will be a public art project taking place in Oregon. It will give visual representation to the insanity caused by alcoholism and how it shrinks the world of alcoholics into cells over a period of time. The goal of the public art project is to inspire alcoholics and their families to take the first step toward recovery, and that is to stop living in denial about the disease. . . .

3 MLA Documentation

MLA AT-A-GLANCE INDEX

MLA AT-A-GLANCE INDEX OF STYLE FEATURES

For research papers and shorter documented essays, always provide detailed information about any books, articles, Web sites, or other sources that you cite. Many courses in English departments ask you to follow the guidelines of the Modern Language Association (MLA) as recommended in the *MLA Handbook*, 8th edition (New York: MLA, 2016), and on the MLA Web site. See chapter 11 for an explanation of MLA style. The following three chapters illustrate this style.

MindTap®
Understand the goals of this part, and complete a warm-up activity.

11 Citing Sources in Your Paper, MLA Style

MindTap®
Read, highlight, and take notes online.

Writers and researchers in various disciplines use documentation styles to present material and acknowledge sources in ways that highlight what is most relevant to colleagues in different fields (see 10h). MLA style is used in humanities fields such as English literature, composition, foreign languages, philosophy, religion, art, theater, and music. A writer in one of these disciplines often undertakes a close study and analysis of a work, considering previous scholarly interpretations to determine how his or her view may offer a new perspective on the work. The writer may also discuss how a work is part of a particular genre.

In MLA style, the focus is on making citations useful to readers. In some cases, you might find more than one "correct" way to document a source, but the most important guideline to keep in mind is that you should focus on the elements that sources share in common (the nine core elements, pp. 231–234) and eliminate redundant or unnecessary information. To accomplish these goals, MLA style uses in-text parenthetical references (see 11a and the Key Points box on pp. 217–218) containing only enough information to help readers find the work's full publication data at the end of the paper (see chapter 12). The conciseness of MLA style is also reflected in its use of shortened forms and abbreviations, such as omitting words such as *Corporation, Company, Limited,* and *Incorporated* from publishers' names and using *P* for the word *Press* (see Source Shot 2, pp. 238–239).

When you refer to, comment on, paraphrase, or quote another author's material, you must indicate that you have done so by inserting what is called a *citation*. In MLA style, you give the name of the author(s) and the page number(s) where you found the material, if available. You can put the author's name in your own text to introduce the material, with the page number in parentheses at the end of the sentence, or, especially for a source you have cited previously, you can put both the author and the page number in parentheses at the place in the sentence where you cite the material. Citations most often appear at the end of the sentence, unless a writer is showing that a certain part of a sentence came from a specific source. All of the more detailed publication information about your sources then goes into a list of works cited at the end of the paper so that readers can retrieve and read the same source.

Sections 11a and 11b show you examples and variations on the basic principle of MLA citation.

11a Basic features of MLA style

KEY POINTS
How to Cite and List Sources in MLA Style

1. *In your paper*
   - Include the **last name(s)** of the author (or authors). Give a title (shortened) if no author is known.
   - Include the **page number(s)** where the information is located (except when the source is only one page long or an online source without page numbers), but do not include the word *page* or *pages* or the abbreviation *p.* or *pp.* For inclusive page numbers over 100 that have the same first number(s), give only the last two digits for the second number in most cases (257-58 but 658-701). In MLA style, put a hyphen rather than a dash between the numbers.

Both author and page number can be given in parentheses (not separated by a comma) at the end of the sentence in which the reference occurs. You can also name the author in your text and put the page number in parentheses at the end of the sentence.

2. *At the end of your paper*
   - Include a **list,** alphabetized by authors' last names or by title (in italics or quotation marks) if the author is not known, of all the sources you refer to in the paper. Also include any other

(Continued)

(Continued)

information relevant to your use of the source, such as the larger container title (such as a periodical title or Web site), other contributors (such as translators or editors), the version, the number, the publisher, the publication date, and the location where it is found. Begin the list on a new page, and title it *Works Cited*. Sections 12d–12i provide many examples of listing different types of sources.

Illustrations of the Basic Features (MLA)

Citation in Your Paper	Entry in List of Works Cited
Author of book named in your text with page(s) given in parentheses The renowned scholar of language David Crystal has promoted the idea of "dialect democracy" (168).	Crystal, David. *The Stories of English*. Overlook, 2004.
Author and pages(s) of book given in parentheses A renowned scholar of language has promoted the idea of "dialect democracy" (Crystal 168).	Crystal, David. *The Stories of English*. Overlook, 2004.
Author of article named in your text with page(s) in parentheses Steel describes the long-term struggle over the future of Viacom when she says "the real fight has only just begun" (A1).	Steel, Emily. "Power Struggle Churns Viacom, Even as a New Leader Is Named." *The New York Times*, late edition, 5 Feb. 2016, pp. A1+.
Author and page(s) of article provided in parentheses The long-term struggle over the future of Viacom shows that "the real fight has only just begun" (Steel A1).	Steel, Emily. "Power Struggle Churns Viacom, Even as a New Leader Is Named." *The New York Times*, late edition, 5 Feb. 2016, pp. A1+.

11b How to cite sources in your paper, MLA author/page style

MLA recommends that you create a draft list of your works cited (see chapter 12) before you begin writing your paper so that you can insert the correct information in your parenthetical references. For example, you will want to plan ahead to correctly cite works by authors with the same last name or two works by the same author. The information in a parenthetical reference must exactly match the information about that source in your works-cited list. The following section gives examples of the various formats used for in-text citations.

THE BASICS OF CITATIONS: INCORPORATING QUOTED MATERIAL INTO YOUR PAPER

A. Author named in your text You can cite an author in a sentence in your paper, or you can put the author and page number in parentheses at the end of your sentence. Naming the author as you introduce the source material allows you to supply information about the author's credentials as an expert and so increases the credibility of your source for readers. Another advantage of naming your source in your text is that readers will know that everything between the mention of the author and the cited page number is a reference to your source material and not your own ideas. Put a page number only within parentheses, not in the text of your paper.

For the first mention of an author in a text sentence, use the full name and any relevant credentials. After that, use only the last name. Generally, use the present tense to cite an author. See Source Shot 2 on pages 238–239 for the entry for the following text in a works-cited list.

author and credentials

National Book Award winner Paul Fussell points out that even people in low-paying jobs show "all but universal pride in a uniform of any kind" (5).

page number

B. Punctuation of the quotation and citation When a quotation ends the sentence, as in the previous example, put the closing quotation marks after the last word and before the parentheses, and place the sentence period after the parentheses. (Note that this rule differs from the one for undocumented writing, which calls for a period before the closing quotation marks.)

When a quoted sentence ends with a question mark or an exclamation point, also include a period after the parenthetical citation:

Paul Fussell reminds us of our equating uniforms with seriousness of purpose when he begins a chapter by asking, "Would you get on an airplane with two pilots who are wearing cut-off jeans?" (85).

For more information on incorporating quotations into your paper, see 10c and 10d. To cite sequential references to the same work in one text paragraph, see item D.

C. Author named in parentheses If you have referred to an author previously or if you are citing statistics, you do not need to mention the author in your text to introduce the reference. Simply include the author's last name before the page number within the parentheses, with no comma between them.

The army retreated from Boston in disarray, making the victors realize that they had defeated the "greatest military power on earth" (McCullough 76).

author page number

D. Sequential references to the same source If you use several quotations from the same page of your source within one of your paragraphs, one parenthetical reference after the last quotation is enough, but make sure that no quotations from other works intervene. If you are paraphrasing from and referring to one work several times in a paragraph, mention the author in your text. Then give the page number at the end of a paraphrase and again if you paraphrase from a different page. Make it clear to readers where the paraphrase ends and your own comments take over (10d).

E. A long quotation For a quotation longer than four lines, indent the quoted material one-half inch, double-space it, and do not enclose it in quotation marks. You may want to introduce the quotation with a text sentence naming the author, followed by a colon. Put the period ending the last sentence of the quotation (and one space) before the parenthetical citation, not after it. For an example and more information on a long quotation, see 10c, pages 194–195.

CITING A WORK WITH AN INDIVIDUAL AUTHOR OR AUTHORS (MLA)

Note: Items A–E give examples of the basic conventions for citing a work by one author. Items F–K that follow provide more details about a wider variety of authored sources.

F. Work written by two or more authors For a work with two authors, include both names either in your text sentence or in parentheses, with no comma between the last name and any available page number.

> Lakoff and Johnson have pointed out . . . (42)
> (Raimes and Miller-Cochran 18-20)

For a work with three or more authors, use the first author's name followed by *et al.* (from the Latin *et alii*, meaning "and others") in your text sentence or in parentheses. Do not include a comma before *et al.*

> (Roberts et al. 10)

See 12e, item 10, for how to list a print work with two or more authors in a works-cited list.

G. Work by author(s) with more than one work cited Include the author and title of the work in your text sentence.

> Alice Walker, in her book *In Search of Our Mothers' Gardens,* describes revisiting her past to discover more about Flannery O'Connor (43-59).

If you do not mention the author in your text, include in your parenthetical reference the author's last name followed by a comma, an abbreviated form of the title (not followed by a comma), and the page number.

> O'Connor's house still stands and is looked after by a caretaker (Walker, *In Search* 57).

comma

abbreviated title page number

H. Work by two authors with the same last name Include each author's first initial or the complete first name if the authors' initials are the same.

> A writer can be seen as both "author" and "secretary," and the two roles can be seen as competitive (F. Smith 19).

I. Author of work in an edited anthology Cite the author of the included or reprinted work (not the editor of the anthology) and the page number(s) you refer to in the anthology (see Source Shot 3, pp. 240-241). Mention the editor of the anthology only in the entry in the works-cited list, as shown in 12e, item 14, page 252.

> Saunders predicts that Bill Clinton will eventually be seen "as the embodiment of a certain strain of ornery, compassionate, complicated American energy" (300).

J. Author of work quoted in another source If an author is quoted in a different source, and you quote or paraphrase that author's words, write *qtd. in* (for "quoted in") in your parenthetical citation, followed by the last name of the author of the source in which you found the reference (the indirect source) and the page number where you found the quotation. List the author of the indirect source in your list of works cited. In the following example, the indirect source Hofstadter, not Harry Williams, would be included in the list of works cited.

> Harry Williams argues that Lincoln waged the war "for the preservation of the status quo which had produced the war" (qtd. in Hofstadter 31).

See 12e, item 14, for this entry in the works-cited list.

However, note that MLA encourages you to quote a direct source whenever possible.

K. More than one work in one citation Use semicolons to separate two or more sources named in the same citation.

> The links between a name and ancestry have occupied many writers and researchers (Waters 65; Antin 188).

To avoid using a long parenthetical citation that disrupts the flow of your text, you can put multiple sources in a bibliographical note (see 11c, p. 228).

However, if you quote sources that refer to different points made in one sentence, cite each source after the point it supports.

CITING A WORK WITH NO INDIVIDUAL AUTHOR(S) NAMED (MLA)

L. Work by a corporation, government agency, or organization as author When you use material authored not by an individual but by a corporation, government agency, or organization, cite that entity as the author, making sure its name corresponds with the alphabetized entry in your works-cited list (see 12i, item 58). Use the complete name in your text sentence or a shortened form in the parenthetical citation. Begin a government source citation with the name or abbreviation of the country or state. Then follow with the name of the agency and any additional divisions. If the author[s] or compiler[s] are named, you may still begin with the name of the government source as author and put *By* and the author[s] or compiler[s] after the document title in the works-cited list. If the corporation, government agency, or organization is also the publisher, list it only as the publisher in the works-cited entry and not as the author. In that case, the title would be listed first, so it should also appear in the in-text citation. The following examples have been listed with the government agency as author in the works-cited entry and a page number cited in the introduction (a specific section) of a PDF version of a government report.

full name

> The United States Department of the Interior US Geological Survey recognizes "a need for clear methods to identify tsunami deposits in the geologic record" since deposit studies are an important element in assessing tsunami risk for localities (Introd. 1).

shortened name

> During the past twenty years, the examination of tsunami deposits has proved to be an essential means of assessing tsunami risk (United States, Dept. of the Interior, USGS Introd. 1).

For United States government offices, separate the individual offices from each other (and from the government as a whole) by commas.

M. No author or editor named If no author or editor is named for a source, refer to the title of the book (italicized), the article title (within quotation marks), or the title of the Web site (italicized).

> *The Chicago Manual of Style* advises that "breaking or bending rules to fit a particular case" when writing is sometimes necessary (xii).

Within a parenthetical citation, shorten the title to the first word (if possible) by which it is alphabetized in the works-cited list.

> When writing, one may find that "breaking or bending rules to fit a particular case" is sometimes necessary (*Chicago* xii).

For help reading a Web site to determine its author, see the Key Points box in 8c on pages 174–175. If no author is indicated, use the name of the site.

N. Unauthored entry in a dictionary or encyclopedia For an unsigned entry, give the title of the entry. A page number is not necessary for an alphabetized work. Begin the entry in the works-cited list with the title of the alphabetized entry.

> Drypoint differs from etching in that it does not use acid ("Etching").

If you are citing a specific definition in a dictionary entry, add a comma after the term and write *def.* and the letter or number: ("Mimesis," def. 3).

CITING A WORK WITH PAGE NUMBERS NOT AVAILABLE OR RELEVANT (MLA)

O. Reference to an entire work and not to one specific page If you are referring not to a quotation or idea on one specific page but rather to an idea that is central to the work as a whole, name the author in your text. Include publication details of the work in your works-cited list.

> Mallon insists that we can learn from diaries about people's everyday lives and the worlds they create.

P. Work only one page long If a print article is only one page long, you may give the author's name alone in your text but include the page number in your works-cited list. However, a page reference in parentheses clearly indicates where quoted or paraphrased material ends, so it may be helpful for readers if you also include the page number in your text.

Q. Web or electronic source with no page numbers Electronic database material and Web sources, which appear on a screen, have no stable page numbers that apply across systems or when printed unless you access them in PDF (portable document format) files.

author named in text

no page citation: online source has no numbered pages or paragraphs

> Science writer Stephen Hart describes how researchers Edward Taub and Thomas Ebert conclude that for musicians, practicing "remaps the brain," thus maybe suggesting that it is better to start practicing at an early age.

With no page number to mark where a parenthetical citation would go (at "brain," above, or at the end of the sentence?), you need to define the point at which the material from your source ends and your own commentary takes over, so it may be advisable to give the author's name in a parenthetical citation to mark the end of the reference.

> Researchers Edward Taub and Thomas Ebert conclude that for musicians, practicing "remaps the brain" (Hart), thus maybe suggesting that . . .

Section 10d shows how to define the boundaries of a citation.

For an online source with no author or page numbers, in your parenthetical citation give the title of the Web page or posting either in full (if short) or abbreviated, to begin with the first word by which it is alphabetized in the works-cited list (see 12g, items 32 and 33).

A list of frequently asked questions about documentation and up-to-date instructions on how to cite online sources in MLA style can be found on the association's Web site (MLA).

If there are no page numbers to refer to, you may cite online scholarly material by the abbreviated internal headings of the source, such as *introduction* (*introd.*), *chapter* (*chap. or ch.*), or *section* (*sec.*) (see example in item L, p. 222). Give paragraph numbers only if they are supplied in the source and you see the numbers on the screen, using the abbreviation *par.* or *pars.*

> Hatchuel discusses how film editing "can change points of view and turn objectivity into subjectivity" (par. 6).

If the parenthetical citation contains the author's name, put a comma after it and before *par.* or *sec.* and the number—something you do *not* do before a page number.

> Film editing provides us with different perceptions of reality (Hatchuel, par. 6).

CITING MULTIMEDIA AND MISCELLANEOUS SOURCES (MLA)

R. Multimedia source For radio or TV programs, interviews, live performances, films, computer software, recordings, works of art, and other multimedia sources, include only the author (or contributor, such as the producer, actor, and so on) or title. Make sure that your text reference corresponds to the first element of the information you provide in the entry in your works-cited list. See 12h, item 51, for examples of documenting the following performance in a works-cited list.

> The audience of *In Paris* may themselves feel isolated while watching Baryshnikov, who portays an aging exiled Russian guard, since translations of the play's sparse Russian dialogue are projected on and behind the actors, along with videos and postcard images of 1930s Paris.

S. Multivolume work If you refer to more than one volume of a work in your paper, in the parenthetical citation give the author's name and the volume number, followed by a colon, a space, and the page number: (Einstein 1: 25). Do not use the word or abbreviation for *volume* or *page*. Give the total number of volumes in the works-cited entry. If you refer to only one volume in your paper, just give the page number in your in-text citation and give the volume number in the works-cited entry (see 12e, item 18, for examples).

T. Lecture, speech, personal communication (letter, e-mail, memo), or interview In your text, give the name of the person delivering the communication. In your works-cited list, state the type of communication at the end of the citation, in this case *E-mail* (see also 12i, items 64 and 65).

> According to Roberta Bernstein, professor of art history at the University of Albany, the most challenging thing about contemporary art is understanding that it is meant to be challenging. This may mean that the artist wants to make us uncomfortable with our familiar ideas or present us with reconceived notions of beauty.

U. Frequently studied literary works: Fiction, poetry, and drama For well-known works published in several different editions, include information in your parenthetical citations that will allow readers to locate the material in whatever edition they are using. For a short story or novel with no divisions or chapters, simply give the author's last name and page number. For other works, particularly classic works appearing in many editions, the following guidelines will allow readers to find your reference in any edition. In your works-cited list, include details about the edition that you used.

For a novel First give the page number(s) in the edition that you used, followed by a semicolon. Then give the chapter or section number (abbreviated): (104; ch. 3).

For a poem Give line numbers, not page numbers (lines 62-73), spelling out the word *lines* in the first citation. Omit the word *lines* and just give the line numbers in subsequent references.

Include up to three lines of poetry sequentially in your text, separating them with a slash (/) with a space on each side (see 49f). For four or more lines of poetry, begin on a new line, indent the whole passage one inch from the left, double-space throughout, and omit quotation marks from the beginning and end of the passage (see 10c).

For classic poems, such as the *Iliad*, with divisions into books or parts Give the book or part number, followed by a period; then, with no space, give the line numbers, not page numbers, separated by a hyphen: (8.21-25).

For a play With dialogue, set off the quotation from your text, indented a half inch, with no quotation marks, and in all capital letters write the name of the character speaking, followed by a period. Indent subsequent lines of the same speech another one-quarter inch. Give act, scene, and line numbers in Arabic numerals (see the following example).

For a new play available in only one published edition, cite author and page numbers as you do for other MLA citations.

For a classic work For classic plays published in several different editions (such as plays by William Shakespeare or Oscar Wilde), omit page numbers and cite in parentheses the act, scene, and line numbers of the quotation in Arabic numerals, separated by periods.

> Shakespeare's lovers in *A Midsummer Night's Dream* appeal to contemporary audiences accustomed to the sense of loss in love songs:
>
> LYSANDER. How now, my love! Why is your cheek so pale?
> How chance the roses there do fade so fast?
> HERMIA. Belike for want of rain, which I could well
> Beteem them from the tempest of mine eyes. (1.1.133-36)

In your works-cited list, list the bibliographical details of the edition you used.

For classic literary works by Shakespeare, Chaucer, and others, MLA style uses abbreviated titles cited in parentheses, such as the following: *Tmp.* for *The Tempest; 2H4* for *Henry IV, Part 2; MND* for *A Midsummer Night's Dream; GP* for the *General Prologue; PrT* for *The Prioress's Tale; Aen. for Aeneid; Beo.* for *Beowulf; Prel.* for Wordsworth's *Prelude.*

V. The Bible and other sacred texts In a parenthetical citation, give the title of the sacred text (italicized), along with the book of the Bible (abbreviated) and chapter and verse numbers. Note, though, that in a reference to a sacred text that is not directing readers to a specific citation in the list of works cited, the title of the sacred text is not italicized, as in the example that follows (see also 50b).

not a reference: no italics

> Of the many passages in the Bible that refer to lying, none is more apt today than the one that says that a wicked person "is snared by the transgression of his lips" (*Holy Bible*, Prov. 12.13).

italics for a reference name of book abbreviated

See 12e, item 24, for this entry and others in a list of works cited.

W. Historical or legal document Cite any article and section number of a familiar historical document, such as the Constitution, in parentheses in your text, with no entry in the works-cited list. Abbreviate the title and section(s), and separate them with commas: (US Const., art. 2, sec. 4).

Italicize the name of a court case (*Citizens United v FEC*) but not the names of laws and acts. List cases and acts in your works-cited list (see 12i, item 66).

X. A footnote or footnotes To cite a footnote in a source, give the page number, followed by *n* or *nn* (as in *65n*). For a footnote in an annotated edition of a sacred text, give the edition (with the word *The* omitted from your citation), book, chapter, and verse(s), followed by *n* or *nn*: (*New Oxford Annotated Bible*, Gen. 35.1-4n). See 12e, item 24, for this entry in a works-cited list.

11c MLA explanatory footnotes and endnotes

The MLA parenthetical style of documentation uses a footnote (at the bottom of the page) or an endnote (on a separate numbered page at the end of the paper before the works-cited list) only for notes giving supplementary bibliographical information or content information that clarifies or expands a point. You can use a note to cite multiple bibliographical sources instead of putting them in an in-text citation that would interrupt the flow of your text (see item K, p. 222) or to evaluate or give additional information about sources. You can also use a note to provide a comment that is interesting but not essential to your argument. Indicate a note with a raised number (superscript) in your text after the word or sentence to which your note refers.

- Begin the first line of each note one-half inch from the left margin. Put the note number (followed by a space) on the same line as the rest of the note content.
- Do not indent subsequent lines of the same note.
- Double-space endnotes.
- Single-space within each footnote, but double-space between notes.

NOTE NUMBER IN TEXT

Ethics have become an important part of many writing classes.[1]

CONTENT FOOTNOTE OR ENDNOTE

one-half inch — number on line followed by a space and text

1. For additional discussion of ethics in the classroom, see Stotsky 799-806; Knoblauch 15-21; Bizzell 663-67; Friend 560-66.

12 The MLA List of Works Cited

The references you make in your text to sources are brief—usually only the author's last name and a page number—so they allow readers to continue reading without interruption. For complete information about the source, readers will use your brief in-text citation to direct them to the full bibliographical reference in the list of works cited at the end of your paper. For formatting instructions for articles, books, databases, Web sources, and multimedia sources, see the sample listings in 12c–12i.

12a How to set up and organize the MLA list

KEY POINTS

How to Format the MLA List of Works Cited

1. **What to list** List only works you actually cite in the text of your paper, not works you read but did not mention, unless your instructor requires you to include all the works you consulted as well as those mentioned in your text.
2. **Format of the list** Begin the list on a new numbered page after the last page of the paper or any endnotes. Center the heading (*Works Cited*) without quotation marks, italicizing, or a period. Double-space within and between entries. Do not number the entries.
3. **Alphabetical order** Alphabetize entries in the list by authors' last names. List works with no stated author by the first main word of the title. Note the following:
   - Alphabetize by the exact letters in the spelling: *MacKay* precedes *McHam*.
   - Let a shorter name precede a longer name beginning with the same letters: *Linden, Ronald* precedes *Lindenmayer, Arnold*.
   - For two authors with the same last name, alphabetize by first names: *Smith, Adam* precedes *Smith, Frank*.
   - With last names using a prefix such as *le, du, di, del,* and *des,* alphabetize by the prefix: *Del Toro, Guillermo*.

(Continued)

(Continued)

- When *de* occurs with French names of one syllable, alphabetize under *D: De Man, Paul.* Otherwise, alphabetize by last name: *Maupassant, Guy de.*
- Alphabetize by the first element of a hyphenated name: *Sackville-West, Vita.*
- Alphabetize by the last name when the author uses two names without a hyphen: *Thomas, Elizabeth Marshall.*
- If you have several works by the same author, alphabetize according to the first significant word in the title. For all entries after the first, replace the name(s) of the author(s) with three hyphens, followed by a period.

  Goleman, Daniel. *Destructive Emotions: A Scientific Dialogue with the Dalai Lama.* Bantam Dell, 2003.

  ---. *Working with Emotional Intelligence.* Bantam, 2000.

4. **Indentation** To help readers find a source and to differentiate one entry from another, indent all lines of each entry—except the first—one-half inch. A word processor can provide these *hanging indents* (go to your Help menu).
5. **Capitals in titles** Capitalize the first letter of all words in titles of books and articles except *a, an, the,* coordinating conjunctions, *to* in an infinitive, and prepositions (such as *in, to, for, with, without, against)* unless they begin the title or subtitle.
6. **Titles in italics** Italicize the titles of books, periodicals, databases, and Web sites as well as the titles of films, CDs, performances, and so on.
7. **Titles in quotation marks** Put in quotation marks shorter titles contained within larger works (articles, stories and poems, Web pages) and unpublished works (letters, speeches).

12b What to include in an MLA works-cited entry

MLA emphasizes the importance of making citations helpful to readers, and the organization of the nine primary elements of citations is consistent to keep citations clear.

KEY POINTS

How to Cite Sources in an MLA List of Works Cited

Following are the nine primary elements of MLA works-cited citations:

1. **Author** Authors are listed first in the citation, followed by a period. Here are guidelines for listing authors:
   - Put the last name first for a single author or the first author: *Fussell, Paul.*
   - For two authors, reverse the names of only the first author: *Hawisher, Gail E., and Cynthia L. Selfe.*
   - For three or more authors, use *et al.* (Latin for "and others") after the reversed name of the first author: *Roen, Duane, et al.*
   - When a corporation, agency, or organization is the author (but not the publisher), begin your entry with that name: *National Science Foundation*. If the publisher is the same as the author, omit the author and alphabetize by title.
   - Include a title such as *Jr.* or a numeral such as *II* after the first name, separating the two with a comma: *King, Martin Luther, Jr.*
   - For a work with no author listed, begin the citation with the first word in the title of the source other than *A*, *An*, or *The*.
2. **Title of source** The title of the source is listed after the author, followed by a period. Here are guidelines for listing titles of sources:
   - Italicize the titles of books, periodicals, databases, and Web sites, as well as the titles of films, CDs, performances, and so on.
   - Put in quotation marks shorter titles contained within larger works (articles, stories and poems, chapters, Web pages, episodes) and unpublished works (letters, speeches).
   - Sometimes a descriptor is used instead of a title (if one doesn't exist) or in addition to a title: *Letter to the Editor*.
   - Sometimes a descriptor is also used to explain which section of a text is being referenced: *Introduction*.

(Continued)

(Continued)

3. **Title of container** The third element of a citation in MLA style is the title of the container in which you found the source you are referencing if the source is part of a larger work. Containers can be books, periodicals, television series, Web sites, and so on. Sometimes you will not include a container at all if the source is not part of a larger work. Here are guidelines for listing titles of containers:
   - Use full titles for all containers, including *A*, *An*, and *The*: *The New York Times.*
   - Containers are followed by a comma because additional information about the container often comes next: *A Rhetoric for Writing Program Administrators,* edited by Rita Malenczyk.
   - Sometimes a source might come from a container that is within another container. For example, if you cite an article from a scholarly journal that you found in an online database, you will list the journal title as the container for the article (the first container) and then work through elements 4–9 for that container. Then you'll go back through elements 3–9 and include the citation information for the second container (in this case, the database).
4. **Other contributors** Other contributors include translators, editors of anthologies, or performers. Not all citations will include other contributors beyond the authors. Here are guidelines for listing other contributors:
   - Spell out the descriptor for the additional contributor's role: *Translated by, edited by, performance by.*
   - Sometimes translators or editors are listed in the first element (author), if a researcher wants to emphasize a specific translation of a work or if no individual author is listed.
5. **Version** Many sources will not include a version. If you are using a source that has multiple versions, though, this is where you would indicate variations such as
   - 7th edition
   - revised edition
   - New International Version
   - director's cut
   - unabridged version

6. **Number** When you are using a source that is part of a sequence (most commonly an issue for a periodical or an episode in a series), you should include the number of the specific source you are using. Here are guidelines for formatting numbers:
   - For journals, list any volume and issue number, abbreviating as *vol.* and *no.*: *WPA: Writing Program Administration*, vol. 31, no. 2.
   - List the season and episode numbers of podcasts, television shows, and so on, spelling out words like *season* and *episode*: *Making a Murderer*, season 1, episode 10.
7. **Publisher** The publisher is the company or organization responsible for making a source available to the public. Examples include university presses, nonprofit organizations, parts of the government, or for-profit companies. Here are guidelines for listing publishers:
   - For presses that include the word *Press* in their title, you can abbreviate it with a *P*. You can also abbreviate *University* with a *U* in the name of university presses: *U of Michigan P*. If the publisher of a source is the same as the title of the container of the source, you do not need to list it twice. For example, you would list *The Washington Post* as the container of an article from that periodical, but you do not need to list the name again as the publisher of the article because it would be redundant and potentially confusing to readers.
   - Cities of publication are no longer included in works-cited entries; the name of the publisher or sponsor/host is enough.
8. **Publication date** Sources can have multiple publication dates. For example, if you cite something that was first published in print and then was published online, you might find two different publication dates. If you see more than one publication date, list the one that is most meaningful for the version of the source you are citing. Here are guidelines for listing publication dates:
   - For periodicals that include a month and/or day of publication, list the day first, then the abbreviated month, and then the year: *27 Mar. 2016*.
   - When relevant (and included on the original source), include the time of publication. For social media and some online resources, time can be an important part of the publication date: *27 Mar. 2016, 9:30 a.m.*

(Continued)

(Continued)

- Include dates of access for online sources only when the source might be altered at some point with no record. For example, an episode of a television series accessed through *Netflix* should have an access date because the episode might not be available at a later time. When in doubt, include an access date. Access dates are listed at the end of the citation: *Accessed 27 Mar. 2016.*

9. **Location** The location of the source gives readers information about where to find the source. For different kinds of sources, the location information can be very different. For articles and chapters, it might be page numbers and/or a DOI (digital object identifier). For a Web site, it would be a URL. Here are guidelines for listing the location of sources:
   - For print sources, include the page numbers as the location if the source is part of a larger print work, preceded by *p.* (for one page) or *pp.* (for multiple pages): *pp. 32-53.* For inclusive page numbers greater than 100 that share the same first number (or more), in most cases use only the last two digits for the second number (for instance, 683-89, but 798-805).
   - Do not include page numbers for online works unless they are in PDF format or are provided on the screen as part of an original print source. If a Web source has sections, then providing the name of a section (*Introd.*) may help readers locate the exact place in the source.
   - For online sources, include the DOI for the location if one is available: *doi:10.1080/21683565.2016.141145.* For a print periodical accessed online, you might have both a DOI and page numbers. In that case, list the DOI as the last part of the citation.
   - If no DOI is available for an online source, list the exact URL where the source was found. Do not include *http://*, and include *www.* only if it is part of the address: *kairos.technorhetoric.net/20.2/topoi/miller-et-al/index.html.* If possible, use a stable link or *permalink*, if one is available.

The nine primary elements of citations are listed in the following table so that you can track them easily as you work with sources.

❶ Author.	
❷ Title of Source.	
❸ Title of Container,	
❹ Other Contributors,	
❺ Version,	
❻ Number,	
❼ Publisher,	
❽ Publication Date,	
❾ Location.	

12c Representative MLA examples (Source Shots)

If you track the nine primary elements of your sources, you will have no difficulty listing their citations in MLA format. Keep in mind that not every source has every element; skip the elements that are not present. For examples of some of the most common types of sources and how to list the nine elements in an MLA citation, look at the source shots that follow. Refer to 12b for definitions of each element.

SOURCE SHOT 1

Print Article in a Scholarly Journal MLA

Table of Contents of a Scholarly Journal

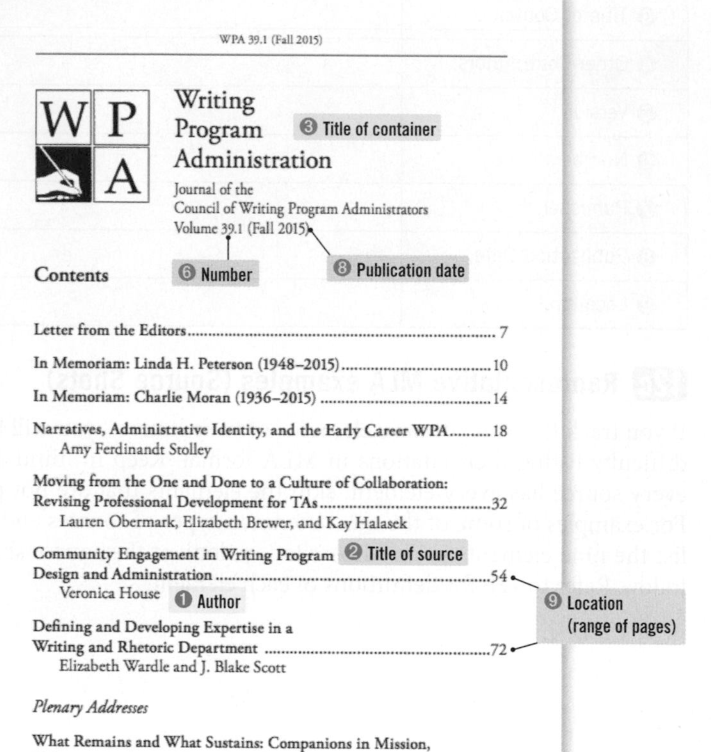

WPA 39.1 (Fall 2015)

Writing Program Administration

Journal of the Council of Writing Program Administrators

Volume 39.1 (Fall 2015)

Contents

Letter from the Editors 7

In Memoriam: Linda H. Peterson (1948–2015) 10

In Memoriam: Charlie Moran (1936–2015) 14

Narratives, Administrative Identity, and the Early Career WPA 18
Amy Ferdinandt Stolley

Moving from the One and Done to a Culture of Collaboration: Revising Professional Development for TAs 32
Lauren Obermark, Elizabeth Brewer, and Kay Halasek

Community Engagement in Writing Program Design and Administration 54
Veronica House

Defining and Developing Expertise in a Writing and Rhetoric Department 72
Elizabeth Wardle and J. Blake Scott

Plenary Addresses

What Remains and What Sustains: Companions in Mission, Colleagues in Action, WPAs for Life 94
Elizabeth Boquet

The elements included in the following table are some that are likely to be relevant when you are citing a scholarly journal article. For a definition of each element in the left-hand column, refer to 12b.

❶ **Author**	House, Veronica.
❷ **Title of Source**	"Community Engagement in Writing Program Design and Administration."
❸ **Title of Container**	*WPA: Writing Program Administration,*
❹ **Other Contributors**	
❺ **Version**	
❻ **Number**	vol. 39, no. 1,
❼ **Publisher**	
❽ **Publication Date**	2015,
❾ **Location**	pp. 54-71.

❶ ❷
House, Veronica. "Community Engagement in Writing Program Design and Administration." *WPA: Writing Program Administration*, vol. 39, no. 1, 2015, pp. 54-71.
❸ ❻ ❽ ❾

SOURCE SHOT 2

Book MLA

Title Page

Copyright Page

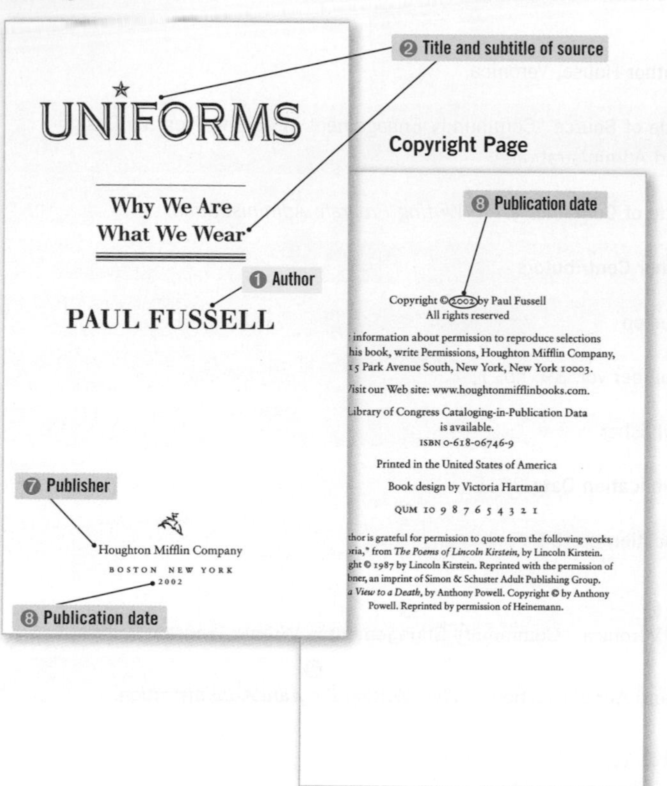

UNIFORMS
Why We Are What We Wear
PAUL FUSSELL
Houghton Mifflin Company
BOSTON NEW YORK
2002
❷ Title and subtitle of source
❶ Author
❼ Publisher
❽ Publication date
❽ Publication date
Copyright © 2002 by Paul Fussell
All rights reserved
information about permission to reproduce selections
his book, write Permissions, Houghton Mifflin Company,
15 Park Avenue South, New York, New York 10003.
Visit our Web site: www.houghtonmifflinbooks.com.
Library of Congress Cataloging-in-Publication Data
is available.
ISBN 0-618-06746-9
Printed in the United States of America
Book design by Victoria Hartman
QUM 10 9 8 7 6 5 4 3 2 1
thor is grateful for permission to quote from the following works:
oria," from The Poems of Lincoln Kirstein, by Lincoln Kirstein.
ght © 1987 by Lincoln Kirstein. Reprinted with the permission of
bner, an imprint of Simon & Schuster Adult Publishing Group.
a View to a Death, by Anthony Powell. Copyright © by Anthony
Powell. Reprinted by permission of Heinemann.

Find the necessary information for documenting a book on its title page. If the date is not on the title page, look on the copyright page. The elements included in the following table are some that are likely to be relevant when you are citing a book. For a definition of each element in the left-hand column, refer to 12b.

❶ **Author**	Fussell, Paul.
❷ **Title of Source**	*Uniforms: Why We Are What We Wear.*
❸ **Title of Container**	
❹ **Other Contributors**	
❺ **Version**	
❻ **Number**	
❼ **Publisher**	Houghton Mifflin,
❽ **Publication Date**	2002.
❾ **Location**	

❶ ❷ ❼

Fussell, Paul. *Uniforms: Why We Are What We Wear*. Houghton Mifflin, 2002.

❽

Modern Language Association MLA

SOURCE SHOT 3

Work in an Anthology MLA

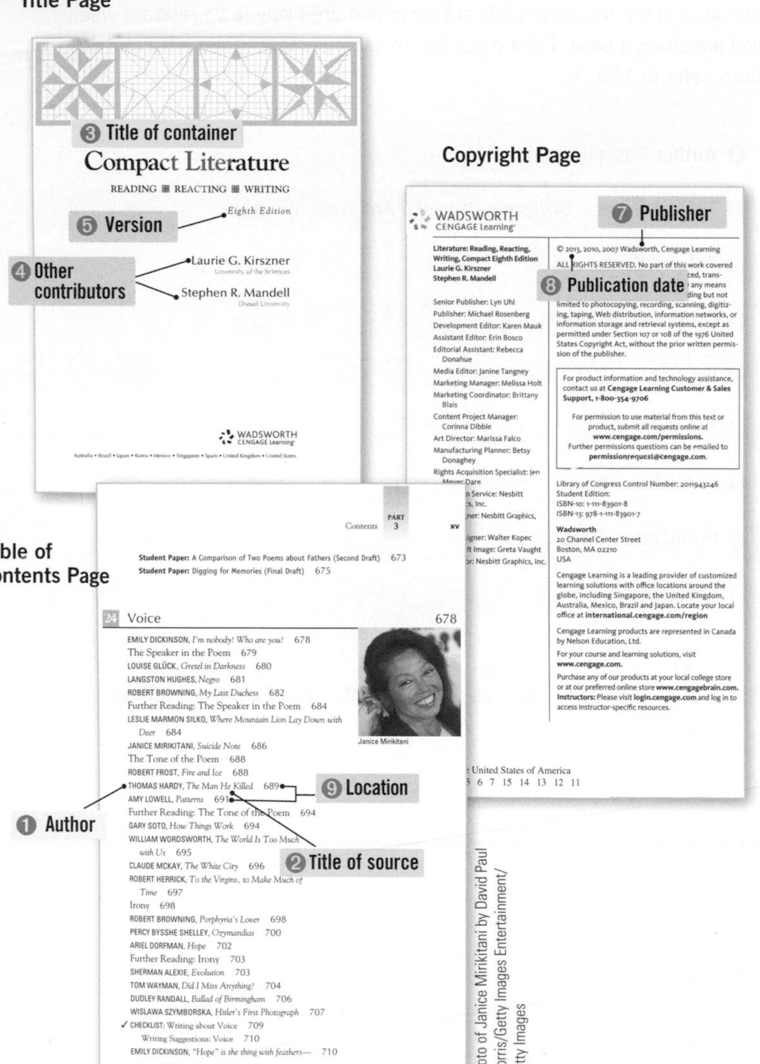

Title Page

Compact Literature

READING ■ REACTING ■ WRITING

Eighth Edition

Laurie G. Kirszner
University of the Sciences

Stephen R. Mandell
Drexel University

WADSWORTH
CENGAGE Learning

Australia • Brazil • Japan • Korea • Mexico • Singapore • Spain • United Kingdom • United States

Copyright Page

WADSWORTH
CENGAGE Learning

Literature: Reading, Reacting, Writing, Compact Eighth Edition
Laurie G. Kirszner
Stephen R. Mandell

Senior Publisher: Lyn Uhl
Publisher: Michael Rosenberg
Development Editor: Karen Mauk
Assistant Editor: Erin Bosco
Editorial Assistant: Rebecca Donahue
Media Editor: Janine Tangney
Marketing Manager: Melissa Holt
Marketing Coordinator: Brittany Blais
Content Project Manager: Corinna Dibble
Art Director: Marissa Falco
Manufacturing Planner: Betsy Donaghey
Rights Acquisition Specialist: Jen Meyer Dare
...n Service: Nesbitt ...s, Inc.
...ner: Nesbitt Graphics,
...igner: Walter Kopec
...t Image: Greta Vaught
...r: Nesbitt Graphics, Inc.

© 2013, 2010, 2007 Wadsworth, Cengage Learning

ALL RIGHTS RESERVED. No part of this work covered ...ced, trans- ... any means ...ding but not limited to photocopying, recording, scanning, digitizing, taping, Web distribution, information networks, or information storage and retrieval systems, except as permitted under Section 107 or 108 of the 1976 United States Copyright Act, without the prior written permission of the publisher.

For product information and technology assistance, contact us at **Cengage Learning Customer & Sales Support, 1-800-354-9706**

For permission to use material from this text or product, submit all requests online at **www.cengage.com/permissions.**
Further permissions questions can be emailed to **permissionrequest@cengage.com.**

Library of Congress Control Number: 2011943246
Student Edition:
ISBN-10: 1-111-83901-8
ISBN-13: 978-1-111-83901-7

Wadsworth
20 Channel Center Street
Boston, MA 02210
USA

Cengage Learning is a leading provider of customized learning solutions with office locations around the globe, including Singapore, the United Kingdom, Australia, Mexico, Brazil and Japan. Locate your local office at **international.cengage.com/region**

Cengage Learning products are represented in Canada by Nelson Education, Ltd.

For your course and learning solutions, visit **www.cengage.com.**

Purchase any of our products at your local college store or at our preferred online store **www.cengagebrain.com.**
Instructors: Please visit **login.cengage.com** and log in to access instructor-specific resources.

...United States of America
...5 6 7 15 14 13 12 11

Table of Contents Page

Contents PART 3 xv

Janice Mirikitani

Photo of Janice Mirikitani by David Paul Morris/Getty Images Entertainment/Getty Images

Look on the title page and copyright page for publication information for the anthology. Look on the appropriate page of the table of contents (and on the pages themselves) for the details and inclusive page numbers of the specific work that you are documenting. List the date of the original publication after the title only if the original publication date will give readers information that is helpful or important (see page 252 for an example). The elements included in the following table are some that are likely to be relevant when you are citing a work found in an anthology. For a definition of each element, refer to 12b.

❶ **Author**	Hardy, Thomas.
❷ **Title of Source**	"The Man He Killed."
❸ **Title of Container**	*Compact Literature: Reading, Reacting, Writing,*
❹ **Other Contributors**	edited by Laurie G. Kirszner and Stephen R. Mandell,
❺ **Version**	8th ed.,
❻ **Number**	
❼ **Publisher**	Cengage Learning,
❽ **Publication Date**	2013,
❾ **Location**	pp. 689-90.

❶ Hardy, Thomas. ❷ "The Man He Killed." ❸ *Compact Literature: Reading, Reacting, Writing*, ❹ edited by Laurie G. Kirszner and Stephen R. Mandell, ❺ 8th ed., ❼ Cengage Learning, ❽ 2013, ❾ pp. 689-90.

SOURCE SHOT 4

Article in an Online Database MLA

***Academic Search Complete* Record for a Magazine Article**

The citation page indicates that the full text of the article is available in HTML or PDF. Always choose PDF as your source when available so that you can provide an exact page number for a citation.

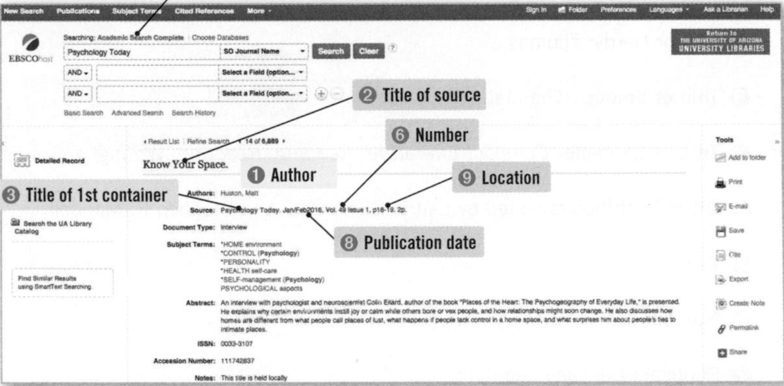

When you access a periodical article through a database, include information for both containers: the periodical itself, as well as the database. To do that, you list all of the nine elements that you can find for the periodical (the first container), and then you start over with the elements that are relevant for the database (the second container). The elements included in the following table are some that are likely to be relevant when you are citing an article found in an online database. For a definition of each element, refer to 12b.

	❶ **Author** Huston, Matt.
	❷ **Title of Source** "Know Your Space."
1st container	❸ **Title of Container** *Psychology Today,*
	❹ **Other Contributors**
	❺ **Version**
	❻ **Number** vol. 49, no. 1,
	❼ **Publisher**
	❽ **Publication Date** Jan/Feb 2016,
	❾ **Location** pp. 18-19.
2nd container	❸ **Title of Container** *Academic Search Complete,*
	❹ **Other Contributors**
	❺ **Version**
	❻ **Number**
	❼ **Publisher**
	❽ **Publication Date**
	❾ **Location** ezproxy.library.arizona.edu/login?url=http://search.ebscohost.com/login.aspx?direct=true&db=a9h&AN=111742837&site=ehost-live.

❶ ❷ ❸ ❻
Huston, Matt. "Know Your Space." *Psychology Today*, vol. 49, no. 1,
❽ ❾ ❸
Jan/Feb 2016, pp. 18-19. *Academic Search Complete*, ezproxy.
❾
library.arizona.edu/login?url=http://search.ebscohost.com/login.
aspx?direct=true&db=a9h&AN=111742837&site=ehost-live.

SOURCE SHOT 5

Article or Page on a Nonperiodical Web Site MLA

Web Site

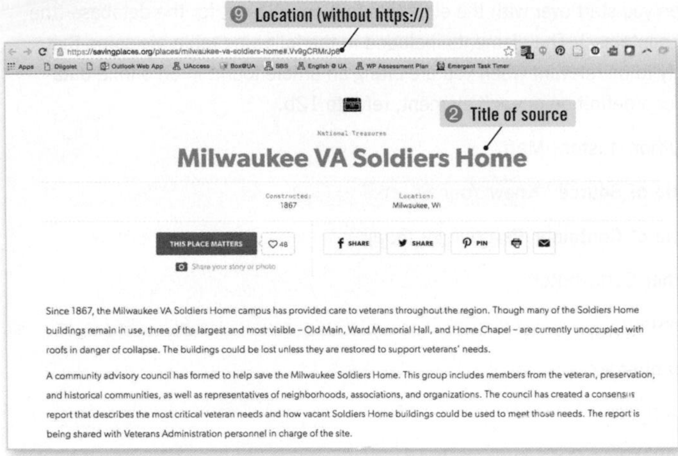

⑨ Location (without https://)
https://savingplaces.org/places/milwaukee-va-soldiers-home#.Vv9gCRMrJp8
② Title of source
National Treasures
Milwaukee VA Soldiers Home
Constructed: 1867
Location: Milwaukee, WI
THIS PLACE MATTERS
Since 1867, the Milwaukee VA Soldiers Home campus has provided care to veterans throughout the region. Though many of the Soldiers Home buildings remain in use, three of the largest and most visible – Old Main, Ward Memorial Hall, and Home Chapel – are currently unoccupied with roofs in danger of collapse. The buildings could be lost unless they are restored to support veterans' needs.
A community advisory council has formed to help save the Milwaukee Soldiers Home. This group includes members from the veteran, preservation, and historical communities, as well as representatives of neighborhoods, associations, and organizations. The council has created a consensus report that describes the most critical veteran needs and how vacant Soldiers Home buildings could be used to meet those needs. The report is being shared with Veterans Administration personnel in charge of the site.

Web Site's Copyright Notice

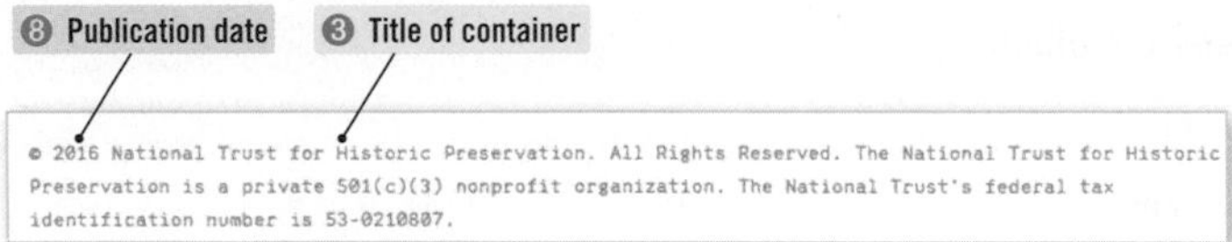

⑧ Publication date
③ Title of container
© 2016 National Trust for Historic Preservation. All Rights Reserved. The National Trust for Historic Preservation is a private 501(c)(3) nonprofit organization. The National Trust's federal tax identification number is 53-0210807.

Source: savingplaces.org/milwaukee-va-soldiers-home

When you are listing sources found on the Web, include the URL as the location. Do not include *http://* or *https://,* and include *www.* only if it is part of the URL. Include the date of access only if the source is one that could be changed without someone seeing a clear history of the change. If you make a copy of the Web page as soon as you find it or save it to your computer, your date of access will appear on your printout or with your saved file. The elements included in the following table are some that are likely to be relevant when you are citing a source from the Web. For a definition of each element, refer to 12b.

❶ **Author**	
❷ **Title of Source**	"Milwaukee VA Soldiers Home."
❸ **Title of Container**	*National Trust for Historic Preservation,*
❹ **Other Contributors**	
❺ **Version**	
❻ **Number**	
❼ **Publisher**	
❽ **Publication Date**	2016,
❾ **Location**	savingplaces.org/places/milwaukee-va-soldiers-home#. Vv9gCRMrJp8.

❷ ❸

"Milwaukee VA Soldiers Home." *National Trust for Historic Preservation*,

❽ ❾

2016, savingplaces.org/places/milwaukee-va-soldiers-home#.

Vv9gCRMrJp8. Accessed 1 Apr. 2016.

Note that when the title of the container and the name of the publisher are the same, you should include that information only one time. MLA style encourages you not to repeat the information so that you don't confuse readers.

SOURCE SHOT 6

Government Publication Online MLA

Online Government Publication

7 Publisher
U.S. Department of Education
Search...
Student Loans
Grants
Laws
Data
King announces guidance to states to help reduce testing
8 Publication date
2 Title of source
FEBRUARY 2, 2016
1 Author
Contact: Press Office, (202) 401-1576, press@ed.gov
Acting U.S. Secretary of Education John B. King Jr. announced today new guidance to help states identify and eliminate low-quality, redundant or unhelpful testing.
"High-quality assessments give parents, educators and students useful information about whether students are developing the critical thinking and problem solving skills they need to succeed in life," said King. "But there has to be a balance, and despite good intentions, there are too many places around the country where the balance still isn't quite right. We hope this guidance will help restore that balance and give back some of the critical learning time that students need to be successful."
The guidance outlines how federal dollars may be used to help reduce testing in schools, while still ensuring that educators and parents have the information they need on students' progress to improve learning. The guidance shines a light on innovative work already happening across the country and provides examples of how states and districts can use their federal funding to explore new strategies for ensuring the use of high-quality, useful and well-constructed assessments, and the elimination of redundant and burdensome assessments.
King talks more about the guidance in a video released today.
The document builds on an October 2015 announcement by President Obama and a set of principles the Department released, outlining that assessments must be worth taking and of high quality; enhance teaching and learning; and give a well-rounded picture of how students and schools are doing.

Source: U.S. Department of Education

The elements included in the following table are some that are likely to be relevant when you are citing a government publication found online. Note that if the publisher were identical to the author, you would list the publisher only, beginning the entry with the title. In this case, the Department of Education's Press Office is the author, while the Department itself is publisher. For a definition of each element, refer to 12b.

❶ **Author**	United States, Department of Education, Press Office.
❷ **Title of Source**	"King Announces Guidance to States to Help Reduce Testing."
❸ **Title of Container**	
❹ **Other Contributors**	
❺ **Version**	
❻ **Number**	
❼ **Publisher**	United States, Department of Education,
❽ **Publication Date**	2 Feb. 2016,
❾ **Location**	www.ed.gov/news/press-releases/king-announces-guidance-states-help-reduce-testing.

❶ United States, Department of Education, Press Office. ❷ "King Announces Guidance to States to Help Reduce Testing." ❼ *United States, Department of Education*, ❽ 2 Feb. 2016, ❾ www.ed.gov/news/press-releases/ king-announces-guidance-states-help-reduce-testing.

SOURCE SHOT 7

Transcript of a Radio or Television Program MLA

Web Page with Transcript of a Television Program

Source: U.S. Department of State

If you have listened to a radio interview or watched an interview on television, you may want to refer to a transcript of the program to quote or paraphrase material from the interview in your paper. Many transcripts of interviews and other programs are archived online and can be downloaded and printed. You can include the word *Transcript* at the end of your citation so that readers know you are working with that version, rather than the audio or video version. Look for the following information on the Web site to include in your citation. For a definition of each element, refer to 12b.

❶ **Author** Clinton, Hillary Rodham.

❷ **Title of Source** "Towntierview with NDTV's Barkha Dutt on 'We the People.'"

❸ **Title of Container** *US Department of State,*

❹ **Other Contributors**

❺ **Version**

❻ **Number**

❼ **Publisher**

❽ **Publication Date** 7 May 2012,

❾ **Location** www.state.gov/secretary/20092013clinton/rm/2012/05/189385.htm.

❶ ❷ ❸ ❽ ❾

Clinton, Hillary Rodham. "Towntierview with NDTV's Barkha Dutt on 'We the People.'" *US Department of State*, 7 May 2012, www.state.gov/secretary/20092013clinton/rm/2012/05/189385.htm. Transcript.

Optional element

12d Additional sample MLA listings: Works in print periodicals

Periodical publications—scholarly journals, magazines, and newspapers—are issued regularly on scheduled dates.

1. Article in a scholarly journal For an example of how to list an article in a scholarly journal, see Source Shot 1, pages 236–237.

2. Article in a magazine

- If the article is on only one page, give that page number.
- If the article covers two or more consecutive pages, list inclusive page numbers.
- If pages are not consecutive, indicate this with a plus sign (+) immediately after the first page number, for example, 16+.

Vogel, Gretchen. "A Race to Explain Brazil's Spike in Birth Defects." *Science,* 8 Jan. 2016, pp. 110-11.

3. Article in a newspaper

- List the full date of publication, including the day, month, and year, in that order, with no commas in between them. Abbreviate all months except May, June, and July.
- If the newspaper is a specific edition (late edition, national edition, international edition), include that information as the version of the newspaper you are listing.
- For a newspaper that uses letters to designate sections, give the letter that appears on the page before the page number: "A23." For a numbered or titled section, write, for example, *section 2. p. 23* or *Arts and Leisure section, p. 3.*

Lieber, Rob. "Catching a College's Eye." *The New York Times*, late edition, 23 May 2015, p. B1.

4. Article that skips pages When a periodical article does not appear on consecutive pages, give only the first page number followed by a plus sign.

Grynbaum, Michael M. "Mayor Wants a Streetcar Line to Link Brooklyn and Queens." *The New York Times,* national edition, 4 Feb. 2016, pp. A1+.

5. Unsigned article If the author's name is not given, begin with the title of the article, ignoring *A*, *An*, or *The* when alphabetizing.

"Put Out to Pasture: Controversy Surrounds the Government's Management of Wild Horses." *The Economist*, 24 Sept. 2011, p. 40.

6. Review Begin with the name of the reviewer and the title of the review article in quotation marks if these are available. Then add *Review of*, the title of the work being reviewed, a comma, the word *by* or *edited by*, and the author or editor of that work. Follow with the publication information for the review.

Delbanco, Nicholas. "Dickens, as Exuberant in Private as in Public." Review of *The Selected Letters of Charles Dickens*, edited by Jenny Hartley. *The Los Angeles Times*, weekend edition, 8 Apr. 2012, p. E6.

7. Editorial (signed or unsigned) Begin with the author (if available) or the title. Include the label *Editorial* after the title. Follow with the rest of the publication information. In alphabetizing, ignore an initial *A*, *An*, or *The* in the editorial title.

"A Bad Bet on Online Gambling." Editorial. *The San Francisco Chronicle*, 13 Apr. 2012, p. A11.

8. Letter to the editor Write *Letter* or *Reply to letter of...* after the name of the author (or after the title, if there is one). Follow with the publication information.

Levin, Michael. "Books with Not Much to Say." Letter. *The Economist*, 24 Sept. 2011, p. 22.

12e Additional sample MLA listings: Works in nonperiodical print publications

9. Book with one author See Source Shot 2 on pages 238–239 for an explanation and example.

10. Book with two or more authors For a book with two authors, list the authors' names in the order in which they appear on the title page. Separate the names with commas. Reverse the order of only the first author's name.

Kamkwamba, William, and Bryan Mealer. *The Boy Who Harnessed the Wind: Creating Currents of Electricity and Hope*. Morrow, 2009.

For a work with more than two authors, list only the first author's name, followed by *et al.* (Latin *et alii*, meaning "and others").

Baumol, William J., et al. *Good Capitalism, Bad Capitalism, and the Economics of Growth and Prosperity*. Yale UP, 2007.

11. Book with editor(s) or compiler(s) For an anthology or compilation, list the editor(s) or compiler(s), a comma, and *editor*, *editors*, or *compilers*.

Gates, Henry Louis, Jr., editor. *Classic Slave Narratives*. NAL, 1987.

For a work with more than two editors or compilers, use the name of only the first, followed by a comma and *et al.*

12. Book with author and editor When an editor has prepared an author's work for publication, list the book under the author's name if you cite the author's work. Then, in your listing, include the name(s) of the editor(s) after the title, introduced by *Edited by* for one or more editors. (See "Other contributors," p. 232.)

Bishop, Elizabeth. *One Art: Letters*. Edited by Robert Giroux. Farrar, Straus and Giroux, 1994.

If you cite a section written by the editor, such as an introduction or a note, list the source under the name of the editor, and give the page numbers for the section.

Giroux, Robert, editor. Introduction. *One Art: Letters,* by Elizabeth Bishop. Farrar, Straus and Giroux, 1994, pp. vii-xxii.

13. One work in an anthology (original or reprinted) See Source Shot 3 on pages 240–241 for an example and an explanation.

14. More than one work in an anthology, cross-referenced If you cite more than one work from the same anthology, list the anthology separately in a complete entry, alphabetized by the name of the editor(s) in the works-cited list. Also list each work in a brief entry with a cross-reference to the anthology. This entry needs only the author's complete name, the title of the work, the last name(s) of the editor(s) of the anthology, and the inclusive page numbers of the work. Alphabetize the entries in the usual way, as in the following examples.

Eggers, Dave, editor. *The Best American Non-Required Reading 2008*. Houghton Mifflin, 2008.

King, Stephen. "Ayana." Eggers, pp. 200-15.

Saunders, George. "Bill Clinton, Public Citizen." Eggers, pp. 267-300.

15. Foreword, preface, introduction, or afterword List the name of the author of the book element cited, followed by the name of the element (*Foreword, Introduction,* and so on), with no quotation marks. Give the title of the work; then use *By* to introduce the name of the author(s) of the book (first name first). Conclude with the inclusive page numbers for the book element cited.

Trillin, Calvin. Foreword. *Eat Me: The Food and Philosophy of Kenny Shopsin*, by Kenny Shopsin and Carolynn Carreño, Alfred A. Knopf, 2008, pp. xiii-xxi.

16. Entry in a reference book Cite an entry in an encyclopedia or other reference work as you would a work in an anthology or collection (shown in Source Shot 3 on pp. 240–241).

Millar, James R., editor. "Caviar." *The Encyclopedia of Russian History*. Vol. 1. Macmillan Reference USA, 2004, pp. 215-16.

17. Book in a second or subsequent edition After the title, give the edition number, using the abbreviation *ed.* for *edition*.

Raimes, Ann, and Susan K. Miller-Cochran. *Pocket Keys for Writers*. 5th ed., Cengage Learning, 2016.

18. Multivolume work If you refer to only one volume of a multivolume work, give the author and page number in your in-text citation, and give only the volume number for that book in the works-cited entry.

Richardson, John. *A Life of Picasso*. Vol. 2, Random House, 1996.

If you refer to more than one volume of a multivolume work in your paper (as in 11b, item S), give the number of volumes (abbreviated *vols.*) at the end of the entry.

Einstein, Albert. *Collected Papers of Albert Einstein*. Princeton UP, 1987-2006. 10 vols.

19. Book in a series If the title page or an earlier page identifies a book as part of a series, you may end the entry with the name of the series and any series number given. This information is optional and should be provided if it would be helpful to readers.

Malenczyk, Rita, editor. *A Rhetoric for Writing Program Administrators*. Parlor P, 2013. Writing Program Administration.

20. Republished book If you are using a book that has been republished but has not changed (so it is not a new edition), you usually just list the publication date of the version that you used. In the following example, the original book was written in 2000, but the listing is for the reprinted version in 2010.

King, Stephen. *On Writing*. Scribner, 2010.

For a book republished under a different title, give the publication information for the version of the book that you referenced.

Raimes, James. *An Englishman's Garden in America*. Frances Lincoln, 2007.

If the original publication date will give readers information that is helpful or important, list the date of the original publication following the title.

Du Bois, W. E. B. *The Souls of Black Folk*. 1903. Modern Library, 1996.

21. Book published under a publisher's imprint If a book lists both a division of a publisher and an imprint of that publisher, list just the name of the division. In the following example, the name of the imprint, Nan A. Talese, is not included.

Atwood, Margaret. *Oryx and Crake*. Doubleday, 2003.

22. Book title including a title Do not italicize a book title (or a journal name) included in the title of the work you list. (However, if the title of a short work, such as a poem or a short story, is included, enclose it in quotation marks.)

Hays, Kevin J., editor. *The Critical Response to Herman Melville's* Moby Dick. Greenwood P, 1994.

23. Book without stated publication information If a book does not provide some publication information, add any details about it that you may have found elsewhere in square brackets to indicate that they were not in the source: *[circa 2008]*.

24. The Bible and other sacred texts Take the information from the title page, and give the usual bibliographical details for a book. Also include the edition or version and the name of a translator or editor where appropriate. Ignore any *The* in the title for alphabetizing purposes in the works-cited list: Alphabetize *The Holy Bible* under *H*.

Enuma Elish. Edited by Leonard W. King. Book Tree, 1998.

The Holy Bible. King James Version. Hendrickson, 2003.

The Koran. Translated by George Sale. F. Warne, 1734.

The New Oxford Annotated Bible. Edited by Michael D. Coogan. 3rd ed., Oxford UP, 2001.

25. Dissertations Cite a published dissertation as you would a book, but also include the dissertation information after the title (for example, *Dissertation, U of Missouri, 2012.*).

Gierdowski, Dana Cockrum. *Geographies of a Writing Space: The Study of a Flexible Composition Classroom*. Dissertation North Carolina State U, 2013. U Microfilm International, 2013.

For an unpublished dissertation, follow the title (in quotation marks) with *Dissertation* and then with the university and year.

Hidalgo, Stephen Paul. "Vietnam War Poetry: A Genre of Witness." Dissertation U of Notre Dame, 1995.

If you cite an abstract published in *Dissertation Abstracts International,* give the volume number, issue number, year, and item or page number.

Hidalgo, Stephen Paul. "Vietnam War Poetry: A Genre of Witness." Dissertation U of Notre Dame, 1995, *Dissertation Abstracts International*, vol. 56, no. 8, 1995, item 0931A.

12f Additional sample MLA listings: Periodical works in online databases or on the Web

Libraries subscribe to large information services to gain access to extensive databases of online articles (such as *Academic Search Premier, InfoTrac, LexisNexis, WorldCat,* and others) as well as to specialized databases (such as *ERIC, Contemporary Literary Criticism, JSTOR,* and *Project Muse).* You can use these databases to locate abstracts and full texts of thousands of articles that were originally published in print. And because many of the articles will have been previously accepted for publication, you will be able to find reliable materials for your papers.

When you access a publication through an online database, you need to list two containers: the container of the original publication and then the container of the database in which you found it. You'll list the nine primary elements for the original source, and then you'll start over again with the database as a container and list the publication information you have. The location for the source in the database will either be a DOI (see Key Points box, pp. 231–234) or a stable URL. DOIs are preferred if they are available, but not all publications in databases have DOIs. See Source Shot 4 (pp. 242–243) for an example of a magazine article from an online database, including a template for listing the elements.

26. Scholarly article in an online database Give the inclusive page numbers only if they are visible on the screen (if the article is in PDF format).

Lowe, Michelle S. "Britain's Regional Shopping Centres: New Urban Forms?" *Urban Studies*, vol. 37, no. 2, 2000, pp. 261-74. *Academic Search Premier*, doi:10.1080/0042098002186.

27. Magazine article in an online database Give the inclusive page numbers if they are visible. See Source Shot 4 on pages 242–243 for more information to include and an example.

28. Newspaper article in an online database Give the inclusive page numbers if they are visible. Instead of a DOI, many print magazine and newspaper articles list an ISSN (International Standard Serial Number), which readers may find helpful as part of the location information.

"A Painful Betrayal." Editorial. *The New York Times,* late ed., 3 Feb. 2012, sec. A. *Academic OneFile,* ISSN 0362-4331.

29. Scholarly article in an online journal List the publication information as you would for an article in a print journal (see Source Shot 1, pp. 236–237). If the publisher is the same as the name of the scholarly journal (which is often the case for online scholarly journals), you do not need to list a publisher. List an exact DOI or URL for the location of the article.

Ferris, Sharmila Pixy. "Writing Electronically: The Effects of Computers on Traditional Writing." *Journal of Electronic Publishing*, vol. 8, no. 1, 2002, doi:10.3998/3336451.0008.104.

Hatchuel, Sarah. "Leading the Gaze: From Showing to Telling in Kenneth Branagh's *Henry V* and *Hamlet*." *Early Modern Literary Studies*, vol. 6, no. 1, 2000, extra.shu.ac.uk/emls/06-1/hatchbra.htm.

30. Article in an online magazine List the publication information as you would for an article in a print magazine. If the publisher or sponsor of the online magazine is the same as the name of the magazine, there is no need to repeat the information. List the full date of publication, and list the exact URL as the location.

Wolk, Alan. "Why Can't Apple Figure Out Television?" *Slate*, 5 Feb. 2016, www.slate.com/articles/technology/technology/2016/02/apple_never_had_a_shot_at_rethinking_tv.html.

31. Article in an online newspaper List the publication information as you would for an article in a print magazine. If the publisher or sponsor of the online magazine is the same as the name of the magazine, there is no need to repeat the information. List the edition of the newspaper, if applicable, as the version of the newspaper that you consulted. Include the full date of publication, and list the exact URL as the location.

Cieply, Michael, and Brooks Barnes. "Why the Film Academy's Diversity Push Is Tougher Than It Thinks." *The New York Times*, 5 Feb. 2016, www.nytimes.com/2016/02/06/business/media/motion-picture-academy-diversity-efforts-a-risk-of-bias.html?_r=0.

12g Additional sample MLA listings: Other Web sources

For nonperiodical sources you find online, you will need to include the exact URL as the location, deleting *http:// https://*, and *www.* unless it is part of the actual address. You may also need to include the date of access if it is a source that is likely to change without any easily accessible history of the change. If you list a date of access, list it at the end of the citation with *Accessed* and the date. Always save or print a copy of a Web source that you are using since it will display your date of access and provide you with the original information you were referencing.

Source Shot 5 (pp. 244–245) shows you how to provide and format the information needed to cite a Web source.

32. Article or page on a nonperiodical Web site Put titles of Web pages and articles in quotation marks, and put titles of reports in italics. Then give the title of the Web site as the container (in italics). Web sites often comprise many pages, each with its own URL, so list the exact URL where you found the page you are referencing.

Rogers, Felisa. "Lessons of a Reluctant Hunter." *Salon.com.* Salon Media Group, 14 Apr. 2012, www.salon.com/2012/04/14/lessons_of_a_reluctant_hunter/. Accessed 16 Apr. 2016.

Source Shot 5 on pages 244–245 shows an example of how to cite a Web page that has no named author.

33. Entire Web site, no author named Begin with the name of the site in italics, and then list the other elements in order.

Penn: University of Pennsylvania. U of Pennsylvania, 2016, www.upenn.edu/. Accessed 28 Mar. 2016.

Modern Language Association. MLA, 2016, www.mla.org.

34. Entry in an online encyclopedia, dictionary, or other reference work When entries are not individually authored, begin with the title of the entry. Give the most recent date of posting as the publication date.

"Vicarious." *Cambridge Dictionaries Online.* Cambridge UP, 2016, dictionary.cambridge.org/us/dictionary/learner-english/vicarious.

35. Government publication accessed online If an author or authors (or compiler or compilers) are named, you may either begin with the government and agency (as illustrated in Source Shot 6 on pp. 246–247) or begin with the author(s) or compiler(s). See Source Shot 6 for an example of how to cite a government publication accessed online.

36. Scholarly project online If the site shows the name of an editor, list it in place of the author. Give the sponsor after the title (or name of the editor), followed by a comma.

Courtney, Angela, and Michelle Dalmau, editors. *Victorian Women Writers Project*. Trustees of Indiana U, 2010, webapp1.dlib.indiana.edu/vwwp/welcome.do.

37. Online book List the publication information as you would for a print book, but include the exact URL as the location of the book. If the online version of the work that you are referencing is available in print, give additional information only for the print version if it is relevant to the work you are doing (see 12e, item 20, which provides guidelines for listing the original publication information for a republished book).

Berry, Patrick, et al., editors. *Provocations: Reconstructing the Archive*. Computers and Composition Digital P / Utah State UP, 2016, ccdigitalpress.org/ebooks-and-projects/reconstructingthearchive.

38. Online poem For a poem accessed on a Web site, list the publication information as you would for a print poem, including the URL as the location of the poem. For the following example, the access date is included in case the poem is taken down or the Web site is altered in the future. If the online version of the work that you are referencing is available in print, only give additional information for the print version if it is relevant to the work you are doing.

Aechtner, Chris D. "Goddess of the Night." *PoetrySoup*, 2011, www.poetrysoup.com/poem/goddess_of_the_night_237294. Accessed 3 Apr. 2016.

39. Review published online After the name of the reviewer and title (if there is one), add *Review of*...and the title of the work being reviewed, a comma, and the author of that work. Then add additional publication information as you would for other online publications.

Miller, Laura. "'The Queen and the Maid': Joan of Arc's Secret Backer." Review of *The Maid and the Queen*, by Nancy Goldstone, *Salon*, 1 Apr. 2012, www.salon.com/2012/04/02/the_queen_and_the_maid_joan_of_arcs_secret_backer/.

40. Personal Web site or home page First list the site creator or editor as the author. If a personal Web site has a title, supply it, in italics. If the home page is part of a larger Web site, use the designation *Home Page* with no italics as the title of the page if it does not have a title separate from the title of the Web site. Then list the title of the Web site as the container in italics.

Ferraro, Janet. *The Art of Janet Ferraro,* 2016, janetferraro.com/.

Pollitzer, Sally. Home page. *Architectural Glass.* Pharus Design, 2006, www.sally-pollitzer.co.uk/.

41. Course or department home page For a course home page, give the name of the instructor(s), the course number and title (in quotation marks), the title of the Web site (if applicable), the institution sponsoring the site (as the publisher), the publication date, the URL, and your date of access. Because course Web sites change frequently, including your date of access is recommended.

Tobin, Beth Fowkes, and Maureen Daly Goggin. "ENG 604: Interdisciplinary Cultural Studies: Material Culture." Arizona State U, 2009, www.public.asu.edu/~mdg42/ENG604MaterialCulture2009.htm. Accessed 3 Apr. 2016.

42. Online posting on a blog, discussion list, social media application, wiki, and so on Give the author's name and the document title (in quotation marks) as visible on-screen or written in the subject line in a discussion list. If there is no title, use the label *Online posting* (not in quotation marks). If the posting is from *Twitter*, include the full message posted as the title and the author's username on *Twitter* as the author's name. You may also include the time of posting after the date.

@stevemartintogo. "I finally found something on the Internet I can believe!" *Twitter*, 3 Apr. 2016, 3:29 p.m. twitter.com/SteveMartinToGo/status/716754410253193216.

Continue with the name of the list or forum or the title of the blog (in italics unless the blog is part of a Web site) or wiki, the name of the sponsor/publisher, the date of posting, and the URL. Include your date of access if the source is one that could be removed without a history of what was posted.

Althouse, Ann. "James Taylor Loves His Echo Chamber." *Althouse*, 5 Feb. 2016, althouse.blogspot.com/2016/02/james-taylor-loves-his-echo-chamber.html.

The following entry by Nick Bilton is a posting on the blog *Bits: The Business of Technology*, which is found on *The New York Times* Web site (an online newspaper; see 12f, item 31). In this case, list the blog as one container and *The New York Times* as the larger container.

Bilton, Nick. "Disruptions: Time to Review FAA Policy on Gadgets." *Bits: The Business of Technology*, 18 Mar. 2012, *The New York Times*, bits.blogs.nytimes.com/2012/03/18/disruptions-time-to-review-f-a-a-policy-on-gadgets/.

If a wiki entry is unsigned, begin with the title of the entry. Because *Wikipedia* entries all have accessible histories, there is no need to list your date of access. You can list the last date that the page was updated as the date of publication, along with the time stamp given.

"Katherine Anne Porter." *Wikipedia.* Wikimedia Foundation, 28 Mar. 2016, 4:14 a.m. en.wikipedia.org/wiki/Katherine_Anne_Porter.

12h Additional sample MLA listings: Visual, audio, and multimedia sources

The same nine primary elements are used for multimedia sources (see Key Points box on pp. 231–234). You might have to search a little to find some elements, and also remember that the goal is to help readers understand the citation and to find the material you are citing. One recommendation made in MLA style is that if you are citing an unusual type of work, you can put a descriptive word or set of words at the end of the citation to explain what the source is (see 12h, item 46, for examples).

43. Work of visual art or photograph (and image reproduction or slide) List the name of the artist; the title of the work (in italics); the date of the work's creation; the medium, if referring to the work itself, rather than a reproduction; the name of the museum, gallery, or private collection; and the city where the work is found.

Duchamp, Marcel. *Bicycle Wheel.* 1951, metal wheel mounted on painted wood stool. Museum of Modern Art, New York.

Johns, Jasper. *Racing Thoughts.* 1983, encaustic and collage on canvas. Whitney Museum of American Art, New York.

For an image of a work of art in another publication (such as a book, a slide, or on the Web), in addition to details about the work and its location, give complete publication information for the place where you found the reproduction, including the number of the page on which the photograph appears in a book or any figure, slide, or plate number.

Johns, Jasper. *Racing Thoughts.* 1983, Whitney Museum of American Art, New York. *The American Century: Art and Culture 1950-2000,* by Lisa Phillips, W. W. Norton, 1999, p. 311.

Wolfgang Volz/Laif/Redux

Christo and Jeanne-Claude. *The Umbrellas.* 1984-1991, *National Gallery of Art,* Washington, D.C., 2016, www.nga.gov/exhibitions/2002/christo/umbrellas.shtm.

44. Museum wall placard For a placard such as a museum wall label, include the name of the exhibition and the label *Placard* after the title or name of the work. Also give the name of the museum, the city in which the museum is located (unless the city is part of the museum name), and the dates of the show.

Aphrodite's Children. Aphrodite and the Gods of Love. Placard. Museum of Fine Arts, Boston, 26 Oct. 2011-20 Feb. 2012.

45. Cartoon or comic strip After the name of the artist and the title (within quotation marks), list the name of the comic strip. Follow this with information about the location of the source. Include the page number for a print source. The word *Cartoon* or *Comic strip* can be given as additional information for readers.

Chast, Roz. "New Chess Pieces." Cartoon. *The New Yorker,* 27 Sept. 2010, p. 65.

46. Advertisement Give the name of the product, company, or organization, followed by the publication information for where the advertisement was found. The word *Advertisement* can be given as a descriptor after the name of the product as additional information for readers.

American Indian College Fund. Advertisement. *The New York Times Style Magazine,* 25 Sept. 2011, p. 91.

Acura automobile. Advertisement. *Comedy Central,* 24 Mar. 2012.

47. Map or chart Italicize the title of the map or chart, and include the genre designation *Map,* if it is helpful for readers, after the title.

Los Angeles Region. Map. Automobile Club of Southern California, 2009.

For a map or chart accessed on the Web, include the date of posting and your date of access.

MLA Language Map. Modern Language Association, 2016.

48. Film or video recording For a film, begin with the title (italicized) unless you are citing the work of a specific contributor (*director, writer,* and so on), whom you would list first. Otherwise, after the title, list the director, performers, and any other contributors relevant for why you are citing the film. Follow with the name of the distributor (and a comma) and the year of distribution.

A Dangerous Method. Directed by David Cronenberg, Sony Pictures Entertainment, 2011.

Cronenberg, David, director. *A Dangerous Method.* Performance by Michael Fassbender, Viggo Mortensen, and Keira Knightley, Sony Pictures Entertainment, 2011.

Cite a DVD, laser disc, videocassette, filmstrip, or slide program as you would a film. Include the date of the original film only if it is relevant. Follow with the name of the distributor of the DVD, laser disc, or other format, and the year of the release of the version you are referencing. If it will help readers, include a description of the medium at the end of the citation.

Casablanca. Directed by Michael Curtiz, performance by Humphrey Bogart and Ingrid Bergman, 1943, MGM Studios, 1998. DVD.

The Iron Lady. Directed by Phyllida Lloyd, Weinstein Company, 2012.

To cite a digitized version of a film that you viewed on the Web, see 12h, item 55.

For an online video, provide the publication information for the original video, followed by information for where you found it. Include the exact URL as the location.

Phillips, Barnaby, narrator. *South Africa's Threatened Rhinos.* AlJazeeraEnglish, 28 Sept. 2010. *YouTube,* www.youtube.com/watch?v=ksLfkvf0U6c.

49. Television or radio program Give the title of the program episode or segment (in quotation marks); the name of the program or series (in italics); the network or distributor for the program; and the date of broadcast. After the title of the episode or program, include any pertinent information about individual additional contributors, such as a performer, narrator, or director.

"The Vaccine War." *Frontline* PBS, 20 Mar. 2012.

Howe, Marie. Interview by Terry Gross. *Fresh Air*, National Public Radio, 20 Oct. 2011.

"Take the Money and Run for Office." *This American Life*, narrated by Ira Glass. Public Radio International, 30 Mar. 2012.

To refer to the work of a particular person, begin the entry with the person's name and contribution (*director*, *narrator*, *performer*, and so on). If there are multiple episodes, you can reference the number at the end of the citation.

Fellowes, Julian, writer. "Downton Abbey: Season Two." Performance by Hugh Bonneville, Maggie Smith, and Elizabeth McGovern, *Masterpiece Theatre*, PBS, 8 Jan.-19 Feb. 2012. 7 episodes.

50. Sound recording Begin the entry with the person whose role you want to emphasize: composer or writer, performer, conductor, and so on. Then list the title of the work (with album titles in italics and song titles in quotation marks), manufacturer (followed by a comma), and the year of issue.

If you cite a specific song on an album, give the song title (in quotation marks) and then the album title (in italics) to indicate a work contained within a larger work (as you would cite a short work contained in an anthology). If you need to give additional information about the source you are referencing (such as a disc number or the number of volumes), include that information at the end of the citation.

Welch, Kevin. "Andaman Sea." *A Patch of Blue Sky*, Music Road Records, 2010.

Brooks, Gwendolyn. "We Real Cool." *The Norton Anthology of African American Literature Audio Companion*, W.W. Norton, 2004. Disc 2.

Walker, Alice. Interview by Kay Bonetti. American Audio Prose Library, 1981.

51. Live performance Give the author, title of the performance (play, concert, dance, and so on), any pertinent information about the director and performers, the theater and city (separated by a comma), and the date of the performance. If you are citing an individual's role in the performance, begin your citation with that person's name, as in the second example that follows.

Bunin, Ivan. *In Paris.* Directed and Adapted by Dmitry Krymov, performance by Mikhail Baryshnikov. Broad Stage, Santa Monica, 15 Apr. 2012.

Baryshnikov, Mikhail, performer. *In Paris*. By Ivan Bunin, directed by Dmitry Krymov. Broad Stage, Santa Monica, 15 Apr. 2012.

52. Podcast (online audio recording) If you listen to or view a podcast online, cite it as you would an article or page on a Web site (12g, item 32). Provide an exact URL as the location.

Cite a podcast that you download and access on an audio player as you would cite a work in its original medium (sound recording, lecture, concert performance, online newspaper, and so on).

Krista Tippet. "Tiffany Shlain: Growing Up the Internet." *On Being*, Krista Tippet Public Productions, 31 Mar. 2016, itunes.apple.com/us/podcast/tiffany-shlain-growing-up/id150892556?i=365953929&mt=2.

53. CD-ROM or DVD-ROM Cite material from a CD-ROM or DVD-ROM published as a single edition (that is, with no regular updating or revising) in the same way you cite a book, an article in a book, or a work of art (see 12h, item 43), but include any version or release number if relevant. Also include information for both containers if you are citing something that has been included in a new container, as is the case for the first example. If you think it will assist readers, include information about the medium at the end of the citation.

Flanner, Janet. "Führer I." *The New Yorker*, 29 Feb. 1934, pp. 20-24. *The Complete New Yorker*, Random House, 2005. DVD-ROM.

Keats, John. "To Autumn." *Columbia Granger's World of Poetry*, Columbia UP, 1999. CD-ROM, Release 3.

If there is more than one disc and you used only one, give the number of that disc (*Disc 3*) at the end of the citation; otherwise, give the total number of discs (*4 discs*).

If you cite a work in a scholarly journal, magazine, newspaper, or reference book that is published periodically in print as well as on CD-ROM or DVD-ROM as a database or as part of a database, you have the option of including the original publication information along with the CD-ROM or DVD-ROM information if you believe it would help readers. If you choose to include the original publication information, first give the publication information for the print source (check the disc's publication booklet for this). Follow with the medium of publication for your source (*CD-ROM* or *DVD-ROM*). Then list the title of the database (italicized), the name of the vendor (such as *Silver Platter*), and the publication date of the database.

54. Digital files A digital file is an image, performance, or document (such as a photograph, video recording of a concert, or typed word processing file) that can exist in digital form on your computer or another device or that can be published on a disc and played without the support of a Web site. For digital files that you download, receive, or create, document the source according to the publication information of the original work.

Byrne, David. "A Walk in the Dark." *Uh-Oh.* Luaka Bop/Warner Bros., 1992.

More, Thomas. *Utopia.* 1516. Read by James Adams, Blackstone Audio, 2008.

Brooks, David. *The Social Animal: The Hidden Sources of Love, Character, and Achievement.* Random House, 2011.

55. Film on the Web For a digitized version of a film that you viewed online, first give all of the film publication information. Then add the title of the Web site or database where you viewed the film and the exact URL.

Hepworth, Cecil, director. *Alice in Wonderland.* Hepworth Mfg., 1903. *Internet Archive,* archive.org/details/Alice_in_Wonderland_1903.

56. Radio or television program on the Web For a live (streaming) radio program accessed online, give all of the broadcast information, including the date of broadcast (see 12h, item 49). Next give the name of the Web site and the exact URL. Give the title of the program episode or segment (in quotation marks), and the name of the program or series (in italics).

Bonnie Simmons Show. KPFA, 31 Mar. 2016. *Archives for the Bonnie Simmons Show*, kpfa.org/program/the-bonnie-simmons-show/. Accessed 3 Apr. 2016.

Follow the same format for a radio or television program accessed from an online archive.

"Mystery of Edwin Drood." *Masterpiece Theatre.* PBS, 16 Apr. 2012, www.pbs.org/wgbh/masterpiece/drood/.

57. Documenting across media The following Key Points box shows seven different publication, performance, and broadcast sources for one song by rap artists Jay-Z and Kanye West, documented in MLA style.

KEY POINTS

Seven Ways to Document a Jay-Z and Kanye West Song

Daniel Boczarski/Getty Images Entertainment/Getty Images

Song on an album

Jay-Z, and Kanye West. "Otis." *Watch the Throne*, Roc-A-Fella, 2011.

Lyrics in print (print booklet with CD)

Carter, Shawn [Jay-Z], et al. "Otis." *Watch the Throne*, Roc-A-Fella, 2011. Booklet.

Lyrics on the Web

Carter, Shawn [Jay-Z], et al. "Otis." *Watch the Throne*, Roc-A-Fella, 2011. *Direct Lyrics*, 2012, www.directlyrics.com/kanye-west-otis-lyrics.html.

Music video on the Web

Jay-Z, and Kanye West. "Otis." *YouTube*, 11 Aug. 2011, www.youtube.com/watch?v=BoEKWtgJQAU.

Live performance

Jay-Z, and Kanye West. "Otis." *Watch the Throne Tour*, Toyota Center, Houston, 5 Dec. 2011

Live performance broadcast on television

Jay-Z, and Kanye West. "Otis." *2011 MTV Video Music Awards*, Nokia Theatre, Los Angeles, 28 Aug. 2011.

Video on the Web of a live performance

Jay-Z, and Kanye West. "Otis (Live)." *2011 MTV Video Music Awards,* Nokia Theatre, Los Angeles, 28 Aug. 2011, www.youtube.com/watch?v=QywO3ogh4O4.

12i Additional sample MLA listings: Other common sources

58. Corporation, organization, or government agency as author Alphabetize by the name of the corporate author or branch of government. However, if the publisher is the same as the author, omit the author and alphabetize by title.

National Research Council, Committee on Economic and Environmental Impacts of Increasing Biofuels Production. *Renewable Fuel Standard: Potential Economic and Environmental Effects of U.S. Biofuel Policy.* National Academies P, 2011.

If no individual author is named for a government publication, begin the entry with the name of the national, state, or local government, followed by the name of the agency.

United States. National Commission on Terrorist Attacks upon the US. *The 9/11 Commission Report.* Norton, 2004.

See 12g, item 35, and Source Shot 6 (pp. 246–247) for an online government publication.

59. Pamphlet, brochure, or press release Document a pamphlet or brochure as you would a book.

Internet Safety: A Computer User's Guide to Privacy and Security. Consumer Action, 2009.

Document a press release similarly, but add the day and month as well as the year.

60. Translation After the title, add *Translated by* and the name of the translator, first name first.

Pastoureau, Michel. *The Bear: History of a Fallen King.* Translated by George Holoch, Harvard UP, 2011.

61. Graphic narrative or illustrated work For collaboratively created graphic narratives, use labels to indicate contributors' roles (for example, *illustrator,* *translator*). Begin your entry with the name of the person(s) whose work you want to emphasize. List other contributors and their roles after the title as relevant, using the order and descriptions of roles given in the source.

McCulloch, Derek. *Gone to Amerikay.* Art by Colleen Doran, colors by José Villarruba, letters by Jared K. Fletcher, DC Comics, 2012.

If the graphic narrative was created by one person, cite it as you would any other nonperiodical print work. In the following example, Corman is both the writer and the illustrator.

Corman, Leela. *Unterzakhn.* Schocken Books, 2012.

If illustrations are part of a literary work and you are citing the writers, give *Illustrated by* and the illustrator's name after the title.

Pekar, Harvey, and Joyce Brabner. *Our Cancer Year.* Illustrated by Frank Stack. Four Walls Eight Windows, 1994.

If you are citing the work of the illustrator, begin the entry with that person's name.

62. Interview (personal, published, broadcast, or online) Begin with the name of the person interviewed. For an interview that you conducted, include the type of interview (telephone, e-mail, personal [in person], and so on).

Earle, Steve. Telephone interview. 4 Apr. 2016.

For a published interview, give the name of the person interviewed and then the title (if any) in quotation marks. Then provide the label *Interview* or *Interview by*... and the name of the interviewer. Then give the publication information.

McCall Smith, Alexander. Interview by Jo Herbert. *Writers and Artists: The Insider Guide to the Media*, 2016, www.writersandartists.co.uk/writers/advice/193/a-writers-toolkit/interviews-with-authors/alexander-mccall-smith.

For a broadcast (television or radio) interview, provide information about the source and date of the interview (see 12h, item 49).

Howe, Marie. Interview by Terry Gross. *Fresh Air,* National Public Radio, 20 Oct. 2011.

Spurlock, Morgan. Interview by Bruce Sylvester. *Troubadour,* 5 May 2011.

63. Transcript of a radio or television program To cite a transcript of a radio or television program, first give all of the program information (see 12h, item 49). Then end the entry with the word *Transcript.*

Howe, Marie. Interview by Terry Gross. *Fresh Air.* National Public Radio, 20 Oct. 2011. Transcript.

64. Lecture, reading, speech, or address Give the author and title, if known. Also give the name of any organizing sponsor, the venue, the city, and the date. At the end of the citation, list the type of source you are referencing to help readers.

Singer, Peter. "Happiness and Ultimate Good." Graduate Council Lectures, Alumni House, U of California, Berkeley, 17 Apr. 2012. Lecture.

65. Letter (published or personal), e-mail, memo, or other personal communication Cite a personal letter by giving the name of the letter writer, the description *Letter to the author* (not in quotation marks), and the date of the letter.

Roen, Duane. Letter to the author. 5 Feb. 2016.

Cite a published letter in a collection as you would cite a work in an anthology. After the name of the author, include any title or number that the editor gives the letter and then the date of the letter. Follow with the inclusive page numbers and the book's publication information.

Bishop, Elizabeth. "To Robert Lowell." 26 Nov. 1951. *One Art: Letters*, edited by Robert Giroux, Farrar, Straus and Giroux, 1994, pp. 224-26.

Cite an e-mail by listing the writer, the title of the message (from the subject line) in quotation marks, a phrase that names the recipient (*Message to the author*), and the date.

Carpenter, Stephanie. "Part 3." Message to the author. 5 Feb. 2016.

Follow the same format for any other type of personal communication or memo.

66. Legal or historical document For a court case, give the name of the case (with no italics or quotation marks) in the short form, listing the first plaintiff and defendant, the number of the case, the name of the court deciding the case, and the date of the decision. End with an exact URL for a Web source. (Note, however, that if you mention the case in the text of your paper, you should italicize the name of the case: "Chief Justice Burger, in *Roe v. Wade,* noted that. . . .")

Roe v. Wade. No. 70-18. Supreme Court of the US. 22 Jan. 1973.

To cite an act, give its Public Law (abbreviated as *Pub. L.*) number, its Statutes at Large volume and inclusive page numbers (abbreviated as *Stat.*), and the date it was enacted.

USA Patriot Act. Pub. L. 107-56. 115 Stat. 272-402. 26 Oct. 2001, www.justice.gov/archive/ll/highlights.htm.

Well-known historical documents (such as the U.S. Constitution) should not be included in your works-cited list (see 11b, item W).

12j Bibliographical software

Your college may provide free access to bibliographical software that can help you compile and format citations and bibliographies in any documentation style. Follow your instructor's directions to see if you should ask a librarian about the availability of a program such as *EndNote* or *RefWorks* or explore the functions of free online software such as *Mendeley* and *Zotero*. With these programs, you enter details in specific fields, and the program then formats your book or journal citations into a bibliography according to MLA, APA, or another documentation style. Some will also transfer the bibliographical references for titles found during a literature search directly into the user's Web-based account (see 9d, 9f). However, whether you use such a program or do the formatting yourself, you still have to find—and type—the information necessary for citations not directly transferred. Such programs sometimes produce incorrect or incomplete citations, so you will still need to learn the specified formats and check any computer-generated entries to be sure that they are correctly styled and contain all of the required information.

13 Sample Paper 4: A Student's Research Paper, MLA Style

Here is Patti Suchan's research paper that she wrote for her first-year composition course at High Point University in North Carolina. For this essay, students were asked to develop an argument that presented a radical perspective, or "re-seeing," on the topic of globalization. The citations and the list of works cited are in the style recommended in the 2016 *MLA Handbook*, 8th edition.

Note: Annotations have been added here to point out features of her paper that you may find useful when you write your own research paper in MLA style. Blue annotations point out issues of content and organization. Red annotations point out MLA format issues.

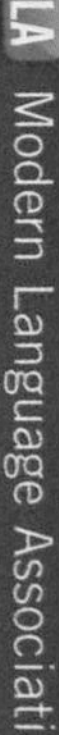

1"

½"

Suchan 1

Last name and page number

Patti Suchan

1"

Dr. Kozma

ENG-1103-10

September 12, 2016

Paper double-spaced throughout

Originality Died and Made Profit King

There was a time when the theater was known for dramatics and creativity, but also for being an unstable and unprofitable way to make a living. Only a few truly gifted people could survive in such an industry, where freedom of expression did not always achieve public resonance and equate to a regular payday, or even an occasional paycheck. The renowned American playwright Arthur Miller remarked, "The theater is so endlessly fascinating because it's so accidental" ("Arthur Miller"), and many believe that this is undoubtedly true. But those days of spontaneity and insecurity have been on the wane, unbeknownst to the world's hoi polloi. Although they are often not included in discussions about how globalization is changing the world, the arts are actually an area that is leading the charge. Back in the Elizabethan age, William Shakespeare created a worldwide theater phenomenon that has resulted in both positive and negative repercussions in modern times. Thomas Friedman, a journalist for *The New York Times*, notes in his book *The Lexus and the Olive Tree* that the present era of globalization began in 1989, with the end of the Cold War (xvii). Jonathan Burston, a

No author named, short form of Web page title, no page number

Establishing argument as chronological

Author, his credentials, and source named in sentence

Page number at end of paraphrase

1"

Blue = content issues, **Red = format issues**

Modern Language Association MLA

Suchan 2

scholar, also connects history and theater to argue that globally driven changes to theater, and "cultural industries in general," began in the early 1980s ("Recombinant" 161). With the advent of globalization, the destruction of the art form that is theater has been almost completely actualized for the benefit of increased profitability and the ruination of originality.

Author with more than one work cited—shortened title in parentheses

Thesis

Globalization is a difficult subject to define. There are many different elements that together create the concept of globalization. The coming together of cultures, ideas, religions, and industries are some of the more essential pieces of globalization. The most important aspect of globalization is the maximizing of profits in a market that has a broader reach than ever before, regardless of what that particular market may be. Michael Moore wrote an article about American business owners who would frequently "tell [him] that 'a company must do whatever is necessary to create the biggest profit possible'" (410). This ideology is not limited to major businesses in the United States, though. It is a mindset that has spread around the world and into atypical market sectors, such as theater, as globalization has become prevalent.

Defining term so that audience can follow argument

Quotation in source quoted by student writer; word changed in brackets within quotation and page numbers in parentheses after quotation and before period

Sentence connects the writer's two main ideas: globalization and the theater.

In the history of theater, going as far back as the origins and as recently as about a half century ago, productions of shows were vastly different from others done previously. The script of the show would be the same, but since the actors would be different, the

Suchan 3

whole show would have a different essence. The sets, costumes, and props could all be different as well, but what would really make the critical difference was the new life that each actor's interpretation breathed into a character. Since this was how the theater worked for such a long period of time, theater became irrevocably known as a creative art form. One of the most important and formative time periods for theater was the Elizabethan age of William Shakespeare. His legacy has been a blessing and a curse to theater worldwide. (See fig. 1.)

Shakespeare greatly contributed to the prominence of theater in not just English-speaking countries but around the globe, which has been very beneficial to the theater community. The popularity becomes a problem when many new shows are just repetitions of common themes. Shakespeare's works have been adapted into many modern works, such as *West Side Story* and *Kiss Me, Kate,* but even his "original" works are not thought to be original ideas. *The Taming of the Shrew*, known as a tale of "achieving rapid dominance" (Fhloinn 188), is based on a common story of the time. Jan Harald Brunvand believes that "Shakespeare's source for the taming plot was most likely an oral text of the folklore" (qtd. in Fhloinn 190), but it has also been suggested that the "story originated in the east" (Fhloinn 191). The possible origin comes from the famous fifth century BC Chinese strategist and philosopher, Sun Tzu, by way of Chinese historian Sima Qian. Sun

Indirect source: cites work in which another author is quoted

Blue = content issues, **Red = format issues**

Suchan 4

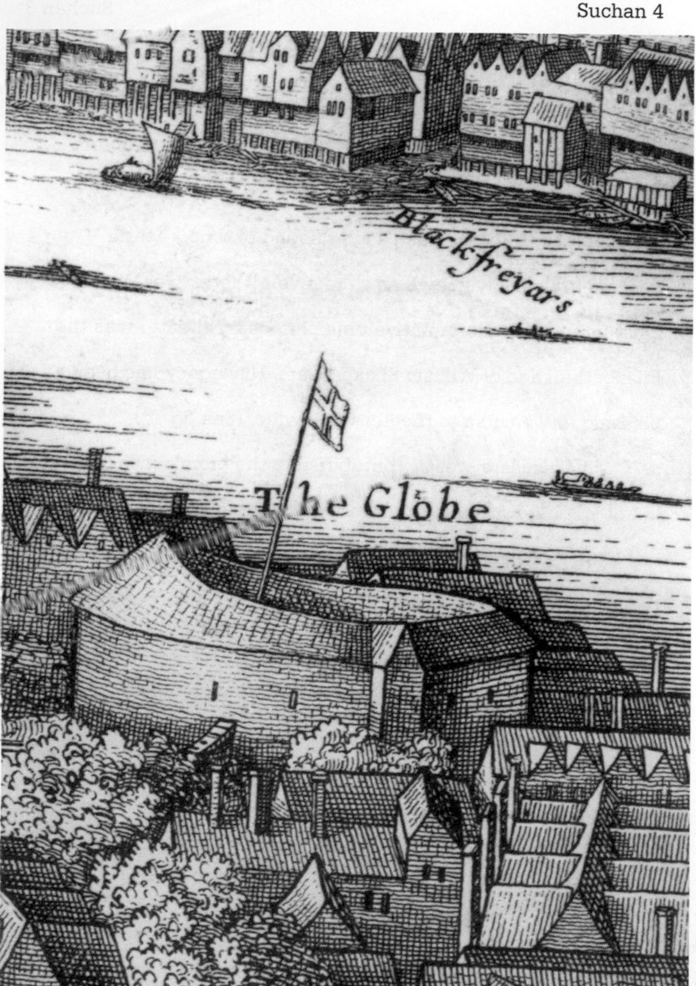

English School/The Bridgeman Art Library/Getty Images

Fig. 1. The First Globe Theatre, where many of Shakespeare's plays were performed, from Visscher's View of London (1616); rpt. in Joseph Quincy Adams, *Shakespearean Playhouses: A History of English Theatres from the Beginnings to the Restoration*, Peter Smith, 1960, p. 254. *Project Gutenberg eBook,* www.gutenberg.org/ebooks/22397.

Blue = content issues, **Red = format issues**

Suchan 5

Tzu, author of *The Art of War*, is said to have performed acts of violence to "achieve rapid dominance," which, in turn, inspired such a tale (Fhloinn 192). Shakespeare's works themselves can therefore be said to represent globalization long before globalization was even acknowledged, which helped with their popularity, but which has also created world-renowned clichés. With the continued success of all things Shakespearean, though, the clichés have been oft-repeated, which is unsurprising. When profit is king, a popular storyline is the surest route to success.

Clear transition from "popular storylines" to "re-creations of well-liked stories." Writer is forming an evidence chain.

There are new shows created every year that are re-creations of already well-liked stories. International blockbusters are frequently being brought to the stage, especially since the Disney Company achieved such wide success with the productions of *Beauty and the Beast* and *The Lion King*. Broadway producers are "choosing bankable titles more and more regularly in order to reduce risk" because, even if the show does poorly, it will attract enough attention to run for an adequate period of time and, more importantly, boost global sales of related products (Burston, "Recombinant" 166). *Shrek the Musical* is a fairly recent adaptation that joined the lineup on the Great White Way (fig. 2). Many negative critiques of the show, by both experts and audience members, revolved around the fact that the storyline of the show was exactly the same as that of the movie. While this is true, it is also true for the Disney musicals, in which no fault is generally found.

Quotation from source and paraphrase both used in sentence

Author's name and short form of work's title (separated by comma) when two works by same author cited

Blue = content issues, **Red = format issues**

ZUMA Press, Inc./Alamy Stock Photo

Fig. 2. Publicity photograph from *Shrek the Musical*. By David Lindsay-Abaire, 2012 Touring Performance.

The difference, I believe, comes from the musical nature of the movie on which a show is based, which Disney has and Dreamworks does not. Regardless, *Shrek the Musical* characters are portrayed in a manner similar to their counterparts in the movie. This is especially surprising since Daniel Breaker, the actor playing Donkey, and possibly the character that was most similar

Suchan 7

between the two mediums, said in an interview that he had "never seen the movies . . . and didn't want to [because he] didn't want to be lost in trying to re-create Eddie Murphy's role." Is his portrayal so similar to that of Eddie Murphy because the part is written in such a way as to lend itself to such an interpretation, or is it that the director of the show was guiding the actor into making the character the same as is found in the movie? Either way, the actor was not organically creating the character. Someone else, either the writer or the director, was pushing him to act in such a way, and it wasn't of his own volition. This repetition of characters from silver screen to stage has become a popular trend, possibly in part because foreign audiences who have seen the movie can enjoy the show despite the language barrier, since they already know the storyline.

Ellipsis points indicate part of quoted sentence omitted

Web source, no page number for quotation

Substituted words in brackets within quotation

Another type of show, those that do not have storylines that are popular from films, is becoming widely famous for another reason: they are being designed for worldwide success. Jonathan Burston, a professor in the Department of Information and Media Studies at the University of Western Ontario who specializes in music, media, globalization, and "social uses of spectacle in contemporary life," wrote an article entitled "Recombinant Broadway" that discusses the changes that have occurred in the field of theater, particularly the changing origins of shows and the methods in which these shows are

Establishing author's credentials is important to demonstrate his ethos and the writer's ethos.

Blue = content issues, **Red = format issues**

reproduced on a global scale ("Faculty Member"). Starting in the early 1980s, when the theater industry was struggling, Andrew Lloyd Webber and Cameron Mackintosh discovered a way to take the theater industry from a risky endeavor and make it into a largely profitable business. Their new musical *Cats* had become a smashing success on Broadway in London's West End and on tours of both North America and Europe, but they realized that the demand to see the show was greater than what they were meeting. They decided to create permanent productions in "emerging major markets like Hamburg, Tokyo, and Toronto" (Burston, "Recombinant" 161) for as long as they were attracting a sufficient audience. The decisive factor about these productions that changed theater forever is that "Lloyd Webber and Mackintosh also concluded that each show should look, feel, and sound *exactly* like the originating production . . . if the producers were to maximize the new levels of profitability" (Burston, "Recombinant" 161). Thus, the megamusical, designed for mega-profits by stifling originality, was born.

Quotation integrated into writer's sentence

Ellipsis points signal part of quoted material omitted

Today, productions of shows that are running in different parts of the world are exactly the same, "based upon a *template* of an original production whose cast and creative team have already completed all the exciting collaborative work of turning written page into breathing performance" (Burston, "Recombinant" 166). The actors and musicians now have greater

Blue = content issues, **Red = format issues**

Suchan 9

First source cited locates the direct quotation. Sources following provide additional evidence for persistence of these ideas.

job security, but they complain about having to work "McTheater jobs," where they are more "acting machines" and less artists (Burston, "Recombinant" 162; also Burston, "Spectacle"; Russell). Have the global audiences' expectations become such that actors can compare their profession to that of a fast-food worker? Sadly, this has become a trending phenomenon in the theater worldwide.

Academic writing can use the first person "I," depending on audience expectation.

I know from experience that people going to a show for a repeat viewing expect the performance to be identical to the first time that they went. When I saw the show Wicked for the first time, I was enraptured by the characters and the story, and I was blown away by the sincerity of the actress playing the main character, Elphaba. When I saw Wicked for the fifth time, I did not enjoy the performance as much. The new leading actress was portraying the character of Elphaba with slightly different emotional motives than I was used to, and these emotions did not fit in with the version of the story, and the character within it, that I had seen four times previously. A person seeing the show for the first time would not have noticed the nuances, but for me the performance wasn't magical. This is not to say that free expression in the theater is a bad thing and that it is good that globalization is making it rare. The point of this anecdote is to illustrate that in order for this actress to make the show feel like her own, she had to change the traits of her character. Originality

Writer builds her credibility as a theatergoer.

Writer's personal experience as primary-source evidence, supported by secondary sources

Blue = content issues, **Red = format issues**

in the theater is getting so rare that it takes theater lovers by surprise.

There is some originality left in the theater, and when it is witnessed it is truly wonderful. Every year there are shows created that are brilliantly pure and unique, but they often go unnoticed. These shows are either not designed for widespread public resonance, or they are simply overshadowed by the unoriginal names lighting up marquees around the world. One such show is *Next to Normal*, which is a mental whirlwind of a show, the likes of which has never been experienced on Broadway before, but it did not achieve lasting success because it did not fit into the category of "megamusical." Even a Pulitzer Prize could not save this theatrical masterpiece.

Having established a pattern of re-creation in the theater, the writer moves to offer examples of shows that seek to defy this trend.

There are also shows that are written in such a way as to inspire creativity, even though they are not new. *Godspell* is an example of a show that exemplifies the joy that is live theater. I was the stage manager when my high school performed this show. The script contains the lines and songs, but ultimately it is up to the cast to decide what the acting in the show will be like. Every parable is performed in a new way by the cast members, who even use their own names on stage. *Godspell* recently reopened on Broadway, and I had the privilege to attend one of the preview showings. The show had all the same stories and songs as what we had performed at school, but it was a

Suchan 11

completely different experience. It was incredible to experience the magic that a small group of people can create on a stage. It was wonderful to see the personalities of the characters and slightly different interpretations of the plot, but this show is a rare exception when it ought to be, and used to be, the rule. Broadway used to be about new drama, but now "for every daring producer risking an *In the Heights* there are two *Legally Blondes* being mounted by corporate suits. All these adaptations are crowding out the authentically *Broadway* Broadway" (Burston, "Recombinant" 166). The Broadway of old is slowly dying to make way for the profitable and unoriginal reproductions that globalization demands.

Writer emphasizes that this kind of show is an exception, further reinforcing her claim.

The magic of theater still exists, but the magic is often not the invention of the actors performing. The story they are acting out is clichéd and the characters are hackneyed. Shakespeare helped the theater become a globally recognized art form and kept it prevalent for many years, but he also damaged theater by starting the trend of reusing ideas to create new shows. The business of Broadway, and its counterparts worldwide, is booming for both the producers and the actors, with profits that were unimaginable several decades ago. Nevertheless, many actors resist the death of creativity and try to keep the originality of the theater alive in our new, globalized world.

Narrow summary sentence restates the writer's claim that originality is dead.

Blue = content issues, **Red = format issues**

1"

Suchan 12

Works Cited

"Arthur Miller Quotes." *BrainyQuote*, 2016, www.brainyquote.com/quotes/authors/a/arthur_miller.html.

Breaker, Daniel. "Daniel Breaker on Fatherhood, Donkey-hood (in *Shrek*), and His Strange New Movie." Interview by Melissa Rose Bernardo. *Broadway.com*, 27 July 2009, www.broadway.com/buzz/133518/daniel-breaker-on-fatherhood-donkey-hood-in-shrek-and-his-strange-new-movie/.

Burston, Jonathan. "Recombinant Broadway." *Continuum: Journal of Media and Cultural Studies*, vol. 23, no. 2, 2009, pp. 159-69. *Academic Search Premier*, doi:10.1080/10304310802710504.

---. "Spectacle, Synergy, and Megamusicals: The Global Industrialisation of Live Theatrical Production." *Media Organisations in Society*, edited by James Curran, Arnold, 2000, pp. 69-81.

"Faculty Member Profile: Jonathan Burston." *Faculty of Information and Media Studies at the University of Western Ontario*, U of Western Ontario, 2016, www.fims.uwo.ca/people/profiles/Jonathan_Burston.html.

Fhloinn, Bairbre Ní. "From Medieval Literature to Missiles: Aspects of ATU 901 in the Twenty-First Century." *Fabula*, vol. 51, no. 3/4, 2010, pp. 187-200. *Academic Search Premier*, doi:10.1515/FABL.2010.019.

Friedman, Thomas L. *The Lexus and the Olive Tree*. Doubleday, 1999.

No author named; entry begins with Web page title

Interview posted on Web site

Two works by same author cited; entries listed by author and then alphabetically by title.

Three hyphens used instead of author's name for second work by same author.

Scholarly journal article accessed in online database

Editor of book named after title.

Sponsor of Web site, date site last updated

Blue = content issues, **Red = format issues**

Suchan 13

Moore, Michael. "Why Doesn't GM Sell Crack?" *The Composition of Everyday Life: A Guide to Writing*, edited by John Mauk and John Metz, 3rd ed., Cengage Learning, 2010, pp. 410-11.

Russell, Susan. "The Performance of Discipline on Broadway." *Studies in Musical Theatre*, vol. 1, no. 1, 2007, pp. 97-108.

Page range for essay in anthology

Journal title, volume and issue numbers listed

Blue = content issues, **Red = format issues**

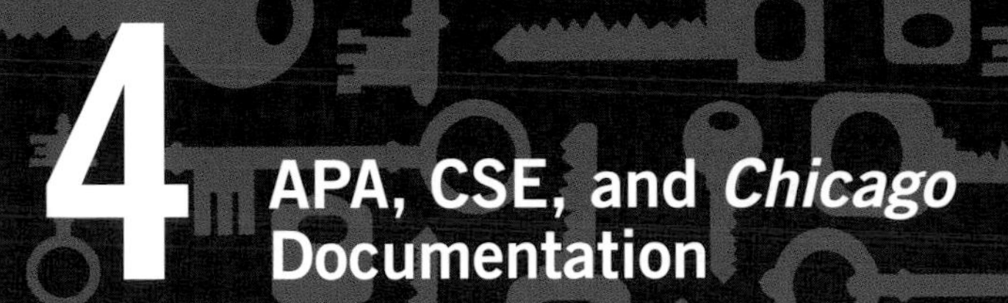

4 APA, CSE, and *Chicago* Documentation

WRITING IN YOUR CAREER

The IT Professional, the Writer

istockphoto.com/Ryan Lane

IT (information technology) professionals don't usually think of themselves as writers, but Gregory Kagan knew that documentation was essential for minimizing troubleshooting time and upgrading information systems. Network documentation such as IP addresses and server documentation show which switch ports connect to what rooms or who needs to be notified (mainly through e-mail) when you need to trace a problem or support a project. The documentation you do in your papers in college does not look like the documentation Kagan works with in his work environment (below), but its purpose is the same. A company's IT policy specifies how documentation is recorded, just as the American Psychological Association or the Modern Language Association specifies how to document an academic report. An organized record provides stability when systems—or papers—need to be modified or rebuilt.

TSAT Project Tasks and Issues

Production Infrastructure outstanding issues

- AD authentication issues utilizing or AD Admin accounts (Resolved)
  Current ticket with TAT support (ISS03422981, 3-Medium SupID:411239). We have narrowed down the problem to the location of the admin accounts within AD.
- What is the impact to the test environment when production is established?
  Is it going to be possible to separate test from production for full testing including policy manager? Segregate test environment from production Wan. Close ports 8448, 5282, 7327.

Production Infrastructure Tasks

- Production TSAT infrastructure installation begins February 2nd
  1. Install Master Transmitter (Complete 2/2/16)
  2. Install CMS Console (Complete 2/2/16)
  3. Configure all internal TSAT products. (Complete 2/8/16)
  4. Install Mirror Transmitter (Nevada) (Complete 2/8/16)
- TSAT production servers
  1. Master Transmitter Server: UTMSA377
  2. CMS console server: UTMSA811
  3. TSAT database server : UTSQL425
  4. Nevada Mirror Transmitter: UTMSA921

4 APA, CSE, and *Chicago* Documentation

APA AT-A-GLANCE INDEX

CSE AT-A-GLANCE INDEX

CHICAGO AT-A-GLANCE INDEX

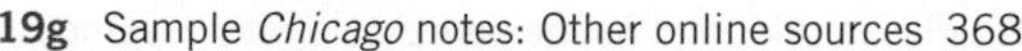

APA AT-A-GLANCE: INDEX OF APA STYLE FEATURES

Part 4 covers documentation styles other than the MLA system. Chapters 14 and 15 focus on the style recommended for the social sciences and some sciences by the *Publication Manual of the American Psychological Association*, 6th edition (Washington, DC: Amer. Psychological Assn., 2010), and on the APA Web site. A student's paper written in APA style is in chapter 16. Chapter 17 describes the citation-sequence and the citation-name styles, two of three documentation styles recommended for all natural and applied sciences by the Council of Science Editors (CSE) in *Scientific Style and Format: The CSE Manual for Authors, Editors, and Publishers*, 8th edition (Chicago: U of Chicago P, 2014). Chapter 18 shows an excerpt from a student's CSE research paper in the citation-sequence style. Chapter 19 illustrates the endnote and footnote style and discusses the bibliography format recommended in *The Chicago Manual of Style*, 16th edition (Chicago: U of Chicago P, 2010), for writing in the humanities, a style sometimes used as an alternative to MLA style. Chapter 20 presents a student's paper with endnotes and bibliography in *Chicago* style. The order of categories in which the citation examples for each style are discussed follows the order of categories in its respective style manual.

MindTap®

Understand the goals of this part, and complete a warm-up activity.

14 Citing Sources in Your Paper, APA Style

MindTap®
Read, highlight, and take notes online.

APA style for documenting and formatting publications, which is described in the *Publication Manual of the American Psychological Association*, 6th edition (2010), is used in the social sciences—psychology, sociology, anthropology, education, management, business, economics, criminal justice, ethnic studies, women's and gender studies, and political science—as well as in geography, communications, nursing, allied health, and other medical disciplines. In these fields, new research results in new theories and interpretations of materials that update and replace earlier ones. Therefore, it is essential for readers to know the publication date of a source when it is introduced so that they can place the information in the continuum of research or views on an issue necessary to understand the writer's analysis or argument.

In order to let readers know when the source's research or theories were presented, APA uses an author-date system. Each time the source is mentioned, the date is given either immediately after the author's name in the text or with the author's name in parentheses (along with any page number) after quoted or paraphrased material. Readers can then refer to an alphabetical list of sources, the References, at the end of the paper for full source information. The prominent placement and repetition of the date in each source citation underscores the need for readers to be aware of the timeliness and relevance of the source's information as they follow the author's presentation.

APA style uses the past or past perfect verb tenses for introducing quoted material: "Smith (2012) reported," "Previous studies have demonstrated." It uses the present tense only when discussing results ("This study illustrates") or generally accepted facts ("Scientists acknowledge"). The passive voice is often used, since the results of a study or experiment are important, whereas the names of the lab assistants who conducted it, for example, are not ("An elevated blood pressure reading was noted for the majority of subjects").

14a Basic features of APA style

KEY POINTS

How to Cite and List Sources in APA Style

1. **In the text of your paper**, include at least two pieces of information each time you cite a source:
   - the last name(s) of the author (or authors) or first words of the title if no author's name is available
   - the year of publication or posting online

Also give the page number(s) (using the abbreviation *p.* or *pp.*) for a quotation, summary, or paraphrase.

2. **At the end of your paper**, on a new numbered page, include a list with the title *References* (centered and not in italics or quotation marks). The list should be double-spaced and arranged alphabetically by authors' last names, followed by the initials of first and the other names (also last name first and with initials), the date in parentheses, and other bibliographical information. See sections 15c–15h for fifty-six sample entries.

Illustrations of APA Style's Basic Features

Citation in Text	Entry in List of References
Print journal article, author's name in text introduces comment [Page number included for quotation]	
In their study Giordano and Giordano (2011) found that despite their profession's concerns about privacy and security, "an overwhelming majority of health students prefer to get their information online" (p. 80).	Giordano, C., & Giordano, C. (2011). Health professions students' use of social media. *Journal of Allied Health, 40*(2), 78–81.

(Continued)

Citation in Text	Entry in List of References
Print journal article, citation in parentheses [Page number included for quotation]	
Although such tools may be useful for recruiting and informing students, "universities may be hesitant to adopt social media due to fear of privacy, security, and inability to measure success and usage with great precision" (Giordano & Giordano, 2011, p. 80).	Giordano, C., & Giordano, C. (2011). Health professions students' use of social media. *Journal of Allied Health, 40*(2), 78–81.
Print book, author and year in your text [Page number included for quotation]	
According to Charles Emmerson (2010), "as the natural environment of the north begins to change out of all recognition, the idea of the Arctic as an impenetrable physical barrier will be overturned" (p. 158).	Emmerson, C. (2010). *The future history of the Arctic.* New York, NY: Public Affairs Press.
Article on a Web site, author paraphrased [no page or paragraph numbers for online source]	
Amanda Enayati (2012) speculates that people may not want to admit that in uncertain times they are biased against creative ideas and instead prefer known procedures and solutions.	Enayati, A. (2012). Is there a bias against creativity? Retrieved from http://www.cnn.com/2012/03/28/health/enayati-uncertainty/index.html?hpt=he_bn2

Citation in Text	Entry in List of References
Journal article with digital object identifier (DOI) in an online database, parenthetical citation	
Research has shown that cross-cultural identification does not begin before eight years of age (Sousa, Neto, & Mullet, 2005).	Sousa, R. M., Neto, F., & Mullet, E. (2005). Can music change ethnic attitudes among children? *Psychology of Music*, *33*(3), 304–316. doi:10.1177/0305735605053735
[See the Key Points box in 15c, pp. 305–306, for more on DOIs, and see the Key Points box in 15a, p. 302, for when to include an issue number.]	

14b How to cite sources (author/date) in your paper

CITING AN AUTHOR OR AUTHORS (APA)

A. Author quoted and named in your text If you mention the author's name in your own text, include the year in parentheses directly after the author's name. Put any page number in parentheses after a quotation or paraphrase; end with a period.

author year

> Martinot (2010) maintains that whenever society seems to be minimizing racism, "it comes back wearing different language, speaking an up-to-date lingo, while creating more of the 'same old' effects" (p. 2).

See 15d, item 17, and Source Shot 11 (pp. 316–317) for this work in a reference list.

B. Author cited in parentheses If you do not name the author in your own text (perhaps because you have referred to the author previously), include both the name and the year, separated by a comma, in parentheses.

> We can only comprehend the full impact of infectious diseases by viewing them in the contexts of culture and history (Reagan, 2010).

author comma year

C. Author quoted or paraphrased If you use a direct quotation or a paraphrase, follow it with parentheses containing the author's name and the date (if not already given in the text, as in item A) and the abbreviation

APA American Psychological Association

p. or *pp.*, a space, and the page number(s). Use commas to separate items within the parentheses, and end the sentence with a period.

> It is important to note that "naming a disease is an essential component of diagnosis and treatment" (Reagan, 2010, p. 25).
>
> comma comma page number

D. A long (block) quotation If you quote more than forty words of prose, do not enclose the quotation in quotation marks. Start the quotation on a new line, and indent the whole quotation half an inch from the left margin. If there are other paragraphs within the block quotation, indent the first line of each paragraph an additional one-half inch. Double-space the quotation. Any necessary parenthetical citation should come after the final period of the quotation. See 10c for more information on quoting long passages.

E. A work with more than one author

Two authors For a work by two authors, name both in the order in which their names appear on the work, and give the year of publication every time that the authors are cited in your text. Use the word *and* between the names for a reference made in your text. Within parentheses, use an ampersand (&) between the names in place of *and*.

> the word *and* in your text
>
> Kanazawa and Still (2000) in their analysis of a large set of data show that the statistical likelihood of being divorced increases if one is male and a secondary school teacher or college professor.
>
> Analysis of a large set of data shows that the statistical likelihood of being divorced increases if one is male and a secondary school teacher or college professor (Kanazawa & Still, 2000).
>
> ampersand in parentheses

See 15c, item 1, for a work by two authors in a reference list.

Three to five authors Identify all authors the first time you mention the work in either your running text or in a parenthetical citation.

> Baumol, Litan, and Schramm (2007) posit the existence of several types of capitalist economies around the world.

In subsequent in-text or parenthetical citations, use the last name of the first author and *et al.* (*et alii*—Latin for "and others") in place of the other names.

> In the United States, the dominant type of capitalism, called "entrepreneurial capitalism," shows significant differences from

> the capitalism in Japan and Europe, which tends to avoid "radical entrepreneurship" (Baumol et al., 2007, p. viii).

See 15d, item 18, for this work in a list of references.

Six or more authors Cite the name of only the first author, followed by *et al.*, for all citations in your text and for all parenthetical citations. However, in your reference list, include the names of up to seven authors. For eight or more authors, list the first six and use ellipsis dots to indicate additional authors; end with the name of the last author. See 15c, item 3, for a reference list entry for more than seven authors.

F. More than one work within same parentheses List the sources by author in alphabetical order as they appear in the list of references (including those that shorten to *et al.*), separated by semicolons. List two or more works by the same author chronologically (earliest source first); give the author's name only once. See item G for citing multiple works by the same author published in the same year.

> Criticisms of large-scale educational testing are anything but new. They have been appearing repeatedly for many years (Crouse & Trusheim, 1988; Nairn, 1978, 1980; Perelman, 2007; Raimes, 1990a, 1990b; Sacks, 2003).

G. Author with more than one work published in the same year In a parenthetical reference, after the author's name, identify each work with a lowercase letter after the year: (Schell, 2007a, 2007b). The letters are assigned in the reference list, where the works are arranged alphabetically by their titles after the author's name and the year (repeated in each entry). Separate the dates with commas. See 15b for how to order such entries in the list of references.

H. Author of work in an edited anthology In your text, refer to the author of the work, not to the editor of the anthology (however, include information about the anthology in your list of references). The essay in the following example is in an anthology of writing about identifying and treating psychiatric problems in general medical environments.

> Geoffrey Lloyd (2007) notes that *post-traumatic stress disorder* (PTSD) is usually defined as "a delayed and/or protracted response to a stressful event or situation of a threatening or catastrophic nature" (p. 73).

In the reference list entry, also include details about the anthology, including its editors (see 15d, item 23, to see how to cite this source).

I. Author's work cited in another source (secondary source) APA advises you to quote primary sources whenever possible. If you do use a secondary source, in your sentence name the author whom you are quoting. After the quoted or paraphrased material, put in parentheses the words *as cited in,* the name of the author of the work in which you found the material (the secondary source), the year, and the page number. List that secondary source in your list of references. In the following example, *Martinot* will appear in the list of references with details of the source; *Goldberg* will not.

> David Goldberg calls this phenomenon the "inherently homogenizing logic of institutions" (as cited in Martinot, 2010, p. 59).

J. Entire work or an idea in a work Use only an author and the year to refer to a complete work. For a paraphrase or a comment on a specific idea, a page number is not required but is recommended.

> Leslie Reagan (2010) recounts the 1960s German measles epidemic to illustrate the extent of society's fear of disability—a fear that is still evident today.

K. Two authors with the same last name Include the authors' initials, even if the publication dates of their works differ, in all citations.

> F. Smith (2011) first described a writer as playing the two competitive roles of author and secretary.

For the order of entries of such works in the list of references, see 15b.

L. Specific part of a source After listing the author and year within parentheses, cite any specific relevant part of the source such as page number, chapter, section, table, or figure. Abbreviate *page* or *pages* (*p.* or *pp.*) but not *Chapter* (capitalizing the first letter). For citing electronic sources that do not have page numbers, see item P on pages 297–298.

> (Cutler, 2011, Introduction)
>
> (Robinson, 2012, Chapter 5)

M. Multivolume work In your citation, give the publication date of the volume you are citing: (Einstein, 1987). If you refer to more than one volume, give inclusive dates for all the volumes you cite: (Einstein, 1998–2004). See 15d, item 28, for how to list this work in your reference list.

CITING A WORK WITH NO INDIVIDUAL AUTHOR NAMED (APA)

N. No author named If a print or Web source has no named individual or organization as author, use the first few words of the title in your text (capitalizing major words). Within the body of the paper (including parenthetical citations), put quotation marks around the title of an article, chapter, or Web page; italicize the title of a book, report, or brochure.

> Many Hurricane Katrina survivors were located to trailers whose materials caused health problems from breathing disorders to cancer (*World Almanac*, 2009, p. 55).

> *Narcolepsy* is defined as "a disabling sleep disorder that mixes the nervous system's messages about when to sleep and when to be awake" ("Narcolepsy," 2011).

See 15d, item 29, and 15f, item 42, for how to list these sources.

O. Work by a corporation, association, government agency, study group, or organization If the first citation is an in-text reference, use the organization's full name and immediately following put in parentheses the abbreviation, a comma, and the year; in subsequent in-text references, just use the abbreviation and the year.

first text mention: full name with abbreviation and year in parentheses

> In its annual survey of college costs, the College Board (CB, 2015) gives examples of rapid increases. In public 4-year colleges, in particular, tuition and fees increased 40% over the last ten years.

In the first parenthetical citation, give the organization's full name, the abbreviation in brackets, a comma, and the year. In subsequent parenthetical citations, just give the abbreviation and year.

> In public 4-year colleges, tuition and fees increased 40% in over the past ten years (College Board [CB], 2015).

first parenthetical citation: full name, abbreviation in brackets, comma, year

Section 15d, item 30, shows how to list this work.

CITING ONLINE VISUAL, MULTIMEDIA, AND MISCELLANEOUS SOURCES (APA)

P. Internet source

Web page or article Give the author's name, if it is available, or a short form of the title, followed by the year of electronic publication or update. In your text, put titles of Web pages in quotation marks as you would an article title. Use *n.d.* if no date is given. Give any page numbers (from the PDF, if it is available in portable document format, which is used for photographed print works available online) or paragraph numbers that you see on the screen (using the abbreviation *para.*). For a section of text you quote, paraphrase, or comment on in a source with no page or paragraph numbers visible on the screen, give any available section heading or a shortened title, and indicate the paragraph within the section (in this case, you would determine the paragraph's number): (Conclusion section, para. 2).

Entire Web site When citing an entire Web site rather than a specific document or page on the site, name only the Web site in your text (not in italics), and give the Web address (URL) in parentheses after the cited material. Do not list the Web site in your reference list.

> The Arthritis Foundation website contains much valuable information about treatments for the disease (http://www.arthritis.org).

E-mail messages Be wary of citing e-mail messages (personal, bulletin board, discussion list, or Usenet group) because they are not peer-reviewed or easily retrievable. If you need to refer to an e-mail message, cite from an archived list whenever possible (see the example in 15f, item 44); otherwise, cite the message in your text as a personal communication (see item R), but do not include it in your list of references.

Q. Visual, multimedia, or nonprint source For a film, television or radio broadcast, podcast, MP3 file, video recording, live performance, map, photo, artwork, or other static object or nonprint source, include in your citation the name of the originator or main contributor (such as the creator, writer, narrator, director, performer, artist, or producer), along with the year of production.

> An Al Jazeera video highlights the plight of the African rhino (Phillips, 2010).

R. Personal communication (telephone conversation, unarchived letter, unpublished interview, e-mail, or unarchived electronic discussion group) Cite only sources that have scholarly content. Mention these sources only in your paper with the label *personal communication* and the date in parentheses; do not include them in your list of references. Give the last name and initial(s) of the author of the communication and the complete date of posting, publication, or occurrence.

> According to V. Sand, former executive director of the Atwater Kent Museum of Philadelphia, "Museums engage our spirit, help us

> understand the natural world, and frame our identities" (personal communication, February 7, 2012).

For including archived sources in the list of references, see 15f, item 44.

S. A classical or religious work If the date of publication of a classical work is not known, cite the year of translation (preceded by *trans.*) or the year of the version you used (followed by *version*): (Plato, trans. 1965). You do not need a reference list entry for major classical works such as ancient Roman and Greek works or religious works such as the Bible or the Qu'ran. Parts of these works are numbered similarly in all editions, so just give information about book, chapter, verse, and line numbers in your text, and identify the version you used in your first citation: Gen. 35: 1–4 (Revised Standard Version).

14c Notes, tables, and figures (APA)

Content notes In APA style, you can use content notes to amplify or supplement information in your text. For example, you might want to indicate where additional material can be found online. Number notes consecutively throughout the paper with superscript Arabic numerals. Footnotes should be double-spaced and placed at the bottom of the page where the material is discussed. Alternately, you can attach a separate page containing your numbered notes after the list of references and title it *Footnotes* (centered). Use notes sparingly and only if they are essential to your analysis; include all important information in your text, not in footnotes.

Tables and figures APA style for manuscripts submitted for publication asks that all tables and figures be placed on separate pages at the end of the paper, after the references and any notes. However, college instructors may prefer that you insert tables and figures within your paper, as shown on pages 329–339 in the sample research paper in chapter 16. Follow your instructor's directions about placement of tables and figures.

Number all tables and figures consecutively with labels containing Arabic numbers (Table 1, Figure 2) in the order in which they appear in your paper. If you include them within the paper, place them close to their discussion in the text.

For tables, include a label (Table 1), followed by a brief title in italics (*Increases in Student Enrollment 2010–2015*) and any explanatory information, such as source information (detailed in "Citing copyrighted material," below).

For graphs, charts, maps, diagrams, drawings, photographs, or other visual elements known as figures, place a caption below the visual. Begin with the numbered label (*Figure 1*) in italics, followed by a period. Then, on the same line, give a brief description (not in italics) of the figure that functions as its title; end with a period. If you did not create the figure yourself, follow with any source information (beginning with the word *From*, as in the sample student paper figure captions in Chapter 16 on pp. 336–337).

Citing copyrighted material When you reproduce a copyrighted table or figure in your paper, you must give complete source details in a specific format in your table notes or figure caption (see examples on pp. 336–337). Notice that this format differs from the one for a citation in a reference list. You can find the copyright information under the original table or figure in your source. If you want to publish your paper or post it online using copyrighted material, you will have to obtain written permission to use it and will have to add these words after the copyright information: *Reprinted* [or *Adapted*] *with permission.*

14d Sections and their headings (APA)

APA-style papers begin with a separate title page; the Abstract and References are also on separate pages, and their titles are centered but not boldfaced. Major headings within the main text, such as Review of the Literature, Experiment, Results, or Conclusion, should be centered and boldfaced. The next level of subheading should be boldfaced and flush left. A third level should be bold, indented to begin a new paragraph, and followed by a period. See chapter 16 for a student's research paper in APA style.

15 APA List of References

15a How to set up an APA reference list

The sixth edition of the APA *Publication Manual* (2010) and the association's Web site www.apastyle.org provide guidelines for submitting professional papers for publication, and many instructors ask students to follow those guidelines to prepare them for advanced work. The following section explains and illustrates APA guidelines for reference list entries. The APA Web site also provides additional citation examples, periodic updates, and tips. Check with your instructor, however, for any specific course requirements for preparation of the paper and the reference list.

KEY POINTS

Guidelines for the APA List of References

- **What to list** List only the works you cited (quoted, summarized, paraphrased, or commented on) in the text of your paper, not every source you examined.
- **Format** Start the list on a new numbered page after the last page of the text of your paper. Center the heading *References,* without quotation marks; not boldfaced, underlined, or italicized; and not followed by a period. Double-space throughout the list, with no additional space between entries.
- **Indentation** Use hanging indents. Begin the first line of each entry at the left margin; indent subsequent lines one-half inch.
- **How to list authors and works** List the works alphabetically by the last names of primary authors or by the name of a corporation or organization that acts as the author. Do not number the entries. Begin each entry with the first author's name, last name first, followed by an initial or initials. Give any additional authors' names after the first in the same inverted form, separated by commas (see 15b and 15c, item 3, for more than seven authors). Connect the last two names with an ampersand (&) instead of the word *and.* List works with no author by title, alphabetized by the first main word.
- **Date** Put the year in parentheses after the authors' names; follow with a period. For magazines, newspapers, and newsletters, also add the month and day (if available) after a comma; do not abbreviate the names of the months: (2012, January 8).
- **Periods** Use a period and one space to separate the main parts of each entry.
- **Titles and capitals** In titles of books, reports, articles, Web documents, and Web pages, capitalize *only* the first word of the title and of any subtitle and any proper nouns or adjectives. For journals, magazines, newspapers, and newsletters, give the periodical title in full, using uppercase and lowercase letters.

(Continued)

(Continued)

- **Titles and italics** Italicize the titles of books, reports, and documents, but do not italicize or use quotation marks around the titles of articles, chapters, or Web pages (however, if the title quotes certain words, as in 15c, item 5, put quotation marks around them). Italicize the titles of newspapers (including the word *The*), newsletters, journals, and magazines. Identify a specific format in square brackets immediately after the title, followed by a period. Do not italicize the format, and capitalize only the first word: [Brochure], [Letter to the editor], [Editorial], [Audio file].
- **Volume and issue numbers** For journals and magazines, also italicize the comma following the title and the volume number (not preceded by *Vol.*), but not the issue number contained next in parentheses (with no space between volume and issue numbers): *Wired, 17*(2). For more information on volume and issue numbers, see 15c, item 1.
- **Page numbers** Give inclusive page numbers for print and PDF articles (portable document format, which is used for photographed print works available online) and for sections of books, repeating all digits and separating the numbers with an en dash: 251–259. Use the abbreviation *p.* or *pp.* only for newspaper articles and sections of books (such as chapters or anthologized short works).
- **Online sources** Give as much information as you would for a print source, with the addition of a DOI or URL to enable readers to find the same source. Use a DOI (digital object identifier)—a permanent identification number that enables easy retrieval—rather than a URL if one is available. See the Key Points box on pages 305–306 for more information on DOIs and URLs. Split a DOI or URL across lines only before a punctuation mark such as a period or a slash (except for the double slash that follows *http:*). Do not underline the URL as a hyperlink unless you are posting the paper online, and do not put a period after a DOI or URL, which will be the last item in the entry. Provide page numbers only for documents accessed as PDF files. Instead, use names of sections for articles written for online use (in HTML): Introduction. See 15f for more on listing online sources.

15b How to list authors in the APA reference list

Name of author(s) Put the last name first, followed by a comma and then the initials.

Gould, S. J.

Reverse the names of all authors listed, except the editors of an anthology or a reference work, and separate them with commas. Use an ampersand (&), not the word *and*, before the last author's name (15c, Source Shot 8 on pp. 308–309). For eight or more authors, give the reversed names of the first six, then use three ellipsis dots and add the name of the last author (as in the example in 15c, item 3).

Alphabetical order Alphabetize letter by letter. Treat *Mac* and *Mc*, literally, by letter.

MacKay, M. D'Agostino, S.
McCarthy, T. De Cesare, P.
McKay, K. DeCurtis, A.

A shorter name precedes a longer name beginning with the same letters, whatever the first initial: *Black, T.* precedes *Blackman, R.*

For a work with no known author, list it by the first word in the title other than *A*, *An*, or *The*. Alphabetize numerals according to their spelling: 5 (*Five*) precedes 2 (*Two*).

Organization or group as author If the author is an organization, corporation, agency, group, or institution, give its official name, alphabetized by the first important word (see 15d, item 30). Use complete names, not abbreviations.

No author named If no author or group is named, alphabetize by the first main word of the title (15d, item 29).

Several works by the same author List the author's name in each entry. Arrange entries chronologically by year of publication from past to present. Entries published in the same year should be arranged alphabetically by title and distinguished with lowercase letters after the date (*a*, *b*, and so on). Note that entries for one author precede entries listing the same author with coauthors.

Goleman, D. (1996a, July 16). Forget money; nothing can buy happiness, some researchers say. *The New York Times*, p. C1.

APA American Psychological Association

Goleman, D. (1996b). *Vital lies, simple truths*. New York, NY: Simon & Schuster.

Goleman, D. (2013). *Focus: The Hidden Driver of Excellence.* New York, NY: HarperCollins.

Goleman, D., Boyatzis, R. E., & McKee, A. (2004). *Primal leadership: Learning to lead with emotional intelligence*. Cambridge, MA: Harvard Business School Press.

Authors with the same last name List the authors alphabetically by their first initial: Smith, A. precedes Smith, F.

15c Sample APA listings: Articles in print and online periodicals with or without a DOI

Periodicals—scholarly journals, magazines, newspapers, and newsletters—are published on a regularly scheduled basis. After the author and year, give the periodical article title. Do not put quotation marks around the title, and capitalize only the first letter of the first word of the title and of any subtitle and proper nouns or adjectives. After the article title, include the italicized periodical name in uppercase and lowercase letters. Items 1–16 describe the rest of the information needed to cite articles in the various types of periodicals.

1. Article in a print scholarly journal For a scholarly journal article, begin with the authors' names, reversed and connected with an ampersand (for more than two authors, see 15b; for more than seven authors, see 15c, item 3). Then give the date (in parentheses), article title, and journal title; add a comma, the volume number, and another comma (all italicized); and then give the inclusive page numbers, repeating all digits and separating the numbers with an en dash (–). Include the issue number only if each issue is paged separately (each issue begins with page 1). Put the issue number (not in italics) in parentheses immediately after the volume number, with no space between them, as in the following example. Then add a comma and the inclusive page numbers, repeating all digits. Do not use *p.* or *pp.* with page numbers.

Giordano, C., & Giordano, C. (2011). Health professions students' use of social media. *Journal of Allied Health, 40*(2), 78–81.

2. Article with a DOI in an online scholarly journal See Source Shot 8 on pages 308–309 for how to locate and cite an article with a DOI found in an online scholarly journal.

KEY POINTS

DOIs and URLs: Locating and Citing Electronic Sources

A DOI (digital object identifier) or URL (uniform resource locator) is listed at the end of a citation for an online source to enable readers to access the same source. Since a URL, a Web address on the Internet, can easily be changed or deleted, resulting in an unreliable link, APA recommends using a DOI, a permanent identification number for a source as published in any medium, rather than a URL if one is available. The DOI for the source will never change, even if its URL does. APA advises listing an available DOI for print as well as electronic sources.

How a DOI Works

The publisher assigns a permanent DOI number to a published article or other work when it is made available electronically. The DOI both identifies the content and provides a link for readers to locate the article on the Internet through registration services such as *CrossRef* (www.crossref.org) or the DOI resolver at www.doi.org. If you give a DOI in your citation, readers can then easily turn the DOI string into a link by going to CrossRef or appending the string to dx.doi.org to access the work. For example, appending the DOI in the citation in Source Shot 9 (pp. 310–311) so that it becomes dx.doi .org/10.1080/03075079.2014.930122 would take readers directly to a page on the Web site of the journal *Studies in Higher Education* containing the article's abstract; they could then either purchase the full text in PDF format there or access the article free by logging into a library database.

The DOI is usually found on the first page of an online journal article near the copyright notice (see Source Shot 8, pp. 308–309) or on the citation page for the article in a library subscription database (see Source Shot 9). A DOI in a database listing or in an electronic document reference may also function as a live direct link to the article. However, the DOI may be lurking behind a button labeled *CrossRef, Article, PubMed,* or the name of a supplier of full-text articles (see item 4). Remember to search the site fully for the DOI.

Listing a DOI or URL

1. Copy and paste a DOI or URL from its source to be sure it is accurate. Many can be long and complex.

(Continued)

(Continued)

2. When a DOI is given, no additional retrieval information is necessary.
3. In your reference list entry, add the DOI after the period following the inclusive page numbers. Write *doi* (lowercase) and add a colon (not followed by a space) and the DOI numbers.
4. If the article has no DOI, list the URL of the home page of the journal. After the inclusive page numbers, write *Retrieved from* and add the URL. Write *Available from* when a URL does not provide the actual source but instead tells how to retrieve it.
5. Split a DOI or URL across lines only before a slash, a period, or other punctuation mark (exception: split after double slashes in *http://*). Do not add a hyphen at the end of the first split line.
6. Do not italicize or underline a DOI or URL, which will be the last item in your reference list entry, and do not follow it with a period. (Underline URLs as hyperlinks only if you are posting your paper online.)

3. Journal article with DOI, more than seven authors If a scholarly journal article has more than seven authors, list the first six (last name, comma, initials), separated by commas. Insert three ellipsis dots, and add the last author's name.

Stoloff, M., McCarthy, M., Keller, L., Varfolomeeva, V., Lynch, J., Makara, K.... Smiley, W. (2010). The undergraduate psychology major: An examination of structure and sequence. *Teaching of Psychology, 37*(1), 4–15. doi:10.1080 /00986280903426274

4. Journal article with DOI in an online database Universities and libraries subscribe to large searchable databases of print publications, such as Gale *InfoTrac*, EBSCO *Academic Search Premier, ERIC, LexisNexis*, ProQuest *PsycINFO*, and WilsonWeb *Education Full Text*, providing access to full-text articles and abstracts. Cite a journal article in an online database the same way that you would cite one found in an online journal (see item 2), listing page numbers if the article is in PDF format. After the publication information, give the DOI for electronic retrieval. Do not give the name of the database. Source Shot 9, pages 310–311, shows the relevant part of the *Academic Search Complete* database citation page that provides information about the journal article needed to create the reference list entry on the opposite page.

5. Article with no DOI in an online-only journal The first article below is published in an online journal with no print version. However, the journal provides downloadable PDF versions of articles, so the inclusive page range is cited. If the article does not have a DOI and a PDF is not available, at the end of the citation, write *Retrieved from* and give the URL of the home page of the journal as in the second example below. Do not list your date of access.

Boudiny, K., & Mortelmans, D. (2011). A critical perspective: Towards a broader understanding of "active ageing." *E-Journal of Applied Psychology, 7*(1), 8–14. Retrieved from http://ojs.lib.swin.edu.au/index.php/ejap

Jacobson, B. (2015). Teaching and learning in an "audit culture": A critical genre analysis of common core implementation. *Journal of Writing Assessment, 8*(1). Retrieved from http://www.journalofwritingassessment.org

6. Abstract of a journal article in a database or online Although it is best to cite full articles, you can use an abstract as a source and cite it in your references. For an abstract in an online database, cite the journal publication details, including the page numbers (but not the DOI). Then add *Abstract retrieved from* and the name of the database. You may add an identifying number (if available).

Ann Cameron, C. (2009). Associations between shyness, reluctance to engage, and academic performance. *Infant and Child Development, 18*, 299–305. Abstract retrieved from ProQuest PsycINFO database.

For an abstract on a Web site, give the URL of the site's home page (not followed by a period).

Hildreth, J.A.D., & Anderson, C. (2016). Failure at the top: How power undermines collaborative performance. *Journal of Personality and Social Psychology, 110*, 261–286. Abstract retrieved from http://psycnet.apa.org

7. Print magazine article Include the year and the exact date of publication in parentheses. Do not abbreviate months. Italicize the name of the magazine, the comma following it, and the volume number. Then give the issue number in parentheses and the page number(s), not italicized. See Source Shot 10 (pp. 312–313) for an example.

SOURCE SHOT 8

Listing an Online Scholarly Journal Article (PDF Format) APA

Online Scholarly Journal Article (PDF Format)

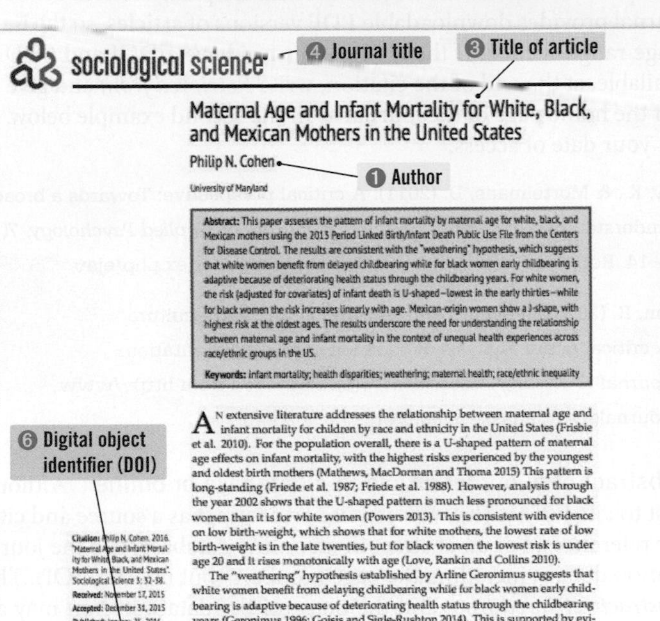

sociological science

Maternal Age and Infant Mortality for White, Black, and Mexican Mothers in the United States

Philip N. Cohen

University of Maryland

Abstract: This paper assesses the pattern of infant mortality by maternal age for white, black, and Mexican mothers using the 2013 Period Linked Birth/Infant Death Public Use File from the Centers for Disease Control. The results are consistent with the "weathering" hypothesis, which suggests that white women benefit from delayed childbearing while for black women early childbearing is adaptive because of deteriorating health status through the childbearing years. For white women, the risk (adjusted for covariates) of infant death is U-shaped—lowest in the early thirties—while for black women the risk increases linearly with age. Mexican-origin women show a J-shape, with highest risk at the oldest ages. The results underscore the need for understanding the relationship between maternal age and infant mortality in the context of unequal health experiences across race/ethnic groups in the US.

Keywords: infant mortality; health disparities; weathering; maternal health; race/ethnic inequality

Citation: Philip N. Cohen. 2016. "Maternal Age and Infant Mortality for White, Black, and Mexican Mothers in the United States". Sociological Science 3: 32-38.

Received: November 17, 2015

Accepted: December 31, 2015

Published: January 25, 2016

Editor(s): Jesper Sørensen, Kim Weeden

DOI: 10.15195/v3.a2

Copyright: © 2016 The Author(s). This open-access article has been published under a Creative Commons Attribution License, which allows unrestricted use, distribution and reproduction, in any form, as long as the original author and source have been credited.

AN extensive literature addresses the relationship between maternal age and infant mortality for children by race and ethnicity in the United States (Frisbie et al. 2010). For the population overall, there is a U-shaped pattern of maternal age effects on infant mortality, with the highest risks experienced by the youngest and oldest birth mothers (Mathews, MacDorman and Thoma 2015) This pattern is long-standing (Friede et al. 1987; Friede et al. 1988). However, analysis through the year 2002 shows that the U-shaped pattern is much less pronounced for black women than it is for white women (Powers 2013). This is consistent with evidence on low birth-weight, which shows that for white mothers, the lowest rate of low birth-weight is in the late twenties, but for black women the lowest risk is under age 20 and it rises monotonically with age (Love, Rankin and Collins 2010).

The "weathering" hypothesis established by Arline Geronimus suggests that white women benefit from delaying childbearing while for black women early childbearing is adaptive because of deteriorating health status through the childbearing years (Geronimus 1996; Goisis and Sigle-Rushton 2014). This is supported by evidence of relative health deterioration for black versus white women on, for example, measures of allostatic load (Geronimu 2006). Subsequent research suggests that the weathering pattern may be seen among women of Mexican origin as well, as they have higher infant mortality rates than whites at advanced maternal ages in older data (Powers 2012).

The recent analysis by Powers (2013) uses the data through 2002, showing the black-white gap in infant mortality narrowing from the 1980s through 2002, but at a stagnating pace (that analysis does not model infant mortality using health-related covariates; see below). In the last decade, the black-white gap has narrowed further

18-24, 25-29, 30-34, 35-39, and 40+. Covariates in the multivariate analysis include plurality (single birth versus twin or higher plurality), birth order (first through fifth or more), maternal education (high school or less, some college, BA or more), timing of prenatal care (began in first trimester, second trimester, third trimester, or not at all), payment source (Medicaid, private insurance, self-pay, or other), and cigarette smoking during pregnancy (no smoking versus smoking).

sociological science | www.sociologicalscience.com 33 January 2016 | Volume 3

5 Page number for the first page; article ends on page 38

2 Date of publication

4 Journal volume number

Source: www.sociologicalscience.com

This scholarly journal article was published in *Sociological Science*, an open-access, online, peer-reviewed journal published by the Society for Sociological Science. Articles are available in downloadable PDF versions, so page numbers of the PDF version are given. (Always use a PDF version if one is available.) When listing a journal article found online either in a database (see Source Shot 9 on pp. 310–311) or on the journal's Web site, include the following information in your reference list entry. Do not list your retrieval date or the name of the database if you found the article there.

❶ **Author(s)** Last name, initials (see Key Points box, pp. 301–302).

❷ **(Date of publication)** In parentheses, give the year of online publication. Put a period after closing parenthesis.

❸ **Title: Subtitle of article** Do not use quotation marks or italics; capitalize only the first word of title and of any subtitle and proper nouns and adjectives. End with a period.

❹ ***Journal Title, volume*** **(issue number)** Capitalize all major words in the title. Italicize the title, comma, and volume number, but not the issue number (contained in parentheses). For journals with each issue paged separately (beginning with page 1), put the issue number immediately following the volume number, with no space between them. Follow with a comma before the page numbers. (The cited journal volume in this example has no issue number.)

❺ **Inclusive range of page numbers** Repeat all digits (as in 167–188) and separate numbers with an en dash. Do not use the abbreviation *p.* or *pp.* End with a period.

❻ **Digital object identifier (DOI)** End with the article's DOI for retrieval information (see Key Points box on pp. 305–306). Break a DOI only before a punctuation mark (such as a slash or a hyphen in this example's DOI), but do not add a hyphen to break a DOI at the end of a line. Do not add a period after the DOI.

Cohen, P. N.❶ (2016).❷ Maternal age and infant mortality for white, black, and Mexican mothers in the United States.❸ *Sociological Science, 3,*❹ 32–38.❺ doi:10.15195/v3.a2❻

SOURCE SHOT 9

Locating a Scholarly Journal Article in an Online Database APA

Online Database Citation Page (from *Academic Search Complete* database)

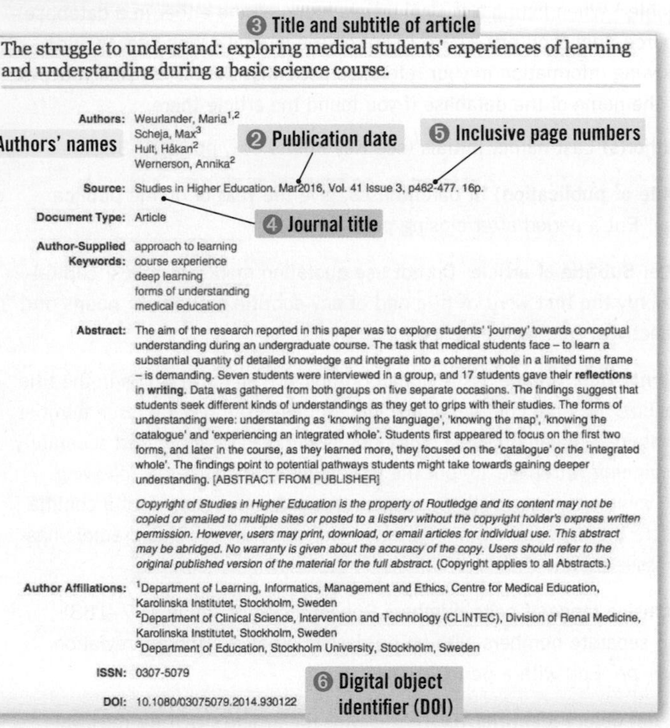

③ Title and subtitle of article
The struggle to understand: exploring medical students' experiences of learning and understanding during a basic science course.
① Authors' names
Authors: Weurlander, Maria[1,2]
Scheja, Max[3]
Hult, Håkan[2]
Wernerson, Annika[2]
② Publication date
⑤ Inclusive page numbers
Source: Studies in Higher Education. Mar2016, Vol. 41 Issue 3, p462-477. 16p.
Document Type: Article
④ Journal title
Author-Supplied Keywords: approach to learning
course experience
deep learning
forms of understanding
medical education
Abstract: The aim of the research reported in this paper was to explore students' 'journey' towards conceptual understanding during an undergraduate course. The task that medical students face – to learn a substantial quantity of detailed knowledge and integrate into a coherent whole in a limited time frame – is demanding. Seven students were interviewed in a group, and 17 students gave their reflections in writing. Data was gathered from both groups on five separate occasions. The findings suggest that students seek different kinds of understandings as they get to grips with their studies. The forms of understanding were: understanding as 'knowing the language', 'knowing the map', 'knowing the catalogue' and 'experiencing an integrated whole'. Students first appeared to focus on the first two forms, and later in the course, as they learned more, they focused on the 'catalogue' or the 'integrated whole'. The findings point to potential pathways students might take towards gaining deeper understanding. [ABSTRACT FROM PUBLISHER]
Copyright of Studies in Higher Education is the property of Routledge and its content may not be copied or emailed to multiple sites or posted to a listserv without the copyright holder's express written permission. However, users may print, download, or email articles for individual use. This abstract may be abridged. No warranty is given about the accuracy of the copy. Users should refer to the original published version of the material for the full abstract. (Copyright applies to all Abstracts.)
Author Affiliations: [1]Department of Learning, Informatics, Management and Ethics, Centre for Medical Education, Karolinska Institutet, Stockholm, Sweden
[2]Department of Clinical Science, Intervention and Technology (CLINTEC), Division of Renal Medicine, Karolinska Institutet, Stockholm, Sweden
[3]Department of Education, Stockholm University, Stockholm, Sweden
ISSN: 0307-5079
⑥ Digital object identifier (DOI)
DOI: 10.1080/03075079.2014.930122

You can use your school library's databases to locate articles for your research (see 7c). The citation page for an article in a database will tell you if the article has been published in a scholarly journal and has been peer-reviewed (see Key Points box in 8b on p. 170) and if it is available in PDF format so that you can cite page numbers. It will also give you the necessary information for your reference list entry.

Include the following in your reference list entry:

❶ **Author(s)** Last name, initials

❷ **(Publication date)** Year in parentheses, followed by a period

❸ **Title of work: Any subtitle** No quotation marks or italics; capitalize only the first word of the title and of any subtitle and proper nouns and adjectives; end with a period.

❹ ***Periodical Title, volume* (issue number)** Capitalize all major words in the title. Italicize the title, comma, and volume number, but not the issue number (contained in parentheses). If each issue of the periodical is paged separately (beginning with page 1, not the case here), put the issue number immediately after the volume number, with no space between them. Follow with a comma.

❺ **Inclusive range of page numbers** Repeat all digits, and separate numbers with an en dash. Do not use the abbreviation *p.* or *pp.* End with a period.

❻ **Digital object identifier (DOI)** End with the article's DOI (see Key Points box on pp. 305–306). Break a DOI only before a punctuation mark, and do not add a hyphen to break a DOI at the end of a line. Do not add a period after the DOI.

Do not list the name of the database or your date of retrieval of the article.

❶ ❷
Weurlander, M., Scheja, M., Hult, H., & Wernerson, A. (2016).

❸
The struggle to understand: Exploring medical students'

experiences of learning and understanding during a basic science

❹ ❺
course. *Studies in Higher Education, 41*, 462–477.

❻
doi:10.1080/03075079.2014.930122

SOURCE SHOT 10

Listing a Print Magazine Article APA

Title page and Table of Contents of a Magazine (APA)

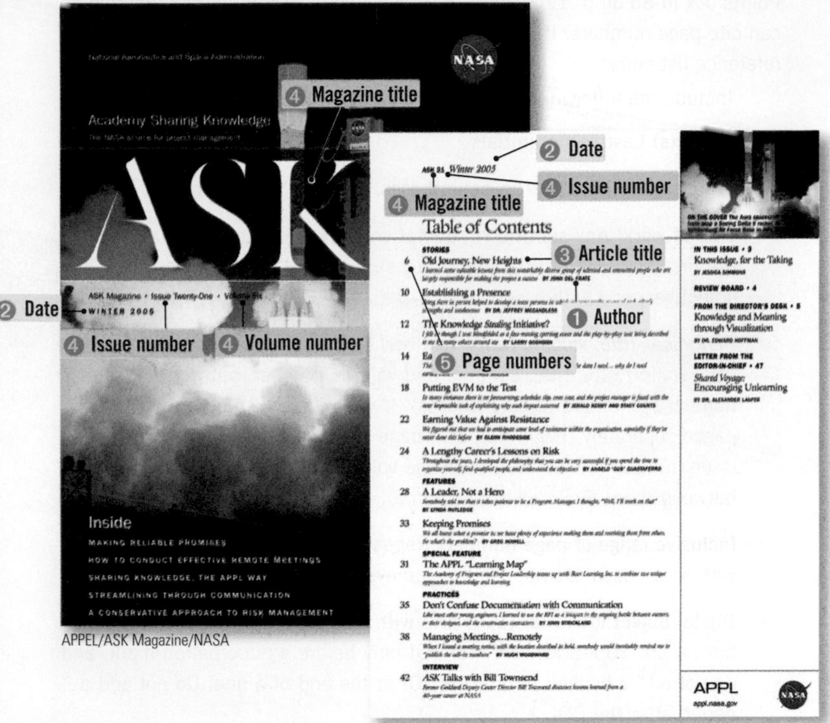

APPEL/ASK Magazine/NASA

8. Online magazine article with no print source If only an HTML version is available, with no page numbers, give the available publication information and the URL.

Solon, O. (2016, February 5). Australia's plan to make a digital representation of everything. *New Scientist*. Retrieved from http://newscientist.com

9. Newsletter article Cite a newsletter article as you would cite an article in a magazine, giving the volume and issue numbers, if available. If no author is named, as in the following citation, begin with the article title. See item 11 for an article that skips pages.

Major fat-burning discovery: Harvard researchers discover a hormone released by exercise. (2012, June). *Harvard Health Letter, 37*(8), 1, 7.

When listing a print magazine article, include the following:

❶ **Author(s)** Last name, initials (see 15b on how to list authors)

❷ **(Date of publication)** In parentheses: year, comma, month (not abbreviated), and day (if given), followed by a period.

❸ **Title of article: Any subtitle** Don't put the title and subtitle in quotation marks or italics; capitalize only the first word of the title and subtitle and proper nouns or adjectives; end with a period.

❹ ***Periodical Title, volume* (issue number)** All italicized, except for the issue number. For periodicals with each issue paged separately, put the issue number in parentheses immediately following the volume number, with no space between. Use a comma (italicized) to separate a periodical title from the volume number, and use another before the page numbers.

❺ **Inclusive range of page numbers** All digits included and separated by an en dash (as in 167–168). Do not use *p.* or *pp.* End with a period.

❶ Del Frate, J. ❷ (2005, Winter). ❸ Old journey, new heights. ❹ *ASK Magazine, 6*(21), ❺ 6–9.

10. Print newspaper article In parentheses, include the month and day of publication after the year. Give the section letter or number before the page, if applicable. Do not omit *The* from the newspaper title. Note that with newspaper articles only, use *p.* and *pp.* with page numbers. See item 13 for an article with no author named.

Tanner, L. (2012, April 10). Study links autism to obesity during pregnancy. *The Washington Post,* A3.

11. Article that skips pages When an article does not appear on continuous pages, give all of the page numbers, separated by commas. Use *p.* and *pp.* for newspapers only.

Strom, S. (2012, April 6). A case long ripening: For two food giants, defining fresh fruit is not cut and dried. *The New York Times,* pp. B1, B3.

12. Online newspaper article Newspaper articles are often available from several sources, in several databases, and in a variety of formats, such as in the newspaper's database or a library subscription database. Give the URL of the newspaper's home page in your entry. Do not insert a period at the end of the URL. A date of retrieval is not necessary.

Belluck, P. (2012, May 15). New drug trial seeks to stop Alzheimer's before it starts. *The New York Times.* Retrieved from www.nytimes.com—no period at end after URL

13. Unsigned article or editorial For an article with no author named, begin with the title and follow with the date in parentheses.

Go with the flow: Removing old dams benefits America's rivers economically and ecologically. (2011, October 1–7). *The Economist, 401*(8753), 35.

For an unsigned editorial, add the label *Editorial* in square brackets after the title.

Who owns the past? [Editorial]. (2012, April). *Scientific American, 306*(4), 9.

If the editorial is signed, begin with the author's name.

14. Review After the title of the review (if any), add in square brackets (with no intervening punctuation) *Review of* and a description of the work reviewed, including the author or creator, and identify the medium: book, film, or video, for example.

Ayala, F. J. (2012, Spring). All for one and one for all? An eminent scientist reconsiders natural selection [Review of the book *The social conquest of Earth,* by E. O. Wilson]. *The American Scholar, 81*(2), 112–113.

15. Published interview Begin with the writer of the published interview and the date. After the title (with no intervening punctuation), in brackets write *Interview with* and the name of the person interviewed.

Jeffery, C. (2009, January/February). The Maddow knows [Interview with Rachel Maddow]. *Mother Jones, 34*(1), 72–73.

16. Letter to the editor Put the label *Letter to the editor* in brackets after the date or the title of the letter, if it has one.

Bogorad, H. C. (2012, April 10). The price of not voting [Letter to the editor]. *The Washington Post,* p. A12.

For an editorial, review, interview, letter to the editor, or other feature in an online periodical, end with *Retrieval from* and the URL.

15d Sample APA listings: Print and online books, parts of books, and reference books

- Look for the necessary information on the title page and the copyright page of a book.
- Use the most recent copyright date or *n.d.* if no date is given.
- Include the city (or the first city if two or more are given) and the state of publication (two-letter U.S. Postal Service abbreviation).
- Write complete names of foreign countries (see item 22).
- Give the publisher's name in a shortened but intelligible form, including *Books* or *Press* but omitting *Publishers*, *Co.*, or *Inc.*
- If a DOI has been assigned to the book, list it. (See the Key Points box on pp. 305–306.)
- If a book or chapter is available only online, either give the DOI or give a retrieval statement and the URL in place of the name and location of the publisher (see item 19).

17. Book with one author Give the last name first, followed by the initial(s). See Source Shot 11 on pages 316–317 for an example.

18. Book with multiple authors For two to seven authors, list all names in the order in which they appear on the book's title page. Reverse the order of each name: last name first, followed by initials. Separate all names with commas, and insert an ampersand (&) before the last name.

Baumol, W. J., Litan, R. E., & Schramm, C. J. (2007). *Good capitalism, bad capitalism, and the economics of growth and prosperity*. New Haven, CT: Yale University Press.

For eight or more authors, list the first six names (reversed), add three ellipsis dots, and list the name of the last author, also reversed (see 15c, item 3).

19. Electronic version of print book (e-book) To cite an electronic version of a print book that can be read on an e-reader such as the Nook, Kindle, iPad, or Sony Reader, give the author, date, and book title. With no intervening punctuation, add in brackets the e-reader version; follow with a period. Then list the book's DOI if available. Do not list the place

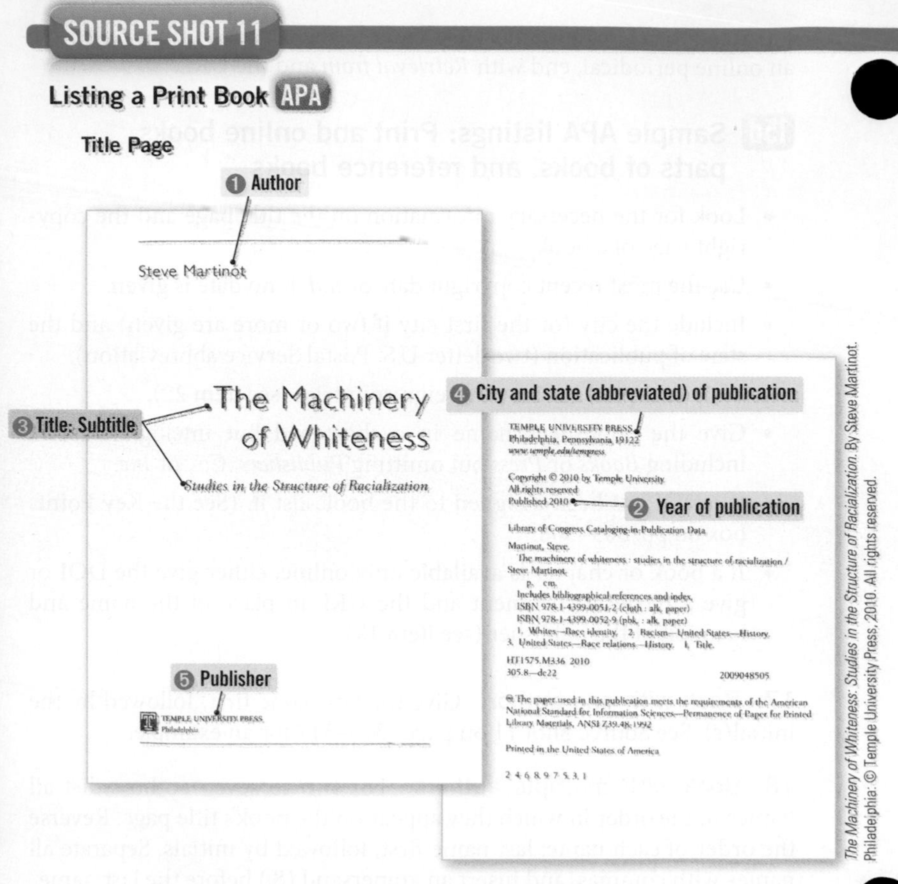

SOURCE SHOT 11
Listing a Print Book APA
Title Page
1 Author
Steve Martinot
3 Title: Subtitle
The Machinery of Whiteness
Studies in the Structure of Racialization
5 Publisher
TEMPLE UNIVERSITY PRESS
Philadelphia
4 City and state (abbreviated) of publication
TEMPLE UNIVERSITY PRESS
Philadelphia, Pennsylvania 19122
www.temple.edu/tempress
Copyright © 2010 by Temple University
All rights reserved
Published 2010
2 Year of publication
Library of Congress Cataloging-in-Publication Data
Martinot, Steve.
The machinery of whiteness : studies in the structure of racialization / Steve Martinot.
p. cm.
Includes bibliographical references and index.
ISBN 978-1-4399-0051-2 (cloth : alk. paper)
ISBN 978-1-4399-0052-9 (pbk. : alk. paper)
1. Whites—Race identity. 2. Racism—United States—History. 3. United States—Race relations—History. I. Title.
HT1575.M336 2010
305.8—dc22
2009048505
The paper used in this publication meets the requirements of the American National Standard for Information Sciences—Permanence of Paper for Printed Library Materials, ANSI Z39.48-1992
Printed in the United States of America
2 4 6 8 9 7 5 3 1

The Machinery of Whiteness: Studies in the Structure of Racialization. By Steve Martinot. Philadelphia: © Temple University Press, 2010. All rights reserved.

of publication or publisher for an electronic book. If you download the e-book from a Web site, and it does not have a DOI, write *Retrieved from* and the URL. Do not give your date of retrieval.

Haws, J. (2015). *Nursing assessment: Head-to-toe assessment in pictures* [Kindle version]. Retrieved from http://www.amazon.com

20. Electronic version of print book in online library If the book was read or accessed through an online library such as NetLibrary, Google Books, or ebrary instead of on an e-reader, just give the retrieval information after the title. Do not give your date of access.

Marshall, T. (2015). *Prisoners of geography: Ten maps that explain everything about the world.* Retrieved from http://books.google.com/books

On the title page and copyright page of the book, you will find the information you need for an entry in the list of references.

❶ **Author(s)** Last name, initials (see 15b on how to list multiple authors).

❷ **(Year of publication)** In parentheses, followed by a period; the most recent copyright (©) date or *n.d.* if no date is supplied.

❸ ***Title of book: Any subtitle*** In italics, with capital letters only for the first word of the title and subtitle and any proper nouns or adjectives.

❹ **Place of publication** City and state (two-letter U.S. Postal Service abbreviation) or country, omitting the state when its name appears in the name of the publisher, as in *University of Illinois Press.* Cite only the first city if more than one is listed. Write complete names of foreign countries. Follow with a colon.

❺ **Publisher** In a short but intelligible form, including *Books* or *Press* but omitting *Publishers, Co.,* or *Inc.* and ending with a period

See 15d, items 18–33, for more examples.

❶ ❷ ❸ ❹ ❺

Martinot, S. (2010). *The machinery of Whiteness: Studies in the structure of racialization*. Philadelphia, PA: Temple University Press.

21. Electronic-only book If a book has been published only online (with no print edition), list the retrieval information after the title. The following book can be downloaded in PDF format.

Shrout, R. N. (2012). *True hypnotism: Understanding its science and mastering its art.* Retrieved from http://www.onlineoriginals.com/showitem.asp?itemID=253

22. Edited book After the reversed name(s) of the editor(s), add *Ed.* or *Eds.* in parentheses and follow with a period. Continue with the year, title, and publication details of the book. Give the city and state (abbreviated) or country (spelled out, as in the example that follows).

Malhotra, S., & Chakrabarti, S. (Eds.). (2015). *Developments in psychiatry in India: Clinical, research, and policy perspectives.* New Delhi, India: Springer.

If the book has both an author and an editor, begin with the author's name (reversed), the date, and the book title. After the title, with no intervening punctuation, in parentheses add the editor's name in normal order, a comma, and the abbreviation *Ed.* (or *Eds.* for more than one editor). Put a period after the closing parenthesis, and continue with the publication details.

23. Work or chapter in an edited book (collection) List the author of the work or chapter, the date of publication of the edited book, and the title of the work. Follow this with *In* and the names of the editors (not inverted), the title of the book, and (in parentheses) the inclusive page numbers (preceded by *pp.*) of the work or chapter. End with the place of publication and the publisher for a print book (as in the following example) or the DOI or URL for an electronic book. If you cite more than one work from an edited book in your reference list, include the full bibliographical details in each entry.

Wig, N. N. (2015). The beginnings of psychiatry in India. In S. Malhotra & S. Chakrabarti (Eds.), *Developments in psychiatry in India: Clinical, research, and policy perspectives* (pp. 3–12). New Delhi, India: Springer.

24. Foreword, preface, introduction, or afterword List in reverse order (last name first, initials) the name(s) of the author(s) of the book element. Follow the date with the name of the element, the word *In,* the names of the author(s) of the book in normal order (initials, last name), the book title, and in parentheses, the page number or numbers of the element, preceded by *p.* or *pp.* In the following example, no state abbreviation appears after the city because the name of the state appears in the publisher's name.

Land, R. (2015). Preface. In L. Adler-Kassner & E. Wardle (Eds.), *Naming what we know: Threshold concepts of writing studies* (pp. xi–xiv). Logan: Utah State University Press.

25. Translated book After the title of the work (with no intervening punctuation), in parentheses give the initials and last name of the translator (in normal order), followed by a comma and the abbreviation *Trans.* Put a period after the closing parenthesis.

Jung, C. G. (1960). *On the nature of the psyche* (R. F. C. Hull, Trans.). Princeton, NJ: Princeton University Press.

26. Edition after the first For an edition of a book after the first, give the edition number in parentheses after the title, with no intervening punctuation.

Raimes, A., & Miller-Cochran, S. K. (2016). *Pocket keys for writers* (5th ed.). Boston, MA: Cengage.

For a revised edition, put *Rev. ed.* in parentheses instead of the edition number.

27. Republished or reprinted work—print and online For a republished book, give the most recent date of publication after the author's name, and at the end in parentheses add *Original work published* and the date. Do not add a final period. In the citation in your paper, give both dates: (Smith, 1793/1976).

Smith, A. (1976). *An inquiry into the nature and causes of the wealth of nations.* Chicago, IL: University of Chicago Press. (Original work published 1793)

For an electronic version of a republished book, give the date of online publication. In place of the location and publisher, give the retrieval information and URL. Add the information about the original publication last.

Freud, S. (2007). *A young girl's diary*. Retrieved from http://books.google.com/books (Original work published 1923)

For a reprint of a work published in a different source, first give the complete publication information for the reprinted work. Begin the details in parentheses with *Reprinted from* and give the title of the original work, inclusive page numbers (if part of a book), *by* and the author or editor, date, place, and publisher.

28. Multivolume work Give the number of volumes after the title, in parentheses. The date should indicate the range of years of publication, when appropriate.

Einstein, A. (1987–2006). *Collected papers of Albert Einstein* (Vols. 1–10). Princeton, NJ: Princeton University Press.

If you cite only one volume, give only that volume number and its date.

29. No author identified Put the title first. Ignore *A*, *An*, and *The* when alphabetizing. Alphabetize the following under *W*.

The world almanac and book of facts 2012. (2012). Pleasantville, NY: World Almanac Books.

30. Print or online book, pamphlet, or brochure by a corporation, government agency, or other organization Give the name of the corporate author first. If the publisher is the same as the author, write *Author* for the name of the publisher. For a brochure or pamphlet, include the format *Brochure* or *Pamphlet* in square brackets after the title.

College Board. (2015). *Trends in college pricing 2015.* Washington, DC: Author.

East Bay Municipal Utility District. (2012). *2011 annual water quality report* [Brochure]. Oakland, CA: Author.

If no author is named for a government publication, begin with the name of the federal, state, or local government department (if given), followed by the agency. If the work is available online (as is the following example in PDF format), give the retrieval information in place of the location and publisher.

U.S. Substance Abuse and Mental Health Services Administration. (2011). *Disaster training and technical assistance* [Brochure]. Retrieved from http://store.samhsa.gov/product

31. Signed entry in a print reference work Cite the entry as you would cite a work in an edited collection, giving complete publication information (see item 23).

Bedford, V. H., & Diderich, M. (2009). Sibling relationships in adulthood. In H. T. Reis & S. Sprecher (Eds.), *Encyclopedia of Human Relationships: Vol. 1* (pp. 41–44). Thousand Oaks, CA: Sage.

32. Signed entry in an online reference work Cite an entry for an online reference work as you would cite one for a print source, but give the retrieval information in place of the location and publisher.

Hilpinen, R. (2011). Artifact. In E. N. Zalta (Ed.), *The Stanford encyclopedia of philosophy* (Spring 2012 ed.). Retrieved from http://plato.stanford.edu /entries/artifact/

33. Unsigned entry in a print or online reference work. Begin an unsigned print entry with the title of the work. Put the edition and page numbers in parentheses after the title, and give complete publication information.

Antarctica. (2000). In *The Columbia encyclopedia* (6th ed., pp. 116–118). New York, NY: Columbia University Press.

For an unsigned online entry, give the edition number in parentheses after the title if the online version of the book is based on a print edition.

Gerrymander. (n.d.). In *Merriam-Webster's online dictionary* (11th ed.). Retrieved from http://www.m-w.com/dictionary/gerrymander

15e Sample APA listings: Reports and presentations—print, online, and live

34. Print report Italicize the title of a technical or research report; list the location and publisher as you would for a print book.

Blash, L., Chapman, S., & Dower, C. (2011). *WellMed's medical assistant training program prepares students for health care career ladder.* San Francisco: Center for the Health Professions, University of California.

35. Online report on a government Web site. If no author is named for a government publication, begin with the name of the federal, state, or local government department, followed by the agency. Provide any identifying number in parentheses after the title. In the retrieval statement, name the publisher (*Retrieved from U.S. Census Bureau Web site*) before the URL, unless it has already been listed as the author, as in the following example.

U.S. Department of Commerce, Economics and Statistics Administration. (2015). *Income and poverty in the United States: 2015* (Report No. P60-252). Retrieved from https://www.census.gov/content/dam/Census/library/publications/2015/demo/p60-252.pdf

36. Task force report on a university Web site If no individual authors are named, give the university and the name of the task force or similar group as the author. In the following example, the name of the task force is capitalized in the report title.

Harvard University, Task Force on University Libraries. (2009). *Report of the Task Force on University Libraries.* Retrieved from http://provost.harvard.edu/reports/Library_Task_Force_Report.pdf

37. Issue brief Cite issue briefs, working papers, and other documents as you would a longer report, giving the document number in parentheses after the title. Give the month as well as the year of publication. Add the retrieval information and URL for documents accessed online.

U.S. Department of Commerce, Census Bureau. (2011, November). *Lifetime mobility in the United States: 2010* (American Community Survey Brief No.10-07). Retrieved from http://www.census.gov/prod/2011pubs/acsbr10-07.pdf

38. Unpublished conference paper Cite unpublished papers or symposia presentations by listing the presenter, date (year and month), title (italicized), name of the meeting, and location (city and state or province/country).

Leavitt, S. (2006, May). *Something to think about when I can't sleep: The development of rubella vaccine.* Paper presented at the American Association for the History of Medicine Annual Meeting, Halifax, Nova Scotia, Canada.

39. Conference paper or proceedings in print or online Cite a conference paper published in a print volume of conference proceedings as you would a work in an edited collection (see 15d, item 23). If the proceedings are published regularly, cite as a journal article. If a DOI is available, include it. If you accessed the work on a Web site, add the retrieval information and URL.

LeMire, S. (2015). *Beyond service: New outreach strategies to reach student veterans.* Presentation to the 2015 annual meeting of the Association of College and Research Libraries, Portland, OR. Retrieved from http://www.ala.org/acrl/sites/ala.org.acrl/files/content/conferences/confsandpreconfs/2015/LeMire.pdf

40. Poster session Give the retrieval information and URL for a poster session accessed online.

Szenher, M. (2005, September). *Visual homing in natural environments.* Poster session presented at the annual meeting of Towards Autonomous Robotic Systems, London, England.

15f Sample APA listings: Other online sources

Include in your citation whatever information is available of the following to enable readers to locate your online source:

1. **Name(s) of author(s)** If not available, begin with the title.
2. **Year and date** of online posting or update in parentheses (or *n.d.* if no date is available).
3. **Title and any subtitle** Italicize titles of documents that stand alone (such as reports) but not items that are part of a larger entity (such as Web pages, articles, or sections). If there is no title, begin with the description of the source contained in brackets (see 4 below).
4. **Format** List the format or other identifying description of the source in square brackets after the title: [Web log post], [Newsgroup message].
5. **Any print publication information** if the document has a print source.
6. **Retrieval statement**: Write *Retrieved from* and the URL. Include your retrieval date (day, month, year) for material from sites that are likely to be frequently updated or changed or are otherwise unstable.

41. Authored article on a Web site Cite a Web page or article as you would a print article, without italics or quotation marks. Do not name the Web site in the entry. Give the date of retrieval only for content that may be changed or updated.

Enayati, A. (2012). Is there a bias against creativity? Retrieved from http://www.cnn.com/2012/03/28/health/enayati-uncertainty/index.html?hpt=he_bn2

42. Web page, no author identified Alphabetize by the first major word of the title. Put identifying information in brackets after the title. Follow the date with the retrieval information.

The heavy burden of arthritis in the U.S. [Prevalence fact sheet]. (2011). Retrieved from http://www.arthritis.org/media/newsroom/Arthritis_Prevalence_Fact_Sheet_5-31-11.pdf

Narcolepsy. (2015). Retrieved from http://www.mayoclinic.org/diseases-conditions/narcolepsy/basics/definition/con-20027429

43. Entire Web site, no author Name the Web site (not italicized) and then give the complete URL in parentheses only in the text of your paper, not in your list of references (see 14b, item P).

44. Blogs, discussion boards, wikis, newsgroups, and archived mailing lists Include in your list of sources only academic material posted on archived lists or blogs. If no archives exist, cite an entry on a discussion or message board as a personal communication (see 14b, item R). List the author's last name and initials, if available. If only a screen name is given, use that. Cite the complete date of posting. Give the subject line (the "thread") of the posting (not in italics), followed by a description in brackets. Always give the retrieval date for wiki pages, which may change constantly.

Myers, P. Z. (2012, June 12). A well-informed citizenry is the only true repository of the public will [Web log post]. Retrieved from http://scienceblogs.com/pharyngula/2012/06/12/a-well-informed-citizenry-is-the-only-true-repository-of-the-public-will/

Love, R. (2012, June 17). Re: Does anyone realistically think that an International Space Agency can be formed and maintained? [Online newsgroup comment]. Retrieved from http://groups.google.com/group/sci.space.policy/browse_thread/thread/e1886d6ddfe9efb9#

Landscape architecture. (2016, January 26, May 2). Retrieved February 6, 2016, from Wikipedia, http://en.wikipedia.org/wiki/Landscape_architecture

15g Sample APA listings: Visual and multimedia sources (live, print, and online)

Multimedia sources include audiovisual media such as motion pictures, television and radio broadcasts, and podcasts; and music recordings such as CDs and LPs. Visual sources include static objects such as artwork and visual representations such as maps, charts, photos, illustrations, and graphs. To cite a multimedia or visual source, begin with the primary contributor, artist, or creator in the author position and identify the person's role in parentheses. In brackets after the title (with no intervening punctuation), give the format or description of the source. If the source was retrieved online, end with *Retrieved from* and the URL.

45. Map in a print book Cite a map included in a print book as you would cite an article contained in one. Give the location and publisher (which is the same as the creator of the map in the following example).

National Geographic Society (Cartographer). (2009). World time zones [Map]. In *Visual atlas of the world* (pp. 310–311). Washington, DC: Author.

46. Online map See Source Shot 12 on pages 326–327 for an example.

47. Film or video Begin with the primary contributors (producer and director, if known). Identify the medium or format (motion picture, videocassette, DVD, and so on) in brackets after the italicized title. Give the country where a film was released, or give the city and state or country for other formats. End with the location and name of the studio or publisher.

Boyle, D. (Director). (2015). *Steve Jobs* [Motion picture]. United States: Universal Pictures.

Jacquet, L. (Director). (2005). *The march of the penguins* [DVD]. Burbank, CA: Warner Home Video.

48. Television or radio program Begin with the writer and director in the author position and the producer as editor, if known. Cite an episode of a television series or radio program as you would an article in a book. Put the description in brackets after the title. End with the location and network of the broadcast.

Knutson, R., & Day, L. (Writers). (2012, May 22). Cell tower deaths [Television series episode]. In D. Fanning (Executive producer), *Frontline*. Boston, MA: WGBH.

49. Music recording Cite a song on an album as you would an article in a book. Begin with the writer, and put the copyright year in parentheses. Give the song title, and put information in brackets if the song was recorded by someone else. Cite the album title (italicized), and put the medium of recording (LP, CD, for example) in brackets. End with the location and record label (publisher). In the following example, the songwriter is also the performing artist, so recording information is not needed.

Ely, J. (2007). July blues. On *Happy songs from Rattlesnake Gulch* [CD]. Austin, TX: Rack 'em Records.

SOURCE SHOT 12

Listing an Online Visual (Figure) APA

An Online Map

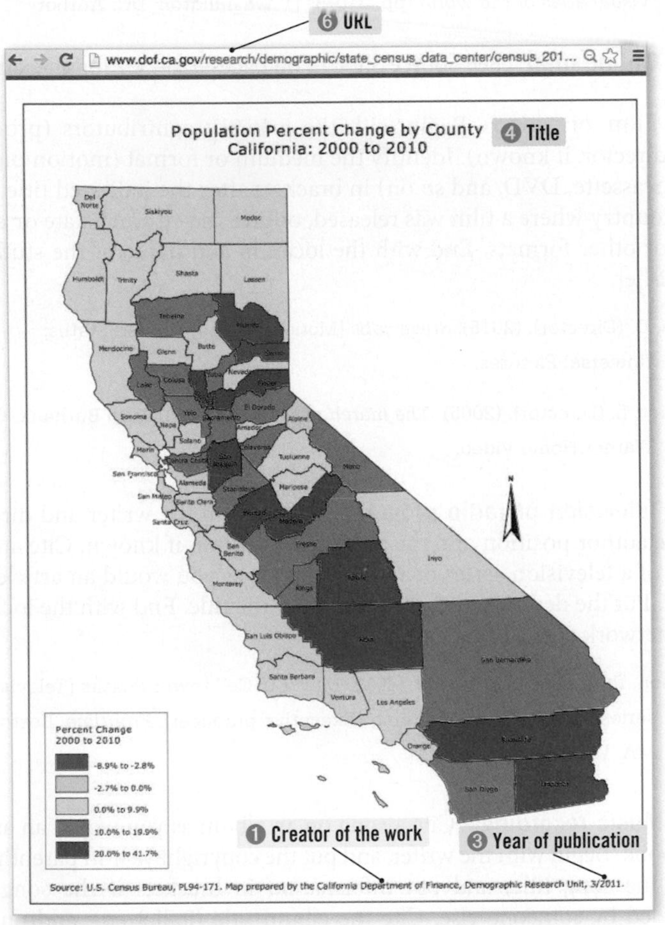

Source: www.dof.ca.gov

APA cites visual elements such as maps, graphs, charts, photographs, illustrations, and cartoons in a format similar to the one used for multimedia sources. Within a paper or published text, these elements are labeled as *figures* and identified by number (see 14c, p. 299). Include the following elements, most of them separated by periods, in your citation.

❶ **Creator of the work** Begin with the creator in the author position.

❷ **(Type of creator)** Follow with a description of the person or organization's role—cartographer, illustrator, and so on—in parentheses, and add a period. In this example, the creator is a cartographer.

❸ **(Year of publication or creation)** contained in parentheses and followed by a period.

❹ **Title of figure or other visual work** No italics for titles of maps, graphs, illustrations, and similar visual elements; italics for works of art (painting, sculpture, artistic photograph) and for visual representations of them (such as a photograph of a painting published in a book or online).

❺ **[Format or description of visual work]** contained in brackets and followed by a period.

❻ **Retrieval information and URL** If the visual work was accessed online, write *Retrieved from* and give the URL, not ending with a period.

The screenshots on the opposite page show you where to find the information necessary to cite a map downloaded from the state of California's online map gallery.

❶

California Department of Finance, Demographic Research Unit

❷ ❸ ❹

(Cartographer). (2011). Population percent change by county

❺

California: 2000 to 2010 [Demographic map]. Retrieved from

No punctuation between title and description in brackets

❻

http://www.dof.ca.gov/research/demographic/state_census

_data_center/census_2010/documents/2010_Map1_PctChange.pdf

No period after URL

50. Podcast or MP3 download For a podcast, give the producer or editor, complete date, italicized title, identification of format, and any other supplementary information in brackets, and *Retrieved from* and the URL.

Koenig, S., Snyder, J., & Chivvis, D. (Producers). (2016, February 4). *Serial* [5 o'clock shadow; Why did Bowe Bergdahl walk off?] [Audio podcast]. Retrieved from https://serialpodcast.org

Davis, A. (2007, October 2). Angela Davis speaks. *Panel discussion with Burnham, Mitchell, and Noble* [MP3 download]. Washington, DC: Folkways Records. Retrieved from http://www.amazon.com

51. Video blog posting Use a screen name if it is the only one available.

nnnicck. (2007, February 7). *The march of the librarians* [Video file]. Retrieved from http://www.youtube.com/watch?v=Td922l0NoDQ

52. CD-ROM or DVD-ROM Identify the format in square brackets after the title.

U.S. Substance Abuse and Mental Health Services Administration. (2012). *Shared decision making in mental health decision aid: Considering the role of antipsychotic medications in your recovery plan* [CD-ROM]. Washington, DC: Author.

15h Sample APA listings: Miscellaneous sources

53. Dissertation or abstract—print, online, multimedia Italicize the dissertation or master's thesis title, and identify the work as such in parentheses. If you retrieved it from a commercial database, add *Available from* here and the database name, with the order or accession number in parentheses at the end of the entry (not followed by a period).

Gierdowski, D. C. (2013). *Geographies of a writing space: The study of a flexible composition classroom* (Doctoral dissertation). Available from ProQuest Dissertation and Theses database. (UMI No. 3575623)

If you retrieved the work from an institutional database or Web site, add the words *Retrieved from* and the URL. For a Web source, add a comma and the granting institution's name after the identifying phrase in the parentheses.

For an abstract published in *DAI,* give the author, date, and dissertation title (not in italics), followed by *Dissertation Abstracts International* and the name of the section (*Section B. Sciences and Engineering*). After a comma, add the volume, issue, and page number: 35(20), 3315.

For a dissertation on microfilm (with the format in brackets), also include in parentheses at the end of the entry the University Microfilms number. For a dissertation on CD-ROM, include CD-ROM in brackets after the title and provide any access number.

54. Presentation slides

Norvig, P. (2000). *The Gettysburg PowerPoint presentation* [PowerPoint slides]. Retrieved from http://norvig.com/Gettysburg/index.htm

55. Personal communication (letter, telephone conversation, unpublished interview, e-mail, message on discussion board) Cite only in the body of your text as *personal communication.* Do not include these communications in your list of references (see 14b, item R).

56. Computer software Do not use italics for the name of the software.

SnagIt (Version 12.0) [Computer software]. (2015). Okemos, MI: TechSmith.

16 Sample Paper 5: A Student's Research Paper, APA Style

The following paper was written by Maria Saparauskaite in a required first-year course at Hunter College. The assignment was to explore a current issue in the news. Using the APA style of documentation, she provides a title page, an abstract, and section headings (see 14d). Her citations and the list of references at the end follow APA guidelines and serve to answer any questions that readers may have about the authors, dates, and publication details of her source material. Her instructor asked for tables and figures to be included within the paper rather than attached separately at the end in normal APA style. See 14c for more on figures and their captions.

Note: Blue annotations point out issues of content and organization; red annotations point out APA format issues.

Title Page (APA)

Running head (brief title) flush left and in capitals on every page

Running head: SECRET OF SAVANT 1

Page number flush right on every page

The Secret of the Savant

Maria Saparauskaite

Hunter College of the City University of New York

Midway on page, centered, capital and lowercase letters

Blue = content issues, Red = format issues

Abstract Page (APA)

SECRET OF SAVANT 2

Heading centered, not in boldface

Double-space throughout paper

Abstract

This paper investigates the phenomenon of savants, people with unusual mental talents, and describes some of their extraordinary feats. Theories of the development of the rare savant syndrome are explored, especially the connection between a savant's abilities and whether the effects of brain damage on the hemispheres of the brain cause savant talents to emerge spontaneously. A study by Snyder, Bahramali, Hawker, and Mitchell (2006) is explored in detail. The researchers wanted to examine how stimulation of the brain affected mental functions, with participants experiencing either brain stimulation or a sham session and then being asked to make judgments about what they saw. The study suggests that the savant condition could be stimulated, thus raising questions about not only whether rewiring of the brain is advisable but also to what ends any newfound intelligence may be applied.

Length: 137 words (aim for 150–250)

Passive voice common in APA style

All four authors named in first text citation to work; year in parentheses

Summary of findings

Blue = content issues, **Red = format issues**

American Psychological Assocation APA

Essay (APA)

SECRET OF SAVANT 3

The Secret of the Savant

Many of us struggle with learning and memorization. We may long to be able to do math problems quickly in our heads, play a favorite song on the piano after hearing it only once, or recapture details from an event we have observed. We may wish we could learn a second language as easily as we did our first. For a few individuals among us, these talents are as natural as breathing. These individuals are *savants,* and they are capable of unusual mental feats. Some recent studies have shown that there may be a savant within all of us, which means that our brains may be capable of the same abilities as those of savants. Through artificial means these talents can in some cases be accessed temporarily.

Background Review of the Literature

Savants and Their Accomplishments

Savants exhibit extraordinary talents. Researchers Treffert and Wallace (2004) have reported that at the age of 14, Leslie Lemke was able to play Tchaikovsky's Piano Concerto No. 1 without a single mistake after hearing it only once. He had never had a piano lesson in his life but today he tours all over the world playing in concerts even though he is blind and developmentally disabled. Lemke even composes his own music. Another savant, Kim Peek, the inspiration for the Oscar-winning film *Rain Man*, has memorized more than 7,600 books. It would take him less than three seconds to tell you which day of the week your birthday fell on and which day of the week you will be

Title centered, not bold or underlined

Indent first line after headings

Double-space text of paper

1" margin

Area of research and hypothesis

Main headings in body of paper bold and centered

No extra space around headings

Subheads in body of paper bold and flush left

Word *and* connects authors' names in text sentence

Blue = content issues, **Red = format issues**

collecting your first pension. Like Lemke, Peek is also developmentally disabled. The artwork of another savant, Richard Wawro, is known all over the world. His childhood oil paintings left people speechless (Treffert & Wallace, 2004). He is an autistic savant, as is David Tammet, who can calculate 37 to the power of four in his head (Heffernan, 2005).

Ampersand (&) connects authors' names in parenthetical citation

The Savant Syndrome

The savant syndrome is an extremely rare condition, most often found in people with IQs ranging from 40 to 70, though sometimes it can occur in people with IQs up to 114 or higher (Treffert & Wallace, 2004). Most savants are physically disabled or suffer from autism, which is a "pervasive development disorder [that] is characterized by a severe disturbance of communication, social, and cognitive skills, and is often associated with mental retardation" (Sternberg, 2004, p. 352). Despite that situation, savants exhibit amazing mental superiority in specific areas, such as arithmetic, drawing, music, or memory. However, their way of thinking is very literal, and they have problems understanding abstract concepts. Their abilities emerge spontaneously and cannot be improved over time. Also savants cannot explain how they do what they do (Snyder et al., 2006).

Word enclosed in brackets added in quotation

Page number for a quotation from a book; period after closing parenthesis

Parenthetical citation uses *et al.* because all authors are named in first citation to work on page 2 of essay

Theories of Development of the Syndrome

Scientists have only a vague idea of how the savant syndrome develops. Recent studies have illustrated that developmental problems in the left brain hemisphere are most commonly seen in savants. Bernard Rimland of the Autism Research Institute

Mentions authority of source

Blue = content issues, **Red = format issues**

Present perfect tense used to introduce source

has observed that most abilities in autistic savants are associated with the right hemisphere, whereas the abilities they are deficient in are associated with the left hemisphere (Treffert & Wallace, 2004). The left hemisphere is thought to be responsible for forming hypotheses and concepts. This observation helps to explain why savants tend to be so literal. Another set of evidence for this theory is the occasional emergence of savantlike talents in people suffering from dementia. Bruce Miller of the University of California observed five elderly patients who spontaneously developed exceptional artistic skills in music and painting. All of these patients had what is called *frontotemporal dementia* (FTD). Miller discovered that most brain damage caused by FTD was localized in the left hemisphere (Treffert & Wallace, 2004). In another case of brain damage, psychologist T. L. Brink reported that a nine-year-old boy developed "unusual savant mechanical skills" (Treffert & Wallace, 2004, p. 18) after a bullet damaged his left hemisphere. According to Treffert and Wallace, these reports of spontaneous emergence of the savant syndrome in people with brain damage could point to a possibility that savant talents may be innate to everyone. So, as reporter Lawrence Osborne (2003) provocatively asked, "Could brain damage, in short, actually make you brilliant?"

Past tense used when discussing a completed research study

Question for research

New section of paper: heading centered

Snyder's Experiment

Credentials of researcher

Allan Snyder of the University of Sydney, "one of the world's most remarkable scientists of human cognition" (Osborne, 2003), became interested in the prospect of hidden genius when observing patients who underwent a procedure called *transcranial magnetic stimulation* (TMS). TMS was "originally developed as a tool for brain surgery:

No page numbers available for quotation from online newspaper article

Blue = content issues, Red = format issues

by stimulating or slowing down specific regions of the brain, it allowed doctors to monitor the effects of surgery in real time" (Osborne, 2003). Interestingly enough, this procedure had very noticeable side effects on the patients' mental functioning. A patient would either temporarily lose his ability to speak or make odd mistakes while speaking. But one side effect intrigued Snyder the most: Some patients undergoing TMS would gain savantlike intelligence for a limited amount of time. With his colleague Mitchell, he came up with the theory that savants have a privileged access to lower levels of cognition, whereas normal persons do not (Snyder & Mitchell, 1999).

Claim of researchers

Participants and Method

To test this theory, Snyder, along with Bahramali, Hawker, and Mitchell (2006), led an experiment that was based on the finding that some savants are able to guess the exact number of items, such as matches, just by glancing at them. He tells of autistic twins who were able to estimate correctly the number of matches (111) fallen on the floor. By using TMS on the brains of 12 volunteers, Snyder wanted to find out if a normal person could accomplish the same thing. The goal was to create virtual lesions in the left anterior temporal lobes of the volunteers, thus suppressing mental activity in that region of the brain (see Figure 1).

First reference to figure in parentheses; figure placed nearby

The participants underwent two sessions. During one of them, they received TMS stimulation, while during the other, or "sham," session, they did not. The participants were not able to tell the difference. During each session, the participants were shown a

Description of the experiment

American Psychological Association APA

SECRET OF SAVANT 7

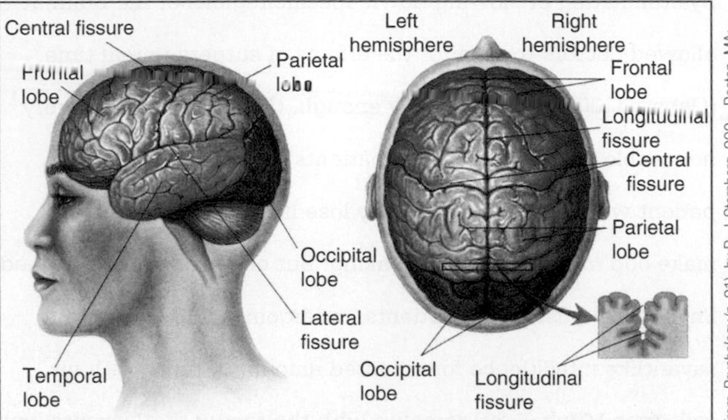

From *Psychology* (p. 91), by R. J. Sternberg, 2004, Boston, MA: Wadsworth. Copyright 2004 by Cengage Learning. Reprinted with permission.

Source information in caption separated by commas; note APA use of capital letters in a caption

Figure 1. Diagram of the brain. From *Psychology* (p. 91), by R. J. Sternberg, 2004, Boston, MA: Wadsworth. Copyright 2004 by Cengage Learning.

random number of dots on a computer screen (as shown in Figure 2) and then told to estimate the number of dots they saw. They were asked to do this before the TMS stimulation, then 15 minutes afterward, and finally an hour later. The same procedure was used in both real and sham sessions.

Results of the Experiment

Purpose of figure explained

The results, summarized in Figure 3, are surprising. Eight of the 12 participants improved their ability to estimate the number of dots within an accuracy range of five after the TMS stimulation. The probability for this to happen merely by chance alone is less than 1 in 1,000. Clearly there is a significant increase in the number of correct estimations after the TMS stimulation. The sham session shows relatively little variation.

Blue = content issues, **Red = format issues**

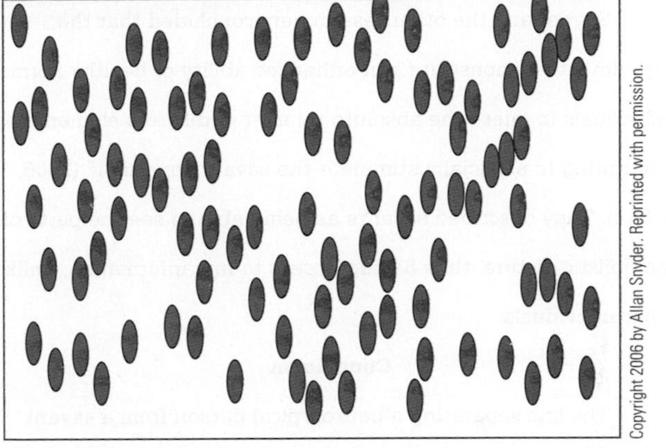

Figure 2. The task—to estimate the number of dots. From A. Snyder et al., 2006, p. 838.

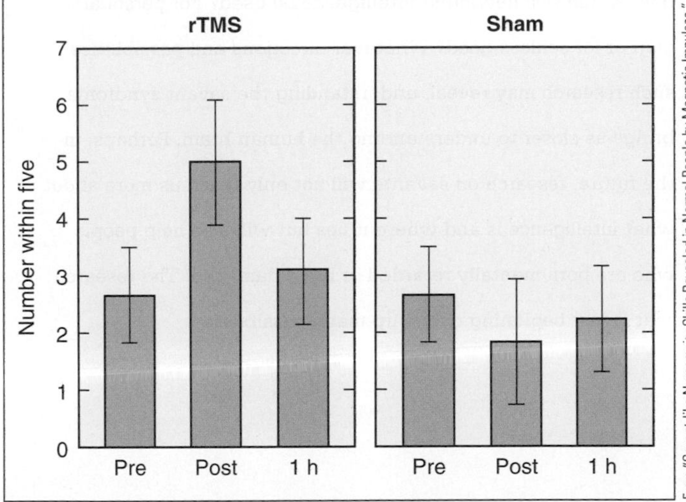

Figure 3. Participants' ability to make guesses within an accuracy range of 5, both with repetitive transcranial magnetic stimulation and without (the sham session). From A. Snyder et al., 2006, p. 841.

Blue = content issues, **Red = format issues**

Confirmation of hypothesis

Authors named at beginning of sentence; year and page number in parentheses after quotation

Snyder and the other researchers concluded that the experiment "demonstrated an enhanced ability of healthy normal individuals to guess the absolute number of discrete elements by attempting to artificially stimulate the savant condition" (2006, p. 842). They described savants as being able to see the parts of the holistic picture, thus having access to raw information, unlike other individuals.

Conclusion

Questions for further research

Thesis

The line separating a neurotypical person from a savant may thus be less "hard wired" than previously assumed. If a person could become brilliant by having his or her brain rewired, how would this newfound intelligence be used? For personal gain or for selfless good? Whatever directions and possibilities such research may reveal, understanding the savant syndrome brings us closer to understanding the human brain. Perhaps, in the future, research on savants will not only teach us more about what intelligence is and where it lies but will also help people who are born mentally retarded or brain damaged. The research that is just beginning opens up many possibilities.

Blue = content issues, **Red = format issues**

SECRET OF SAVANT 10

Heading centered, not in boldface

References

New page, double-spaced

Heffernan, V. (2005, February 23). A savant aided by the sparks that he sees inside his head. *The New York Times.* Retrieved from http://www.nytimes.com

Osborne, L. (2003, June 22). Savant for a day. *The New York Times Magazine*. Retrieved from http://www.nytimes.com

Snyder, A. W., Bahramali, H., Hawker, T., & Mitchell, D. J. (2006). Savant-like numerosity skills revealed in normal people by magnetic impulses. *Perception, 35,* 837–845. doi:10.1068/p5539

Snyder, A. W., & Mitchell, D. J. (1999). Is integer arithmetic fundamental to mental processing? The mind's secret arithmetic. *Proceedings of the Royal Society B: Biological Sciences, 266,* 287–292. doi:10.1098/rspb.1999.0676

Sternberg, R. J. (2004). *Psychology* (4th ed.). Boston, MA: Wadsworth.

Treffert, D. A., & Wallace, G. L. (2004, January). Islands of genius. Mind [Special issue]. *Scientific American, 14*(1), 14–23. Retrieved from http://scientificamerican.com

Entries organized alphabetically by author

Complete date given in parentheses for newspaper article

All four authors' names (reversed) listed in entry; ampersand (&) before last author's name

Scholarly journal title, comma, and volume number italicized

Volume and issue numbers and page range of print magazine article

Retrieval information: URL for home page of online newspaper

No period after URL

All digits repeated in page range

DOI of the article given last in entry, not followed by period

Edition of book in parentheses after title

Name of special issue followed by label in brackets

Blue = content issues, Red = format issues

Council of Science Editors CSE

CSE Style of Documentation

CSE AT-A GLANCE: INDEX OF CSE STYLE FEATURES

MindTap®
Read, highlight, and take notes online.

This chapter describes the documentation style recommended for all natural and applied science disciplines by the Council of Science Editors (CSE) in *Scientific Style and Format: The CSE Manual for Authors, Editors, and Publishers*, 8th edition (Chicago: University of Chicago Press, 2014). This edition describes three systems of documentation citing references in research and other academic texts:

- a *name-year system* similar to APA style (see chapters 14 and 15), in which the in-text citation includes the author(s) and year of publication, and the reference list is arranged alphabetically by author
- a *citation-sequence system* that numbers and lists sources in the order in which they are cited in the paper
- a *citation-name system* that also gives numbers to citations but organizes and numbers the list of references alphabetically by author or title, differing from the citation-sequence system only in the method of assigning numbers to the entries (both systems use the same number when citing a source throughout the paper)

This last option is the one used in *The CSE Manual* itself. Because the name-year system is so similar to APA and because citations for the citation-sequence and citation-name systems differ only in the ordering of the reference list, this chapter concentrates on examples of entries for those last two citation systems.

17a Basic features of CSE style

Always check with your instructors about documentation style guidelines. Some may not specify a particular style but will ask you to select one and use it consistently.

KEY POINTS

How to Number and List Sources in the CSE Citation-Sequence or Citation-Name Style

1. **In the text of your paper**, number each reference with a superscript number in a smaller size than the font for the text, or place the reference number on the line within parentheses. Place punctuation *after* the superscript number.
2. **At the end of your paper**, list the references on a new page titled *References, Cited References, Literature Cited,* or *Bibliography.*

For the *citation-sequence system*, arrange and number the references in your list in the order in which you cite them in your paper. The first citation that appears in your paper will be *1*, and the first reference in your list (also number *1*) will give information about that first citation.

Therefore, an author's name beginning with *Z* could be number *1* and listed first if it is the first source cited in your paper. Each time you cite this source in your paper, you will use the same number (in this case, *1*).

For the *citation-name system*, first arrange your list of references alphabetically by author (or by title if no author is known); then number that list. Whenever you cite the source numbered *1* in your paper, you will insert a superscript *1* (and so on). Therefore, a source with an author's name beginning with *Z* is likely to appear near the end of your list and be numbered accordingly.

Example of Documenting a Print Periodical Article

In-Text Number Citation	Numbered Entry in List of References
Clinical, dopominergic treatment, and MRI data were collected from seventeen PD patients with excessive daytime sleepiness and seventeen PD patients without excessive daytime sleepiness to determine potential causes[6].	6. Chondrogiorgi M, Tzarouchi LC, Zikou AK, Astrakas LG, Kosta P, Argyropoulou MI, Konitsiotis S. Multimodal imaging evaluation of excessive daytime sleepiness in Parkinson's disease. Int J Neurosci. 2016;126(5): 422–428.

17b How to cite CSE sources in your paper (citation-sequence and citation-name styles)

Use superscript numbers to refer readers to the list of references at the end of your paper. Note that the superscript number goes before a punctuation mark.

superscript number

A recent fruit fly study has produced interesting results[2].

One summary of studies of the life span of the fruit fly[3] has shown . . .

Refer to more than one entry in the reference list as follows:

Two studies of the life span of the fruit fly[1,5] have shown that . . .

Several studies of the life span of the fruit fly[1–4] have shown that . . .

Studies of the fruit fly are plentiful[1–6], but the most revealing is . . .

17c How to list CSE references (citation-sequence and citation-name systems)

KEY POINTS

Setting Up the CSE List of Cited References

1. After the last page of your paper, include the list of references, titled *References, Cited References, Literature Cited,* or *Bibliography.*
2. Arrange and number the works either (1) consecutively in the order in which you mention them in your paper (citation-sequence system) or (2) alphabetically (citation-name system). Invert all authors' names, and use the initials of first and middle names. Use no punctuation between last names and initials, leave no space between initials, and do not use *and* or *&* before the last author's name.
3. Begin each entry with the note number followed by a period and a space. Do not indent the first line of each entry; indent subsequent lines to align beneath the first letter of the previous line.
4. Do not italicize, underline, or use quotation marks for the titles of articles, books, or journals and other periodicals.
5. Capitalize only the first word of a book or article title and any proper nouns.
6. Abbreviate titles of journals, organizations, and words such as *volume* (*vol.*) or *series* (*ser.*) according to the International Standard Serial Number's List of Title Word Abbreviations (www.issn.org).
7. Use a period between major divisions of each entry.
8. Put a semicolon and a space between the name of the publisher (not abbreviated) and the publication year of a book. Use a semicolon with no space between the date and the volume number of a journal.
9. For books, you may give the total number of pages, followed by a space and *p.* For journal articles, give inclusive page spans, using all digits: 135–136.
10. For online sources, provide (as applicable) the author; title; edition (if applicable); publication information (place of publication, publisher, date); date updated; date accessed; and a DOI or URL (see the Key Points box in 15c on pp. 305–306). Break a DOI or URL only after a slash.

CSE Council of Science Editors

17d Sample CSE listings: Print and online books and parts of books (citation-sequence or citation-name system)

1. Whole book with one author

no punctuation — title not italicized; only first word capitalized

1. Volobuev AN. Mathematical genetics. New York: Nova Science Publishers; 2015. 145 p.

initials with no period between — publisher — semicolon — number of pages in book (optional)

Give the city of publication, and include the state in parentheses if the city is not well known (see item 3).

2. Book with two or more authors For up to ten authors, list all names (separated by commas). For eleven authors or more, list the first ten and follow with a comma and *et al.*

all authors' names reversed — edition after the first

2. Siebert L, Simkin T, Kimberly P. Volcanoes of the world. 3rd ed. Berkeley: University of California Press; 2011. 568 p.

3. Book with editor(s) Spell out the word *editors.*

3. Wusirika R, Bohn M, Lai J, Kole C, editors. Genetics, genomics, and the breeding of maize. Boca Raton (FL): CRC Press; 2015. 307 p.

4. Part of a book For a work in an edited book, first give the author and name of the work. Then write *In* (followed by a colon) and give the publication information for the edited book. End with the page numbers for the work.

4. Tallacchini M. Risks and rights in xenotransplantation. In: Jasanoff S, editor. Reframing rights: bioconstitutionalism in the genetic age. Cambridge: MIT Press; 2011. p. 169–192.

For a chapter or section of a book written by the author(s), first give the book's regular publication details (but not the total number of pages); then give the name of the chapter or section and its inclusive page numbers.

5. Online book (e-book) Give the publication information as you would for a print book, and then provide the date updated (if applicable) and the date accessed in brackets, followed by the DOI or URL.

5. Macdougall D. Nature's clocks: how scientists measure the age of almost everything. Berkeley: University of California Press; 2008 [accessed 2016 Feb 12]. http://www.ucpress.edu/ebook.php?isbn=9780520933446.

17e Sample CSE listings: Articles in print and online periodicals

6. Article in a print scholarly journal

6. Bonar EE, Young KM, Hoffman E, Gumber S, Cummings JP, Pavlick M, Rosenberg H. Quantitative and qualitative assessment of university students' definitions of binge drinking. Psych Add Behav. 2012;26:187–193.

volume complete page span

no spaces in information about journal

For a journal paginated by issue, include the issue number in parentheses after the volume number.

7. Newspaper or magazine article Give the name of the newspaper (not including *The*), the edition, the complete date, the section, and the first page and column numbers of the article. Abbreviate months to three letters with no period.

7. Gorman J. In the human genome, hearing echoes of opera's intricacies. New York Times (National Ed.). 2012 Apr 10;Sect D:3 (col. 1).

For a magazine article, give the complete date but not volume and issue numbers. Give the complete page span.

8. Article with no author identified Begin with the title of the article.

9. Online journal article with a print source and DOI Cite as for a print journal article, but after the publication date, give your date of access (*cited . . .*) in brackets, followed by a semicolon. Then give the volume and issue numbers and inclusive page numbers. End with the DOI. (See the Key Points box on p. 343.)

9. Pawitan JA. Prospect of cell therapy for Parkinson's disease. Ant Cell Biol. 2011 [accessed 2016 Feb 12];44(4):256–264. doi:10.5115/acb.2011.44.4.256.

10. Online journal article with no print source If no print source is available, after the volume or issue number provide in square brackets an estimate of the article's length in paragraphs, screens, lines, or bytes: [15 paragraphs], [172 lines].

10. Russo C. A neurological virus. Vectors Journ. 2007 [accessed 2016 Feb 12];2(2); [about 2 screens]. http://vectors.usc.edu/issues/4/malperception/virus.html.

11. Article in an online database Provide any identifying document number at the end of the citation, after the URL.

11. Verhoeven JTA, Setter TL. Agricultural use of wetlands: opportunities and limitations. Ann Bot. 2010 [accessed 2016 Feb 12];105(1):155–163. http://www.ncbi.nlm.nih.gov/pmc/articles/PMC2794053/. Document no. PMC 2794053.

17f Sample CSE listings: Other online and audiovisual sources

For other online sources provide the author, title, city, publisher or site sponsor, and the full date of publication or copyright year. In brackets put any update or modification date and your date of access. Indicate in brackets the number of screens, paragraphs, lines, or bytes. End with the URL.

12. Web page Give full dates (abbreviating months).

12. Hill LO. Seizures: when "electrical brainstorm" hits. Atlanta: Cable News Network; 2012 Jun 21 [accessed 2016 Feb 12]. [about 5 screens]. http://www.cnn.com/2012/06/18/health/seizures-epilepsy-myths/index.html?hpt=he_bn2.

13. Posting to social media After the username, group, or page name, list the name of the social media platform, and in brackets give descriptive information for the type of page or post you are citing. Next, list the date and time of the posting (if available), your date of access in brackets, and the URL where the posting can be found.

13. Matt Shipman. Twitter [status update, shared link]. 2016 Apr 19, 5:08 a.m. [accessed 2016 Apr 19]. https://twitter.com/ShipLives/status/722396394242383872.

14. DVDs, CD-ROMs, and other audiovisual sources Begin with the title, and include the medium in brackets. Follow this with details of the producer, author, or editor; place; publisher; and date. Include a brief description, such as length (of a film), color (of a work of art), number of discs, and type of accompanying material. End with the URL for online sources.

18 Sample Paper 6: Excerpt from a Student's Research Paper, CSE Style

The following excerpt from a paper titled "Longaeva: The Scientific Significance of the Ancient Bristlecone Pine" was written by Andrew Dillon for a first-year course on "Volcanoes of the Eastern Sierra Nevada" at Indiana University. He uses the CSE citation-sequence documentation style as required by his instructor and divides his paper into sections with headings: Abstract, Introduction, Phenotype and Physiology, Natural Range and Growing Adversities, Contributions to Science, Conclusion, and References. He also illustrates his twenty-one-page paper with photographs and images that show some features and settings of the huge ancient trees. Dillon's title page, numbered page 1, provides the essay title, the running head (*Bristlecone Pine*), his name, the name of the course, the instructor, and the date. Shown here are pages excerpted from the paper: the abstract, the beginning of the Phenotype and Physiology section, and the references, all of which demonstrate key features of the CSE citation-sequence system.

Note: Blue annotations point out issues of content and organization. Red annotations point out CSE format issues.

Council of Science Editors CSE

Abstract

Running head and page number on every page (title page is page 1)

Bristlecone Pine 2

Section heading centered

Abstract

More than any other species of tree, the bristlecone pine (*Pinus longaeva*), of the White Mountains in California, helps scientists to understand the environmental conditions of the past. With some living specimens attaining ages nearing 5,000 years, and dead matter persisting for another several thousand, these ancient trees have provided climatologists, geologists, and dendrochronologists with a continuous tree-ring chronology that dates back to the last Ice Age. This paper examines the complex physiology and habitat of the species and considers what scientists have learned from the bristlecone about the earth's history. Research from the past half century illuminates the magnificence of bristlecone pines as living evidence of past millennia.

Summary of paper

Blue = content issues, **Red = format issues**

Excerpt from third section of paper, pages 6 and 7

Bristlecone Pine 6

Phenotype and Physiology

Section heading centered

1" margins

Like all pines, bristlecones belong to the phylum *Coniferophyta*: the conifers. Classified within this phylum are almost 50 genera and roughly 550 species. Evidence suggests that the *Coniferophyta* developed some 300 million years ago in the Carboniferous Period, developing the pine family after 165 million years. Now approximately 135 million years old, this family includes bristlecones and coastal redwoods, respectively holding records for the oldest and tallest trees in the world[1].

Includes data on age and size

Superscript number referring to source #1 in references (citation-sequence style)

Although maintaining easily identifiable conifer traits, the bristlecone pine has a distinctive, even odd, appearance. Many of these trees have been gnarled, bent, and twisted over time, resulting in ghostly entangled forms of both living and dead material. Some researchers believe that in fact, "over the millennia bristlecones genetically programmed to twist may have been better adapted to survive"[2], potentially explaining the unusual contortions, as shown in Figure 1.

Figure placed near first mention in text

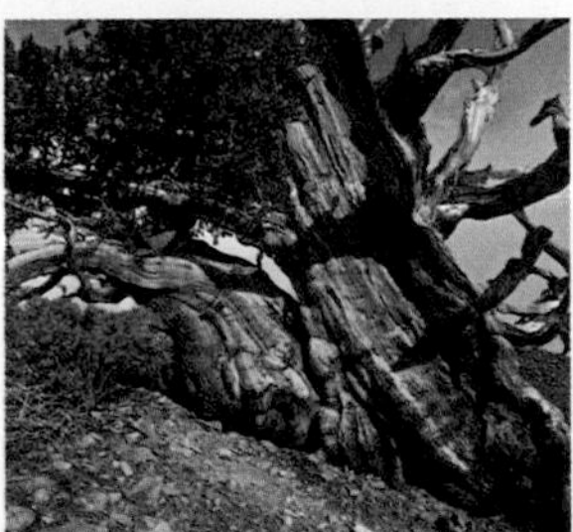

Rinusbaak/Dreamstime

Figure 1. Bristlecone Pine (*Pinus aristata*), among the oldest known trees (Lola B. Graham, The National Audubon Society Collection/Photo Researchers).

Blue = content issues, **Red = format issues**

Bristlecone Pine 7

Punctuation mark after superscript citation number

Deadwood colors range from white to dark gray or black, living from light to dark brown. Because these trees grow for so long and at such slow rates, wood tends to be tightly compact, resinous, and highly resistant to disease, infestation, or rot[3]. For their old age they are also remarkably small, hardly ever exceeding thirteen meters tall by four meters around[4].

Blue = content issues, **Red = format issues**

List of references (selected here to match the excerpt)

Bristlecone Pine 20

References

1. Allaby M. Plants and plant life. Vol. 8, Conifers. Danbury (CT): Grolier; 2001. 49 p.
2. Little JB. Timeline. Amer Forests. 2004;109(4):22–27.
3. Ferguson CW. Bristlecone pine: science and esthetics. Science New Ser. 1968;159(3817):839–846.
4. Gidwitz T. Telling time. Archaeology. 2001 [accessed 2016 Feb 12];54(2):36–41. http://www.archaeology.org/0103/abstracts/time.html.

Issue number in parentheses

Online source: date of access in brackets and URL at the end

Blue = content issues, Red = format issues

Chicago Manual of Style CHICAGO

19 *Chicago Manual of Style:* Endnotes, Footnotes, and Bibliography

CHICAGO AT-A-GLANCE: INDEX OF *CHICAGO* STYLE FEATURES

MindTap®
Read, highlight, and take notes online.

The Chicago Manual of Style, 16th ed. (Chicago: U of Chicago P, 2010) describes two documentation systems, an author-year parenthetical system of references similar to the APA system and a system in which sources are documented in footnotes or endnotes and usually listed in a bibliography. This second system, sometimes called *Chicago* humanities style, discussed in this chapter and in chapter 20, is used widely in the humanities, especially in history, art history, literature, and the arts. Because works in these fields are most concerned with presenting content without interruption, sources are cited within the text with only superscript numbers that refer readers to footnotes or endnotes for source information. All publication details are given either in a complete first footnote or endnote for the source or in a bibliography at the end of the work.

19a Basic features of the *Chicago* note style

KEY POINTS

How to Number and Document Sources in the *Chicago* Endnote/Footnote Style

1. **In your text,** place a superscript numeral at the end of the quotation or the clause or sentence in which you mention source material; place the number after all punctuation marks except a dash.

(Continued)

(Continued)

2. **On a separate numbered page at the end of the paper,** list all endnotes, and number the notes sequentially, as they appear in your paper. If you use footnotes, a word processing program will automatically place them at the bottom of a page (see 21g on using computer programs such as *Word* for formatting an academic paper).

Example of an Endnote or Footnote for a Book

In-text Citation with Numeral	Numbered Endnote or Footnote
Numeral only Mondrian planned his compositions with colored tape.[3] **Source mentioned in your paper** According to Arnason and Prather, Mondrian planned his compositions with colored tape.[3]	3. H. Harvard Arnason and Marla F. Prather, *History of Modern Art* (New York: Abrams, 1998), 393.

19b How to cite sources and prepare notes (*Chicago*)

To cite a source in your paper Use the following format, and number your notes sequentially. If you use endnotes and not footnotes, mention the source in your text whenever possible so that readers do not have to flip to the end to find the source.

> George Eliot thought that *Eliot* was a "good, mouthfilling, easy to pronounce word."[1]

First note for a source when no bibliography is attached Long-form source notes can supply full publication details of a source, so a separate list of references is not necessary. However, if your instructor requires one, see 19d and the sample student paper in chapter 20. See the Key Points box on pages 353–354 for more on the format of a note.

author's name in normal order | comma | book title italicized; all major words capitalized | place, publisher, and date in parentheses

1. Margaret Crompton, *George Eliot: The Woman* (London: Cox and Wyman, 1960), 123.

page number | comma

Short-form first note for a source if a bibliography is provided If you are required to attach a separate bibliography listing the complete publication information for all the sources you cited or consulted, the note citation can be concise. It gives just enough information to enable readers to find the source in the bibliography.

1. Crompton, *George Eliot*, 123.

For the format of a bibliography entry, see 19d; for a sample bibliography, see chapter 20.

Note referring to the immediately preceding source In a reference to the immediately preceding source, you may use *Ibid.* (Latin *ibidem*, meaning "in the same place") instead of repeating the author's name and the title of the work; follow with a comma and the page number(s). All the details except the page number(s) must be the same as those in the previous citation. If the page number is the same, too, just write *Ibid.*

2. Ibid., 127.

However, avoid using a series of *Ibid.* notes. These are likely to irritate readers. Instead, place additional page references within your text: *As Crompton points out (127), . . .*

Any subsequent reference to a previously cited source For a reference to a source cited in a previous note but not in the immediately preceding note, give only the author and page number:

6. Crompton, 124.

If you cite more than one work by the same author, however, include a short title to identify the source.

19c How to format *Chicago* endnotes and footnotes

KEY POINTS

Guidelines for *Chicago* Endnotes and Footnotes

1. **Numbering** In the list of endnotes, place each number on the line (not as a superscript), followed by a period and one space. Follow the same format for a footnote. For footnotes, word processing software will often automatically make the number a superscript—just be consistent with whatever format you use.

(Continued)

(Continued)

2. **Spacing and indentation** Indent the first line of each note as you would the first line of a paragraph. Single-space within a note and double-space between notes unless your instructor prefers double-spacing throughout.
3. **Author's name** Use the author's full name, not inverted, followed by a comma and the title of the work.
4. **More than one author** In section 19e, items 2–3 show how to cite multiple authors of books. Follow these examples for articles, online sources, multimedia, and miscellaneous works.
5. **Titles of works** Put quotation marks around titles of articles and Web pages, and italicize titles of books, periodicals, and blogs. Capitalize all first letters of words in the titles of books, periodicals, and articles except *a*, *an*, *the*; coordinating conjunctions such as *and*, *but*, and *so*; *to* in an infinitive; and prepositions. These words are capitalized only when they are the beginning words of titles.
6. **Publishing information** After a book title, in parentheses give the city (and state for a city not well known), name of publisher, and year. Follow this with a comma and the page number(s), with no *p.* or *pp.* After an article title, give the name of the periodical and pertinent publication information (volume, issue, date, and page numbers where appropriate). You may abbreviate or spell out months in the date of publication—just be consistent.
7. **Punctuation** Separate major parts of the citation with commas, not periods.
8. **Online sources** Provide a DOI or a URL and date of posting or revision. If there is none, list your access date (not otherwise needed) before the URL.
9. **Quotations and specific references** Provide the page number(s) for cited material following the publication details and after a comma, as in Source Shot 13 (pp. 360–361). No page numbers are needed when referring to a work as a whole.

19d The *Chicago* bibliography

A bibliography is an alphabetical list arranged by author (or by title if no author is named) of all the works cited (or consulted) in your paper. It is placed at the end of the paper after any endnotes. A bibliography contains the same elements as those listed in a long-form note (see 19c), but they are separated by periods rather than commas. In entries, the first author's name is inverted, and a book's publication details are not put in parentheses (see Source Shot 13 on pp. 360–361). Inclusive page numbers are given for periodical articles and for short works and chapters in books, but no page range or total is given for complete books. Entries are single-spaced, with a double-space between them. The first line of an entry begins flush left, and subsequent lines are indented (called a *hanging indent*).

If you include a bibliography, you need to use only short-form notes (see 19b), but check to see what your instructor prefers. See an example of a bibliography in the sample student paper in chapter 20.

Note how the bibliography form differs from the note form:

Note Form	Bibliography Form
commas separate 3 major parts of note; note number, first line indented	periods separate 3 major parts of entry; no note number, indented after first line
7. Andrea Pappas, "Configuring and Contesting Jewish Identities in the Visual Field," *Journal of Modern Jewish Studies* 15, no. 1 (2016): 2.	Pappas, Andrea. "Configuring and Contesting Jewish Identities in the Visual Field." *Journal of Modern Jewish Studies* 15, no. 1 (2016): 1–5.
page number of cited material	page range of article

19e Sample *Chicago* notes: Print and online books, parts of books, and reports

1. Print book with one author See Source Shot 13 (pp. 360–361). Always include a page number or numbers to cite a specific page or specific pages of a book.

2. Book with two or three authors

2. George Lakoff and Mark Johnson, *Metaphors We Live By*, 2nd ed. (Chicago: University of Chicago Press, 2003), 55–61.

List two or three authors in the order in which they appear on the title page, separated by commas. In a bibliography entry, invert only the first author's name.

3. Book with four or more authors In a note for a book with multiple authors, use the name of only the first author, followed by *et al.* (abbreviation for Latin *et alli,* "and others").

3. Randolph Quirk et al., *A Comprehensive Grammar of the English Language* (London: Longman, 1985), 132.

In a bibliography, for a work with ten authors or fewer, include all the names; for a work with more than ten authors, list only the first seven names, followed by *et al.*

4. Book with no author identified For a note, begin with the title.

4. *Chicago Manual of Style*, 16th ed. (Chicago: University of Chicago Press, 2010).

5. Book with editor, translator, or compiler

5. John Updike, ed., *The Best American Short Stories of the Century* (Boston: Houghton Mifflin, 1999).

For a translated or compiled work, after the title write *trans.* or *comp.* and the name of the translator or compiler. For more than one editor, translator, or compiler, add the appropriate abbreviation and treat as multiple authors (see items 2 and 3).

If the book has both an author and an editor or translator, begin with the author; then add *ed.* or *trans.* after the title of the book, and give that person's name.

6. Work in an edited volume or anthology (essay, story, chapter, poem, letter) Begin with the author and title of the work, and follow with the title of the anthology. Include *ed.* for *edited by*. For a letter, also include the addressee and the date (Elizabeth Bishop to Marianne Moore, January 5, 1945). End with any relevant page number(s).

6. Adrienne Rich, "Split at the Root," in *The Art of the Personal Essay*, ed. Phillip Lopate (New York: Anchor/Doubleday, 1994), 649.

7. Preface, introduction, foreword, or afterword Give the name of the writer of the material when this is different from the author of the book.

7. David Remnick, introduction to *Politics*, by Hendrik Hertzberg (New York: Penguin, 2004), xviii.

8. Subsequent and reprint editions For an edition after the first, add the number and *ed.* (for *edition*) after the title. Use *rev. ed.* for a revised edition.

8. Jim Leach, *Film in Canada,* 2nd ed. (New York: Oxford University Press, 2010), 40.

If a work has been reprinted, in a note in parentheses, give the year of the original publication and a semicolon, and then add the abbreviation *repr.*, a comma, and the publication details for the work.

9. Multivolume work Give the number of any specific volume you cite, followed by a colon (with no space) and the page number. If the author's name is part of the title, the note may begin with the title.

9. *Collected Papers of Albert Einstein,* ed. John Stachel, David C. Cassidy, and Robert Schulmann (Princeton, NJ: Princeton University Press, 1987), 1:107.

If you refer to the work as a whole, the part of the citation after the title should look like this: *13 vols. (Princeton, NJ: Princeton University Press, 1987–2012).*

10. Author's work quoted in another work (secondary source) List both works in your bibliography, giving *quoted in* and the name of the secondary source in the entry for the author's work. Note, however, that *The Chicago Manual of Style* recommends that whenever possible a reference be cited from the original work.

10. E. M. Forster, *Two Cheers for Democracy* (New York: Harcourt, Brace, and World, 1942), 242, quoted in Phyllis Rose, *Woman of Letters, A Life of Virginia Woolf* (New York: Oxford University Press, 1978), 219.

11. E-book (electronic book) Cite an e-book downloaded from a bookseller or library as you would a print book, but add the format: *Kindle edition, Microsoft Reader e-book,* and so on. Because page numbers are usually not stable, cite a chapter, section heading, or other division of the work.

11. Jane Blocker, *Becoming Past: History in Contemporary Art* (Minneapolis: University of Minnesota Press, 2016), MyiLibrary e-book, chap. 1.

12. Book accessed online Cite as you would a print book, but end with the DOI (if available) or URL (see Key Points box on p. 363). For citing specific material, give a chapter number or section heading (as in item 11).

12. Mary Wollestonecraft Shelley, *Frankenstein, or, the Modern Prometheus* (London: Dent, 1912), http://ota.ahds.ac.uk.

13. Religious works and classics Provide the citation in parenthetical text references or in a note. For the Bible, include the book (in abbreviated form, along with chapter and verse, but no page number), and in parentheses give the version used (spelled out in full on first mention).

13. Gen. 27:29 (New Revised Standard Version).

For Greek and Roman works and for classic plays in English, put a comma between the author and title, but add no punctuation after the title. Locate the work by the number of book, section, and line or by act, scene, and line (separated by periods with no space following). Cite a

Continued on page 362

CHICAGO

Chicago Manual of Style

SOURCE SHOT 13

Listing a Print Book in *Chicago* Style

Find the necessary information for documenting a book on its title page or copyright page.

Title Page of Print Book

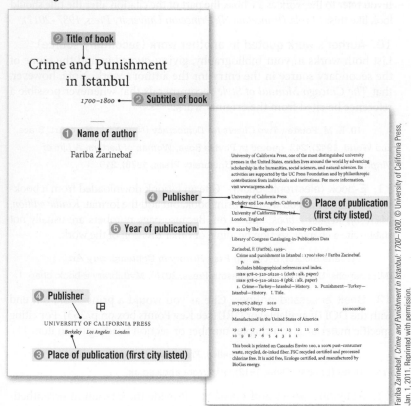

❷ Title of book

Crime and Punishment in Istanbul

1700–1800 ❷ Subtitle of book

❶ Name of author

Fariba Zarinebaf

❹ Publisher

UNIVERSITY OF CALIFORNIA PRESS

Berkeley Los Angeles London

❸ Place of publication (first city listed)

University of California Press, one of the most distinguished university presses in the United States, enriches lives around the world by advancing scholarship in the humanities, social sciences, and natural sciences. Its activities are supported by the UC Press Foundation and by philanthropic contributions from individuals and institutions. For more information, visit www.ucpress.edu.

❹ Publisher

University of California Press
Berkeley and Los Angeles, California ❸ Place of publication (first city listed)

University of California Press, Ltd.
London, England

❺ Year of publication

© 2010 by The Regents of the University of California

Library of Congress Cataloging-in-Publication Data

Zarinebaf, F. (Fariba), 1959–.
Crime and punishment in Istanbul : 1700/1800 / Fariba Zarinebaf.
p. cm.
Includes bibliographical references and index.
ISBN 978-0-520-26220-1 (cloth : alk. paper)
ISBN 978-0-520-26221-8 (pbk. : alk. paper)
1. Crime—Turkey—Istanbul—History. 2. Punishment—Turkey—Istanbul—History. I. Title.

HV7076.7.Z8Z37 2010
394.94961'809033—dc22 2010020820

Manufactured in the United States of America

19 18 17 16 15 14 13 12 11 10
10 9 8 7 6 5 4 3 2 1

This book is printed on Cascades Enviro 100, a 100% post-consumer waste, recycled, de-inked fiber. FSC recycled certified and processed chlorine free. It is acid free, Ecologo certified, and manufactured by BioGas energy.

Format for a footnote or endnote:

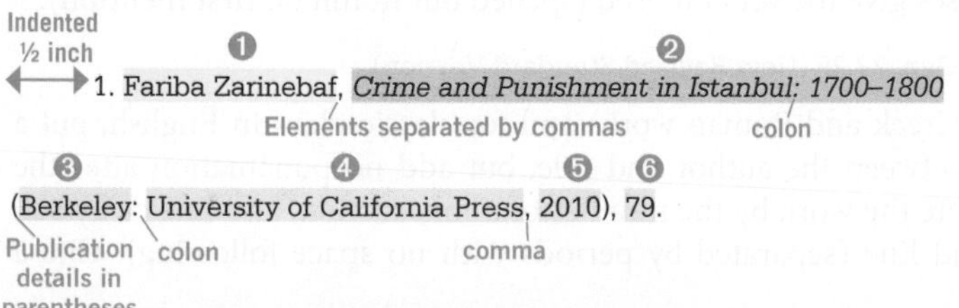

❶ **Name of author** First and last name in normal order, followed by a comma

❷ ***Title of Book: Subtitle*** In italics, with capitals for main words (see the Key Points box on pp. 355–356); not followed by punctuation

In parentheses after the title (or subtitle if there is one), list items 3–5.

❸ **City of publication** The first city mentioned on the title page, followed by a colon. Give the state (two-letter postal abbreviation) or country (abbreviated) only if the city is not well known or could be confused with another one.

❹ **Name of publisher** Either give the name in full or in a somewhat shortened form, omitting abbreviations such as *Co.* and *Inc.* (*Little, Brown,* not *Little, Brown & Co.*), followed by a comma. (***Note:*** Usually list the word *Books* (*Basic Books*) and list *Press* if omitting it could cause misunderstanding (*New Press*). Always list *Press* for a university press.

❺ **Year of publication** Available after © on the copyright page. Give the most recent year if several are listed. End with closing parentheses.

❻ **To cite a page or pages** in the source, put a comma after the closing parentheses and add the number(s) and a period.

Format for a bibliography entry

In a bibliography entry, invert the first author's name, separate the elements with periods instead of commas, and do not put the publishing details in parentheses. Do not list the total page numbers of the book. Begin the first line flush left (at the margin), and indent all subsequent lines.

Author's name inverted **Elements separated by periods**

Zarinebaf, Fariba. *Crime and Punishment in Istanbul: 1700–1800.*

First line begins at left margin

Berkeley: University of California Press, 2010.

classic poem by book, canto, stanza, and line, whichever is appropriate. Specify the edition used only in the first note referring to the work.

Do not include the Bible or classical works in a bibliography.

14. Entry in a print reference work Begin with the work's title and edition, but include no page number, publication information, or date. Precede the title of an alphabetized entry with the initials *s.v.* (*sub verbo*—Latin for "under the word").

14. *Chambers Biographical Dictionary,* 9th ed., s.v. "Fuller, Margaret."

Do not include dictionary or encyclopedia entries in a bibliography.

15. Entry in an online reference work Cite an online reference work entry as you would cite one in a print reference work (see item 14), and give the date of posting or update and the URL. If there is no date, give your date of access before the URL.

15. *Encyclopaedia Brittanica* s.v. "symbolism," accessed February 6, 2016, http://www.britannica.com/art/realism-art.

16. Print organization or government report Cite reports, pamphlets, and similar documents as you would cite books. If no individual author is named, list the organization or government department and agency as author. Give any report number after the title.

16. US Department of Education, National Center for Education Statistics, *The National Indian Education Study: 2011,* Report No. 2012466 (Washington, DC: Government Printing Office, 2012), 15.

17. Online organization or government report Cite as you would a print report (see item 16), but give the date of online publication and the URL.

17. US Department of Education, National Center for Education Statistics, *Trends in High School Dropout and Completion Dates in the United States 1972–2009,* Report No. 2012006, 2011, http://nces.ed.gov/pubsearch/pubsinfo.asp?pubid=2012006.

19f Sample *Chicago* notes: Articles in print and online periodicals

When citing periodicals (scholarly journals, magazines, and newspapers), give the full name of the author or authors, title and subtitle of the article (in quotation marks), italicized title of the periodical, volume and issue numbers (for journals), date (complete dates for newspapers), specific page numbers (for notes) or inclusive page numbers (for bibliography entries), and the DOI or URL for online periodicals (see Key Points box on p. 363). Most online journals have page numbers. When there are none, you may cite material by visible paragraph number or section heading. Cite multiple authors for articles as you would cite them for books (see 19e, items 2 and 3).

18. Article in a print scholarly journal, continuously paged If journal volumes are paged continuously through issues (for example, if issue 1 ends on page 188 and issue 2 of the same volume begins with page 189), you need to give only the volume number, not the issue number (although in *Chicago* style, it is never wrong to list it as well), and year (in parentheses). If you refer to a specific page, put a colon and a space after the year, and then add the page number(s). To cite an abstract, include the word *abstract* after the title of the article. For more on scholarly journals, see 8b.

18. Meir Zamir, "MI6: The History of the Secret Intelligence Service: 1909–1949," *Middle Eastern Studies* 48 (2012): 682.

19. Article in a print scholarly journal, each issue paged separately When each issue of a journal begins on page 1, after the volume number, add a comma, *no.* (for *number*), and the issue number. Follow with the year in parentheses, a colon and space, and the specific page number(s) of the cited material. See Source Shot 14 on pages 366–367 for an example.

KEY POINTS

Using DOIs and URLs in *Chicago* Style

Chicago recommends using a DOI (digital object identifier) or URL (uniform resource locator) for any electronic source, including periodicals, accessed online. Use a DOI, a unique, permanent identifying number that applies to a work in any medium in which it is published, rather than a URL, if one is available. Put a DOI at the end of an entry, with *doi* (lowercase) and a colon (with no intervening space) before the number. See the Key Points box in 15c on pages 305–306 for more on using a DOI to locate sources.

When citing a URL, put the date of posting or update before the URL. You do not need to give your date of access (placed immediately before the URL) unless there is no date of posting or update, the site material changes frequently, or your instructor or field requires it.

Break a DOI or URL that continues to a second line only **after** a colon or double slash; **before** a single slash, a comma, period, hyphen, or most other punctuation marks; or **before** or **after** an ampersand or equals sign. Never add a hyphen at the end of a line. Put a period after the DOI or URL, which will end the citation.

20. Article with a DOI in an online scholarly journal Most articles published in online journals have DOIs, which go at the end of the citation. See the Key Points box on p. 363.

20. Paul Jenkins, "Frederick Grant: Ghanaian Photographer," *African Arts* 49, no. 1 (2016): 4, doi:10.1162/AFAR_a_00266.

21. Scholarly journal article in an online database Many articles published in print are also archived and available through free or subscription databases. To cite one, use a DOI rather than a URL, if one is available. Otherwise, cite a stable or persistent, shorter URL that is listed with the article (as in the following example) instead of the URL you see in your browser's address bar when viewing the article. If listing the DOI or stable URL, do not name the database. If no stable URL is given, list just the name of the database and (in parentheses) any identification number.

21. Dianne Sachko Macleod, "Rossetti's Two Ligeias: Their Relationship to Visual Art, Music, and Poetry," special issue on the works of Dante Gabriel Rossetti, *Victorian Poetry* 20, no. 3/4 (1982): 93, http://www.jstor.org/stable/40002989.

Put information about a special issue (often a double issue, as in this example) before the journal title.

22. Online scholarly journal article with URL If an article published in an online journal does not have a DOI (sometimes the case if a journal does not also have a print version), give the URL. The following example cites an article in an online-only journal with numbered paragraphs rather than page numbers.

22. Anna Feuer, "Fair Foul and Right Wrong: The Language of Alchemy in *Timon of Athens*," *Early Modern Literary Studies* 16, no. 1 (2012): paragraphs 5–6, http://extra.shu.ac.uk/emls/16-1/feuetimo.htm.

23. Article in a print magazine Do not give volume or issue numbers, even if they are available. Include the month (abbreviated or spelled out) for monthly magazines and the complete date (with commas) for weekly magazines (month, day, year). Cite only a specific page number in a note (after a comma), not the range of pages. In a bibliography, provide the range of pages of the whole article.

23. Sam Tanenhaus, "The Electroshock Novelist," *Newsweek,* July 2 and 9, 2012, 52.

24. Article in an online magazine Cite as for a print publication, but add the URL. Add the name of a department or section (not in quotation marks) before the magazine title.

24. Brian Palmer, "Living Legends: Do Mythical Creatures Like Bigfoot Ever Turn Out to Be Real?," Explainer, *Slate,* May 23, 2012, http://www.slate.com/articles/health_and_science/explainer/2012/05/bigfoot_dna_analysis_how_often_do_scientists_discover_mythical_creatures_.htm.

25. Article in a print newspaper Cite newspaper articles in notes or in parentheses in running text but not in a bibliography. Do not include an initial *The* in the newspaper title. If the city is not part of the title, add it (italicized). Add the state (abbreviated) or province in parentheses (italicized) if the city is not well known. You may give an edition or section number, but do not give page numbers.

25. Jenny Anderson, "New Rules Seek to Stop Cheating on SAT and ACT," *New York Times*, March 28, 2012, national edition, sec. A.

26. Article in an online newspaper Cite as for a print publication, adding the URL. See Source Shot 15 on pages 368–369 for an example.

27. Editorial For an unsigned editorial, begin with the title. Cite a signed editorial as you would an article.

27. "A Rockier Pathway to Work," Editorial, *New York Times,* April 10, 2012, national edition, sec. A.

28. Letter to the editor Do not list a title even if one is given.

28. Robert Appin, letter to the editor, *Economist*, June 30, 2012, 10.

29. Review (of a book, play, film, performance, etc.) Give the name of the reviewer (if signed); title (if any); words *review of* and title of the reviewed work; name of the author, director, or other creator; location and date (for a performance); and publication details of the periodical.

29. Joe Morgenstern, "'Tattoo': Raw, Rousing and Rather Redundant," review of *The Girl with the Dragon Tattoo,* directed by David Fincher, *Wall Street Journal,* December 23, 2011, sec. D.

SOURCE SHOT 14

Listing a Scholarly Print Journal Article in *Chicago* Style

Journal Table of Contents

FOREIGN AFFAIRS

❸ Journal title

❻ Year of publication

SEPTEMBER / OCTOBER 2010

❹ Volume number — VOLUME 89, NUMBER 5 — ❺ Issue number

Comments

❷ Title of article

❼ Page span

Out of Order *Matthew Moten* 2

The ouster of General Stanley McChrystal for his disparaging comments about civilian leaders does not suggest that U.S. political-military relations are in crisis. But it should remind the military's highest officers of the the need for, and the requirements of, appropriate professional behavior.

❶ Author

Smaller and Safer *Bruce Blair, Victor Esin, Matthew McKinzie, Valery Yarynich, and Pavel Zolotarev* 9

The proposed nuclear arms reductions in the New START treaty are sensible, but the United States and Russia can and should go much further. In the next round of negotiations, the two countries should pursue deep cuts in their stockpiles and agree on maintaining a lower level of launch readiness.

Essays

Beyond Moderates and Militants
Robert Malley and Peter Harling 18

When it comes to the Middle East, U.S. policymakers tend to apply yesterday's solutions to today's problems. In doing so, they miss realistic chances to help reshape the region. President Barack Obama must recognize that there is not a clean divide between a moderate, pro-American camp and an extremist, militant axis and take into account the Middle East's rapidly shifting dynamics—including the complex and competing interests of newly engaged players, such as Iran, Syria, and Turkey.

Endnote or footnote format for a print article

First line indented ½ inch

19. Matthew Moten, "Out of Order," *Foreign Affairs* 89, no. 5 (2010): 5.

❶ ❷ ❸ ❹ ❺ ❻ ❼

Elements separated by commas

Colon and space

In a note, include the following when listing an article in a scholarly print journal with each issue paged separately:

❶ **Name of author** First and last names in normal order, followed by a comma

❷ **"Title of Article: Any Subtitle."** In quotation marks, with major words capitalized, followed by a comma

❸ ***Title of journal*** In italics, omitting *The* with no comma following

❹ The **volume number** (with no abbreviation *vol.*) in regular (Roman) print, followed by a comma

❺ The abbreviation *no.* and the **issue number**, not followed by a comma

❻ **(Year of publication)** in parentheses, followed by a colon

❼ **Specific page number** or **numbers** of cited material, followed by a period

Bibliography entry format

In a bibliography entry, separate the elements with periods. Begin the first line flush left, and indent all other lines. List the author's last name, a comma, and first name (for alphabetizing). End with the range of pages for the article.

Author's name inverted

Moten, Matthew. "Out of Order." *Foreign Affairs* 89, no. 5 (2010): 2–8.

First line begins at left margin

Elements separated with periods

Complete page range of article

SOURCE SHOT 15

Listing an Article in an Online Newspaper in *Chicago* Style

An Article in an Online Newspaper

Top of Article Web Page

Bottom of Web Page

Source: www.washingtonpost.com

19g Sample *Chicago* notes: Other online sources

See the Key Points box on page 363 on formatting URLs and publication dates. Do not give an access date unless there is no date of posting or update, site material is frequently updated, or your instructor or discipline requires one.

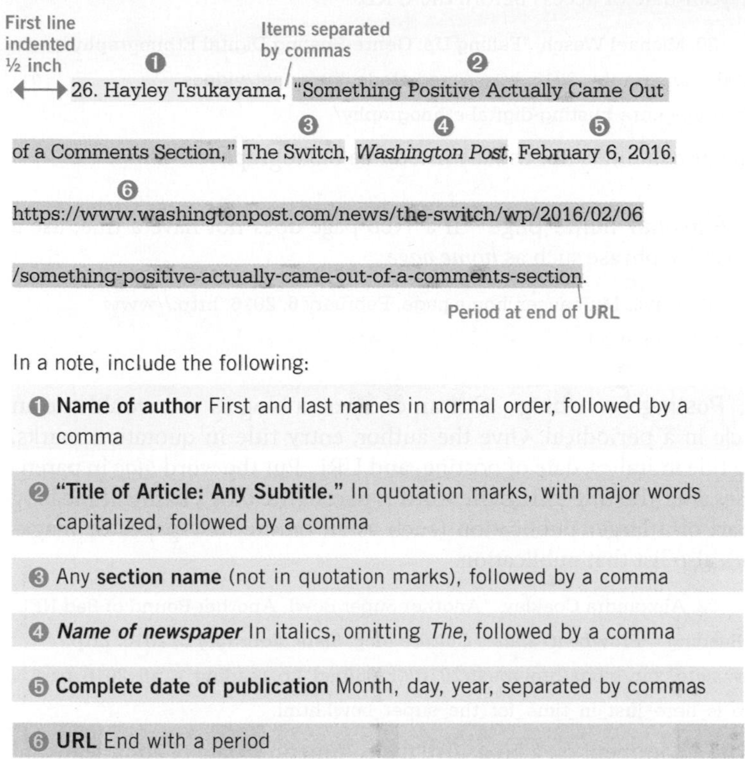

First line indented ½ inch
Items separated by commas
26. Hayley Tsukayama, "Something Positive Actually Came Out of a Comments Section," The Switch, *Washington Post*, February 6, 2016, https://www.washingtonpost.com/news/the-switch/wp/2016/02/06/something-positive-actually-came-out-of-a-comments-section.
Period at end of URL
In a note, include the following:
❶ **Name of author** First and last names in normal order, followed by a comma
❷ **"Title of Article: Any Subtitle."** In quotation marks, with major words capitalized, followed by a comma
❸ Any **section name** (not in quotation marks), followed by a comma
❹ ***Name of newspaper*** In italics, omitting *The*, followed by a comma
❺ **Complete date of publication** Month, day, year, separated by commas
❻ **URL** End with a period

30. Web page or article To cite a Web page or article that is not a formally published document, give the author of the content, if known; the title of the page or article (in quotation marks); the Web site name, if necessary (not in quotation marks and italics only if the name of a publication); the owner or sponsor of the site; the date of posting or update; and the URL. If there is no publication date or if the material is often updated, give your date of access before the URL.

30. Michael Wesch, "Falling Up: Genre-Busting Digital Ethnography," Digital Ethnography, 2015, http://mediatedcultures.net/videos /falling-up-genre-busting-digital-ethnography/.

Web site content is not usually listed in a bibliography.

31. Personal home page If a Web page does not have a title, use a descriptive phrase such as *home page.*

31. Travis Mulhauser, home page, February 6, 2016, http://www .travismulhauser.com.

32. Posting on a blog Cite an entry on a blog as you would cite an article in a periodical. Give the author, entry title in quotation marks, blog title in italics, date of posting, and URL. Put the word *blog* in parentheses after the title unless the word is part of the blog's name. If the blog is part of a larger publication (such as an online newspaper or magazine), also list that publication.

32. Alexandra Coakley, "Another Super Bowl, Another Round of Bad NFL Lip Reading," *Browbeat: Slate's Culture Blog, Slate,* February 6, 2016, http:// www.slate.com/blogs/browbeat/2016/02/06/bad_lip_reading_s_nfl_2016_part _two_is_here_just_in_time_for_the_super_bowl.html.

To cite a comment on a blog, give the commenter, date of comment, and words *comment on* with information about the related entry. Blog entries are usually only cited in notes, but you may list a blog you cite often in a bibliography.

33. Posting on a discussion board, archived electronic mailing list, or wiki Whenever possible, include the name of the list, date of posting, and URL for archived material.

33. Duane Roen to WPA-L mailing list, February 6, 2016, https://lists.asu .edu/cgi-bin/wa?AO=WPA-L.

34. E-mail or other personal communication Mention within your text or in a note, noting the type of message (telephone, etc.).

34. Stephanie Carpenter, e-mail message to the author, February 6, 2016.

19h Sample *Chicago* notes: Visual, multimedia, and miscellaneous sources

35. Sound recording (MP3, LP, compact disc, audiocassette, audiobook, etc.) Give the performer, writer, or other creator of the content; title; name of recording company or publisher; any identifying number; date of copyright, publication, or recording; medium (LP, etc.), and any optional supplementary information (number of discs, etc.). If accessed online, include a URL or DOI.

35. Ta-Nehisi Coates, *Between the World and Me,* read by the author, Random House Audio, 2015, MP3 audiobook.

36. Video recording (DVD, CD-ROM, videocassette, film, filmstrip, etc.) List pertinent identifying details (see item 35), and identify the medium (DVD, slides, etc.). Give the facts of publication as for print media where needed.

36. Davis Guggenheim, *He Named Me Malala,* Century City, CA: Fox Searchlight, 2015, DVD.

37. Podcast and other online multimedia Cite a podcast, video blog, or other electronic format as you would cite a blog posting (see item 32). List performers, writers, or other creators of the content; pertinent identifying and publication or broadcast details (including information about the original performance or source); the medium (MPEG video, MP3 file, etc.); and the URL.

37. John S. Allen, author of *The Omnivorous Mind: Our Evolving Relationship with Food,* interview with Chris Gondek, Harvard University Press website, podcast audio, July 15, 2012, http://www.hup.harvard.edu/news/audio/HUP_Allen.mp3.

38. Interview Treat a published interview like a periodical article or book chapter, including the phrase *interview with.*

38. Rachel Maddow, "The Maddow Knows," interview with Clara Jeffery, *Mother Jones,* January/February, 2009, 72–73.

For an interview conducted online, include the URL. If it is on an audiovisual source, indicate the medium (see item 37).

For an unpublished interview, include in your text the names of the interviewer and person interviewed, date, and type of interview (such as *telephone interview*).

39. Lecture, speech, or debate In addition to the speaker(s) and title, in parentheses give the type of presentation, sponsor, location, and date.

39. Susan Miller-Cochran, "Placement and Curricular Designs for FYC Multilingual Realities" (paper presented at the 2016 Conference on College Composition and Communication, Houston, April 7, 2016).

20 Sample Paper 7: A Student's Research Paper, *Chicago* Style

Here is a paper in *Chicago* style written by Ashley Hanson for Dr. Erik Trump's political science course, Race and the US Political System, at Saginaw Valley State University in Michigan. The assignment was to write an introduction to Richard Wright's autobiographical book, *American Hunger,* analyzing it as a political work rather than as an emotional record, as Wright calls it. Wright's complete text, which recounts his early life in Mississippi and his experiences after moving to Chicago in 1927, was to be published in 1944 with the original title, *American Hunger.* However, after the Book-of-the-Month Club requested that the politically focused second half be dropped, only the first part was published in 1945 as *Black Boy.* The second part was published posthumously in 1977 as *American Hunger.* In it, Wright tells of the social isolation, economic distress, and political concerns of black southerners who had moved north. Hanson's class was asked to examine how the surrounding political context of the 1920s and 1930s affected the plight of African Americans and, more specifically, how the book reveals the political unrest of the time.

The paper is formatted and documented in *Chicago* style. Note that a *Chicago*-style paper begins with a title page, which is unnumbered, containing the paper's title (centered and in all capital letters) and the author's name, course title, and date. The first full page of the text of the paper is numbered 1. Some instructors also request that the title be put above the first paragraph on page 1, as is done here. Because the paper contains a bibliography, short-form endnotes are used. The endnotes and bibliography pages are numbered consecutively after the text pages. For more information on formatting college papers in *Chicago* style, see Kate L. Turabian, *A Manual for Writers of Research Papers, Theses, and Dissertations,* 7th ed. (Chicago: U of Chicago P, 2007).

Note: Blue annotations point out issues of content and organization. Red annotations point out formatting features in *Chicago* style.

No page number on title page

Title (all capitals) centered, 1/3 way down page

AMERICAN HUNGER: A POLITICAL INTRODUCTION

Ashley Hanson

Political Science 270: Race and the US Political System

Fall 2015

Author's name, course title, date (centered, capital and lowercase letters)

Blue = content issues, **Red = format issues**

1

Title centered, capital and lowercase letters, double-space below

Page number in top right-hand corner of every page

American Hunger: A Political Introduction

"Politics was not my game; the human heart was my game, but it was only in the realm of politics that I could see the depths of the human heart."

1" margins on all four sides

—Richard Wright, *American Hunger*[1]

Superscript note numbers refer readers to citations in endnotes

Paper double-spaced throughout

Introduction establishes context

In his book *American Hunger,* author Richard Wright describes himself as a conveyer of human emotions, especially those shared by African Americans, rather than a political writer. This book, set in the late 1920s and 1930s, describes Wright's experiences and hardships as a young African American man in Chicago. On the surface, it is obvious that Wright delivers his story in an emotional context. However, when one examines the book from a deeper perspective, it becomes clear that this text not only is an emotional depiction of African American life in the 1930s but also is set in a much larger political context that greatly influences the structure and transformation of the African American community.Through his descriptions of his experiences, Wright exposes much of the political unrest that African Americans endured during this time, which resulted in political transformations, Communist allegiance, and new artistic visions shaped by the New Deal programs.

Thesis

American Hunger begins with Wright's journey from the South to the northern city of Chicago. Between 1920 and 1930, the time that Wright migrated north, approximately 872,000 African Americans left the South to move northward. Much

Blue = content issues, **Red = format issues**

2

Background information telling why black people moved north

of this move could be attributed to the extreme political disenfranchisement, segregation, and violence that black people suffered in the southern states. Many black people believed that the North held more opportunity and possibility than they would ever be able to obtain in the South. Wright's recounting of his journey gives his reasoning for leaving the South and describes his adjustment to the northern city of Chicago.[2]

Superscript note number placed after punctuation mark

Like most black people, Wright believed that the North held greater opportunities; however, once he settled in Chicago, he quickly discovered that the North, too, was extremely racist. Although the North was not quite as openly prejudiced as the South, black people were still segregated into ghettos and suffered political limitations such as excessive unemployment.[3] In addition, the political significance of the migration had a potentially much more devastating effect on the black community. Just as Wright describes, once the African Americans began to settle into their northern homes, they became increasingly conscious of their race. In his book, Wright states that "color hate defined the place of black life as below that of white life; and the black man . . . strove to bury within his heart his awareness of this difference because it made him lonely and afraid."[4] As Wright explains, although black people migrated north to escape the hate and disenfranchisement, the harsh political effects of the move still overwhelmed them and left them feeling helpless and isolated.

Quotes Wright to illustrate point

Ellipsis dots indicate part of quotation omitted

As black Southerners began to experience isolation even in the northern cities, they also began to feel neglected by

Chicago Manual of Style CHICAGO

3

the Republican Party. For years, African American allegiance had remained with the Republican Party because of Lincoln's support for ending slavery during the Civil War.[5] However, in the years following, the Republican Party disregarded the support of its black constituents, an action that forced them to rethink their loyalty to the party. Richard Wright himself wrote on a ballot for Republican candidate "Big Bill" Thompson the words *I protest this fraud!*[6] African Americans all over the country felt as though their loyalty to the party was being taken for granted, and they grew bitter toward the failed promises of the Republican Party.

In 1928, black allegiance to the Republican Party began to shift.[7] Slowly, the Democratic Party gained more support from the black community. In 1932, presidential candidate Franklin Delano Roosevelt promised to impose national relief programs and make "Negro" appointments to provide benefits to African Americans and promote their equality. In addition to stressing the relief programs in his campaign, he also appointed black cabinet members, and his wife, Eleanor Roosevelt, sat with the leading members of national African American groups.[8] To black people, FDR became known as a symbol of economic and political freedom.

Presents examples found through research to illustrate point

In a 1936 African American journal, a campaign advertisement was published for the reelection of Roosevelt under the slogan "Not Promise but Performance."[9] The advertisement outlined his relief programs and black appointments and encouraged black people to "Read what he has done . . . [and] vote for his re-election!"[10] One political cartoon, also published in 1936, showed FDR physically

Word in brackets added to quotation

Blue = content issues, **Red = format issues**

4

Figure placed near text reference (in parentheses) to it

Fig. 1: FDR Promises Economic Freedom.
Source: Originally published in *New York Amsterdam News*, October 1936. Reprinted in Weiss, *Farewell to the Party of Lincoln* (Princeton, NJ: Princeton University Press, 1983), 215.

leading a suppressed African American to economic freedom (see Fig. 1). This shift of African American allegiance from the Republican to the Democratic Party depicted a major change that influenced blacks in the 1930s, and the hardships and neglect that are so vividly illustrated in Wright's book accurately coincide with the reason for the African Americans' political party shift. The disregard and inequality they suffered forced them to shift their political loyalty from the Republicans to the Democrats in search of a much needed feeling of unity and usefulness.

Explains significance of New Deal programs and cites examples

One significant reason for African Americans' political change from the Republicans to the Democrats was the New Deal programs initiated by President Franklin Delano Roosevelt; the

Blue = content issues, **Red = format issues**

experiences described in *American Hunger* are deeply intertwined with many of these programs. The New Deal programs that were established by FDR were essentially an attempt by the federal government to manage the economy and provide assistance to unemployed and poor citizens, including African Americans. Organizations such as the Works Progress Administration (WPA) and the Public Works Administration (PWA) were established and employed a large number of black people in the country.[11] For example, a Democratic campaign advertisement that was published in an African American journal confirmed that the "unemployment relief inaugurated by the Roosevelt Administration saved millions of Negro men, women, and children from extreme want by direct relief, WPA and PWA."[12] These New Deal programs created by Roosevelt provided many new economic and political opportunities for African American citizens in the United States.

Transition: Expands discussion to show significance of New Deal arts programs for black people's artistic aspirations

Wright's experiences with the New Deal programs not only coincided with the greater political context of the era but also provide a window to view how these programs intersected with African Americans' artistic visions. For example, one of the jobs Wright was given by the government was working in the Federal Negro Theater, an art division under the WPA. While working in this theater, Wright describes his larger goal, one of great political importance, which was to create a genuine Negro theater to depict the realities of African American life. He believed that the "heart of the Negro actor was pining for adult expression in the American theater,"[13] and he wanted to be able to help black people express their feelings.

Quotation incorporated into sentence

6

Wright's goal was shared by the overall objective found in these Federal Arts relief programs. These political arts programs did many things to document the experience of the African American. For example, the theater produced all-black performances of *Macbeth,* the writing division produced an oral history project that included southern ex-slaves' stories, and guidebooks were created by black people that included a history of African Americans.[14] Overall, Wright's explanation of his experiences with the relief programs and his artistic visions that resulted from his experiences intersect with the New Deal programs and the larger political framework of the time period.

Provides transition from discussion of New Deal art programs to Communist support of African American art and broader political support of African Americans

Despite these New Deal programs and the exposure to art that Wright and other African Americans received, many black people began to turn to the Communist Party as a means to pursue their artistic endeavors. The Communist Party was a great supporter of African American art. Wright himself said, "I owe my literary development to the Communist Party and its influence, which has shaped my thoughts and creative growth."[15] In a sense, African Americans turned to the Communist Party because it gave them a feeling of hope within America when everyone else had abandoned them. For example, the lynching of black people became a very prominent issue in the early 1900s, yet the response of the Democratic Party to brutal lynchings was one of disregard. Although Roosevelt claimed to oppose lynching, his fear of losing the support of southern Democrats kept him from pushing any anti-lynching bills through the Senate.[16] Conversely, in 1928,

Blue = content issues, **Red = format issues**

the Communist Party publicly denounced lynching in its party platform and urged black people to organize against the practice.

In a 1934 election leaflet titled *Why Every Negro Should Vote Communist,* the author points out that "[the Communist Party] is the only party that fights against lynching, jim-crowism, [and] discrimination, and for complete equality and freedom of the Negro people."[17] In addition, in 1925 the Communist Party integrated their black and white memberships, long before the two major parties did so, in order to advance the Communist Party's political well-being. As a result, some African Americans began to show greater allegiance to the Communist Party in the 1930s. In Wright's discussion of his ties to the Communist Party, he states, "It was not the economics of Communism, nor the great power of trade unions, nor the excitement of underground politics that claimed me; my attention was caught by the similarity of the experiences of workers in other lands, by the possibility of uniting scattered but kindred peoples into a whole."[18] Just as Wright's search for unity and integration, as recounted in this book, led him to the Communist Party, African Americans as a whole in the 1930s were drawn to the Communist Party because of the support it provided for black artists and because of its sense of unity and kinship, a feeling many African Americans had never known before.

Words in brackets added in quotation

Transition: Expands discussion and presents examples to show why black people, including Wright, turned to the Communist Party

Superscript note number placed after period and closing quotation mark

Overall, the early 1900s were a time of unrest and political turmoil for many African Americans. Even those who had moved north to escape the hatred and isolation of the South were still unhappy and felt abandoned. Wright's book *American Hunger*

8

does an excellent job of shaping this feeling and opening the reader's eyes to the larger issues of the era. Although Wright claims he is neither a political person nor a political writer, the issues he exposes in his book seem to express the overall plight of African Americans in a largely political manner. Wright's words and experiences resonate in a way that allows his readers not only to sympathize with the emotions and sentiments he felt but also to understand his hardships, and those of other African Americans, in a much broader political culture. Just as African Americans in the 1930s continued searching for a feeling of unity and equality even during times of struggle, Wright's main goal when writing this book was to "send other words to tell, to march to fight, to create a sense of the hunger for life that gnaws in us all, to keep alive in our hearts a sense of the inexpressibly human."[19] And he succeeded.

Conclusion restates thesis and expands on it to discuss significance of Wright's book for readers

Blue = content issues, **Red = format issues**

Chicago Manual of Style CHICAGO

Double-space twice between head and first note

9

Notes page numbered consecutively

NOTES

Short-form notes used because complete details of sources in bibliography

1. Wright, *American Hunger,* 46.

2. Trump, class lecture.

3. Ibid.

4. Wright, *Black Boy,* 266.

Ibid. indicates source is same as one in previous note

5. Trump, class lecture.

6. Wright, *Black Boy,* 298.

Indent first line of note ½ inch (paragraph indent)

7. Trump, class lecture.

8. Ibid.

9. Democratic campaign advertisement, in Weiss, *Farewell to the Party,* 188.

Source contained within a larger source

Short-form note: Author's last name, shortened title, page number

10. Ibid.

11. Trump, class lecture.

12. Democratic campaign advertisement, in Weiss, *Farewell to the Party,* 188.

Single-space notes; double-space between notes

13. Wright, *Black Boy,* 365.

Secondary source: Author quoted in another source; both sources listed in bibliography

14. Trump, class lecture.

15. Wright, *Daily Worker*, February 25, 1938, quoted in Naison, *Communists in Harlem*, 210–11.

16. Trump, class lecture.

17. Communist Party, *Why Every Negro.*

No page number for Web source

18. Wright, *Black Boy,* 318.

19. Ibid., 384.

Blue = content issues, **Red = format issues**

10

Page number (consecutive) in right-hand corner

Head centered, all capital letters

BIBLIOGRAPHY

Entries listed alphabetically

Periods separate major components

Double-space twice between head and first entry

Hanging indent: First line flush left; subsequent lines indented ½ inch

Access date given when no date of posting or update; period after URL ends entry

Communist Party. *Why Every Negro Should Vote Communist.* Leaflet, 1934. A. E. Forbes Communist Collection. Archives Service Center. Digital Research Library, University of Pittsburgh. Accessed November 30, 2015. http://images.library.pitt.edu/a/aeforbes/.

Democratic campaign advertisement, in *Opportunity,* October 1936. Reprinted in Nancy J. Weiss, *Farewell to the Party of Lincoln: Black Politics in the Age of FDR,* 188. Princeton, NJ: Princeton University Press, 1983.

"FDR Promises Economic Freedom." Political Cartoon. *New York Amsterdam News*, October 1936. Reprinted in Weiss, *Farewell to the Party of Lincoln,* 188.

Naison, Mark. *Communists in Harlem During the Depression.* New York: Grove, 1984.

Trump, Erik. Class lecture. Political Science 270: Race and the U.S. Political System, Fall 2015. Saginaw Valley State University, University Center, MI. October 7, 2015.

Weiss, Nancy. *Farewell to the Party of Lincoln: Black Politics in the Age of FDR.* Princeton, NJ: Princeton University Press, 1983.

Wright, Richard. *American Hunger: The Compelling Continuation of Richard Wright's Autobiographical Work, Black Boy.* New York: Harper, 1977.

———. *Black Boy*. 60th anniversary ed. New York: Harper Perennial Modern Classics, 2007.

———. [Unknown article title]. *Daily Worker.* February 25, 1938.

Organization as author

Entry lists information about leaflet and details about collection, archive, online source, and sponsor

Source reprinted in another source

Single-space entries; double-space between entries

Author's name inverted for alphabetizing

No periods in abbreviations in notes or bibliography

Only sources used in the paper are listed

CHICAGO Chicago Manual of Style

Blue = content issues, **Red = format issues**

5 Design, Media, and Presentation

WRITING IN YOUR CAREER

The Industrial Designer, the Writer

Photo courtesy of Kate Tsyrlin

You might think the word *artist* applies only to individuals who paint or draw, but some artists do their work primarily on computers. The visual skills of painters and sculptors are also required by those who need to design a Web site or a computer game. They, too, are primarily engaged in the creation of visual design. But whether individuals are traditional artists or designers who work on the computer, designers and artists will need to communicate effectively with the written word. At least that's what art student Kate Tsyrlin found when she was applying for a degree in industrial design. In her application, she needed to put together a portfolio of works just as she would if she were trying to get a show in an art gallery. Her portfolio was accompanied by a written explanation for each work. She also provided a general statement about her vision as an artist. Think of words, in these instances, as frames for each piece or series of work. Tsyrlin accompanied her college application with a written inventory of her portfolio and the statement displayed below. A professional and engaging presentation is as important in the arts as it is in any other career; and the consequences of writing well—acceptance into a program, by a gallery, in a collective show, for example—are significant. For information on writing a cover letter for a portfolio, see the section in the Assignment Guide titled "Portfolio Cover Letters."

From Kate Tsyrlin's artist's statement accompanying her portfolio

> My father liked to grab my arm and my mother was a screamer. Still, I did manage to concentrate in those early weeks of driving, and the idea of judging distances was on my mind. It applied to everything—distance from car to curb, or bumper to bumper; distance in the classroom, and why people choose the front, middle, or back rows; distance in personal relationships, in how close you stand and how much you hold back. I am drawn to working in 3D because spatial relationships can be so packed with meaning. . . .

5 Design, Media, and Presentation

There's no getting around it: medium (such as print, online, video, and so on) is an important part of your writing context, which is why it's part of the Critical Thinking Framework introduced in part 1. Your choice of medium, and how well you use its capabilities, will leave an impression on your audience. Your audience will have expectations about what a particular type of communication should look like, and, to make an impression that inspires their interest and confidence in what you have to say, you will need to fulfill those expectations. Straying from those expectations is also an option, but you want to do that only if you have a specific reason for doing so that will communicate with your audience. Whether it's an academic essay or a scientific report, a Web-based résumé, or a post on a community-based blog, the design and presentation of your writing communicates to readers that you understand the conventions required by your writing context. Equally important, the design and presentation of your writing can help you communicate your message as effectively as possible.

MindTap®
Understand the goals of this part, and complete a warm-up activity.

While the design of texts and presentation of information have always been important, the expansion of digital media has enhanced our ability to make strong, media-rich impressions and to skillfully convey information to readers and listeners. It's not unusual to see text (in words) joined by pictures, photographs, tables, graphs, sound, and video to convey information and emotion, often more immediately and dramatically than is possible with words alone. During presentations, audiences are accustomed to visuals that are digital slides, often with other media embedded into the slides to enhance and illustrate what they are hearing and seeing in the presentation.

Whether you are tweeting to readers around the globe or sending a message to an older family member who just discovered *Facebook*, whether you are formatting your English professor's six-page essay assignment or putting the final touches on your e-portfolio before sending the link to a prospective employer, you will want to ask yourself (or your professor) this: What medium is most appropriate for my writing context, what will my audience's expectations be for that medium, and how can I communicate my message with the most impact?

21 Document Design

21a Formatting academic writing in print

MindTap®
Read, highlight, and take notes online.

As you draft, revise, and edit your writing, you can think about how you'll prepare it for presentation to readers. Guides are available for presenting academic essays in specific disciplines and media. Frequently used style guides are those published by the Modern Language Association (MLA), American Psychological Association (APA), Council of Science Editors (CSE), and *The Chicago Manual of Style*. The features of these guides are covered in parts 3 and 4 of this handbook. However, commonalities exist among the differences. Basic guidelines are in the Key Points box for preparing your essay on paper, whichever style guide you follow. See 21g for a table and detailed instructions for *MS Word* functions that can help with formatting academic writing, including tips for navigating the function in whichever version you may have installed on your computer.

KEY POINTS

Guidelines for College Essay Format (Printed)

- **Paper** White bond, unlined, 8½" × 11". Clip or staple the pages.
- **Print** Dark black printing ink.
- **Margins** One inch all around. In some styles, one and one-half inches may be acceptable. Lines should be justified left but should have ragged right margins.
- **Space between lines** Uniformly double-spaced, including any list of works cited. Footnotes (in *Chicago* style) may be single-spaced.
- **Spaces after a period, question mark, or exclamation point** One space, as suggested by most style manuals. Your instructor may prefer two in the text of your essay.
- **Type font and size** Standard type font (such as Times New Roman or Arial), not a fancy font that looks like handwriting. Select a regular size of 10 to 12 points.

- **Page numbers** In the top right margin. (In MLA style, put your last name before the page number. In APA style, put a short version of the title, called a "running head," on the left and the page number on the right.) Use Arabic numerals with no period. (See p. 389; 21g shows the header formatting tools that are available in *Word*.)
- **Paragraphing** Indent one-half inch (five spaces) from the left.
- **Title and identification** On the first page or on a separate title page. See the examples that follow and on pages 271 and 330.
- **Parentheses around a source citation** MLA and APA style, for any source you refer to or quote, including the textbook for your course; then add at the end an alphabetical list of works cited.

Note: Your instructor may prefer a separate title page or ask you to include the identification material on the first page of the essay.

Title and identification on the first page The sample in Figure 21.1 of part of a first page shows one format for identifying a paper and giving it a title. The MLA recommends this format for papers in the humanities.

Figure 21.1 Recommended format for first page of essay in MLA style

Croasdale 1

Yulanda Croasdale

Professor Raimes

English 120, Section 13

5 April 2016

Jamaican-American: A New Culture

To outsiders, the emergence of a strong Jamaican-American community is probably not a noticeable occurrence, though insiders are all too well aware of their growing population and spread of notoriety.

At the top of subsequent pages, write the page number in the upper-right corner, preceded by your last name (21g shows you how to make this header).

Title and identification on a separate title page In the humanities, include a title page only if your instructor requires one or if you include an outline. (For the social sciences or other academic areas, see part 4.) On the title page, include the following, all double-spaced:

Title: Centered, about one-third of the way down the page. Do not enclose the title in quotation marks, do not italicize or underline it, and do not put a period at the end.

Name: Centered, after the word *by*, on a separate line.

Course information: College course and section, instructor, and date, each centered on a new line, either directly below your name or at the bottom of the title page.

With a title page, you do not need the title and identification on your first page.

21b Formatting academic writing online

You may be required to submit an essay for a course online rather than in hard copy. Your instructor may ask you to e-mail an attachment, or in a hybrid or distance-learning course, you may be required to submit your essays in a dropbox or post them on a class online discussion board for the instructor and other students to read and comment on. Alternatively, you may have your own e-portfolio (25b) where you display your work. In any of these cases, keep in mind the following general guidelines, and ask your instructor for instructions specific to the course, format, and type of posting.

Guidelines for posting academic writing online Word processing programs can automatically convert a document and save it as an HTML file for the Web. In *Word*, for example, you simply produce your document in the usual way, but when you save it, you choose "Save As" and change "File Format" from "Word" to "HTM." The automatic coding can create some formatting issues because the code is not clean, but it can be a useful alternative if you do not know how to code in HTML yourself. If you prefer to write the document in an HTML editor instead of *Word*, *KompoZer* is a free, open-source application you can download that is easy to use.

KEY POINTS

Posting Academic Writing Online

- **Structure** Set up a structure with sections and subsections, all with headings, that allows each section to be accessed directly through a link—for example, from your table of contents (see the next point) and from any other part of your paper as well. So, instead of saying "See above" or "See below," you can provide a specific link that will allow readers to jump directly to this part of your paper (see the *internal hyperlinks* list entry).
- **Links to sections from a table of contents** Provide a table of contents, with an internal link to each section. Readers can then click and go directly to any section they are interested in.
- **Internal hyperlinks** Use internal hyperlinks (Insert/Bookmark) to connect readers directly to relevant sections of your text, content notes, and visuals. Also provide a link from a source cited in the body of your paper to the entry in your list of works cited.
- **External hyperlinks** Use external hyperlinks (Insert/Hyperlink) to connect to Web documents from references in the body of your paper and from your list of works cited. *Word* has a function that will automatically convert any string starting with *http://* or *www.* into a hyperlink, which is useful for preparing your works-cited list.
- **No paragraph indentation** Do not indent new paragraphs when you are writing online. Instead, leave a line space between paragraphs.
- **Attribution of sources** Make sure that the link you give to an online article in a database is a persistent link, not a link that works for only a few hours or days. Typically, you shouldn't just link to where you got an article in a library database, but you should find the link to get to the article directly without going through the database. You might need to copy the link, open a new browser, and try it. It is often difficult to determine at first glance whether a link is persistent. Some databases are explicit; others are not. Double-check your links after a few days to see

(Continued)

(Continued)

whether they are still working. Some sites such as *Thomas* at the Library of Congress (http://thomas.loc.gov) and *EBSCO* databases provide persistent links.

- **List of works cited or list of references** Give a complete list, even if you provide some external links to the sources from the body of your paper. If readers print your paper, the exact references will then still be available.

21c Typefaces

What's in a typeface? A lot. It's not just what you write that is important but also how it looks when it's read. Fitting the typeface to the content of a public document can be seen as an aesthetic challenge, as it was for the choice of the simple and legible Gotham typeface for the Freedom Tower cornerstone at the site of the former World Trade Center (Figure 21.2). The silver-leaf letters with strokes of uniform width with no decorative touches, have been described by David Dunlap in the *New York Times* as conjuring "the exuberant, modernist, midcentury optimism of New York even as they augur the glass

James Estrin/The New York Times/Redux

Figure 21.2 Gotham typeface on the Freedom Tower cornerstone and stainless-steel tower to come." That's what's in a typeface. The cornerstone, according to Dunlap, looks "neutral enough so that viewers could impose their own meanings" on a site of profound historical and emotional impact.

Of course, designing the presentation of a college essay is not the same as designing a historic monument. However, you can still make a choice that emphasizes simplicity and legibility.

For college essays in hard copy, consider using the following:

For the body of the text: Times New Roman or some other *serif* font. (A *serif* font has little strokes—serifs—at the top and bottom of individual characters.)

For captions and headings: Arial or some other *sans serif* font. (The word *sans* is French for "without"; a sans serif font does not have the little strokes at the top and bottom of the characters.)

Avoid ornamental fonts such as *Monotype Corsiva* and ***Brush Script***. They are distracting and hard to read. Also avoid fonts that appear overly playful, such as Comic Sans, which could make your work appear less serious than you intend.

Note that, if you are designing a Web page or other online communication, readers' computer settings determine which fonts can be displayed. The simpler the font that you choose (Times, Arial, Georgia, and Verdana all work well on both PC and Mac browsers), the more likely readers are to see your chosen font.

For the body of your text in a college essay or a piece of business communication, stick to 10- to 12-point type. Use larger type only for headings and subheadings in business, technical, or Web documents (see 21b and chapter 24). Never increase or decrease the font size (or margins) to achieve a required page length. You will convey desperation, and you will certainly not fool your instructor.

Note: MLA and APA guidelines do not recommend typeface changes or bold type for titles and headings.

21d Color

Color printers and online publication have made the production of documents an exciting enterprise for both writers and readers. You can include graphs and illustrations in color, and you can highlight headings or parts of your text by using a different color typeface. However, simplicity and readability should prevail. Use color only when its use will enhance your message. Certainly, in the design of business reports, newsletters, brochures, and Web pages, color can play an important and eye-catching role. Color can be expensive to print, however, so minimize the use of color for documents that must be reproduced for a large number of people. For college essays, the leading style manuals ignore and implicitly discourage the use of color. Also, keep in mind that many people may not have a color printer, and printing color charts on a black-and-white printer may produce shades that are difficult to distinguish.

21e Headings

Headings divide text into helpful chunks and give readers a sense of your document's structure. Main divisions are marked by first-level headings, and subdivisions are marked by second-level and third-level headings. In the heading structure of chapter 21, for example, the main heading is "Document Design," and the subheadings include "Formatting academic writing in print," "Formatting academic writing online," "Typefaces," "Color," "Headings," "Lists," and "Academic design features in *MS Word*."

For headings, bear in mind the following recommendations:

- If you use subheadings, use at least two—not just one. If you think you need only one subheading, the point can probably be incorporated under the main heading.
- Whenever possible, use your word processing program's Style feature to determine the level of heading you need: heading 1, 2, 3, and so on. This will make it easy to produce a Table of Contents with internal links when your document is finished and will help you maintain consistency throughout the document.
- Style manuals, such as the one for APA style, recommend specific formats for typeface and position on the page for levels of headings. Follow these recommended formats. See chapter 16 for an APA paper with headings.
- Keep headings clear, brief, and parallel in grammatical form (for instance, all commands: "Set Up Sales Strategies"; all beginning with *-ing* words: "Setting Up Sales Strategies"; or all noun-plus-modifier phrases: "Sales Strategies").

21f Lists

Lists are particularly useful in business reports, proposals, and memos. They direct readers' attention to the outlined points or steps. Decide whether to use numbers, dashes, or bullets to set off the items in a list.

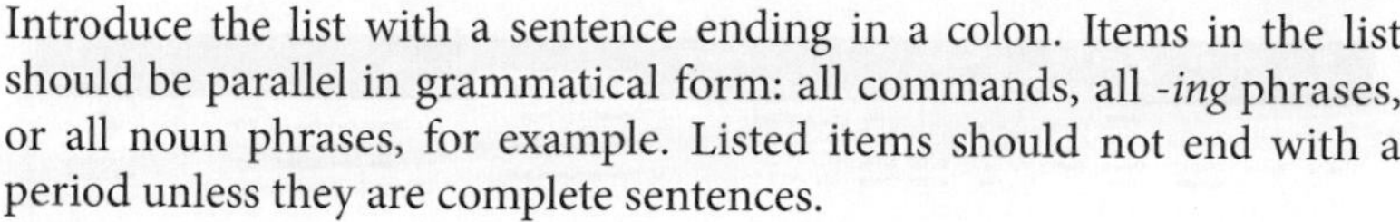
Introduce the list with a sentence ending in a colon. Items in the list should be parallel in grammatical form: all commands, all *-ing* phrases, or all noun phrases, for example. Listed items should not end with a period unless they are complete sentences.

21g Academic design features in *MS Word*

As a college student in the twenty-first century, you probably find it second nature to use the functions of a word processing program to add, delete, move material, and check your spelling. But a word processor also can help you fulfill the conventions of academic writing and the formatting functions that your audience may expect.

This section outlines the features of *Word* that are most useful in academic writing. You'll find a table on page 398 with brief instructions for accessing the formatting options in *MS Word*. (For full details on the following list of tasks, consult your word processing program's written documentation, built-in "Help" menu, or online training and customer support.)

1. Formatting a document using templates and styles *Word* provides useful ready-made design formats called *templates* for an MLA essay, APA paper, and a term paper. It also has templates for many other documents you may need to produce in college and beyond, including résumés, brochures, and newsletters. In addition, you can create and save your own templates. Most word processing programs also use *styles*—a mechanism for setting document format choices that apply to the entire document rather than to individual parts. Using the Styles feature lets you establish the default look and feel of your document and maintain a consistency of design so that you don't have to worry about formatting choices while you are writing or editing.

2. Adding a header or footer on every page The Header and Footer options that are useful for academic writing are those that allow you to (1) include a page number along with any text, such as your name or a short running head; (2) include the date and time; and (3) toggle between the choice of headers or footers (see Figure 21.3). Headers and footers will adjust automatically to any changes in the pagination of your document (screens shown in Figures 21.3, 21.4, and 21.5 are taken on a Mac; placement of the menus and tabs is very similar for computers running a Windows version).

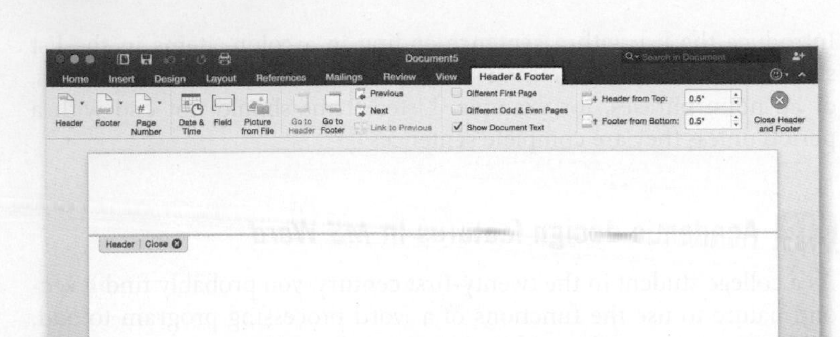

Figure 21.3 Header and Footer screen in *Word 2016*

3. Inserting visuals, charts, and graphs The Insert menu and the Insert tab on the ribbon provide access to useful functions. Here, you can insert into your text a page number, a footnote, or a hyperlink to a URL. It is also possible to insert into your text a picture, screenshot, caption, diagram, or chart. For presentation of data, the chart feature is particularly helpful and easy to use: you simply type your data into a data grid and then choose from a wide variety of charts, such as bar, line, pie, doughnut, scatter, and pyramid. One click, and your chart appears.

4. Inserting a table Tables can help you organize your data into easy-to-read columns and rows. Figure 21.4 shows options for formatting a table in *Word 2016*.

5. Formatting your document As you move toward your final draft, you will want to format your document using some of the following features:

- **Font** Options are available for changing typeface, styles, and size as well as using superscripts, which are useful for *Chicago Manual of Style* citations; see also 21c.
- **Paragraph** Options are given for line spacing and indenting (see Figure 21.5 for how to set the special command for the hanging indents used in an MLA list of works cited).

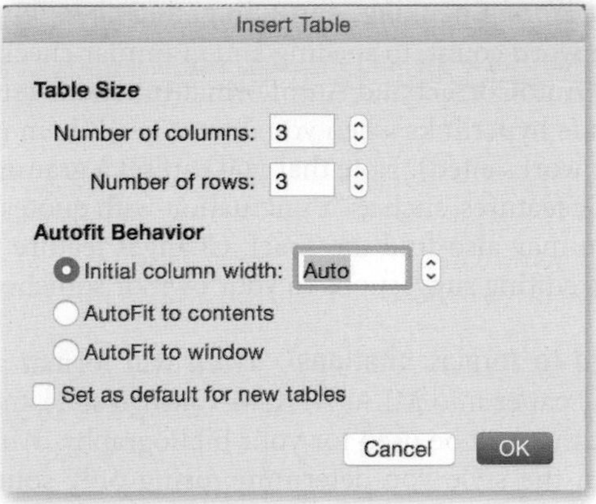

Insert Table

Table Size

Number of columns: 3

Number of rows: 3

Autofit Behavior

Initial column width: Auto

AutoFit to contents

AutoFit to window

Set as default for new tables

Cancel OK

Figure 21.4 Insert Table options for *Word 2016*

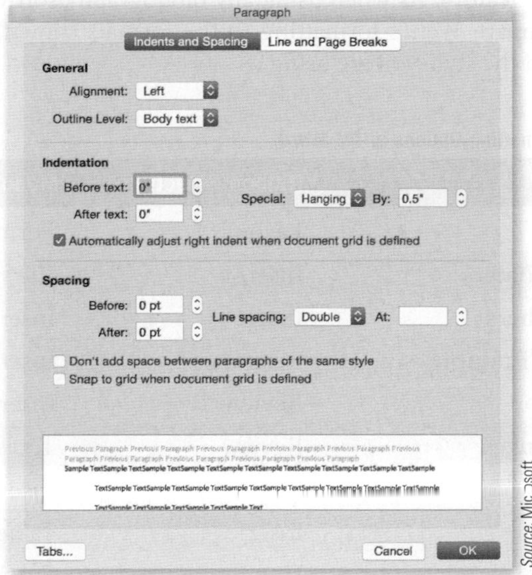

Source: Microsoft

Figure 21.5 The hanging indent paragraph function is shown in *Word 2016*

- **Bullets and Numbering** Options are given for lists, Borders and Shading, Columns, Tabs, and Dropped Capitals (just highlight the text to be formatted).
- **Change Case** Options are provided for changing text from capital letters to lowercase, or vice versa.

6. Editing with *Word*: Checking, correcting, and changing *Word* gives you access to a word count, to spelling and grammar checkers and a thesaurus, and to AutoCorrect and AutoFormat functions (such as turning off the automatic hyperlinks when you do not need them underlined for an MLA list of works cited). Note that you can set a grammar checker to look for specific features, such as "Punctuation with quotes" and "Passive sentences." You may also find the Track Changes feature to be a useful tool for adding editing suggestions to your own or somebody else's text.

7. Using *Word* to format citations *Word* will format a citation you include in your paper into MLA, APA, or *Chicago* style and will add the source to a list that will be used for your bibliography. *Word* will form a bibliography in the style you determine, using only sources you have cited in your paper via the Bibliography command on the References tab. Other word processors, such as *OpenOffice*, also include the citation/bibliography feature. As when using any bibliography software, you will want to compare *Word*'s formatting to the formats shown in the latest guidelines of the style you are using.

Accessing Formatting Options in *MS Word*

	Ribbon Selection	Menu Selection
Margins	Layout	Format
Headers/Footers	Insert	View
Page Numbers	Insert	Insert
Footnotes/Endnotes	References	Insert
Comments	Review	Insert
Track Changes	Review	Tools
Visuals	Insert	Insert
Tables	Insert	Table
Font Style	Home	Format
Paragraph Formatting	Layout	Format
Bullets/Numbering	Home	Format
Word Count	Review	Tools
Citations	References	
Spelling and Grammar Check	Home	Tools

22 Visuals

The technology of scanners, photocopiers, smartphones, digital cameras, and downloaded images provides the means of making documents more functional and more attractive by allowing the inclusion of visual material. Frequently, when you are dealing with arguments using complicated data, the best way to get information across to readers is to display it visually.

MindTap®
Read, highlight, and take notes online.

For a college paper, you can download visuals from the Web (with a source acknowledgment) to strengthen an argument or to present data clearly and efficiently. Alternatively, computers make it easy for you to take data from your own research and present the data in a table, graph, or chart (22a, 22b).

KEY POINTS
On Using Visuals

1. **Plan** Decide which type of visual presentation best fits your data, and determine where to place your visuals; these are usually best placed within your text. However, APA style for printed papers requires visuals to be placed in an appendix.
2. **Introduce** Whenever you place a visual in your text, introduce it and discuss it fully before readers come across it. Do not just make a perfunctory comment like "The results are significant, as seen in Figure 1." Rather, say something like "Figure 1 shows an increase in the number of accidents since 2010." Keep in mind that the visual should supplement your words but not replace them. In your discussion, indicate where the visual appears ("In the table below" or "In the pie chart on page 8"), and carefully interpret or analyze the visual for readers, using it as an aid that supports your points, not as something that can stand alone.
3. **Compress** When you include a visual in an online document, make sure the image file is not so large that it will take a long time for readers to download.
4. **Identify** Number each visual if you use more than one of the same type, give each visual a title, and credit the source.

(Continued)

(Continued)

5. **Avoid filler** Do not include visuals simply to fill space or to make your document look colorful. Every visual addition should enhance your content and provide an interesting and relevant illustration.

22a Tables

Tables are useful for presenting data in columns and rows. They help readers keep track of and comprehend data that might otherwise be confusing if the data were included just in the text itself. Tables can be created easily with word processing programs using figures from large sets of data, as in Table 22.1.

Table 22.1 Party Affiliation among Hispanic Registered Voters in Florida, 2006 to 2012

	Republicans	Democrats	Other Party	No Party Affiliation	Total
2012*	452,619	564,513	25,657	431,131	1,473,920
2010	445,353	550,799	25,082	404,570	1,425,804
2008	445,526	513,252	23,500	372,992	1,355,270
2006	414,185	369,902	16,915	312,881	1,113,883

Note: *Data for 2012 as of January 3, 2012, the presidential preference primary book closing date. The Florida presidential preference primary election date is Tuesday January 31, 2012. For all other years, data reflect general election book closing dates.

Source: Florida Division of Elections, http://election.dos.state.fl.us/voter-registration/statistics/elections.shtml.

22b Graphs and charts

Graphs and charts are useful for presenting data and comparisons of data. Many software products allow you to produce graphs easily, and even standard word processing software gives you several ways to present your numbers in visual form. In *Microsoft Office*, you can create graphs and charts in *Word* or *Excel*. In *Word*, you are able to select a type of chart, such as a pie chart or a bar chart, and enter your own details, such as title, labels for the vertical and horizontal axes of a bar chart, numbers, and data labels (see Figure 22.1).

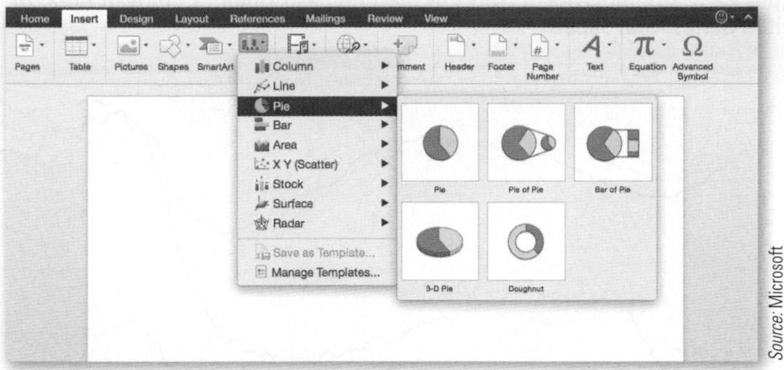

Figure 22.1 Chart options, *Word 2016*

Simple line graph Use a line graph to show changes over time. Figure 22.2 has a clear caption and is self-explanatory.

Figure 22.2 Relationship of Income to Education

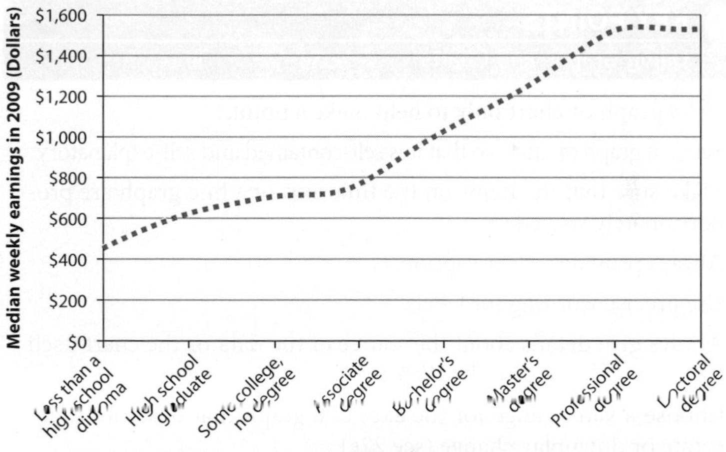

Source: Data are 2009 annual averages for persons age 25 and over. Earnings are for full-time wage and salary workers. Bureau of Labor Statistics, Current Population Survey. BLS has some data on the employment status of the civilian noninstitutional population 25 years and over by educational attainment, sex, race, and Hispanic origin online. The Bureau of the Census also has some data on the educational attainment online at http://www.bls.gov/emp/p_chart_001.txt.

Comparative line graph Line graphs are especially useful for comparing data over time. Figure 22.3, for example, compares unemployment rates in the European Union, European Area, the United States, and Japan from 2000 to 2012.

Figure 22.3 Unemployment Rates in the European Union, European Area, the United States, and Japan

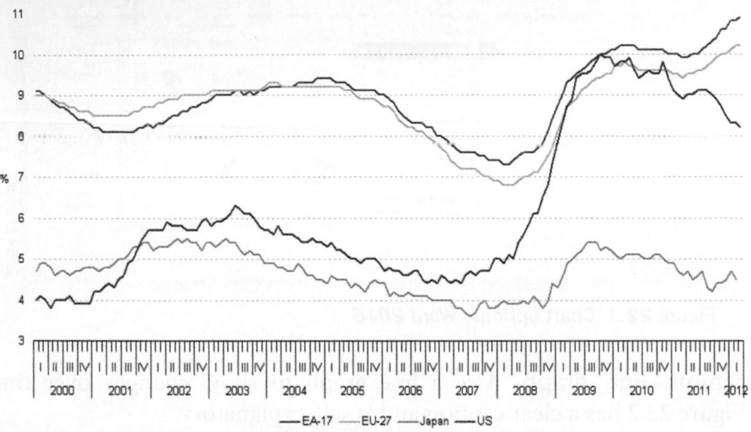

Source: http://epp.eurostat.ec.europa.eu/statistics_explained/index.php/Unemployment_statistics

KEY POINTS

Using Graphs and Charts

- Use a graph or chart only to help make a point.
- Set up a graph or chart so that it is self-contained and self-explanatory.
- Make sure that the items on the time axis of a line graph are proportionately spaced.
- Always provide a clear caption.
- Use precise wording for labels.
- Always give details about the source of the data or the chart itself if you download from the Web.
- Choose a value range for the axes of a graph that does not exaggerate or downplay change (see 22e).

Pie chart Use a pie chart to show how fractions and percentages relate to one another and make up a whole. Figure 22.4 shows petroleum imports in the United States in 2011.

Bar chart A bar chart is useful to show comparisons and correlations and to highlight differences among groups. The bar chart in Figure 22.5, created in *MS Word*, displays the level of competence that teachers and

Figure 22.4 Sources of US Net Petroleum Imports, 2011

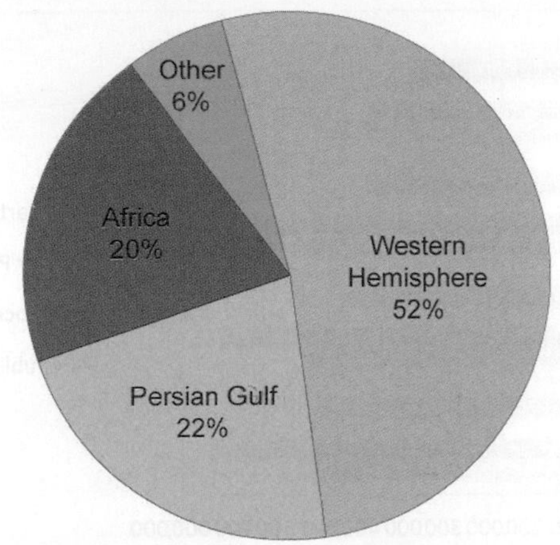

Source: U.S. Energy Information Administration, *Petroleum Supply Monthly* (February 2012), preliminary data.

students felt that the students in online and face-to-face courses had achieved in documenting sources in their writing on a scale of 0 (low) to 4 (high). The chart shows that teachers perceived slightly lower competence in documenting sources in the face-to-face course than in the online course, while students perceived a similar level of competence.

Figure 22.5 Student Competence in Documenting Sources

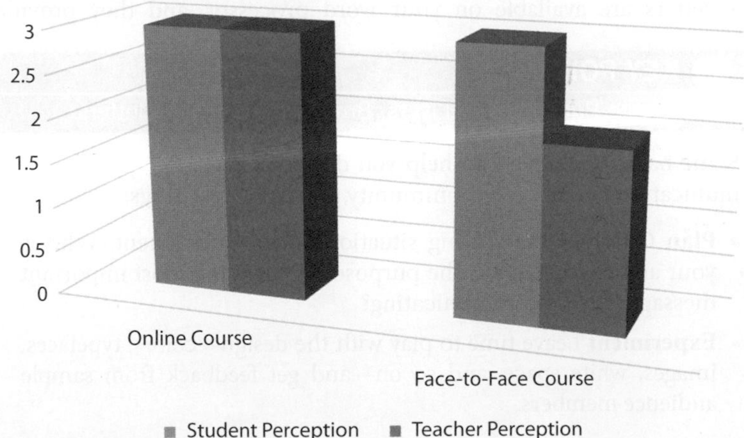

Figure 22.6 Party Affiliation among Hispanic Registered Voters in Florida

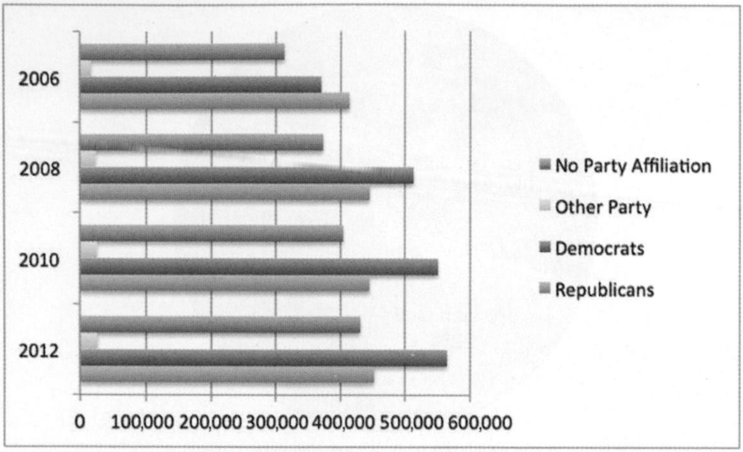

Source: Data are from the Florida Division of Elections, http://election.dos.state.fl.us/voter-registration/statistics/elections.shtml

A bar chart can also be presented horizontally, which makes it easier to attach labels to the bars. Figure 22.6 was produced in *MS Office* using the data from Table 22.1 on page 400.

22c Flyers, brochures, and newsletters

Although it is generally better to use document design software (such as *Adobe InDesign*) for creating publishable document formats, it is certainly possible to create simple flyers, brochures, and newsletters using word processing software. Templates for flyers, brochures, and newsletters are available on your word processor, and they provide

KEY POINTS

Design Principles for Flyers, Brochures, and Newsletters

Some basic principles can help you design a successful print communication in academic, community, or business settings.

- **Plan** Consider the writing situation of your document. Who is your audience? What is the purpose? What is the most important message you are communicating?
- **Experiment** Leave time to play with the design—colors, typefaces, images, white space, and so on—and get feedback from sample audience members.

- **Value readability and clarity** Give priority to important information.
- **Be consistent** Keep all design elements consistent (headers, margins, typefaces, captions, and so on).
- **Consider standard design principles.**
  - **Type size and font** Choose a readable type size. Serif typefaces (the ones with the little strokes at the top and bottom of individual characters) are more readable and are thus the best choice for the main body of the document. For headlines and headings, use a limited number of other larger type sizes.
  - **Use of white space** Allow for a generous amount of white space in your margins and borders. Adequate line spacing is important, too, to make the text easy to read.
  - **End-of-line alignment** Justified lines (lines that are all the same length to create a squared-off box of text) appear more formal, have a greater type density, and can create a lot of hyphenated words; lines that are ragged right create a less formal and more open look.
  - **Column width and line length** Shorter columns and shorter lines of type are easier to read (but too many columns on one page may overwhelm readers).
  - **Boxes and sidebars** Boxing a part of your document can give it extra emphasis or attention.

layouts that must be customized with text and images. Careful attention to the elements of design increases the chance that your flyer, brochure, or newsletter will be read and have the effect you hoped.

22d Images and copyright issues

Your computer software provides many standard images (clip art) and photographs that you can use free in your documents without any copyright concerns. Web sites offer images to download, either free or at a small cost. Keep in mind, however, that unless the creator of the image has explicitly stated that it is free for noncommercial use (either by a statement on the Web site or by using a Creative Commons license), you should assume that the image is copyrighted and not free for the taking.

Note that if your document is to be posted on the Web, readers who have slow Internet connections may find it time-consuming or even impossible to download images with a large file size. Use a lower quality setting for .jpg files or the .gif or .png format instead (resave if necessary).

Sophisticated and original graphics are usually copyrighted, so if you intend to use an image in a document that you post on the Web or make widely available in print, you must do more than download the image and cite the source. The "fair use" principle of copyright law allows use of a small portion of a source in a noncommercial work, but you may need to write to the originator for permission to use an image or text.

For a college paper intended for your classmates and instructor alone and not posted publicly on the Web, you may want to include an illustration you find on the Web, such as a graph, a map, a photograph of an author or artist, a work of art, or an illustration from an online encyclopedia. You can do so without getting permission, but you must cite the source in your paper.

22e Honesty in visuals

With the ability to use software programs such as *Photoshop* to crop, combine, juxtapose, erase, and enhance images come attendant dangers and innumerable opportunities for comedy. Late night talk-show hosts show edited photos and video clips from the day's news to hilarious effect. Image manipulation can also be used for political effect (such as Josef Stalin's order to delete Leon Trotsky from photographs that show Lenin). In academic work, the changing of images is never acceptable. Falsifying data can reach the level of fraud, as in the case of a scientist who manipulated images of stem cells to achieve personal ambition. Scientific journals are beginning to check photos that are submitted with research to ensure that they have not been manipulated to remove images, change the contrast, or combine images from several slides into one.

The lesson here is a simple one: Be ethical in your use of visuals.

Charts and graphs can also be manipulated, not by changing the original data, but simply by selectively plotting the axes of a graph. Take care when choosing the value range for the axes to avoid exaggerating or downplaying changes over time. For example, for comparative data on population projections ranging between a 50% and 60% increase, a vertical axis of 0% to 100% will show the lines as almost flat, indicating little change over time. However, a vertical axis of 40% to 70% will emphasize and maybe exaggerate the small projected increase—one that could be attributable solely to a sampling fluctuation.

23 Online Communication Forums

23a E-mail in academic and business settings

MindTap
Read, highlight, and take notes online.

E-mail is used frequently in academic and business settings. If you use personal e-mail frequently, you should keep in mind that communicating online to professors or supervisors in academic or business contexts is different from writing a personal e-mail or a text message. Observe the following conventions.

Salutations Although e-mail can seem like an informal medium, when communicating with your professor or with individuals you do not know well, you should begin your e-mail with an appropriate salutation. Unless your instructor tells you otherwise, you should use "Dear Professor [Name]:" to start your e-mail. If you are addressing an individual in an organization, find out and use that person's title. Don't address someone who is not your peer and whom you don't know well by a first name unless instructed to do so.

Subject line Be clear and concise when composing a subject line so that readers will know at a glance what your message is about. Well-written subject lines will also make it easier to find a message if you want to refer to it later.

Length and readability Be brief, and state your main points clearly at the start of your e-mail. One screen holds about 250 words, and online readers do not want to scroll repeatedly to find out what you are saying. Keep paragraphs short and manageable so that readers can take in the information at a glance. Use numbered or bulleted lists to present a sequence of points as brief items that can be readily seen and absorbed. Avoid multiple colors, fonts, and graphics unless you are certain readers can receive and read these features.

Capitals Avoid using all capital letters in an e-mail message. To readers, it looks as if you are SHOUTING. But do use capitals when appropriate, especially for "I."

Accuracy Use a spelling checker, and edit your e-mail before sending it if you are writing to people you do not know well and you want them to take your ideas seriously.

Signing off Always put your actual name (not just Steelers.Rule@gmail.com) at the end of your e-mail message. You can also construct a "signature file," which will appear automatically at the end of every message you send. Find out how to do this from the Help or Tools menu of your e-mail program.

E-mail accounts If possible, send your e-mail from an account that the receiver will take seriously. Beware of e-mailing important information from accounts with addresses that seem fitting in one context (like the preceding Steelers.Rule@gmail.com address) but may appear unprofessional in an academic or business context. In an academic setting, use your account from the school if you have one. If not, you can easily set up separate e-mail accounts for social and professional/academic contexts.

Attachments Attachments can harbor computer viruses, so always be cautious about opening any attachments to an e-mail message. Open attachments only from known senders, and keep your own antivirus software up to date so that you will not spread a virus. If you need to send a large attachment, condense it or send it as a zipped file so that you don't overload the inbox of the receiver.

Spam Make sure you add your instructor or business associates to your safe list so that their messages are not classified as spam.

The two e-mail examples in Figures 23.1 and 23.2 show some of these principles in action. See if you can identify the ways in which the first e-mail is an improvement over the second.

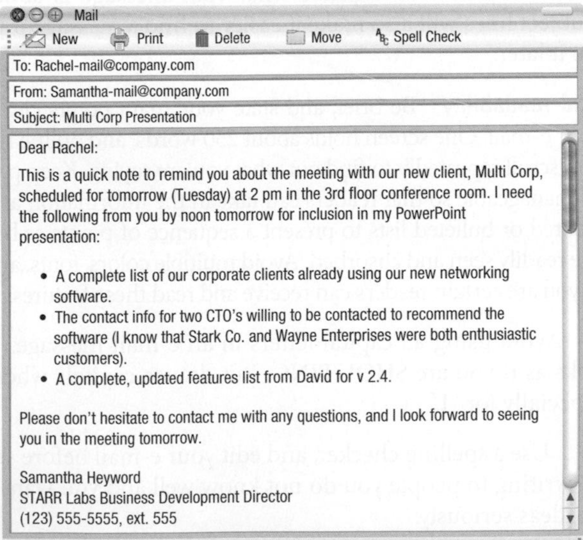

Figure 23.1 Example of an e-mail that follows the guidelines in this chapter

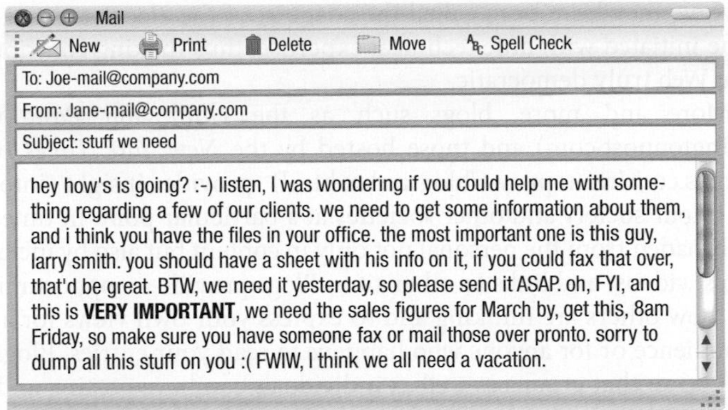

Figure 23.2 Example of an e-mail that does not follow the guidelines in this chapter

E-mail discussion lists, discussion boards on the Web and within course sites (such as *Blackboard, Moodle, Canvas,* or *D2L*), and online communities provide a forum for a virtual community of people sharing interest in a topic. Thousands of these forums exist—some public, some private—providing opportunities for you to find information and to enter discussions with others and make your own contributions. Since many of the groups and forums may not be moderated or refereed in any way, you must always be careful about evaluating the reliability of a source of information. However, any discussion group can be valuable not only for the information it provides but also for the ideas that emerge as participants discuss an issue and tease out its complexities. As a general rule, e-mail lists to which it is necessary to first subscribe or register tend to be more substantive and professional than lists or boards with no access control.

23b Other forums: Blogs, wikis, and virtual classrooms

Blogs Blogs are publicly posted observations on a topic initiated by the author or authorized group; they cover a range from personal diaries, family photos, and stories about pets to statements of political/religious/cultural views and observations of social issues. Typically open to everyone, they have been called the soapbox of the electronic age; they can be initiated with little technical expertise, thus making contributing to the Web truly democratic.

More and more, blogs such as the *Huffington Post* (www.huffingtonpost.com) and those hosted by the *New York Times* (www.nytimes.com/ref/topnews/blog-index.html) provide insight into the state of our society and other societies at a particular point in time, and they broaden from the personal not only in content but also by including images, videos, and links to other sites. Blogs provide an opportunity to learn how others are thinking and to express your own views for a special audience or for anyone who happens to read your entries. Blogs can be set up so that groups as well as individuals can have posting and discussion rights, so they are useful and affordable discussion venues for student course sites and clubs (for a student's blog for a course, see 2a). Several providers, such as *Blogger, Wordpress,* and *Edublogs*, offer free server space for blogs.

Wikis Wikis are dynamic Web texts that are open to editing by anyone, allowing information to be instantaneously added and corrected or otherwise changed with minimal technical expertise. Pages are created as a team or community effort. Some college instructors use wikis in their courses as a venue for student-instructor discussion, to support collaborative writing or to serve as the platform for course portfolios. Some course management systems such as *Blackboard, Moodle, Canvas,* and *D2L* offer wikis in the course Web site, and these are generally restricted to editing and viewing only by other students who are enrolled in the course.

You are probably familiar with the collaborative encyclopedia *Wikipedia,* one of the best-known wikis. In collaborative writing situations, such as a report assigned to a group of students or a team of employees, wikis can be a fast way to work together on generating and editing text. Most wikis can be set up so that contributors have to log in; this is useful for tracking who made specific changes. One of the key features of wikis is that you can easily see what changes have been made and can even compare versions throughout the entire history of a document using the "page history" function. In a word processing program, you have to be careful to keep copies of the iterations of your revised work; a wiki will take care of that aspect of composition for you. However, because wikis are server based, it is a good idea to always draft text in your word processor and save it before posting it to the wiki (that way, in the event of a server crash or a network disconnect, you won't lose your work). See 8c for guidelines on using wikis as a research source.

Virtual classrooms Course management systems such as *Blackboard, Moodle, Canvas,* and *D2L* provide synchronous cyberspaces in which a whole class or a group of students can log in at the same time and communicate synchronously. Virtual classrooms exist at different levels of sophistication:

- no more than a chat room, but typically archiving all entries
- adding a "whiteboard," a display/draw space that can be used by both instructor and student (upon permission)
- adding an audio channel to allow verbal exchange
- adding a two-way video (including live feed from instructor to students, and vice versa)
- adding slide show capability for presentations

Virtual classrooms are used for serious instruction in distance learning, with some providing videoconferencing tools for group projects and opportunities for online discussions.

23c Social media: *Twitter, Instagram,* and *Facebook*

Some instructors use social media such as *Twitter, Instagram,* and *Facebook* as instructional spaces. Although you probably use social media for a more informal purpose, you may find that you need to think about multiple audiences when you're posting in spaces like *Instagram*. This poses a challenge for many students, so keep a few guidelines in mind.

- If your instructor sets up a virtual space in a social media site for your class, follow the same guidelines for writing that we mention in 23a when you are communicating with your teacher and other students in your class in these spaces.
- When you post images, status updates, and other information in social media, everyone can see them (unless you have altered your privacy settings). Because images of you can be posted and tagged by others, they can be especially compromising. Consider whether you want your teacher or other students in your class (or a future employer, for that matter) seeing images and information about you posted online. Stay vigilant, and keep track of what you are sharing about yourself publicly.
- Take advantage of privacy controls. Various social media platforms have sophisticated privacy settings, but you need to keep up to date because they change frequently.

24 Oral and Multimedia Presentations

You may be asked to give oral presentations in writing courses, in other college courses, and in the working world. Usually, you will do some writing as you prepare your oral presentation, and you may deliver your oral report either from notes or from a manuscript text written especially for oral presentation.

MindTap®
Read, highlight, and take notes online.

24a Preparing an oral presentation

Use the Critical Thinking Framework in chapter 1 to consider the background and expectations of your audience and other elements of your writing situation. Jot down what you know about listeners and what stance and tone will best convince them of the validity of your views. For example, what effect do you want to have on the members of your audience? Do you want to inform, persuade, move, or entertain them? What do you know about your listeners' age, gender, background, education, occupation, political affiliation, beliefs, and knowledge of your subject? What do listeners need to know? In a college class, your audience will be your classmates and instructor. You can often help build a sense of community with your audience by asking questions and using the inclusive pronoun *we*.

Making an effective oral presentation is largely a matter of having control over your material, deciding what you want to say, and knowing your subject matter well. Preparation and planning are essential.

KEY POINTS

Tips for Preparing an Oral Presentation

1. **Select a topic you are committed to, and decide on a clear focus.** If you are assigned a topic, concentrate on what aspect of the topic is most interesting and relevant to you. Think about ways you can help your audience connect with your topic.
2. **Prepare a strong introduction.** Quickly capturing your audience's attention will increase your confidence and help ensure that your entire talk gets heard.

3. **Make a few strong points.** Back up your ideas with specific details. Have a few points that you can expand on and develop with interesting examples, quotations, and stories.
4. **Provide listening cues.** Include signposts and signal phrases to help your audience follow your ideas (*first, next, finally; the most important point is…*).
5. **Structure your talk clearly.** Present the organizational framework of your talk along with illustrative materials in handouts, *PowerPoint* slides (24e), posters, charts, or other visuals (22a and 22b).
6. **Use short sentences, accessible words, memorable phrases, and natural language.** In writing, you can use long sentences with one clause embedded in another, but these are difficult for listeners to follow.
7. **Use repetition.** An audience listening, rather than reading, will appreciate being reminded of the structure of the talk and of points you referred to previously.
8. **Follow the guidelines.** To be effective, you will want to meet the requirements set for the presentation in terms of time available for preparation, length of presentation, and possible questions from the audience.
9. **Prepare a strong ending.** To ensure that you make an impact on the audience, deliver a strong conclusion. Do not simply stop or trail off. Consider connecting your introduction to your conclusion to frame your presentation for the audience.

24b Speaking from notes or manuscript

Speaking from notes You will be able to be more spontaneous and to look your audience in the eye if you speak from notes instead of a full manuscript. Think of your presentation as a conversation. For this method, notes or a key-word outline must be clear and organized so that you feel secure about which points you will discuss and in what order. Also, practice is essential so that you don't lose your place in your notes. Here are a speaker's notes for a presentation on paternity leave.

PATERNITY LEAVE

1. Children's needs
   Benefits
   Bonding
2. Issue of equity
   Equal treatment for men and women
   Cost

Your notes or outline should make reference to specific illustrations and quotations to help you keep your place as you present your speech (as in Key Points box, p. 413, item 4). You can also use *PowerPoint*, *Prezi*, or *Google Drive* slides to guide the direction and structure of your presentation (24e). For a short presentation on a topic that you know very well, use notes with or without the visual aid of slides. Do not read aloud the text on your slides, though, especially in front of a small audience. Try to limit the amount of text you put on slides, and use them primarily for visual support to your presentation.

Speaking from a manuscript Writing out a complete speech may be necessary for a long, formal presentation. Still, even if you do this, you should practice and prepare so that you do not have to labor over every word. Remember, too, to build in places to pause and make spontaneous comments. This gives you the opportunity to make frequent eye contact with the audience. The advantages of speaking from a prepared manuscript are that you can time the presentation exactly and that you will never wonder what to say next. The disadvantage is that you have to read the text, and reading aloud is not easy, especially if you want to maintain eye contact. If you prefer to speak from a complete manuscript text, prepare the text for oral presentation as follows:

- Triple-space your text, and use a large font.
- When you reach the bottom of a page, begin a new sentence on the next page. Do not start a sentence on one page and finish it on the next.
- Highlight key words in each paragraph so that you will be able to spot them easily.
- Underline words and phrases that you want to stress.
- Use slash marks (/ or //) to remind yourself to pause. Read in "sense groups" (parts of a sentence that are read as a unit—a phrase or a clause, for example—often indicated by a pause when spoken and by punctuation when written). Mark your text at the end of a sense group.

- Number your pages so that you can keep them in the proper sequence.
- Do not staple the pages, but rather place them face down as you finish each page.

24c Practicing and presenting

Whether you speak from notes or from a manuscript, practice is essential.

- **Practice not just once, but many times.** Try recording yourself, watching or listening to the recording, and asking a friend for comments.
- **Speak at a normal speed and at a good volume.** Speaking too quickly and too softly is a common mistake.
- **Imagine a full audience.** Use gestures, and practice looking up to make eye contact with people in the audience. Practice in front of a mirror and critique yourself, or practice in front of a friend and ask for feedback.
- **Beware of filler words and phrases.** Avoid terms such as *OK, well, you know*, and *like.* These verbal tics, when repeated during a presentation, annoy and distract the audience.
- **Do not punctuate pauses with "er" or "uhm."** These verbalized pauses may undermine your confidence, and they will almost certainly annoy and distract your audience.
- **Beware of nervous habits when you speak.** Avoid pacing too quickly, playing with your hair, or other nervous habits. They can be distracting to your audience.

It is natural to feel some anxiety before the actual presentation, but most people find that their jitters disappear as soon as they begin talking, especially when they are well prepared.

Look frequently at your listeners. Work the room so that you gaze directly at people in all sections of the audience. In *Secrets of Successful Speakers,* Lilly Walters points out that when you look at one person, all the people in a V behind that person will think you are looking at them. Bear in mind that no matter how well prepared a report is, listeners will not respond positively if the presenter reads it too rapidly or in a monotone or without looking up and engaging the audience. If your topic is lighthearted, remember to smile.

24d Preparing a multimedia presentation

The possibilities for supplementing a presentation with multiple media can seem almost limitless. You can use slide presentation software such as *PowerPoint, Prezi,* or *Google Drive* to embed graphics, photos, charts, video, audio, or any combination of these to support and enhance your presentation. Many audiences expect some type of multimedia presentation as part of the listening experience, and it is important to pay attention to what your audience's expectations are.

Charlie Schuck/Photodisc/Jupiter Images

When you prepare an oral presentation, think about your writing and *speaking* situation: what type of media would be appropriate and effective for your purpose, your audience, the length of your presentation, and the media you have available? The goal of your presentation is to effectively communicate to your audience. You want them to leave thinking about *what* you said and not only *how* you said it. Use multimedia aids to help your audience grasp an important point, and eliminate them when they are not legitimately needed.

KEY POINTS

Common Types of Multimedia Aids

- **Digital slides of video** are run directly from a computer and are shown on a screen via a digital projector. On the one hand, digital slides are flexible and provide the possibility of easily embedding other media such as photographs, video, and audio. On the other hand, you are limited by your equipment and the facility where you will be giving your presentation.
- **Video clips, audio clips, and DVDs** require a moderate amount of production but can be particularly effective for orientations and training purposes. Presentation software makes integrating

audio and video quite easy, as it eliminates a speaker's need to transport and manage additional equipment.

- **Flip charts** are best used in informal presentations with a smaller audience. They are easy to prepare, easy to update, and require no equipment.
- **Posters** are common for presentations in the sciences and social sciences, especially during "poster sessions" when several speakers display their posters at the same time and the audience circulates to hear informal presentations of the speakers' research. Posters typically contain visuals or graphics to represent the research with limited amounts of texts so that the audience can see the main points without reading too much up close.
- **Handouts** can provide the audience with printed copies of notes, tables, or illustrations from your presentation. They also can provide the audience with a permanent record of the presentation's major points and bibliographic information for any sources you cite. Not only do they help your audience follow your presentation, but also they can provide a review and new information for the audience after the presentation is over. Many presenters will provide a URL to their audience so that participants can access materials online.

Using multimedia equipment smoothly does not come naturally, so be sure to practice giving your presentation. And because bulbs can burn out, cords can be forgotten, and computers can crash, always be prepared to give your presentation without visuals if necessary. Use the following guidelines to prepare yourself for any presentation situation:

- **Use multimedia to enhance what you have to say, not to replace it.** Your words should still be the star of your presentation, and the media should enhance and support what you have to say.
- **Keep it simple.** Flashy doesn't always mean effective. Sometimes the simplest media can make the most effective impact.
- **Know the technical requirements and limitations.** Don't plan a presentation that requires Internet access if there's no Internet connection available. If you use a Mac, find out whether you need to bring an adapter if you are projecting images. Avoid using platform-specific software (like *Keynote* for the Mac) if you don't know whether it will be available for your presentation. Instead, use something that works across platforms, like *Google Drive* (but only if you have an Internet

connection). If you are using common software such as *PowerPoint*, make sure a compatible version is available.

- **Have a backup plan.** You never know what might go wrong, so have a backup plan in case your technology does not work. Handouts are the safest backup in case all technology fails. An alternate presentation technology (like *Google Drive*, which works on any platform with Internet access) is helpful if you have compatibility issues or the right software isn't available.

When you are preparing a live or online multimedia presentation, consider the effectiveness of positioning images near your words and of conveying emotion and meaning through pictures. Imagine, for instance, how you might present an argument against genetic engineering of food crops to classmates or colleagues. In addition to your well-formed argument, you could show graphs of public opinion data on the issue, pictures of chemicals that are used on crops and how they are applied, and a video clip of interviews with shoppers as they read labels and buy produce. If you use media imaginatively, you can do what writing teachers have long advised for printed essays: Show; don't tell.

KEY POINTS

Multimedia Presentation Design

An excellent online resource that covers a wide range of issues for designers of multimedia presentations is Garr Reynolds's *Presentation Zen* site, www.presentationzen.com/. For examples of compelling multimedia presentations, check out *TED*: "Riveting talks by remarkable people, free to the world," www.ted.com/.

24e Using *PowerPoint, Prezi,* and *Google Drive*

Using presentation software like *PowerPoint, Prezi,* and *Google Drive* gives you access to organizing and design tools. It also allows you to seamlessly integrate audio and visual components to produce a dynamic multimedia presentation.

Presentation software as an organizational tool Presentation software allows you to prepare slides that illustrate the logic of your presentation and helps you separate the main points from the supporting details. That way, the slides keep you focused as you give your presentation. Your audience follows your ideas not only because you have established a clear principle of organization but also because the slide on the presentation screen reminds people of where you are in your talk, what point you are addressing, and how that point fits into your total scheme.

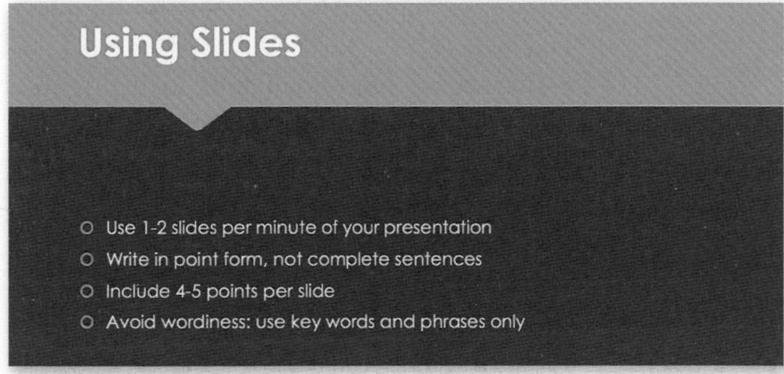
Using Slides
Use 1-2 slides per minute of your presentation
Write in point form, not complete sentences
Include 4-5 points per slide
Avoid wordiness: use key words and phrases only

Figure 24.1 ***PowerPoint*** **slide**

Slides as visual evidence and support Many speakers incorporate slides in their presentations as evidence, support, and even as counterpoints to their presentations. Slides containing well-timed quotes, visual images, graphs, and charts can have the same rhetorical effect as well-placed visuals in an argument essay (4j). If you decide to include sound, music, and video clips to illustrate and drive home the points you want to make, be careful not to overdo these effects. Embedded media can easily become distracting bells and whistles, and your audience may suspect you have used them to make up for lack of content. They should enhance your work, not dominate it.

Creating Slides* When you create slides, keep in mind the following:

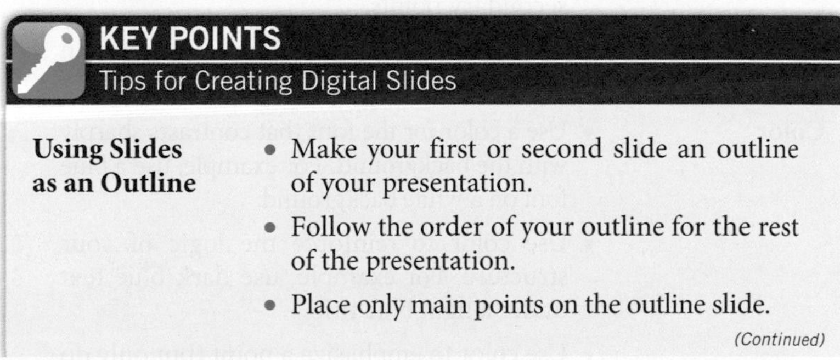

KEY POINTS

Tips for Creating Digital Slides

Using Slides as an Outline	• Make your first or second slide an outline of your presentation. • Follow the order of your outline for the rest of the presentation. • Place only main points on the outline slide.

(Continued)

*Adapted from *Making PowerPoint Slides: Avoiding the Pitfalls of Bad Slides* at: http://www.iasted.org/conferences/formatting/Presentations-Tips.ppt.

(Continued)

Slide Structure	• When possible, choose visuals instead of text.
	• Write in bulleted form, never in complete sentences.
	• Include no more than four to five points per slide.
	• Consider the 6 × 6 rule:
	  ○ No more than six words across.
	  ○ No more than six lines down.
	• Avoid wordiness: use key words and phrases only.

Slide Timing	Use one or two slides per minute of your presentation, and show one point at a time to: • help your audience concentrate on what you are saying • prevent your audience from reading ahead • help you keep your presentation focused
Animation	• Do not use distracting animation. • Do not go overboard with the animation. • Be consistent with the animation that you use.
Fonts	• Use at least an 18-point font. • Use different size fonts for main points and secondary points. • Use a standard font like Times New Roman or Arial.
Color	• Use a color for the font that contrasts sharply with the background. For example, use a blue font on a white background. • Use color to reinforce the logic of your structure. For example, use dark blue text under a light blue title. • Use color to emphasize a point (but only do so occasionally).

Background	• Use backgrounds that are attractive but simple. • Use backgrounds that are light. • Use the same background consistently throughout your presentation.
Graphs	• Use graphs rather than just charts and words because ○ data in graphs are easier to comprehend and retain than are raw data ○ trends are easier to visualize in graph form • Always title your graphs.
Spelling and Grammar	• Proofread your slides for ○ spelling mistakes ○ the use of repeated words ○ grammatical errors • If English is not your first language, have someone else check your presentation.

25 Portfolios

25a Preparing a hard-copy portfolio

MindTap®
Read, highlight, and take notes online.

Portfolios are used by artists, writers, and job hunters to demonstrate their range of skills and accomplishments. In your college writing courses, your instructors may ask you to select work to include in a portfolio that allows you and your instructor an opportunity to review and assess your progress over time. If your instructor does not issue specific guidelines for presenting your portfolio, use the guidelines in the following Key Points box.

KEY POINTS

Presenting a Course Writing Portfolio

- Number and date your drafts; clip or staple all drafts and final copy together.
- Include a cover sheet describing the contents of the package for each separate package in your portfolio (for example, "In-class essay" or "Documented paper with three prior drafts").
- Include a brief cover letter to introduce the material and yourself.
- Pay special attention to accuracy and mechanics. Your semester grade may depend on the few pieces of writing that you select for evaluation, so make sure that the ones you include are carefully edited and well presented.

Regardless of whether a portfolio is required, consider collecting in your own portfolio academic writing that indicates both the range of topics covered in your courses and the types of writing you have done. To show prospective professors, graduate schools, or employers that you are able to produce several kinds of writing, use the list in the following Key Points box (adapted from Carleton College's writing portfolio requirements for its graduates) as a guideline in preparing your portfolio. Don't leave it up to readers to deduce what you have accomplished. Be sure to include at the beginning of your portfolio a cover letter, an essay, and/or a table of contents that explicitly states what you have included and why.

KEY POINTS

Preparing a Portfolio of Your Academic Writing

An effective academic writing portfolio will demonstrate to readers

- your breadth of interests by showing writing that you have produced in multiple courses from a range of departments or disciplines: the humanities, business, education, social sciences, mathematics, and the natural sciences
- your ability to construct, develop, and effectively support an argument

- your ability to observe and report by showing writing such as interviews from a sociology class, field notes from an education class, a laboratory report from the natural sciences, a description of a work of art you observed, or a concert you attended
- your ability to analyze complex information by showing writing that includes, for example, numeric data, multiple texts, or multiple observations
- your ability to interpret diverse material, whether it's a film you saw, a poem you read, or a set of data you analyzed
- your ability to conduct effective research by including writing that shows a range of well-identified, integrated, and documented sources

25b Preparing an e-portfolio

Increasingly, individual instructors as well as college-wide programs require or strongly encourage students to construct an e-portfolio. Space is allotted on a server where students can store writing samples, a résumé, information about their experience, and relevant images. Students can also reflect on their work as they present it to readers. The specific charges or tasks vary with the course. While an English instructor will probably focus on writing samples, a social science instructor may ask students to locate primary sources about a specific research topic (like the environment or laws and court cases related to civil unions). In education, e-portfolios have become quite common to document a student's progress through a course of study—for example, to file lesson plans, lesson evaluations, and so on.

KEY POINTS

Additional Resources for E-portfolios

For examples of college programs that assign e-portfolios, see the following:

- Penn State includes instructions on building e-portfolios and examples of students' e-portfolios (including video and audio clips) that they used when applying for jobs. See http://portfolio.psu.edu/.

(Continued)

(Continued)

- LaGuardia Community College includes a useful e-portfolio flowchart, instructions for developing an e-portfolio, resources, student samples, and advice about the language to use, the information to provide, and ways to avoid plagiarizing images and sounds found on the Web. See http://www.eportfolio.lagcc.cuny.edu.
- Florida State University has a useful Career Portfolio guide to help students develop online portfolios to show instructors and prospective employers what they have learned and what skills they possess. See http://career.fsu.edu.

Whatever software your school may use to support e-portfolios, typically you will have control over the material that goes onto your pages on the (Web) server. In your private storage area, you'll be able to make material available to your instructors and/or other students for review so that these reviewers can add their comments to the material. Also, you may have the option of publishing the document online so that future employers or friends and family can also see the work. You can make specific documents—aimed at particular audiences—available for viewing at any time. One advantage of e-portfolios is that you have the flexibility to remix the materials for different purposes. In addition, you can include a variety of materials that you produce, such as HTML documents, graphics, images, audio files, and film clips, rather than simply printed college essays that make up more conventional portfolios. If you use an e-portfolio system at your school to upload and design your portfolio, find out what access you'll have to it after you graduate.

25c A student's e-portfolio

Hannah Lynne Sims prepared an e-portfolio to showcase the work she had done to prepare for a career in nursing at Auburn University. Figures 25.1 and 25.2 show an excerpt from two pages—her home page and a page that outlines her professional goals—both of which combine text and images, and provide internal links to her work and to other sections of her Web site. The five tabs on the menu of her home page provide information about her goals (Home), a bio (About Me), her nursing philosophy, additional professional information and work (Professional), and a link for her contact information. Note that the links to the home page and all the other pages appear across the top of each screen, allowing easy access to all parts of the site at all times.

Figure 25.1 A student's e-portfolio home page

Source: http://hannahlynnes.wix.com/hannahsims

Figure 25.2 A student's e-portfolio page, showing her goals

26 Résumés and Letters of Application

In business, knowing how to prepare documents for the screen and for the page is a valuable skill, whether you are applying for a job or communicating with colleagues and clients.

MindTap®
Read, highlight, and take notes online.

26a How to write a résumé

Résumés can be presented on paper, posted on the Web, or delivered electronically through e-mail or a dropbox. Designs differ, and no one format works for everybody. However, in all formats, you need to convey to a prospective employer what you have accomplished and when, providing details of your education, work experience, honors or awards, interests, and special skills. Above all, you need to show that your qualifications and experience make you suitable for the job that you are applying for.

KEY POINTS
Writing a Résumé

1. Decide how to deliver your résumé, or follow a prospective employer's instructions: on paper, posted online, sent as an e-mail attachment, uploaded to a dropbox—or all of these. Start with a word-processed version, and save it as .rtf or .docx. Convert it to HTML or PDF to post online. If you send it as an e-mail attachment or upload it to a dropbox, save it as a PDF first to preserve the formatting.
2. For a hard-copy version, print on white or off-white standard-size paper of good quality.
3. Use headings to indicate the main sections.
4. Highlight section headings and important information with boldface, italics, bullets, indentation, or different fonts. Use a clear, simple design. Do not use overly elaborate fonts, colors, or design features. Keep a print résumé at one or two pages. Do not include extraneous information to add length, but do not cram the page by single-spacing between sections or by using a small font or tiny margins.
5. Include information and experience relevant to the job you are applying for. Use reverse chronological order (begin with your most recent work experience and education).
6. Proofread your résumé several times, and ask someone else to examine it carefully as well. Make sure it contains no errors. Avoid howlers such as "rabid typist" and "responsible for ruining a five-store chain."
7. Accompany your résumé with a cover letter (26c), also carefully checked to avoid an error such as "Thank you for considering me. I look forward to hearing from you shorty."

Note: *Microsoft Word* provides résumé templates that set up headings for you—a useful guide. If you are converting your résumé to HTML, however, the formatting may not translate exactly.

26b Sample print or Web page résumé

Notice how Marcus Benini organized his résumé into clear divisions, using bold headings and a space between sections (Figure 26.1). This résumé presents his most recent education and job experience first and works backward.*

Use a simple, creative design; includes clear contact information and a professional e-mail address

Marcus C. Benini
1445 College Avenue
Palos Hills, IL 60465
708.555.453S
mbenlnK8555.com

Education

Starts with educational background, most relevant for a graduating student

Moraine Valley Community College, Palos Hills, IL

- Associate in Science Degree (A.S.), 3.8 G.P.A., Expected Graduation 2016
- Dean's List All Semesters
- Coursework: International Business, Fundamentals of Accounting, Business Mathematics, Financial Accounting, Computer Applications in Accounting

The American International University in Rome
Study Abroad, High School Program, Summer 2012

- Lived with a host family for three weeks
- Studied Italian and Introduction to Business Management

Employment

Highlights experience to differentiate his candidacy

Uses bold type to emphasize job title, which is more important than the names of his employers

Moraine Valley Community College
Teaching Assistant, Computer Applications in Accounting, (2015–present)

Chooses present tense verbs to describe current responsibilities

- Assist professor with grading 150 papers each semester
- Hold daily office hours for students
- Provide tutoring on challenging course material

Lakewatch Apartments
Property Accountant (2013–2015)

Chooses past tense verbs to describe previous experience

- Processed all accounts payable including taxes, mortgages, and monthly bills
- Maintained cash receipt journals for various properties
- Processed and deposited rental income
- Maintained general ledger and reconciled all bank statements
- Produced special reports for the partners and investors

Other

Includes relevant skills and hobbies (optional)

- Notary Public, State of Illinois
- Proficient in Peachtree and Microsoft Word, Excel, and Outlook
- Proficient Italian
- Hobbies include guitar, tennis, model airplanes

Figure 26.1 Sample résumé

*Sample documents in 26b, 26c, and 27b are adapted from Amy Newman and Scot Ober's *Business Communication: In Person, in Print, Online*, 8th edition (Boston: South-Western, 2012). Used with permission.

26c Cover letter and sample

Accompany your print or e-mail résumé with a cover letter that explains what position you are applying for and why you are a good candidate. Find out as much as you can about the potential employer and type of work; then, in your letter, emphasize the connections between your experience and the job requirements. (Figure 26.2 is an example of a

October 13, 2016

Ms. Jane Wu, Partner
Ross, Russell & Weston
452 S. Michigan Avenue
Chicago, IL 60605

Addresses the letter to a specific person

Dear Ms. Wu:

Subject: EDP Specialist Position (Reference No. 103-G)

Identifies the job position (EDP, or Electronic Data Processing, Specialist) and source of advertising

My varied work experience in accounting, coupled with my associate's degree earned in May 2016, has prepared me for the position of EDP specialist that you advertised in the October 9 *Chicago Sun-Times*.

In addition to taking required courses in accounting and international business at Moraine Valley Community College, I took an elective course in EDP auditing and control. The training I received in this course in applications, software, systems, and service-center records would enable me to immediately become a productive member of your EDP consulting staff.

Emphasizes a qualification that might distinguish him from other applicants

My college training has been supplemented by experience as a teaching assistant in computer applications in accounting, a position that gave me leadership experience among my fellow business and accounting students. I also noticed that you have a branch office in Milan, and I hope that my native fluency in Italian and my training in international business would be of use as you continue to grow your overseas accounts.

Relates his work experience to the specific needs of the employer

After you have reviewed my enclosed résumé I would appreciate having the opportunity to discuss with you why I believe I have the right qualifications and personality to serve you and your clients. I can be reached by e-mail or phone after 3 p.m. daily.

Sincerely,

Marcus C. Benini

Marcus C. Benini
1445 College Avenue
Palos Hills, IL 60465
Phone: 708.555.4539
E-mail: mbenini@555.com

Provides a telephone number and an e-mail address (may be done either in the body of the letter or at the end of the address block)

Figure 26.2 Sample cover letter

solicited application letter; it accompanies the résumé on p. 427.) Let the employer see that you understand what type of person he or she is looking for. State when, where, and how you can be contacted. As you do with the résumé itself, proofread the letter carefully.

Once you have had an interview, write a short note to thank the interviewer and emphasize your interest in the position.

27 Business Letters and Memos

27a Features of a business letter

MindTap®
Read, highlight, and take notes online.

A good business letter usually has the following qualities:

1. It is brief.
2. It clearly conveys to readers information and expectations for action or response.
3. It lets readers know how they will benefit from, or be affected by, the proposal or suggestion.
4. It is polite.
5. It is written in relatively formal language.
6. It contains no errors.

27b Sample business letter

LANGUAGE AND CULTURE

Business Letters across Cultures

The basic features of business letters vary from culture to culture. Business letters in English avoid both flowery language and references to religion, elements that are viewed favorably in some other cultures. Do not assume that there are universal conventions. When writing cross-cultural business letters, follow these suggestions:

1. Use a formal style; address correspondents by title and family name.

(Continued)

(Continued)

2. If possible, learn about the writing conventions of your correspondent's culture.
3. Use clear language and a summary to get your point across.
4. Avoid humor; it may fall flat and could offend.

The sample letter in Figure 27.1 uses a block format, with all parts aligned at the left. This format is commonly used with business stationery.

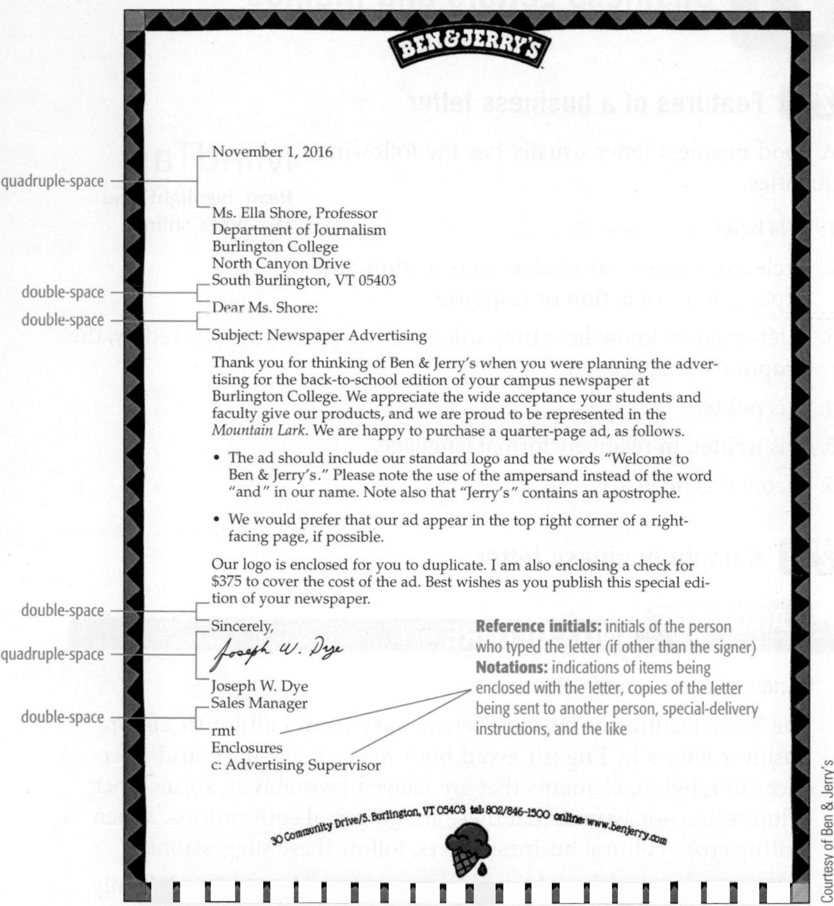
quadruple-space
double-space
double-space
double-space
quadruple-space
double-space
Reference initials: initials of the person who typed the letter (if other than the signer)
Notations: indications of items being enclosed with the letter, copies of the letter being sent to another person, special-delivery instructions, and the like
Courtesy of Ben & Jerry's

BEN&JERRY'S

November 1, 2016

Ms. Ella Shore, Professor
Department of Journalism
Burlington College
North Canyon Drive
South Burlington, VT 05403

Dear Ms. Shore:

Subject: Newspaper Advertising

Thank you for thinking of Ben & Jerry's when you were planning the advertising for the back-to-school edition of your campus newspaper at Burlington College. We appreciate the wide acceptance your students and faculty give our products, and we are proud to be represented in the *Mountain Lark*. We are happy to purchase a quarter-page ad, as follows.

- The ad should include our standard logo and the words "Welcome to Ben & Jerry's." Please note the use of the ampersand instead of the word "and" in our name. Note also that "Jerry's" contains an apostrophe.
- We would prefer that our ad appear in the top right corner of a right-facing page, if possible.

Our logo is enclosed for you to duplicate. I am also enclosing a check for $375 to cover the cost of the ad. Best wishes as you publish this special edition of your newspaper.

Sincerely,

Joseph W. Dye

Joseph W. Dye
Sales Manager

rmt
Enclosures
c: Advertising Supervisor

30 Community Drive/S. Burlington, VT 05403 tel: 802/846-1500 online: www.benjerry.com

Figure 27.1 Sample business letter using block format

27c Technical requirements of a business letter

Paper and page numbering Use 8½" × 11" white unlined paper. If your letter is longer than one page, number the pages beginning with page 2 in the top right margin.

Spacing Type single-spaced, on one side of the page only, and double-space between paragraphs. Quadruple-space below the date. Double-space below the inside address and the salutation. Double-space between the last line of the letter and the closing. Quadruple-space between the closing and the typed name of the writer, and then double-space to *Enclosure* (or *Enc.*) or *c*: (indicating that you are enclosing materials or are sending a copy to another person, respectively).

Left and right margins The sample letter on letterhead in 27b uses a block format: the date, inside address, salutation, paragraphs, closing, and signature begin at the left margin. The right margin should not be justified; it should be ragged (with lines of unequal length) to avoid awkward gaps in the spacing between words. A modified block format places the date, closing, and signature on the right.

Return address If you are not using business letterhead, give your address as the return address, followed by the date. Do not include your name with the address. (If you are using business letterhead on which an address is printed, you do not have to write a return address.)

Inside address The inside address gives the name, title, and complete address of the person you are writing to. With a word processing program and certain printers, you can use this part of the letter for addressing the envelope.

Salutation In the salutation, mention the recipient's name if you know it, with the appropriate title (*Dr., Professor, Mr., Ms.*) or just the recipient's title (*Dear Sales Manager*). If you are writing to a company or institution, use a more general term of address (*Dear Sir* or *Madam*) or the name of the company or institution (*Dear British Airways*). Use a colon after the salutation in a business letter.

Closing phrase and signature Capitalize only the first word of a closing phrase, such as *Yours truly* or *Sincerely yours*. Type your name four lines below the closing phrase (omitting *Mr.* or *Ms.*). If you have a title (*Supervisor, Manager*), type it underneath your name. Between the closing phrase and your typed name, sign your name in blue or black ink.

Other information Indicate whether you have enclosed materials with the letter (*Enclosure* or *Enc.*) and to whom you have sent copies (*cc: Ms. Amy Ray*). The abbreviation *cc:* previously referred to "carbon copy" but now refers to "courtesy copy" or "computer copy." You may, however, use a single *c:* followed by a name or names to indicate who besides your addressee is receiving the letter.

The envelope Choose an envelope that fits your letter when folded from bottom to top in thirds. Use your computer's addressing capability to place the name, title, and full address of the recipient in the middle of the envelope and your own name and address in the top left corner. Remember to include ZIP codes. Word processing programs include a function that allows you to create labels for envelopes.

27d Basic features of a memo

A memo (from the Latin *memorandum,* meaning "to be remembered") is a message from one person to someone else within an organization. It can be sent on paper or by e-mail. A memo usually reports briefly on an action, raises a question, or asks permission to follow a course of action. It addresses a specific question or issue in a quick, focused way, conveying information in clear paragraphs or numbered points.

Begin what will be a hard-copy memo with headings such as *To*, *From*, *Date*, and *Subject*; such headings are frequently capitalized and in boldface type. If you will be sending a memo via e-mail, be sure to fill in the "Subject" field. For both formats, tell readers what your point is in the first sentence. Then briefly explain and give reasons or details. Single-space the memo. If the body of your memo is long, divide it into short paragraphs, or include headings and numbered or bulleted lists (see 21e and 21f) to draw attention to and organize essential points. Most computer programs provide a standard template for memo format. The design and headings are provided; you just fill in what you want to say. Keep in mind that the features of a memo pertaining to considerations such as tone and correctness are essentially the same as for a business letter (27a).

Exercises on Design, Media, and Presentation

EXERCISE 1 Format a piece of academic writing in print. 21a

Select a piece of writing that you've completed for one of your courses. Format and print the piece according to the guidelines in this chapter. Check with your instructor, or the style guide for your discipline, about variables such as documentation style and whether to use a title page. Have a peer check your work for style and accuracy.

EXERCISE 2 Format a piece of academic writing to be published online. 21b

Select a piece of writing that you've completed for one of your courses, and adapt the piece to be published on a Web site. Follow the instructions in the Key Points box for creating section headings, internal hyperlinks, and external hyperlinks (p. 385). Format paragraphs in a block style, attribute sources with persistent links, and provide a list of references or works cited. Have a peer check the paper and test the links. Consider submitting the piece to a Web-based publication that is related to your topic, or publish it on your own or in a class blog.

EXERCISE 3 Suggest visuals to support a paper. 22

Read the following list of college papers. Then suggest visuals that would add to or support each paper.

- an argument that CPR training should be compulsory for every United States citizen
- a critical review comparing the success and artistic achievement of Johnny Cash's albums to other artists' recordings of his songs
- an analysis of the change in traffic that would result from building a shopping mall where there is now a school
- instructions for creating a compost pile
- an explanation of the failure of NASA's first Orbiting Carbon Observatory satellite

EXERCISE 4 Create a pie chart and a bar chart. 22b

Suppose that, at a college, 43 percent of the students live on campus, 29 percent commute by car, 18 percent commute by bicycle, and 10 percent live near enough to walk to the campus. Using your word processing program, create a pie chart to display these data. Then create a bar chart using the same data.

EXERCISE 5 Consider sources for visuals. 22d–22e

Look back at your answers for Exercise 3. Indicate which of these visuals you would create and where you would find the others. Then indicate which items would require permission, a source credit, or a copyright line.

EXERCISE 6 Revise an e-mail message. 23a

Rewrite the second message in section 23a so that it follows the guidelines for e-mail in a business setting. Create any details that you need to complete the message.

EXERCISE 7 Create a plan for an oral presentation. 24a

Select one aspect of your school or community that you think needs to be changed. Then write up a plan for convincing the people who can make this change:

1. Identify where the audience currently stands on your issue.
2. Decide on the main points that you should make to bring decision makers around to your point of view.
3. Select the right medium for the presentation (in-person talk, video, slides, podcast).
4. Assess what visuals you would need.
5. Choose a tone that would alert listeners to the need for change without alienating them, and draft a sample paragraph of the presentation.

EXERCISE 8 Select items for an academic portfolio. 25a

Choose five items that you would put in a college portfolio (either print or online). Select items that demonstrate your interests and abilities, as described in the Key Points box "Preparing a Portfolio of Your Academic Writing." Write a cover letter describing each assignment and why you've selected it.

EXERCISE 9 Select items for a résumé. 26a

Decide on a job or training program that you would like to apply for, either this year or in the near future. Select five or six experiences that you believe qualify you for this opportunity, and expand them into items for a résumé. Exchange your list of items with a classmate, and critically evaluate how well your classmate presents herself or himself. Which items are most relevant and compelling? What improvements would you suggest?

6 Style: The Five C's

THE BRAND MANAGER

The Writer

Brand management is the application of marketing techniques to a particular product line. Recognizable logos for Nike and Apple are just one outcome of brand management. Expressive verbs, exact and vivid word choices, and clean, direct sentences are critical to marketing a product or service. Because consumers won't spend a lot of time deciphering a marketing piece, each word has to carry its weight in a message, as does the overall design of the marketing material.

Not surprisingly, revising for style is an essential part of a brand manager's job. As product director for 4LTR Press, a company that produces learning materials, Steven Joos is responsible for the success of the larger brand. He needs to craft a consistent message about that brand while communicating with vastly different readers. On any given day, Joos might deliver a message three different ways for as many different audiences. For example, his technology team needs a clear set of requirements so that they can build an effective quiz; instructors assigning those quizzes want to know the right content is being covered, among other things; and students ultimately want to maximize the effectiveness of their study time. Word choice, tone, and structure must work together in each message to achieve the target response. The following screen shot shows one of 4LTR Press's products, with some of the options for creating quizzes outlined for the user.

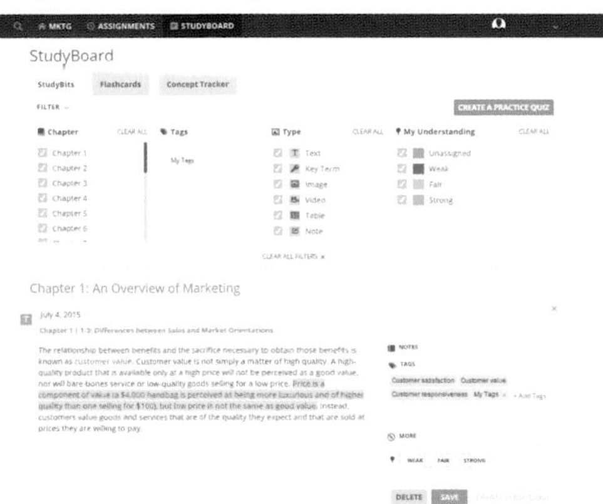

6 Style: The Five C's

Sometimes style can obscure meaning, even when ideas are well organized and there are no grammatical errors. This happens when readers are turned off by a style that is characterized by wordiness, flatness, inappropriate word choice, clichés, or sentences constructed without interesting variations. Do readers a favor: When you read your own draft prior to revision, use the convenient mnemonic of the five C's to remind you what to consider for revision: **C**ut, **C**heck for Action, **C**onnect, **C**ommit, and **C**hoose the Best Words. Keep clarity and directness in mind as the basics of academic writing. Of course, graceful and elegant writing may ultimately be your aim, but grace and elegance always need an underlay of clarity.

MindTap®

Understand the goals of this part, and complete a warm-up activity.

Try this quick test: read your draft aloud. If you have to pause anywhere to make sense of what you have written (watch out for a stumble, a pause, discomfort, or the occasions when "huh?" flashes through your mind), use the five C's to revise for style and to get rid of the glitch.

LANGUAGE AND CULTURE

Style across Cultures

It is impossible to identify one style as the best. What is considered good (or appropriate) style varies according to the writer's purpose and the expectations of the anticipated readers. Country, culture, region, ethnic heritage, language, gender, and class can all play a role in influencing what readers define as *style*. What may please readers in one language and culture, in one setting, in one part of the world may seem too flat or too adorned in another. Good style is relative and culture-bound. The Japanese novelist Junichuro Tanizaki, for example, gives writers this advice: "Do not try to be too clear; leave some gaps in the meaning." Western cultures, on the other hand, tend to value clarity.

With acknowledgment to Joseph Williams's *Style: Lessons in Clarity and Grace*, 11th edition, chapters 28 to 32 examine five strategies, called here the "five C's of style": cut, check for action, connect, commit, and choose the best words. Chapters 33 and 34 provide a sample of a passage revised for style and some handy tips for writers.

28 The First C: Cut

MindTap®
Read, highlight, and take notes online.

When you write, do not underdevelop your ideas because you fear taxing readers' patience. Work on developing ideas and presenting material that has substance, persuasive detail, explanation, and original expression, and make sure you don't pad your work to fill an assigned number of pages. However, once you have a draft that has ideas and content you are happy with, scrutinize it for obvious redundancies, fumbling phrases, weak expressions, and obscurities that can easily creep into a first draft.

28a Cut repetition and wordiness

Say something only once and in the best place.

- **The Lilly Library ~~contains many rare books.~~**

  s

  ~~The books in the library are~~ carefully preserved~~,~~

  many rare books and manuscripts.

  ~~The library also houses a manuscript collection.~~

- **~~In my own personal opinion,~~ I believe that bail should never be granted to anyone who has ~~ever~~ committed a violent crime ~~in which a gun was used by the criminal.~~** .

- **In 1998, California residents voted to abolish bilingual education~~,~~ ~~The main reason for their voting to abolish~~**

  because

  ~~bilingual education was that~~ many children were being placed indiscriminately into programs and kept there too long.

If your draft says something like "As the first paragraph states" or "As previously stated," beware. Such phrases indicate that you are repeating yourself.

28b Cut formulaic phrases

Replace wordy phrases with shorter and more direct expressions.

Formulaic	Concise
at the present time at this point in time in this day and age in today's society	now
because of the fact that due to the fact that	because
are of the opinion that	believe
have the ability to	can
in spite of the fact that	although, despite
last but not least	finally
prior to	before
concerning the matter of	about

Be watchful for the phrase "the fact that." Edit when you can.

- **Few people realize ~~the fact~~ that the computer controlling the *Eagle* lunar module in 1969 had less memory than a cheap wristwatch does today.**

28c Cut references to your intentions

Eliminate references to the organization of your text and your own planning, such as *In this essay, I intend to prove* . . . or *In the next few paragraphs, I hope to show* . . . or *In conclusion, I have demonstrated*. . . . In a short essay, there's no need to announce a plan.

However, in the social or physical sciences, information is often provided in a set order, so such signals are more appropriate and occur more frequently: *This paper describes three approaches to treating depression.*

28d Cut redundant words and phrases

Trim words that simply repeat an idea expressed by another word in the same phrase: *basic* essentials, *true* facts, circle *around*, cooperate *together*, *final* completion, return *again*, refer *back*, *advance* planning, consensus *of opinion, completely* unanimous, *free* gift. Also edit redundant pairs: *various and sundry, hopes and desires, each and every.*

- ▶ **Before deciding to cancel classes, the program director sought a consensus ~~of opinion~~ among the teachers.**
- ▶ **His surgeon ~~is a doctor with~~ ^has^ a great deal of clinical experience.**
- ▶ **~~A total of 97~~ ^Ninety-seven^ students completed the survey.**

29 The Second C: Check for Action

Vigorous sentences show clearly who or what is doing the action. Use vivid, expressive verbs when you can. Do not overuse the verb *be* (*be, am, is, are, was, were, being, been*) or verbs in the passive voice.

29a Show "Who's doing what" as subject and verb

In the following sentence, the subject (*approval*) and verb (*was*) tell readers very little:

MindTap®
Read, highlight, and take notes online.

Wordy **The mayor's approval of the new law was due to voters' suspicion of the concealment of campaign funds by his deputy.**

The subject and verb of this dull thud of a sentence tell us that "the . . . approval . . . was"—not a very powerful statement! Ask "Who's doing what?" and you come up with a tougher, leaner sentence.

Who's Doing What?

Subject	Verb
the mayor	approved
the voters	suspected
his deputy	had concealed

Revised **The mayor approved the new law because voters suspected that his deputy had concealed campaign funds.**

The revision is shorter and more direct; it gets rid of three nouns formed from verbs (*approval, suspicion,* and *concealment*) as well as five phrases using prepositions (words used before nouns and pronouns): *of, to, of, of, by.*

29b Scrutinize sentences beginning with *there* or *it*

For a lean, direct style, rewrite sentences in which *there* or *it* occupies the subject position (as in *there is, there were, it is, it was*). Revise by using verbs that describe an action and subjects that perform the action.

Wordy **There was a discussion of the health care system by the politicians. [Who's doing what here?]**

Revised **The politicians discussed the health care system.**

Wordy **There is a statue of a lion standing in the center of the square.**

Revised **A statue of a lion stands in the center of the square.**

Wordy **It is a fact that Arnold is proudly displaying a new tattoo.**

Revised **Arnold is proudly displaying a new tattoo.**

KEY POINTS

Searching for *There* and *It*

Use the Find function on your computer to locate all instances in your draft of *it is, there is,* and *there are* in the initial position in a clause. If you find a filler subject with little purpose, revise.

29c Avoid unnecessary passive voice

The *passive voice* tells what is done to someone or something: "The turkey *was cooked* too long." Extensive use of the passive voice can make your style seem pedantic and wordy, especially if you use a "by . . ." phrase to tell about who is doing the action.

Passive **The problem will be discussed thoroughly by the committee.**

Active **The committee will discuss the problem thoroughly.**

Note: The passive voice occurs frequently in scientific writing because readers are primarily interested in data, procedures, and results, not in who developed or produced them. In a scientific report, you are likely to read, for example, *The rats were fed,* not *The researchers fed the rats.* For other acceptable uses of the passive voice, see section 30a and chapter 40.

30 The Third C: Connect

When you read your draft, pay attention to whether or not it flows smoothly with clear connections between sentences and paragraphs. Avoid a series of grasshopper-like jumps.

MindTap®
Read, highlight, and take notes online.

30a Connect with consistent subjects and topic chains

Readers need a way to connect the ideas beginning a sentence with what has gone before. So when you move from one sentence to the next, avoid jarring shifts of subjects by maintaining a topic chain of consistent subjects, as in the revised example that follows.

Shift of subject **Memoirs are becoming increasingly popular. *Readers* all over North America are finding them appealing.**

Revised ***Memoirs* are becoming increasingly popular. *They* appeal to readers all over North America.**

In the revised version, the subject of the second sentence, *they*, refers to the subject of the previous sentence, *memoirs*; the new information about "readers all over North America" comes at the end, where it receives more emphasis.

Examine your writing for awkward topic switches. Note that preserving a connected topic chain may mean using the passive voice, as in the last sentence of the revision that follows (see also 40c).

Frequent topic **I have lived all my life in Brooklyn, New York. Park Slope is a neighborhood that has many different ethnic** switches **cultures. *Harmony* exists among the people, even though it does not in many other Brooklyn neighborhoods. *Many articles in the press* have praised the Slope for its ethnic variety.**

Revised with topic chain **_Many different ethnic cultures_ flourish in Park Slope, Brooklyn, where I have lived all my life. _These different cultures_ live together harmoniously, even though they do not in many other Brooklyn neighborhoods. In fact, _the ethnic variety_ of the Slope has often been praised in the press.**

30b Use logical connections with coordination, subordination, and transitions

When you write sentences containing two or more clauses, consider where you want to place the emphasis.

Coordination You give two or more clauses equal emphasis when you connect them with one of the following coordinating conjunctions: *and, but, or, nor, so, for,* or *yet*. (For more on coordination, see 30c, 35d, and 45b.)

independent clause — independent clause

▶ **The waves were enormous, but the surfers approached them with glee.**

Subordination When you use subordinating conjunctions such as *when, if,* or *because* to connect clauses, you give one idea more importance by putting it in the independent clause (35d and 36c).

▶ **We cannot now end our differences. At least we can help make the world safe for diversity. [Two sentences with equal importance]**

dependent clause — independent clause

▶ **If we cannot now end our differences, at least we can help make the world safe for diversity.** —John F. Kennedy
[Two clauses connected by _if_; emphasis on the independent clause at the end of the sentence]

Transitional expressions Use words such as *however, therefore,* and *nevertheless* (known as *conjunctive adverbs*) and phrases such as *in addition, as a result,* and *on the other hand* to signal the logical connection between independent clauses (for a list of transitional expressions, see 2f). A transitional expression can move around in its own clause—yet another stylistic option for you to consider.

- **The children collected bags full of candy on Halloween; *however*, their parents would allow them to eat only one piece per day.**
- **The children collected bags full of candy on Halloween; their parents, *however*, would allow them to eat only one piece per day.**

KEY POINTS

Options for Connecting Clauses

COORDINATING CONJUNCTION	SEMICOLON AND TRANSITIONAL EXPRESSION	SUBORDINATING CONJUNCTION
and (addition)	also, further, furthermore, moreover, in addition	
but, yet (contrast)	however, nevertheless, on the other hand	although, even though, whereas, while
or, nor (alternative)	instead, otherwise, alternatively	unless
so, for (result)	therefore, as a result, hence, consequently, thus, accordingly, then	because, as, since, so/such that, now that, once

Know your options To avoid a series of short, choppy sentences, consider the logical connection between ideas. Frequently, you will have several alternatives: a transition, a coordinator (*and, but, or, nor, so, for,* or *yet*), or a subordinator (a word such as *because, if, although, while, who,* or *which* used to introduce a dependent clause), as in the following examples. Note the punctuation in each.

- **Grant has traveled all over South America and Asia. He has seen little of his own country.**

Transition **Grant has traveled all over South America and Asia; *however*, he has seen little of his own country.**

Grant has traveled all over South America and Asia; he has seen little of his own country, *however*.

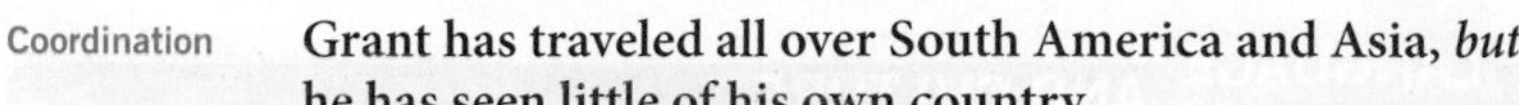

Coordination — **Grant has traveled all over South America and Asia, *but* he has seen little of his own country.**

Subordination — ***Although* Grant has traveled all over South America and Asia, he has seen little of his own country.**

Avoid excessive coordination or subordination Too much of any one stylistic feature will become tedious to readers.

Excessive coordination with *and* — **I grew up in a large family, and we lived on a small farm, and every day I had to get up early and do farm work, and I would spend a lot of time cleaning out the stables, and then I would be exhausted in the evening, and I never had the energy to read.**

Revised — **Because I grew up in a large family on a small farm, every day I had to get up early to do farm work, mostly cleaning out the stables. I would be so exhausted in the evening that I never had the energy to read.**

Excessive subordination — **Because the report was weak and poorly written, our boss, who wanted to impress the company president by showing her how efficient his division was, to gain prestige in the company, decided, despite the fact that work projects were piling up, that he would rewrite the report over the weekend.**

Revised — **Because the report was weak and poorly written, our boss decided to rewrite it over the weekend, even though work projects were piling up. He wanted to impress the company president by showing her how efficient his division was; that was his way of gaining prestige.**

30c Perhaps begin a sentence with *and* or *but*

People who consider *and* and *but* conjunctions whose purpose is join two or more independent clauses within a sentence may frown when they see these words starting a sentence. Nevertheless, examples of this usage can be found in literature from the tenth century onward. As with any other stylistic device, it is not wise to begin a sentence with *and* or *but* too often. And, given the difference of opinion on this usage, check with your instructor, too.

LANGUAGE AND CULTURE

Sentences Beginning with *And* or *But*

Occasionally, writers choose to start a sentence with *and* or *but*, either for stylistic effect of emphasis or contrast or to make a close connection to the previous sentence:

▸ **You can have wealth concentrated in the hands of a few, or democracy. But you cannot have both.** —Justice Louis Brandeis

The usage is found often in journalism. Note, though, that the culture of academia is more conservative, and some readers may raise an eyebrow when they see *and* or *but* starting a sentence in an academic paper, especially if it happens often.

 Connect paragraphs

Just as readers appreciate a smooth flow of information from sentence to sentence, they also look for transitions—word bridges—to move them from paragraph to paragraph. A new paragraph signals a shift in topic, but careful readers will look for transitional words and phrases that tell them *how* a new paragraph relates to the paragraph that precedes it. Provide readers with stepping-stones; don't ask them to leap over chasms.

KEY POINTS

A Checklist for Connecting Paragraphs

- **Read your draft aloud.** When you finish a paragraph, make a note of the point you made in the paragraph. Then, check your notes for the flow of ideas and logic.
- **Refer to the main idea of the previous paragraph as you begin a new paragraph.** After a paragraph on retirement, the next paragraph could begin like this, moving from the idea of retirement to saving: *Retirement is not the only reason for saving. Saving also provides a nest egg for the unexpected and the pleasurable.*
- **Use adjectives like *this* and *these* to provide a link.** After a paragraph discussing urban planning proposals, the next paragraph might begin like this: *These proposals will help. However, ...*
- **Use transition words.** Words and phrases such as *also, too, in addition, however, therefore,* and *as a result* signal the logical connection between ideas (2f).

31 The Fourth C: Commit

MindTap®
Read, highlight, and take notes online.

Ultimately, what you write needs to reflect *you*—that is, it should consistently and confidently include details that reflect who you are. This chapter focuses on ways to be detailed, bold, colorful, and resolute so that your writing is something that you can commit to.

31a Commit to a personal presence

Academic writing is certainly not the same as writing personal accounts of feelings, events, and opinions. But it is not writing from which you as the writer should fade from sight. The best academic writing reveals personal engagement with the topic and details of what you (the writer) have observed and read—an unmistakable *you*. Always ask yourself: Where am *I* in this draft? What picture of me and my world do readers get from my writing? Do they see clearly what I base my opinions on? If you use sources, readers should be able to perceive you in conversation with your sources; they should see not just a listing of what your sources say but also your responses to and comments on those sources.

Showing a personal presence does not necessarily mean always using *I* or repeatedly saying "in my opinion." It means writing so that readers see *you* in what you write and recognize that you have integrated any research findings into your views on a topic. See 1b for more on voice.

31b Commit to an appropriate and consistent tone

PURPOSE AUDIENCE
VOICE MEDIUM

See the full model on page 7.

Readers will expect the tone of your document to fit its purpose. The tone of your piece of writing reflects your attitude toward your subject matter and is closely connected to your audience's expectations and your purpose in writing. If you were, for example, writing about a topic such as compensation for post-traumatic stress disorder suffered by soldiers who have served on active duty, anything other than a serious, respectful tone would be inappropriate.

For most academic writing, commit resolutely to an objective, serious tone. Avoid sarcasm, colloquial language, name calling, or pedantic words and structures, even for the sake of variety. Make sure you dedicate a special reading of a draft to examining your tone; if you are reading along and a word or sentence strikes you as unexpected and out of place, flag it for later correction. In formal college essays, watch out especially for sudden switches to a chatty and conversational tone (see 32d), as in "Willy Loman surprises his family and the theater audience when his frustration makes him suddenly become *mad as all hell.*" Since tone is really an indicator of how you anticipate readers' expectations, ask a tutor or a friend to read your document and note any lapses in consistency of tone.

31c Commit to a confident stance

Your background reading, critical thinking, and drafting will help you discover and decide upon a perspective and thesis that seem correct to you (2a–2c). Once you have made those decisions, commit to that point of view. When you are trying to persuade readers to accept your point of view, avoid the ambivalence and indecisiveness evident in words and phrases like *maybe, perhaps, it could be, it might seem*, and *it would appear*.

Hedging will not heighten readers' confidence in what you say:

▸ **~~You may not agree with me, but~~ I believe it ~~might be~~ is time for the city council to replace Chief Yates with a leader who is unafraid to crack down on corruption in the ranks.**

Aim for language that reflects accountability and commitment: *as a result, consequently, of course, believe, need, demand, should, must.* It's important, however, to use the language of commitment only after thoroughly researching your topic and satisfying yourself that the evidence is convincing.

In addition, convey to readers an attitude of confidence in your own abilities and judgment. Make an ethical appeal to readers by stressing your evenhanded expertise (4f). Avoid apologies. One student ended a first draft this way:

Too apologetic **I hope I have conveyed something about our cultural differences. I would like my reader to note that this is just my view, even if a unique one. Room for errors and prejudices should be provided. The lack of a total overview, which would take more time and expertise, should also be taken into account.**

If you really have not done an adequate job of making and supporting a point, try to gather more information to improve the draft instead of adding apologetic notes. The writer revised the ending after reading section 2h on conclusions.

Revised version **The stories I have told and the examples I have given come from my own experience; however, my multicultural background has emphasized that cultural differences do not have to separate people but can bring them closer together. A diverse, multicultural society holds many potential benefits for all its members.**

31d Commit to sentence variety

Variety in sentence length Readers appreciate variety, so aim for a mix of long and short sentences. If your editing program can print out your text in a series of single numbered sentences, you will easily be able to examine the length and structure of each. Academic writing need not consist solely of long, heavyweight sentences—in fact, it should not. Short sentences interspersed among longer ones can have a dramatic effect.

This passage from a student's course blog demonstrates the use of short sentences to great effect:

> I once had a baseball team-mate who said to me, "Mathematics is like whipped cream." I never fully understood what he meant, but I knew I liked whipped cream on anything, and as far as I was concerned mathematics could get lost. It was one of the very few disagreements I ever had with him. He was a nice guy, but he had a problem. He loved math.

Variety in sentence functions: Statements, questions, commands, and exclamations *Declarative* sentences make statements (such as "Poems are to be read slowly with concentration"), *interrogative* sentences ask questions (such as "What does the author intend?"), *imperative* sentences give commands (such as "Forget about trying to understand Barthelme"), and *exclamatory* sentences express surprise or some other strong emotion (such as "The ending was a total shock!"). Most of the sentences in your college writing will be declarative. However, the occasional question or command provides a sense of contact between writer and reader. Beware, though, of sprinkling an academic text with exclamations.

Variety of sentence types Vary the structure of your sentences throughout any piece of writing. Aim for a mix of simple, compound, complex, and compound-complex sentences.

A *simple sentence* contains one independent clause.

▶ **Kara raised her hand.**

A *compound sentence* contains two or more independent clauses connected with one or more coordinating conjunctions (*and, but, or, nor, so, for, yet*), with a semicolon alone, or with a semicolon and a transitional expression (2f).

- **Kara raised her hand, and the whole class was surprised.** [independent clause: "Kara raised her hand," / independent clause: "the whole class was surprised."]
- **Kara raised her hand, but nobody else responded.** [independent clause: "Kara raised her hand," / independent clause: "nobody else responded."]
- **Kara raised her hand; the whole class was surprised.** [independent clause: "Kara raised her hand;" / independent clause: "the whole class was surprised."]
- **Kara raised her hand; as a result, the whole class was surprised.** [independent clause: "Kara raised her hand;" / independent clause: "the whole class was surprised."]

If you read these sentences aloud, you may notice the longer pause in the last two; consider how that pause may affect readers. Consider, too, how your expectations as a reader change as you see a comma or a semicolon.

A *complex sentence* contains an independent clause and one or more dependent clauses.

- **When Kara raised her hand, the whole class was surprised.** [dependent clause: "When Kara raised her hand," / independent clause: "the whole class was surprised."]
- **The whole class was surprised when Kara raised her hand.** [independent clause: "The whole class was surprised" / dependent clause: "when Kara raised her hand."]

When you decide which of the two previous types of complex sentences to write, also consider the sentences that precede and follow. Avoiding repetition or following through with a subject or topic chain (see 30a) may help you determine which element should come first and which should come last.

A *compound-complex sentence* contains at least two independent clauses and at least one dependent clause.

- **When Kara raised her hand, the whole class was surprised,** [dependent clause: "When Kara raised her hand," / independent clause: "the whole class was surprised,"]
  and the professor waited eagerly as she began to speak. [independent clause: "the professor waited eagerly" / dependent clause: "as she began to speak."]

Sentences structured with several clauses are common in academic writing. Just make sure that you keep track of where you are in the sentence and check the relationship between dependent and independent clauses.

In addition, be aware of *cumulative* and *periodic sentences*. Cumulative (or loose) sentences begin with the independent clause and add on to it. Periodic sentences begin with words and phrases that lead to the independent clause, giving emphasis to the end of the sentence.

The cumulative sentence is the norm in English prose. Use a periodic sentence to make a specific stylistic impact.

Cumulative *The experienced hunter stood stock still for at least five minutes,* **sweat pouring from his brow, all senses alert, and waiting to hear a twig snap.**

Periodic **Sweat pouring from his brow, all senses alert, and waiting to hear a twig snap,** ***the experienced hunter stood stock still for at least five minutes.***

Variety of word order in a sentence Sometimes, inverted word order of verb followed by subject (v + s) helps achieve coherence, consistent subjects, emphasis, or a smooth transition:

▸ **Next to the river runs a superhighway.**

▸ **Never have I laughed so hard.**

▸ **Not only does the novel entertain, but it also raises our awareness of poverty.**

▸ **So eager was I to win that I set off before the starter's gun.**

▸ **Rarely has a poem achieved such a grasp of the times.**

Using an occasional rhetorical question will also help drive a point home:

▸ **How did she think she could get away with such a lie?**

Variety of sentence beginnings Consider using some of these variations to begin a sentence, but remember that beginning with the subject will always be clear and direct for readers. Any of the following beginnings repeated too often will seem like a stylistic tic and may annoy readers.

Begin with a dependent or condensed clause

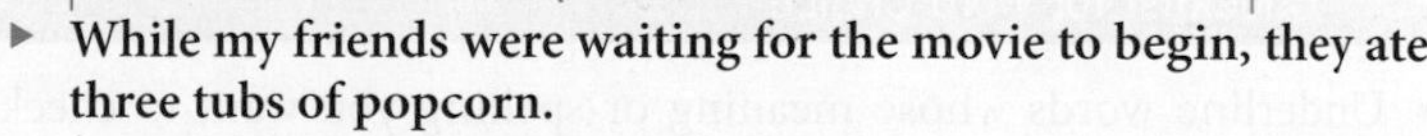

▸ **While my friends were waiting for the movie to begin, they ate three tubs of popcorn.**

clause condensed to phrase

▸ **While waiting for the movie to begin, my friends ate three tubs of popcorn.**

Begin with a participle or an adjective A sentence can begin with a participle or an adjective, but only if the word is in a phrase that refers to the subject of the independent clause. If the phrase does not refer to the subject, the result is a *dangling modifier* error (38c).

-ing participle

▶ **Waiting for the movie to begin, my friends ate popcorn.**

past participle

▶ **Wanted by Interpol, the spy fled Europe and hid out in South America.**

adjective

▶ **Aware of the problems, they nevertheless decided to continue.**

Begin with a prepositional phrase

prepositional phrase

▶ **With immense joy, we watched our team win the pennant.**

You can also occasionally use inverted word order after a prepositional phrase (but see 41d on agreement of subject and verb).

prepositional phrase — verb — subject

▶ **At the bottom of the trunk lay a satin wedding dress.**

32 The Fifth C: Choose the Best Words

Word choice, or *diction*, contributes a great deal to the effect your writing has on readers. Do not give readers puzzles to solve.

MindTap®
Read, highlight, and take notes online.

32a Word choice checklist

KEY POINTS
Checklist for Word Choice

- Underline words whose meaning or spelling you want to check and words that you might want to replace. Then spend some time with a dictionary and a thesaurus (32b).

- Look for words that might not convey exactly what you mean (*thrifty* vs. *stingy*, for example), and look for vague words (32c).
- Check figurative language for appropriateness, think about where a simile (a comparison) might help convey your meaning, and find original substitutes for any clichés (32e, 32g).
- Check for level of formality and for the appropriateness of any colloquial, regional, ethnic, or specialized work terms (32d).
- Check for gender bias in your use of *he* and *she* and other gender-related words (32f).
- Look for language that might exclude or offend (such as *normal* to mean people similar to you). Build community with your readers by eliminating disrespectful or stereotyping terms referring to race, place, age, politics, religion, abilities, or sexual orientation (32f).

32b Use a dictionary and a thesaurus

Dictionary The dictionary built into your word processing program informs you about spelling, pronunciation, and definitions. Sometimes, though, you need more than that. Don't forget about the comprehensive dictionaries such as the *Oxford English Dictionary* (OED), available online in many libraries or in print form. In the OED, you can explore the historical development of the meaning and usage of a word (its etymology), find synonyms and antonyms (words of similar and opposite meaning), and learn about grammatical functions and current usage. If you have no easy online access to the OED, invest in a good desk dictionary such as *The Merriam-Webster Dictionary*.

Use a dictionary to learn or confirm the *denotation*—the basic meaning—of a word. Some words that appear similar are not interchangeable. For example, *respectable* has a meaning that is very different from *respectful*; *emigrant* and *immigrant* have different meanings; and so do *defuse* and *diffuse*, *uninterested* and *disinterested*, and *principal* and *principle*.

Thesaurus A thesaurus is useful when you want to find alternatives to words that you know. Exercise caution, however, to make sure that the word you choose fits your context. Suppose you use the word *privacy* a few times and want an alternative in the sentence, "She values the privacy of her own home." You could consult a thesaurus, and you might find words such as *aloofness, seclusion,* and *isolation* listed. The word *aloofness* would not work as a replacement for *privacy* in the example sentence, and the others do not capture the idea of *privacy*. You might, in the end, want to use two words to convey your meaning: *She values the* safety *and* seclusion *of her own home*, or you might stick with *privacy*.

"YES," SHE MUMBLED?...SIGHED?... MUTTERED?...SNARLED?... HISSED?...GROWLED?...

Thesaurus programs built into word processing programs typically offer lists of synonyms but little guidance on *connotation*—the meaning associated with a word beyond its literal definition. Using a thesaurus alone is not enough. Always check a word in a dictionary that provides examples of usage.

32c Use exact words and connotations

When you write, use words that convey exactly the meaning you intend. Two words that have similar dictionary definitions (*denotation*) can also have additional positive or negative implications and emotional overtones (*connotation*). Readers will not get the impression you intend if you describe a person as *lazy* when the more positive *relaxed* is what you have in mind.

Select words with appropriate connotations. Hurricanes *devastate* neighborhoods; construction workers *demolish* buildings. Writing "Construction workers devastated the building" would be inappropriate. Note how the connotations of words can affect meaning in the following examples:

Version 1 **The crowd consisted of young couples holding their children's hands, students in well-worn clothes, and activist politicians, all voicing support of their cause.**

Version 2 **The mob consisted of hard-faced workers dragging children by the hand, students in leather jackets and ragged jeans, and militant politicians, all howling about their cause.**

Some words do little more than fill space because they are so vague. The following oh-so-general words signal the need for revision: *area, aspect, certain, circumstance, factor, kind, manner, nature, seem, situation, thing.*

Vague **Our perceptions of women's roles differ as we enter new *areas*. The girl in Kincaid's story did many *things* that are commonly seen as women's work.**

Revised **Our perceptions of women's roles differ as we learn more from what we *see, hear, read, and experience*. The girl in Kincaid's story did many *household chores* that are commonly seen as women's work. She washed the clothes, cooked, swept the floor, and set the table.**

Some words are abstract and general; other words are concrete and specific. Notice the increasing concreteness and specificity in this list: *tool, cutting instrument, knife, penknife. Tool* is a general term; *penknife* is more specific. If you do not move away from the general and abstract, you will give readers too much imaginative leeway. "Her grandmother was shocked by the clothing she bought" leaves a great deal to readers' imaginations. What kind of clothing do you mean: a low-necked dress, high-heeled platform shoes, and black fishnet stockings or a conservative navy blue wool suit? Choose words that convey exact images and precise information.

32d Monitor the language of speech, region, and workplace

The language of speech In a formal college essay, avoid using colloquial language and slang unless you are quoting someone's words. Use the level of diction that is appropriate for the academic world, not for the world of hip-hop, social media, or texting unless you are using that language to make a very specific point. Don't enclose a slang expression in quotation marks to signal to readers that you know it is inappropriate. Instead, revise to reach an appropriate level of formality.

- **The solution to the problem ~~was a no-brainer~~** ^required little thought^**.**
- **The jury returned the verdict that the ~~guy~~** ^defendant^ **was guilty.**
- **Nutrition plays a large part in whether people ~~hang on to~~** ^retain^ **their own teeth as they age.**

▸ **The music at the party was ~~dope~~ excellent.**

▸ **The class was ~~a drag~~ tedious, so I stopped attending after the second week.**

In formal writing, avoid colloquial words and expressions, such as *folks, guy, OK, okay, pretty good, hassle, kind of interesting/nice, a ways away, no-brainer.*

Note that the synonyms of the italicized words listed next convey different eras, attitudes, and degrees of formality:

child: kid, offspring, progeny

friend: dog, peeps, buddy, mate, brother/sister, comrade

jail: slammer, cooler, prison, correctional institution

angry: pissed off, ticked off, furious, mad, fuming, wrathful

computer expert: geek, hacker, techie, programmer

threatening: spooky, scary, eerie, menacing

fine: rad, sick, dope, fly, cool, first-rate, excellent

Some of these words—*kid, slammer, ticked off, geek, spooky, rad*—are so informal that they would rarely, if ever, be appropriate in formal academic writing or business letters, though they would raise no eyebrows in most journalism, advertising, or e-mail. Overuse of formal words—*progeny, comrade, wrathful*—on the other hand, could produce a tone that suggests a stuffy, pedantic attitude (see 32g).

For more on levels of diction and Standard English, see 35c.

Regional and ethnic language Use regional and ethnic dialects in your writing only when you are quoting someone directly (*"Your car needs fixed," the mechanic grunted.*) or you know that readers will understand why you are using a nonstandard phrase.

▸ **I bought ~~me~~ myself a backpack.**

▸ **They ~~done~~ have finished painting the house.**

▸ **~~They're~~ They have been here three years already.**

▸ **She used to ~~could~~ be able to run two miles, but now she's out of shape.**

LANGUAGE AND CULTURE

Dialect and Dialogue in Formal Writing

Note how Paule Marshall uses Standard English for the narrative thread of her story while reproducing the father's Barbadian dialect and idioms in the dialogue, thus combining the formal and the informal, the academic and the personal into a rich whole:

> She should have leaped up and pirouetted and joined his happiness. But a strange uneasiness kept her seated with her knees drawn tight against her chest. She asked cautiously, "You mean we're rich?"
>
> "We ain rich but we got land."
>
> "Is it a lot?"
>
> "Two acres almost. I know the piece of ground good. You could throw down I-don-know-what on it and it would grow. And we gon have a house there—just like the white people own. A house to end all house!"
>
> "Are you gonna tell Mother?"
>
> His smile faltered and failed; his eyes closed in a kind of weariness.
>
> —Paule Marshall, *Brown Girl, Brownstones*

The jargon of the workplace People engaged in most areas of specialized work and study use technical words that outsiders perceive as jargon. A sportswriter writing about baseball will refer to *balks, ERAs, brushbacks*, and *cutters*. A linguist writing about language for an audience of linguists will use terms like *phonemics, sociolinguistics, semantics, kinesics*, and *suprasegmentals*. If you know that your audience is familiar with the technical vocabulary of a field, specialized language is acceptable. But, if you are writing for a more general audience, try to avoid jargon. If you must use technical terms, provide definitions that will make sense to your audience.

32e Use figurative language for effect, but don't overuse it

Figures of speech can enhance your writing and add to imaginative descriptions. Particularly useful are similes and metaphors. A simile is a comparison in which both sides are stated explicitly and linked by the words *like* or *as*. A metaphor is an implied comparison in which the two sides are indirectly compared. When figurative language is overused, however, it can become tedious and contrived.

Simile: An explicit comparison with both sides stated

- **America is *not like a blanket*—one piece of unbroken cloth, the same color, the same texture, the same size. America is more *like a quilt*—many pieces, many colors, many sizes, all woven and held together by a common thread.** —Rev. Jesse Jackson
- **He was reading, leaning so far back in the chair that it was balanced on its two hind legs *like a dancing dog*.** —Barbara Kingsolver

Metaphor: An implied comparison, without *like* or *as*

- **All the world's a stage,**
  And all the men and women merely players
  —William Shakespeare, *As You Like It*
- **Some television programs are so much chewing gum for the eyes.** —John Mason Brown

Mixed metaphors Take care not to mix (illogically combine) metaphors.

- **As she walked onto the tennis court, she was ready to sink or swim. [Swimming on a tennis court?]**
- **You need to wake up and smell the music. [The mix of metaphors—*wake up and smell the coffee* and *face the music*—creates a confusing clash for readers.]**
- **He was a whirlwind of activity, trumpeting defiance whenever anyone crossed swords with any of his ideas. [The three metaphors—*whirlwind, trumpet, crossed swords*—obscure rather than illuminate.]**

For more examples of figurative language in literature, see 5e.

32f Avoid sexist, biased, and exclusionary language

You cannot avoid writing from perspectives and backgrounds that you know about, but you can avoid divisive terms that reinforce stereotypes or belittle other people. Be sensitive to differences. Consider the feelings of members of the opposite sex, racial or ethnic minorities (now sometimes called "world majorities"), and special-interest groups. Do not emphasize differences by separating society into *we* (people like you) and *they* or *these people* (people different from you). Use *we* only to be truly inclusive of yourself and all readers. Be aware, too, of terms that are likely to offend.

Gender The writer of the following sentence edited to avoid gender bias and sexist language in the perception of women's roles and achievements.

▶ **Running for the position of ~~councilman~~ council member were Stan Foster, an accountant, and ~~Mrs.~~ Julia Estes, a community organizer ~~and mother.~~**

Choice of words can reveal gender bias, too.

Avoid	Use
chairman	chairperson
female astronaut	astronaut
forefathers	ancestors
foreman	supervisor
mailman	mail carrier
male nurse	nurse
man, mankind (meaning any human being)	person, people, our species, human beings, humanity, humankind
poetess	poet
policeman, policewoman	police officer
salesman	sales representative, salesclerk
veterans and their wives	veterans and their spouses

Pronouns *he* or *she* Pronoun use is especially vulnerable to gender bias. See 42e for more on gender pronouns, the use of the phrase *he or she*, and the use of *they* to avoid tricky decisions and gender bias.

Race Mention a person's race only when it is relevant. If you write, "Attending the meeting were three doctors and an Asian computer programmer," you reveal more about your own stereotypes than you do about the meeting.

Aside from avoiding gratuitous comments about race, try to use the names that people prefer for their racial or ethnic affiliations. The *Columbia Guide to Standard American English* advises: "It is good manners (and therefore good usage) to call people only by the names they wish to be called." Consider, for example, that *black* and *African American* are preferred terms; *American Indian*, or better still, the particular group (*Sioux*, for example) is now often preferred to *Native American*, though this usage has swung back and forth. *Asian* is preferred to *Oriental*, while *Latino/Latina* vies with *Hispanic* to refer to Americans originating in Latin America.

Place Avoid stereotyping people according to where they come from. Some British people may be stiff and formal, but not all are (one of the authors of this book is from London, so take her word for it). Not all Germans eat sausage and drink beer; not all North Americans carry cameras and chew gum.

Be careful, too, with the way you refer to countries and continents. The Americas include both North and South America, so you need to make the distinction. England, Scotland, Wales, and Northern Ireland make up Great Britain, or the United Kingdom. In addition, shifts in world politics and national borders have resulted in the renaming of many countries. Always consult a current atlas, almanac, or reliable reference Web site.

Age Avoid derogatory or condescending terms associated with age. Refer to a person's age or condition neutrally if at all: not *well-preserved little old lady* but *woman in her eighties* or just *woman*.

Politics Words referring to politics are full of connotations. Consider, for instance, the positive and negative connotations of *liberal* and *conservative* in various election campaigns. Take care when you use words like *radical, left-wing, right-wing,* and *moderate*. How do you want readers to interpret them? Are you identifying with one group and implicitly criticizing other groups?

Religion An older edition of an encyclopedia referred to "devout Catholics" and "fanatical Muslims." A newer edition refers to both Catholics and Muslims as "devout," thus eliminating the bias of a sweeping generalization. Examine your use of the following: words that sound derogatory or exclusionary, such as *cult* or *fundamentalist*; expressions, such as *these people*, which emphasize difference; and even the word *we* when it implies that all readers share your beliefs.

Health and abilities Avoid expressions such as *confined to a wheelchair* and *AIDS victim* so as not to focus on difference and disability. Instead, write *someone who uses a wheelchair* and *a person with AIDS*, but only if the context makes it necessary to include that information. Do not unnecessarily draw attention to a disability or an illness.

Sexual orientation Mention a person's sexual orientation only if the information is relevant in context. To write that someone accused of stock market fraud was "defended by a homosexual lawyer" would be to provide gratuitous information. The sexual orientation of the attorney might be more relevant in a case involving discrimination against homosexuals. Since you may not know the sexual orientation of readers, do not assume it is the same as your own.

The word *normal* Be especially careful about using the word *normal* when referring to your own health, ability, or sexual orientation. Some readers might justifiably find that usage offensive.

32g Avoid clichés and pretentious language

Avoiding clichés *Clichés* are tired, overly familiar expressions that anyone can complete: *as cool as a* ________. Common clichés are *hit the nail on the head, crystal clear, better late than never,* and *easier said than done.* They never contribute anything fresh or original. Avoid or eliminate them as you revise your early drafts.

- ▸ **~~Last but not least~~ [Finally], the article recommends the TeleZapper.**

- ▸ **My main ambition in life is not to make a fortune, since I know that~~, as they say, "money is the root of all evil."~~ [having money does not guarantee a good life.]**

- ▸ **After five months of daily exercise and twice-weekly sessions with a trainer, Mallick is ~~fit as a fiddle~~ [physically fit] and healthy.**

Distinguishing the formal from the stuffy *Formal* does not mean stuffy and pretentious. Writing in a formal situation does not require you to use obscure words and long sentences. In fact, convoluted writing is not a sign of brilliance or of a powerful mind. It is usually just a sign of bad writing. Pretentious language makes reading difficult, as the following example shows:

- ▸ **When a female of the species ascertains that a male with whom she is acquainted exhibits considerable desire to extend their acquaintance, that female customarily will first engage in protracted discussion with her close confidantes.**

Simplify your writing if you find sentences like that in your draft. Aim for clear, direct expression of ideas. Here are some words to watch out for:

Stuffy	Direct	Stuffy	Direct
ascertain	find out	optimal	best
commence	begin	prior to	before
deceased	dead	purchase	buy
endeavor	try	reside	live
finalize	finish	terminate	end
implement	carry out	utilize	use

Avoiding euphemisms *Euphemisms* are expressions that try to conceal a forthright meaning and make the concept seem more delicate, such as *change of life* for *menopause* or *downsized* for *fired*. Because euphemisms often sound evasive or are unclear, avoid them in favor of direct language. Similarly, avoid *doublespeak* (evasive expressions that seek to conceal the truth, such as *incendiary device* for *firebomb, combat situation* for *battle*, and *collateral damage* for *civilian casualties*). Examples of such language are easy to find in advertising, business, politics, and especially in war reporting. Do not equate formality with these indirect expressions.

▶ **Six ~~freedom fighters~~ ^terrorists^ were intercepted as they attempted to set ~~an~~ ^a^ ~~incendiary device~~ ^bomb^ under the general's car.**

33 Revising for Style: A Student's Drafts

One of the biggest challenges writers face is revising a draft (chapter 3). Seeing your writing through new eyes (re-vision) is incredibly hard when you've spent a lot of time and effort on a draft. The suggestions for revising content in 3a provide helpful ideas for developing your own revision process.

MindTap®
Read, highlight, and take notes online.

Many writers also find it helpful to have a systematic process for revision that helps them focus on different aspects of style, such as the five C's outlined in chapters 28–32. Once you have a completed draft, try working through the five C's as a revision heuristic.

KEY POINTS
Revising for Style: A Checklist

Take a look at the following stylistic elements from the five C's, and select at least one from each area to look for in your draft. If you can't decide which elements to select, ask your instructor for suggestions about areas of your writing that you might work on. Try reading your draft anew for each element you select so that you can focus your attention as you revise.

Cut:

- ☑ Repetition and wordiness (28a)
- ☑ Formulaic phrases (28b)
- ☑ References to your intentions (28c)
- ☑ Redundancy (28d)

Check for Action:

- ☑ Who's doing what? (29a)
- ☑ Sentences beginning with *there* or *it* (29b)
- ☑ Unnecessary passive voice (29c)

Connect:

- ☑ Consistent subjects and topic chains (30a)
- ☑ Logical connections (30b)
- ☑ Beginning a sentence with *and* or *but* (30c)
- ☑ Paragraph connections (30d)

Commit:

- ☑ Personal presence (31a)
- ☑ Appropriate and consistent tone (31b)
- ☑ Confident stance (31c)
- ☑ Sentence variety (31d)

Choose the Best Words:

- ☑ Word choice checklist (32a)
- ☑ Dictionary and thesaurus (32b)
- ☑ Exact words and connotations (32c)
- ☑ Language of speech, region, and workplace (32d)
- ☑ Figurative language (32e)
- ☑ Avoiding sexist, biased, and exclusionary language (32f)
- ☑ Avoiding clichés and pretentious language (32g)

KEY EXAMPLE

Revising for Style

While focusing on the style features discussed in this chapter, several classmates analyzed one of their peer's writing on the topic of taking online courses. The writer's paragraphs and analysis, along with his classmates' responses, are shown below.

Student's passage for peer review	Classmates' analysis, using part 6 on style
Lots of colleges are offering classes online.	Switch in subject
More and more students are turning to online classes. Online classes are taken when	Unnecessary passive; switch in subject
people need some schedule flexibility or even when they just want to be able to kick back and relax while taking a class.	Formulaic cliché
In this paragraph, I will turn to explaining	Reference to intentions
the many advantages of online classes. At this point in time, online classes are becoming	Formulaic phrase
more and more popular because they fit into students' busy schedules. The main reason for	Wordy
the fact that some people prefer online classes is that they can fit them around their work,	Good examples here
practice, and social schedules. You can also do the work anywhere with technology you're already using.	Tone too conversational with "you"
A friend of mine takes classes on his iPad. He sends messages to his friends on his iPad. It is very versatile. It's a pretty awesome tool for everyday life.	No sentence variety in this part of paragraph Slang
Last but not least, despite the many	Formulaic cliché
advantages to online classes, people still like to take classes in person with a teacher. There is	"There is"—action verb better
so much advantage to being in class with a teacher and other students. You can ask questions of a teacher at the moment you're	Good point here
confused. And you can talk to classmates that you meet outside of class if you have questions.	Unnecessary "And" at beginning of sentence

The student worked with his group to revise the paragraphs for style. This is a better version, which the student took as the basis for his next two revisions.

Revised passage

Students across the country are finding that colleges offer an increasing number of courses online. Many of those students turn to online classes because they need flexibility in their schedules, but they have to weigh the advantages against the disadvantages of not being in a classroom with a teacher and other students.

Many students prefer online classes because they fit into busy, complex schedules. In addition to managing coursework, students must find time for work, athletic practice, and a social life. They can do work in an online class anywhere, and they can often use technology they would already use for everyday communication. A friend of mine takes classes on his iPad, and he also communicates with his friends and his work supervisor on the same device. His iPad is a versatile tool that helps him succeed at school and work.

Despite the many advantages to online classes, some students still like to take classes in person with a teacher. When students are in a classroom with a teacher, they can ask questions at the moment they need help, and they can talk to classmates outside of class for additional study help.

Questions

1. As you compare the two drafts, do you notice any advice that the writer did not follow? What do you think were the best improvements to the draft? Explain your thoughts to a classmate.
2. What style elements in chapters 28–32 do you think you struggle with the most in your writing?
3. Can you imagine a situation in which revising for style might have been helpful to you in the past? In what kind of writing situation might you use this kind of revision process in the future?
4. What strategies have you used in the past to revise for style? What strategies were useful? What strategies might you try the next time you need to revise a draft before turning it in?

34 Style Tips

As you write and revise, keep in mind the five C's of style, and aim for sentence variety. For a final, quick review of your style, read your draft aloud and use these tips.

MindTap®
Read, highlight, and take notes online.

KEY POINTS
Tips for Style

1. **Be adaptable.** Consider the style readers will expect. Don't work on developing a figurative style for short stories and then continue to use the same style in business communications or e-mail. Choose a style as you choose your clothes: the right outfit for the occasion.
2. **When in doubt, favor a plain style.** Be clear and straightforward. Don't search for the big words or the obscure turn of phrase. The following sentences, part of an e-mail message to the author of this book from an online service provider, are decidedly overdressed and stuffed with bureaucratic nothings: "It has been a pleasure assisting you. It is my hope that the information provided would be of great help with regards to your concern."
3. **Less is often better.** Details and descriptions are interesting, but don't overload your writing with adjectives and adverbs: *The perky little redheaded twin sat languidly in the comfortable overstuffed green-striped armchair and bit enthusiastically into a red and yellow fleshy, overripe peach.* Such prose is as overripe as the peach. Also avoid intensifying adverbs such as *very, really, extremely, terribly,* and *enormously.* Find a stronger word to use in place of the two words, such as *terrified* in place of *extremely scared.*
4. **Focus on rhythm, not rules.** Heed the advice of *The New York Times Manual of Style and Usage:* "One measure of skill is exceptions, not rules." And keep in mind this remark by novelist Ford Madox Ford: "Carefully examined, a good—and interesting—style will be found to consist in a constant succession of tiny, unobservable surprises." Ask yourself how you can provide pleasant surprises for readers.

Exercises on Style: The Five C's

EXERCISE 1 Cut wordiness and formulaic phrases. 28a, 28b

Edit the following sentences to eliminate wordiness and formulaic phrases.

Example ~~In spite of the fact that~~ [Although] Michael Jordan retired from basketball twice, fans held out hope that their hero would return ~~back~~ to the court ~~again~~.

1. Michael Jordan first retired from basketball in 1993 and tried to begin a career in the game of baseball, but he returned to the Chicago Bulls in the spring of 1995 because of the fact that he had not been successful enough in baseball to reach the major leagues.
2. When Jordan retired again in 1999, he told reporters that he was "99.9 percent" sure that he would never return to basketball, but basketball fans who loved the game were of the opinion that he had meant to leave himself a loophole.
3. Jordan bought for himself a part of the Washington Wizards, a team with a poor record of wins and losses in the 2000–2001 season.
4. At the point in time when Jordan began working out on a basketball court again, many people thought he was planning a comeback, but Jordan insisted that he was simply and solely trying to lose weight.
5. Then, in the fall of 2001, Jordan, who at the time was then thirty-eight years old, revealed that he would sell his stake in the Wizards and reprise his role as a player in the game of basketball.
6. He played with the Wizards for two seasons and called his 2009 induction into the Hall of Fame "bittersweet" because it meant he had undoubtedly retired for sure.

EXERCISE 2 Cut redundant words and phrases. 28d

Edit to eliminate redundant words and phrases.

Example The Strangler cases terrified ~~and unnerved~~ Bostonians until 1965, when Albert DeSalvo confessed to the eleven murders.

1. The nephew of one of the Boston Strangler's murder victims began to investigate his aunt's case in 1999 to prove to his own mother that the Strangler had been caught, but he eventually became mentally certain that Albert DeSalvo, the confessed killer of the victims, was not guilty.
2. In the 1960s, the public was told that DeSalvo had admitted details in his confession that only the murderer or killer would have known.
3. DeSalvo was never convicted of the Strangler murders, but he went to prison, where he was jailed for another crime and was fatally stabbed there in 1973.

4. DeSalvo seemed to have exclusive and inside knowledge of the murders, but others have since noted that he had heard many details from lawyers and police officials, and DeSalvo was known for his complete and total recall of each and every thing he had been told.
5. Once the victim's nephew got involved, lawyers and forensic specialists began cooperating together to investigate new leads and DNA evidence that could either exonerate DeSalvo or finally prove him guilty at last.

EXERCISE 3 Revise sentences beginning with *there* or *it*. 29b

Rewrite each sentence to eliminate *there* or *it* wherever possible.

Example ~~There are families~~ [Families] known as "travelers" ~~who~~ live in mobile homes in Ireland and are constantly on the move.

1. It is traditional for some families in Ireland to travel from place to place instead of settling permanently in one location.
2. There are deep-seated prejudices among many Irish people against the traveler families.
3. Although most travelers share the Catholic faith and the Celtic background of the majority of Irish people, it is not unusual for travelers to face discrimination and accusations of thievery.
4. There have been instances in which parents have removed children from local schools after traveler children arrived.
5. There was a law instituted in Ireland requiring communities to begin providing water and other basic services to traveler populations by 2004, but few districts made plans to comply.

EXERCISE 4 Avoid unnecessary passive voice constructions. 29c

Rewrite any passive voice constructions in the active voice.

Example ~~Wild animals~~ [Poachers] have ~~been~~ hunted ~~by poachers~~ [wild animals] in national parks all over the world.

1. In some wildlife preserves abroad, a radical new strategy has been adopted by conservationists.
2. Even in preserves that are supposed to be safe, many threatened wild species are either captured by poachers for the thriving black market in exotic pets or killed for their valuable body parts.
3. Poachers have been asked by wildlife organizations to use their knowledge of animals and animal habitats to contribute to wildlife preservation.
4. Many poachers have agreed to stop hunting endangered animals in exchange for a living wage and health benefits for themselves and their families; instead, information about the animals in the preserves is now collected by former poachers.

5. Local economies in poor areas near the preserves have long been supported by poaching, but with this new approach, local young people can see that working to support wildlife conservation is a better and safer way to earn a living than illegal poaching.

EXERCISE 5 Use different options for connecting ideas. 30b

In each of the following sentences, rewrite the two independent clauses as a single sentence, giving the information appropriate emphasis by using coordination, subordination, or a transitional expression. Then identify the method that you used.

Example Environmental groups have often portrayed American Indians as conservationists. ~~Some~~ , but some tribes feel that such portrayals are simplistic and culturally insensitive. [coordination]

1. Environmentalists believe that drilling for oil in the Arctic National Wildlife Refuge will damage a wilderness area. They have also cast drilling for oil as a human rights issue.
2. The Gwich'in Indians rely on a caribou herd in the wildlife refuge. Drilling for oil on the caribou's calving ground could disrupt the herd and the tribe's way of life.
3. The Gwich'in are not categorically opposed to oil drilling on tribal lands. They have permitted an oil company to drill on their lands in Canada.
4. Many tribes around the United States have turned to allowing drilling for oil and gas, gambling, and even nuclear waste storage on their reservations in an effort to achieve economic independence. The Gwich'in are not alone in trying to use their land to make money.
5. The view of American Indians as stewards of the land may be based more on myth than on fact. Some feel that this view denies American Indians a place in the modern world.

EXERCISE 6 Commit to sentence variety. 31d

Select a piece of your own writing. Using your word processing program, print out your text in a series of single numbered sentences. Examine the length, word order, and sentence beginnings, and consider how they might be revised for greater effect.

EXERCISE 7 Monitor word choices. 32a–32d

Revise the following sentences to eliminate inappropriately colloquial language, regional or community dialect, non-Standard English, or workplace jargon. Some sentences may not need revision.

Example Organic farmers have ~~a rough time~~ [difficulty] protecting their corn crops from genetic contamination by corn ~~produced through bioengineering~~ [that has been genetically modified] because ~~corn is open-pollinating.~~ [wind and insects carry pollen from one plant to other plants that can be miles away.]

1. A common agricultural genetic modification introduces *Bacillus thurengensis* into corn plants.
2. These bacteria bump off caterpillars; the bacteria, also called *Bt,* are sometimes spread on organic corn plants to rid them of corn borers and other destructive insects.
3. Organic farmers have been testing their corn crops for the presence of genetic modifications, and many of these guys are discovering that their crops have been contaminated by genetically modified corn grown up the road.
4. Some farmers are getting stuck with unsold corn, and others are selling it on the open market for less than half the price they would have gotten for a purely organic crop.
5. The problem of cross-pollination of genetically modified corn with organic corn—known as "genetic drift"—troubles many nonfarmers as well.
6. A lot of other countries buy organic produce from the United States, and few of them countries allow genetically modified foods to cross their borders.
7. If genetically modified corn can contaminate organic corn naturally, pretty soon there won't be hardly any corn without genetic modifications, and exports of American corn will be greatly reduced.
8. Genetic drift also bugs people who believe that maintaining crops' genetic diversity is important to avoid massive crop failures caused by disease and pests.
9. Most of the dozens of unique corn types found in the world come from Central America.
10. Genetic drift has gotten to lots of the unique corn types in parts of Mexico that scientists have studied, and some folks fear that eventually there will be no untainted corn.

EXERCISE 8 Use figurative language appropriately. 32e

Revise any of the following items that contain mixed metaphors or other inappropriate figurative language. Some sentences may not need revision.

Example Grade inflation may have begun as a ~~salve to~~ [way to promote] students' self-esteem, but some professors believe that it has now become ~~a tidal wave.~~ [a self-perpetuating force.]

1. Dr. Harvey C. Mansfield, a professor at Harvard University, argued that college students are too often allowed to coast easily along in the sea of courses and arrive in a harbor protected by unrealistically high grade point averages.

2. According to Mansfield's article in the *Chronicle of Higher Education,* half of the grades given at Harvard are either A's or A-minuses, so some professors, and even students, complain that there is no way to distinguish the cream from the chaff or to tell where students stand in relation to one another.
3. Faculty members who lack tenure are often handicapped in their grading because they know that good student evaluations can help them in the ceaseless competition for scarce teaching appointments.
4. Instructors who do not offer the carrot of A's and B's to students whose work is below par are likely to be bludgeoned with poor evaluations.
5. Mansfield wards off the minefield of grade inflation by keeping two grades for each student, an official inflated one that appears on the transcript and a privately communicated one that tells the student how well his or her work compared with that of other students in the class and with Dr. Mansfield's standards.

EXERCISE 9 Avoid biased language. 32f

In each of the following sentences, revise any biased or exclusionary language.

Example Some comic strips, such as *Doonesbury,* written by Garry Trudeau, and *The Boondocks,* created by ~~the African American~~ Aaron McGruder, can be considered political satires.

1. Many normal people have found *Doonesbury* offensive throughout its long history, for Trudeau has depicted premarital sex and drug use and criticized respectable politicians from Richard Nixon to Rick Perry.
2. The radical leftist Aaron McGruder's comic strip offended some readers with its claim that the United States had helped to arm and train Osama bin Laden.
3. In the fall of 2001, the main character in McGruder's comic strip argued that the ultraconservative Reagan administration had aided Osama bin Laden and other fanatical Muslims fighting against the Soviet Union.
4. In March of 2012, Trudeau published a series of strips criticizing new laws that required promiscuous women to have ultrasounds before undergoing an abortion.
5. Several papers chose not to run the strip that week, displaying their squeamish midwestern sensibilities.

EXERCISE 10 Avoid tired expressions (clichés) and pretentious language. 32g

Edit the following sentences to eliminate clichés and pretentious language.

Example I have found a new ~~employment opportunity~~ *job* that is ~~truly a dream come true.~~ *exactly what I wanted.*

1. It is with a heavy heart that I terminate my employment situation at Liberty Fixtures.
2. I have accepted a new position at Holt Manufacturing that not only fits me like a glove but is more remunerative.
3. My new position in the credit department involves making "friendly reminders" to customers who are allowing our bills to collect dust.
4. I will everlastingly recollect my years with my Liberty "band of brothers," and I hope that our paths cross often.
5. If you are ever within proximity of my new office, please don't be a stranger.

MindTap®

- **Practice skills that you have learned in this part and receive automatic feedback.**

7 Common Sentence Problems

WRITING IN YOUR CAREER

The Paralegal, the Writer

Courtesy of Eartha Hinds

A paralegal is an important member of a legal team who may be called upon to research, draft, and edit legal documents for an attorney. Outstanding research and writing skills are core competencies for a paralegal. NALA (the National Association of Legal Assistants) in its *NALA Manual for Paralegals* (6th ed., Delmar/Cengage, 2015) stresses that a paralegal should be able to interview and maintain contact with clients; draft correspondence, pleadings, and other legal documents; and summarize depositions, interrogatories, and testimony.

In an article in *Paralegal Today* titled "The Consequences of Bad Legal Writing" (2007), certified legal assistant Christy Hall Denson presents the following example to show why "your documents should be written in complete sentences, have subjects and verbs that agree with one another and contain properly placed modifiers":

> In Mississippi, a defendant appealed a district attorney's burglary indictment, stating that it didn't charge him with anything because it contained bad grammar. In part, the indictment charged that the "goods, ware, and merchandise unlawfully, feloniously and burglariously did break and enter."

Eartha Hinds, a paralegal in the Legal Department at Cengage Publishing, says, "Clarity is critical for legal correspondence because grammatical errors can create confusion." What can you do to make sure your writing is clear? Hinds recommends using short sentences, choosing active verbs, and avoiding legal jargon. "There is no room for error in a legal document," she warns.

7 Common Sentence Problems

35 Trouble Spots and Terms

MindTap®

Understand the goals of this part, and complete a warm-up activity.

MindTap®

Read, highlight, and take notes online.

35a Students' FAQs—and where to find answers

Questions	Short Answer	More Information
Can I begin a sentence with *and* or *but*?	Occasionally, yes	30c, p. 446
Can I interchange *but* and *however*?	No. Meanings are similar; usage and punctuation differ.	37c, 45e: pp. 490, 573
Is it *would have drank* or *would have drunk*?	*Drunk:* past participle verb form after *have*	39a, p. 498
How do I know whether to use *I* or *me* with *and*? (The boss promoted *Tom and I* or *Tom and me*?)	Use the "drop the noun in the *and* phrase" test: The boss promoted *me.*	42a, p. 528
When do I use *who, whom, which,* or *that*?	For people: *who, whom* For things: *which, that* This is a complex issue; turn to the sections in column 3.	44a, 44b, 44d: pp. 546, 548, and 550
What is the difference between *who* and *whom*?	Use *whom* in formal writing as an object form.	42i, 44a: pp. 538, 546
When do I use *good* or *well, bad* or *badly*?	*Good* and *bad* modify nouns. *Well* and *badly* modify verbs. But there are tricky exceptions.	43a, 43b, 43c: pp. 540, 541, and 542

Questions	Short Answer	More Information
What are the errors called fragments, run-ons, and comma splices?	A fragment is an incomplete sentence; a run-on or a comma splice is wrongly written as one sentence but needs to be separated or rewritten.	chapters 36 and 37: pp. 484, 488
What is the difference between		
a. *it's* and *its*?	*It's* stands for *it is* or *it has. Its* is a possessive adjective.	46f, p. 579
b. *who's* and *whose*?	*Who's* stands for *who is* or *who has. Whose* is a possessive relative pronoun.	Glossary of Usage, p. 675
c. *lay* and *lie*?	*Lay* is used only with a direct object, and *lie* with no direct object.	39b, p. 503

35b Grammar-check programs: Uses, dangers, and suggestions

Set aside time for a separate reading of your draft to check for the common problem areas covered in this part of the book and to make corrections. Do not rely on computer tools for editing. Spelling checkers and grammar-check programs are not complete or sophisticated enough to cover all the options. Spelling checkers will catch typographical errors, such as *teh* in place of *the*, but they will not catch missing *-s* or *-ed* endings, nor will they find a misspelled word that forms another word: *affect/effect, expect/except, then/than*, or *peek/peak/pique,* for example. In addition, auto-complete features in some word processing programs might change a word that you didn't intend, so you need to edit carefully. You can check out many of these problem areas in the Glossary of Usage at the end of this book.

A grammar-check program analyzes sentences and makes suggestions about what might need to be fixed, tightened, or polished. But technology has not advanced enough for it to be able to take context, meaning, and cultural diversity into account.

KEY POINTS

Grammar-Check Programs: Uses, Dangers, and Suggestions

Uses

A grammar-check program provides helpful observations about simple mechanical matters, such as pointing out

- commas and periods that you may need to place inside quotation marks
- quotation marks or parentheses that you may need to close
- passive verbs that you may wish to revise as active
- clichés
- verb problems such as in the sentence, "Can the mayor wins?"
- You may find it worthwhile to activate a grammar-check program solely to catch these basic errors. But before you do, be aware of the following dangers.

Dangers

The capabilities of grammar-check programs are limited. They cannot recognize some errors because they do not "understand" the context or your intention. For example, if you wrote "The actors were boring" but meant to write "The actors were bored," a grammar-check program would not reveal your mistake. Some correct sentences can even be made wrong upon the advice of such a program, as shown in the Note for Multilingual Writers in 3c, page 45.

Suggestions

If you use a grammar-check program, review all its points of advice before you make any changes based on its recommendations. Never make a suggested change in your draft before verifying that the change is really necessary. Or, more radically, consider deactivating the grammar-check program while you write. Its constant reminders may interrupt your train of thought, introduce errors, and keep you from developing confidence in your own judgment and grammatical expertise.

35c Standard English/Edited American English

Science fiction writer and editor Teresa Neilson Hayden, in *Making Book*, characterizes English as "a generous, expansive, and flexible language" but adds, "a less charitable description would characterize it as drunk and disorderly." The task of editing, she claims, is to try to impose "a degree of regularity on something that is inherently irregular." A set of conventions referred to as Standard English can help you move away from irregularities in your writing; the term *Edited American English* more directly relates to academic writing in the United States.

The American Heritage Dictionary (*AHD*), Fifth Edition, defines *Standard English* as "the variety of English that is generally acknowledged as the model for the speech and writing of educated speakers."* A Usage Note in the *AHD,* however, continues, "A form that is considered standard in one region may be nonstandard in another" and points out that *standard* and *nonstandard* are relative terms, depending largely on context.

In short, the concept of Standard English is complex. It is entwined with the region, race, class, education, and gender of both the speaker (or writer) and the listener (or reader). Standard English is far from monolithic. It is constantly supplemented and challenged by other ways of speaking and writing, such as those coming from technology, hip-hop, the worlds of gender and sexual politics, popular culture, and conventions in use in different parts of the English-speaking world. Sometimes what is identified as Standard English changes, too, complicating the concept even more.

Nevertheless, Standard English, with all its quirks, irregularities, rules, and exceptions, is politically and sociologically branded as the language of those in power. Its practices are what most readers still expect in the academic and business worlds. However insightful and original your ideas may be, readers will soon become impatient if those ideas are not expressed in sentences that follow conventions determined by the history of the language and the prescriptive power of its educated users.

Attention to accuracy is important in the business world as well as in college. A study of 120 corporations found that one-third of the employees of major companies had poor writing skills, leading an executive to say, "It's not that companies want to hire Tolstoy. But they need people who can write clearly."

To meet readers' expectations in academic and business settings, use the version of Edited American English represented in this book and stressed in parts 7–10.

---

*Definition of "Standard English," Copyright © 2011 by Houghton Mifflin Harcourt Publishing Company. Adapted and reproduced by permission from *The American Heritage Dictionary of the English Language*, Fifth Edition.

35d Terms for the parts of a sentence

To think about and discuss how sentences work, it is useful to have a shared vocabulary. Here are some of the basic terms covering the parts of speech and the parts of a sentence. The Glossary of Grammatical Terms (64, p. 689) provides further definitions and examples.

Parts of speech Words are traditionally classified into eight categories, called *parts of speech.* Note that the part of speech refers not to the word itself but to its function in a sentence. Some words can function as different parts of speech.

▸ **They respect the orchestra manager.** (verb: respect)

▸ **Respect is a large part of a business relationship.** (noun: Respect)

Nouns Words that name a person, place, thing, or concept—*teacher, valley, furniture, Hinduism*—are called *nouns.* When you use a noun, determine the following: Is it a proper noun, requiring a capital letter? Does it have a plural form? If so, are you using the singular or plural form?

Pronouns A pronoun represents a noun or a noun phrase. In writing, a pronoun refers to its antecedent—that is, a noun or noun phrase appearing just before it in the text.

▸ **My sister loves *her* new car, but *she* dented *it* last week.**

Pronouns fall into seven types: personal (42a), possessive (42b), demonstrative (41j), intensive or reflexive (42h), relative (44a), interrogative (42i), and indefinite (41h). When you use a pronoun, determine the following: What word or words in the sentence does the pronoun refer to? Does the pronoun refer to a noun or pronoun that is singular or plural?

Verbs Words that tell what a person, place, thing, or concept does or is—*smile, throw, think, seem, become, be*—are called *verbs.* Verbs change form, so when you use a verb, determine the following: What time period does the verb refer to? What auxiliary or modal verbs are needed for an appropriate tense? Is the subject of the verb singular or plural? Is the verb in the active voice or passive voice? What are the five forms of the verb (*sing, sings, singing, sang, sung*), and are you using the correct form?

Main verbs often need auxiliary verbs (*be, do, have*) or modal auxiliaries (*will, would, can, could, shall, should, may, might, must*) to complete the meaning.

Adjectives Words that describe nouns—*purple, beautiful, big*—are called *adjectives*. An adjective can precede a noun or follow a linking verb:

- ▶ **Renee Fleming has a *magnificent* singing voice.**
- ▶ **Her singing voice is *magnificent*.**

Descriptive adjectives have comparative and superlative forms: *short, shorter, shortest*. Also functioning as adjectives (before a noun) are *a, an,* and *the,* as well as possessives and demonstratives: *a* cabbage, *an* allegory, *their* poems, *this* book. For more on adjectives, see chapter 43.

Adverbs Words that provide information about verbs, adjectives, adverbs, or clauses are called *adverbs*. Many but not all adverbs end in *-ly: quickly, efficiently.* Adverbs also provide information about how or when: *very, well, sometimes, often, soon, never.* Adverbs modify verbs, adjectives, other adverbs, or clauses.

modifies verb — modifies adverb

- ▶ **Federer served brilliantly. He played spectacularly well.**

modifies adjective — modifies whole clause

- ▶ **He is a very energetic player. Undoubtedly, he is a genius.**

Conjunctive adverbs—such as *however, therefore, furthermore*—make connections between independent clauses.

Conjunctions Words that connect words, phrases, and clauses are called *conjunctions*.

- ▶ **Martin loves ham *and* eggs**
- ▶ **Kathryn requested an aisle seat *and* a vegetarian meal.**
- ▶ **To brighten up her room, she bought a red bowl, a blue jug, *and* yellow cushions.**
- ▶ **The magazine was published, *and* his article won acclaim.**

The seven coordinating conjunctions—*and, but, or, nor, so, for, yet*—connect ideas of equal importance. Subordinating conjunctions—*because, if, when, although,* for instance—make one clause dependent on another. Consider meaning and style when deciding whether to use a conjunction or a transition.

Prepositions Words used before nouns and pronouns to form phrases that usually do the work of an adjective or adverb are called *prepositions.*

preposition preposition

▸ **A bird with a red crest flew onto the feeder.**

Some common prepositions are *against, around, at, behind, between, except, for, from, in, into, like, on, over, regarding, to,* and *without.* Prepositional phrases are often idiomatic: *on occasion, in love.* To understand their use and meaning, consult a good dictionary. See also chapter 61, a useful resource on this topic for all writers, regardless of whether or not English is your first language.

Interjections Words that express emotion and can stand alone—*Ha! Wow! Ugh! Ouch! Say!*—are called *interjections.* Interjections are not used frequently in academic writing. The more formal ones (such as *alas, oh*) are sometimes used in poetry:

> But she is in her grave, and, Oh,
> The difference to me!
> —William Wordsworth, "She Dwelt among the Untrodden Ways"

A sentence and its parts You have probably heard various definitions of a *sentence,* the common one being that "a sentence is a complete thought." Sometimes it is. Sometimes it is not, depending on what one expects by "complete." In fact, that definition is not particularly helpful. How complete is this thought?

▸ **He did not.**

You probably do not regard it as complete in the traditional sense because it relies on text around it, on other sentences, to tell who he is and what it was he did not do, as in the following example.

▸ **Sarah was always competitive with her brother. She studied hard. He did not.**

However, each of these sentences can be said to be *grammatically* complete, containing a subject and a verb in an independent clause.

Subject and predicate A sentence needs at the very least a *subject* (the person or thing doing or receiving the action) and a *predicate* (a comment or assertion about the subject). Only a command (such as "Run!") will not state the subject (*you*). A predicate must contain a complete verb, expressing action or state.

subject predicate

▸ **Babies cry.**

verb

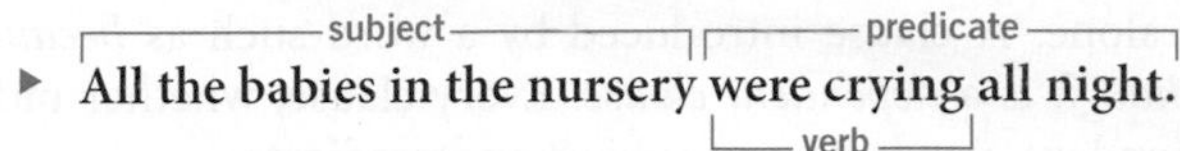

subject
predicate
▸ All the babies in the nursery were crying all night.
verb

Direct and indirect object Some verbs are followed by a *direct object*, a word that receives the action of a verb.

direct object

▸ **Many people wear glasses.** [A verb that is followed by a direct object is known as a *transitive verb. Intransitive verbs* such as *sit, happen, occur,* and *rise* are never followed by a direct object.]

Verbs such as *give, send,* and *offer* can be followed by both a direct and an *indirect object* (see 60c).

indirect object — direct object

▸ **He gave his leading lady one exquisite rose.**

Complement Verbs such as *be, seem, look,* and *appear* are *linking verbs,* not action verbs. They are followed by a *subject complement* that renames or describes the subject.

subject complement

▸ **The instructor seems troubled.**

An *object complement* renames or describes the direct object.

direct object — object complement

▸ **We appointed a student the chairperson of the committee.**

Phrase A *phrase* is a group of words that lacks a subject, a verb, or both. A phrase is only a part of a sentence. It cannot be punctuated as a sentence.

an elegant evening gown
singing in the rain
on the corner
worried by the news
with her thoughts in turmoil
to travel around the world

Clause Clauses can be independent or dependent. A sentence must contain a *main clause,* also called an *independent clause,* which is one that can stand alone. A clause introduced by a word such as *because, when, if,* or *although* is a *dependent clause.* Every clause, whether independent or dependent, needs its own subject and predicate.

▸ **Because her eyesight is deteriorating,** [dependent (subordinate) clause] **she wears glasses.** [independent clause]

Dependent clauses can function as adverbs, adjectives, or nouns.

▸ ***When the sun shines,*** **the strawberries ripen.** [Adverbial clause expressing time]

▸ **The berries** ***that we picked yesterday*** **were delicious.** [Adjective clause modifying *berries*]

▸ **The farmers know** ***what they should do.*** [Noun clause functioning as a direct object]

See 36c for more on dependent clause fragments.

36 Fixing a Sentence Fragment

A *fragment* is a group of words incorrectly punctuated as if it were a complete sentence.

36a What a sentence needs

Check that your sentences contain the following:

1. a **capital letter** at the beginning
2. an **independent (main) clause**—one that can stand alone—containing both a **subject** and a **complete verb** and not introduced by a word such as *when, because, although, which,* or *until* (such words, known as *subordinators* or *subordinating conjunctions,* introduce dependent clauses and are common culprits in fragments)
3. appropriate **end punctuation:** period, question mark, exclamation point, or semicolon

Note that a semicolon indicates the end of one independent clause with a close meaning attached to another independent clause: *The senator explained the budget items; her assistants helped by displaying explanatory charts.*

Most problems occur when what is presented as a sentence has no complete independent clause.

a phrase fragment: no subject or verb

▶ **He wanted to make a point. To prove his competence.**

not an independent clause

▶ **The *Titanic* sank in 1912. Because it hit an iceberg.**

[*Because* is a subordinating conjunction connecting to an idea in the previous sentence.]

36b How to fix a phrase fragment with no subject and/or verb

1. Connect the phrase fragment to what comes before or after, removing a period and the following capital letter:

   ▶ **Architects recommend solar panels/ ~~To~~ to save on heating bills.**

   ▶ **In a valiant attempt to save some money/ ~~The~~ , the family moved into their RV and rented their house.**

   ▶ **The police found a knife and an Uzi/ ~~An~~ , an Israeli-made submachine gun.**

   ▶ **The sculptor described his ~~proposal. An~~ innovative plan for an abstract fountain in the middle of the town square.**

   ▶ **A prize was awarded to Ed/ ~~The~~ , the best worker in the company.**

2. Revise so that each group of words between a capital letter and a period contains a subject and a verb.

   ▶ **Many people try to lose weight. ~~Is~~ It is wise for them to avoid sugary snacks.**

36c How to fix a dependent clause fragment

A *dependent clause* begins with a word that makes the clause subordinate to and dependent upon another clause. Unable to stand alone, a dependent clause must be attached to an independent clause. Here are the words that introduce dependent adverbial clauses:

SUBORDINATING CONJUNCTIONS

time: when, whenever, until, till, before, after, while, once, as soon as, as long as

place: where, wherever

cause: because, as, since

condition: if, even if, unless, provided that

contrast: although, though, even though, whereas, while

comparison: than, as, as if, as though

purpose: so that, in order that

result: so…that, such…that

Whenever you begin a sentence with one of these words, make sure you see a comma at the end of the clause and then the subject and verb of the independent clause:

- **When Jane Austen describes people, she emphasizes all their little foibles.**

Words introducing other types of dependent clauses (adjective or noun clauses) include *who, whom, whose, which, that, what, when,* and *whoever.*

Methods of correcting a dependent clause fragment Two methods are available:

1. Connect the fragment to an independent clause before or after it.

- **Lars wants to be a stand-up comic/ ~~Because~~ he likes to make people laugh.** (inserted: because)
- **Comedians like to perform in small clubs/ ~~In~~ which they can connect with their audience.** (inserted: in)
- **She made many promises to her family./ ~~That~~ she would write to them every day.** (inserted: that)
- **The name *Google* comes from the word *googol*./ ~~Which~~ is the mathematical term for a one followed by a hundred zeros.** (inserted: which, with comma)

For the use of commas before clauses beginning with *who, whom,* or *which,* see 44b and 45d.

2. Delete the subordinating conjunction. The dependent clause then becomes an independent clause, which can stand alone.

   ▸ **Lars plans to become a stand-up comic. ~~Because he~~ He likes to make people laugh.**

Note: It is a myth that a sentence should never begin with *because*. A word like *because* at the beginning of a sentence does not always signal a fragment. The following sentence is perfectly grammatical, beginning with a dependent clause and ending with an independent clause.

▸ **Because Lars likes to make people laugh, he plans to become a stand-up comic.**

36d How to fix a fragment with a missing subject after *and*, *but*, or *or*

Two separate sentences need two separate subjects. In Standard academic English, one subject is enough for a compound predicate (two verbs after the subject in the same sentence), but it cannot do the work of a subject across two sentences.

Fragment

▸ **After an hour, the dancers changed partners. And easily adapted from rock and roll to the tango.**
fragment: no subject of *adapted*

Possible revisions

▸ **After an hour, the dancers changed partners and easily adapted from rock and roll to the tango.**

▸ **After an hour, the dancers changed partners. They easily adapted from rock and roll to the tango.**

▸ **After an hour, the dancers changed partners, adapting easily from rock and roll to the tango.**

▸ **After an hour, the dancers changed partners. And they adapted easily from rock and roll to the tango.** [See the Language and Culture box in 30c for more on sentences beginning with *and* or *but*.]

36e Intentional fragments

Fragments are used frequently in advertisements to keep the text short. In academic writing, you will sometimes see a fragment used intentionally for emphasis, after a question, as an explanation, or at a point of transition.

▸ **Man is the only animal that blushes. Or needs to.**

—Mark Twain, *Following the Equator*

▸ **He** [Dylan Thomas] **lived twenty-four years after he began to be a poet. Twenty-four years of poetry, dwindling rapidly in the last decade.**

—Donald Hall, *Remembering Poets*

By all means, use fragments to achieve a specific effect. However, edit fragments that serve no identifiable rhetorical purpose.

37 Run-ons and Comma Splices

37a How to identify run-on (or *fused*) sentences and comma splices

A writer who takes two independent clauses and rams them up against each other, end to end, creates the error of a *run-on sentence*, also known as a *fused sentence*. Academic readers expect two independent clauses to be separated by more than a comma alone.

RUN-ON ERROR

▸ **Blue jeans were originally made as tough work clothes they became a fashion statement in the 1970s.**

(independent clause: they became a fashion statement in the 1970s.)

Inserting a comma between the two clauses is no help. That would then be a *comma splice* error.

COMMA SPLICE ERROR

▸ **Blue jeans were originally made as tough work clothes, they became a fashion statement in the 1970s.**

Note: Comma splices are often used in advertising and journalism for stylistic effect to emphasize a contrast: *Barack Obama and Hillary Clinton campaigned on different issues. He looked for ways to create change in the future, she looked back to her time in the Senate.* Take this stylistic risk only if you are sure of the effect you want to achieve.

 Five ways to correct run-on sentences and comma splices

You can correct run-ons and comma splices in the following five ways. Select the one that works best for the sentence you are editing.

KEY POINTS

Options for Editing a Run-on or Comma Splice

1. When the two clauses are quite long, simply separate them.

   ▸ **Blue jeans were originally made as tough work clothes. *They* became a fashion statement in the 1970s.**

   ▸ **Blue jeans were originally made as tough work clothes; *they* became a fashion statement in the 1970s.**

2. Include a comma, but make sure it is followed by *and, but, or, nor, so, for,* or *yet.*

   ▸ **Blue jeans were originally made as tough work clothes, *but* they became a fashion statement in the 1970s.**

3. If you are switching direction or want to stress the second clause, separate the clauses with a period or a semicolon, followed by a transitional expression such as *however* or *therefore,* followed by a comma (see also 37c and 43f).

   ▸ **Blue jeans were originally made as tough work clothes; *however*, they became a fashion statement in the 1970s.**

4. Rewrite the sentences as one sentence by using, for example, *because, although,* or *when* to make one clause introduce or set up the clause containing the important point.

   ▸ ***Although* blue jeans were originally made as tough work clothes, they became a fashion statement in the 1970s.**

5. Condense or restructure the sentence.

   ▸ **Blue jeans, *originally* made as tough work clothes, became a fashion statement in the 1970s.**

37c How to avoid a run-on or a comma splice when using a transition

Run-ons and comma splices often occur with transitional expressions such as *in addition, however, therefore, for example,* and *moreover* (you'll find a list in 2f). When one of these expressions precedes the subject of its own clause, end the previous sentence with a period or a semicolon. Put a comma after the transitional expression, not before it.

Corrected run-on error — **Martha cleaned her closets ~~in~~ In addition, she reorganized the kitchen.** [period inserted after "closets"; "in" replaced by "In"]

The house was remodeled ~~moreover~~ Moreover, the new owners added a guest wing. [period inserted after "remodeled"; "moreover" replaced by "Moreover,"]

Corrected comma splice error — **The doctor prescribed new pills; however, she did not alert the patient to the side effects.** [comma after "pills" replaced by semicolon; comma inserted after "however"]

Note: You can use the coordinating conjunctions *and, but,* and *so* after a comma to connect two independent clauses, but *in addition, however,* and *therefore* do not follow the same punctuation pattern.

- **The stock market was falling, so he decided not to invest his savings.**
- **The stock market was falling; therefore, he decided not to invest his savings.**

Commas should both precede and follow a transitional expression that does not appear at the beginning of its own clause:

- **The weekend guest apologized for breaking a vase. She did not, however, offer to pay for a replacement.**

38 Sentence Snarls

Snarls, tangles, and knots are as difficult to deal with on a bad writing day as on a bad hair day, though they may not be as painful. Sentences with structural inconsistencies give readers trouble. They make readers work to untangle the meaning.

38a Tangles: Mixed constructions, confusing comparisons, and convoluted syntax

Mixed constructions A mixed construction is a sentence with parts that do not match grammatically. The sentence begins one way and then veers off in an unexpected direction. Check to ensure that the subject and verb in your sentence are clear and work together, and note that a phrase beginning with *by* can never be the subject of a sentence. Do not use a pronoun to restate the subject, as shown in the third example that follows.

- ▶ ~~In the~~ ^The^ **excerpt by Heilbrun and the story by Gould are similar.**
- ▶ ~~By working~~ ^Working^ **at night can create tension with family members.**
- ▶ **My neighbors ~~they~~ speak Farsi among themselves.**

When you start a sentence with a dependent adverbial clause (beginning with a word like *when, if, because,* and *since*), make sure you follow that clause with an independent clause. A dependent clause cannot serve as the subject of a verb.

- ▶ ~~Because she swims~~ ^Swimming^ **every day does not guarantee she is healthy.**
- ▶ ~~When~~ ^Trading^ **a baseball player ~~is traded~~ every few years causes family problems.**

Confusing comparisons When you make comparisons, readers need to know clearly what you are comparing. See also 42a for faulty comparisons with personal pronouns.

Confusing comparison	**When you finish the exercise, compare your answers with a partner.** [Don't compare your answers with your partner; compare them with your partner's answers.]
Revised	**When you finish the exercise, compare your answers with your partner's.**

Convoluted syntax Revise sentences that ramble on to such an extent that they become tangled. Make sure they have clear subjects, verbs, and connections between clauses.

Tangled	**The way I feel about getting what you want is that when there is a particular position or item that you want to**

try to get to do your best and not give up because if you give up you have probably missed your chance of succeeding.

Possible revision **To get what you want, keep trying.**

38b Misplaced modifiers: Phrases, *not*, *only*, split infinitives

A modifier is a word or words describing a noun, verb, or clause. A misplaced modifier is a word, phrase, or clause that is wrongly placed so that it appears to modify the incorrect word or words.

Place a phrase or clause close to the word it modifies

Misplaced **She proudly showed the iPhone to her colleagues that her boss had given her.**

Revised **She proudly showed her colleagues the iPhone that her boss had given her.**

Take care with modifiers such as *only* and *not* Place a word such as *only, even, just, nearly, not, merely,* or *simply* immediately before the word it modifies. The meaning of a sentence can change significantly as the position of a modifier changes, so careful placement is important.

- **Next year, ^not everyone in the company will ~~not~~ get a raise.** [The unrevised sentence says that nobody at all will get a raise. If you move *not*, the sentence now says that although not all workers will get a raise, some will.]
- ***Only* Rafael planned to visit Disney World.** [no one else]
- **Rafael *only* planned to visit Disney World.** [planned but didn't visit]
- **Rafael planned to visit *only* Disney World.** [and nowhere else]

What you need to know about splitting an infinitive When you place a word or a phrase between *to* and the verb (the infinitive), the result can be awkward. Avoid splitting an infinitive when the split is unnecessary or clumsy, as in the following:

- **Upon hearing the news, she began ~~to uncontrollably cry.~~ ^to cry uncontrollably.**

▸ We want ~~to honestly and in confidence inform~~ you of our plans. [to inform … honestly and in confidence.]

Traditionally, a split infinitive was frowned upon, but it is now acceptable, as in the *Star Trek* motto, "To boldly go where no man has gone before...." Sometimes, however, splitting an infinitive may be necessary to avoid ambiguity.

▸ **We had *to stop* them from talking *quickly*.** [Were they talking too quickly? Did we have to stop them quickly? The meaning is ambiguous.]

▸ **We had *to quickly stop* them from talking.** [The split infinitive clearly says that we were the ones who had to do something quickly.]

38c Dangling modifiers

When a modifier beginning with a word ending in *-ing* or *-ed* is not grammatically connected to the noun or phrase it is intended to describe, it is said to *dangle*.

Dangling **_Driving_ across the desert, the saguaro _cactus_ appeared eerily human.** [Who or what was driving? The cactus?]

Usually, you can fix a dangling modifier by either (1) making the modifier refer to the person or thing performing the action or (2) rewriting the modifier as a dependent clause.

Possible revisions **_Driving_ across the desert, _the naturalists_ thought the saguaro cactus appeared eerily human.**

When the naturalists were driving across the desert, the saguaro cactus appeared eerily human.

38d Shifts: From statements to commands, from indirect to direct quotation, and in point of view

Sudden shifts in your sentences can be disconcerting to readers. See also 39h on avoiding unnecessary shifts in verb tense.

Do not shift abruptly from statements to commands

▸ **Participants should discuss the questions in small groups. ~~Inform~~ [They should inform] the facilitator if there are questions.**

Do not shift from indirect to direct quotation See 39i and 60d for more on tenses in indirect quotations.

▸ **The client told us that he wanted to sign the lease and ~~would we~~ [asked us to] prepare the papers.**

▸ **She wanted to find out whether any interest had accumulated on her account and ~~was she~~ [whether she was] receiving any money.**

Do not shift point of view in pronouns Be consistent when you are using first, second, or third person pronouns. For example, if you begin by referring to *one,* do not switch to *you* or *we.* Also avoid shifting unnecessarily between third person singular and plural forms.

Shift — ***One*** **needs a high salary to live in a city because** ***you*** **have to spend so much on rent and transportation.**

Possible revisions — ***One*** **needs a high salary to live in a city because** ***one*** **has to spend so much on rent and transportation.**

Possible — ***We all*** **need high salaries to live in a city because we have to spend so much on rent and transportation.**

A high salary is necessary in a city because rent and transportation cost so much.

38e Mismatch of subject and predicate

To avoid confusing readers, never use a subject and predicate that do not make sense together (see 35d, p. 482, for the definition of a predicate). This error is known as *faulty predication.*

▸ **~~The decision to build~~ [Building] an elaborate extension onto the train station made all the trains arrive late.** [It was not the decision that delayed the trains; building the extension did.]

▸ **According to the guidelines, ~~people in~~ dilapidated public housing will be demolished this year.** [Surely the housing, not the people, will be demolished!]

38f Definitions and reasons

When you write a definition of a term, use parallel structures on either side of the verb *be*. In formal writing, avoid defining a term by using *is when* or *is where* (or *was when, was where*).

▸ **A tiebreaker in tennis *is when there is* a final game to decide a set.**

In giving reasons in both speech and writing, the expression *the reason is because* is becoming common. However, many readers of formal prose traditionally prefer *the reason is that* or simply *because* by itself. Decide what readers may expect, and consider your options.

▸ ***The reason* the young executive lost the account *is* ~~*because*~~ that clients had little confidence in his judgment.**

▸ **~~*The reason* the~~ The young executive lost the account *because* ~~that~~ clients had little confidence in his judgment.**

38g *Because* and *when* clauses as subject

A dependent adverbial clause (35d) beginning with *because* or *when* cannot function as the subject of a sentence.

▸ **~~Just because she swims~~ Swimming every day does not mean she is healthy.**

[The subject is now a noun phrase, *Swimming every day*, instead of a clause, *Because she swims every day*.]

▸ **When people eat too much fat, they increase~~s~~ their cholesterol.**

[The dependent clause *When people eat too much fat* is now attached to an independent clause with its own subject, *they*.]

38h Omitted words

Include necessary words in compound structures If you omit a verb form from a compound verb, the main verb form must fit into each part of the compound; otherwise, you must use the complete verb form (see 38j on parallelism).

▸ **The person we could hear coughing has always been and will always be a cigar smoker.** [*Be* fits only with *will*, not with *has*.]

Include necessary words in comparisons

▸ **The volleyball captain is as competitive** *as* **or even more competitive than her teammates.** [The comparative structures are *as competitive as* and *more competitive than*. Do not merge them.]

If you omit the verb in the second part of a comparison, ambiguity may occur.

▸ **He liked baseball more than his son~~.~~** *did.* [Omitting *did* implies he liked baseball more than he liked his son.]

For more on faulty comparisons, see 43i. For sentence snarls caused by omitting an apostrophe, see 46c.

38i Unnecessary restated subject

Do not insert a pronoun between the subject and the verb to restate the subject (see also 60f).

▸ **The voters** (subject) **who supported the candidate ~~they~~ felt** (verb) **betrayed when he lost the election.** [The stated subject is "*The voters.*"]

▸ **What may seem funny to some** (subject) **~~it~~ can** (verb) **be deadly serious to others.** [The subject is the clause "*What may seem funny to some.*"]

38j Structures not parallel

Parallel structures are words, phrases, or clauses that use similar grammatical form. Balance your sentences by using similar grammatical constructions in each part of a sentence.

Not parallel	**The results of reform were that class size decreased, more multicultural courses, and being allowed to choose a pass/fail option.**
Parallel clauses after *that*	**The results of reform were that class size decreased, more multicultural courses were offered, and students were allowed to choose a pass/fail option.**
Parallel noun phrases	**The results of reform were a decrease in class size, an increase in the number of multicultural courses, and the introduction of a pass/fail option for students.**

The use of parallel structures helps produce cohesion and coherence in a text. Aim for parallelism in sentences and in longer passages, too. The structures can be clauses or phrases, as shown in the following passages from "Maintenance" by Naomi Shihab Nye. (Italics have been added.)

PARALLEL STRUCTURES: CLAUSES

> We saw one house *where walls and windows had been sheathed in various patterns of gloomy brocade*. We visited another *where the kitchen had been removed* because the owners only ate in restaurants.

PARALLEL STRUCTURES: VERB PHRASES

> Sometimes I'd come home to find her *lounging* in the bamboo chair on the back porch, *eating* melon, or *lying* on the couch with a bowl of half-melted ice cream balanced on her chest.

Use parallel structures with paired (correlative) conjunctions When your sentence contains *correlative conjunctions* (pairs such as *either...or, neither...nor, not only...but also, both...and, whether...or,* and *as...as*) the structure after the second part of the pair should be exactly parallel in form to the structure after the first part.

- ▶ **He made up his mind *either* to paint the van *or* to sell it to another buyer.** [*To paint* follows *either*; therefore, *to sell* should follow *or*.]
- ▶ **She loves *both* singing in a choir *and* ~~to dance~~ dancing with a folk-dance troupe.** [An *-ing* form follows *both*; therefore, an *-ing* form should also follow *and*.]
- ▶ **The drive to Cuernavaca was *not only* too expensive *but also* ~~was~~ too tiring to do alone.** [*Too expensive* follows *not only*; therefore, *too tiring* should follow *but also*.]

Use parallel structures in comparisons with *as* or *than* and in lists

- ▶ **Talking to a child in a stroller is more important than ~~to text~~ texting and ~~check~~ checking e-mails.**
- ▶ **~~To find~~ Finding a life partner is infinitely more complex than choosing a new pair of shoes.**

▸ **Writing well demands the following: (1) planning your time, (2) paying attention to details, (3) ~~the need for revision,~~ revising, and (4) proofreading.**

39 Verbs

A verb expresses what the subject of the sentence is or does. Verbs may change form according to person, number, and tense; can be regular or irregular; and may require auxiliary verbs (forms of *be, do,* or *have*) or modal verbs (*will, would, can, could, shall, should, may, might,* and *must*) to complete their meaning.

A verb will fit into all four of the following:

1. They want to __________.
2. They will __________.
3. It is going to __________.
4. It might __________.

Identify a verb by checking that the *base form* (that is, the form listed as a dictionary entry) fits these sentences. Note, however, that modal or auxiliary verbs (see 39c) follow a different pattern. Although you may use a variety of verb forms when you speak, readers generally expect verbs in formal writing to follow predictable patterns.

39a Regular and irregular verb forms in Edited American English

Regular Verbs Regular verbs follow a predictable pattern. From the base form—that is, the dictionary form—you can construct all the forms.

Regular Verbs

Base	-*s*	-*ing* Present Participle	Past Tense	Past Participle
paint	paints	painting	painted	painted
smile	smiles	smiling	smiled	smiled

Irregular verbs Irregular verbs also have the -*s* and the present participle (-*ing*) forms, but they do not use -*ed* to form the past tense and the past participle. (For *be, do,* and *have,* see 39c; for *rise, lie,* and *sit/set,* see 39b.)

However, there are many more verbs, so use a dictionary to check irregular past tense and past participle forms if you are unsure. Always refer to 39c for help in deciding which form to use in tenses after auxiliary verbs (such as *has swam* or *has swum*?—the latter is correct).

Note, too, that verbs such as *bet, burst, cost, cut, hit, hurt, let, put, quit, set, slit, split, spread*, and *upset* are irregular only in that they make no change for their past tense or past participle form.

Common Irregular Verbs

Base Form	Past Tense	Past Participle
arise	arose	arisen
be	was/were	been
bear	bore	born, borne
beat	beat	beaten
become	became	become
begin	began	begun
bend	bent	bent
bind	bound	bound
bite	bit	bitten
bleed	bled	bled
blow	blew	blown
break	broke	broken
bring	brought	brought
build	built	built
buy	bought	bought
catch	caught	caught
choose	chose	chosen
cling	clung	clung
come	came	come
creep	crept	crept
deal	dealt	dealt
dig	dug	dug
do	did	done

(Continued)

(Continued)

Base Form	Past Tense	Past Participle
draw	drew	drawn
drink	drank	drunk
drive	drove	driven
eat	ate	eaten
fall	fell	fallen
feed	fed	fed
feel	felt	felt
fight	fought	fought
find	found	found
flee	fled	fled
fly	flew	flown
forbid	forbad(e)	forbidden
forget	forgot	forgotten
forgive	forgave	forgiven
freeze	froze	frozen
get	got	gotten, got
give	gave	given
go	went	gone
grind	ground	ground
grow	grew	grown
hang*	hung	hung
have	had	had
hear	heard	heard
hide	hid	hidden
hold	held	held
keep	kept	kept
know	knew	known
lay	laid	laid (39b)

**Hang* meaning "put to death" is regular: *hang, hanged, hanged.*

Base Form	Past Tense	Past Participle
lead	led	led
leave	left	left
lend	lent	lent
lie	lay	lain (39b)
light	lit, lighted	lit, lighted
lose	lost	lost
make	made	made
mean	meant	meant
meet	met	met
ride	rode	ridden
ring	rang	rung
rise	rose	risen (39b)
run	ran	run
say	said	said
see	saw	seen
seek	sought	sought
sell	sold	sold
send	sent	sent
shake	shook	shaken
shine	shone, shined	shone, shined
shoot	shot	shot
shrink	shrank	shrunk
sing	sang	sung
sink	sank	sunk
sit	sat	sat (39b)
sleep	slept	slept
slide	slid	slid
speak	spoke	spoken

(Continued)

(Continued)

Base Form	Past Tense	Past Participle
spend	spent	spent
spin	spun	spun
spit	spit, spat	spit
spring	sprang	sprung
stand	stood	stood
steal	stole	stolen
stick	stuck	stuck
sting	stung	stung
stink	stank, stunk	stunk
strike	struck	struck, stricken
swear	swore	sworn
sweep	swept	swept
swim	swam	swum
swing	swung	swung
take	took	taken
teach	taught	taught
tear	tore	torn
tell	told	told
think	thought	thought
throw	threw	thrown
tread	trod	trodden, trod
understand	understood	understood
wake	woke	waked, woken
wear	wore	worn
weave	wove	woven
weep	wept	wept
win	won	won

Base Form	Past Tense	Past Participle
wind	wound	wound
wring	wrung	wrung
write	wrote	written

39b Verbs commonly confused

Give special attention to verbs that are similar in form but different in meaning. Some of them, called *transitive verbs,* can take a direct object. Others, called *intransitive verbs*, never take a direct object (see 60c).

1. *rise:* to get up, to ascend (intransitive; irregular)
   raise: to lift, to cause to rise (transitive; regular)

Base	-s	-ing	Past Tense	Past Participle
rise	rises	rising	rose	risen
raise	raises	raising	raised	raised

▸ **A strong wind *rose* out of the west.**

▸ **The historian *raised* the issue of accuracy.** [The direct object answers the question "raised what?"]

2. *sit:* to occupy a seat (intransitive; irregular)
   set: to put or place (transitive; irregular)

Base	-s	-ing	Past Tense	Past Participle
sit	sits	sitting	sat	sat
set	sets	setting	set	set

▸ **The audience *sat* on hard wooden seats.**

▸ **The server *set* the steaming plates in front of the diners.**

3. *lie:* to recline (intransitive; irregular)
   lay: to put or place (transitive; regular)

Base	-s	-ing	Past Tense	Past Participle
lie	lies	lying	lay	lain
lay	lays	laying	laid	laid

▸ **She ~~laid~~ lay down for an hour after her oral presentation.**

▸ I was just ~~laying~~ lying down for a nap when the phone rang.

▸ ~~Lie~~ Lay the map on the floor.

In addition, note the verb *lie* ("to say something untrue"), which is intransitive and regular.

Base	-s	-ing	Past Tense	Past Participle
lie	lies	lying	lied	lied

▸ **He *lied* when he said he had won three trophies.**

39c Auxiliary verbs

An auxiliary verb is used with a main verb and sometimes with other auxiliaries. The auxiliary verbs are *do, have,* and *be,* and the nine modal verbs are *will, would, can, could, shall, should, may, might,* and *must* (59b). Note the irregular forms of *do, have,* and *be.*

Base	Present Tense Forms	-ing	Past	Past Participle
do	do, does	doing	did	done
have	have, has	having	had	had
be	am, is, are	being	was, were	been

See 41a for agreement with present tense forms of *do, have,* and *be.*

LANGUAGE AND CULTURE

Language and Dialect Variation with *Be*

In some languages (Chinese and Russian, for example), forms of *be* used as an auxiliary verb ("She *is* singing") or as a linking verb ("He *is* happy") can be omitted. In some spoken dialects of English (African American Vernacular, for example), subtle linguistic distinctions that are not possible in Standard English can be achieved: The omission of a form of *be* and the use of the base form in place of an inflected form (a form that shows number, person, mood, or tense) signal entirely different meanings.

VERNACULAR		STANDARD
He busy.	(temporarily)	He is busy now.
She be busy.	(habitually)	She is busy all the time.

Edited American English always requires the inclusion of a form of *be*.

▶ **Latecomers ^ always at a disadvantage.** [inserted: are]

Auxiliary verbs can be used in combination. Whatever the combination, the form of the main verb is determined by the auxiliary that precedes it.

Verb Forms Following Auxiliaries

Last Auxiliary and Its Forms	+ Base	+ *ing* Present Participle	+ Past Participle
do	*did* write		
modals (*can, could, will, would, shall, should, must, might, may*)	*might* go *would* fall		
have			*has/have/had* written should *have* seen would *have* gone
be (active)		*is* writing *were* singing might *be* driving has *been* running should have *been* thinking	
be (passive)			*are* grown *was* taken was *being* stolen would *be* eaten has *been* written might have *been* worn

Pay careful attention to the tricky editing points that follow:

1. Make sure you use a past participle form after *have*. In speech, we run sounds together, and the pronunciation may be mistakenly carried over into writing.

▸ **He could ~~of~~ ^have run faster.**

▸ **We should ~~of~~ ^have replaced the roof before it started leaking.**

The contracted forms *could've, should've, would've,* and so on are probably responsible for the nonstandard substitution of the word *of* in place of *have.* Watch out for this as you edit.

2. With modal verbs and the verbs *do* and *have,* the verb form following is fixed. It is only with *be* that a conscious choice of active or passive voice comes into play.

▸ **Laura *is taking* her driving test.** [active]

▸ **Laura *was taken* to the hospital last night.** [passive]

● **NOTE FOR MULTILINGUAL WRITERS**

What Comes before *Be*, *Been*, and *Being*

Be requires a modal auxiliary verb before it to form a complete verb (*could be jogging; will be closed*). *Been* requires *have, has,* or *had* (*have been driving; has been eaten*). *Being* must be preceded by *am, is, are, was,* or *were* to form a complete verb and must be followed by an adjective or a past participle: *You are being silly. He was being followed.*

39d Verb tenses: Overview

Tenses indicate time as perceived by the speaker or writer. The following examples show active voice verbs referring to past, present, and future time. For passive voice verbs, see chapter 40.

PAST TIME

Simple past	They *arrived* yesterday./They *did* not *arrive* today.
Past progressive	They *were leaving* when the phone rang.
Past perfect	Everyone *had left* when I called.
Past perfect progressive	We *had been sleeping* for an hour before you arrived.

PRESENT TIME

Simple present	He *eats* Wheaties every morning./ He *does* not *eat* eggs.
Present progressive	They *are working* today.
Present perfect	She *has* never *read* Melville.
Present perfect progressive	He *has been living* here for five years.

FUTURE TIME (USING *WILL*)

Simple future	She *will arrive* soon.
Future progressive	They *will be playing* baseball at noon tomorrow.
Future perfect	He *will have finished* the project by Friday.
Future perfect progressive	By the year 2025, they *will have been running* the company for twenty-five years.

Other modal auxiliaries can substitute for *will* and thus change the meaning: *must arrive, might be playing, may have finished, should have been running* (see also 59b).

NOTE FOR MULTILINGUAL WRITERS

Verbs Not Using -*ing* Forms for Progressive Tenses

Use simple tenses, not progressive forms, with verbs expressing mental activity referring to the senses, preference, or thought, as well as with verbs of possession, appearance, and inclusion (for example, *smell, prefer, understand, own, seem, contain*).

- **Sorry, I ~~am not understanding~~ don't understand the point of the story.**
- **They ~~are possessing~~ possess different behavior patterns.**

39e Present tenses

Simple present Use the simple present tense for the following purposes:

1. to make a generalization

- **Gardening *nourishes* the spirit.**

2. to indicate a permanent or habitual activity

   ▸ **The poet *uses* rhyme and meter in an innovative way.**

   ▸ **Young snakes *shed* their skins as often as once every two weeks.**

3. to express future time in dependent clauses (clauses beginning with words such as *if, when, before, after, until, as soon as*) when *will* is used in the independent clause

   ▸ **When the newt colony *dies* in the cold weather, building construction will begin.**

4. to discuss literature and the arts (called the *literary present*) even if the work was written in the past or the author is no longer alive

   ▸ **In *Zami*, Audre Lorde *describes* how a librarian *introduces* her to the joys of reading.**

   However, when you write a narrative of your own, use past tenses to tell about past actions.

   ▸ **Then the candidate ~~walks~~ walked up to the crowd and ~~kisses~~ kissed all the babies.**

● NOTE FOR MULTILINGUAL WRITERS

No *Will* in Time Clause

In a dependent clause beginning with a conjunction such as *if, when, before, after, until,* or *as soon as,* do not use *will* to express future time. Use *will* only in the independent clause. Use the simple present in the dependent clause.

▸ **As soon as they ~~will~~ get married, they will return to their hometown.**

Present progressive Use the present progressive to indicate an action in progress at the moment of speaking or writing.

▸ **Publishers *are getting* nervous about Internet copyright issues.**

However, do not use progressive forms with intransitive verbs such as *believe, know, like, prefer, want, own, seem, appear,* and *contain.*

▸ **Many people ~~are believing~~ believe that there may be life on other planets.**

Present perfect and present perfect progressive Use the present perfect in the following instances:

1. to indicate that an action occurring at some unstated time in the past is related to the present time

▸ **They *have worked* in New Mexico, so they know its laws.**

2. to indicate that an action beginning in the past continues to the present

▸ **She *has worked* for the same company since I *have known* her.**

If you state the exact time when something occurred, use the simple past tense, not the present perfect.

▸ **Sandra ~~has planted~~ planted tulips, hyacinths, and daffodils last fall.**

3. to report research results in APA style

▸ **Feynmann *has shown* that science can be fun.**

Use the present perfect progressive when you indicate the length of time an action has been in progress up to the present time.

▸ **Researchers *have been searching* for a cure for arthritis for many years.** [This implies that they are still searching.]

39f Past tenses

Use past tenses consistently. Do not switch from past to present or future for no reason (see 39h).

Simple past Use the simple past tense when you specify a past time or event.

▸ **The tornado *destroyed* hundreds of structures and *left* three people dead.**

When the sequence of past events is indicated with words like *before* or *after,* use the simple past tense for both events.

▸ **She *knew* how to write her name before she *went* to school.**

Use the past tense in an indirect quotation (a reported quotation, not in quotation marks) introduced by a past tense verb.

▸ **His chiropractor *told* him that the adjustments *were* over.**

Past progressive Use the past progressive for an activity in progress over time or at a specified point in the past.

▸ **Abraham Lincoln *was attending* the theater when he was assassinated.**

Past perfect and past perfect progressive Use the past perfect or the past perfect progressive only when one past event was completed before another past event or stated past time.

▸ ***Ben had cooked* the whole meal by the time Sam arrived.** [Two events occurred: Ben cooked the meal; then Sam arrived.]

▸ **He *had been cooking* for three hours when his sister finally offered to help.** [An event in progress—cooking—was interrupted in the past.]

Make sure that the past tense form you choose expresses your exact meaning.

▸ **When the student protesters marched into the building at noon, the administrators *were leaving*.** [The administrators were in the process of leaving. They began to leave at, say, 11:57 a.m.]

▸ **When the student protesters marched into the building at noon, the administrators *had left*.** [There was no sign of the administrators. They had already left at 11 a.m.]

▸ **When the student protesters marched into the building at noon, the administrators *left*.** [The administrators saw the protesters and then left at 12:01 p.m.]

39g -*ed* endings: Past tense and past participle forms

Both the past tense form and the past participle of regular verbs end in -*ed*. Edited American English (see 35c) requires the -*ed* ending in the following instances:

1. to form the past tense of a regular verb

   ed
   ▸ **The new trainee ask^ to take on more responsibility.**

2. to form the expression *used to,* indicating past habit

   d
   ▸ **Laptops use^ to be larger and heavier than they are now.**

3. to form the past participle of a regular verb after the auxiliary *has, have,* or *had* in the active voice or after forms of *be* (*am, is, are, was, were, be, being, been*) in the passive voice (see chapter 40)

- **The sheriff has live^d in this town for over thirty years.** [active]
- **Their work will not be finish^ed soon.** [passive]

4. to form a past participle used as an adjective

- **The nurses rushed to help the injure^d toddler.**
- **The trainer was surprise^d to learn that the skier had been hurt.**

NOTE FOR MULTILINGUAL WRITERS

The *-ed* Ending

The *-ed* ending is particularly troublesome for learners of English because in speech the ending is difficult to hear and may seem to be dropped—particularly when it blends into the next sound.

- **They wash^ed two baskets of laundry last night.**

This is an area that will always need careful editing.

The following *-ed* forms are used with *be: concerned, confused, depressed, divorced, embarrassed, married, prejudiced, satisfied, scared, supposed (to), surprised, used (to), worried.* Some can also be used with *get, seem, appear,* and *look.* Do not omit the *-d* ending.

- **People are often confuse^d when driving around a rotary in England.**
- **The candidate was embarrass^ed not to know the answer to the reporter's question.**

Do not confuse the past tense and past participle forms of an irregular verb (39a). A past tense form occurs alone as a complete verb, and a past participle form must be used with a *have* or *be* auxiliary verb.

- **He ~~drunk~~ ^drank the liquid before his medical tests.**
- **She ~~done~~ ^did her best to learn how to count in Japanese.**

▸ The explorers could have ~~went~~ gone alone.

▸ The employees were badly ~~shook~~ shaken up after the unexpected news.

39h Tense shifts

If you use tenses consistently throughout a piece of writing, you help readers understand what is happening and when. Check that your verbs consistently express present or past time, both within a sentence and from one sentence to the next. Avoid unnecessary tense shifts.

Tense shifts **Selecting a jury *was* very difficult. The lawyers *ask* many questions to discover bias and prejudice; sometimes, the prospective jurors *had* the idea they *are acting* in a play.**

Revised **Selecting a jury *was* very difficult. The lawyers *asked* many questions to discover bias and prejudice; sometimes, the prospective jurors *had* the idea they *were acting* in a play.**

When you write about events or ideas presented by another writer, use the literary present consistently (see 39e).

▸ **The author ~~illustrated~~ illustrates the images of women in two shows using advertisements and dramas on TV. One way shows women who advance~~d~~ their careers by themselves, and the other shows those who use~~d~~ beauty to gain recognition.**

Tense shifts are appropriate in the following instances:

1. when you signal a time change with a time word or phrase

   ▸ **We *bought* our house at the wrong time, and *now*** [signal for switch from past to present] **it *is* worth less than we *paid* for it *ten years ago*.** [signal for switch back to the past]

2. when you follow a generalization (present tense) with a specific example of a past incident

   ▸ **Some bilingual schools *offer* intensive instruction in English.** [generalization] **My sister, for example, *went* to a bilingual school where she *studied* English for two hours every day.** [specific example]

39i Tenses in indirect quotations

An indirect quotation reports what someone said. It does not use quotation marks, and it follows the tense of the introductory verb. For example, when the verb introducing an indirect quotation is in the present tense, the indirect quotation should preserve the tense of the original direct quotation (see also 60d).

Direct **"The economic outlook has improved."**

Indirect **Only one reporter *says* that the economic outlook has improved.** [present: *says*; indirect quotation: that the economic outlook has improved]

When the introductory verb is in the past tense, use forms that express past time in the indirect quotation.

Direct **"The banks are lending, and the economic outlook has improved."**

Indirect **The reporter *announced* that the banks were lending and the economic outlook *had improved.*** [past: *announced*; indirect quotation: that the banks were lending and the economic outlook had improved]

In a passage of more than one sentence, preserve the sequence of tenses showing past time throughout the whole passage.

- **The reporter announced that the banks were lending and the economic outlook *had improved.* His newspaper *had reassigned* him to another case, so he *was ending* his daily reports on the crisis.**

Note: Use a present tense after a past tense introductory verb only if the statement is a general statement that holds true in present time.

- **The reporter *announced* that he *is* happy with his new assignment.**

39j Verbs in conditional sentences, wishes, requests, demands, and recommendations

Conditions When *if* or *unless* introduces a dependent clause, the sentence expresses a condition. There are four types of conditional sentences: two refer to actual or possible situations, and two refer to speculative or hypothetical situations.

KEY POINTS

Verb Tenses in Conditional Sentences

MEANING EXPRESSED	*IF* CLAUSE	INDEPENDENT CLAUSE
1. Fact	Simple present	Simple present

▸ **If mortgage rates *go* down, house sales *increase*.**

MEANING EXPRESSED	*IF* CLAUSE	INDEPENDENT CLAUSE
2. Prediction/possibility	Simple present	*will, can, should, might* + base form

▸ **If I *hear* someone misuse the word "literally" one more time, I *will scream*.**

▸ **If we *don't speak* ill of the dead, who *will*?** —Harold Bloom

MEANING EXPRESSED	*IF* CLAUSE	INDEPENDENT CLAUSE
3. Speculation about present or future	Simple past or subjunctive *were*	*would, could, should, might* + base form

▸ **If he *had* a smartphone, he *would stream* music.** [But he does not have one.]

▸ **If she *were* my lawyer, I *might win* the case.** [But she is not.]

MEANING EXPRESSED	*IF* CLAUSE	INDEPENDENT CLAUSE
4. Speculation about past	Past perfect (*had* + past participle)	*would have* / *could have* / *should have* / *might have* } + past participle

▸ **If Jane *had attended* the book signing, she *could have met* her favorite author.** [But she did not attend.]

Use of subjunctive *were* in place of *was* With speculative conditions about the present and future using the verb *be*, *were* is used in place of *was* in the dependent *if* clause. This use of *were* to indicate hypothetical situations involves what is called the *subjunctive mood*.

▸ **If my aunt *were* sixty-five, she *could get* a discount airfare.** [My aunt is sixty.]

Blending Some blending of time and tenses can occur, as in the case of a condition that speculates about the past in relation to the effect on the present.

▸ **If we *hadn't taken out* a second mortgage, we *would own* the house free and clear by now.**

Use of *would* When writing in an academic setting, use *would* only in the independent clause, not in the conditional clause. However, *would* occurs frequently in the conditional clause in speech and in informal writing.

▸ **If the fish-fry committee ~~would show~~ showed more initiative, people might attend their events more regularly.**

▸ **If the driver ~~would have~~ had heard what the pedestrian said, he would have been angry.**

▸ **If you ~~would have~~ had paid attention in class, you wouldn't have done the wrong assignment.**

***Would*, *could*, and *might* with conditional clause understood** *Would, could,* and *might* are used in independent clauses when no conditional clause is present. These are situations that are contrary to fact, and the conditional clause is understood.

▸ **I *would* never *advise* her to leave college without a degree. She *might come back* later and blame me for her lack of direction.**

Wishes Like some conditions, wishes deal with speculation. For a present wish—about something that has not happened and is therefore hypothetical and imaginary—use the past tense or subjunctive *were* in the dependent clause. For a wish about the past, use the past perfect: *had* + past participle.

A wish about the present

▸ **I wish I *had* your attitude.**

▸ **I wish that Shakespeare *were* still alive.**

A wish about the past

▸ **Addicted to cigarettes, the patient wishes she *had* never *taken* that first puff.**

Requests, demands, and recommendations The subjunctive also appears after certain verbs, such as *request, command, insist, demand,* *move* (meaning "propose"), *propose,* and *urge.* In these cases, the verb in the dependent clause is the base form regardless of the person and number of the subject.

▸ **The dean suggested that students *be* allowed to vote.**

▸ **He insisted that she *submit* the report.**

▸ **The boss is demanding that everyone *work* overtime.**

Some idiomatic expressions preserve the use of the subjunctive, for example, *far* be *it from me, if need* be, *as it* were.

40 Passive Voice

In the active voice, the grammatical subject is the doer of the action, and the sentence tells "who's doing what." The passive voice tells what "is done to" the subject of the sentence. The person or thing doing the action may or may not be mentioned but is always implied: "My car was repaired" (by somebody at the garage).

ACTIVE

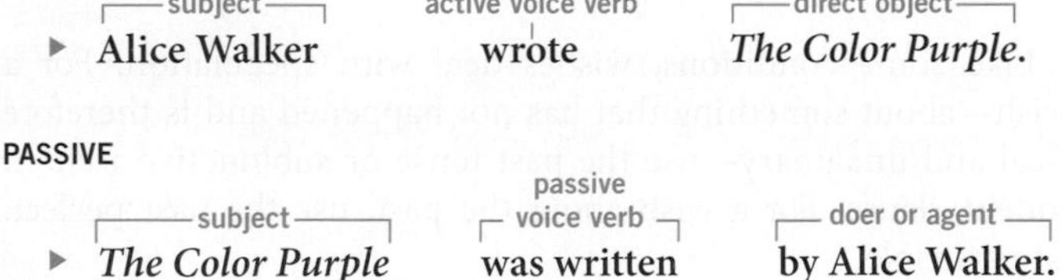

40a How to form the passive voice

The complete verb of a passive voice sentence consists of a form of the verb *be* followed by a past participle.

receiver as subject | verb: *be* + past participle | doer omitted or named after *by*

▸ **The windows *are cleaned* [by someone] every month.**

▸ **The windows *were being cleaned* yesterday afternoon.**

▸ **The windows *will have been cleaned* by the end of the workday.**

Auxiliaries such as *would, can, could, should, may, might,* and *must* can also replace *will* when the meaning demands it.

▸ **The windows *might be cleaned* next month.**

40b When to use the passive voice

Use the passive voice sparingly. A general rule is to use the passive voice only when the doer or agent in your sentence (the person or thing acting) is unknown or is unimportant or when you want to connect the topics of two clauses (see 30a and 40c).

▸ **The pandas are rare. Two of them *will be returned* to the wild.**

▸ **He had a lot of people working for him, maybe sixty, and most of them liked him most of the time. Three of them *will be* seriously *considered* for his job.** —Ellen Goodman, "The Company Man"

Notice how in the first example, the pandas are the topic of the sentences. It doesn't really matter who is returning them to the wild—only that they are being returned.

In scientific writing, the passive voice is often preferred to indicate objective procedures. Scientists and engineers are interested in analyzing data and in performing studies that other researchers can replicate. The individual doing the experiment is therefore relatively unimportant and usually is not the subject of the sentence.

▸ **Sixty volunteers *were given* a placebo while another sixty received the experimental treatment. Participants *were not told* which group they had been assigned to.**

NOTE FOR MULTILINGUAL WRITERS

Passive Voice with Transitive Verbs

Use the passive voice only with verbs that are transitive in English (that is, they can be followed by a direct object). Intransitive verbs such as *happen*, *occur*, and *try* (*to*) are not used in the passive voice.

▸ **The accident ~~was~~ occurred on a deserted street.**

▸ **Morality is an issue that ~~was~~ have tried to explain ~~by~~ many philosophers.**

40c The passive voice as connector

In the following passage, notice how the passive voice (indicated with added italics) preserves the topic chain of *I* subjects (see also 30a):

▸ **I remember to start with that day in Sacramento . . . when I first entered a classroom, able to understand some fifty stray English words. The third of four children, I *had been preceded* to a Roman Catholic school by an older brother and sister.**

—Richard Rodriguez, *Hunger of Memory*

40d Overuse of the passive voice

In the humanities, your writing will generally be clearer and stronger if you name the subject and use verbs in the active voice to explain who is doing what. If you overuse the passive voice, the effect will be heavy and impersonal (see 29a).

Unnecessary passive **He *was alerted* to the danger of using drugs by his doctor and *was persuaded* by her to enroll in a treatment program.**

Revised **His doctor alerted him to the danger of using drugs and persuaded him to enroll in a treatment program.**

41 Subject-Verb Agreement

The principle of agreement means that when you use the present tense of any verb or the past tense of the verb *be* in academic writing, you must make the subject and verb agree in person (first, second, or third) and number (singular or plural): *A baby cries. Babies cry.*

41a Basic principles for an -*s* ending

The ending -*s* is added to both nouns and verbs but for very different reasons.

1. An -*s* ending on a noun is a plural signal: *her brothers* (more than one).
2. An -*s* ending on a verb is a singular signal; -*s* is added to a third person singular verb in the present tense: *Her plumber wears gold jewelry.*

KEY POINTS

Two Key Points about Agreement

1. Follow the "one -*s* rule" in the present tense. Generally, you can put an -*s* on a noun to make it plural, or you can put an -*s* on a verb to make it singular. (But see the irregular forms *is* and *has* in the following table.) Do not add an -*s* to both subject and verb.

   No — **The articles explains the controversy.** [Violates the "one -*s* rule"]

   Possible revisions — **The article explains the controversy.**
   The articles explain the controversy.

2. Do not omit a necessary -*s*.

   ▸ **Whitehead's novel ~~deal~~ deals with issues of race and morality.**

   ▸ **The ~~report~~ reports in the files describe the housing project in detail.**

Most simple present verbs show agreement with an -*s* ending. The verb *be*, however, has three instead of two present tense forms. In addition, *be* is the only verb to show agreement in the past tense, where it has two forms: *were* and the third person singular *was*. The table shows agreement forms for a regular verb and for the three auxiliary verbs *have*, *be*, and *do*.

Subject-Verb Agreement

Base Form	like (regular)	have	be	do
Simple Present: Singular				
First person: I	like	have	am	do
Second person: you	like	have	are	do
Third person: he, she, it	likes	has	is	does
Simple Present: Plural				
First person: we	like	have	are	do
Second person: you	like	have	are	do
Third person: they	like	have	are	do

LANGUAGE AND CULTURE

Issues of Subject-Verb Agreement

Many languages make no change in the verb form to indicate number and person, and several spoken versions of English, such as African American Vernacular (AAV), Caribbean Creole, and London Cockney, do not observe the standard rules of agreement.

- ▶ **AAV: She *have* a lot of work experience.**
- ▶ **Cockney: He *don't* never wear that brown whistle.** [The standard form is *doesn't;* other nonstandard forms in this sentence are *don't never* (a double negative) and *whistle*—short for *whistle and flute,* rhyming slang for *suit.*]

Use authentic forms like these when quoting direct speech; for your formal academic writing, though, follow the subject-verb agreement conventions used in academic English.

41b What to do when words come between the subject and verb

When words separate the subject and verb, find the verb and ask "who?" or "what?" about it to determine the subject. Ignore any intervening words.

- ▶ **The general discussing the attacks looks tired.** [Who looks tired? The subject, *general*, is singular.]
- ▶ **A box containing valuable old books was accidentally tossed into the dumpster.** [What was tossed? The subject, *box*, is singular.]
- ▶ **The government's proposals about preserving the environment cause controversy.** [What things cause controversy? The subject, *proposals*, is plural.]

Do not be confused by intervening words ending in *-s,* such as *always* and *sometimes.* The *-s* ending still must appear on a present tense verb if the subject is singular.

- ▶ **A school play always get**^s **the parents involved.**

Phrases introduced by *as well as, along with, together with,* and *in addition to* that come between the subject and the verb do not change the number of the verb.

▸ **The dog, as well as the two cats, spend most of the day outdoors.**

▸ **The article, together with the books, make a significant contribution to the topic.**

41c Agreement with linking verbs (*be, seem, appear,* etc.)

Linking verbs such as *be, become, look,* and *appear* are followed by what is called a *complement*, and a subject complement should not be confused with a subject (see 35d). Make the verb agree with the subject.

plural subject / plural verb / singular complement

▸ **The drinks *were* the most expensive item on the restaurant bill.**

singular subject / singular verb / plural complement

▸ **The most expensive item on the restaurant bill *was* the drinks.**

▸ **My favorite part of dorm life *has become* the parties.**

▸ **Parties *have become* my favorite part of dorm life.**

41d What to do when the subject follows the verb

When the subject follows the verb in the sentence, you must still make the subject and verb agree.

1. Questions In a question, make the auxiliary verb agree with the subject, which follows the verb.

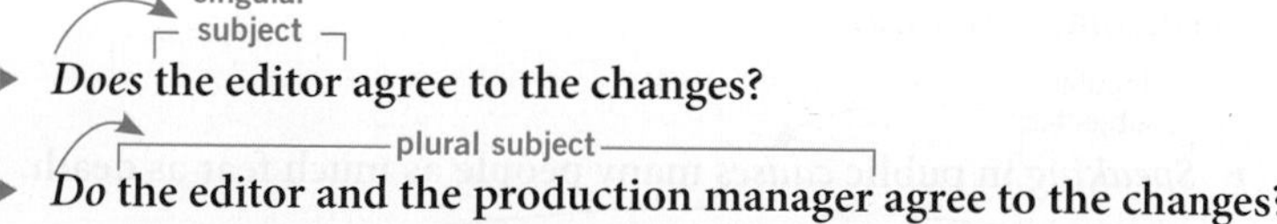

▸ ***Does* the editor agree to the changes?**

▸ ***Do* the editor and the production manager agree to the changes?**

2. Initial *here* or *there* When a sentence begins with *here* or *there*, make the verb agree with the subject.

singular subject

▸ **There *is* a reason to rejoice.**

plural subject

▸ **There *are* many reasons to rejoice.**

However, avoid excessive use of an initial *there* (see 29b): *We have a reason to rejoice.*

NOTE FOR MULTILINGUAL WRITERS

Singular Verb after *It*

It does not follow the same pattern as *here* and *there*. The verb attached to an *it* subject is always singular.

- **It *is* hundreds of miles away.**

---

3. Inverted word order When a sentence begins with a phrase placed before the verb, not with the subject, the verb still agrees with the subject (see also 31d, p. 451).

prepositional phrase — plural verb — plural subject

- **In front of the library sit two stone lions.** [Who or what performs the action of the verb? Two stone lions do.]

41e Eight tricky subjects with singular verbs

1. *Each* and *every* *Each* and *every* may seem to indicate more than one, but grammatically, they are singular words. Use them with a singular verb, even if they are parts of a compound subject (41g) using *and* or *or*.

- ***Each* of the poems *employs* a different rhyme scheme.**
- ***Every* seat in the theater *has* a good view of the stage.**
- ***Every* essay and quiz *counts* in the grade.**

2. *-ing* or infinitive form as subject With a subject beginning with the *-ing* verb form used as a noun (a *gerund*) or with an infinitive, always use a singular verb form.

singular subject

- ***Speaking* in public *causes* many people as much fear as death.**
- ***To fly* across the country with small children *requires* patience and stamina.**

3. Singular nouns ending in *-s* Some names of disciplines that end in *-s* (*economics, physics, politics, mathematics, statistics*) are not plural. Use them and the noun *news* with a singular verb.

- ▸ **The news *has* been bad lately.**

- ▸ **Politics *is* a dirty business.**

4. Phrases of time, money, and weight When the subject is regarded as one unit, use a singular verb.

- ▸ **Fifteen pounds *is* a lot of weight to lose in one month.**

- ▸ **Seven years *was* a long time to spend at college.**

But

- ▸ **Seven years *have* passed.**

5. Uncountable nouns An uncountable noun (such as *furniture, jewelry, equipment, advice, happiness, honesty, information*, and *knowledge*) encompasses all the items in its class. An uncountable noun does not have a plural form and is always followed by a singular verb (58b).

- ▸ **That advice *makes* me nervous.**

- ▸ **The information found in the press *is* not always accurate.**

6. *One of* *One of* is followed by a plural noun (the object of the preposition *of*) and a singular verb form. The verb agrees with the subject *one*.

- ▸ ***One* of her friends *loves* to tango.**

- ▸ ***One* of the reasons for his difficulties *is* that he spends too much money.**

For agreement with *one of* and *the only one of* followed by a relative clause, see 44c, page 549.

7. *The number of/a number of* The phrase *the number of* is followed by a plural noun (the object of the preposition *of*) and a singular verb form.

- ▸ **In the United States, the number of television sets *exceeds* the number of people.**

However, with the phrase *a number of*, meaning "several," use a plural verb.

- ▸ **A number of reasons *are* listed in the letter.**

8. The title of a long work or a word referred to as the word itself Use a singular verb with the title of a long, whole work or a word referred to as the word itself. Use a singular verb even if the title or word is plural in form (see also 50a and 50d).

▸ ***Cats was*** **based on a poem by T. S. Eliot.**

▸ **In her story, the** ***word*** **"dudes"** ***appears*** **five times.**

41f Collective noun as subject

A collective noun names a collection of people or things: *class, government, family, jury, committee, group, couple,* or *team*. If you refer to the group as a whole, use a singular verb.

▸ **The class** ***begins*** **every school day with a song.**

Use a plural verb if you wish to emphasize differences among the individuals or if members of the group are thought of as individuals.

▸ **His family** ***are*** **mostly artists and musicians.**

▸ **The committee** ***are*** **taking on many different jobs around the county.**

If that seems awkward to you, revise the sentence.

▸ **His close relatives** ***are*** **mostly artists and musicians.**

▸ **The members of the committee** ***are*** **taking on many different jobs around the county.**

However, with the collective nouns *police, poor, elderly,* and *young,* always use plural verbs.

▸ **The elderly** ***deserve*** **our respect.**

41g Subjects containing *and*, *or*, or *nor*

Subjects with *and* When a subject consists of two or more parts joined by *and,* treat the subject as plural and use a plural verb.

▸ **His instructor and his advisor** ***want*** **him to change his major.**

However, if the parts of the compound subject refer to a single person or thing, use a singular verb.

singular subject (one person) — singular verb

▸ **The film's director and producer *has* a fearsome temper.**

singular subject — singular verb

▸ **Fish and chips *is* a popular dish in England, but it is no longer served wrapped in newspaper.**

Also use a singular verb with a subject beginning with *each* or *every*.

▸ **Every claim and conclusion *deserves* consideration.**

With *or* or *nor* When the parts of a compound subject are joined by *or* or *nor*, the verb agrees with the part nearer to it.

▸ **Her sister or her parents *look* after her children every Friday.**

▸ **Neither her colleagues nor her boss *remembers* her name.**

41h Indefinite pronouns (*anyone, everybody, nobody,* etc.)

Words that refer to nonspecific people or things (indefinite pronouns) can be tricky. Most of them take a singular verb. Usage may differ in speech and writing, so when you write, it is important to pay attention to the conventions of agreement between subject and verb.

Indefinite pronouns used with a singular verb

someone, somebody, something
anyone, anybody, anything
one, no one, nobody, nothing
everyone, everybody, everything
each, either, neither

▸ **Nobody *knows* the answer.**

▸ **Everyone *agrees* on the author's intention.**

▸ **Everything about the story *makes* me suspicious.**

▸ **Both films are popular; neither *contains* gratuitous violence.**

▸ **Each of the chess games *promises* to be exciting.**

See 42d, page 533, on the personal pronouns to use (*he*? *she*? *they*?) to refer to indefinite pronouns.

A note on *none* and *neither*

None Some writers prefer to use a singular verb after *none* (of) because *none* means "not one": *None of the contestants has smiled.* However, as *The American Heritage Dictionary* (5th ed.) points out, a singular or a plural verb is technically acceptable: *None of the authorities has* (or *have*) *greater tolerance on this point than H. W. Fowler.* Check to see if your instructor prefers the literal singular usage.

Neither The pronoun *neither* is, like *none*, technically singular: *The partners have made a decision; neither wants to change the product.* In informal writing, however, you may come across *neither* with a plural verb, especially when followed by an *of* phrase: *Neither of the novels reveal a polished style.*

41i Quantity words

Some quantity words are singular, and some are plural. Others can be used to indicate either singular or plural depending on the noun they refer to.

Words Expressing Quantity

With Singular Nouns and Verbs	With Plural Nouns and Verbs
much	many
(a) little	(a) few
a great deal (of)	several
a large amount of	a large number of
less	fewer
another	both

See 62c for more on the difference between *few* and *a few*.

- **Much *remains* to be done before our departure.**
- **Much of the machinery *needs* to be repaired.**
- **Many *have* gained from the recent economic swings.**
- **Fewer celebrities than anticipated *have* agreed to attend the gala.**

You will see and hear *less* used in place of *fewer*, especially with numbers ("five items or less"), but in formal writing, use *fewer* to refer to a plural word.

- **More *movies* have been made this year than last, but *fewer have* made a large profit.**

Quantity words used with both singular and plural nouns and verbs The following quantity words take their cue from the number (singular or plural) of the noun they refer to: *all, any, half (of), more, most, no, other, part (of), some.*

▸ You gave me *some information. More is* necessary.

▸ You gave me *some facts. More are* needed.

▸ *All the water is* contaminated.

▸ *All the students look* healthy.

41j Agreement with *this, that, these, those, mine, ours,* etc.

Demonstrative pronouns agree in number with a noun: *this solution, these solutions; that problem, those problems.*

plural

▸ The mayor is planning changes. These will be controversial.

Singular	Plural
this	these
that	those

Possessives such as *mine, his, hers, ours, yours,* and *theirs* can refer to both singular and plural antecedents (see 42d).

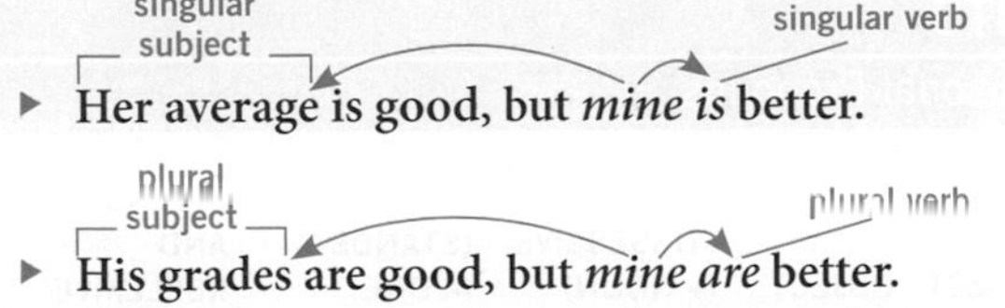

▸ Her average is good, but *mine is* better.

▸ His grades are good, but *mine are* better.

41k Agreement with subject clauses beginning with *what* or other question words

When a clause introduced by *what* or other question words, such as *how, who,* and *why,* functions as the subject of an independent clause, use a third person singular verb in the independent clause.

subject

▸ What you eat in the morning *affects* your mood all day long.

subject
▸ **How the players train *makes* all the difference.**

When the verb is followed by the linking verb *be* and a plural complement, some writers use a plural verb. However, some readers may object.

▸ **What I need *are* black pants and an orange shirt.**

You can avoid the issue by revising the sentence to eliminate the *what* clause.

▸ **I need black pants and an orange shirt.**

42 Pronouns

A pronoun is a word that substitutes for a noun, a noun phrase, or another pronoun.

▸ **Rebecca's headaches are so bad that *they* are affecting *her* ability to function.**

42a Forms of personal pronouns (*I* or *me, he* or *him*?)

Personal pronouns change form to indicate person (first, second, or third), number (singular or plural), and function in a clause.

KEY POINTS

Forms of Personal Pronouns

PERSON	SUBJECT	OBJECT	POSSESSIVE (+ NOUN)	POSSESSIVE (STANDS ALONE)	INTENSIVE AND REFLEXIVE
1st person singular	I	me	my	mine	myself
1st person plural	we	us	our	ours	ourselves
2nd person singular and plural	you	you	your	yours	yourself/ yourselves

3rd person singular	he	him	his	his	himself
	she	her	her	hers	herself
	it	it	its	its [rare]	itself
3rd person plural	they	them	their	theirs	themselves

In a compound subject or compound object with *and*: *I* or *me*; *he* or *him*? In speech, the forms *I* and *me*, *he* and *him*, *she* and *her* are often interchanged even by educated people, but you should take care to edit them in formal writing. To decide which pronoun form to use with a compound subject or compound object, mentally recast the sentence with only one pronoun in the subject or object position.

- **Richard and ~~me~~ ^I play in our school's marching band.** [Drop the words *Richard and*. Then you will have *I play*, not *me play*. Here you need the subject form, *I*.]
- **~~Him~~ ^He and his whole family decided to move to Oregon.** [He decided to move.]
- **~~Her~~ ^She and ~~me~~ ^I tried to solve the problem.** [She tried. I tried.]
- **The teacher invited Stacey and ~~I~~ ^me to join the class.**

  [If the words *Stacey and* are dropped, the sentence would be *The teacher invited me*, not *The teacher invited I*. The object form is needed here. The teacher invited *me*, not "The teacher invited I."]

After a preposition After a preposition, you need an object form.

- **Between you and ~~I~~ ^me, the company is in serious trouble.**
- **Rachid stared at my colleague and ~~I~~ ^me.** [He stared at my colleague. He stared at me.]

After a linking verb In formal academic writing, use the subject form of a personal pronoun after a linking verb, such as *be*, *seem*, *look*, or *appear*.

▸ **Was that Oprah Winfrey? It was *she*.** [Informal: "It was her."]

▸ **It was *they* who hosted the benefit.** [Many writers would revise this sentence to sound less formal: "They were the ones who hosted the benefit" or simply "They hosted the benefit."]

After a verb and before an infinitive Use the object form of a personal pronoun after a verb and before an infinitive. When a sentence has only one object, this principle is easy to apply.

▸ **The dean wanted *him* to lead the procession.**

Difficulties occur with compound objects.

▸ **The dean wanted ~~he and I~~ him and me to lead the procession.**

In appositive phrases and with *we* or *us* before a noun When using a personal pronoun in an appositive phrase (a phrase that gives additional information about a preceding noun), determine whether the noun that the pronoun refers to functions as subject or as object in its own clause.

▸ **The supervisor praised only two employees, Ramón and me.** [She praised me.] (direct object: two employees; appositive phrase: Ramón and me)

▸ **Only two employees, Ramón and I, received a bonus.** [I received a bonus.] (subject: two employees; appositive phrase: Ramón and I)

Similarly, when you consider whether to use *we* or *us* before a noun, use *us* when the pronoun is the direct object of a verb or preposition; use *we* when it is the subject.

▸ **LL Cool J waved to us fans.** (object of preposition: us)

▸ **We fans have decided to form a club.** (subject: We)

In comparisons In comparisons with *than* and *as*, decide when to use the subject or object form of the personal pronoun by mentally completing the meaning of the comparison.

▸ **You have more information about the project than I.** [. . . than I do.]

▸ **Matt and Juanita work in the same office; Matt criticizes his boss more than she.** [. . . more than Juanita does.]

▸ **Matt and Juanita work in the same office; Matt criticizes his boss more than her.** [. . . more than he criticizes Juanita.]

42b Possessive forms of pronouns (*my* or *mine, her* or *hers?*)

Distinguish between adjective and pronoun forms (*her* and *hers*)

▸ **The large room with three windows is *her* office.** [*Her* is an adjective.]

▸ **The office is *hers*.** [*Hers,* the possessive pronoun, can stand alone.]

When a possessive pronoun functions as a subject, the word it refers to (its antecedent) determines singular or plural agreement for the verb (see 41j).

▸ **My purse is leather; hers *is* plastic.** [*purse* is singular; it needs a singular verb.]

▸ **My gloves are black; hers *are* yellow.** [plural antecedent and plural verb]

Note: The word *mine* does not follow the pattern of *hers, theirs, yours,* and *ours.* The form *mines* is nonstandard.

▸ **The little room on the left is *mine*.**

No apostrophe with possessive personal pronouns Even though they are possessive in meaning, the pronouns *yours, ours, theirs, his,* and *hers* should never be spelled with an apostrophe. Use an apostrophe only with the possessive form of a noun.

▸ **That swim cap is *Nancy's*.**

▸ **That is *her* swim cap.**

▸ **That swim cap is *hers*.**

▸ **These books are the *twins'*.** (46c)

▸ **These are *their* books.**

▸ **These books are *theirs*.**

No apostrophe with *its* as a possessive pronoun The word *it's* is not a pronoun; it is the contraction of *it is* or *it has.* An apostrophe is never used with *its*, the possessive form of the pronoun *it* (see also 46f).

- **The paint has lost *its* gloss.**
- ***It's* not as glossy as it used to be.** [It is not as glossy. . . .]

Possessive pronoun before an *-ing* form Generally, use a possessive personal pronoun before an *-ing* verb form used as a noun.

- **I appreciate *your* thinking of me.**
- ***Their* winning the marathon surprised us all.**

Sometimes, the *-ing* form is a participle functioning as an adjective. In that case, the pronoun preceding the *-ing* form should be in the object form.

- **I saw *him* rummaging through the trash.**

Comparisons using possessive forms Note how using *them* in place of *theirs* in the following sentence would change the meaning by comparing suitcases to roommates, not suitcases to suitcases.

- **It's really hard to be roommates with people if your suitcases are much better than *theirs*.** —J. D. Salinger, *The Catcher in the Rye*

Forgetting to use the appropriate possessive form in the next example, too, could create a misunderstanding. Is the writer comparing a house to a person or his house to her house?

- **I like his house more than I like her~~.~~s.**

42c Pronoun reference to a clear antecedent

A pronoun substitutes for a noun, a noun phrase, or a pronoun already mentioned. The word or phrase that a pronoun refers to is known as the pronoun's *antecedent*. Antecedents should always be clear and explicit.

- **Psychiatrist Edward Hallowell, a leading expert on ADD, suspects that some of the greatest minds in history had the condition and that *it* enhanced *their* creativity.**

State a specific antecedent Be sure to give a pronoun such as *they*, *this*, or *it* an explicit antecedent.

No specific antecedent **When Mr. Rivera applied for a loan, they outlined the procedures for him.** [The pronoun *they* lacks an explicit antecedent.]

Revised **When Mr. Rivera applied to bank officials for a loan, *they* outlined the procedures for him.**

When you use a pronoun, make sure it does not refer to a possessive noun or to a noun within a prepositional phrase.

▶ **In ~~George Orwell's~~ "Shooting an Elephant," ~~he~~ George Orwell reports an incident that shows the evil effects of imperialism.** [The pronoun *he* cannot refer to the possessive noun *Orwell's*.]

▶ **~~In the essay by Lance Morrow, it~~ Lance Morrow's essay points out the problems of choosing a name.** [*It* refers to *essay*, which functions as the object of the preposition *in* and therefore cannot function as an antecedent.]

Avoid ambiguous pronoun reference Readers should never be left wondering which *this*, *they*, or *it* is being discussed.

Ambiguous **My husband told my father that he should choose the baby's name.** [Does *he* refer to *husband* or *father*?]

Revised **My husband told my father to choose the baby's name.**

Revised **My husband wanted to choose the baby's name and told my father so.**

42d Making a pronoun agree with its antecedent

A plural antecedent needs a plural pronoun; a singular antecedent needs a singular pronoun.

▶ **Listeners heard *they* could win free tickets. The ninth caller learned *she* was the winner.**

Make a demonstrative pronoun agree with its antecedent The demonstrative pronouns *this* and *that* refer to singular nouns; *these* and *those* refer to plural nouns: *this/that house, these/those houses* (41j).

▶ **He published his autobiography two years ago. This was his first book.** [singular antecedent: autobiography] plural antecedent

▸ **One reviewer praised his honesty and directness. These were qualities he had worked hard to develop.**

Make a pronoun agree with a generalized (generic) antecedent Generic nouns name a class or type of person or object, such as *a student* meaning "all students" or *a company* meaning "any company" or "all companies." Sometimes, writers use *they* to refer to a singular generic noun, but the singular/plural mismatch annoys some readers.

singular antecedent / plural pronoun

Mismatch **When a student is educated, they can go far in the world.**

singular antecedent / singular pronoun

Revised but somewhat stilted **When a student is educated, he or she can go far in the world.**

plural antecedent / plural pronoun

Best **When students are educated, they can go far in the world.**

Increasingly, in advertising, journalism, and informal writing you will see (and you will certainly hear this usage in speech, too) a plural pronoun referring to a singular antecedent, as in the following station wagon advertisement:

▸ **One day *your child* turns sixteen, and you let *them* borrow the keys to the wagon.**

However, in formal academic writing, many readers may still expect a pronoun to agree with its antecedent. Even though usage may be changing, you can avoid problems by making the antecedent plural.

▸ I respect ~~a person~~ *people* who ~~stands~~ *stand* by their word.

Make a pronoun agree with an indefinite pronoun Indefinite pronouns, such as *everyone, somebody, each,* and *nothing* (see the list in 41h), are singular in form. A singular antecedent traditionally needs a singular pronoun to refer to it, but which one: *he, she,* or *he or she*? The *Oxford English Dictionary* points out that for centuries, *they* has often been used "in reference to a singular noun made universal by *every, any, no,* etc., or applicable to one of either sex (= 'he or she')."

Despite the increasingly widespread use of *they,* some readers may still object to it, so you might choose to revise the sentence.

Singular pronoun	***Everyone*** **picked up** ***his*** **assignment and raced off to write** ***his*** **part of the report.** [Sentence needs revision because of the sexist bias.]
Revised but clumsy	***Everyone*** **picked up** ***his or her*** **assignments and raced off to write** ***his or her*** **parts of the report.**
Revised but some may object	***Everyone*** **picked up** ***their assignments*** **and raced off to write** ***their*** **parts of the report.** [The plural pronoun *their* refers to a singular antecedent, *everyone*.]
Probably best	**The lawyers all picked up** ***their*** **assignments and raced off to write** ***their*** **parts of the report.**

Make a pronoun agree with the nearer antecedent when you use *or* or *nor* When an antecedent includes *or* or *nor*, a pronoun agrees with the element that is nearer to it. If one part of the compound is singular and the other part is plural, put the plural antecedent closer to the pronoun and have the pronoun agree with it.

▸ **Either my tutor or my professor has left** ***his*** **wallet on the table.**

▸ **Neither Bill nor the campers could find** ***their*** **soap.**

Make a pronoun agree with a collective noun Use a singular pronoun to refer to a collective noun (*class, family, jury, committee, couple, team*) if you are referring to the group as a whole.

▸ **The jury reached** ***its*** **decision in less than an hour.**

▸ **The committee has not yet completed** ***its*** **report.**

Use a plural pronoun if members of the group named by the collective noun are considered to be acting individually.

▸ **The committee began to cast** ***their*** **ballots in a formal vote.**

42e Gender bias

For many years, the pronoun *he* was used routinely in generic references to unspecified individuals in certain roles or professions, such as student, teacher, doctor, lawyer, and banker, and *she* was used routinely in generic references to individuals in roles such as nurse, secretary, or typist. This usage is now considered sexist language.

Not appropriate **When an accountant learns a foreign language, *he* gains access to an expanded job market.**

To revise such sentences that make general statements about people, roles, and professions, use one of the following methods:

1. Use a plural antecedent plus *they* (see also 32f and 42d). While it is becoming more accepted to use *they* with a singular antecedent to avoid gender bias, it is not yet universally accepted.

   ▸ **When accountants learn a foreign language, *they* gain access to an expanded job market.**

2. Avoid the issue by rewriting the sentence to eliminate the pronoun.

   ▸ **An accountant who learns a foreign language gains access to an expanded job market.**

3. Use a singular antecedent and the phrase *he or she*.

   ▸ **When an accountant learns a foreign language, *he or she* gains access to an expanded job market.**

The problem with option 3 is that awkward and repetitive structures can result when such a sentence is expanded.

▸ **When an accountant learns a foreign language, *he or she* gains access to an expanded job market once *he or she* has decided on *his or her* specialty.**

That's clumsy. Use the *he or she* option only when a sentence is relatively short and does not repeat the pronouns. On the whole, though, revision is usually the best option.

▸ **Accountants who learn a foreign language gain access to expanded job markets once they choose a specialty.**

See also pronoun agreement with indefinite pronouns (42d, p. 533).

42f Consistent point of view

Always write from a consistent perspective. Pronouns can help maintain consistency. Consider the person and number of the pronouns you use:

- Are you emphasizing the perspective of the first person (*I* or *we*)?
- Are you primarily addressing readers as the second person (*you*)?

- Are you, as is most common in formal academic writing, writing about the third person (*he, she, it, one,* or *they*)?

Avoid confusing readers by switching from one perspective to another.

Inconsistent **The company decided to promote only three midlevel managers. *You* had to have worked there for ten years to qualify.**

Revised **The company decided to promote only three midlevel managers. *The employees* had to have worked there for ten years to qualify.**

42g The use of the pronoun *you*

In formal writing, do not use the pronoun *you* when you mean "people generally." Use *you* only to address readers directly and to give instructions.

Not appropriate **Credit card companies should educate students about how to handle credit. *You* should not have to find out the problems the hard way.** [A reader addressed directly in this way might think, "Who, me? I don't need to be educated about credit, and I have no problems."]

Appropriate **Turn to the next page, where *you* will find an excerpt from Edith Wharton's novel that will help *you* appreciate the accuracy of the details in this film.**

Edit uses of *you* if you are making a generalization about a group or if using *you* entails a switch from the third person.

▸ **While growing up, ~~you~~ [teenagers] face arguments with ~~your~~ [their] parents.**

▸ **It doesn't matter if young professionals are avid music admirers or comedy fans since ~~you~~ [they] can find anything ~~you~~ [they] want in the city.**

42h Intensive and reflexive pronouns

Intensive pronouns emphasize a previously mentioned noun or pronoun. Reflexive pronouns identify a previously mentioned noun or pronoun as the person or thing receiving the action (see the Key Points box in 42a).

Intensive **The chancellor *himself* appeared at the gates.**

Reflexive **He introduced *himself*.**

Do not use an intensive pronoun in place of a personal pronoun in a compound subject:

▸ **Joe and ~~myself~~ I will design the brochure.**

Forms such as *hisself, theirself,* and *theirselves* occur in spoken dialects but are not Standard English.

42i *Who/whom, whoever/whomever*

In all formal writing situations, distinguish between the subject and object forms of the pronouns used to form questions (interrogative pronouns) or to introduce a dependent noun clause.

Subject	Object
who	whom (or informally, *who*)
whoever	whomever

In questions In a question, ask yourself whether the pronoun is the subject of its clause or the object of the verb. Test the pronoun's function by rephrasing the question as a statement, substituting a personal pronoun for *who* or *whom.*

▸ **Who wrote that fascinating book?** [*He* wrote that fascinating book. Subject: use *who.*]

▸ **Whoever could have written it?** [*She* could have written it. Subject: use *whoever.*]

▸ **Who[m] were they describing?** [*They* were describing *him.* Object: *whom* (formal), though *who* is common in such contexts both in speech and in writing.]

When you are introducing a dependent clause with a pronoun, determine whether to use the subject or object form by examining the pronoun's function in the clause. Ignore expressions such as *I think* or *I know* when they follow the pronoun; they have no effect on the form of the pronoun.

▸ **They want to know who runs the business.** [who: subject of clause]

▸ **They want to know who I think runs the business.** [who: subject of clause (who runs the business)] object of *to* (the manager reports to him or her)

▶ **They want to know whom the manager reports to.**

subject of clause

▶ **I will hire whoever is qualified.**

object of *recommends*

▶ **I will hire whomever my boss recommends.**

For uses of *who* and *whom* in relative clauses, see 44a.

43 Adjectives and Adverbs

Adjectives describe, or modify, nouns or pronouns. They do not add -*s* or change form to reflect number or gender. For the order of adjectives, see 60g.

▶ **A recent article in the journal *Nature* discussed the *toxic* effects of sugar on our health.**

▶ **The director tried a *different* approach to a documentary.**

▶ **The depiction of rural life is *accurate*.**

▶ **The reporter keeps her desk *tidy*.**

● NOTE FOR MULTILINGUAL WRITERS

No Plural Form for Adjectives

Do not add -*s* to an adjective that modifies a plural noun.

▶ **Only *bilinguals* candidates will be interviewed for the job.**

Adverbs modify verbs, adjectives, and other adverbs, as well as whole clauses.

▶ **The financial analyst settled down *comfortably* in her new job.**

▶ **The patient is demanding a *theoretically* impossible treatment.**

▸ *Inevitably*, **the projector failed five minutes before the start of our presentation.**

43a Forms of adjectives and adverbs

No single rule indicates the correct form of all adjectives and adverbs.

Adverb: adjective + *-ly* Many adverbs are formed by adding *-ly* to an adjective: *soft/softly; intelligent/intelligently*. Sometimes, when *-ly* is added, a spelling change occurs: *easy/easily; terrible/terribly*.

Adjectives ending in *-ic* To form an adverb from an adjective ending in *-ic*, add *-ally* (*basic/basically; artistic/artistically*), except for *public*, whose adverb form is *publicly*.

Adjectives ending in *-ly* Some adjectives, such as *friendly, lovely, timely,* and *masterly*, already end in *-ly* and have no distinctive adverb form.

adjective

▸ **She is a friendly person.**

adverbial phrase

▸ **She spoke to me in a friendly way.**

Irregular adverb forms Certain adjectives do not add *-ly* to form an adverb:

Adjective	Adverb
good	well
fast	fast
hard	hard

adjective

▸ **He is a hard worker.**

adverb

▸ **He works hard.** [*Hardly* is not the adverb form of *hard*. Rather, it means "barely," "scarcely," or "almost not at all": *I could* hardly *breathe in that stuffy room.*]

Note: *Well* can also function as an adjective, meaning "healthy" or "satisfactory": *A* well *baby smiles often. She feels* well.

43b When to use adjectives and adverbs

In speech, adjectives (particularly, *good, bad,* and *real*) are often used to modify verbs, adjectives, or adverbs. This is nonstandard usage. Use an adverb to modify a verb or an adverb.

- **The webmaster fixed the link ~~good~~ well.**
- **The chorus sings ~~real good~~ really well.**
- **She sings ~~nice~~ nicely.**
- **They dance ~~bad~~ badly.**

43c Adjectives after linking verbs

After linking verbs (*be, seem, appear, become*), use an adjective to modify the subject.

- **Sharon Olds's poems are *lyrical.***
- **The book seems *repetitive.***

Some verbs (*appear, look, feel, smell, taste*) are sometimes used as linking verbs and other times as action verbs. If the modifier tells about the subject, use an adjective. If the modifier tells about the action of the verb, use an adverb.

Adjective **The analyst looks *confident* in her new job.**

Adverb **The lawyer looked *confidently* at all the assembled partners.**

Adjective **The server feels *bad.***

The steak smells *bad.*

Adverb **The chef smelled the lobster *appreciatively.***

Note: Use a hyphen to connect two words used as an adjective when they appear before a noun. Do not use a hyphen when the words follow a linking verb with no noun complement.

▸ **Wynton Marsalis is a *well-known* trumpet player.**

▸ **Wynton Marsalis is *well known*.**

43d Compound adjectives

A compound adjective consists of two or more words used as a unit to describe a noun. Many compound adjectives contain the past participle *-ed* verb form: *flat-footed, barrel-chested, broad-shouldered, old-fashioned, well-dressed, left-handed*. Note the form when a compound adjective is used before a noun: hyphen, past participle (*-ed*) form where necessary, and no noun plural (*-s*) ending.

▸ **They have a *five-year-old* daughter.** [Their daughter is five years old.]

▸ **She gave me a *five-dollar* bill.** [She gave me five dollars.]

▸ **The actress was accompanied by a *well-dressed* older man.** [The man was dressed well.]

For more on hyphenation with compound adjectives, see 54b.

43e Position of adverbs

An adverb can be placed in various positions in a sentence.

▸ ***Enthusiastically*, she ate the sushi.**

▸ **She *enthusiastically* ate the sushi.**

▸ **She ate the sushi *enthusiastically*.**

NOTE FOR MULTILINGUAL WRITERS

Adverb Placement

Do not place an adverb between a verb and a short direct object (60b).

▸ **She ate *enthusiastically* the sushi.**

Put adverbs that show frequency (*always, usually, frequently, often, sometimes, seldom, rarely, never*) in one of four positions:

1. at the beginning of a sentence

▸ ***Sometimes*, he rides his bike to work instead of driving.**

When *never, seldom*, or *rarely* occurs at the beginning of the sentence, word order is inverted (see also 41d).

▸ ***Never* will I let that happen.**

2. between the subject and the main verb

▶ **They *always* arrive half an hour late.**

3. after a form of *be* or any auxiliary verb (such as *do, have, can, will, must*)

▶ **The writing center is *always* closed on Saturdays.**

▶ **The tutors are *seldom* late for training.**

▶ **There has *never* been an available computer during exam week.**

4. in the final position

▶ **Amira checks her e-mail *frequently*.**

Note: Don't place the adverb *never* in the final position.

43f Conjunctive adverbs (*however, therefore,* etc.)

There are two important points to remember about conjunctive adverbs such as *however, therefore,* and *moreover*.

1. When a conjunctive adverb occurs in the middle of a clause, set it off with commas.

▶ **The mayor's course of action has, therefore, been severely criticized.**

2. When it occurs between independent clauses, use a semicolon to end the first clause and put a comma after the adverb.

▶ **The hearings were contentious; however, the Supreme Court justice was approved.**

See also 2f, 30b, 37c, and 45e.

43g No double negatives

Adverbs like *hardly, scarcely,* and *barely* are considered negatives, and the contraction *-n't* stands for the adverb *not*. Some languages and dialects allow the use of more than one negative to emphasize an idea, but the standard form is for only one negative in a clause. Avoid double negatives.

Double negative **We *don't* have *no* excuses.**

Revised **We *don't* have *any* excuses. [or] We have *no* excuses.**

Double **She did*n't* say *nothing*.**

Revised **She did*n't* say *anything*. [or] She said *nothing*.**

Double negative **City residents ca*n't hardly* afford the sales tax.**

Revised **City residents can *hardly* afford the sales tax.**

43h Comparative and superlative forms of adjectives and adverbs

Adjectives and adverbs have three forms: positive, comparative, and superlative. Use the comparative form when comparing two people, places, things, or ideas; use the superlative form when comparing more than two.

Regular forms Add the ending *-er* (or just *-r* for an adjective already ending in *-e,* such as *feeble*) to form the comparative and *-(e)st* to form the superlative of both short adjectives (those that have one syllable or those that have two syllables and end in *-y* or *-le*) and one-syllable adverbs. (Change *-y* to *-i* if *-y* is preceded by a consonant: *icy, icier, iciest.*) Generally, a superlative form is preceded by *the* (*the shortest distance*).

Positive	Comparative (Comparing two)	Superlative (Comparing more than two)
short	shorter	shortest
pretty	prettier	prettiest
simple	simpler	simplest
fast	faster	fastest

With longer adjectives and with adverbs ending in *-ly,* use *more* (for the comparative) and *most* (for the superlative). Note that *less* (comparative) and *least* (superlative) are used with adjectives of any length (*less bright, least bright; less effective, least effective*).

Positive	Comparative	Superlative
intelligent	more intelligent	most intelligent
carefully	more carefully	most carefully
dangerous	less dangerous	least dangerous

If you cannot decide whether to use *-er/-est* or *more/most*, consult a dictionary. If there is an *-er/-est* form, the dictionary will say so.

Note: Do not use the *-er* form along with *more* or the *-est* form along with *most*.

▸ **The pizza from the store is ~~more~~ better than the pizza we make at home.**

▸ **Boris is the ~~most~~ fittest person I know.**

Irregular forms The following common adjectives and adverbs have irregular comparative and superlative forms:

Positive	Comparative	Superlative
good	better	best
bad	worse	worst
much/many	more	most
little	less	least
well	better	best
badly	worse	worst

***Than* with comparative forms** To compare two people, places, things, or ideas, use the comparative form and the word *than*. If you use a comparative form in your sentence, you need the word *than* to let readers know what items you are comparing.

▸ **This course of action is more efficient~~.~~** ^than the previous one.^

Comparative forms are also used without *than* in an idiomatic way.

▸ **The *longer* the wait, the *more anxious* she becomes.**

▸ **The *more*, the *merrier*.**

Absolute adjectives Do not use comparative and superlative forms of adjectives that imply absolutes: *complete, empty, full, equal, perfect, priceless,* or *unique*. In addition, do not add intensifying adverbs such as *very, totally, completely,* or *absolutely* to these adjectives. To say that something is "perfect" implies an absolute rather than something measured in degrees.

▸ **He has ~~the most~~** ^a^ **perfect view of the ocean.**

▸ **They bought a ~~totally~~ unique quilt at an auction.**

43i Faulty or incomplete comparisons

Make sure that you state clearly what items you are comparing. Some faulty comparisons can give readers the wrong idea (see 38h and 42b).

Incomplete **He likes the parrot better than his wife.**

Do you really want to suggest that he prefers the parrot to his wife? If not, clarify the comparison by completing the second clause.

Revised **He likes the parrot better *than his wife does.***

Edit sentences like the following:

▶ **In winter, New York's weather is colder than London.** ['s inserted after "London"] [Compare the weather in both places, not the weather in New York and the city of London.]

▶ **Williams's poem gives a more objective depiction of the painting than Auden.** ['s inserted after "Auden"] [To compare Williams's poem with Auden's poem, you need to include an apostrophe and *-s*; otherwise, you compare a poem to the poet W. H. Auden.]

Comparisons must also be complete. If you say that something is "more efficient," readers wonder, "More efficient than what?"

▶ **Didion shows us a home that makes her feel more tied to her roots.** [inserted after "roots": than her home in Los Angeles does] [Include the other part of the comparison.]

44 Relative Clauses and Relative Pronouns (*who, whom, whose, which, that*, etc.)

A relative clause relates to an antecedent in a nearby clause.

▶ **The girl *who* can't dance says the band can't play.** [label: relative clause] —Yiddish proverb

44a Relative pronouns

When you are deciding whether to use *who, whom, which,* or *that*, use the following table as a guide. Your choice of pronoun will depend on these three factors:

1. the function of the relative pronoun in its clause
2. whether the relative pronoun refers to a human or nonhuman antecedent
3. whether the clause is restrictive or nonrestrictive (see 44b for this distinction)

Relative Pronouns and Antecedents

	Function of Relative Pronoun		
Antecedent	**Subject**	**Object**	**Possessive**
Human antecedent	*who*	*whom* (can be omitted)	*whose*
Nonhuman antecedent	*that* or *which* (see 44b)	*that* (can be omitted) or *which* (see 44b)	*of which* (formal); *whose* (informal)

Examples: Human

Subject	**The teachers *who* challenge us are the ones we remember.**
Object	**The players [*whom*] the spectators boo often end up in the minor leagues.**
Possessive	**Spectators *whose* cell phones ring will be asked to leave.**

Examples: Nonhuman

Subject	**The dog *that* kept barking all night drove the neighbors crazy.**
Object	**They stayed at a hotel [*that*] their friends had recommended.**
Possessive	**We stayed in a picturesque town the name *of which* I can't remember.** **We stayed in a picturesque town *whose* name I can't remember.**

Watch out! Do not rename the subject in the independent clause.

▸ **The teachers who challenge us ~~they~~ are the ones we remember.**

Remember that an inserted phrase does not affect the function of a pronoun.

▸ **Let's reward contestants who we realize have not been coached.**

Do not use *what* as a relative pronoun.

- **The deal ~~what~~ that the CEO was trying to make turned out to be crooked.**

44b Restrictive and nonrestrictive relative clauses

The two types of relative clauses, restrictive and nonrestrictive, fulfill different functions and need different punctuation (45d).

Restrictive **The people *who live in the apartment above mine* make a lot of noise at night.**

Nonrestrictive **The Sullivans, *who live in the apartment above mine,* make a lot of noise at night.**

Restrictive relative clause A restrictive relative clause provides information that is essential for identifying the antecedent and restricting its scope.

Features

The clause is not set off with commas. It is needed to understand what the subject is.

An object relative pronoun can be omitted.

That (rather than *which*) is used for reference to nonhuman antecedents.

- **The teachers *who challenge us* are the ones we remember.** [The independent clause—"The teachers are the ones we remember"—leads us to ask, "Which teachers?" The relative clause provides information that is essential to completing the meaning of the subject; it restricts the meaning from "all teachers" to "the teachers who challenge us."]

- **The book [*that*] *you gave me* was fascinating.** [The relative pronoun *that* is the direct object in its clause ("You gave me the book") and can be omitted.]

Nonrestrictive relative clause A nonrestrictive relative clause provides information that merely adds descriptive information.

Features

The antecedent is a unique, designated person or thing.

The clause is set off by commas; it provides additional nonessential information, a kind of aside. It could be omitted, and the sentence would make sense without it.

Which (not *that*) is used to refer to a nonhuman antecedent.

An object relative pronoun cannot be omitted.

▸ **The book *War and Peace*, which you gave me, was fascinating.** [The independent clause—"The book *War and Peace* was fascinating"—does not promote further questions, such as "Which book?" The information in the relative clause ("which you gave me") is almost an aside and not essential for understanding the independent clause.]

A nonrestrictive relative clause with a quantity word Relative clauses beginning with a quantity word such as *some, none, many, much, most*, or *one* followed by *of which* or *of whom* are always nonrestrictive.

▸ **They selected five candidates, *one of whom* would get the job.**

▸ **The report mentioned five names, *none of which* I recognized.**

NOTE FOR MULTILINGUAL WRITERS

Relative versus Personal Pronouns

Do not add a personal pronoun in addition to the relative pronoun.

most of which

▸ **We harvested fifty pounds of tomatoes, ~~which most of them~~ we plan to give away.**

44c Agreement of verb with relative pronoun

Determine subject-verb agreement within a relative clause by asking whether the antecedent of a subject relative pronoun is singular or plural.

relative clause

▸ **The book that *is* at the top of the bestseller list gives advice about health.** [The singular noun *book* is the antecedent of *that*, the subject of the singular verb *is* in the relative clause.]

relative clause

▸ **The books that *are* at the top of the bestseller list give advice about health, success, and making money.** [The plural noun *books* is the antecedent of *that*, the subject of the plural verb *are* in the relative clause.]

Note: The phrase *one of* is followed by a plural noun phrase. However, the verb can be singular or plural depending on the meaning.

relative clause

- **Juan is one of the employees who *work* long hours.** [Several employees work long hours. Juan is one of them. The plural noun *employees* is the antecedent of *who*, the subject of the plural verb *work* in the relative clause.]

antecedent — singular verb

- **Juan is the only one of the employees who *works* long hours.** [Only Juan works long hours.]

44d Relative clauses with prepositions

When a relative clause contains a relative pronoun within a prepositional phrase, do not omit the preposition. Keep in mind these three points:

1. Directly after the preposition, use *whom* or *which*, never *that.*

relative clause

- **The family *to whom* the package is addressed no longer lives here.**

2. In a restrictive clause (44b), if you place the preposition after the verb, use *that* (or you can omit *that*), but do not use *whom* or *which.*

[that]

- **The security measures ~~which~~ the mayor had insisted on made him unpopular.**

3. Do not add an extra personal pronoun object after the preposition at the end of the relative clause.

- **The theater company [that] they are devoted to ~~it~~ has produced six new plays this season.**

44e Position of relative clause

To avoid ambiguity, place a relative clause as close as possible to its antecedent (see also 38b on misplaced modifiers).

Ambiguous **He searched for the notebook all over the house that his friend had forgotten.** [Had his friend forgotten the house?]

Revised **He searched all over the house for the notebook that his friend had forgotten.**

44f *Where* and *when* as relative pronouns

When you refer to actual or metaphoric places and times, you can use *where* to replace *in which, at which,* or *to which,* and you can use *when* to replace *at which, in which,* or *on which.* Do not use a preposition with *where* or *when.*

▶ **The day on which I was born was cold and snowy.**

▶ **The day *when* I was born was cold and snowy.**

▶ **The village in which he was born honored him last year.**

▶ **The village *where* he was born honored him last year.**

Use *where* or *when* only if actual time or physical location is involved.

▶ **The influence of the Sapir-Whorf hypothesis, ~~where~~ according to which behavior is regarded as influenced by language, has declined.**

Exercises on Common Sentence Problems

EXERCISE 1 Identify the subject and predicate in a simple sentence. 35d

In each of the following sentences, underline the complete subject once and underline the predicate twice. Then write *S* over the simple subject and *V* over the verb. Remember that the verb may consist of more than one word and that sentences can have more than one subject or verb.

Example Many people (S) in the United States carry (V) too much credit-card debt.

1. Most experts consider some types of debt, such as a mortgage, financially necessary.
2. However, credit-card debt never benefits an individual's long-term financial goals.
3. Today, even college students without jobs or credit records can usually acquire credit cards easily.
4. Unfortunately, many students charge expensive purchases and pay only the minimum balance on their cards every month.
5. Graduating from college with a large credit-card debt can severely limit a person's opportunities.

EXERCISE 2 Identify and correct phrase fragments. 36a–36e

In each of the following items, identify any phrase fragment, and correct it either by attaching it to a nearby independent clause or by changing it to an independent clause. Some sentences may be correct.

Example American popular music has had an enthusiastic following around the world~~. Since~~ since the early days of rock and roll.

1. Every country has its own musical styles. Based on the traditional music of its people.
2. Having its own tradition as the birthplace of jazz, blues, and rock music. The United States has long been one of the world's leading exporters of popular music.
3. In spite of enjoying enormous popularity in their own countries. Many performers from Europe, South America, Africa, and Asia have had a hard time attracting American fans.
4. Some American musicians have championed their favorite artists from abroad. Examples include the hip-hop artist Jay-Z's collaboration with South Asian artist Punjabi MC on the song "Beware of the Boys" and Beck's tribute to the late French singer-songwriter Serge Gainsbourg.

5. Although some US music fans pay attention to foreign musical styles, most Americans buy the music they know from American top-40 radio and MTV. Songs also loved by fans around the world for sounding typically American.
6. However, not all Americans are native English speakers. Listening exclusively to English-language music.
7. Latin music has had some crossover success in the United States. Propelled, at least at first, by the high percentage of Spanish-speaking people in this country.
8. On American radio and television today, some of the most popular male acts are Latin pop stars. Singing sensations such as Marc Anthony, Ricky Martin, and Enrique Iglesias.
9. These singers are considered crossover artists because they have achieved mainstream success by singing in English. After making earlier recordings in Spanish.
10. Perhaps there will be a time when artists can have big hits with songs sung in a foreign language. At present, however, singing in English is almost always required for being successful in America.

EXERCISE 3 Identify run-on sentences and comma splices. 37a, 37b

For each of the following items, write *CS* on the line before the sentence if it is a comma splice, *RO* if it is a run-on sentence, and *OK* if the sentence is correctly written.

Example CS Many consumers want to buy American cars, unfortunately, choosing an American car is not as easy as it sounds.

1. ___ Often a car's parts are made in one country and assembled in another, can the car be considered American if the whole thing is not manufactured in this country?
2. ___ Sometimes car companies manufacture parts in the United States and also put cars together here however, these companies may have their headquarters in Japan.
3. ___ People who buy cars sold by Ford, an automaker whose name implies "made in the United States" to many Americans, may not know that the vehicles may have been assembled in Mexico.
4. ___ On the other hand, most Honda Accords are made in Ohio in fact, the Honda Corporation now manufactures more cars in the United States than in Japan.
5. ___ As several American auto manufacturers have become part of multinational corporations, globalization has made "buying American" increasingly difficult, consumers can no longer simply rely on the make of a car to determine its country of origin.

EXERCISE 4 Avoid a run-on or comma splice when using a transition. 37c

Correct the run-ons and comma splices in each of the following sentences by changing punctuation and capitalization.

Example If you have a proper place for everything in your house or apartment, you may be able to turn that knack into a profit; ~~,~~ that is, you may want to consider becoming a professional organizer.

1. Many people need help making the most of their space and eliminating clutter from their homes and offices in fact the demand is so great that the National Association of Professional Organizers (NAPO) now has 4,200 members in thirteen countries.
2. Many of NAPO's clients are businesspeople, however, organizers also create plans for homemakers, retired adults, hobbyists, and school-age children.
3. Paper is the major source of clutter in most homes, says organizer Jennifer Hunter, incidentally, Hunter's business has the humorous name of "Find Your Floor."
4. Disorganized people often waste time searching for keys, documents, and other items they've misplaced as a result, organizers help their clients save not only space but time.
5. Getting organized can be a matter of life and death accordingly, for several years NAPO has joined with the US Department of Homeland Security to educate the public about how households can prepare for emergencies.

EXERCISE 5 Correct sentence "tangles." 38a

In each of the following items, correct mixed constructions and faulty comparisons.

Example Adopting ~~By adopting~~ the poetic techniques popular in colonial America enabled Phillis Wheatley to find an audience for her writings.

1. Phillis Wheatley's education, which was remarkable mainly because she received one, a rare luxury for a slave girl in the American colonies.
2. Wheatley, kidnapped from her homeland and sold into slavery when she was about seven, an experience that must have been traumatic.
3. By learning to read and write gave Phillis an opportunity to demonstrate her aptitude for poetry.
4. Like Alexander Pope, iambic pentameter couplets were Phillis Wheatley's preferred poetic form.
5. Publishing a book of poems, Phillis Wheatley, becoming famous partly because she was an African slave who could compete as a poet with well-educated white men.

6. Her work, poems in a very formal eighteenth-century style that found aristocratic admirers in America and England.
7. With the deaths of Mr. and Mrs. Wheatley, when Phillis was in her twenties, left her free but also penniless.
8. Like Zora Neale Hurston in the twentieth century, an impoverished, lonely death followed a loss of public interest in Wheatley's writings, but scholars discovered her work posthumously and realized her contribution to American literature.

EXERCISE 6 Correct inappropriate shifts: mood, pronoun person and number, and direct and indirect quotations. 38d

On the line after each of the following sentences, identify inappropriate shifts in mood by writing *M*, inappropriate shifts in pronoun person by writing *PP*, inappropriate shifts in pronoun number by writing *PN*, and inappropriate shifts in direct and indirect quotations by writing *Q*. Then revise each inappropriate shift.

Example Sharks do occasionally attack swimmers, but ~~you~~ people are more likely to be killed by a falling television than by a shark bite. PP

1. When a tourist in Florida wants an underwater adventure, you can swim in the ocean with sharks.___
2. A series of shark attacks on the east coast of the United States made Florida Fish and Wildlife Conservation commissioners ask whether swimmers were being too careless or were tourist attractions that feature swimming with sharks the cause of the problem? ___
3. When a tour operator puts bait in the water before a shark swim, they may be teaching sharks to associate people with food. ___
4. If sharks were fed too frequently by human beings, the commissioners wondered, will the big fish be more likely to endanger swimmers? ___
5. The curator of the International Shark Attack File told commissioners that the feeding probably didn't contribute to the attacks and would they tell people more about the good behavior of sharks. ___
6. The shark attacks shocked people around the country, and you heard about the attacks constantly at the beach and in coastal regions. ___
7. A shark can seem ferocious, but they are often in more danger from humans than humans are from the sharks. ___
8. People should not be frightened by the shark's torpedo-like body, scaly skin, and sharp teeth. Try to learn about the shark's habits instead. ___
9. Some scientists believe that if a person studies sharks, they will understand ocean ecosystems better. ___
10. Some species of sharks have become endangered because so many people like the taste of it. ___

EXERCISE 7 Use the correct form of regular and irregular verbs. 39a

Replace any incorrect verb forms with the correct form in the following sentences. Some sentences may be correct as written.

Example Kenrick ~~broken~~ ^broke his elbow when he ~~fall~~ ^fell off his skateboard.

1. I lent Miranda my *Divergent* books, and she red all three of them.
2. Sacha ment to leave the party early.
3. Sir William Wallace led the Scots in their rebellion against English rule.
4. Surgeons were pleased that the tumor had shrunken considerably.
5. Some of the campers were bitten by snakes or stang by bees.

EXERCISE 8 Use auxiliary verbs correctly. 39c

Revise the following two paragraphs to eliminate errors in auxiliary verbs or the verb forms following auxiliaries. Some sentences may be correct.

Example Syria ~~be~~ ^is located north of Jordan.

Paragraph 1

We living in an era when antibiotics and other antimicrobial medicines can be use to treat diseases that just a few decades ago would of been fatal. Nevertheless, the world health community is still concern about the rise of "superbugs"—microorganisms that have develop resistance to the medications that are most commonly prescribe to treat them. Antimicrobial resistance may occur when medicines are used inappropriately: for example, a tuberculosis patient might of taken substandard doses of a medication or fail to finish a prescribed course of treatment. Superbugs must become a worldwide health priority, because a resistant infection can spread uncontrollably, imposing huge costs on individuals and society. On April 7, World Health Day, the World Health Organization will calls for a greater global commitment to educating people about the correct use of antimicrobials so that these drugs will continues to be effective.

Paragraph 2

Todd's Market in Silverlake, California, has became slightly less friendly now that cashiers have been instruct not to refer to customers by the name printed on the customers' credit cards. One shopper complained that a man who had been standen behind her in line followed her out of the store and used her first name to try to strike up a conversation. Cashiers can see the name of any shopper who pays with a debit or credit card, and the store manager had instruct cashiers to use a customer's name in order to personalize the shopping experience and make a good impression. The woman in the Silverlake incident was not harm, but she did felt worried enough to tell the company it should discontinued the practice. "When someone uses your name, you think they know you, and you let down your guard," said the woman, who preferred to remain anonymous. "I'm lucky," she added, noting that the situation could of ended differently. Todd's Market has announce that although cashiers will no longer say aloud the name on a credit card, they will continue to wish departing customers a good day.

EXERCISE 9 Use present tenses correctly. 39e

In each of the following sentences, correct any errors in the use of present tense verb forms. Some sentences may be correct.

do observe

Example What ~~did~~ babies ~~observed~~ when they look at faces?

1. Within a few hours of birth, newborn babies are showing a preference for looking at human faces.
2. Cognitive psychologists determine what has interested babies by measuring how long they look at certain patterns or objects.
3. Recent studies have shown that babies' brains have been forming the ability to differentiate faces by the time the babies are a few months old.
4. Scientists have not yet come to an agreement on whether babies are born with the ability to recognize faces or whether they are simply born with a preference for certain shapes and contours.
5. Scientific debate on the subject is raging, but as further studies will be completed, our understanding of how humans learn face recognition will continue to grow.

EXERCISE 10 Identify active and passive voices. 40a–40d

In each of the following sentences, write *P* on the line before each sentence that is in the passive voice and *A* before each sentence that is in the active voice. Then rewrite each passive voice sentence as active whenever it is possible or advisable to do so, and underline the verb that you changed.

Each acre of the fertile rice fields of southern China yields more

Example _P_ ~~More~~ than a thousand pounds of rice. ~~is yielded by each acre of fertile rice fields of southern China.~~

1. ___ The sticky rice that brings the highest prices in China is often attacked by rice blast, a fungus that destroys the rice crop.
2. ___ A farmer in Yunnan province discovered that he could nearly eliminate rice blast by planting alternating rows of sticky rice and long-grain rice.
3. ___ The technique of alternating rows of rice was then adopted widely.
4. ___ The application of expensive and toxic fungicides that had been used to fight the rice blast was discontinued by most farmers.
5. ___ Healthier fields, bigger rice yields, and more money for the farmers were subsequently produced by this low-tech, environmentally sound agricultural method.

EXERCISES

EXERCISE 11 Make subjects and verbs agree, and identify linking verbs. 41c

In the following passage, underline the subject in each independent clause. Then correct any errors in subject-verb agreement. Write *LV* over any linking verbs.

Example There ~~is~~ are many security questions involved in cryptography.

Do the government have the right to keep certain kinds of information out of the hands of the public? There is no easy answers to this question. When the science of cryptography was being developed, the National Security Agency (NSA) wanted to restrict access to powerful, unbreakable codes. After all, using codes are one way that a government keeps information from its enemies, and breaking codes allows a government to find out what its enemies are planning. NSA agents worried that unbreakable codes would allow enemies of the United States to conceal their activities from US intelligence. Cryptographers won the right to develop and distribute their new codes to the general public, and unbreakable codes have certainly been a boon to the computer science and communications industries. Does these codes also hamper efforts to discover what terrorists are doing? Probably, say cryptographers. However, technologies that scientists decide not to develop out of fear of the results is a potential danger: if someone else develops these technologies, they can be used against anyone who has not considered their potential. There is dangers in cryptography, but perhaps there is even more problems in avoiding the issue. Somewhere in the future is the answers to these and other urgent security questions.

EXERCISE 12 Make the subject and the verb agree when the subject follows the verb. 41d

Correct the subject-verb agreement in the following sentences. Some sentences may be correct as written.

Example ~~Do~~ Does every civilization have some kind of horticulture?

1. At the US National Arboretum is the miniature trees that are called *bonsai* in Japanese.
2. There is three pavilions where visitors can view specimens from Japan, China, and several other Asian countries.
3. On display in the gardens and pavilions are approximately 150 perfect miniature trees.
4. For example, there are a Japanese white pine that was presented to the people of the United States in celebration of the US bicentennial in 1976.
5. It are hundreds of years old.
6. In the Special Exhibits Wing is seasonal displays of bonsai, flower arrangements, stones, and wood block prints.

EXERCISE 13 Correct the subject-verb agreement in sentences with indefinite pronouns (*anyone*, *nobody*, etc.). 41h

Correct the following sentences so that the verb agrees with the subject in number. Some sentences may be correct as written.

Example Nobody ~~have~~ ^has^ to be afraid to sing in public.

1. Do everybody have the ability to sing?
2. Not everyone are born with great natural talent.
3. However, most voice teachers believe no one has to avoid singing.
4. The key is to find the range of notes in which someone feel most comfortable.
5. Somebody who sing professionally probably have a wide range.
6. Each of us amateurs need a range of only fifteen notes to sing most songs.

EXERCISE 14 Use the correct form of personal pronouns. 42a

In the following passage, correct any errors in the form of personal pronouns.

Example Although Marie and Pierre Curie made important scientific discoveries, both ~~her~~ ^she^ and ~~him~~ ^he^ spent years being unable to afford a decent laboratory to work in.

Marie Curie, born Maria Sklodowska in Poland in 1867, devoted her life to pure science in the hope that humans would benefit from what she discovered. Her parents, poor teachers, wanted she and her siblings to get an education. Marie went to Paris to study at the Sorbonne when she was twenty-four; her work as a governess had earned her enough money to educate she and her older sister. Marie struggled to learn French and overcome her deficient early education in physics and mathematics—subjects that girls in Poland such as her and her sister had not been allowed to study. When she completed her master's degree in physics in 1894, she placed first in her class. Pierre Curie, who was doing research on magnetism, and her met when Marie was searching for a laboratory she could use. Although Pierre did not have space for Marie in his lab, him and her fell in love and married.

The Curies did much of their innovative research in a small lab set up in an abandoned shed because both she and him believed that scientists should not waste valuable research time trying to make money. Marie did work on uranium and thorium, and it was her who invented the term *radioactivity*. In 1903, three scientists, Pierre and her, along with Henri Becquerel, shared the Nobel Prize in Physics. At around the same time, Pierre and Marie discovered the elements polonium (named after Marie's homeland) and radium. In 1911, after her husband's death, an unprecedented second Nobel Prize, this time in chemistry, was awarded to she alone. Marie Curie died in 1934 as a result of years of exposure to radiation, but her legacy continued. The Curies' daughter Irene, who had learned physics and chemistry from Marie and was nearly as skilled in scientific research as her, shared a Nobel Prize in Chemistry with her husband, Frederic Joliot-Curie, in 1935.

EXERCISE 15 Use the correct possessive pronoun form. 42b

In the following sentences, correct any errors in the use of possessive forms of pronouns. Some sentences may be correct.

Example Bonhoeffer tried to convince other Germans to oppose Nazi views of racial purity, and ~~him~~ his playing gospel records in Nazi Germany required courage.

1. When Dietrich Bonhoeffer was a visiting pastor at Harlem's Abyssinian Baptist Church in 1931, the congregation was pleased with him learning to love gospel music.
2. As a white German Protestant among African American worshippers, Bonhoeffer at first worried that his life was too different from them.
3. When Bonhoeffer returned to Germany, something of their's went with him: members of the church gave him several gospel records.
4. Dietrich Bonhoeffer's opposition to the Nazi regime led to him putting his life on the line by participating in the plot to assassinate Hitler in 1944; it's failure resulted in his imprisonment and execution.
5. Bonhoeffer's influence still appears in today's Germany, where the popularity of gospel music is still growing as a result of his championing of it decades ago.

EXERCISE 16 Use correct pronoun-antecedent agreement. 42c, 42d

In each of the following sentences, correct any errors in pronoun-antecedent agreement, revising sentences as necessary. Some sentences may be correct.

Example In wartime, the work of a country's intelligence community ~~finds that their work~~ has tremendous importance and urgency.

1. If a historian studies World War II, they will learn how important intelligence was for the Allied victory.
2. At first, however, US intelligence was unable to identify the risk of a Japanese attack, and their failure brought the country into the war.
3. Neither the head of the FBI nor his counterparts at the State Department, Army, and Navy allowed other government officials access to secrets their agents had discovered, and the result was American unpreparedness for the attack on Pearl Harbor.

4. In December 1941, an American could easily have felt that his country might lose the war against the Japanese military and the still-undefeated German army.
5. Everyone involved in decoding German and Japanese messages deserves their share of the credit for the ultimate defeat of the Axis powers in 1945.

EXERCISE 17 Use the correct forms of adjectives and adverbs. 43a

In each of the following sentences, correct any errors in adjective or adverb forms. Some sentences may be correct.

Example Amish adolescents face issues of independence and conformity that are ~~basicly~~ basically the same as those confronting other young Americans.

1. People in Amish communities live without electricity or cars, in isolation from the modern world, where technology makes activities such as work and travel go swift.
2. Members of the church live strict by its rules, but a young person in an Amish household does not join the church until adulthood.
3. Amish teenagers are allowed to break church rules and experiment with the outside world; many non-Amish are shocked to learn how widely accepted such behavior is in the Amish community.
4. The great majority of young Amish people do eventually join the church, and those who feel that they are not suited good to a highly regulated life may decide to join a more tolerant Amish group in another area.
5. A church member who breaks the rules faces excommunication and shunning by others in the community, so Amish groups try hardly to encourage young people to get over their interest in experimentation before they join the church.

EXERCISE 18 Use adjectives and adverbs correctly after linking verbs. 43c

In each of the following sentences, correct any errors in adjective and adverb use. Some sentences may be correct.

Example The aurora borealis appeared ~~sudden~~ suddenly in the sky.

1. The Norwegian scientist Kristian Birkeland felt certainly about the cause of the aurora borealis (or northern lights).
2. The lights, which hang like a brightly colored curtain in the night sky, look spookily to most observers.
3. Birkeland looked careful at the lights from a Norwegian mountaintop in midwinter during his 1899 expedition to study the phenomenon.

4. His two expeditions to observe the northern lights appeared successful, but some members of his scientific teams were badly injured or killed in the severe winter conditions.
5. He appeared madly to some colleagues, but Birkeland finally determined that sunspots caused the aurora borealis.

EXERCISE 19 Identify restrictive and nonrestrictive clauses. 44b

In the following sentences, underline each relative clause and write *R* (restrictive) or *NR* (nonrestrictive) on the line before the sentence. There may be more than one relative clause in a sentence. Then edit to make sure that each clause is punctuated correctly and that the correct form of the relative pronoun is used.

Example R People <u>who speak a pidgin language</u> are finding a way to bridge the communication gap.

1. ___ When a person who speaks only English and a person, who speaks only Spanish, must communicate, they will find common ground by using the simple grammar and vocabulary of pidgin.
2. ___ Pidgin which is not spoken as a native tongue by anyone is different from creolized language.
3. ___ When a language, that started out as pidgin, becomes the common speech of a community, that language has been creolized.
4. ___ For example, Haitian Creole that is a language with its own complex grammar and vocabulary came from the pidgin speech created by slaves from many cultures, who were forced to live and work together.
5. ___ Creolized languages which often develop when pidgin speakers raise children in a multicultural community demonstrate both the creativity of human beings—even in terrible hardship—and the depth of the human need to communicate with other people.

EXERCISE 20 Make the verb and the antecedent of subject relative pronouns agree. 44c

In each of the following sentences, correct any subject-verb agreement errors within the relative clauses. Then draw an arrow from any subject relative pronoun to its antecedent. Some sentences may be correct.

Example Keeping costs down is one of the reasons that ~~makes~~ make most health maintenance organizations require approval for certain treatments.

1. Most people who participate in group insurance plans now use some form of managed care.
2. Many insurance companies require any patients who participates in managed care plans to get a referral from their primary care physician before seeing an expensive specialist.
3. This practice, which are known as "gatekeeping," often infuriates both patients and physicians.

4. In some cases, patients may believe that a particular specialist is the only one of the doctors in the group who know how to treat a particular condition.
5. Everyone in the plan who need to see a specialist must first make an appointment with a primary care physician to get his or her referral; many patients resent having to make this extra visit.
6. In addition, many insurance companies pay lower fees to any doctor in a managed care plan who refer patients to a specialist for treatment, so doctors are often reluctant to make referrals.
7. Any patients in managed care who sees a specialist without a referral usually have to pay for the full cost of the visit.
8. According to some analysts, feeling angry about being forced to get a primary care physician's permission to see a specialist is one of the situations that causes patients to sue their doctors.
9. One of the surprises that has come from a recent study of health maintenance organizations is the finding that few patients made unnecessary visits to specialists when referrals were not required.
10. In spite of this finding, many experts still support some version of gatekeeping because they think that patients who get a specialist's care should nevertheless let the primary care physicians who knows them best participate in decisions about treatment.

EXERCISE 21 Use *where* and *when* appropriately. 44f

In each of the following sentences, revise any inappropriate uses of *where* and *when* as relative pronouns. Some sentences may be correct.

Example Spelunking is one name for the profession or hobby ~~where~~ [in which] people explore caves, but most cave explorers prefer the term *caving*.

1. In 1838, Stephen Bishop, a seventeen-year-old slave, arrived at Kentucky's Mammoth Cave, to where he had been sent to work as a guide.
2. Bishop was a popular guide, but he was also a fearless explorer, squeezing through tight passages in which no humans had been for centuries.
3. In a single year where Bishop explored previously unknown parts of the cave, he doubled the explored portion of Mammoth Cave, earning fame—but not freedom—and attracting hundreds of tourists to the site.
4. Bishop discovered the underground river in Mammoth Cave, in which blind fish and crustaceans live, and in 1842 he drew a careful map of the cave that was used by explorers for the next forty years.
5. In 1972, cave explorers found a passage called Hanson's Lost River that led from another Kentucky cave system into Mammoth Cave; the explorers later discovered that the passage through where they had crawled to make the connection was marked on Bishop's 130-year-old map.

MindTap®

▶ **Practice skills that you have learned in this part, and receive automatic feedback.**

8 Punctuation, Mechanics, and Spelling

WRITING IN YOUR CAREER

The Police Officer, the Writer

Hill Street Studio/BlendRF/Glowimages

After every crime, a police officer sits down and puts together a written incident report. Sometimes "the importance of a single word can make the difference between a dismissal and a judgment," write Robert E. Grubb, Jr., and K. Virginia Henby *in Effective Communication for Criminal Justice Professionals.* Police cadet Johanna Jackson has learned that she must write clearly and coherently so that her reports will be credible in a courtroom. See how Jackson edited the following incident report (from Grubb and Henby's *Effective Communication for Criminal Justice Professionals*).

UNEDITED VERSION

> I, Officer Jackson, arrived at the location. . . . And apon my arrivel spoke to the victim a Mr. Mike Parks. I asked Mr. Parks what happened and Mr. Parks stated that he was walking home from work, when he crossed the alley way between Little's Bookstore and Dr. Greens florist a noise startiled Mr. Parks so he turned to see what the noise was and at that momement Mr. Parks states that a man with a gun pulled Mr. Parks into the alley way and toled Mr. Parks to give him all of his money and watch. The man then pistol wiped Mr. Parks. . . .

EDITED VERSION

> I, Officer Jackson, arrived at the location. . . . Upon arrival, I spoke to the victim, a Mr. Mike Parks. Mr. Parks stated that when he was walking home from work a noise startled him as he crossed the alley way between Little's Bookstore and Dr. Green's florist. Mr. Parks stated that he turned to see what the noise was, and at that moment, a man with a gun pulled Mr. Parks in the alley way and told Mr. Parks to give him all of his money and his watch. The man then pistol whipped Mr. Parks. . . .

8 Punctuation, Mechanics, and Spelling

MindTap®

Understand the goals of this part, and complete a warm-up activity.

Punctuation serves to regulate the flow of information through a sentence, showing readers how to read your ideas. The following headline from the *New York Times*, "Stock Fraud Is Easier, and Easier to Spot," says that stock fraud is not only easy to engage in but also easy to detect. Without the comma, however, the sentence would send a different message: It would say that detecting stock fraud is becoming increasingly easy.

Try reading the following without the benefit of the signals readers usually expect:

> When active viruses especially those transmitted by contact can spread easily within the world health organization hard working doctors are continually collaborating to find treatments for several infectious diseases sars avian flu and hepatitis.

Conventional punctuation and mechanics clarify the meaning:

> When active, viruses—especially those transmitted by contact—can spread easily; within the World Health Organization, hard-working doctors are continually collaborating to find treatments for several infectious diseases: SARS, avian flu, and hepatitis.

45 Commas

A comma separates parts of a sentence. It does not separate one sentence from another. When readers see a comma, they know that the parts of the sentence are separated for a reason. When you really can't decide whether to use commas, follow this general principle: "When in doubt, leave them out." Readers find excessive use of commas more distracting than a few missing ones.

MindTap® Read, highlight, and take notes online.

45a Checklists: Comma yes and comma no

Use the guidelines in the following Key Points box, but note that variations can occur. Details and more examples follow in the rest of the chapter. Throughout chapter 45, note the comma where there is blue shading.

KEY POINTS

Comma Yes

1. between two independent clauses connected by a coordinating conjunction: *and, but, or, nor, so, for,* or *yet*, but optional in British English (45b)

   ▸ **The food was beautifully displayed, but no one felt like eating.**

   A comma is optional if the clauses are short.

   ▸ **She finished speaking and she left.**

2. after most introductory words, phrases, or clauses (45c)

   ▸ **After the noisy party, the neighbors complained. When the police came, the guests left.**

3. to set off extra (nonrestrictive) information included in a sentence ("extra commas with extra information"—see 45d)

   ▸ **Her husband, a computer programmer, works late at night.**

4. to set off a transitional expression or an explanatory insert (45e)

   ▸ **The ending of the film, however, is disappointing. In fact, it is totally predictable.**

5. to separate three or more items in a series (45f)
   - ▸ **The robot vacuums, makes toast, and plays chess.**
6. between adjectives that can be reversed and connected with *and* (coordinate adjectives—45g)
   - ▸ **When people move, they often discard their worn, dilapidated furniture.**
7. before or after a direct quotation (45h)
   - ▸ **"Whales are color-blind," the professor declared. The student replied, "I didn't know that."**

In the following Key Points box and in 45b–45i, yellow shading indicates "no comma here."

KEY POINTS
Comma No

1. not between subject and verb
   - ▸ **The debate between the two contestants became more acrimonious as the evening wore on.**

Note: Use paired commas, however, to set off any extra information inserted between the subject and verb (see 45d).

- ▸ **The fund manager, a billionaire, has been married five times.**

2. not before the word *and* that connects two verbs to the same subject
   - ▸ **She won the trophy and accepted it graciously.**
3. not *after* a coordinating conjunction (*and, but, or, nor, so, for, yet*) connecting two independent clauses, but *before* it (see 45b)
   - ▸ **The prisoner begged for mercy, but the judge was unmoved.**
4. not between two independent clauses without any coordinating conjunction such as *and* or *but* (use either a period or a semicolon instead)
   - ▸ **The harvest was meager; it had been a dry winter.**

Some writers, however, use a comma between two independent clauses when the clauses use parallel structures (38j) to point out a contrast.

- ▸ **She never insults, she just criticizes.**

(Continued)

(Continued)

5. not between an independent clause and a following dependent clause introduced by *after, before, because, if, since, unless, until,* or *when* (no comma before the subordinating conjunction)

    ▶ **Test results tend to be good when students study in groups.**

6. not before a clause beginning with *that*

    ▶ **The dean warned the students that the speech would be long.**

Note: A comma can appear before a *that* clause when it is the second comma of a pair before and after extra information inserted as a nonrestrictive phrase.

▶ **He skates so fast, despite his size, that he will probably break the world record.**

7. not before or after essential, restrictive information (see 45d)

    ▶ **Alice Walker's essay "Beauty: When the Other Dancer Is the Self" discusses coping with a physical disfigurement.** [Walker has written more than one essay. The title restricts the noun *essay* to one specific essay.]

Similarly, a restrictive relative clause introduced by *who, whom, whose, which,* or *that* is never set off by commas. The clause provides essential, identifying information (see 45b and 45d).

▶ **The teachers praised the children who finished on time.** [The teachers didn't praise all the children. The clause "who finished on time" restricts the meaning to only those who finished on time.]

8. not between a verb and its object or complement

    ▶ **The best gifts are food and clothes.**

9. not after *such as*

    ▶ **Popular fast-food items such as hamburgers and hot dogs tend to be high in cholesterol.**

10. not separating cumulative adjectives (adjectives that cannot be connected by *and* and whose order cannot be reversed—see 45g for more examples)

    ▶ **many little white ivory buttons**

45b Use a comma before a coordinating conjunction (*and, but*, and so on) that connects independent clauses

When you connect independent clauses with a coordinating conjunction (*and, but, or, nor, so, for, yet*), place a comma before the conjunction.

▸ **The managers are efficient, but personnel turnover is high.**

▸ **The winner was announced, and the audience erupted in cheers.**

However, when the clauses are short, many writers omit the comma.

45c Use a comma after most introductory phrases and clauses

The comma signals to readers that the introductory part of the sentence has ended. It says, in effect, "Now wait for the main point in the independent clause."

▸ **Just as we began eating, there was a knock at the door.**

▸ **As recently as twenty-five years ago, very few students had computers or cell phones.**

The comma after the introductory material tells readers to expect the subject and verb of the independent clause. After one word or a short phrase, the comma can be omitted: *Immediately the fun began*. However, in some sentences, omitting the comma can lead to a serious or humorous misreading:

▸ **While the guests were eating a mouse ran across the floor.**

45d Use commas to set off an extra (nonrestrictive) phrase or clause

A phrase or clause may provide extra information that can be omitted without changing the meaning of the independent clause by restricting its meaning. Such information may be included almost as an aside—a "by the way." If the insertion comes midsentence, think of the commas as handles that can lift the extra information out without inconveniencing readers.

Nonrestrictive **We'll attend, even though we'd rather not.** [We will definitely attend. The *even though* clause does not restrict the meaning of the independent clause.]

Restrictive **We'll attend if we have time.** [We will attend only if circumstances permit. The *if* clause restricts the meaning.]

Commas around appositive phrases Use commas to set off a descriptive or explanatory phrase, called an *appositive phrase*. If the phrase were omitted, readers might lose some interesting details but would still be able to understand the message.

appositive phrase

▶ **She loves her new phone, a Droid.**

appositive phrase

▶ **His dog, a big Labrador retriever, is afraid of mice.**

▶ **Salinger's first novel, *The Catcher in the Rye*, captures the language and thoughts of teenagers.** [The commas are used because the title provides supplementary information about the first novel, not information that identifies which novel the writer means.]

Commas around nonrestrictive participle phrases Nonrestrictive participle phrases add extra descriptive, but not essential, information.

▶ **My boss, wearing a red tie and a green shirt, radiated the holiday spirit.** [The participle phrase does not restrict the meaning of *boss* by distinguishing one boss from another.]

Commas around extra information in nonrestrictive relative clauses When you give nonessential information in a relative clause introduced by *who, whom*, or *which* (never *that*), set off the clause with commas.

▶ **The trainee's new shoes, which cost more than $300, were too fancy to wear to work.** [The independent clause "The trainee's new shoes were too fancy to wear to work" does not lead readers to ask "Which shoes?" The relative clause does not restrict the meaning of *shoes*.]

Note: Do not use commas to set off essential, restrictive information.

restricts *people* to a subgroup

▶ **People who wear bright colors send an optimistic message.** [The relative clause, beginning with *who*, restricts "people" to a subgroup: Not all people send an optimistic message; those who wear bright colors do.]

45e Use commas to set off transitional expressions and explanatory insertions

Transitional expressions and conjunctive adverbs connect or weave together the ideas in your writing and act as signposts for readers. See 2f for a list of these transitional expressions. Use commas to set off a transitional expression from the rest of the sentence.

▸ **Most Labrador retrievers, however, are courageous.**

Note: When you use a transitional expression such as *however, therefore, nevertheless, above all, of course*, or *in fact* at the beginning of an independent clause, end the previous clause with a period or a semicolon. Then place a comma after the transitional expression.

▸ **The patient suffered from both diabetes and high blood pressure. Nevertheless, she lived to be 93.**

You may sometimes choose to insert a phrase or a clause to make a comment, offer an explanation, drive a point home, or indicate a contrast. Insertions used for these purposes are set off by commas.

▸ **The consequences will be dire, I think.**

▸ **The best, if not the only, solution is to apologize and start over.**

▸ **Seasonal allergies, such as those caused by ragweed, are common.**

▸ **Unlike silver, gold does not tarnish.**

45f Use commas to separate three or more items in a series

Readers see the commas between items in a series (words, phrases, or clauses) and realize that "this is a list." If you said the sentence aloud, you would pause between items; when writing, you use commas to separate them. However, journalists and British writers often omit a comma before the final *and*.

▸ **In the hour between appointments, the salesperson managed to eat lunch, phone his mother, buy a potted plant, and have his shoes shined.**

See also 48a for when to use semicolons in place of commas in a list.

45g Use commas to separate certain (coordinate) adjectives

Adjectives are *coordinate* when their order can be reversed and the word *and* can be inserted between them without any change in meaning. Coordinate adjectives (such as *beautiful, delicious, exciting, noisy*) make subjective and evaluative judgments rather than provide objectively verifiable information about, for instance, size, shape, color, or nationality. Separate coordinate adjectives with commas.

▸ **Buyers like to deal with energetic, efficient, and polite salespeople.**

Do not, however, put a comma between the final adjective of a series and the noun it modifies.

▸ **Energetic, efficient, and polite salespeople are in demand.**

Note that no comma is necessary to separate adjectives that are cumulative, modifying the whole noun phrase that follows (see 60g for the order of these adjectives).

▸ **An old blue Persian rug sold for the auction's highest price.**

45h Use a comma between a direct quotation and the preceding or following clause

The independent clause may come either before or after the quotation.

▸ **When asked what she wanted to be later in life, she replied, "An Olympic swimmer."**

▸ **"I want to be an Olympic swimmer," she announced confidently.** [The comma is inside the quotation marks.]

However, omit the comma if the quotation is a question or exclamation.

▸ **"Would you like to sit down?" the interviewer asked.**

In addition, do not insert a comma before a quotation that is integrated into your sentence:

▸ **In our family, a ten-year-old car was considered "new."**

45i Special uses of commas

To prevent misreading Use a comma to separate elements in a sentence that may otherwise be confusing.

▸ **It's one of the greatest gifts you can give, to forgive yourself.**

—Maya Angelou

[Usually, a comma is not used to separate a subject from the verb. Here, the comma is necessary to prevent confusion.]

With an absolute phrase Use a comma to set off a phrase that modifies the whole sentence (an absolute phrase).

absolute phrase

▸ **Her arms folded defiantly across her chest, the four-year-old announced that she would not take a bath.**

With a date Use a comma to separate the day from the year in a date.

▸ **On May 14, 1998, the legendary singer Frank Sinatra died.** [Do not use a comma before the year when the day precedes the month: 14 May 1998.]

With numbers Use a comma (never a period) to divide numbers into thousands.

▸ **1,200** ▸ **515,000** ▸ **34,000,000**

No commas are necessary in years (*2012*), numbers in addresses (*3501 East 10th Street*), or page numbers (*page 1008*).

With titles Use commas around a person's title or degree when it follows the name.

▸ **Stephen L. Carter, PhD, gave the commencement speech.**

With the parts of an address

▸ **Ronald Reagan was born in Tampico, Illinois, in 1911.**

However, do not use a comma before a ZIP code: Newton, MA 02159.

With a conversational tag, tag question, or insert

▸ **Yes, Salinger's daughter, like others before her, has produced a memoir.**

▸ **Mark Zuckerberg is the chief executive of Facebook, isn't he?**

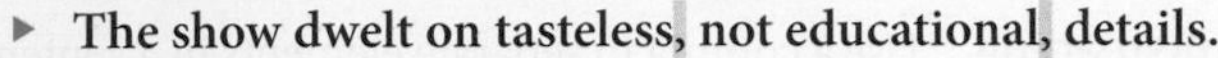

▸ **The show dwelt on tasteless, not educational, details.**

With a direct address or salutation

▸ **Thank you, Mr. Carter, for attending this evening.**

46 Apostrophes

An apostrophe indicates ownership or possession: *Fred's books, the government's plans, a year's pay* (the books belonging to Fred, the plans of the government, the pay for a year). It can also signal omitted letters in contractions.

46a Checklists: Apostrophe yes and apostrophe no

KEY POINTS

Apostrophe Yes

1. Use *-'s* for the possessive form of all nouns except plural nouns that end with *-s: the hero's misfortunes, the nation's capital, the people's advocate.*
2. Use an apostrophe alone for the possessive form of plural nouns that end with *-s: the heroes' misfortunes, the states' governors, liberal politicians' efforts.*
3. Use an apostrophe to indicate the omission of letters in contracted forms such as *didn't, they're, can't,* and *let's.* However, some readers of formal academic writing may object to such contractions.

Note: If you do use a contraction, use *it's* only for "it is" or "it has": *It's a good idea; it's been a slow process* (see 46f).

KEY POINTS

Apostrophe No

1. Generally, do not use an apostrophe to form the plurals of nouns (see 46e for rare exceptions).
2. Never use an apostrophe before an *-s* ending on a verb. Note that *let's* is a contracted form for *let us*; the *-s* is not a verb ending.
3. Do not write possessive pronouns (*hers, its, ours, yours, theirs*) with an apostrophe.
4. Do not use an apostrophe to form the plural of names or numbers: *the Browns; the 1990s* [not *1990's*]; *the '90s* [not *90's*].
5. With inanimate objects and concepts, *of* is often preferred to an apostrophe: *the cost of service, the top of the mountain, the back of the desk.*

46b When to use -'*s* to signal possession

As a general rule, to signal possession, use -'*s* with singular nouns, with indefinite pronouns (41h), with names, and with plural nouns that do not form the plural with *-s*: *the gardener's tools, anybody's opinion, the men's department, today's world, this week's schedule, Mr. Jackson's voice, someone else's idea, their money's worth.* Also note the following uses:

With individual and joint ownership To indicate individual ownership, make each owner possessive.

▸ **Sam's and Pat's houses are across the street from each other.**

To show joint ownership, make only the last owner possessive: *Sam and Pat's house.*

With compound nouns Add -'*s* to the last word in a compound noun.

▸ **her sister-in-law's purse**

With singular proper nouns ending in *-s* When a name ends in *-s*, add -'*s* as usual for the possessive.

▸ **Dylan Thomas's imagery conjures up the Welsh landscape.**

When a name has more than one syllable and ends in *-s* with a *z* pronunciation, you can use an apostrophe alone: *Moses'* law, *Euripides' dramas.*

In all words that need an apostrophe to signal possession

- ▶ **Yosemite National Park's vegetation differs from Sequoia's.** [meaning the vegetation of Sequoia National Park]

46c Use only an apostrophe to signal possession in plural nouns already ending in *-s*

Add only an apostrophe when a plural noun already ends in *-s*.

- ▶ **the students' suggestions** [more than one student]
- ▶ **my parents' friends** [more than one parent]

Remember to include an apostrophe in comparisons with a plural noun that is understood:

- ▶ **His views are different from other professors'.** [...from other professors' views]

46d Use an apostrophe in contractions

In a contraction (*shouldn't, don't, haven't*), the apostrophe appears where letters have been omitted. To test whether an apostrophe is in the correct place, mentally replace the missing letters. The replacement test, however, will not help with the following:

won't will not

Note: Some readers may object to contractions in formal academic writing, especially scientific writing, because they view them as colloquial and informal. It is safer not to use contractions unless you know the conventions of the genre and readers' preferences.

can't	cannot	'd	had, would, did (They'd already left. I'd try. Where'd you go?)
didn't	did not		
he's	he is *or* he has	're	are (you're, we're, they're)
's	is, has, does (He's happy. She's moved. How's it taste?)	it's	it is *or* it has
		let's	let us (as in "Let's go.")

Never place an apostrophe before the *-s* ending of a verb.

▶ **The author let's his characters take over.**

An apostrophe can also take the place of the first part of a year or a decade.

▶ **the radical rebellion of the '60s** [the 1960s]

▶ **the floods of '04** [the year 2004]

Note: Fixed forms spelled with an apostrophe, such as *o'clock* and the poetic *o'er*, are contractions ("of the clock," "over").

46e Two occasions to use *-'s* to form a plural

1. Use *-'s* for the plural form of letters of the alphabet Italicize only the letter, not the plural ending (50d).

▶ **Maria picked all the *M*'s out of her alphabet soup.**

▶ **Georges Perec's novel called *A Void* has no *e*'s in it at all.**

2. Use *-'s* for the plural form of a word referred to as the word itself Italicize the word named as a word, but do not italicize the *-'s* ending (50d).

▶ **Her speech was punctuated with *um*'s.**

MLA and APA prefer no apostrophe in the plural form of numbers, acronyms, and abbreviations (52f).

the 2000s the terrible twos DVDs FAQs MAs

However, you may see such plurals spelled with *-'s*. In all cases, be consistent in your usage.

Never use an apostrophe to signal the plural of common nouns or personal names: *big bargains, the Jacksons.*

46f Distinguish between *it's* and *its*

Its is the possessive form of the pronoun *it* and means "belonging to it." Use the apostrophe only if you intend *it is* or *it has* (see also 42b, p. 531).

▶ **It's a hilarious play.** ▶ **The committee took its time.**

Many writers slip up with these forms. Use your spell checker to search your entire document for both *its* and *it's*. Then check each one by asking, "Am I saying *it is* or *it has* here?" If the answer is yes, use *it's* or *it is*. If the answer is no, use *its*.

47 Quotation Marks

In American English, double quotation marks indicate where someone's exact words begin and end. (British English, however, uses single quotation marks.) For long quotations, see 47f.

47a Guidelines for using quotation marks

KEY POINTS

Quotation Marks: Basic Guidelines

1. Quote exactly the words used by the original speaker or writer.
2. Pair opening quotation marks with closing quotation marks to indicate where the quotation ends and your ideas begin.
3. Use correct punctuation to introduce and end a quotation, and place other marks of punctuation carefully in relation to the quotation marks.
4. Enclose the titles of articles, short stories, songs, and poems in quotation marks.
5. Enclose any added or changed material in square brackets (49e); indicate omitted material with ellipsis dots (49g).

47b Punctuation introducing and ending a quotation

After an introductory verb, such as *say*, *state*, or *write*, use a comma followed by a capital letter to introduce a direct quotation

- ▸ **It was Tolstoy who wrote, "Happy families are all alike, [but] every unhappy family is unhappy in its own way."** —*Anna Karenina*

Use a colon after a complete sentence introducing a quotation, and begin the quotation with a capital letter

▸ **Woody Allen always tries to make us laugh even about serious issues like wealth and poverty: "Money is better than poverty, if only for financial reasons."** —*Without Feathers*

When a quotation is integrated into the structure of your own sentence, use no special introductory punctuation other than the quotation marks

▸ **Phyllis Grosskurth says of Lord Byron that "anxiety over money was driving him over the brink."** —*Byron*

Put periods and commas inside quotation marks, even if these punctuation marks do not appear in the original quotation

▸ **When Henry Rosovsky characterizes Bloom's ideas as "mind-boggling," he is not offering praise.** —*The University*

In a documented paper, when you use parenthetical citations after a short quotation at the end of a sentence, put the period at the end of the citation, not within the quotation. See 10c and 47f for how to handle long quotations.

▸ **Geoffrey Wolff observes that when his father died, there was nothing to indicate "that he had ever known another human being" (11).** —*The Duke of Deception*

Put question marks and exclamation points inside the quotation marks if they are part of the original source, with no additional period When your sentence is a statement, do not use a comma or period in addition to a question mark or exclamation point.

▸ **The attorney asked her secretary, "Where did you put my report?"**

Put a question mark, exclamation point, semicolon, or colon outside the closing quotation marks If your sentence contains punctuation that is your own, not part of the original quotation, do not include it within the quotation marks.

▸ **What does the author mean when she describes the heroine as a "carnivorous spider"?**

47c Quotation marks in dialogue

Do not add closing quotation marks until the speaker changes or you interrupt the quotation. Begin each new speaker's words with a new paragraph.

interruption of quotation

▸ **"I'm not going to work today," he announced. "Why should I? I worked all weekend. My boss is away on vacation. And I have a headache."**

change of speaker

▸ **"Honey, your boss is on the phone," his wife called from the bedroom.**

If a quotation from one speaker continues for more than one paragraph, place *closing* quotation marks only at the end of the *final* paragraph of the quotation. However, place *opening* quotation marks at the beginning of every paragraph so that readers realize that the quotation is continuing.

47d A quotation within a quotation

Enclose quotations in double quotation marks. Use single quotation marks to enclose a quotation or a title of a short work within a quotation. (The reverse is the case in British English.)

▸ **"I read 'The Turn of the Screw' in ninth grade," Jorge recalled.**

▸ **The comedian Steven Wright once said, "I have an existential map. It has 'You are here' written all over it."**

47e Quotation marks with titles, definitions, and translations

For a translation or definition, use quotation marks:

▸ **The abbreviation *p.m.* means "after midday."**

KEY POINTS

Titles: Quotation Marks or Italics/Underlining?

1. **Quotation marks** for the title of an article, short story, poem, song, or chapter: "Ode on a Grecian Urn"; "Candle in the Wind"; "The Yellow Wallpaper"; "America: The Multinational Society"

2. **Italics** (or underlining in a handwritten manuscript) for the title of a book, journal, magazine, newspaper, film, play, or long poem published alone: *The Atlantic, Time, District 9, Beowulf* (50a)
3. **No quotation marks and no italics or underlining** for the title of your own essay

For more on capital letters with titles, see 51d.

47f When not to use quotation marks

In the sample sentences, yellow shading means "no quotation marks here."

1. Do not put quotation marks around indirect quotations

▸ **Some astrophysicists claim that the world is headed for a new Ice Age.**

2. Do not put quotation marks around clichés, slang, or trite expressions

Instead, revise. See also 32d and 32g.

▸ **All they want is ~~"a piece of the action."~~** involvement.

3. Do not put quotation marks at the beginning and end of long indented quotations

When you use MLA style to quote more than three lines of poetry or more than four typed lines of prose, indent the whole passage one-half inch from the left margin. For 40 or more words in APA style or for 100 words (eight lines or two or more paragraphs) in *Chicago* style, indent the passage one-half inch as well. Do not enclose the quoted passage in quotation marks, but retain any internal quotation marks. See 10c, 13, and 14b, item R for examples.

4. On the title page of your own paper, do not put quotation marks around your essay title

Use quotation marks in your title only when your title contains a quotation or the title of a short work.

Charles Baxter's "Gryphon" as an Educational Warning

48 Semicolons and Colons

A colon (:) looks somewhat like a semicolon (;). However, they are used in different ways, and they are not interchangeable.

48a Checklists: Semicolon yes and semicolon no

A period separates independent clauses with finality; a semicolon, such as the one you just saw in this sentence, provides a less distinct separation and indicates that an additional related thought or item will follow immediately. As essayist Lewis Thomas comments in his "Notes on Punctuation":

> The period tells you that that is that; if you didn't get all the meaning you wanted or expected, anyway you got all the writer intended to parcel out and now you have to move along. But with a semicolon there you get a pleasant little feeling of expectancy; there is more to come.

KEY POINTS

Semicolon Yes

1. between closely connected independent clauses when no coordinating conjunction (*and, but, or, nor, so, for, yet*) is used

   ▸ **Biography tells us about the subject; biographers also tell us about themselves.**

   Do not overuse semicolons in this way. They are more effective when used sparingly. Do not use a capital letter to begin a clause after a semicolon.

2. between independent clauses connected with a transitional expression like *however, moreover, in fact, nevertheless, above all,* or *therefore* (see the list in 2f)

   ▸ **Chocolate may have some benefit as a mood enhancer; however, it is high in calories.**

   (If the transitional expression is in the middle or at the end of its clause, the semicolon still appears between the clauses:

The results support the hypothesis; further research, however, is necessary.)

3. to separate items in a list containing internal commas

   ▶ **When I cleaned out the refrigerator, I found a chocolate cake, half-eaten; some canned tomato paste, which had a blue fungus growing on the top; and some possibly edible meat loaf.**

KEY POINTS

Semicolon No

1. not in place of a colon to introduce a list or an explanation

   ▶ **Ellsworth Kelly has produced a variety of works of art; drawings, paintings, prints, and sculptures.**

2. not after an introductory phrase or dependent clause, even if the phrase or clause is long. A semicolon would produce a fragment. Use a comma instead.

   ▶ **Because the training period was so long and arduous for all the players; the manager allowed one visit by family and friends.**

3. not before an appositive phrase

   ▶ **The audience cheered the Oscar winner; Leonardo DiCaprio.**

4. not in place of a comma before *and, but, or, nor, so, for,* or *yet* joining independent clauses

   ▶ **The thrift shop in the church basement needed a name; and the volunteers chose Attic Treasures.**

48b Checklists: Colon yes and colon no

A colon signals anticipation. It follows an independent clause and introduces information that readers will need. A colon tells readers, "What comes next will define, illustrate, or explain what you have just read." Use one space after a colon.

KEY POINTS
Colon Yes

1. after an independent clause to introduce items in a list

   ▸ **The students included three pieces of writing in their portfolios: a narrative, an argument, and a documented paper.**

2. after an independent clause to introduce an explanation, expansion, or elaboration

   ▸ **After winning seven Tour de France cycling titles, Lance Armstrong was deprived of his titles: he was accused of taking part in a doping program.**

   Note: Some writers may prefer to use a capital letter after a colon introducing an independent clause. Whatever you choose to do, be consistent in your usage.

3. to introduce a rule or principle (a capital is usually used here)

   ▸ **The main principle of public speaking is simple: Look at the audience.**

4. to introduce a quotation not integrated into your sentence and not introduced by a verb such as *say*

   ▸ **Emily Post has provided an alternative to attempting to outdo others: "To do *exactly as your neighbors do* is the only sensible rule."**

   Note the capital for the first word of a sentence quotation. A colon also introduces a long quotation set off from your text (see 10c).

5. in salutations, precise time notations, titles, and biblical citations of chapter and verse

   ▸ **Dear Doctor Faber:**

   ▸ **To: The Chancellor**

   ▸ **8:30 p.m.**

   ▸ ***Backlash: The Undeclared War against American Women***

   ▸ **Exodus 3:11–14** [In MLA style, a period is used in place of the colon.]

KEY POINTS

Colon No

(Note that in the sample sentences, yellow shading means "no colon here.")

1. not directly after a verb (such as a form of *be* or *include*)

   ▶ **The two main effects were the improvement of registration and an increase in the numbers of advisors.**

   ▶ **A classical sonata typically includes exposition, development, recapitulation, and coda sections.**

2. not after a preposition (such as *of, for, except,* and *regarding*) or the phrase *such as*

   ▶ **Southern California is known for its beautiful beaches, mild weather, crowded freeways, and dirty air.**

   ▶ **The novel will please many readers except linguists and lawyers.**

   ▶ **They packed many different items for the picnic, such as taco chips, salsa, bean salad, pita bread, and egg rolls.**

3. not after *for example, especially,* or *including*

   ▶ **His varied taste is shown by his living room furnishings, including antiques, modern art, and art deco lighting fixtures.**

49 Other Punctuation Marks

49a Periods

In British English, a period is descriptively called a "full stop." The stop at the end of a sentence is indeed full—more of a stop than a comma provides. Periods are also used with abbreviations, decimals, and amounts of money, as in items 3 and 4 below.

1. Use a period to end a sentence that makes a statement or gives a command

▸ **The interviewer asked the manager about the company's finances.**

▸ **Remember to log out at the end of the day.**

Leave one space after a period, unless your instructor requests two spaces. For periods used with sentences within parentheses, see 51a.

2. Use a period, not a question mark, to end a sentence concluding with an indirect question

▸ **The reporter asked the company treasurer how much the company had spent on gifts.**

3. Use a period to signal an abbreviation

Mr. Dr. Rev. Tues. etc.

Use only one space after the period: Mr. Lomax. When abbreviations contain internal periods, do not insert a space after any internal periods.

e.g. i.e. a.m. p.m. (or A.M. P.M.)

Note: For some abbreviations with capital letters, you can use periods or not. Just be consistent.

A.M. or AM P.M. or PM U.S.A. or USA (but note that MLA style prefers USA)

When you end a sentence with an abbreviation, do not add an extra period: *The plane left at 7 a.m.*

However, MLA style recommends that no periods be used with initials of names of government agencies (HUD) or other organizations (ACLU), acronyms (abbreviations pronounced as words: NASA, AIDS), Internet abbreviations (URL), abbreviations for states (CA, NJ), or common time indicators (BC, AD). See also 52c.

4. Use a period with decimals and with amounts of money over a dollar

▸ 3.7, $7.50

49b Question marks and exclamation points

Question marks (?) A question mark at the end of a sentence signals a direct question. Do not use a period in addition to a question mark.

▸ **Was anyone hurt in the accident?**

If questions in a series are not complete sentences, you still need question marks. A question fragment may begin with a capital letter or not. Just make your usage consistent.

▸ **Are the characters in the play involved in the disaster? Indifferent to it? Unaware of it?**

▸ **Are the characters in the play involved in the disaster? indifferent to it? unaware of it?**

However, after an indirect question, use a period, not a question mark (49a, item 2).

▸ **We'd like to know what you expect us to do.**

Questions are useful devices to engage readers' attention. You ask a question and then provide an answer.

▸ **Many cooks nowadays are making healthier dishes. How do they do this? For the most part, they use unsaturated oil.**

A question mark is sometimes used to express uncertainty about a date or a query about an incident.

▸ **"A noise outside woke her up?" the detective wondered.** [Note that no comma is needed after a question mark that is part of a quotation.]

▸ **Plato (427?–347 BC) founded the Academy at Athens.**

Exclamation points (!) An exclamation point at the end of a sentence indicates that the writer considers the statement amazing, surprising, or extraordinary. As novelist F. Scott Fitzgerald said, "An exclamation point is like laughing at your own joke." Let your words and ideas carry the force of any emphasis you want to communicate.

No **The last act of her play is really impressive!**

Yes **The last act of her play resolves the crisis in an unexpected and dramatic way.**

If you feel you absolutely have to include an exclamation point to get your point across in dialogue or with an emphatic command or statement, do not use it along with an additional comma or period.

▸ **"Get off my property!" the farmer yelled at the teenage couple.**

Note: An exclamation point (or a question mark) *can* be used with a period that signals an abbreviation:

▸ **The match didn't end until 1 a.m.!**

Avoid using a question mark or an exclamation point enclosed in parentheses to convey irony or sarcasm.

No **My father, Mr. Diplomatic (!), regularly insulted my sister by commenting on her weight.**

Yes **My father, who could be tactless, regularly insulted my sister by commenting on her weight.**

49c Dashes

A dash (—) alerts readers to an explanation, to something unexpected, or to an interruption. Form a dash by typing two hyphens with no extra space before, between, or after them. Some word processing software will transform the two hyphens into one continuous dash. Dashes should enclose a phrase, not a clause.

▸ **She bragged that her dog--a Pomeranian--had a complete wardrobe of sweaters.**

▸ **The accused gasped, "But I never—" and fainted.**

▸ **In America there are two classes of travel—first class and with children.**

—Robert Benchley, in Robert E. Drennan, *The Algonquin Wits*

Commas can be used to set off an appositive phrase, but a pair of dashes is preferable when appositive phrases form a list already containing commas.

▸ **The contents of his closet—torn jeans, frayed jackets, and suits shiny on the seat and elbows—made him reassess his priorities.**

Overusing the dash may produce a staccato effect. Use it sparingly.

49d Parentheses

Use parentheses to mark an aside or to provide additional information.

▶ **Everyone admires Rafael Nadal's feat (winning Grand Slam finals on all court surfaces).**

Also use parentheses to enclose citations in a documented paper and to enclose numbers or letters preceding items in a list.

▶ **(3) A journalist reports that in the course of many interviews, he met very few people who were cynical about the future of the country (Lamb 5).**

At the end of a sentence, place the period inside the last parenthesis only when a separate new sentence is enclosed (see examples in 51a).

▶ **Meryl Streep burst out laughing when it was announced that she had won the 2012 Oscar for Best Actress. (Her previous win had taken place almost 30 years earlier.)**

49e Brackets

When you insert words or comments or make changes to words within a quotation, enclose the inserted or changed material in square brackets. Be careful to insert only words that help the quotation fit into your sentence grammatically or that offer a necessary explanation. Do not insert words that substantially change the meaning.

▶ **According to Ridley, "the key to both of these features of life [the ability to reproduce and to create order] is information."**

On occasion, you may need to use brackets to insert the Latin word *sic* (meaning "thus") into a quoted passage in which an error occurs. Using *sic* tells readers that the word or words that it follows were present in the original source and are not your own.

▶ **Richard Lederer tells of a man who did "exercises to strengthen his abominable [sic] muscles."**

Brackets can also be used in MLA style around ellipsis dots that you add to signal an omission from a source that itself contains ellipsis dots (49g).

49f Slashes

Use a slash (/) to separate two or three lines of poetry quoted within your own text. For quoting more than three lines of poetry, see 10c and 49g.

▸ **Elizabeth Barrett's most romantic poem begins with the famous question: "How do I love thee? / Let me count the ways."**

Slashes are also used in expressions such as *and/or* and *he/she* to indicate options. Be careful not to overuse these expressions.

49g Ellipsis dots

When you omit material from a quotation, indicate the omission—the ellipsis—by three dots with a space between each dot (. . .). (MLA style recommends using square brackets around ellipsis dots if the passage you quote from already contains an ellipsis.) The following passage by Ruth Sidel, on page 27 of *On Her Own,* is used in some of the examples that follow.

> These women have a commitment to career, to material well-being, to success, and to independence. To many of them, an affluent life-style is central to their dreams; they often describe their goals in terms of cars, homes, travel to Europe. In short, they want their piece of the American Dream.

Words omitted from the middle of a quotation Use three ellipsis dots when you omit material from the middle of a quotation.

▸ **Ruth Sidel reports that the women in her interviews "have a commitment to career . . . and to independence" (27).**

Words omitted at the end of your sentence When you omit part of a quotation and the omission occurs at the end of your own sentence, insert ellipsis dots after the sentence period, followed by the closing quotation marks, making four dots in all.

▸ **Ruth Sidel presents interesting findings about jobs and money: "These women have a commitment to career, to material well-being. . . ."**

When a parenthetical reference follows the quoted passage, put the final sentence period after the parenthetical reference.

▸ **Ruth Sidel presents interesting findings about jobs and money: "These women have a commitment to career, to material well-being . . ." (27).**

Complete sentence omitted When you omit a complete sentence or more, insert three ellipsis dots.

- **Sidel tells us how "an affluent lifestyle is central to their dreams; . . . they want their piece of the American Dream" (27).**

Line of poetry omitted When you omit one or more lines of poetry from a long, indented quotation, indicate the omission with a line of dots.

> My good Lysander!
> I swear to thee, by Cupid's strongest bow,
> By his best arrow with the golden head,
> By the simplicity of Venus' doves,
> By that which knitteth souls and prospers loves,
> ....
> By all the vows that ever men have broke,
> In number more than ever women spoke,
> In that same place thou hast appointed me,
> To-morrow truly will I meet with thee.
>
> —William Shakespeare, *A Midsummer Night's Dream*

When not to use ellipsis dots Do not use ellipsis dots when you quote only a word or a phrase because it will be obvious that material has been omitted:

- **The women Sidel interviewed see an "affluent lifestyle" in their future.**

Note: Use three dots to indicate a pause in speech or an interruption.

- **Professor Lang got as far as "Economists disagree on the wisest course . . ." before he was overtaken by a fit of coughing.**

50 Italics/Underlining

Italics and underlining serve the same function: to highlight a word, phrase, or title. Use underlining only in a handwritten or typed manuscript. In all other material written with a word processor or online, use italics. In some e-mail postings and discussion lists, you may need to indicate italics by a single underscore at the beginning and end of the passage you would usually italicize.

50a When to italicize the titles of long, whole works

In the body of an essay, italicize the titles of books, journals, magazines, newspapers, plays, films, TV series, long poems, musical compositions, Web sites, online databases, and works of art

- *Pride and Prejudice*
- *The Daily Show*
- *Mad Men*
- *American Gothic*
- *Newsweek*
- *About.com*

50b When not to italicize titles

- In the body of your text, do not italicize the names of sacred works such as the Bible and the Koran (Qur'an). Note, though, that these will be italicized in an MLA citation (11b, item V) and in an MLA works-cited list (12e, item 24).
- Do not italicize the books of the Bible (Genesis, Psalms) or the titles of documents and laws, such as the Declaration of Independence, the Constitution, and the Americans with Disabilities Act. However, follow style guides for the use of italics for titles of works in bibliographical lists or notes: CSE, for example, does not use italics for titles.
- Do not italicize the titles of short works, such as poems, short stories, essays, and articles. (MLA and *Chicago* styles use quotation marks for short works in their list of works cited or notes.)
- Do not italicize the title of your own essay (see 47f).
- See MLA, APA, CSE, and *Chicago* styles for the conventions of using italics and quotation marks in a list of references (chapters 11–20).

50c Italicize names of ships, trains, airplanes, and spacecraft

- *Titanic*
- *Silver Meteor*
- *Mir*
- *Gemini*

However, do not italicize any abbreviation preceding the name: USS *Constitution.*

50d Italicize letters, numerals, and words referring to the words themselves, not to what they represent

- The sign had a large *P* in black marker and a *3* in red.
- Many publications now write *website* as one word, uncapitalized.

50e Italicize words from other languages not yet adopted in English

Expressions that are not commonly used in English should be italicized. Do not overuse such expressions because they tend to sound pretentious.

▸ **The Marshall Plan was instrumental in creating the *Wirtschaftswunder* in West Germany after World War II.**

Do not italicize common expressions: et al., croissant, film noir, and so on.

50f Do not use italics for emphasis

Select a word that better conveys the idea you want to express.

hilarious.

▸ **The joke was ~~*too funny!*~~** ^

51 Capitalization

51a Capitalize *I* and the first word of a sentence

Always use a capital letter for the pronoun *I* and for the first letter of the first word of a sentence. E-mail correspondence without any capitals may look sloppy and annoy some readers (see also 55b). However, do not use a capital letter for the first word after a semicolon even when it begins a complete sentence. In addition, do not use a capital letter if you insert a complete sentence into another sentence using parentheses:

▸ **Dr. Elana Fisher was recently appointed Chief of Surgery (previously, she was a staff surgeon at the Cleveland Clinic).**

If you want to give the material within the parentheses a little more emphasis, make it a sentence with a capital letter and place the period before the closing parenthesis.

▸ **Dr. Elana Fisher was recently appointed Chief of Surgery. (Previously, she was a staff surgeon at the Cleveland Clinic.)**

51b Capitalize proper nouns and proper adjectives

Begin the names of specific people, places, and things with a capital letter. For the use of *the* with proper nouns, see 58f.

Types of Proper Nouns and Adjectives	Examples
People	Albert Einstein, Adele, T. S. Eliot, Bill Gates, Selena Gomez (but bell hooks)
Nations, continents, planets, stars, and galaxies	Hungary, Asia, Mercury, the North Star, the Milky Way
Mountains, rivers, and oceans	Mount Everest, the Thames, the Pacific Ocean
Public places and regions	Golden Gate Park, the Great Plains, the Midwest, the South (but no capital for direction, as in "Drive south on the turnpike")
Streets, buildings, and monuments	Rodeo Drive, the Empire State Building, the Roosevelt Memorial
Cities, states, and provinces	Toledo, Kansas, Nova Scotia
Days of the week and months	Wednesday, March
Holidays	Labor Day, the Fourth of July
Organizations, companies, and search engines	the Red Cross, Microsoft Corporation, eBay (internal capital), Yahoo!
Institutions (including colleges, departments, schools, government offices, and courts of law)	University of Texas, Department of English, School of Business, Department of Defense, Florida Supreme Court
Historical events, named periods, and documents	the Civil War, the Renaissance, the Roaring Twenties, the Declaration of Independence
Religions, deities, revered persons, and sacred texts	Buddhism, Islam, Muslim, Baptist, Jehovah, Mohammed, the Torah, the Koran (Qur'an)
Races, tribes, nations, nationalities, and languages	the Navajo, Greece, Greek, Spain, Spanish, Syrian, Farsi
Registered trademarks	Kleenex, Apple, iPod, Nike, Xerox
Names of ships, planes, and spacecraft	the USS *Kearsarge*, the *Spirit of St. Louis*, the *Challenger*
Titles of courses	English Composition, Introduction to Sociology

Note: Do not capitalize nouns naming general classes or types of people, places, things, or ideas: *government, jury, mall, prairie, utopia, traffic court, the twentieth century, goodness, reason.* Also, do not capitalize the names of seasons (*next spring*) or subjects of study, except for languages (*She is interested in geology and Spanish.*). For the use of capital letters in online writing, see 55b.

51c Capitalize a title before a person's name

▸ **Voters were surprised to hear of Senator Snowe's retirement.**

▸ **The residents cheered Grandma Jones.**

Do not use a capital letter when a title is not attached to a person's name.

▸ **Maine has had the same senator since 1994.**

▸ **My grandmother is ninety years old.**

When a title substitutes for the name of a known person, a capital letter is often used.

▸ **Have you spoken with the Senator [senator] yet?**

51d Capitalize major words in a title

In titles of published books, journals, magazines, essays, articles, films, poems, and songs, use a capital letter at the beginning of all words. Exceptions: articles (*the, a, an*), coordinating conjunctions (*and, but, or, nor, so, for, yet*), *to* in an infinitive (*to stay*), and prepositions unless they begin or end the title or subtitle.

▸ **"With a Little Help from My Friends"**

▸ ***Reflections from the Keyboard: The World of the Concert Pianist***

For more on titles, see the Key Points box in 47e, pages 582–583.

51e Capitals with colons and quotations

Writers often ask how to use capital letters with colons and quotations.

Should a capital letter be used at the beginning of a clause after a colon? Usage varies. Usually, a capital letter is used if the clause states a rule or principle (p. 586, item 3). Make your usage consistent.

Should a capital letter be used at the beginning of a quotation? Capitalize the first word of a quoted sentence if it is capitalized in the original passage.

- **When Quindlen writes, "The world is full of women blindsided by the unceasing demands of motherhood, still flabbergasted by how a job can be terrific and torturous," is she writing from experience?**

Do not capitalize when you quote part of a sentence.

- **When Quindlen writes that motherhood can be both "terrific and torturous," it makes me wonder how her own children turned out.**

52 Abbreviations

For abbreviations commonly used in online writing, see 55c.

52a Abbreviate titles used with people's names

Use an abbreviation, followed by a period, for titles before or after names. The following abbreviated titles precede names: *Mr., Mrs., Ms., Prof., Dr., Gen.,* and *Sen.* The following abbreviated titles follow names: *Sr., Jr., PhD, MD, BA,* and *DDS.* Do not use a title both before and after a name: *Dr. Benjamin Spock* or *Benjamin Spock, MD.* Do not abbreviate a title if it is not attached to a specific name.

- **The ~~prof.~~ professor is supposed to hold office hours twice a week, but he never shows up.**

52b Abbreviate the names of familiar institutions, countries, tests, diseases, diplomas, individuals, and objects

Use capitalized abbreviations of the names of well-known institutions (*UCLA, YWCA, FBI, UN*), countries (*USA* or *U.S.A.*), tests and diplomas (*SAT, GED*), diseases (*MS, HIV*), individuals (*FDR*), TV and radio networks and stations (*PBS, WQXR*), and objects (*DVD*). If you use a specialized abbreviation, first use the term in full, followed by the abbreviation in parentheses; then use the abbreviation.

- **The Test of English as a Foreign Language (TOEFL) is taken by more than 800,000 students a year. However, our college does not offer a TOEFL preparation class.**

52c Abbreviate terms used with numbers

Use abbreviations such as *BC, AD, a.m., p.m., $, mph, wpm, mg, kg,* and other units of measure only when they occur with specific numbers.

- **35 BC** [meaning "before Christ," now often replaced with *BCE,* "before the Common Era"]
- **AD 1776** [*anno domini,* "in the year of the Lord," now often replaced with *CE,* "Common Era," used after the date: *1776 CE*]
- **2:00 a.m./p.m.** [*ante* or *post meridiem,* Latin for "before or after midday"] Alternatives are A.M./P.M. or AM/PM. Be consistent.

Do not use these abbreviations and other units of measure when no number is attached to them.

- **The keg weighed about forty ~~lbs.~~** pounds.
- **They arrived late in the ~~p.m.~~** afternoon.

52d Abbreviate common Latin terms

In notes, parentheses, and source citations, use abbreviations for common Latin terms. In the body of your text, use the English meaning.

ABBREVIATION	LATIN	ENGLISH MEANING
etc.	et cetera	and so on
i.e.	id est	that is
e.g.	exempli gratia	for example
cf.	confer	compare
NB	nota bene	note well
et al.	et alii	and others

52e Do not abbreviate familiar words to save time and space

In formal writing, write out full expressions such as the following:

&	and
bros.	brothers [Use "Bros." only if it is part of the official name of a business, such as Warner Bros. Studio.]

chap. chapter

lb. pound

Mon. Monday

nite night

NJ New Jersey [Abbreviate the name of a state only in an address, a note, or a reference.]

no. number [Use the abbreviation only with a specific number: "No. 17 on the list was deleted."]

Oct. October [Write names of days and months in full, except in some works-cited lists, such as in MLA format.]

soc. sociology [Write names of academic subjects in full.]

thru through

w/ with

52f Use -*s* (not -*'s*) for the plural form of an abbreviation

Do not use an apostrophe to make an abbreviation plural (46e).

- ▸ We packed away our old Springsteen LPs.
- ▸ Both his SUVs are at the repair shop.

53 Numbers

Conventions for using numerals (actual figures) or words vary across the disciplines.

53a Use the conventions of the discipline in which you are writing

In the humanities and in business letters

Use words for numbers expressible in one or two words and for fractions (*nineteen, fifty-six, two hundred, one-half*).

Use numerals for longer numbers (*326; 5,625; 7,642,000*).

Use a combination of words and numerals for whole millions, billions, and so on (*45 million, 1 billion*).

In scientific and technical writing

Use numerals for all numbers above nine.

Use numerals for numbers below ten only when they show precise measurement, as when they are grouped and compared with other larger numbers (*5 of the 39 participants*) or when they precede a unit of measurement (*6 cm*), indicate a mathematical function (*8%; 0.4*), or represent a specific time, date, age, score, or number in a series.

Use words for fractions: *two-thirds.*

53b Spell out numbers that begin a sentence

- **One hundred twenty-five members voted for the new bylaws.**
- **Three thousand residents were evacuated in anticipation of the flood.**

NOTE FOR MULTILINGUAL WRITERS

Number before *Hundred, Thousand,* and *Million*

Even after plural numbers, use the singular form of *hundred, thousand,* and *million.* Add *-s* only when there is no preceding number.

- **Five *hundred* books were damaged in the flood.**
- ***Hundreds* of books were damaged in the flood.**

53c Use numerals for giving the time and dates and in other special instances

In nonscientific writing, use numerals for the following:

Time and dates	6 p.m. on 31 May 2009
Decimals	20.89
Statistics	median score 35
Addresses	16 East 93rd Street
Chapter, page, scene, and line numbers	chapter 5, page 97

Quantities appearing with abbreviations or symbols	6°C (for temperature Celsius), $21, 6′7″
Scores	The Yankees beat the Orioles 3–2 to win the Division Series.

For percentages and money, numerals and the symbol (*75%, $24.67*) are usually acceptable, or you can spell out the expression if it is fewer than four words (*seventy-five percent, twenty-four dollars*).

53d Use -*s* (not -*'s*) for the plural form of numerals

- ▸ **Housing prices skyrocketed in the 1980s.**
- ▸ **Most of the graduating class scored in the 700s on the SATs.**

54 Hyphens

Use hyphens to divide a word or to form a compound.

54a Hyphens with prefixes

Many words with prefixes are spelled without hyphens: *cooperate, nonrestrictive, unnatural.* Others are hyphenated: *all-inclusive, anti-intellectual, self-effacing.* Always use a hyphen when the main word is a number or a proper noun: *all-American, post-2010.* If you are unsure about whether to insert a hyphen after a prefix, check a big dictionary to see if it lists the word as hyphenated.

54b Hyphens in compound words

Some compound nouns are written as one word (*toothbrush*), others as two words (*coffee shop*), and still others with one or more hyphens (*role-playing, father-in-law*). Always check an up-to-date dictionary. Similarly, check a dictionary for compound verbs (*cross-examine, overemphasize*).

Hyphenate compound adjectives preceding a noun: *a well-organized party, a law-abiding citizen, a ten-page essay.* When the modifier follows the noun, no hyphen is necessary: *The party was well organized. Most citizens try to be law abiding. The essay was ten pages long.*

Do not insert a hyphen between an *-ly* adverb and the word it modifies or after an adjective in its comparative (*-er*) or superlative (*-est*) form: *a tightly fitting suit, an expertly written essay, a sweeter sounding melody.*

Treat a series of hyphenated prefixes like this:

▸ **A verdict of either first- or second-degree murder was expected.**

54c Hyphens in spelled-out numbers

Use hyphens when spelling out two-word numbers from twenty-one to ninety-nine. (See 53b for more on spelling out numbers.)

▸ **Twenty-two applicants arrived early in the morning.**

Also use a hyphen in spelled-out fractions: *two-thirds of a cup.*

54d End-of-line hyphens

Most word processors either automatically hyphenate words or automatically wrap words around to the next line. Choose the latter option to avoid the strange and unacceptable word division that sometimes appears with automatic hyphenation. Do not insert a hyphen into a URL to split it across lines.

55 Online Guidelines

55a Punctuation in URLs

Punctuation marks communicate essential information in Web site addresses—uniform resource locators (URLs)—and in e-mail addresses. Be sure to include all marks when you write an address, and if you need to spread a URL over more than one line in your text, split it after a slash (MLA, CSE, and *Chicago* styles) or before a punctuation mark such as a period (APA and *Chicago* styles).

55b Capital letters online

Don't let the speed and informal nature of e-mail delude you into thinking that no rules or conventions matter anymore. Especially in academic and business settings, e-mail messages written with no capitals for the first letter of the first word of a sentence, for proper nouns, or for *I* will send readers the somewhat insulting signal that you have not bothered to check what you send them.

Overdoing capitals is as bad as (maybe worse than) including none at all. Writing a whole message in capital letters can be perceived by readers as the online equivalent of shouting. In order not to offend readers in e-mail communications and online discussion groups, avoid the prolonged use of capital letters.

55c Abbreviations online

Many abbreviations in the electronic world have become standard fare: DVD, RAM, PIN, and more. In addition, the informal world of online communication leads to informal abbreviations, at least in personal e-mail and text messages. Abbreviations such as *BTW* ("by the way"), *IMHO* ("in my humble opinion"), and *TBH* ("to be honest") are used in texting and informal e-mails, but you should avoid them in formal contexts.

55d Italics online

If you are using a social networking Web site or other technology that provides no italics, you can indicate a title and other types of words that are usually italicized by inserting an underscore before and after the words to be italicized:

▸ **I loved the cinematography in Scorsese's film _Hugo_.**

56 Spelling

Get into the habit of using a dictionary and a word processor with a spelling-check program. Even if you check your spelling with computer software, you still need to proofread. A program will not alert you to a correctly spelled word used in the wrong place (such as *cite* used in place of *sight* or *site*). However, you may be called upon to write spontaneously without access to a spelling program or a dictionary, so learn the basic rules in this chapter.

56a Plurals of nouns

Regular plural forms The regular plural of nouns is formed by adding *-s* or *-es* to the singular word.

essay, essays   match, matches

To form the plural of a compound noun, attach the *-s* to the main noun in the phrase.

mothers-in-law   passersby

Proofread carefully for words that form the plural with *-s* but make other changes, too, such as the following:

-f* or *-fe* → *-ves

thief, thieves

wife, wives

Exceptions: beliefs, roofs, chiefs

-o* → *-oes	***-o* → *-os***
potato, potatoes	hero (sandwich), heros
tomato, tomatoes	photo, photos
hero (human), heroes	piano, pianos
Consonant + *-y* → *-ies*	**Vowel + *-y* → *-ys***
family, families	toy, toys
party, parties	monkey, monkeys

Irregular plural forms (no -s ending)

man, men	foot, feet
woman, women	tooth, teeth
child, children	mouse, mice

Plural forms borrowed from other languages Words borrowed from other languages, particularly Greek and Latin, frequently borrow the plural form of the language, too.

basis, bases	nucleus, nuclei
thesis, theses	vertebra, vertebrae
hypothesis, hypotheses	alumnus (m.), alumni
criterion, criteria	alumna (f.), alumnae

Plural forms with no change Some words have the same form in singular and plural: *moose, deer, sheep, species.*

56b Doubling consonants

Doubled consonants form a link between spelling and pronunciation because the doubling of a consonant signals a short vowel sound.

Double the consonant when the verb stem contains one vowel plus one consonant in one syllable

slip, slipping, slipped hop, hopping, hopped

The doubled consonant preserves the short vowel sound. Compare the pronunciation of *hop, hopping, hopped* with *hope, hoping, hoped.* Compare the vowel sounds in *write, writing,* and *written.*

Double the consonant when the verb stem contains two or more syllables with one vowel plus one consonant in the final stressed syllable

refer, referring, referred control, controlling, controlled

Compare *traveling* and *traveled* with the stress on the first syllable. (British English usage, however, is *travelling* and *travelled.*)

Double the consonant when the suffix *-er* or *-est* is added to one-syllable adjectives ending in one vowel plus one consonant

big, bigger, biggest hot, hotter, hottest

Double the *l* when adding *-ly* to an adjective that ends in one *-l*

careful, carefully successful, successfully

56c Spelling with *-y* or *-i*

Verb Ends in Consonant + *-y*	*-ies*	*-ying*	*-ied*
cry	cries	crying	cried
study	studies	studying	studied

Verb Ends in Vowel + *-y*	*-ys*	*-ying*	*-yed*
play	plays	playing	played

Exceptions: pay/paid, say/said, lay/laid

Verb Ends in Vowel + *-e*	*-ies*	*-ying*	*-ied*
die	dies	dying	died

Two-Syllable Adjective Ends in *-y*	*-i* with a Suffix
happy	happier, happily, happiness

Two-Syllable Adjective Ends in *-ly*	*-lier*	*-liest*
friendly	friendlier	friendliest

56d Internal *ie* or *ei*

This traditional rhyme helps with the decision about whether to use *ie* or *ei:* "*I* before *e* / Except after *c* / Or when sounded like *ay* / As in *neighbor* and *weigh*." The following examples illustrate those guidelines:

i before *e*	*e* before *i* after *c*	*e* before *i* when sounded like *ay*
believe	receive	vein
relief	ceiling	reign
niece	deceive	sleigh

But note the exceptions:

i before *e* even after *c*	*e* before *i*, not after *c*	
conscience	height	seize
science	either/neither	foreign
species	leisure	weird

56e Adding a suffix

Keep a silent *-e* before an *-ly* suffix

immediate, immediately   sure, surely

Exceptions: true, truly; whole, wholly; due, duly

Keep a silent *-e* before a suffix beginning with a consonant

state, statement   force, forceful   rude, rudeness

Exceptions: acknowledge, acknowledgment; judge, judgment; argue, argument

Drop a silent *-e* before a suffix beginning with a vowel

hope, hoping   observe, observant

write, writing   remove, removable

Exceptions: enforce, enforceable; change, changeable. Retaining the *-e* preserves the soft sound of the preceding consonant.

With adjectives ending in *-le*, drop the *-le* when adding *-ly*

sensible, sensibly

With adjectives ending in *-ic*, add *-ally* to form the adverb

basic, basically   characteristic, characteristically

Exception: public, publicly

Pay attention to the suffixes *-able, -ible, -ant, -ent, -ify,* and *-efy*

More words end in *-able* than in *-ible*. Here are some of the most common *-ible* words:

eligible	incredible	irresistible	legible
permissible	responsible	terrible	visible

Unfortunately, there are no rules of thumb to help you decide whether to use the suffix *-ant* or *-ent*. Learn common words with these suffixes, and have your dictionary handy for others.

-ant	***-ent***
defiant	confident
observant	convenient

relevant existent
reluctant imminent
resistant independent

The suffix *-ify* is more common than *-efy*. Learn the four *-efy* words:

liquefy putrefy rarefy stupefy

56f Multinational characters: Accents, umlauts, tildes, and cedillas

Words and names in languages other than English may be spelled with special marks over or under a letter, such as an accent (é or è), an umlaut or dieresis (ö), a tilde (ñ), or a cedilla (ç). Your word processing program probably provides these characters (in Microsoft Word, go to/Insert> Symbol). If it does not, insert them by hand.

EXERCISES

Exercises on Punctuation, Mechanics, and Spelling

EXERCISE 1 Use commas after introductory material or with nonrestrictive elements 45c

Add any necessary commas. Some sentences may be correct.

Example Working for a major chemical manufacturer, Charles Baldwin, an engineer, helped to develop the symbol that identifies biohazards.

1. Realizing that laboratories and medical facilities around the world all needed to dispose of biohazards researchers wanted a symbol that would indicate to everyone which material was infectious.
2. Designers who create symbols want them to be memorable.
3. However the biohazard symbol needed to be unlike any other symbol.
4. In 1966 the symbol which is three-sided so that it looks the same if seen upside-down or sideways was chosen.
5. With its vivid orange color, a shade determined to be the most visible of all colors under most conditions the symbol was soon accepted by the Centers for Disease Control and Prevention, the Occupational Safety and Health Administration, and the National Institutes of Health.

EXERCISE 2 Use commas in special situations 45i

Add commas to the correct places in the following sentences.

Example The Mayan calendar ends a major sequence on December 21, 2012, and then begins a new sequence.

1. Yes some people believed that this date also known as the winter solstice signalled the end of human civilization.
2. Many books and Internet sites said that a planet called Nibiru discovered by the Sumerians would collide with Earth at that time.
3. The village of Bugarach France was overrun by visitors who believed aliens in the mountains there would lead them to safety.
4. Scientists such as Mary A. Voytek PhD of NASA sought to reassure the public that the frightening predictions were unfounded.
5. It's exciting to speculate about cataclysmic events isn't it?

EXERCISE 3 Know when to use an apostrophe 46a

Correct the use of the apostrophe in the following sentences.

Example Some of Rihanna's fans applauded her songs about domestic violence.

1. The farmer's market offers the freshest honeydew melon's, watermelon's, and cantaloupe's.

2. Let's jump in the water before it get's too cold.
3. The orange parka is Sara's, and the blue one is your's.
4. When we're in New Orleans, we can stay with my friends the Abbott's.
5. The mountain's sides are beginning to erode.

EXERCISE 4 Use apostrophes to signal possession 46b, 46c

Correct any errors in the use of apostrophes in the following sentences.

Example In parts of Africa that have been devastated by AIDS, doctors who practice Western-style medicine are looking at traditional ~~healer's~~ healers' roles in treating the sick.

1. Doctors and healers' ideas about useful treatments for people infected with the AIDS virus sometimes conflict with each other.
2. For example, traditional healers often prescribe emetics to cause vomiting, and if a patients' treatment also includes retroviral drugs, the patient may expel the drugs before they take effect.
3. Because many doctors in Africa understand their patients faith in traditional healing, some doctors are trying to work with healers rather than fighting them.
4. Some healers have agreed to attend conferences' at hospitals, where they learn to wear latex gloves when treating patients and to use alcohol to clean razor blades' edges and porcupine quills that have contacted any patients' body fluids.
5. Many patients trust healer's more than they trust doctor's, so hospitals in some areas have deputized traditional healers to monitor their patients intake of AIDS drugs and their mental well-being.

EXERCISE 5 Use apostrophes correctly with contractions in special instances and with *it's* 46d, 46f

Correct any errors in the use of apostrophes in the following sentences.

Example Trainspotting has ~~it's~~ its fans in Great Britain, and airplane spotters ~~are'nt~~ aren't unusual either.

1. Although theyre often regarded as geek's by people who do'nt share their passion, trainspotters are devoted to their hobby of watching trains and noting engine numbers.
2. Planespotting, a variation of trainspotting, resulted in legal difficulties for a group of vacationing Briton's who were arrested and accused of spying on airfields in Greece.
3. The arrests led to a diplomatic rift between Great Britain and Greece, with the Britons claiming that theyd merely been enjoying the Greek Air Force celebrations and the Greeks claiming that the spotters were illegally

monitoring pilots conversations and observing high-security military installations.

4. Its not surprising that the Greek police were unfamiliar with planespotting, since the hobby attracts few people outside of it’s British birthplace.
5. “Its an embarrassment,” said one Greek official; the detained Britons may have been accustomed to seeing their passions ridiculed at home, but they probably were’nt expecting to meet such a reception abroad.

EXERCISE 6 Use quotation marks in dialogue 47c

Correct the use of quotation marks in the following sentences.

> **Example** “Are you going to the play this weekend?” Marj asked.

1. Bao isn’t coming to the theater,” Aidan said. “He can’t stand comedies.
2. “Why didn’t he say that, Marj asked, before I paid for the tickets?”
3. “When you said this was a Shakespeare play, Bao assumed you meant a tragedy.” Aidan explained. “You should have been more specific.”
4. But no big tragedy, he joked. “Right?
5. “Small tragedy, grumbled Marj. “I’m still out fifteen dollars.

EXERCISE 7 Punctuate a quotation within a quotation 47d

Correct the use of quotation marks in the following sentences. Some sentences may be correct as written.

> **Example** The article stated, “Indiana University’s eight-minute flag routine has been called ‘the best timeout in college basketball.’”

1. “I get chills when I hear the song “Lay Your Head Down,”” Pam said.
2. Randy asked, ‘Do you like that song better than “Molly Malone”?’
3. Writes Jack De Bellis in *The John Updike Encyclopedia,* “Updike has explained that he writes every day but Sunday for three hours in the morning. As he notes, Like snowflakes falling an accumulation will result.”
4. Jayne’s dating book advised, “When a man says ‘I’ll call you, reply, No, I’ll call you.’”
5. I was fascinated by this *Huffington Post* headline: ‘Mirlande Wilson, McDonald’s Worker, ‘Loses’ Mega Millions Ticket.’

EXERCISE 8 Use quotations with titles, definitions, and translations 47e

Use quotation marks and italics to correct the following sentences.

> **Example** My grandfather used the word *stripling* to mean “young man.”

1. Did you know that alfresco means in the fresh air?
2. A. M. Homes’s short story The Safety of Objects became a film with the same name.

3. After Joao heard the song Mamma Mia on the radio, he found himself singing it all day.
4. The article Unsinkable in this week's issue of The New Yorker reviews Jeannette Winterson's memoir Why Be Happy When You Could Be Normal?
5. The word that means government by a few is oligarchy.

EXERCISE 9 Know when to use and when not to use a semicolon 48a

Add semicolons and change commas to semicolons as needed in the following sentences.

Example Jan Harold Brunvald is the man who coined the term *urban legend*,/; he once said that the truth never stands in the way of a good story.

Many urban legends are the kinds of stories that people use to frighten one another around a campfire. Some of the best-known ones are about escaped lunatics and murderers such as the man with a hook for a hand who terrorizes a young couple who, while parked on a deserted road, hear a radio broadcast about him, the man who telephones a babysitter with dire warnings, finally revealing that he is calling from another extension in the same house, and the killer who hides in the back seat of a woman's car or under the bed in her dorm room. These stories are chilling but faintly unbelievable, we all realize, eventually, that they are not true.

EXERCISE 10 Know when to use and when not to use a colon 48b

Make any changes in the following sentences so that colons and semicolons are used correctly.

Example Turtles are a unique life form for one reason,/: no other creature has a rigid shell made of vertebrae and ribs.

1. The professor required each student to have a copy of *Herpetology An Introductory Biology of Amphibians and Reptiles.*
2. Turtles are divided into two main types according to the way they retract their necks into their bodies, the *cryptodire*, or "hidden neck," turtles can pull their heads completely into their shells, but the *pleurodire*, or "side neck," turtles can only partially retract their heads.
3. Turtles are different from other reptiles because: their chest cavities cannot expand when they inhale.
4. Turtles can survive without air much longer than other reptiles; sometimes as long as thirty-three hours.
5. Many species of turtles can take in oxygen through sacs which emerge from the turtle's digestive and urogenital cavity; turtles share this unusual method of breathing with life forms such as: dragonfly nymphs and sea cucumbers.

EXERCISE 11 Use end punctuation correctly 49a, 49b

Mark with an "X" the sentence (A or B) that uses more appropriate end punctuation. Explain your choice to your classmates.

Example

___ A. The Web site asks users whether they are so afraid of flying that they avoid airplanes in all circumstances?

_X_ B. The Web site asks users whether they are so afraid of flying that they avoid airplanes in all circumstances.

1. ___ A. With modern technology come modern fears, and thousands of people in industrial societies are terrified of air travel.

   ___ B. With modern technology come modern fears, and thousands of people in industrial societies are terrified of air travel!

2. ___ A. If people who must fly for business or family reasons are too frightened to board an airplane, where can they turn for help.

   ___ B. If people who must fly for business or family reasons are too frightened to board an airplane, where can they turn for help?

3. ___ A. Although most fearful fliers know that flying is statistically safer than driving a car, many of them cannot overcome the part of the mind that says, "What if the plane crashes?"

   ___ B. Although most fearful fliers know that flying is statistically safer than driving a car, many of them cannot overcome the part of the mind that says, "What if the plane crashes?".

4. ___ A. Self-help classes and Web sites help fearful fliers to become more familiar with airplanes; the idea is that familiar things are less frightening.

   ___ B. Self-help classes and Web sites help fearful fliers to become more familiar with airplanes; the idea is that familiar things are less frightening!

5. ___ A. After a plane crash has been in the news, enrollment in self-help classes for fearful fliers tends to decline; psychologists believe that such events convince people that their irrational fears are based in reality, so they say to themselves, "See? I was right to avoid airplanes."

   ___ B. After a plane crash has been in the news, enrollment in self-help classes for fearful fliers tends to decline; psychologists believe that such events convince people that their irrational fears are based in reality, so they say to themselves, "See? I was right to avoid airplanes!"

EXERCISE 12 Use italics and underlining correctly 50a–50f

Underline any words that need italicization or underlining, and remove any unnecessary underlining or quotation marks.

In the nineteenth century, phrenology—the study of bumps on the skull and their relation to the personality—was a popular pseudoscientific practice, and one of the best-known phrenologists was Lorenzo Fowler. Along with his brother Orson, Lorenzo Fowler headed the Phrenological Institute in New York City, where the two trained other phrenologists, and Lorenzo gave readings to celebrities such as Julia Ward Howe, author of The Battle Hymn of the Republic. The Fowler brothers saw themselves as leaders of a progressive movement; they ran the publishing company that put out the first edition of Walt Whitman's "Leaves of Grass." They also published the Phrenological Journal, hoping that phrenological analysis could lead people to correct defects of character that had been revealed by their cranial protrusions.

In 1872, Samuel Clemens, who had written Huckleberry Finn and many other works under the nom de plume Mark Twain, visited Fowler under an assumed name and obtained a reading and a phrenological chart. Clemens, who was an early champion both of scientific innovations like fingerprinting (which is featured in his novel "Pudd'nhead Wilson") and of inventions that proved to be dismal failures, wanted to put phrenology to the test. The results amused him: in "The Autobiography of Mark Twain," Clemens notes that Fowler found a spot on his skull that "represented the total absence of the sense of humor." Months later, Clemens returned for a second reading, identifying himself both as Clemens and as Mark Twain, and was given a reading and a chart that "contained several sharply defined details of my character, but [...] bore no recognizable resemblance to the earlier chart."

Clemens remained convinced that phrenology was quackery, and others soon agreed. By 1900, phrenology had fallen out of favor. Even in the twenty-first century, however, the use of terms such as highbrow and lowbrow, which came from phrenology, demonstrates the influence that this idea once had.

EXERCISE 13 Use capital letters correctly 51a–51e

Capitalize any letters that are incorrectly lowercase, and change any incorrect capital letters to lowercase letters.

Example During the ~~civil war~~ [Civil War], a ~~Doctor~~ [doctor] from Kentucky tried to spread a ~~Virus~~ [virus] to cities in the ~~north~~ [North].

1. Biological warfare may strike modern Americans as Barbaric, but during the French and Indian war, smallpox-infected blankets given to Native Americans helped to decimate their numbers.
2. in the 1860s, Dr. Luke blackburn tried the same tactic, giving or selling clothing from patients with Yellow fever to Soldiers in the Union Army.
3. According to some historians, the Doctor hoped to spread Yellow Fever in washington and new York; president Jefferson Davis of the confederate States of America probably knew about and approved of the plan.
4. Fortunately for citizens of the north, yellow fever cannot be passed from one person to another by skin contact. although Dr. Blackburn's plot was

discovered on the day of Lincoln's Assassination, he was never prosecuted in a Court of Law.

5. Blackburn eventually became the Governor of Kentucky, where he worked for penal and educational reform. A statue of the good samaritan marks his grave in frankfort cemetery.

EXERCISE 14 Use abbreviations correctly 52a–52f

Correct any errors in the use of abbreviations in the following sentences.

Example According to ~~Mister~~ [Mr.] Sid Green, who teaches ~~H.S. hist.~~ [high school history] in ~~CA~~ [California], some US colleges and universities no longer require students to take the SAT.

1. An early adopter—someone who buys new devices and gadgets as soon as they are available—probably downloaded music when most people still bought CDs, rented streamed movies on Netflix while others still watched movies on DVDs, and picked out smartphones as holiday gifts when most people still had landlines.
2. The acupuncturist's receptionist referred to him as Doctor Loren Selwyn, but I later discovered that he was Loren Selwyn, doctor of philosophy, not Loren Selwyn, medical doctor.
3. Ms Krebs could type so many w.p.m. that the computer printer was spewing out pp. long after she had stopped working for the eve.
4. Sen Hammond helpfully told us that the New Year's Eve party would be held on Dec. 31, but he neglected to say what time we should arrive.
5. Akhenaton, orig. known as Amenhotep, ruled ancient Egypt until his death in about 1358 before the Common Era.

EXERCISE 15 Use hyphens correctly 54a–54d

Correct the use of hyphens in the following sentences.

Example My friend Suzette is great at do [-] it [-] yourself projects.

1. Suzette's mother- and father-inlaw got a postHalloween visit from their grand-children.
2. Suzette dressed her kids in home-made were-wolf costumes.
3. They were un-recognizable in heavy, furcovered masks.
4. Their lethal-looking paws were creatively-designed too.
5. Their grandfather pretended to be terror-stricken.

EXERCISE 16 Correct misspelled words 56a–56e

In each of the following sentences, correct any misspelled words. Some sentences may not contain any errors.

Example In the wake of ~~violant~~ violent incidents at high schools, many schools have adopted a "zero ~~tolerence~~ tolerance" policy toward weapons.

1. After a slew of school shootings in Arkansas, Kentucky, and elsewhere, some schools decided to crack down on students carrieing weapons.
2. In many schools, students face suspension if they are caught with guns, knifes, or any potential weapon.
3. One seven-year-old boy was suspended when other childrens saw a two-inch toy gun on a keychain fall out of his pocket.
4. His mother made the arguement that suspending students for carrying toys was a violation of common sense.
5. Schools have also been declareing zero-tolerance policys toward possession of drugs and other controled substances.
6. It's hard to beleive, but one child was suspended for shareing candy with friends when teachers did not recognize the brand.
7. A declareation of zero tolerance means that a school automaticly punishs any student who even appears to have broken the rules.
8. These policys allow employees no leeway to decide for themselfs whether the student's behavior warrants punishment.
9. Some of the grislyest incidants of school violence have occured in schools that had already adopted zero-tolerance policies, such as Columbine High School in Littleton, Colorado.
10. Can a zero-tolerance policy realy help schools, familys, and nieghborhoods avoid tragedy?

MindTap®

▸ **Practice skills that you have learned in this part, and receive automatic feedback.**

9 Writing across Languages and Cultures

WRITING IN YOUR CAREER

The Engineer, the Writer

Courtesy of Lisa Zhang Wharton

Engineering today is an international profession. Electrical engineer Lisa Zhang Wharton, for example, was born in China and educated at Beijing University before she started working at Boston Scientific on cardiac devices such as pacemakers. She's not the only one who is far from home. Almost half—45 percent—of those studying to be engineers in the United States are from somewhere else (National Science Board, 2006). Global interdependence means engineers can find themselves studying or working abroad. In a 2008 article for the *Online Journal of Global Engineering Education*, Carol Del Vitto quotes Thomas Tischhauser, vice president of the Powertrain & Chassis Division of Continental Automotive Systems: "The engineer of the future must be prepared to 'champion cultural diversity' by understanding that 'cultures are diverse' and that 'diversity drives the best ideas.'" Del Vitto also quotes the president and CEO of Corporate Research for the Siemens Corporation: "New skills will be needed, skills that go beyond the traditional technical capabilities." As an engineer, Wharton has written protocols, results, reports, and requirement documents. "Navigating disagreements can be the biggest challenge, so understanding your colleagues, whatever their cultural background, is important," Wharton says. "Being around Americans has made me a different person. In China, I was very shy. I was a good student, but I would have been embarrassed if I spoke up. In America, actually, speaking up means you are actively interested. So, I'm more open, more ready to speak my mind."

Sample Paper 2 (section 5c) examines what makes a report in the natural sciences different from one in the social sciences—and from an academic article in the humanities.

9 Writing across Languages and Cultures

MindTap®

Understand the goals of this part, and complete a warm-up activity.

57 Language Diversity and Edited American English: Challenges for Multilingual Writers

MindTap®

Read, highlight, and take notes online.

College students in North America are a linguistically diverse group: monolingual English-speaking students who have little experience with other cultures and who may speak a local dialect of English; students who grew up in North America among family and friends with their own languages and cultures; students who learned English in formal or informal situations either in their own countries or after they emigrated from other countries; students who speak several languages fluently; and various mixes and remixes of these categories. For college students, Edited American English consists of the language used in formal written documents, for example, in course essays, assignments, and term papers. The rigorous editing required for those tasks is not as necessary in more informal writing, such as journal entries, freewriting, blogs, and first drafts—nor on social media such as *Twitter* or *Instagram*. The chapters in this part of the handbook are specifically designed to help you write and edit your college work.

57a Englishes and other languages

At the same time that travel and the Internet make us more aware of diversity and other countries' languages and cultures, we are also experiencing a spread in the use of English. According to David Crystal, in 2003 non-native speakers of English outnumbered native speakers of English three to one. It is estimated that more than 400 million people speak English as their native language, and more than a billion use English as a common language for special communicative, educational, and business purposes within their own communities. And by 2017, the estimated number of people speaking English will be about 3 billion—that is, half the world.

But languages are not fixed and static, and the users of English in their various locations adapt the language for their own purposes.

The concept of one English or a "standard" language is becoming more fluid; it is more focused on the situation and the readers of a

The Circle of World English (used with permission)

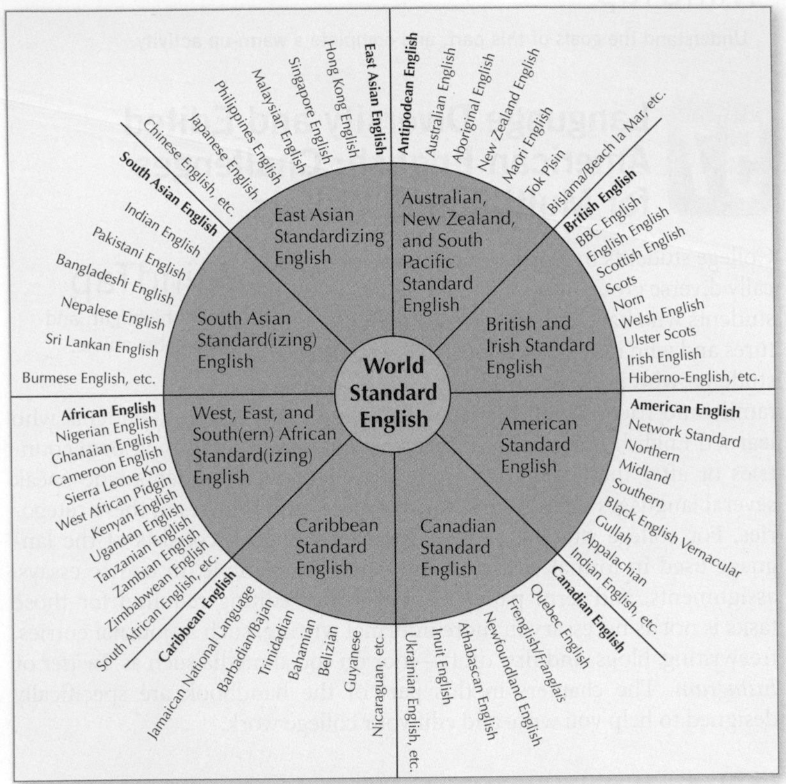

Source: Tom McArthur, "The English Languages?" *English Today* (July 1987), p. 11. Reprinted with the permission of Cambridge University Press.

particular piece of writing rather than on one set of rules. Consequently, the English regarded as standard in North America is not necessarily standard in Australia, the United Kingdom, Hong Kong, Singapore, Indonesia, India, or Pakistan. Even the versions of "standard" English in North America vary. Scholars see Englishes—varieties of English—in place of one monolithic language, and these Englishes sometimes claim their own names, such as Spanglish, Singlish, Hindlish, and Taglish. English is constantly being reinvented around the world, sometimes to the dismay of academics and government officials and sometimes with the approval of individuals who see the adaptation as an act of freedom, even rebellion. The Filipino poet Gemino Abad has gone so far as to make this claim: "The English language is now ours. We have colonized it."

In the United States, too, the Conference on College Composition and Communication as early as 1974 passed a resolution on *Students' Right to Their Own Language* (http://www.ncte.org/library/NCTEFiles/Groups/CCCC/NewSRTOL.pdf). The report on this resolution stresses the differences between speech and writing, affirming the viability of spoken dialects. However, the report makes the point that students "who want to write EAE [Edited American English] will have to learn the forms identified with that dialect as additional options to the forms they already control." The concept of *addition* and not *replacement* is important.

Therefore, despite the complexity and fluidity of varieties of English, with all their quirks, irregularities, rules, and exceptions, in the academic and business worlds, the conventions of what is often called "Edited American English" remain relatively constant in grammar, syntax, and vocabulary (though not in spelling), with only subtle variations from country to country, region to region. Whether you are monolingual—familiar only with American English—or grew up multilingual or learned English in classes designated for English as a Second Language (ESL) students, in everyday life you, too, constantly switch the Englishes you use, depending on whether you are texting a friend, tweeting, compiling a report for a supervisor, or writing a research paper in college. In all instances, it is *you* in the writing, but they are different *you*s, different voices of you. The formal voice of Edited American English is the one to use in most academic contexts. More on the importance of voice can be found in sections 1b and 1c.

57b Difference, not deficit, in academic writing

Students in colleges in North America who grew up speaking another language are often called "English as a Second Language learners," and the ESL abbreviation is commonly used in college curricula, professional literature, and the press. However, this term is not broad enough. Many so-called second-language students speak three or more languages, depending on their life and educational circumstances and the languages spoken at home. Along with being bilingual or multilingual, such students frequently are multicultural, equipped with all the knowledge and experience that those terms imply.

Whether your first language is a variety of English or a totally different language, it is a good idea to view your knowledge of language and culture as an advantage rather than a problem. Unlike many monolingual writers (individuals who know only one version of one language), you are familiar with different cultures in depth and can switch at will among varied linguistic and rhetorical codes. Rather than having only one language, one culture, and one culturally bound type of writing, you have a broader perspective—more to think about, more to write about, more resources to draw on as you write, and far more comparisons to make among languages, writers, writing, and culture. You bring your culture with you into your writing, and as you do so, you help shape and reshape the culture of North America.

Remember, too, that in many situations, the readers you write for will be culturally and linguistically diverse, not all emerging from one educational background. In formal settings, always aim to make your ideas clear to *all* readers by using standard forms of Edited American English, avoiding slang and jargon, and choosing a style that is appropriate to your subject matter.

57c Learning about difference as you write

Even for students who have been learning a new language or the conventions of academic writing for some time, departures from the standard language forms are inevitable. Welcome and embrace what others describe as "errors." Study them and learn from them. Having errors pointed out can help you become aware of differences among languages. In fact, errors show learning in progress. If you make no errors while you are learning to speak or write a new language or a standard version of English, perhaps you are being too careful and using only what you know is correct. Be willing to take risks and try new words, new expressions, new combinations. Expand your repertoire.

KEY POINTS

Web Sites on Language and Writing

The Web sites listed here provide useful information.

- Resources for ESL Instructors and Students from Purdue University's Online Writing Lab at http://owl.english.purdue.edu/owl/resource/678/1/.
- Guide to Grammar and Writing at http://grammar.ccc.commnet.edu/grammar. On this Capital Community College site, you will find information and quizzes on words, paragraphs, and essays. The Grammar Logs in "Ask Grammar" contain questions and answers and cover interesting points.

When somebody points out an error in your writing, write a note about it. Consider why you made the error—was it, for example, a transfer from your home language, a guess, a careless mistake? Or was it the

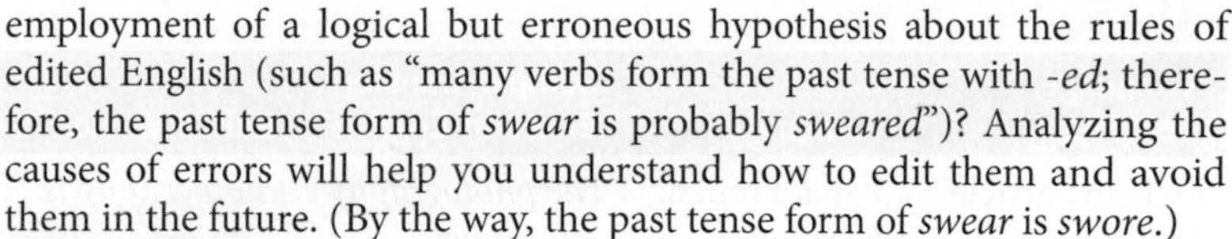

employment of a logical but erroneous hypothesis about the rules of edited English (such as "many verbs form the past tense with *-ed*; therefore, the past tense form of *swear* is probably *sweared*")? Analyzing the causes of errors will help you understand how to edit them and avoid them in the future. (By the way, the past tense form of *swear* is *swore*.)

57d Editing guide to multilingual transfer patterns

Nonstandard forms can occur while you are writing in a new language, especially when you are grappling with new subject matter and difficult subjects. You concentrate on ideas and clarity, but because no writer can do everything at once, you fail to concentrate on editing.

The editing guide that follows identifies several problem areas for multilingual writers. It shows grammatical features (column 1) of specific languages (column 2) and features that lead to an error when transferred to English (column 3). An Edited American English version appears in column 4. Of course, the guide covers neither all linguistic problem areas nor all languages. Rather, it lists a selection, with the goal of being useful and practical. Use the guide to raise your awareness about your own and other languages.

Editing Guide

Language Features	Languages	Sample Transfer Errors in English	Edited Version
Articles (58c–58f)			
No articles	Chinese, Japanese, Russian, Swahili, Thai, Urdu	*Sun is hot. I bought book.* *Computer has changed our lives.*	*The sun is hot. I bought a book.* *The computer has changed our lives.*
No indefinite article with profession	Arabic, French, Japanese, Korean, Vietnamese	*He is student.* *She lawyer.*	*He is a student.* *She is a lawyer.*
Definite article with days, months, places, idioms	Arabic	*She is in the bed.* *He lives in the Peru.*	*She is in bed.* *He lives in Peru.*

(Continued)

(Continued)

Language Features	Languages	Sample Transfer Errors in English	Edited Version
Definite article used for generalization	Farsi, French, German, Greek, Portuguese, Spanish	*The photography is an art.* *The books are more expensive than the disks.*	*Photography is an art.* *Books are more expensive than disks.*
Definite article used with proper noun	French, German, Portuguese, Spanish	*The Professor Brackert teaches in Frankfurt.*	*Professor Brackert teaches in Frankfurt.*
No definite article	Hindi, Turkish	*Store on corner is closed.*	*The store on the corner is closed.*
No indefinite article	Korean (uses *one* for *a*; depends on context)	*He ran into one tree.*	*He ran into a tree.*
Verbs and Verb Forms (chapter 59)			
A form of the verb *be* can be omitted	Arabic, Chinese, Greek, Russian	*India hotter than Britain.* *They working now.* *He cheerful.*	*India is hotter than Britain.* *They are working now.* *He is cheerful.*
No progressive forms	French, German, Greek, Russian	*They still discuss the problem.* *When I walked in, she slept.*	*They are still discussing the problem.* *When I walked in, she was sleeping.*
No tense inflections	Chinese, Thai, Vietnamese	*He arrive yesterday.* *When I was little, I always walk to school.*	*He arrived yesterday.* *When I was little, I always walked to school.*

Language Features	Languages	Sample Transfer Errors in English	Edited Version
No inflection for third person singular	Chinese, Japanese, Korean, Russian, Thai	*The singer have a big band.* *She work hard.*	*The singer has a big band.* *She works hard.*
Past perfect formed with *be*	Arabic	*They were arrived when I called.*	*They had arrived when I called.*
Different tense boundaries from English	Arabic, Chinese, Farsi, French	*I study here for a year.* *He has left yesterday.*	*I have been studying here for a year.* *He left yesterday.*
Different limits for passive voice	Japanese, Korean, Russian, Thai, Vietnamese	*They were stolen their luggage.* *My name base on Chinese characters.* *The mess clean up quick.* *A miracle was happened.*	*Their luggage was stolen.* *My name is based on Chinese characters.* *The mess was cleaned up quickly.* *A miracle (has) happened.*
No *-ing* (gerund)/ infinitive distinction	Arabic, Chinese, Farsi, French, Greek, Portuguese, Spanish, Vietnamese	*She avoids to go.* *I enjoy to play tennis.*	*She avoids going.* *I enjoy playing tennis.*
Infinitive not used to express purpose	Korean	*People exercise for losing weight.*	*People exercise to lose weight.*
Overuse of progressive forms	Hindi, Urdu	*I am wanting to leave now.*	*I want to leave now.*

(Continued)

(Continued)

Language Features	Languages	Sample Transfer Errors in English	Edited Version
Sentence Structure and Word Order (chapter 60)			
Verb precedes subject	Arabic, Hebrew, Russian, Spanish (optional), Tagalog	*Good grades received every student in the class.*	*Every student in the class received good grades.*
Verb-subject order in dependent clause	French	*I knew what would propose the committee.*	*I knew what the committee would propose.*
Verb after subject and object	Bengali, German (in dependent clause), Hindi, Japanese, Korean, Turkish	*... (when) the teacher the money collected.*	*... (when) the teacher collected the money.*
Coordination favored over subordination	Arabic	Frequent use of *and* and *so*	
Relative clause or restrictive phrase precedes noun that it modifies	Chinese, Japanese, Korean, Russian	*The enrolled in college student...* *A nine-meter-high impressive monument...* *He gave me a too difficult for me book.*	*The student (who was) enrolled in college...* *An impressive monument that is nine meters high...* *He gave me a book that was too difficult for me.*

Language Features	Languages	Sample Transfer Errors in English	Edited Version
Adverb can occur between verb and object or before verb	French, Spanish, Urdu (before verb)	*I like very much clam chowder.* *They efficiently organized the work.*	*I like clam chowder very much.* *They organized the work efficiently.*
That clause rather than an infinitive	Arabic, French, Hindi, Russian, Spanish	*I want that you stay.* *I want that they try harder.*	*I want you to stay.* *I want them to try harder.*
Inversion of subject and verb (rare)	Chinese	*She is leaving, and so I am.*	*She is leaving, and so am I.*
Conjunctions occur in pairs	Chinese, Farsi, Vietnamese	*Although she is rich, but she wears simple clothes.* *Even if I had money, I would also not buy that car.*	*Although she is rich, she wears simple clothes.* *Even if I had money, I would not buy that car.*
Subject (especially *it* pronoun) can be omitted	Chinese, Italian, Japanese, Portuguese, Spanish, Thai	*Is raining.*	*It is raining.*
Commas set off a dependent clause	German, Russian	*He knows, that we are right.*	*He knows that we are right.*
No exact equivalent of *there is/there are*	Japanese, Korean, Portuguese, Russian, Thai (adverb of place and *have*)	*This article says four reasons to eat beans.* *In the garden has many trees.*	*This article says [that] there are four reasons to eat beans.* *There are many trees in the garden.*

(Continued)

(Continued)

Language Features	Languages	Sample Transfer Errors in English	Edited Version
Nouns, Pronouns, Adjectives, Adverbs (chapters 42, 43, 58)			
Personal pronouns restate subject	Arabic, Gujarati, Spanish (optional)	*My father he lives in California.*	*My father lives in California.*
No human/nonhuman distinction for relative pronoun (*who/which*)	Arabic, Farsi, French, Russian, Spanish, Thai	*Here is the student which you met her last week.* *The people which arrived…*	*Here is the student [whom] you met last week.* *The people who arrived…*
Pronoun object included in relative clause	Arabic, Chinese, Farsi, Hebrew	*The house [that] I used to live in it is big.*	*The house that I used to live in is big.*
No distinction between subject and object forms of some pronouns	Chinese, Gujarati, Korean, Thai	*I gave the forms to she.*	*I gave the forms to her.* Or *I gave her the forms.*
Nouns and adjectives have same form	Chinese, Japanese	*She is beauty woman.* *They felt very safety on the train.*	*She is a beautiful woman.* *They felt very safe on the train.*
No distinction between *he* and *she, his* and *her*	Bengali, Farsi, Gujarati, Spanish (*his* and *her* only), Thai	*My sister dropped his purse.*	*My sister dropped her purse.*
No plural form after a number	Creole, Farsi	*He has two dog.*	*He has two dogs.*
No plural (or optional) forms of nouns	Chinese, Japanese, Korean, Thai	*Several good book…*	*Several good books…*

Language Features	Languages	Sample Transfer Errors in English	Edited Version
No relative pronouns	Korean	*The book is on the table is mine.*	*The book that is on the table is mine.*
Different perception of countable/ uncountable	Japanese, Russian, Spanish	*I bought three furnitures.*	*I bought three pieces of furniture.* Or *I bought three chairs.*
		She has red hairs.	*She has red hair.*
Adjectives show number	Russian, Spanish	*I have helpfuls friends.*	*I have helpful friends.*
Negative before verb	Spanish	*Jack no like meat.*	*Jack does not like meat.*
Double negatives used routinely	Spanish	*They don't know nothing.*	*They don't know anything.* Or *They know nothing.*

57e Editing guide to vernacular Englishes

Many of the varieties of English shown in the Circle of World English in section 57a differ from what is known as a standard form of the language in their use of words and grammatical conventions. Speakers of these Englishes have to do a kind of translating, called "code switching," when they speak or write, just as we all switch codes between levels of formality when we interact with different audiences. Consider, for example, situations in which you might say, "'Sup?" ("What's up?") rather than "Good morning." As David Crystal, author of *The Stories of English*, points out, "We need to be very sure of our ground (or very drunk) before we say, 'Yo, Officer.' "

The following table shows some of the common language features that confront speakers of African American Vernacular (AAV), Creole, and other varieties of English in North America when they move back and forth between their home culture and the academic world.

Vernaculars and Standard English

Linguistic Feature of Vernacular	Example (Nonstandard)	Edited for Standard English
Omitted form of *be*	*Maxine studying.*	*Maxine is studying.*
Use of *be* for habitual action	*Ray be working at home.*	*Ray usually works at home.*
Use of *been* without *have*	*I been sleeping all day.*	*I have (I've) been sleeping all day.*
Omitted *-ed*	*The books arrive this morning.*	*The books arrived this morning.*
No *-s* ending for third person singular present tense verb	*That model have a big smile.*	*That model has a big smile.*
No plural form after a plural number	*Jake own two dog.*	*Jake owns two dogs.*
Verb inversion before indefinite pronoun subject	*Can't nobody do that.*	*Nobody can do that.*
They instead of possessive *their*	*The players grabbed they gear.*	*The players grabbed their gear.*
Hisself instead of *himself*	*That musician promote hisself too much.*	*That musician promotes himself too much.*
Personal pronoun restates subject	*His instructor, she strict.*	*His instructor is strict.*
No apostrophe + *-s* for possessive	*She my brother wife.*	*She is my brother's wife.*
It used in place of *there*	*It's a gate at the entrance.*	*There is (There's) a gate at the entrance.*
Double negative	*You don't know nothing.*	*You don't know anything.* Or *You know nothing.*

57f Tips for multilingual writers

Get help Use the resources available at your college. Librarians and Writing Center tutors are there to assist you. Don't be afraid to ask. And make sure that you go to your instructor during assigned office hours to get advice and clarification on any of the assignments and on your progress in the course.

Participate in class It isn't always easy to join a discussion with a group of students who speak English fluently, but if you prepare well for class, you will find that your fellow students will be eager to hear the comments and observations of somebody who knows more than one language and has lived in more than one country. In class or in a group, listen attentively to others and offer informative responses. Your instructor and classmates will be delighted to hear comments from a cross-cultural perspective.

Follow the conventions Be aware of the conventions associated with writing papers in North America. Readers expect you to take a stand on a controversial issue, and they value direct expression of your opinions, authoritatively backed up by appropriately cited evidence. Academic readers will expect you to express your point of view clearly in a thesis statement somewhere close to the beginning of your paper and back up your claim with concrete points of evidence. Some students find that making an outline helps with organizing a paper. See section 2d for sample outlines.

Don't lapse into informality and slang It is often difficult for learners of a language to decide exactly how and when to use the new language forms they hear and read. By all means, try out new words and expressions, but do so in safe situations before you use them in an academic setting where they might be inappropriate or even cause offense. When you are in doubt about whether you should use a new expression, check its connotations first with a friend, tutor, or your instructor.

Keep a learning log In a notebook or a computer file, keep a log of language errors that your instructor or peer editors comment on. If you enter in your log a sentence with an error and then correct the error on the page in your log, you will create a record of your own editing and learning. In addition, keep special logs of prepositions (rely *on*, afraid *of*) and of idioms—those expressions that defy rules and follow no patterns, such as *burn up* and *burn down*. The tabbed page at the beginning of Part 10 has an example of such a log.

Consult learners' dictionaries Make use of an English dictionary specifically designed for multilingual writers, such as *Cambridge Learner's Dictionary* (http://dictionary.cambridge.org/us/dictionary/learner-english/) or *Oxford ESL Dictionary for Students of American English*. Such dictionaries provide useful information to language learners, including example sentences.

Learn from Web sites Use sites specially designed for language learners, such as the ones listed on page 624. In addition, go to *Activities for ESL Students* at http://a4esl.org, which includes quizzes and crossword puzzles in English as well as bilingual quizzes in more than forty languages.

Acknowledge sources In some cultures, the citing of classic, often memorized texts without acknowledgment of the exact source is accepted and common. However, academic conventions in North America require all writers to cite their sources of information other than the common knowledge of dates and events in the lives of public figures. Failing to do so can lead to a serious charge of academic plagiarism. Whatever you do, always cite your sources to avoid plagiarism. For more on the important issues of textual ownership and plagiarism, go to 9a–9c.

58 Nouns and Articles

58a Categories of nouns

MindTap®
Read, highlight, and take notes online.

Nouns in English fall into two categories: proper nouns and common nouns. A *proper noun* names a unique person, place, or thing and begins with a capital letter: *Walt Whitman, Lake Superior, Grand Canyon, Vietnam Veterans Memorial, Tuesday* (51b, 58f).

A *common noun* names a general class of persons, places, or things and begins with a lowercase letter: *bicycle, furniture, plan, daughter, home, happiness*. Common nouns can be further categorized as countable and uncountable.

- A *countable noun* has a plural form. Countable nouns frequently add *-s* to indicate the plural: *picture, pictures; plan, plans*. Singular countable nouns are used after *a, an, the, this, that, each, every*. Plural countable nouns are used after *the, these, those, many, a few, both, all, some, several.*
- An *uncountable noun* cannot be directly counted. It has no plural form: *furniture, advice, information*. Uncountable nouns are used after *the, this, that, much, some*, and other singular expressions of quantity.

Common Nouns

Countable	Uncountable
tool, hammer (tools, hammers)	equipment
chair, desk (chairs, desks)	furniture
necklace, earring (necklaces, earrings)	jewelry
view, scene (views, scenes)	scenery
tip, suggestion (tips, suggestions)	advice

The concept of countability varies across languages. Japanese, for example, makes no distinction between countable and uncountable nouns. In French, Spanish, and Chinese, the word for *furniture* is a countable noun; in English, it is not. In Russian, the word for *hair* is countable and used in the plural.

58b Uncountable nouns

Some nouns are usually uncountable in English and are commonly listed as such in a language learners' dictionary such as *The American Heritage English as a Second Language Dictionary*. Learn the most common uncountable nouns, and note the ones that end in *-s* but are nevertheless singular:

A mass made up of parts: clothing, equipment, furniture, garbage, homework, information, jewelry, luggage, machinery, money, scenery, traffic, transportation

Abstract concepts: advice, courage, education, fun, happiness, health, honesty, information, knowledge

Natural substances: air, blood, cotton, heat, ice, sunshine, water, wood, wool

Diseases: diabetes, influenza, measles

Games: checkers, chess, soccer, tennis

Subjects of study: biology, economics, history, physics

Note the following features of uncountable nouns.

1. An uncountable noun has no plural form:

▶ **She gave me ~~several~~ some informations.** [edited: "several" crossed out, "some" inserted; "s" of "informations" struck]

▶ **The couple bought a lot of new furnitures.** [edited: "s" of "furnitures" struck]

2. An uncountable noun subject is always followed by a singular verb:

   ▸ **Their advice ~~are~~ ^is^ useful.**

3. You can give an uncountable noun a countable sense—that is, indicate a quantity of it—by adding a word or phrase that indicates quantity. The noun itself will always remain singular: three pieces of *furniture*, two items of *information*, many pieces of *advice*.

4. Some nouns can be countable in one context and uncountable in another. Always examine the context.

General class (uncountable)

▸ **He loves *chocolate*.** [all chocolate, in whatever form]

▸ ***Time* flies.**

▸ **He has red *hair*.**

A countable item or items

▸ **She gave him a *chocolate*.** [one piece of candy from a box of many chocolates]

▸ **They are having *a good time*.**

▸ **There is a *long gray hair* on her pillow.**

KEY POINTS

What to Use before an Uncountable Noun

Use	
The zero article (generalization)	Furniture is expensive.
The (specific reference)	*The* furniture in the new office is hideous.
This, that	*This* furniture is tacky.
A possessive pronoun: *my, his, their*, etc.	*Their* furniture is modern.
A quantity word: *some, any, much, less, more, most, a little, a great deal (of), all, other* (41i)	She has bought *some* new furniture.

Do not use	
A/an (except in phrases *a little* or *a great deal of*)	The room needs ~~a~~ new furniture.
Each, every, another	All furniture ~~Every furniture~~ should be practical.
These, those	That furniture is ~~Those furnitures are~~ elegant.
Numerals: *one, two, three,* etc.	They bought two pieces of furniture. ~~two furnitures.~~
A plural quantity word: *several, many, a few*	She took only a little furniture ~~a few furniture~~ with her to her new apartment.

58c Basic rules for *a, an,* and *the*

1. Use *the* whenever a reference to a common noun is specific and unique for both the writer and readers (see 58d).
   - ▸ **He loves the museum that Rem Koolhaas designed.**
2. Do not use *a* or *an* with a plural countable noun.
   - ▸ **They cited ~~a~~ reliable surveys.**
3. Do not use *a* or *an* with an uncountable noun.
   - ▸ **He gave ~~a~~ helpful advice.**
4. Use *a* before a consonant sound: *a bird, a house, a sonnet*. Use *an* before a vowel sound: *an egg, an ostrich, an hour, an ugly vase*. Take special care with the sounds associated with the letters *h* and *u*, which can have either a consonant or a vowel sound: *a housing project, an honest man; a unicorn, an uprising*.
5. To make a generalization about a countable noun, do one of the following:
   - Use the plural form: *Lions are majestic.*
   - Use the singular with *a* or *an*: *A lion is a majestic animal.*

- Use the singular with *the* to denote a classification: *The lion is a majestic animal.*

6. Make sure that a countable singular noun is preceded by an article or by a demonstrative pronoun (*this, that*), a number, a singular word expressing quantity, or a possessive.

   A (Every, That, One, Her) nurse
   ▸ ~~**Nurse**~~ **has a difficult job.**

7. In general, although there are many exceptions, use no article with a singular proper noun (*Mount Everest*), and use *the* with a plural proper noun (*the Himalayas*) (see 58f).

58d *The* for a specific reference

When you write a common noun that both you and your readers know refers to one or more specific persons, places, things, or concepts, use the article *the.*

▸ **I study *the* earth, *the* sun, and *the* moon.** [the ones in our solar system]

▸ **She closed *the* door.** [of the room she was in]

▸ **Her husband took *the* dog out for a walk.** [the dog belonging to the couple]

▸ ***The* song that won *the* prize was written by a first-year student.** [a specific song—the one that won a specific prize]

▸ **Jorge wrote *a* song last night for his music class assignment. He was delighted when he was asked to perform *the* song in class.**

▸ **He bought *the most expensive* bicycle in the store.** [A superlative makes a reference to one specific item.]

58e Which article? Four basic questions to ask

Multilingual writers often have difficulty choosing among the articles *a*, *an*, and *the* and the *zero article* (no article at all). Languages vary greatly in their representation of the concepts conveyed by English articles (see 57d, editing guide to multilingual transfer patterns). The following Key Points box should provide a useful guide.

KEY POINTS

Articles at a Glance: Four Basic Questions about a Noun

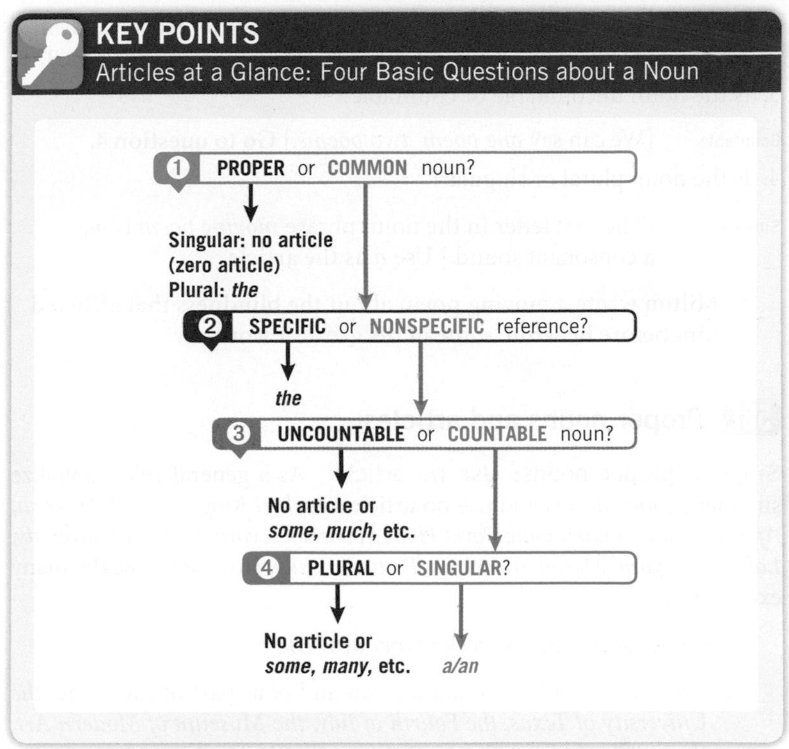

You can use the four basic questions about a noun to decide which article, if any, to use with the noun *poem* as you consider the following sentence:

▸ **Milton wrote ___?___ moving poem about the blindness that afflicted him before he wrote some of his greatest works.**

1. Is the noun (*poem*) a proper noun or a common noun?

Common **Go to question 2.**

2. Does the common noun refer to a specific person, place, thing, or idea known to both writer and readers as unique, or is the reference nonspecific?

Nonspecific [*Poem* is not identified to readers in the same way that *blindness* is. We know the reference is to the blindness that afflicted Milton before he wrote some of his greatest works. However, there is more than one "moving poem" in literature. The reference would be specific for readers only if the poem had been previously discussed.] **Go to question 3.**

3. Is the noun uncountable or countable?

Countable [We can say *one poem, two poems.*] **Go to question 4.**

4. Is the noun plural or singular?

Singular [The first letter in the noun phrase *moving poem* is *m*, a consonant sound.] **Use *a* as the article.**

▶ **Milton wrote *a* moving poem about the blindness that afflicted him before he wrote some of his greatest works.**

58f Proper nouns and articles

Singular proper nouns: Use no article As a general rule, capitalize singular proper nouns and use no article: *Stephen King, Central America, Africa, Islam, Golden Gate Park, Hollywood Boulevard, Cornell University, Lake Temagami, Mount St. Helens, Thursday, July*. However, note the many exceptions.

EXCEPTIONS: SINGULAR PROPER NOUNS WITH *THE*

Proper nouns with a common noun and *of* as part of the name: *the University of Texas, the Fourth of July, the Museum of Modern Art, the Statue of Liberty*

Highways: *the New Jersey Turnpike, the Long Island Expressway*

Buildings: *the Eiffel Tower, the Prudential Building*

Bridges: *the Golden Gate Bridge*

Hotels and museums: *the Stanley Hotel, the Guggenheim Museum*

Countries named with a phrase: *the United Kingdom, the Dominican Republic, the People's Republic of China*

Parts of the globe: *the North Pole, the West, the East, the Riviera*

Seas, oceans, gulfs, rivers, and deserts: *the Dead Sea, the Atlantic Ocean, the Persian Gulf, the Yangtze River, the Mojave Desert*

Historical periods and events: *the Enlightenment, the October Revolution, the Cold War*

Groups: *the Taliban, the Chicago Seven*

Plural proper nouns: Use *the* Examples are *the United States, the Great Lakes, the Himalayas, the Philippines, the Chinese* (people) (51b).

59 Verbs and Verb Forms

A clause needs a complete verb consisting of one of the five verb forms (39a) and any necessary auxiliaries. Forms derived from a verb (*verbals*) cannot serve as the main verb of a clause; such forms are an *-ing* form, a past participle (ending in *-ed* for a regular verb), or an infinitive (*to* + base form). Because readers get so much information from verbs, they have a relatively low level of tolerance for error, so make sure you edit with care and use auxiliary verbs whenever necessary.

MindTap®
Read, highlight, and take notes online.

59a The *be* auxiliary

Inclusion The *be* auxiliary must be included in a verb phrase in English, though in languages such as Chinese, Russian, and Arabic it can be omitted (see also 39c).

▸ **They ^are studying this evening.**

▸ **They have ^been studying since dinner.**

Sequence What comes after a *be* auxiliary? (see also 39c)

- The *-ing* form follows a verb in the active voice: He *is sweeping* the floor.
- The past participle follows a verb in the passive voice: The floor *was swept* yesterday.

59b Modal auxiliary verbs: Form and meaning

The nine modal auxiliary verbs are *will, would, can, could, shall, should, may, might,* and *must*. Note the following three important points:

1. The modals do not change form.
2. The modals never add an *-s* ending.
3. The form immediately following a modal is always a base form of a verb without *to: could go, should ask, must arrive, might have* seen, *would be* sleeping.

- **The committee must ~~to~~ vote tomorrow.**
- **The proposal might improve~~s~~ the city.**
- **The residents could disapprove~~d~~.**

Meanings of Modal Verbs

Meaning	Present and Future	Past
1. Intention	*will, shall* She *will* explain. [*Shall* is used mostly in questions: *Shall I buy that big green ceramic horse?*]	*Would* She said that she *would* explain.
2. Ability	*can (am/is/are able to)* He *can* cook well. [Do not use *can* and *able to* together: *He is able to cook well.*]	*could (was/were able to)* He *could* not read until he was eight. [He was not able to read until he was eight.]
3. Permission	*may, might, can, could* *May* I refer to Auden again? [*Might* or *could* is more tentative.]	*might, could* Her instructor said she *could* use a dictionary.
4. Polite question	*would, could* *Would* readers please indulge me for a moment? *Could* you try not to read ahead?	
5. Speculation	*would, could, might* If he had more talent, he *could* become a professional pianist. [See also 39j.]	*would* or *could* or *might* + *have* + past participle If I had studied, I *might have* passed the test.

Meaning	Present and Future	Past
6. Advisability	*should* You *should* go home and rest.	*should* + *have* + past participle You *should have* taken your medication. [Implied here is "but you did not."]
7. Necessity (stronger than *should*)	*must* (or *have to*) Applicants *must* apply for a mortgage.	*had to* + base form Theo van Gogh *had to* support his brother.
8. Prohibition	*must* + *not* Participants *must not* leave until all the questions have been answered.	
9. Expectation	*should* The author *should* receive a check soon.	*should* + *have* + past participle You *should have* received your check a week ago.
10. Possibility	*may, might* The technician *may* be working on the problem now.	*might* + *have* + past participle She *might* already *have* revised the ending.
11. Logical assumption	*must* She's late; she *must* be stuck in traffic.	*must* + *have* + past participle She *must have* taken the wrong route.
12. Repeated past action		*would* (or *used to*) + base form When I was a child, I *would* spend hours drawing.

59c Infinitive after verbs and adjectives

Some verbs are followed by an infinitive (*to* + base form) or a base form alone. Some adjectives also occur with an infinitive. Such combinations are highly idiomatic. You need to learn each one individually as you come across it in your reading.

Verb + infinitive The following verbs are commonly followed by an infinitive (*to* + base form):

agree	choose	fail	offer	refuse
ask	claim	hope	plan	venture
beg	decide	manage	pretend	want
bother	expect	need	promise	wish

Note any differences between English and your native language. For example, in Spanish, the word for *refuse* is followed by the equivalent of an *-ing* form. In English, you need *to* + the base form.

to criticize

▸ **He refused ~~criticizing~~ the system.**

Position of a negative In a verb + infinitive pattern, the position of the negative affects meaning. Note the difference in meaning that the position of a negative (*not, never*) can create.

▸ **He did *not* decide to buy a new car. His wife did.**

▸ **He decided *not* to buy a new car. His wife was disappointed.**

Verb + noun or pronoun + infinitive Some verbs are followed by a noun or pronoun and then an infinitive. See also 42a (p. 528) for a pronoun used before an infinitive.

V pron. inf.

▸ **The librarian *advised them to use* a better database.**

Verbs that follow this pattern are *advise, allow, ask, cause, command, convince, encourage, expect, force, help, need, order, persuade, remind, require, tell, urge, want, warn.*

Spanish and Russian use a *that* clause after verbs like *want*. In English, however, *want* is followed by an infinitive.

to

▸ **Rose wanted ~~that~~ her son ~~would~~ become a doctor.**

Make, let, and have After these verbs, use a noun or pronoun and a base form of the verb (without *to*).

- ▶ **He *made his son practice* for an hour.**
- ▶ **They *let us leave* early.**
- ▶ **The editor *had her secretary write* the rejection letter.**

Note the corresponding passive voice structure with *have:*

- ▶ **She usually *has the car washed* once a month.**

Adjective + infinitive Some adjectives are followed by an infinitive. The filler subject *it* often occurs with this structure.

- ▶ **It is dangerous to hike alone in the woods.** (infinitive: *to hike*)

These are some of the adjectives that can be followed by an infinitive: *anxious, correct, dangerous, eager, essential, foolish, happy, (im)possible, (in)advisable, likely, lucky, powerless, proud, right, silly, sorry, (un)fair, (un)just, (un)kind, (un)necessary, wrong.*

- ▶ **They were foolish to think they could climb to the top of the mountain.**

59d Verbs followed by an -*ing* verb form used as a noun

- ▶ **I can't help *laughing* at Jimmy Fallon.**

The verbs that are systematically followed by an -*ing* form (known as a *gerund*) make up a relatively short and learnable list.

admit	consider	enjoy	miss	resist
appreciate	delay	finish	postpone	risk
avoid	deny	imagine	practice	suggest
be worth	discuss	keep	recall	tolerate
can't help	dislike			

- ▶ **We considered ~~to invite~~ inviting his parents.**
- ▶ **Most people dislike ~~to hear~~ hearing cell phones at concerts.**

Place a negation between the verb and the -*ing* form:

- **On weekends, drivers enjoy *not* sitting in traffic jams.**

Note: An -*ing* form can also be used as a noun in the subject position of a sentence:

- ***Swimming* helps people maintain their weight.**

59e Verbs followed by an infinitive or an -*ing* verb form

Some verbs can be followed by either an infinitive or an -*ing* verb form (a gerund) with almost no discernible difference in meaning: *begin, continue, hate, like, love, start.*

- **She loves *cooking*.**
- **She loves *to cook*.**

The infinitive and the -*ing* form of a few verbs (*forget, remember, try, stop*), however, signal different meanings:

- **He remembered *to mail* the letter.** [an intention]
- **He remembered *mailing* the letter.** [a past act]

59f -*ing* and -*ed* forms used as adjectives

Both the present participle (-*ing* verb form) and the past participle (ending in -*ed* in regular verbs) can function as adjectives (see 39a and 39g). Each form has a different meaning: The -*ing* adjective indicates that the word modified produces an effect; the past participle adjective indicates that the word modified has an effect produced on it.

- **The *boring* cook served baked beans yet again.** [The cook produces boredom. Everyone is tired of baked beans.]
- **The *bored* cook yawned as she scrambled eggs.** [The cook felt the emotion of boredom as she did the cooking, but the eggs could still be appreciated.]

Produces an Effect	Has an Effect Produced on It
amazing	amazed
amusing	amused

annoying	annoyed
confusing	confused
depressing	depressed
disappointing	disappointed
embarrassing	embarrassed
exciting	excited
interesting	interested
satisfying	satisfied
shocking	shocked
surprising	surprised
worrying	worried

Note: Do not drop the *-ed* ending from a past participle. Sometimes in speech, it blends with a following *t* or *d* sound, but in writing, the *-ed* ending must be included.

▸ **I was surprise^d to see her wild outfit.**

▸ **The researchers were ~~worry~~ ^worried that the results were contaminated.**

60 Sentence Structure and Word Order

60a A subject in every clause

MindTap®
Read, highlight, and take notes online.

In some languages, a subject can be omitted. In English, you must include a subject in every clause, even just a filler subject such as *there* or *it*.

▸ **When the director's business partners lost money, ^there were immediate effects on the share prices.**

▸ **The critics hated the movie because ^it was too sentimental.**

Do not use *it* to point to a long subject that follows. Put the long subject in the subject position before the verb.

- **We can say that ~~it~~ does not matter the historical period of the society.**

The editing mark here points to reversing the order: *We can say that the historical period of the society does not matter.*

60b Order of sentence elements

Subject, verb, object Languages vary in their basic word order for the sentence elements of subject (S), verb (V), and direct object (DO). In English, the most commonly occurring sentence pattern is S + V + DO ("Children like candy") (see also 35d).

- **~~Good grades received every~~ student in the class.** (Every ... received good grades.)

Expressions of time and place Do not put an adverb or a phrase between the verb and its direct object.

- **The quiz show host congratulated ~~many times~~ the winner.** (many times.)

Descriptive adjective phrases Put a descriptive adjective phrase after, not before, the noun it modifies.

- **I would go to known only to me places.**

60c Direct and indirect objects

Some verbs—such as *give, send, show, tell, teach, find, sell, ask, offer, pay, pass,* and *hand*—can be followed by both a direct object (DO) and an indirect object (IO). The indirect object is the person or thing to whom or to which, or for whom or for which, something is done. It follows the verb and precedes the direct object (35d).

- **He gave his mother some flowers.** (IO: his mother; DO: some flowers)
- **He gave her some flowers.** (IO: her; DO: some flowers)

An indirect object can be replaced with a prepositional phrase that *follows* the direct object:

- **He gave some flowers to his mother.** (DO: some flowers; prepositional phrase: to his mother)

Some verbs—such as *explain, describe, say, mention,* and *open*—are never followed by an indirect object. Rather, they are followed by a direct object and a prepositional phrase with *to* or *for:*

▸ **She explained ~~me~~ the election process** to me.

Note that *tell*, but not *say*, can take an indirect object.

▸ **She ~~said~~** told **him the secret.**

60d Direct and indirect quotations and questions

The sentence structure and word order that you use relates directly to whether your quotations and questions are direct or indirect.

In a direct quotation or direct question, the exact words used by the speaker are enclosed in quotation marks. In an indirect quotation or indirect question, commonly used in expository writing, the writer reports what the speaker said, and quotation marks are not used. Changes also occur in pronouns, time expressions, and verb tenses. See also 38d and 39i for problems to avoid with shifts and with the use of tenses.

▸ **He said, "I have forgotten my password."** (direct quotation)

▸ **He said that he had forgotten his password.** (indirect quotation)

▸ **He asked, "Do you know it?"** (direct question)

▸ **He asked if anyone knew it.** (indirect question)

Direct and indirect quotations Usually, you must make several changes when you report a direct quotation as an indirect quotation. You will do this often when you write college papers and report the views of others.

Note: Style guides vary in the tenses they recommend for reporting the words of others, so in formal research papers, always follow the style of the discipline (chapter 5) for reporting authors' words.

Be careful to avoid shifting randomly between direct and indirect quotations (38d). For expository writing in college essays, as a general rule use indirect rather than direct quotation. However, to make a significant point, a direct quotation can pack a punch.

Direct and Indirect Quotations

Change	Direct/ Indirect Quotation	Example	Explanation
Punctuation and tense	Direct	Oscar Wilde said of his era, "Whatever *is* popular is wrong."	Exact words within quotation marks
	Indirect	Oscar Wilde said of his era that whatever was popular was wrong.	No quotation marks; tense change (39i)
Pronoun and tense	Direct	He insisted, "*I understand* the figures."	First person pronoun and present tense
	Indirect	He insisted that *he understood* the figures.	Change to third person pronoun; tense change
Command to statement	Direct	"Cancel the payment," her lawyer said.	
	Indirect	Her lawyer *advised* her *to* cancel the payment.	Verb (*tell, instruct*) + *to*
Expressions of time, place, and tense	Direct	The bankers promised, "We *will* work on *this* deal *tomorrow*."	
	Indirect	The bankers promised *they would* work on *that* deal *the next day*.	Expressions of time and place not related to speaker's perspective; tense change (39i); change to third person pronoun

Change	Direct/ Indirect Quotation	Example	Explanation
Colloquial to formal	Direct	The clients said, "Well, no thanks; *we won't* wait."	
	Indirect	The clients thanked the bankers but said *they would not* wait.	Spoken words and phrases omitted or rephrased; also a tense change

The sample essays in this book in parts 1, 3, and 4 show examples of direct and reported quotation from sources.

Direct and indirect questions When a direct question is reported indirectly in writing, it loses the word order of a question (V + S) and the question mark. Sometimes, changes in tense are necessary, too (see also 39i).

Direct question — V S — **The buyer asked, "*Are* the goods ready to be shipped?"**

Indirect question — S V — **The buyer asked if the goods *were* ready to be shipped.**

Direct question — V S — **The boss asked, "What *are* they doing?"**

Indirect question — S V — **The boss asked what they *were* doing**

Direct question — V S V — **"Why *did* they *send* a letter instead of an e-mail?" her secretary asked.**

Indirect question — S V V — **Her secretary asked why they [*had*] *sent* a letter instead of an e-mail.**

Use only a question word such as *why* or the word *if* or *whether* to introduce an indirect question. Do not use *that* as well.

- **Her secretary asked ~~that~~ why they had sent a letter instead of an e-mail.**

Direct and Indirect Questions

	Introductory Words	Auxiliary Verb	Subject	Auxiliary Verb(s)	Main Verb and Rest of Clause
Direct	What	are	they		thinking?
Indirect	Nobody knows what		they	are	thinking.
Direct	Where	does	he		work?
Indirect	I can't remember where		he		works.
Direct	Why	did	she		write that poem?
Indirect	The poet does not reveal why		she		wrote that poem.
Direct		Have	the diaries	been	published yet?
Indirect	The Web site does not say if (whether)		the diaries	have been	published yet.
Direct		Did	the space program		succeed?
Indirect	It is not clear if		the space program		succeeded.

60e Clauses beginning with *although* and *because*

In some languages, a subordinating conjunction (such as *although* or *because*) can be used along with a coordinating conjunction (*but, so*) or a transitional expression (*however, therefore*) in the same sentence. In English, only one is used.

No **_Although_ he loved his father, _but_ he did not have much opportunity to spend time with him.**

Possible revisions **_Although_ he loved his father, he did not have much opportunity to spend time with him.**

He loved his father, _but_ he did not have much opportunity to spend time with him.

No **_Because_ she had been trained in the church, _therefore_ she was sensitive to the idea of audience.**

Possible revisions **_Because_ she had been trained in the church, she was sensitive to the idea of audience.**

She had been trained in the church, _so_ she was sensitive to the idea of audience.

She had been trained in the church; _therefore_, she was sensitive to the idea of audience.

See 45e for punctuation with transitional expressions.

60f Unnecessary pronouns

Do not restate the simple subject of a sentence as a pronoun (see also 38i).

- ▶ **Visitors to the Statue of Liberty ~~they~~ have worn down the steps.**
- ▶ **The counselor who told me about dyslexia ~~he~~ is a man I will never forget.**

In a relative clause introduced by *whom, which,* or *that*, do not include a pronoun that the relative pronoun has replaced (see also 44d).

- ▶ **The house that I lived in ~~it~~ for ten years has been sold.**

60g Order of adjectives

Put adjectives after an article (*a*, *an*, *the*), a numeral (such as *four*), or a possessive (such as *my*, *his*). Cumulative adjectives cannot have the word *and* inserted between them, as each modifies the whole noun phrase that follows it. With cumulative adjectives, follow the conventional sequence before the main noun: (1) size, (2) shape, (3) age, (4) color, (5) region or geographical origin, (6) architectural style or religion, (7) material, (8) noun used as adjective to modify the head noun.

1 3 5 7 main noun

▶ **the big old Italian stone house**

2 4 6 8 main noun

▶ **our rectangular green Art Deco storage chest**

Do not use commas between cumulative adjectives. For punctuation with other types of adjectives (coordinate adjectives), see 45g.

61 Prepositions and Idioms

MindTap®
Read, highlight, and take notes online.

Prepositions appear in phrases with nouns and pronouns, and they also combine with adjectives and verbs in specific and set ways, as illustrated in 61a–61e. An idiom is a group of words that takes on a special, not necessarily literal, meaning, such as "kick the bucket" (die) and "smell a rat" (suspect). Learn idioms like these one by one as you come across them, and keep your own list.

61a Expressions with three common prepositions

Learn the uses of prepositions by writing them in lists when you come across them in your reading. Here is a start:

IN + YEAR, MONTH, PART OF DAY, STATE, COUNTRY, CITY, LANGUAGE, ETC.

in 2016, in July, in the morning, in Ohio, in the United States, in Milwaukee, in Spanish, in the drawer, in the closet, in the cookie jar, in the library stacks, in a book, in the rain, in his pocket, in bed, in school, in class, in time (to participate in an activity), in the envelope, in the newspaper, in love

ON + DAY, DATE, STREET NAME, ETC.

on Saturday, on 9 September, on Union Street, on the weekend, on the moon, on Earth, on the menu, on the library shelf, on the roof, a ring on her finger, an article on education, on occasion, on time (punctual), on foot, on the couch, knock on the door, the address on the envelope

AT + TIME, ETC.

at eight o'clock, at home, at a party, at night, at work

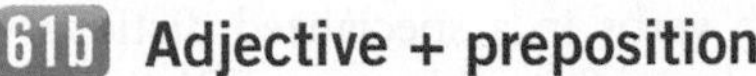

61b Adjective + preposition

When you are writing, use a dictionary to check the specific prepositions that are used with an adjective.

- ▸ **The botanist is *afraid of* spiders.**
- ▸ **E. O. Wilson was *interested in* ants.**

Some adjective + preposition combinations are *afraid of, ashamed of, aware of, fond of, full of, jealous of, proud of, suspicious of, tired of, interested in, grateful to* (someone), *grateful for* (something), *responsible to* (someone), *responsible for* (something), *anxious about, content with,* and *satisfied with.*

61c Verb + preposition

Some idiomatic verb + preposition combinations are *apologize to* (someone), *apologize for* (an offense or error), *arrive in* (a country or city), *arrive at* (a building or an event), *blame* (someone) *for* (an offense or error), *complain about, concentrate on, congratulate* (someone) *on* (success or good fortune), *consist of, depend on, explain* (facts) *to* (someone), *insist on, laugh at, rely on, smile at, take care of, thank* (someone) *for* (a gift or favor), *throw* (an object) *to* (someone waiting to catch it), *throw* (an object) *at* (someone not expecting it), and *worry about*. Keep a list of others you notice.

61d Phrasal verbs

Prepositions and a few adverbs (such as *away* and *forward*) can combine with verbs in such a way that they no longer function as prepositions or ordinary adverbs. They are then known as *particles*. Only a few languages other than English—Dutch, German, and Swedish, for example—have this verb + particle (preposition or adverb) combination, which is called a *phrasal verb*.

The meaning of a phrasal verb is entirely different from the meaning of the verb alone. Note the idiomatic meanings of some common phrasal verbs.

break down [stop functioning]	get over [recover from]
put off [postpone]	put up with [tolerate, endure]
run out [become used up]	run across [meet unexpectedly]
look into [examine]	take after [resemble]

Always check the meanings of such verbs in a specialized dictionary such as *The American Heritage English as a Second Language Dictionary.*

A particle can be followed by a preposition to make a three-word combination:

▸ **She *gets along with* everybody.** [She is friendly toward everybody.]

Other three-word verb combinations are

catch up with [draw level with]	look up to [admire]
look down on [despise]	put up with [endure]
look forward to [anticipate]	stand up for [defend]

Position of direct objects with two-word phrasal verbs Some two-word transitive phrasal verbs are separable. The direct object of these verbs can come between the verb and the accompanying particle.

▸ **She *put off* her dinner party.** [She postponed her dinner party.]

▸ **She *put* her dinner party *off*.**

When the direct object is a pronoun, however, always place the pronoun between the verb and the particle.

▸ **She *put* it *off*.**

Some commonly used phrasal verbs that follow this principle are listed here. They *can* be separated by a noun as a direct object, but they *must* be separated when the direct object is a pronoun.

call off [cancel]	give up [surrender]	make up [invent]
fill out [complete]	leave out [omit]	turn down [reject]
find out [discover]	look up [locate]	turn off [stop]

Most dictionaries list phrasal verbs that are associated with a particular verb along with their meanings and examples. Develop your own list of such verbs from your reading.

61e Preposition + -*ing* verb form used as a noun

The -*ing* verb form that functions as a noun (the *gerund*) frequently occurs after a preposition.

▸ **They congratulated him *on winning* the prize.**

▸ **The school principal expressed interest *in participating* in the fundraiser.**

▸ **He ran three miles *without stopping.***

▸ **The cheese is the right consistency *for spreading.***

Note: Take care not to confuse *to* when used as a preposition with *to* used in an infinitive. When *to* is a preposition, it is followed by an object—a noun, a pronoun, a noun phrase, or an *-ing* verb form, not by the base form of a verb.

infinitive

▸ **They want *to adopt* a child.**

preposition + *-ing* form (gerund)

▸ **They are looking forward *to adopting* a child.**

Determine which to use by testing whether a noun replacement fits the sentence:

▸ **They are looking forward to *parenthood.***

Note also *be devoted to, be/get used to* (see 62h).

62 Language Learners' FAQs

The following are commonly asked questions. For more on sentence-level topics, see parts 7 and 8.

MindTap®
Read, highlight, and take notes online.

62a When do I use *no* and *not*?

Not is an adverb that negates a verb, an adjective, or another adverb. *No* is an adjective and therefore modifies a noun.

▸ **She is *not* wealthy.**

▸ **She is *not* really poor.**

▸ **The author does *not* intend to deceive the reader.**

▸ **The author has *no* intention of deceiving the reader.**

62b What is the difference between *too* and *very*?

Both *too* and *very* intensify an adjective or adverb, but they are not interchangeable. *Too* indicates excess. *Very* indicates degree and means "extremely."

- **It was *very* hot.**
- **It was *too* hot to sit outside.** [*Too* occurs frequently in the pattern *too* + adjective or adverb + *to* + base form of verb.]
- **The Volvo was *very* expensive, but he bought it anyway.**
- **The Volvo was *too* expensive, so he bought a Ford instead.**

62c Does *few* mean the same as *a few*?

A few is the equivalent of *some*. *Few* is the equivalent of *hardly any*; it has more negative connotations than *a few*. Both expressions are used with countable plural nouns. Although *a* is not generally used with plural nouns, the expression *a few* is an exception.

- **She feels fortunate because she has *a few* [some] helpful colleagues.**
- **She feels depressed because she has *few* [hardly any] helpful colleagues.**

You might prefer to use only the more common *a few* and use *hardly any* in sentences in which the context demands *few*. Similar expressions used with uncountable nouns are *little* and *a little*.

- **She has *a little* [some] time to spend on work-related projects.**
- **She has *little* [hardly any] time to spend on recreation.**

62d How do I distinguish *most, most of*, and *the most*?

Most expresses a generalization, meaning "nearly all."

- ***Most* young children like ice cream.**

When a word like *the, this, these, that*, or *those* or a possessive pronoun (such as *my, their*) precedes the noun to make it specific, *most of* is used. The meaning is "nearly all of."

- **Her assistant wrote *most of* the report.**
- ***Most of his colleagues* work long hours.**

The most is used to compare more than two people or items.

▸ **Bill is *the most* efficient of all the technicians.**

62e What structures are used with *easy*, *hard*, and *difficult*?

The adjectives *easy, hard*, and *difficult* cause problems for speakers of Japanese and Chinese. All of the following patterns are acceptable in English.

▸ **It is *difficult* for some people to learn a new language.**

▸ **It is *difficult* to learn a new language.**

▸ **To learn a new language isn't *easy*.**

▸ **Learning a new language is *hard* for some people.**

▸ **Learning a language can be *difficult*.**

▸ **Her students find it *difficult* to learn Chinese.**

However, a sentence like the following needs to be edited in English into one of the patterns listed previously or as follows:

think it is
▸ **I ~~am~~ *easy* to learn a new language.**

62f How do I use *it* and *there* to begin a sentence?

Use *there* to indicate that something exists (or existed) or happens (or happened) (see also 29b).

There
▸ **~~It~~ was a royal wedding in London in April 2011.**

There
▸ **~~It~~ is a tree on the corner of my block.**

Use *it* for weather, distance, time, and surroundings.

▸ **It is a long way to Tipperary.**

▸ **It is hot.**

Use *it* also in expressions such as *it is important*, *it is necessary*, and *it is obvious*, emphasizing the details that come next (see also 29b).

▸ **It is essential for all of you to sign your application forms.**

It or *there* cannot be omitted as a filler subject.

▸ **As you can see, ^it is dark out already.**

62g Which possessive adjective do I use: *His* or *her*?

In English and some other languages, the form of the adjective used to indicate possession changes according to the gender of the noun that precedes it.

▸ **Mary and *her* mother**

▸ **Peter and *his* mother**

▸ **Peter and *his* father**

Note that Spanish uses one possessive adjective (*su*) for both *his* and *her*, with the gender inferred from the antecedent:

▸ **Maria y su madre.**

▸ **Pedro y su madre.**

▸ **Pedro y su padre.**

In French, however, *son* or *sa* can both mean "his" or "her," with the gender determined not by the noun that *son* or *sa* refers back to but by the word that follows the possessive adjective:

▸ **Marie et sa mère** [Marie and her mother]

▸ **Pierre et sa mère** [Pierre and his mother]

▸ **Pierre et son père** [Pierre and his father]

With all this variability across languages, if English is not your native language, always check your writing for the accurate use of *his* and *her*.

62h What is the difference between *be/get used to* and *used to*?

For multilingual writers of English, understanding the distinction between *used to* + base form and *be/get used to* + *-ing* (gerund) is difficult.

- **The bankers *used to eat* lunch at a fancy restaurant.** [They don't anymore.]
- **Now they are *getting used to eating* lunch in the cafeteria.** [They are getting accustomed to it.]

Exercises on Writing across Languages and Cultures

EXERCISE 1 Identify transfer errors. 57d

From samples of your writing marked by instructors, gather examples of transfer errors that you know you need to be aware of. Use a language notebook or blog to keep a list of transfer errors that you make, with an edited version.

EXERCISE 2 Use proper and common nouns. 58a

Decide which nouns are proper and which are common. Then edit the following sentences so that all the proper nouns are capitalized and the common nouns are lowercased.

Example The store on ~~hudson~~ ^Hudson ~~street~~ ^Street has slashed its prices on ~~Clothing,~~ ^clothing, ~~Sunglasses,~~ ^sunglasses, and French perfume.

1. Have you seen Stores with Signs saying "Going out of business" and "Everything must go"? According to the magazine *consumer reports,* some of these Stores may not offer real Bargains.
2. Many stores bring in a Company that specializes in selling off Stock, says *the washington Post.* This second company, known as a *liquidator,* may jack up the prices in order to make a Profit.
3. When the circuit city chain went bankrupt, liquidators charged up to 100 Percent more than the store's Regular Prices.
4. *Time* magazine reporter brad tuttle writes that Investigators who visited a closing sale at a Borders store in new york city found Prices higher than they were before the Sale.
5. Usually, a Customer cannot return anything bought at a Liquidation Sale. Be sure you really want the Item and are not just reacting to the false promise of a Bargain.

EXERCISE 3 Use uncountable nouns correctly. 58b

Correct any errors in the use of countable and uncountable nouns. Remember to check for subject-verb agreement when correcting errors.

Example Until about 1810, ~~papers~~ ^paper made from ~~piece~~ ^pieces of cloth ~~were~~ ^was used for printing books.

1. In most cases, the page of books made before 1840 is still flexible and well preserved.

2. Between 1840 and 1950, however, publishers began to use less expensive paper that was made from wood pulps instead of from cloth.
3. To turn wood into paper, manufacturers added acidic chemicals that could break down and soften the wood. The pages created from these paper still contained some of the acid.
4. The pages of many books printed between 1840 and 1950 are beginning to crumble into dusts because acid is eating away the wood fiber in the pages.
5. The Library of Congress, which owns a huge collection of books, has begun to soak books made with acid paper in chemical bath to remove any remaining acid from the pages; books treated in this way can last for another several hundred years.

EXERCISE 4 Use articles, including *the*, correctly. 58c, 58d

In each of the following sentences, correct any errors in article use.

Example Many inactive people suffer from ~~the~~ depression.

1. Many scientific studies have proved that exercise helps the people sleep better and lose a weight.
2. A active lifestyle seems to improve not only a person's health but also his or her mood.
3. Endorphins, which are chemicals in human brain that are linked to feelings of well-being, increase when people get the enough exercise.
4. People who do not exercise are twice as likely as active people to suffer a symptoms of depression.
5. However, the scientists are not certain whether people do not exercise because they are depressed or whether they are depressed because they do not exercise.

EXERCISE 5 Use nouns and articles correctly. 58f

In the following passage, correct any errors in article use.

Name of Emmanual "Toto" Constant may not be familiar to everyone in United States, but to Haitian immigrants in this country, he is familiar and controversial figure. Constant, the son of an powerful Haitian military leader, was raised as a aristocrat in the impoverished Caribbean nation. In 1991, he formed political party known as FRAPH. Purpose of FRAPH was to fight against return of exiled president Jean-Bertrande Aristide, whom most poor Haitians supported as a their leader. FRAPH men, armed with the machine guns and machetes, roamed country, terrorizing Aristide supporters with torture, rape, and murder. Constant encouraged Haitians to fear him, claiming that he had the voodoo powers. Observers from United Nations said that FRAPH had been "linked to assassinations and rapes," and a American military official in Haiti warned that FRAPH was turning into "a sort of Mafia."

Even after a American peacekeeping force helped Aristide return to power in the 1994, Toto Constant remained the powerful man in Haiti. He apparently cooperated with an American intelligence officers, revealing details about his group's terrorist activities. Somehow, Toto Constant got out of Haiti and migrated to the New York, where he lived in an Haitian immigrant neighborhood and became real estate broker. Many of his neighbors recognized a face of Toto Constant.

In 2000, the most Haitian immigrants in New York wanted Toto Constant deported to Haiti. A trials were being held there to determine if he and other FRAPH members were guilty of the murder and torture. Although Constant did not return to Haiti, the Haitian court convicted him of murder and sentenced him to the life imprisonment. However, Constant remained free, and United States Immigration and Naturalization Service did not deport him. In 2001, after terror attacks on New York City, Haitians in a city demanded that the United States stop sheltering man who had terrorized his own people. Constant is currently serving prison term of twelve to thirty-seven years in United States for the mortgage fraud, and he had still not returned to Haiti.

EXERCISE 6 Use the *be* auxiliary and modal auxiliary verbs correctly. 59a, 59b

Correct any errors in the use of the *be* auxiliary and modal auxiliaries.

Example Young people who ^are learning to play an instrument ~~would~~ ^should practice if they want to improve.

Most people believe that musicians must to have talent in order to succeed. However, a 1998 study by British psychologist John Sloboda may indicates that the number of hours spent practicing affects musical ability more than inborn talent does. The study included musicians aged ten to sixteen years, from both public and private schools. Sloboda investigated how much each young musician practiced, whether parents and teachers involved in helping each musician improve, and how well each student scored on the British national music examination. Young musicians who had practicing most frequently were most successful on the exam; students whose parents and teachers working closely with them also received high scores. After looking at the exam results, Sloboda cannot help noticing that the students with the highest scores practiced 800 times more than the students with the lowest scores. Sloboda believes that individual differences in musical ability would be related to the amount students practice and the amount of support they get from teachers and parents. According to Sloboda's research, even people who do not believe they have musical talent became excellent musicians if they practiced hard enough.

EXERCISE 7 Use verbs and adjectives followed by infinitives and *-ing* or *-ed* forms. 59c–59f

Example A respected pop singer was ~~sentence~~ ^sentenced to twenty days of community service.

1. The United States Constitution prohibits force someone to work, except as punishment for a crime. Therefore, the corrections system can make criminals to provide labor without pay.
2. True, some convicted criminals may dislike performing their required tasks. Others may be relieve to have an occupation.
3. Prisoners at the Washington State Corrections Center for Women practice to groom dogs and to train them as service animals. Teams of male prisoners enjoy rehabilitate troubled dogs so that the dogs can be adopted.
4. In California, about 4,300 inmates risk to be injured at their jobs fighting wildfires. Women and juvenile offenders live in fire camps so they can remove brush from the perimeter of a blazed fire to prevent the fire from spread.
5. It is common for celebrities choose work when they wish shortening a jail term. Actor Lindsay Lohan chose working ten days for the American Red Cross to avoid spend more than two days in jail.

EXERCISE 8 Use correct verbs and verb forms. 59 and 39

In the following passage, correct any errors in verbs and verb forms.

Can money makes people happy? A well-known proverb says, "Money can't buy happiness," but some people probably would to agree that money is important for a happy life. Andrew Oswald and Jonathan Gardner of the University of Warwick in England has investigating the connection between money and happiness over eight years. The results are not surprised. If people suddenly get money that they not expecting—from the lottery, for example—they generally feel more satisfying with their lives.

In general, according to the study, receiving about $75,000 must mean the difference between being fairly happy and being very happy. However, people who admitted to be miserable before they had money needed to get $1.5 million before they considered themselves happy. But Oswald and Gardner advise to recognize that the study is not finished. They not admit knowing whether the happiness from receiving unexpected money lasts for a long time.

People who do not expect getting a large amount of money can find other reasons not to despair. The researchers say that money is not the most important factor in whether a person is happy or not. People who married are happier than those who are not: the researchers estimate that a lasting marriage makes the partners as happy as an extra $100,000 a year can. Perhaps looking for love is as important as trying to make—or win—a large amount of money.

EXERCISE 9 Correct errors in inclusion of a subject, order of elements, direct and indirect objects. 60a–60c

Correct any errors in the inclusion of a subject, in the order of elements, and in the use of direct and indirect objects. Some sentences may be correct.

Example In the United States, more people are having ~~every year~~ plastic surgery ^every year^ even though ^there^ are sometimes side effects from the surgery.

1. Cosmetic surgery had in the past a stigma, but now many people consider changing their appearance surgically.
2. In addition, the price of such surgery was once high, but it has declined in recent years.
3. In 2009, cosmetic surgeons 10 million procedures of one kind or other performed.
4. Six percent of those procedures were performed on African Americans, and African Americans represent a growing percentage of wanting plastic surgery people.
5. Cosmetic surgery gives to some people an improved self-image.
6. However, can be drawbacks to changing one's appearance.
7. Psychologists are concerned that some African American women reject their African features because they accept the most commonly seen in magazines standards of beauty.
8. Such women might say, for example, that it is a universal standard of beauty a narrow nose.
9. Some middle-class African Americans may also consider plastic surgery when they see that certain African American celebrities have changed their features.
10. Many psychologists say a patient considering cosmetic surgery that beauty comes from inside.

EXERCISE 10 Rewrite direct quotation as indirect (reported) quotation. 60d

Rewrite the following sentences as indirect (reported) quotation, making any necessary changes. In each case, use the given tag followed by *that, if,* or a question word.

Example "The soup is too spicy." (She complained)
She complained that the soup was too spicy.

1. "I cannot abide such pretentious prose." (The critic announced)
2. "Who is in charge?" (The mayor wanted to know)
3. "What is the square root of 2209?" (The contestant cannot work out)
4. "The economy will rebound." (The broker predicted)
5. "Will I lose all my savings?" (Investors constantly wonder)
6. "I understand the problems." (The candidate assured everyone)
7. "Who knows the answer?" (The game-show host asked)
8. "We will leave early tomorrow." (The guests hinted)
9. "Did my sweater shrink in the wash?" (Her son asked)
10. "We are going to a new French restaurant this evening." (The committee members said)

EXERCISE 11 Use adjectives in the correct order. 60g

In each of the following sentences, make any necessary changes in the order of adjectives and the use of commas. Some sentences may be correct.

Short, dark winter
Example ~~Dark, winter, short~~ days can cause some people to become depressed.

1. In northern states in wintertime, many office workers spend most of the daylight hours indoors.
2. Architects are beginning to design some new big buildings to admit as much natural light as possible.
3. A building with features such as skylights, large windows, or an atrium reduces the need for artificial light, but the most one money-saving benefit of outside light is its effect on many workers.
4. A recent architectural study demonstrated that workers in buildings with natural light were happier, more productive employees than workers in dark or artificially lighted offices.
5. Concerned employers can help their office workers maintain a positive outlook through winter dreary months by ensuring that workplaces are brightly lit, preferably with natural light.

EXERCISE 12 Use correct word order and sentence structure. 60a, 60b

Correct any errors in word order, missing words, or sentence structure in the following passage.

Many people fear in China and Japan the number *four*. Is a good reason for this fear: in Japanese, Mandarin, and Cantonese, the word for *four* and the word for *death* are nearly identical. A study in the *British Medical Journal* suggests that cardiac patients from Chinese and Japanese backgrounds they may literally die of fear of the number four. According to the study, which looked at US mortality statistics over a twenty-five-year period, Chinese and Japanese hospitalized for heart disease patients were more likely to die on the fourth day of the month. Although Chinese and Japanese cardiac patients across the country were all statistically more likely to die on that day, but the effect was strongest among Californian Chinese and Japanese patients. Is not clear why Californians are more at risk. However, one researcher suggested that because California's large Asian population includes many older people, the older generation may therefore teach to younger generations traditional beliefs.

Chinese and Japanese patients with other diseases they were no more likely to die on the fourth of the month than at any other time. White patients, whether they had heart disease or any other illness, they were no more likely to die on the supposedly unlucky thirteenth of the month than on any other day. Psychiatrist Jiang Wei of Duke University Medical School said, "She still didn't know the biological reason for the statistical effect" on Chinese and Japanese cardiac patients. David P. Phillips, the sociologist who conducted the study, said that the only explanation that makes sense is that the number four causes extra stress in Chinese and Japanese heart patients. More research may someday prove whether or not the stress on the fourth of the month it can be enough to kill.

EXERCISE 13 Use adjective + preposition, verb + preposition. 61b, 61c

In each of the following sentences, correct any errors in the choice of prepositions.

Example Many Americans have been worried ~~from~~ *about* the possibility of biological terrorism, but some doctors are more afraid ~~from~~ *of* the naturally caused influenza than any biological agent.

1. Although some Americans wanted to take antibiotics as a precaution against anthrax in the fall of 2001, the percentage of people who asked their doctors of flu shots at that time was no higher than normal.
2. Influenza has been responsible to the deaths of many healthy people in the past century, and doctors do not know when a dangerous strain of flu may appear.
3. Doctors in 1918 were unable to prevent the flu epidemic to killing millions of people around the world; more people died of the flu than as a result of World War I that year.
4. Many people may not be aware to the dangers of influenza.
5. Medical specialists are studying genetic samples from people who died with influenza in 1918 to try to find ways to prevent such a deadly flu from recurring.

EXERCISE 14 Use prepositions in phrasal verbs. 61d

Correct the preposition in each phrasal verb. A clue to the verb's meaning appears in brackets.

Example My car broke ~~off~~ *down*, but I kept putting ~~down~~ *off* the repairs.

1. When Fran needed to move out from [vacate] her apartment early, she looked onto [researched] subletting the apartment to another student. She checked the details on the application she filled over [completed] when she had moved along [inhabited].
2. Fran looked forward at [anticipated] leaving town without giving in [sacrificing] another month's rent. Luckily, she ran over [met unexpectedly] a classmate who had just found on [discovered] that he was losing his apartment.
3. Unfortunately, the landlord turned around [rejected] the new tenant and called out [cancelled] the deal. Fran gave away [surrendered] trying to sublet the place; she would allow her lease to run away [expire].
4. Because she had put across [delayed] making her arrangements for so long, she would have to put on with [endure] the extra expense.
5. It pained Fran to make down [compensate for] the several hundred dollars she was wasting, but she told herself to get under [recover from] it.

EXERCISE 15 Use preposition + *-ing* form as a noun (gerund). 61e

Edit the following sentences so that prepositions are followed by gerunds when appropriate. Do not use the *–ing* form with infinitives.

Example Many states have decided to ~~participating~~ ^participate in a program for ~~accept~~ ^accepting tolls electronically.

1. The E-ZPass can save time for US motorists who do a great deal of drive. The pass allows drivers to paying at a toll booth without stop.
2. Upon enroll in E-ZPass, drivers attach an electronic tag to their windshield. Then they set up a prepaid account for cover their toll expenses.
3. After detect the tag, an antenna at the toll station debits the driver's account. If widely used, the pass can prevent long lines from form at the entrance to major highways.
4. The Interagency Group, which oversees E-ZPass, plans on expand the system through the entire I-95 corridor of the eastern United States.
5. Some states are not averse to implement E-ZPass, but they need time to integrating it with their own toll systems.

EXERCISE 16 Use *no* and *not*, *too* and *very*, *few* and *a few* correctly. 62a–62c

Correct any errors in the use of *no* and *not, too* and *very*, or *few* and *a few*.

Example A wildfire in a wilderness area is ~~no~~ ^not necessarily a disaster.

1. Natural disasters such as fires, floods, and storms are usually seen as terrible events, but sometimes they have few positive results.
2. For example, a forest with many tall trees may be very dark for new plant growth, but fires can change the situation to allow sunlight to reach the ground.
3. A river that has no flooded for many years collects silt, which often means that a few fish can spawn.
4. Few human attempts to control disasters have been successful, and trying to ensure that not fire or flood can occur often means that fires and floods are more damaging when they do happen.
5. Although many ecologists have found it too difficult to stop trying to prevent natural disasters, they are now working instead to keep disasters from being too devastating.

EXERCISE 17 Use *most, most of*, and *the most*. 62d

Correct the phrases that use *most, most of,* and *the most* incorrectly.

Example Obesity is becoming one of ^the most dangerous health problems in the world.

1. Most of Americans would be better off if they lost a little weight. But most the world is now in the same boat.
2. Developing nations such as China and India are seeing most rapid rise in obesity. Most of this increase occurs when people move to cities.
3. Rural lifestyles are often healthier, because people are more active and the most of their food is locally grown.
4. City life means less exercise and more exposure to processed foods, which can be the most of unhealthy.
5. The countries with most obese people are in the South Pacific. Some health experts believe that most that problem is due to an influx of Western-style junk food.

EXERCISE 18 Use *easy*, *hard*, and *difficult*. 62e

Correct the following sentences that use the patterns for *easy, hard,* and *difficult.*

Example ~~Easy~~ ^It is easy for many people on the Autism spectrum to talk at length about a favorite subject.

1. People on the Autism spectrum are hard to know what another person is feeling. Reading body language and tone of voice difficult for people with this disorder.
2. Maintaining eye contact during a conversation can also difficult. Easy for people with autism to simply avoid looking at others while they are speaking.
3. While talking about their favorite subjects is often easy, they may be hard for them to join a conversation initiated by someone else.
4. Because of an upcoming change in the way this disorder is defined, people with autism may be more difficult to get the support they need.
5. To raise a child not easy for any parent. To find adequate services for a child with autism a challenge for parents in the next few years.

EXERCISE 19 Use *it* and *there* appropriately. 62f

Correct the use of *there* and *it* in the following sentences. Make sure that every sentence has a subject.

Example In my opinion, ^there was not enough food at the banquet.

1. It dry and dusty in parts of Oklahoma.
2. Is about 500 miles from here to Houston.
3. It was a religious festival in my town last weekend.
4. Necessary to bring your passport when you sign up for insurance.
5. If you don't like the movie, is no point in staying to the end.

EXERCISE 20 Use the possessive pronouns *his* and *her*. 62g

Make sure that the gender of each possessive pronoun matches the antecedent elsewhere in the sentence.

Example Rosa is always losing things in ~~its~~ her desk drawers.

1. Tomas wants to visit her mother.
2. Adèle needs to call his husband this afternoon.
3. Did Raúl show you her aunt's military medals?
4. Sarah drove his daughter's car back home.
5. Gabrielle and his sister are both pregnant.

EXERCISE 21 Use phrasal verbs, preposition + *-ing*, *get used to*, and *used to* correctly. 61d–61e, 62h

Correct any errors in the use of phrasal verbs, gerunds after prepositions, and the phrases *get used to* and *used to*.

Example AIDS ~~is used to being~~ used to be a death sentence, but more people now survive for years with the disease.

Since scientists began to learn about AIDS more than thirty years ago, many people have been counting up a cure for the disease. The cure has not yet been found, but today many people with AIDS in this country used to live with the medications and other treatments that allow them to having a reasonably healthy life. In poorer countries, unfortunately, fewer people can look forward on living with AIDS, but AIDS researchers are excited about a recent discovery in the central African country of Rwanda. In Kigali, Rwanda's capital, a study followed a group of sixteen people who tested positive for HIV more than ten years ago but have neither taken medicine to treating the illness nor gotten sick. In most AIDS patients, the virus breaks out the immune system; in many patients in the Rwandan study, however, the virus shows an unusual mutation that seems to allow the body to put the virus up with. Researchers do not yet know whether this discovery will assist them in find a cure for the AIDS virus, but every new piece of information in this puzzle may be helpful in fight the disease.

10 Glossaries

WRITING IN YOUR CAREER

All writers have words or grammatical concepts that cause them difficulties. It can be helpful to have a system for tracking your own trouble spots, somewhere you can note that you confuse *accept* and *except*, for example, or that *comma splices* are what trip you up when you end up writing run-on sentences. This way, you can identify patterns in your writing and have a customized checklist to refer to as you edit your academic and workplace writing. You may also find that having such a list, either in a form similar to the table below or some other format that makes sense to you, can show you where you've made progress over time.

Word or Grammar Term	*Keys for Writers* Page Number or Section	Notes or Example

10 Glossaries

MindTap®

Understand the goals of this part, and complete a warm-up activity.

63 Words to Watch For: Glossary of Usage

Listed in this glossary are words that are often confused (*affect/effect, elicit/illicit*) or misspelled (*it's/its*). Also listed are nonstandard words (*irregardless, theirself*) and colloquial expressions (*OK*) that should be avoided in formal writing.

MindTap®

Read, highlight, and take notes online.

a, an Use *an* before words that begin with a vowel sound (the vowels are *a, e, i, o,* and *u*): *an apple, an hour* (*h* silent). Use *a* before words that begin with a consonant sound: *a planet, a yam, a ukulele, a house* (*h* pronounced).

accept, except, expect *Accept* is a verb: *She accepted the salary offer. Except* is usually a preposition: *Everyone has gone home except my boss. Expect* is a verb: *They expect to visit New Mexico on vacation.*

adapt, adopt *Adapt* means "to adjust" and is used with the preposition *to: It takes people some time to adapt to the work routine after college. Adopt* means "to take into a family" or "to take up and follow": *The couple adopted a three-year-old child. The company adopted a more aggressive policy.*

adverse, averse *Adverse* is an adjective describing something as hostile, unfavorable, or difficult. *Averse* indicates opposition to something and usually takes the preposition *to: The bus driver was averse to driving in the adverse traffic conditions.*

advice, advise *Advice* is a noun: *Take my advice and don't start smoking. Advise* is a verb: *He advised his brother to stop smoking.*

affect, effect In their most common uses, *affect* is a verb, and *effect* is a noun. To *affect* is to have an *effect* on something: *Pesticides can affect health. Pesticides have a bad effect on health. Effect,* however, can be used as a ver meaning "to bring about": *The administration hopes to effect new health c legislation. Affect* can also be used as a noun in psychology, meaning "a fe or emotion."

aisle, isle You'll walk down an *aisle* in a supermarket or a churc an island.

all ready, already *All ready* means "totally prepared": *The students were all ready for their final examination. Already* is an adverb meaning "by this time": *He has already written the report.*

all right, alright *All right* (meaning "satisfactory") is standard. *Alright* is nonstandard. *All together* is used to describe acting simultaneously: *As soon as the boss had presented the plan, the managers spoke up all together. Altogether* is an adverb meaning "totally," often used before an adjective: *His presentation was altogether impressive.*

allude, elude *Allude* means "to refer to": *She alluded to his height. Elude* means "to avoid": *He eluded her criticism by leaving the room.*

allusion, illusion The noun *allusion* means "reference to": *Her allusion to his height made him uncomfortable.* The noun *illusion* means "false idea": *He had no illusions about being Mr. Universe.*

almost, most Do not use *most* to mean *almost: Almost* [not *Most*] *all my friends are computer literate.*

alot, a lot of, lots of *Alot* is nonstandard. *A lot of* and *lots of* are regarded by some as informal for *many* or *a great deal of: Students send lots of text messages.*

aloud, allowed *Aloud* is an adverb meaning "out loud": *She read her critique aloud. Allowed* is a form of the verb *allow: Employees are not allowed to participate in the competition.*

ambiguous, ambivalent *Ambiguous* is used to describe a phrase or act with more than one meaning: *The ending of the movie is ambiguous; we don't know if the butler really committed the murder. Ambivalent* describes uncertainty and the coexistence of opposing attitudes and feelings: *The committee is ambivalent about the proposal for restructuring the company.*

among, between Use *between* for two items, *among* for three or more: *I couldn't decide between red or blue. I couldn't decide among red, blue, or green.*

amoral, immoral *Amoral* can mean "neither moral nor immoral" or "not caring about right or wrong," whereas *immoral* means "morally wrong": *Some consider vegetarianism an amoral issue, but others believe eating meat is immoral.*

unt, number *Amount* is used with uncountable expressions: *a large t of money, work, or effort. Number* is used with countable plural expres- *arge number of people, a number of attempts.* See 58b.

ante-, anti- *Ante-* is a prefix meaning "before," as in *anteroom. Anti-* means "against" or "opposite," as in *antiseptic* or *antifreeze.*

anyone, any one *Anyone* is a singular indefinite pronoun meaning "anybody": *Can anyone help me? Any one* refers to one from a group and is usually followed by *of* + plural noun: *Any one* [as opposed to any two] *of the suggestions will be acceptable.*

anyplace The standard *anywhere* is preferable.

anyway, anywhere, nowhere; anyways, anywheres, nowheres *Anyway, anywhere,* and *nowhere* are standard forms. The others, ending in *-s,* are not.

apart, a part *Apart* is an adverb: *The old book fell apart. A part* is a noun phrase: *I'd like to be a part of that project.*

as, as if, like See *like.*

as regards See *in regard to.*

assure, ensure, insure All three words mean "to make secure or certain," but only *assure* is used in the sense of making a promise: *He assured us everything would be fine. Ensure* and *insure* are interchangeable, but only *insure* is commonly used in the commercial or financial sense: *We wanted to ensure that the rate we paid to insure our car against theft would not change.*

awful Avoid using *awful* to mean "bad" or "extremely": not *He's awful late,* but *He's extremely late.*

a while, awhile *A while* is a noun phrase: *a while ago; for a while. Awhile* is an adverb meaning "for some time": *They lived awhile in the wilderness.*

bad, badly *Bad* is an adjective, *badly* an adverb. Use *bad* after linking verbs (such as *am, is, become, seem*): *They felt bad after losing the match.* Use *badly* to modify a verb: *They played badly.*

bare, bear *Bare* is an adjective meaning "naked": the *bare* facts, a *bare*faced lie. *Bear* is a noun (the animal) or a verb meaning "to carry" or "to endure": *He could not bear the pressure of losing.*

barely Avoid creating a double negative (such as *can't barely type*). *Barely* should always take a positive verb: *She can barely type. They could barely keep their eyes open.* See *hardly.*

because, because of *Because* is a subordinating conjunction used to introduce a dependent clause: *Because it was raining, we left early. Because of* is a two-word preposition: *We left early because of the rain.*

being as, being that Avoid. Use *because* instead: *Because* [not *Being as*] *I was tired, I didn't go to class.*

belief, believe *Belief* is a noun: *She has radical beliefs. Believe* is a verb: *He believes in an afterlife.*

beside, besides *Beside* is a preposition meaning "next to": *Sit beside me. Besides* is a preposition meaning "except for": *He has no assistants besides us. Besides* is also an adverb meaning "in addition": *I hate horror movies. Besides, there's a long line.*

better See *had better.*

between See *among.*

brake, break To slow down, we *brake* by applying the *brake(s)* in a car. We can *break* a window or even get a bad *break.*

breath, breathe *Breath* is a noun: *Take three deep breaths. Breathe* is a verb: *Breathe in deeply.*

bring, take Use *bring* to suggest carrying something from a farther place to a nearer one, and use *take* for any other transportation: *First bring me a cake from the store, and then we can take it to the party.*

can't hardly This expression is nonstandard. See *hardly.*

censor, censure The verb *censor* refers to editing or removing from public view. *Censure* means "to criticize harshly." *The new film was censored for graphic content, and the director was censured by critics for his irresponsibility.*

cite, site, sight *Cite* means "to quote or mention"; *site* is a noun meaning "location"; *sight* is a noun meaning "view": *She cited the page number in her paper. They visited the original site of the abbey. The sight of the skyline from the plane produced applause from the passengers.*

compare to, compare with Use *compare to* when implying similarity: *They compared the director to Alfred Hitchcock.* Use *compare with* when examining similarities or differences: *She wrote an essay comparing Hitchcock with Orson Welles.*

complement, compliment As verbs, *complement* means "to complete or add to something," and *compliment* means "to make a flattering comment about someone or something": *The wine complemented the meal. The guests complimented the hostess on the fine dinner.* As nouns, the words have meanings associated with the verbs: *The wine was a fine complement to the meal. The guests paid the hostess a compliment.*

compose, comprise *Compose* means "to make up"; *comprise* means "to include." *The conference center is composed of twenty-five rooms. The conference center comprises twenty-five rooms.*

conscience, conscious *Conscience* is a noun meaning "awareness of right and wrong": *Conscious* is an adjective meaning "awake" or "aware." *Her conscience troubled her after the accident. The victim was still not conscious.*

continual, continuous *Continual* implies repetition; *continuous* implies lack of a pause: *The continual interruptions made the lecturer angry. Continuous rain for two hours stopped play.*

could care less This expression is often used but is regarded by some as nonstandard. In formal English, use it only with a negative: *They could not care less about their work.*

council, counsel A *council* is a group formed to consult, deliberate, or make decisions. *Counsel* is advice or guidance. *The council was called together to help give counsel to the people. Counsel* can also be a verb: *We counseled the students to withdraw from the course.*

credible, creditable, credulous *Credible* means "believable": *The jury found the accused's alibi to be credible and so acquitted her. Creditable* means "deserving of credit": *A B+ grade attests to a creditable performance. Credulous* means "easily taken in or deceived": *Only a child would be so credulous as to believe that the streets are paved with gold.* See also *incredible, incredulous.*

criteria, criterion *Criteria* is the plural form of the singular noun *criterion*: *There are many criteria for a successful essay. One criterion is sentence clarity.*

curricula, curriculum *Curricula* is the plural form of *curriculum. All the departments have well-thought-out curricula, but the English Department has the best curriculum.*

custom, customs, costume All three words are nouns. *Custom* means "habitual practice or tradition": *a family custom. Customs* refers to taxes on imports or to the procedures for inspecting items entering a country: *go through customs at the airport.* A *costume* is a style of dress: *a Halloween costume.*

dairy, diary *Dairy* is associated with cows and milk, and *diary* is associated with a daily journal.

decease, disease *Decease* is a verb or noun meaning "die" or "death." *Disease* is an illness: *The disease caused an early decease.*

decent, descent, dissent *Decent* is an adjective meaning "good" or "respectable": *decent clothes, a decent salary. Descent* is a noun meaning "way down" or "lineage": *She is of Scottish descent. Dissent,* used both as a noun and a verb, refers to disagreement: *The dissent about freedom led to civil war.*

desert, dessert *Desert* can be pronounced two ways. It can be a noun with the stress on the first syllable (*the Mojave Desert*) or on the second syllable as in the expression derived from the verb "to deserve": *They got their just deserts.* It can also be a verb with the stress on the second syllable meaning "to abandon": *When did he desert his family? Dessert* (with the stress on the second syllable) is the sweet course at the end of a meal.

device, devise *Device* is a noun: *He said they needed a device that could lift a car. Devise* is a verb: *She began to devise a solution to the problem.*

different from, different than Standard usage is *different from*: *She looks different from her sister.* However, *different than* appears frequently in speech and informal writing, particularly when *different from* would require more words: *My writing is different than* [in place of *different from what*] *it was last semester.*

differ from, differ with To *differ from* means "to be unlike": *Lions differ from tigers in several ways, despite being closely related.* To *differ with* means to "disagree with": *They differ with each other on many topics but are still good friends.*

discreet, discrete *Discreet* means "tactful": *Be discreet when you talk about your boss. Discrete* means "separate": *He writes on five discrete topics.*

disease See *decease.*

disinterested, uninterested *Disinterested* means "impartial or unbiased": *The mediator was hired to make a disinterested settlement. Uninterested* means "lacking in interest": *He seemed uninterested in his job.*

dissent See *decent.*

do, due *Do* is a verb. Do not write "*Do* to his absences, he lost his job"; instead use the two-word preposition *due to* or *because of. Due* is also an adjective meaning "expected at a certain time": *When will the final payment be due?*

drag, dragged Use *dragged* for the past tense of the verb *drag. Drug* is nonstandard.

drown, drowned The past tense of the verb *drown* is *drowned; drownded* is not a word: *He almost drowned yesterday.*

due to the fact that, owing to the fact that Wordy. Use *because* instead: *They stopped the game because* [not *due to the fact that*] *it was raining.*

each, every These are singular pronouns; use them with a singular verb. See also 41h and 42d.

each other, one another Use *each other* with two; use *one another* with more than two: *The twins love each other. The triplets all love one another.*

effect See *affect.*

e.g. Use *for example* or *for instance* in place of this Latin abbreviation.

elicit, illicit *Elicit* means "to get or draw out": *The police tried in vain to elicit information from the suspect's accomplice. Illicit* is an adjective meaning "illegal": *Their illicit deals landed them in prison.*

elude See *allude.*

emigrate, immigrate *Emigrate from* means "to leave a country"; *immigrate to* means "to move to another country": *They emigrated from Ukraine and immigrated to the United States.* The noun forms *emigrant* and *immigrant* are derived from the verbs.

eminent, imminent *Eminent* means "well known and noteworthy": *an eminent lawyer. Imminent* means "about to happen": *an imminent disaster.*

ensure See *assure.*

etc. This abbreviation for the Latin *et cetera* means "and so on." Do not let a list trail off with *etc.* Rather than *They took a tent, a sleeping bag, etc.*, write *They took a tent, a sleeping bag, cooking utensils, and a stove.*

every, each See *each.*

everyday, every day *Everyday* (one word) is an adjective meaning "usual": *Their everyday routine is to break for lunch at 12:30. Every day* (two words) is an adverbial expression of frequency: *I get up early every day.*

except, expect See *accept.*

explicit, implicit *Explicit* means "direct": *She gave explicit instructions. Implicit* means "implied": *A tax increase is implicit in the proposal.*

farther, further Both words can refer to distance: *She lives farther (further) from the campus than I do. Further* also means "additional" or "additionally": *The management offered further incentives. Further, the union proposed new work rules.*

few, a few *Few* means "hardly any": *She feels depressed because she has few helpful colleagues. A few* means "some"; it has more positive connotations than *few*: *She feels fortunate because she has a few helpful colleagues.* See 62c.

fewer, less Formal usage demands *fewer* with plural countable nouns (*fewer holidays*), *less* with uncountable nouns (*less sunshine*). However, in informal usage, *less* with plural nouns commonly occurs, especially with *than: less than six items, less than ten miles, fifty words or less.* In formal usage, *fewer* is preferred.

first, firstly Avoid *firstly, secondly,* and so on, when listing reasons or examples. Instead, use *first, second.*

flammable, inflammable, nonflammable Both *flammable* and *inflammable* mean the same thing: able to be ignited easily. *Nonflammable* means "unable to be ignited easily." *Dry wood is flammable*, or *Dry wood is inflammable. Asbestos is nonflammable.*

flaunt, flout *Flaunt* means "to show [something] off" or "to display in a proud or boastful manner." *Flout* means "to defy or to show scorn for." *When she flaunted her jewels, she flouted good taste.*

former, latter These terms should be used only in reference to a list of two people or things: *We bought lasagna and rhubarb, the former for dinner and the latter for dessert.* For more than two items, use *first* and *last: I had some pasta, a salad, and rhubarb; though the first was very filling, I still had room for the last.*

get married to, marry These expressions can be used interchangeably: *He will get married to his fiancée next week. She will marry her childhood friend next month.* The noun form is *marriage: Their marriage has lasted thirty years.*

go, say Avoid replacing the verb *say* with *go,* as this is nonstandard usage: *Jane says* [not *goes*], *"I'm tired of this game."*

good, well *Good* is an adjective; *well* is an adverb: *If you want to write well, you must use good grammar.* See 43a.

had better Include *had* in Standard English, although it is often omitted in advertising and in speech: *You had better* [not *You better*] *try harder.*

hardly This is a negative word. Do not use it with another negative: not *He couldn't hardly walk*, but *He could hardly walk.*

have, of Use *have,* not *of,* after *should, could, might,* and *must: They should have* [not *should of*] *appealed.*

height Note the spelling and pronunciation: not *heighth.*

heroin, heroine Do not confuse these words. *Heroin* is a drug; *heroine* is a brave woman. *Hero* may be used for an admirable person of either sex.

hisself Nonstandard; instead, use *himself.*

hopefully This word is an adverb meaning "in a hopeful manner" or "with a hopeful attitude": *Hopefully, she e-mailed her résumé.* Avoid using *hopefully* in place of *I hope that:* not *Hopefully, she will get the job*, but *I hope that she will get the job.* The former usage is, however, quite common.

I, me Do not confuse *I* and *me*. Use *I* only in the subject position, and use *me* only in the object position. To check subjects and objects using *and,* simply drop any additional subject or object so that only the pronoun remains: not *The CFO and me were sent to the conference,* but *The CFO and I were sent* (I was sent); not *Please send copies to my secretary and I,* but *Please send copies to my secretary and me* (send copies to me). See 42a.

illicit See *elicit.*

illusion See *allusion.*

immigrate See *emigrate.*

imminent See *eminent.*

implicit See *explicit.*

imply, infer *Imply* means "to suggest in an indirect way": *He implied that further layoffs were unlikely. Infer* means "to guess" or "to draw a conclusion": *I inferred that the company was doing well.*

incredible, incredulous *Incredible* means "difficult to believe": *The violence of the storm was incredible. Incredulous* means "skeptical, unable to believe": *They were incredulous when he told them about his daring exploits in the whitewater rapids.*

infamous *Infamous* is an adjective meaning "notorious": *Blackbeard's many exploits as a pirate made him infamous along the American coast.* Avoid using it as a synonym for "not famous."

inflammable See *flammable.*

in regard to, as regards Use one or the other. Do not use the nonstandard *in regards to.*

insure See *assure.*

irregardless Nonstandard; instead, use *regardless: He selected a major regardless of the preparation it would give him for a career.*

it's, its The apostrophe in *it's* signals not a possessive but a contraction of *it is* or *it has. Its* is the possessive form of the pronoun *it: The city government agency has produced its final report. It's available upon request.* See also 46f.

kind, sort, type In the singular, use each of these nouns with *this* and a singular noun: *this type of book.* Use each of them in the plural with *these* and a plural noun: *these kinds of books.*

kind of, sort of Do not use these to mean "somewhat" or "a little." *The pace of the baseball game was somewhat* [not *kind of*] *slow.*

knew, new *Knew* is the past tense of the verb *know. New* is an adjective meaning "not old": *He knew that the book was new.*

lend, loan *Lend* is a verb, and *loan* is ordinarily used as a noun: *Our cousins offered to lend us some money, but we refused the loan.*

less See *fewer.*

lie, lay Be sure not to confuse these verbs. *Lie* does not take a direct object; *lay* does. See 39b.

like, as, as if In formal usage, *as* and *as if* are subordinating conjunctions and introduce dependent clauses: *She walks as her father does. She looks as if she could win the contest. Like* is a preposition and is followed by a noun or a pronoun, not by a clause: *She looks like her father.* In speech, however, and increasingly in writing, *like* is often used where formal usage dictates *as* or *as if*: *She walks like her father does. He looks like he needs a new suit.* Know your audience's expectations.

likely, liable *Likely* means "probably going to," while *liable* means "at risk of" and is generally used to describe something negative: *Eddie plays the guitar so well that he's likely to start a band. If he keeps playing that way, he's liable to break a string. Liable* also means "responsible": *The guitar manufacturer cannot be held liable.*

literally Avoid overuse: *literally* is an adverb meaning "actually" or "word for word" and should not be used in conjunction with figurative expressions such as *My jaw literally hit the floor* or *He was literally bouncing off the walls. Literally* should be used only when the words describe exactly what is happening: *He was so scared that his face literally went white.*

loan See *lend.*

loose, lose *Loose* is an adjective meaning "not tight": *This jacket is comfortable because it is so loose. Lose* is a verb (the past tense form and past participle are *lost*): *Many people lose their jobs in a recession.*

lots of See *alot.*

man, mankind Avoid using these terms, as they are gender specific. Instead, use *people, human beings, humankind, humanity,* or *men and women.*

marital, martial *Marital* is associated with marriage; *martial* is associated with war: *Their marital relationship was sometimes martial.*

may be, maybe *May be* consists of a modal verb followed by the base form of the verb *be; maybe* is an adverb meaning "perhaps." If you can replace the expression with *perhaps,* make it one word: *They may be there already, or maybe they got caught in traffic.*

me, I See *I.*

media, medium *Media* is the plural form of *medium: Television and radio are both useful communication media, but his favorite medium is the written word.*

most See *almost.*

myself Use *myself* only as a reflexive pronoun (*I told them myself*) or as an intensive pronoun (*I myself told them*). Do not use *myself* as a subject pronoun: not *My sister and myself won,* but *My sister and I won.*

no, not *No* modifies a noun: *The author has no intention of deceiving readers. Not* modifies a verb, adjective, or adverb: *She is not wealthy. He does not intend to deceive.*

nonflammable See *flammable.*

nowadays All one word. Be sure to include the final *-s.*

nowhere, nowheres See *anyway.*

number See *amount.*

off, off of Use only *off,* not *off of: She drove the car off* [not *off of*] *the road.*

oftentimes Do not use. Use *often* instead.

OK, O.K., okay Reserve these forms for informal speech and writing. Choose another word in a formal context: not *Her performance was OK,* but *Her performance was satisfactory.*

one another See *each other.*

owing to the fact that See *due to the fact that.*

passed, past *Passed* is a past tense verb form: *They passed the deli on the way to work. He passed his exam. Past* can be a noun (*in the past*), an adjective (*in past years*), or a preposition (*She walked past the bakery*).

peak, peek, pique *Peak* is the top of a summit: *She has reached the peak of her performance. Peek* (noun or verb) means "glance": *A peek through the window is enough. Pique* (also a noun or a verb) has to do with being indignant: *Feeling insulted, he stormed out in a fit of pique.*

personal, personnel *Personal* is an adjective meaning "individual," while *personnel* is a noun referring to employees or staff: *It is my personal belief that a company's personnel should be treated like family.*

phenomena, phenomenon *Phenomena* is the plural form of the noun *phenomenon: Outer space is full of celestial phenomena, one spectacular phenomenon being the Milky Way.*

plus Do not use *plus* as a coordinating conjunction or a transitional expression. Use *and* or *moreover* instead: *He was promoted, and* [not *plus*] *he received a bonus.* Use *plus* as a preposition meaning "in addition to": *His salary plus his dividends placed him in a high tax bracket.*

pore, pour To *pore* is to read carefully or to ponder: *I saw him poring over the want ads before he poured himself a drink.*

precede, proceed *Precede* means "to go or occur before": *The Roaring Twenties preceded the Great Depression. Proceed* means "to go ahead": *After you pay the fee, proceed to the examination room.*

prejudice, prejudiced *Prejudice* can be a noun (*Prejudice is harmful to society*) or a verb, with *prejudiced* as its past participle: *He is prejudiced against ethnic minorities.*

pretty Avoid using *pretty* as an intensifying adverb. Use *really, very, rather,* or *quite: The stew tastes very* [not *pretty*] *good.*

principal, principle *Principal* is a noun (*the principal of a school*) or an adjective meaning "main" or "most important": *His principal motive was monetary gain. Principle* is a noun meaning "standard or rule": *He always acts on his principles.*

quite, quiet Do not confuse the adverb *quite,* meaning "very," with the adjective *quiet* ("still" or "silent"): *We were all quite relieved when the audience became quiet.*

quote, quotation *Quote* is a verb. Do not use it as a noun; use *quotation: The quotation* [not *quote*] *from Walker tells readers a great deal.*

real, really *Real* is an adjective; *really* is an adverb. Do not use *real* as an intensifying adverb: *She acted really* [not *real*] *well.*

reason is because Avoid *the reason is because.* Instead, use *the reason is that* or rewrite the sentence. See 38f.

regardless Use this to mean "in spite" or "anyway": They finished the game *regardless* of the weather. It rained, but they finished the game *regardless.* See also the nonstandard *irregardless.*

respectable, respectful, respective *Respectable* means "presentable, worthy of respect": *Wear some respectable shoes to your interview. Respectful* means "polite or deferential": *Parents want their children to be respectful to adults. Respective* means "particular" or "individual": *The friends of the bride and the groom sat in their respective seats in the church.*

respectfully, respectively *Respectfully* means "showing respect": *He bowed respectfully when the queen entered. Respectively* refers to items in a list and means "in the order mentioned": *Horses and birds gallop and fly, respectively.*

rise, raise *Rise* is an intransitive verb: *She rises early every day. Raise* is a transitive verb: *We raised alfalfa last summer.* See 39b.

sale, sell *Sale* is a noun: *The sale of the house has been postponed. Sell* is a verb: *They are still trying to sell their house.*

should (could, might) of Nonstandard; instead use *should have: You should have paid.* See 39c.

since Use this subordinating conjunction only when time or reason is clear: *Since you insist on helping, I'll let you paint this bookcase.* Unclear: *Since he got a new job, he has been happy. Since* here may refer to time or to reason (*because*).

site, sight See *cite.*

sometimes, sometime, some time The adverb *sometimes* means "occasionally": *He sometimes prefers to eat lunch at his desk.* The adverb *sometime* means "at an indefinite time": *I read that book sometime last year.* The noun phrase *some time* consists of the noun *time* modified by the quantity word *some: After working for Honda, I spent some time in Brazil.*

sort, type See *kind.*

sort of See *kind of.*

stationary, stationery *Stationary* is an adjective meaning "not moving" (*a stationary vehicle*); *stationery* is a noun referring to writing paper.

supposedly Use *supposedly,* not *supposably: She is supposedly a great athlete.*

taught, thought Do not confuse these verb forms. *Taught* is the past tense and past participle form of *teach*; *thought* is the past tense and past participle form of *think: The students thought that their professor had not taught essay organization.*

than, then *Then* is a time word; *than* must be preceded by a comparative form: *bigger than, more interesting than.*

their, there, they're *Their* is a pronoun indicating possession; *there* indicates place or is used as a filler in the subject position in a sentence; *they're* is the contracted form of *they are: They're over there, guarding their luggage.*

theirself, theirselves, themself Nonstandard; instead, use *themselves.*

threat, treat A *threat* is a "possible danger": *The threat of an earthquake was alarming.* A *treat* is a "source of pleasure": *She gave the children some cookies as a treat.*

thusly Incorrect form of *thus.*

to, too, two Do not confuse these words. *To* is a sign of the infinitive and a common preposition; *too* is an adverb meaning *also*; *two* is the number: *She is too smart to agree to report to two bosses.*

undoubtedly The correct word is *undoubtedly*, not *undoubtably.*

uninterested See *disinterested.*

unique The adjective *unique* means "the only one of its kind" and therefore should not be used with qualifying adjectives like *very* or *most: His recipe for chowder is unique* [not *most unique* or *quite unique*]. See 43h.

used to, get (become) used to These expressions share the common form *used to.* But the first, expressing a past habit that no longer exists, is followed by the base form of a verb: *He used to wear his hair long.* (Note that after *not,* the form is *use to: He did not use to have a beard.*) In the expression *get* (*become*) *used to, used to* means "accustomed to" and is followed by a noun or an *-ing* verb form: *She couldn't get used to driving on the left when she was in England.* See also 62h.

way, ways Use *way* to mean "distance": *He has a way to go. Ways* in this context is nonstandard.

wear, were, we're *Wear* is a verb meaning "to have on as covering, adornment, or protection" (*wearing a helmet*); *were* is a past tense form of *be*; *we're* is a contraction for *we are.*

weather, whether *Weather* is a noun; *whether* is a conjunction: *The weather will determine whether we go on the picnic.*

whose, who's *Whose* is a possessive pronoun: *Whose goal was that? Who's* is a contraction of *who is* or *who has: Who's the player whose pass was caught? Who's got the ball?*

your, you're *Your* is a pronoun used to show possession. *You're* is a contraction for *you are: You're wearing your new shoes today, aren't you?*

64 Glossary of Grammatical Terms

MindTap®
Read, highlight, and take notes online.

absolute phrase A phrase consisting of a noun phrase followed by a verbal or a prepositional phrase and modifying an entire sentence: *Flags flapping in the wind,* the stadium looked bleak. 45i.

acronym A pronounceable word formed from the initials of an abbreviation: *NATO, MADD, NOW.* 49a.

active voice The attribute of a verb when its grammatical subject performs the action: The dog *ate* the cake. See also 40a on the passive voice.

adjective The part of speech that modifies a noun or pronoun: She wears *flamboyant* clothes. His cap is *orange.* 35d, 43a, 60g. See also *comparative; coordinate adjective; cumulative adjective; parts of speech; superlative.*

adjective clause A dependent clause beginning with a relative pronoun (*who, whom, whose, which,* or *that*) and modifying a noun or pronoun: The writer *who won the prize* was elated. Also called a *relative clause.* 35d, 44a.

adverb The part of speech that modifies a verb, an adjective, another adverb, or a clause: She ran *quickly.* He will *inevitably* become a success. The children were *well* liked. Many adverbs end in *-ly.* 35d, 43a, 43b. See also *comparative; conjunctive adverb; frequency adverb; parts of speech; superlative.*

adverbial clause A dependent clause that modifies a verb, an adjective, or an adverb and begins with a subordinating conjunction: He left early *because he was tired.* 35d.

agent The person or thing doing the action, described by a verb: *His sister* won the marathon. The marathon was won by *his sister.* 40b.

agreement The grammatical match in person, number, and gender between a verb and its subject or between a pronoun and its antecedent (the word the pronoun refers to): The *benefits continue; they are* pleasing. The *benefit continues; it is* pleasing. 41a, 42d.

antecedent The noun that a pronoun refers to: My son who lives nearby found a *kitten. It* was black and white. 42c, 42d, 44a.

appositive phrase A phrase occurring next to a noun and used to describe it: His father, *a factory worker,* is running for office. 45d.

article *A, an* (indefinite articles), or *the* (definite article). Also called a *determiner.* 58c–58e.

auxiliary verb A verb that joins with another verb to form a complete verb. Auxiliary verbs are forms of *do, be,* and *have,* as well as the modal auxiliary verbs. 35d, 39c. See also *modal auxiliary verb.*

base form The dictionary form of a verb, used in an infinitive after *to: see, eat, go, be.* 39, 39a.

clause A group of words that includes a subject and a verb. 35d. See also *dependent clause; independent clause.*

cliché An overused, predictable expression: *as cool as a cucumber.* 32g.

collective noun A noun naming a collection of people or things that are regarded as a unit: *team, jury, family.* For agreement with collective nouns, see 41f, 42d.

comma splice The error that results when two independent clauses are incorrectly joined with only a comma. 37a–37c.

common noun A noun that does not name a unique person, place, or thing. 58a, 58b. See also *proper noun.*

comparative The form of an adjective or adverb used to compare two people or things: *bigger, more interesting.* 43h. See also *superlative.*

complement A *subject complement* is a word or group of words used after a linking verb to refer to and describe the subject: Harry looks *happy.* An *object complement* is a word or group of words used after a direct object to complete its meaning: They call him a *liar.* 35d, 41c.

complete verb A verb that shows tense. Some verb forms, such as *-ing* (present) participles and past participles, require auxiliary verbs to make them complete verbs. *Going* and *seen* are not complete verbs; *are going* and *has been seen* are complete. 36a, 39c.

complex sentence A sentence that has one independent clause and one or more dependent clauses: *He wept when he won the marathon.* 31d.

compound adjective An adjective formed of two or more words often connected with hyphens: a *well-constructed* house. 43d, 54b.

compound-complex sentence A sentence that has at least two independent clauses and one or more dependent clauses: *She works in Los Angeles, but her husband works in San Diego, where they both live.* 31d.

compound noun A noun formed of two or more words: *toothbrush, merry-go-round.* 54b.

compound predicate A predicate consisting of two or more verbs and their objects, complements, and modifiers: He *whistles and sings in the morning.* 36d, 38h.

compound sentence A sentence that has two or more independent clauses: *She works in Los Angeles, but her husband works in San Diego.* 31d.

compound subject A subject consisting of two or more nouns or pronouns and their modifiers: *My uncle and my aunt* are leaving soon. 41g, 42a.

conditional clause A clause introduced by *if* or *unless,* expressing conditions of fact, prediction, or speculation: *If we earned more,* we would spend more. 39j.

conjunction The part of speech used to link words, phrases, or clauses. 35d, 36c. See also *coordinating conjunction; correlative conjunctions; parts of speech; subordinating conjunction.*

conjunctive adverb A transitional expression used to link two independent clauses. Some common conjunctive adverbs are *moreover, however,* and *furthermore.* 2f, 35d.

connotation The meanings and associations suggested by a word, as distinct from the word's denotation, or dictionary meaning. 32c.

contraction The shortened form that results when an apostrophe replaces one or more letters: *can't* (for *cannot*), *he's* (for *he is* or *he has*), *they're* (for *they are*). 46d.

coordinate adjective An evaluative adjective modifying a noun. When coordinate adjectives appear in a series, their order can be reversed, and they can be separated by *and.* Commas are used between coordinate adjectives: the *comfortable, expensive car.* 45g.

coordinating conjunction The seven coordinating conjunctions are *and, but, or, nor, so, for,* and *yet.* They connect sentence elements that are parallel in structure: He couldn't call, *but* he sent an e-mail. 30b, 35d, 45b.

coordination The connection of two or more ideas to give each one equal emphasis: *Sue worked after school, so she didn't have time to jog.* 30b.

correlative conjunctions A pair of conjunctions joining equivalent elements. The most common correlative conjunctions are *either . . . or, neither . . . nor, both . . . and,* and *not only . . . but also: Neither* my sister *nor* I could find the concert hall. 38j.

countable noun A common noun that has a plural form and can be used after a plural quantity word (such as *many* or *three*): one *book,* three *stores,* many *children.* 58a, 58e.

cumulative adjective An adjective that modifies a noun and occurs in a conventional order with no comma between adjectives: a *new red plastic* bench. 60g.

cumulative sentence A sentence that adds elements after the independent clause. 31d.

dangling modifier A modifier that fails to modify the noun or pronoun it is intended to modify: not *Turning the corner,* the lights went out, but *Turning the corner, we* saw the lights go out. 38c.

demonstrative pronoun The four demonstrative pronouns are *this, that, these,* and *those: That* is my glass. 41j.

denotation A word's dictionary meaning. See also *connotation.* 32b, 32c.

dependent clause A clause that cannot stand alone as a complete sentence and needs to be attached to an independent clause. A dependent clause begins with a subordinating word such as *because, if, when, although, who, which,* or *that: When it rains,* we can't take the children outside. 35d, 36c.

diction The choice of appropriate words and tone. 32a–32g.

direct object The person or thing that receives the action of a verb: They ate *cake* and *ice cream.* 35d, 60c.

direct quotation A person's words reproduced exactly and placed in quotation marks: *"I won't be home until noon,"* she said. 10c, 38d, 60d.

double negative The use of two negative words in the same sentence: He does *not* know *nothing.* This usage is nonstandard and needs to be avoided: *He does not know anything. He knows nothing.* 43g.

Edited American English The variety of English that is used in formal academic writing. 35c, 57a.

ellipsis The omission of words from a quotation, indicated by three dots: "I pledge allegiance to the flag...and to the republic for which it stands...." 49g.

etymology The origin of a word. 32b.

euphemism A word or phrase used to disguise literal meaning: She *is in the family way* [meaning "pregnant"]. 32g.

faulty predication The error that results when the subject and verb do not match logically: not The *decrease* in stolen cars *has diminished* in the past year, but The *number* of stolen cars *has decreased* in the past year. 38e.

figurative language The use of unusual comparisons or other devices to draw attention to a specific meaning. See *metaphor; simile.* 5e, 32e.

filler subject *It* or *there* used in the subject position of a clause, followed by a form of *be: There are* two elm trees on the corner. 29b, 41d, 62f.

first person The person speaking or writing: *I* or *we.* 42a.

fragment A group of words that is punctuated as if it were a sentence but is grammatically incomplete because it lacks a subject or a predicate or begins with a subordinating word: *Because it was a sunny day.* 36a–36e.

frequency adverb An adverb that expresses time (such as *often, always,* or *sometimes*). It can be the first word in a sentence, or it can be placed between the subject and the main verb, after an auxiliary verb, or as the last word in a sentence. 43e.

fused sentence See *run-on sentence.*

gender The classification of a noun or pronoun as masculine (*Uncle John, he*), feminine (*Ms. Torez, she*), or neuter (*book, it*). 42e, 62g.

generic noun A noun referring to a general class or type of person or object: A *student* has to write many papers. 42d.

gerund The *-ing* verb form used as a noun: *Walking* is good for your health. 41e, 59d, 59e, 61e. See also *verbal.*

helping verb See *auxiliary verb.*

imperative mood The verb mood used to give a command: *Follow* me. 31d.

indefinite pronoun A pronoun that refers to a nonspecific person or thing: *anybody, something.* 41h, 42d.

independent clause A clause that has a subject and a predicate and is not introduced by a subordinating word. An independent clause can function as a complete sentence. *Birds sing. The old man was singing a song.* Hailing a cab, *the woman used a silver whistle.* 30b, 35d.

indicative mood The verb mood used to ask questions or make statements. It is the most common mood, used for declarative statements and questions. See also *subjunctive mood.*

indirect object The person or thing to whom or to which, or for whom or for which, an action is performed. It comes between the verb and the direct object: He gave his *sister* some flowers. 35d, 60c.

indirect question A question reported by a speaker or a writer, not enclosed in quotation marks: They asked *if we would help them.* 60d.

indirect quotation A description or paraphrase of the words of another speaker or writer, integrated into a writer's own sentence and not enclosed in quotation marks: He said *that they were making money.* 38d, 60d.

infinitive The base form, or dictionary form, of a verb, preceded by *to: to see, to smile.* 39a, 59c, 59e.

infinitive phrase An infinitive with its objects, complements, or modifiers: *To wait for hours* is unpleasant. He tries hard *to be punctual.* 36b, 41e.

intensive pronoun A pronoun ending in *-self* or *-selves* and used to emphasize its antecedent: They *themselves* will not attend. 42h.

interjection The part of speech that expresses emotion and is able to stand alone: *Aha! Wow!* Interjections are seldom appropriate in academic writing. 35d.

interrogative pronoun A pronoun that introduces a direct or indirect question: *Who* is that? I don't know *what* you want. 42i.

intransitive verb A verb that does not take a direct object: Exciting events *have occurred.* He *fell.* 35d, 40b. See also *transitive verb.*

inverted word order The presence of the verb before the subject in a sentence; used in questions or for emphasis: *Do you expect* an award? Not only *does she do* gymnastics, but she also wins awards. 29b, 41d.

irregular verb A verb that does not form its past tense and past participle with *-ed: sing, sang, sung; grow, grew, grown.* 39a.

linking verb A verb connecting a subject to its complement. Typical linking verbs are *be, become, seem,* and *appear:* He *seems* angry. A linking verb is intransitive; it does not take a direct object. 35d, 39c, 42a, 43c.

mental activity verb A verb not used in a tense showing progressive aspect: *prefer, want, understand:* not He *is wanting to leave*, but He *wants* to leave. 39d.

metaphor A figure of speech implying a comparison but not stating it directly: a *gale* of laughter. 5e, 32e.

misplaced modifier An adverb (particularly *only* and *even*) or a descriptive phrase or clause positioned in such a way that it modifies the wrong word or words: She showed the ring to her sister *that her aunt gave her.* 38b.

mixed construction A sentence with two or more types of structures that clash grammatically: *By doing* her homework at the last minute *caused* Meg to make many mistakes. 38a, 38e, 38f.

modal auxiliary verb The nine modal auxiliary verbs are *will, would, can, could, shall, should, may, might,* and *must.* They are followed by the base form of a verb: *will go, would believe.* Modal auxiliary verbs do not change form. 39c, 59b.

modifier A word or words that describe another noun, adverb, verb, phrase, or clause: He is a *happy* man. He is smiling *happily.* 43a–43e.

mood The mood of a verb tells whether the verb states a fact (*indicative:* She *goes* to school); gives a command (*imperative: Come* back soon); or expresses a condition, wish, or request (*subjunctive:* I wish you *were* not leaving). 39j. See also *imperative mood; indicative mood; subjunctive mood.*

nonrestrictive phrase or clause A phrase or clause that adds extra or nonessential information to a sentence and is set off with commas: His report, *which he gave to his boss yesterday,* received enthusiastic praise. 44b, 45d.

noun The part of speech that names a person, place, thing, or idea. Nouns are proper or common and, if common, countable or uncountable. 35d, 58a, 58b. See also *collective noun; common noun; compound noun; countable noun; generic noun; noun clause; parts of speech; proper noun; uncountable noun.*

noun clause A dependent clause that functions as a noun: I like *what you do. Whoever scores a goal* will be a hero. 35d.

noun phrase A noun with its accompanying modifiers and articles: *a brilliant, hard-working student.* 35d.

number The indication of a noun or pronoun as singular (one person, place, thing, or idea) or plural (more than one). 41a, 42d.

object of preposition The noun or pronoun (along with its modifiers) that follows a preposition: on *the beach.* 35d.

paragraph A group of sentences set off in a text, usually on one topic. 2e, 2g.

parallelism The use of coordinate structures that have the same grammatical form: She likes *swimming* and *playing* tennis. 38j.

participle phrase A phrase beginning with an *-ing* verb form or a past participle: The woman *wearing a green skirt* is my sister. *Baffled by the puzzle,* he gave up. 31d. See also *verbal.*

particle A word (frequently a preposition or adverb) that combines with a verb to form a phrasal verb, a verb with an idiomatic meaning: get *over,* take *after.* 61d.

parts of speech Eight traditional categories of words used to form sentences: noun, pronoun, verb, adjective, adverb, conjunction, preposition, and interjection. See 35d and the entry for each in this glossary.

passive voice The attribute of a verb when its grammatical subject is the receiver of the action that the verb describes: The book *was written* by my professor. 29c, 40a–40d. See also *active voice.*

past participle A verb form that in regular verbs ends with *-ed.* The past participle needs an auxiliary verb to function as the complete verb of a clause: *has chosen, was cleaned, might have been told.* The past participle can function alone as an adjective. 39a, 39c, 39d, 39g, 59f.

perfect progressive tense forms The verb tenses that show actions in progress up to a specific point in present, past, or future time. For active voice verbs, use forms of the auxiliary *have been,* followed by the *-ing* form of the verb: *has/have been living, had been living, will have been living.* 39d.

perfect tense forms The verb tenses that show actions completed by a present, past, or future time. For active voice verbs, use forms of the auxiliary verb *have,* followed by the past participle of the verb: *has/have arrived, had arrived, will have arrived.* 39d.

periodic sentence A sentence that uses words and phrases to build up to the independent clause. 31d.

person The form of a pronoun or verb that indicates whether the subject is doing the speaking (first person, *I* or *we*), is spoken to (second person, *you*), or is spoken about (third person, *he, she, it,* or *they*). 42a.

phrasal verb An idiomatic verb phrase consisting of a verb and a preposition or adverb, called a *particle*: *put off, put on.* 61d.

phrase A group of words that lacks a subject or a predicate and functions as a noun, verb, adjective, or adverb: *under the tree, has been singing, amazingly simple.* 35d. See also *absolute phrase; appositive phrase; infinitive phrase; participle phrase; prepositional phrase.*

possessive The form of a noun or pronoun that indicates ownership. Possessive pronouns include *my, his, her, their, theirs,* and *whose: my* boat, *your* socks. The possessive form of a noun is indicated by an apostrophe or an apostrophe and *-s: Mario's* car, the *children's* nanny, the *birds'* nests. 41j, 42b, 46a, 46b, 46c.

predicate The part of a sentence that contains the verb and its modifiers and that comments on, or makes an assertion about, the subject. To be complete, a sentence needs a subject and a predicate. 35d.

prefix The letters attached to the beginning of a word that change the word's meaning: *un*necessary, *re*organize, *non*stop. 54a.

preposition The part of speech used with a noun or pronoun in a phrase to indicate time, space, or some other relationship. 35d, 44d, 61a–61e. The noun or pronoun is the object of the preposition: *on the table, after dinner, to her.*

prepositional phrase A phrase beginning with a preposition and including the object of the preposition and its modifiers: The head *of the electronics company* was waiting *for an hour.* 31d, 35d, 44d.

present participle The *-ing* form of a verb, showing an action as being in progress or continuous: They are *sleeping.* Without an auxiliary verb, the *-ing* form cannot function as a complete verb but can be used as an adjective:

searing heat. When the *-ing* form is used as a noun, it is called a *gerund*: *Skiing* can be dangerous. 39a, 41e, 59d, 59f. See also *verbal*.

progressive tense forms The verb tenses that show actions in progress at a point or over a period of time in past, present, or future time. They use a form of *be* + the *-ing* form of the verb: They *are working;* he *will be writing.* 39d–39f.

pronoun The part of speech that takes the place of a noun, a noun phrase, or another pronoun. 35d, 41h, 42a, 42b. See *parts of speech*.

pronoun reference The connection between a pronoun and its antecedent. Reference should be clear and unambiguous: Mr. Estern picked up *his* hat and left. 42c.

proper noun The capitalized name of a specific person, place, or thing: *Golden Gate Park, University of Kansas.* 35d, 51b, 58f. See also *common noun*.

quantity word A word expressing the idea of quantity, such as *each, every, several, many,* and *much.* Subject-verb agreement is tricky with quantity words: *Each* of the students *has* a different assignment. 41i. See also *agreement.*

reflexive pronoun A pronoun ending in *-self* or *-selves* and referring to the subject of a clause: They incriminated *themselves.* 42h.

regular verb A verb that ends with *-ed* in its past tense and past participle forms. 39a.

relative clause See *adjective clause.*

relative pronoun A pronoun that introduces a relative clause: *who, whom, whose, which, that.* 44a.

restrictive phrase or clause A phrase or clause that provides information that is essential for identifying the word or phrase it modifies. A restrictive phrase or clause is not set off with commas: The book *that is first on the best-seller list* is a memoir. 44b, 45d.

run-on sentence The error that results when two independent clauses are not separated by a conjunction or by any punctuation: not *The dog ate the meat the cat ate the fish,* but *The dog ate the meat; the cat ate the fish.* Also called a *fused sentence.* 37a–37c.

second person The person addressed: *you.* 42a, 42g.

shifts The inappropriate switches in grammatical structure such as from one tense to another or from statement to command or from indirect to direct quotation: not *Joan asked whether I was warm enough and did I sleep well,* but *Joan asked whether I was warm enough and had slept well.* 38d, 39h.

simile A figure of speech that makes a direct comparison: She has a laugh *like a fire siren.* 5e, 32e.

simple tense forms The verb tenses that show present, past, or future time with no perfect or progressive aspects: they *work,* we *worked,* she *will work.* 39d–39g.

split infinitive An infinitive with a word or words separating *to* from the base verb form: *to successfully complete.* This structure has become acceptable. 38b.

Standard English "The variety of English that is generally acknowledged as the model for the speech and writing of educated speakers." This *American Heritage Dictionary,* 5th edition, definition warns that the use of the term is "highly elastic and variable" and confers no "absolute positive evaluation." 32d, 35c, 57a. See also *Edited American English.*

subject The noun or pronoun that performs the action of the verb in an active voice sentence or receives the action of the verb in a passive voice sentence. To be complete, a sentence needs a subject and a verb. 35d, 36d, 38i, 60a.

subjunctive mood The verb mood used in conditions and in wishes, requests, and demands: I wish he *were* here. She demanded that he *be* present. 39j.

subordinate clause See *dependent clause.*

subordinating conjunction A conjunction that is used to introduce a dependent adverbial clause: *because, if, when, although, since, while.* 30b, 35d, 36c.

suffix The letters attached to the end of a word that change the word's function or meaning: gentle*ness,* humor*ist,* slow*er,* sing*ing.* 56e.

superlative The form of an adjective or adverb that is used to compare three or more people or things: *biggest; most unusual; least effectively.* 43h, 58d. See also *comparative.*

synonym A word that has the same or nearly the same meaning as another word. 32b.

tense The form of a verb that indicates time. Verbs change form to distinguish present and past time: he *goes;* he *went.* Various structures are used to express future time, mainly *will* + the base form, or *going to* + the base form. 39d. See also *perfect progressive tense forms; perfect tense forms; progressive tense forms; simple tense forms.*

third person The person or thing spoken about: *he, she, it, they,* or nouns. 41a, 42a.

topic chain The repetition of key words or related words throughout a passage to aid cohesion. 30a, 40c.

transitional expression A word or phrase used to connect two independent clauses, such as *for example, however,* and *similarly.* 2f, 45e, 48a.

transitive verb A verb that takes an object—the person or thing that receives the action (in the active voice): Dogs *chase* cats. When transitive verbs are used in the passive voice, the subject receives the action of the verb: Cats *are chased* by dogs. 35d, 39b, 40b. See also *intransitive verb.*

uncountable noun A common noun that cannot follow a plural quantity word (such as *several* or *many*), is never used with *a* or *an,* is used with a singular third person verb, and has no plural form: *furniture, happiness, information.* 41e, 58b.

verb The part of speech that expresses action or being and tells (in the active voice) what the subject of the clause is or does. The complete verb in a clause may require auxiliary or modal auxiliary verbs to complete its meaning. 35d, 39a–39j, 59a–59f.

verbal A form, derived from a verb, that cannot function as the main verb of a clause. The three types of verbals are the infinitive, the *-ing* participle, and the past participle (for example, *to try, singing, stolen*). A verbal can function in a phrase as a noun, adjective, or adverb. 59c–59f, 61e.

verb chain The combination of an auxiliary verb, a main verb, and verbals: She *might have promised to leave;* they *should deny having helped* him. 59a–59e.

verb phrase A complete verb formed by auxiliaries and the main verb: *should have waited.* 35d.

voice Transitive verbs (verbs that take an object) can be used in the active voice (*He is painting the door*) or the passive voice (*The door is being painted*). 40a, 40b.

zero article The lack of an article (*a, an,* or *the*) before a noun. Uncountable nouns are used with the zero article when they make no specific reference. 58b, 58d, 58e.

Text Credits

This page constitutes an extension of the copyright page. We have made every effort to trace the ownership of all copyrighted material and to secure permission from copyright holders. In the event of any question arising as to the use of any materials, we will be pleased to make the necessary corrections in future prints. Thanks are due to the following authors, publishers, and agents for permission to use the material indicated.

p. 12: © Cengage Learning
p. 15: © 2018 Cengage Learning
p. 19: © Cengage Learning
p. 29: Winifred Gallagher, *Rapt* (p. 37)
p. 29: Deborah Tannen, *You Just Don't Understand*
p. 30: David McCullough, *Truman*
pp. 30–31: Dawn O. Braithwaite, "Viewing Persons with Disabilities as a Culture"
p. 31: Ruth Reichl, *Tender at the Bone: Growing Up at the Table*
p. 31: Geoffrey C. Ward, *The Civil War: An Illustrated History*
p. 32: Thomas Mallon, *A Book of One's Own: People and Their Diaries*
pp. 32–33: *Columbia Encyclopedia,* ed. Paul Lagasse, © 2006 Columbia University Press. Reprinted with the permission of the publisher.
p. 33: Laurie Helgoe, "Revenge of the Introvert"
p. 34: Phyllis Rose, *Parallel Lives: Five Victorian Marriages*
p. 36: Joe Bageant, *Deer Hunting with Jesus: Dispatches from America's Class War*
p. 36: Jane Austen, *Pride and Prejudice*
p. 36: Ruth Reichl, *Garlic and Sapphires*
p. 37: George Orwell, *1984*
p. 37: Eric Schlosser, *Fast Food Nation*
p. 60: "Crisis in the Kindergarten," Alliance for Childhood, March 2009, http://www.nytimes.com/2009/05/03/magazine/03wwln-lede-t.html.
p. 70: Used by permission of Bibi Bhani Khalsa.
p. 89: John Keats
p. 89: Jerome K. Jerome
p. 89: David Wells (when a Yankees pitcher)
p. 89: William Wordsworth
p. 89: William Shakespeare
p. 89: William Shakespeare
p. 89: Alfred, Lord Tennyson
p. 89: William Shakespeare, *Julius Caesar*
p. 89: Elizabeth Warren
p. 90: Alice Moore-Dunbar Nelson
p. 95: Used with permission of Andrew Dillon.
p. 145: © Cengage Learning
p. 164: © Cengage Learning
p. 165: © Cengage Learning
pp. 188–189: Robillard, Amy E. "We Won't Get Fooled Again: On the Absence of Angry Responses to Plagiarism in Composition Studies." *College English*, vol. 70, no. 1, 2007, pp. 10–31.

p. 189: Flora, Carlin. "The Beauty Paradox." *Psychology Today,* vol. 47, no. 1, 2014, pp. 36–37. Academic Search Complete, ezproxy.library.arizona.edu/login?url=http://search.ebscohost.com/login.aspx?direct=true&db=a9h&AN=93288156&site=ehost-live.

p. 199: *North American Journal of Psychology* 14.2 (2012): 281–291.

p. 199: Times Higher Education Supplement: THE 14 May 2015: 34.

p. 218: Steel, Emily. "Power Struggle Churns Viacom, Even as a New Leader Is Named." *The New York Times,* late edition, 5 Feb. 2016, pp. A1+.

p. 218: Crystal, David. *The Stories of English.* Overlook, 2004.

p. 220: Fussell, Paul, Uniforms: *Why We Are What We Wear,* pp. 85 (Boston: Houghton Mifflin 2002).

p. 223: United States, Dept. of the Interior, USGS Introd. 1).

p. 225: Bunin, Ivan. *In Paris.* Directed and Adapted by Dmitry Krymov, performance by Mikhail Baryshnikov. Broad Stage, Santa Monica, 15 Apr. 2012.

p. 227: Shakespeare, William, *A Midnight Summer's Dream.*

p. 336: From *Psychology* (p. 91), by R. J. Sternberg, 2004, Boston, MA: Wadsworth. Copyright 2004 by Cengage Learning.

p. 337: From A. Snyder et al., 2006, p. 838.

p. 337: From A. Snyder et al., 2006, p. 841.

p. 375: Wright, Richard. *American Hunger: The Compelling Continuation of Richard Wright's Autobiographical Work, Black Boy.* New York: Harper, 1977, p. 266.

p. 401: Data are 2009 annual averages for persons age 25 and over. Earnings are for full-time wage and salary workers. Bureau of Labor Statistics, Current Population Survey. BLS has some data on the employment status of the civilian noninstitutional population 25 years and over by educational attainment, sex, race, and Hispanic origin online. The Bureau of the Census also has some data on the educational attainment online at http://www.bls.gov/emp/p_chart_001.txt.

p. 402: http://epp.eurostat.ec.europa.eu/statistics_explained/index.php/unemployment_statistics

p. 403: U.S. Energy Information Administration, Petroleum Supply Monthly (February 2012), preliminary data.

p. 404: Data are from the Florida Division of Elections, http://election.dos.state.fl.us/voter-registration/statistics/elections.shtml

p. 427: Sample documents in 26b, 26c, and 27b are adapted from Amy Newman and Scot Ober's *Business Communication: In Person, In Print, Online,* 8th edition (Boston: South-Western, 2012). Used with permission.

p. 428: © Cengage Learning

p. 430: Courtesy of Ben & Jerry's

p. 458: Barbara Kingsolver

p. 458: John Mason Brown

p. 458: Rev. Jesse Jackson

p. 475: Maya Angelou

p. 482: Steven Wright

p. 620: Tom McArthur, "The English Languages?" *English Today* (July 1987), p. 11. Reprinted with the permission of Cambridge University Press.

p. 620: Gemino Abad

p. 620: David Crystal

Index

Note: An asterisk (*) refers to a page number in the Glossary of Grammatical Terms.

A

B

C

E

G

J

K

L

N

S

U

V

Y

Z

Key to Featured Content

Writing

Planning and Critical Thinking

Drafting

Revising

Editing

Reading

Research

Documentation

Grammar and Punctuation

For Multilingual Writers

Design and Media

Common Editing and Proofreading Marks

SYMBOL	EXAMPLE (CHANGE MARKED)	EXAMPLE (CHANGE MADE)
o	Correct a typu.	Correct a typo.
r/m/o	Cornect nore than one typu.	Correct more than one typo.
t	Insert a leer.	Insert a letter.
or words	Insert a word.	Insert a word or words.
	Make a a deletion.	Make a deletion.
	Delette and close up space.	Delete and close up space.
	Close up ex tra space.	Close up extra space.
#	Insertproper spacing.	Insert proper spacing.
#/	Inserts pace and close up.	Insert space and close up.
tr	Transpose letters inidcated.	Transpose letters indicated.
tr	Transpose as words indicated.	Transpose words as indicated.
tr	Reorder shown as words several.	Reorder several words as shown.
[	Move text to left.	Move text to left.
]	Move text to right.	Move text to right.
¶	Indent for paragraph.	Indent for paragraph.
no ¶	No paragraph indent.	No paragraph indent.
run in	Run back turnover lines.	Run back turnover lines.
	Break line when it runs far too long.	Break line when it runs far too long.
⊙	Insert period here	Insert period here.
,	Commas commas everywhere.	Commas, commas everywhere.
'	Its in need of an apostrophe.	It's in need of an apostrophe.
" / "	Add quotation marks, he begged.	"Add quotation marks," he begged.
;	Add a semicolon don't hesitate.	Add a semicolon; don't hesitate.
:	She advised "You need a colon."	She advised: "You need a colon."
?	How about a question mark	How about a question mark?
=	Add a hyphen to a bill like receipt.	Add a hyphen to a bill-like receipt.
(/)	Add parentheses as they say.	Add parentheses (as they say).
lc	Sometimes you want Lowercase.	Sometimes you want lowercase.
caps	Sometimes you want upperCASE.	Sometimes you want UPPERCASE.
ital	Add italics instantly.	Add italics *instantly*.
rom	But use *roman* in the main.	But use roman in the main.
bf	Add boldface if necessary.	Add **boldface** if necessary.
sp	Spell out all 3 terms.	Spell out all three terms.
stet	Let stand ~~as is.~~	Let stand as is. (This retracts a change already marked.)

Correction Guide

Note: Numbers refer to chapters and sections in the book.

ABBREVIATION	MEANING/ERROR
ab or abbr	abbreviation, 52, 55c
adj	adjective, 35d, 43
adv	adverb, 35d, 43
agr	agreement, 41, 42d
apos	apostrophe, 46
arg	argument error, 4e–4i
art	articles, 58
awk	awkward, 28, 29, 38
bias	biased or sexist language, 32f, 42e
ca or case	case, 42a
cap (tom)	use capital letter, 51, 55b, 58f
coh	coherence, 2f
comp	comparative, 43h, 43i
coord	coordination, 2b, 30c, 45b
cs	comma splice, 37
d	diction, 32
db neg	double negative, 43g
dev	development, 2g
dm	dangling modifier, 38c
doc	documentation, 11–20
-ed	error with *-ed* ending, 39g, 59f
exact	exactness, 32c
frag	sentence fragment, 36
fs	fused sentence, 37
gen	gender bias, 32f, 42e
hyph	hyphenation, 54
id	idiom, 61
inc	incomplete sentence or construction, 38h, 60a
ind quot	indirect quotation, 39i, 60d
-ing	error with *-ing* ending, 59
ital	italics/underlining, 12a, 15a, 19c, 50
jar	jargon, 32d
lc (M/e)	use a lowercase letter, 51
log	logic, 4h, 4j
mix or mixed	mixed construction, 38a
mm	misplaced modifier, 38b
ms	manuscript form, 21, 25, 26, 27
nonst	nonstandard usage, 35c, 36–44
num	faulty use of numbers, 53
//	parallelism, 38j
p	punctuation, 45–49, 55a
pass	passive voice, 29c, 40
prep	preposition, 35d, 61
pron	pronoun, 35d, 42
quot	quotation, 10d, 47
ref	pronoun reference, 42c
rel cl	relative clause, 44
rep or red	repetitive or redundant, 28a, 28d
-s	error with *-s* ending, 41
shift	needless shift, 38d, 39h
sp	spelling, 56
s/pl	singular/plural, 41a, 41h, 56a
sub	subordination, 30b, 60e
sup	superlative, 43h
s-v agr	subject-verb agreement, 41
t	verb tense, 39d
trans	transition, 2f, 45e
und	underlining/italics, 50
us	usage, 63
v or vb	error with verb, 39
var	[sentence] variety, 31d
w	wordy, 28
wc	word choice, 32
wo	word order, 31d, 60b, 60g
ww	wrong word, 32

CONTENTS